THE PELICAN HISTORY OF ART

EDITED BY NIKOLAUS PEVSNER

Z22

BAROQUE ART AND ARCHITECTURE IN CENTRAL EUROPE

EBERHARD HEMPEL

EBERHARD HEMPEL

BAROQUE ART AND ARCHITECTURE
IN CENTRAL EUROPE

GERMANY / AUSTRIA / SWITZERLAND / HUNGARY
CZECHOSLOVAKIA / POLAND

Painting and Sculpture: Seventeenth and Eighteenth Centuries
Architecture: Sixteenth to Eighteenth Centuries

PENGUIN BOOKS
BALTIMORE · MARYLAND

WRITTEN FOR THE PELICAN HISTORY OF ART
TRANSLATED FROM THE GERMAN BY ELISABETH HEMPEL AND MARGUERITE KAY

★

Penguin Books Ltd, Harmondsworth, Middlesex
Penguin Books Inc., Baltimore, Maryland, U.S.A.
Penguin Books Pty Ltd, Ringwood, Victoria, Australia

★

Text printed by Richard Clay (The Chaucer Press), Ltd, Bungay, Suffolk
Plates printed by Balding & Mansell Ltd, London
Made and printed in Great Britain

★

CONTENTS

Part One

Introduction

Part Two

The Heroic Age 1600–39

CONTENTS

Part Three

The Years of Recovery after the Thirty Years War 1640–82

Part Four

The Baroque Period 1683–1739

CONTENTS

Part Five

Rococo and its End 1740–80

CONTENTS

The Plates

LIST OF FIGURES

LIST OF FIGURES

Unless otherwise marked in the text, all plans are reproduced at the scale of 1 : 750

The drawings and adaptations in the text were made, and the maps drawn, by Donald Bell-Scott

LIST OF PLATES

FOREWORD

CENTRAL European art of the seventeenth and eighteenth centuries tends
to be not only unknown to the English-speaking world, but also alien in
content and feeling to such an extent that it is frequently resented as an aber-
ration. Having throughout my life lived in this Baroque world, I regarded it
therefore as my best plan to present my subject in such a way as to rely as far
as possible on its own evidence. To do this welcome service to an English
public, I had to look for people familiar both with the material and with life
in both countries. I was fortunate in finding two such helpers in my sister,
to whom I dedicate this book, and in Frau Veronika Schubert, a friend of
many years' standing. My gratitude to them, and also to my indefatigable
secretary Fräulein Hanna von Littrow, will be foremost in my mind whenever I look at this book in its published form. My thanks are also due to my
old friend from student days, the editor of the Pelican History of Art, a series
which I interpret as endeavouring to combine the character of the textbook
with that of the receptacle for progressing research. It is pleasant for me to
remember in connexion with this book that the German Baroque stood at
the beginning of Nikolaus Pevsner's career. As for the many others who have
helped me, I want to single out for recognition Major Máté and his collaborators in Budapest, Viktor Kotrba, Hugo Rokyta, and Miroslav Korecký
in Prague, Stanislaw Lorentz in Warsaw, Gerhard Woeckel in Munich,
Hans Reuther in Hanover, Herbert Wolfgang Keiser in Oldenburg,
Walter Hantschel in Dresden, Walter Frodl and Erwin Hainisch in
Vienna, Gerhard Franz in Graz, and Elisabeth Figdor in
Heiligenkreuz-Gutenbrunn.

THE MAPS

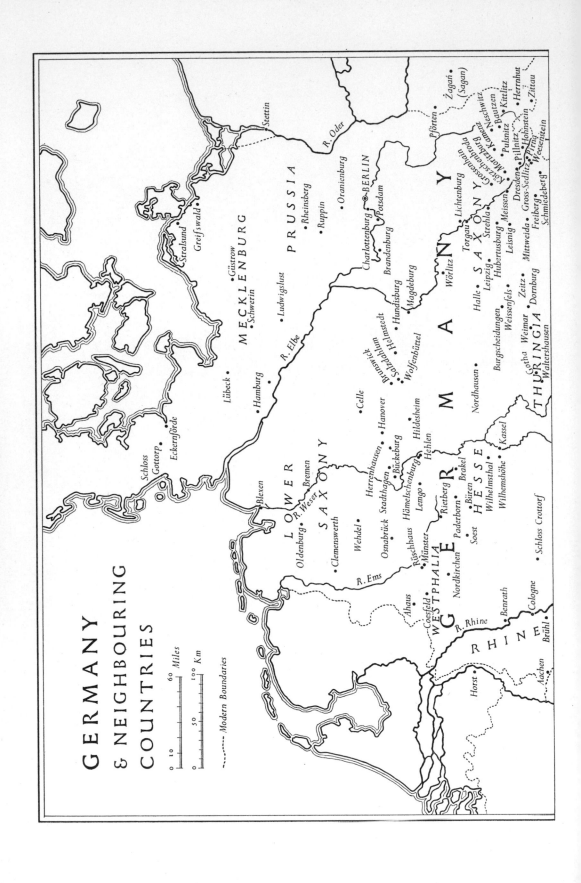

GERMANY
& NEIGHBOURING
COUNTRIES

Miles
60

0 10   Km
          50   100

----- Modern Boundaries

Stettin

R. Oder

Pförten

Żagań
(Sagan)

PRUSSIA

Rheinsberg
Ruppin
Oranienburg

BERLIN
Charlottenburg Potsdam
Brandenburg

Grossenhain Herrnhut
Königsbrück Neschwitz Zittau
Kamenz Bautzen
Moritzburg Pulsnitz Kittlitz
Meissen Dresden Pillnitz Hohnstein
Leisnig Gross-Sedlitz Pirna Weesenstein
Mittweida Freiberg Schmiedeberg

SAXONY

Torgau Lichtenburg
Halle Leipzig Strehla
Hubertusburg
Burgscheidungen Weissenfels
Zeitz Weimar Dornburg
Gotha THURINGIA
Waltershausen

Wörlitz

Greifswald
Stralsund

MECKLENBURG

Güstrow
Schwerin
Ludwigslust

R. Elbe

Magdeburg
Hundisburg
Salzdahlum Helmstedt
Brunswick Wolfenbüttel
Celle

Nordhausen

Lübeck
Hamburg

Schloss
Gottorp
Eckernförde

Blexen
Bremen
R. Weser
Oldenburg

LOWER
SAXONY

Wehdel
Clemenswerth
Stadthagen
Osnabrück
Herrenhausen Hanover
Hämelschenburg Hildesheim
Bückeburg
Lemgo Hehlen
Rietberg Brakel
Büren
Paderborn
Soest

Kassel
Wilhelmsthal
Wilhelmshöhe

HESSE

Schloss Crottorf

GERMANY

WESTPHALIA

R. Ems
Rüschhaus Münster
Nordkirchen
Coesfeld
Ahaus

Benrath
Cologne
Brühl

RHINE

R. Rhine

Horst

Aachen

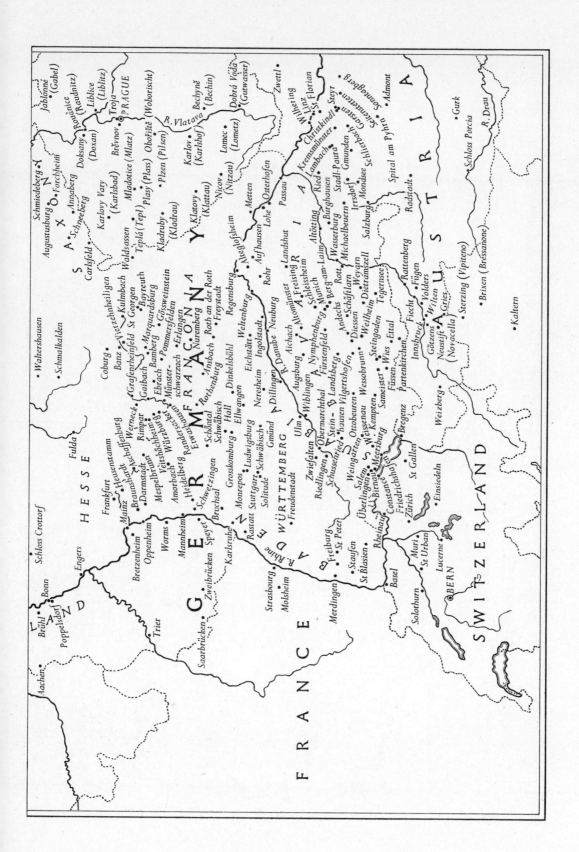

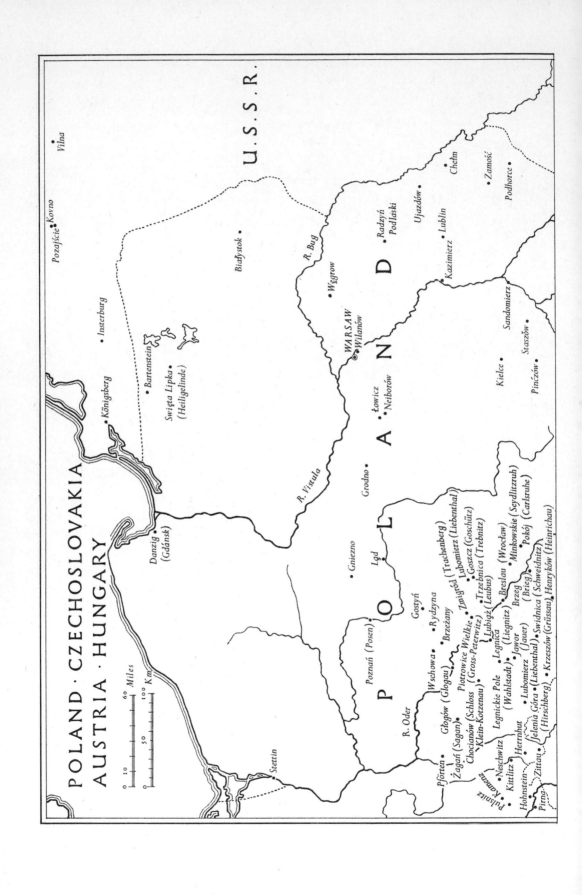

POLAND · CZECHOSLOVAKIA
AUSTRIA · HUNGARY

Miles
Km

U.S.S.R.

Vilha

Pozajście • Kovno

Insterburg

Königsberg

Bartenstein •
• Święta Lipka
  (Heiligelinde)

Danzig
(Gdánsk)

Stettin

R. Oder

Pförten •
Żagań (Sagan) •
Głogów (Glogau) •
Chocianów (Schloss •
Klein-Kotzenau) •
Pulsnitz •
Kamenz •
Neschwitz •
Kittlitz •
Hohnstein •
Pirna •
Herrnhut •
Zittau •
Jelenia Góra (Liebenthal) •
(Hirschberg) •
Krzeszów (Grüssau) Henryków (Heinrichau) •

Wschowa •
Rydzyna •
Brzezany •
Piotrowice Wielkie •
(Gross-Peterwitz) •
Legnickie Pole •
(Wahlstadt) •
Legnica •
(Liegnitz) •
Lubomierz •
(Liebenthal) •
Jawor •
(Jauer) •
Świdnica (Schweidnitz) •

Gostyń •
Znigród (Trachenberg) •
Lubomierz (Liebenthal) •
Goszcz (Goschütz) •
Trzebnica (Trebnitz) •
Lubiąż (Leubus) •
Breslau (Wrocław) •
Brzeg
(Brieg) •
Minkowskie (Seydlitzruh) •
Pokój (Carlsruhe) •

Poznań (Posen) •

Gniezno •

Lgd
•

Grodno •

R. Vistula

Białystok •

Węgrow •

WARSAW
Wilanów

Łowicz •
Nieborów

Kielce •

Pińczów •

Staszów •

Sandomierz •

Radzyń •
Podlaski

Ujazdów •

Lublin •

Kazimierz •

Chełm •

Zamość •

Podhorce •

P   O   L   A   N   D

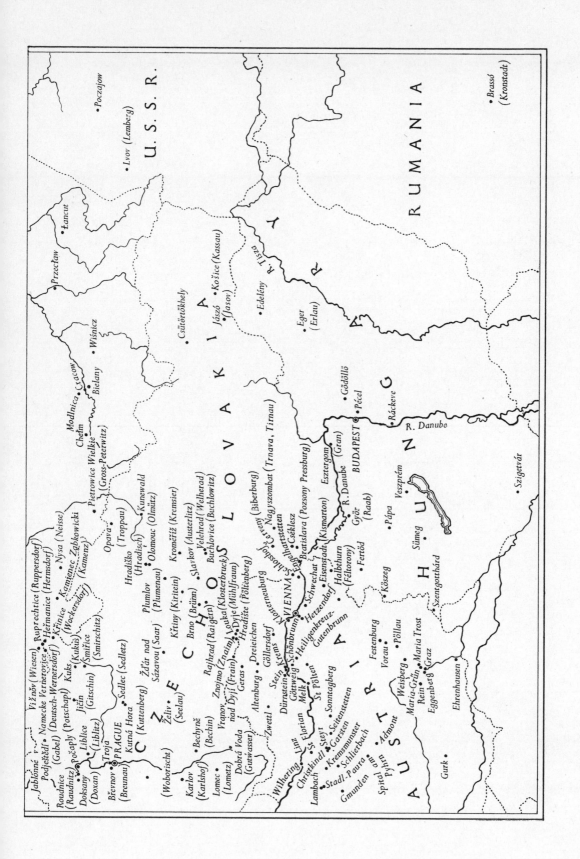

PART ONE

INTRODUCTION

CHAPTER I

CHARACTERISTICS AND ANTECEDENTS

THE Central European countries, although quite distinct from each other in character, developed a homogeneous climate in regard to art during the seventeenth and eighteenth centuries. The situation was determined by their acceptance of the Baroque, a late variety of the Renaissance style, which had originated in Italy. (In western and northern Europe it was considered degenerate and rejected.) There must have been fundamental reasons for this favourable climate: and indeed the cause was this. The roots of the new style grew out of the culmination reached at the point of transition from the Late Gothic to the Renaissance style, in the sixteenth century, when Late Gothic motifs and mood were not yet lost in the new classical forms. During these decades the eyes of all Europe turned to towns like Nuremberg, Augsburg, Basel, Budapest, Cracow. The attitude towards culture became akin in a large area of Central Europe. Albrecht Dürer and Hans Holbein took their places alongside the great masters of the Renaissance. Such favourable conditions never occurred again. The cause of this flowering was to a considerable extent the fact that, from the middle of the fourteenth century onwards, certain forces which had been latent in the middle class came gradually into the open, and became a decisive factor in politics and culture. This period of specially favourable conditions lasted for two hundred years, until the middle of the sixteenth century.

Already since the end of the fourteenth century the individual had grown in importance within the community of the masons' lodges and guilds. One indication of this is the fact that the trade name 'Parlier' (i.e. foreman) became the family name 'Parler'. This higher evaluation of the individual occurred especially when, as at Prague, there was contact with the Italian Renaissance. Peter Parler of Schwäbisch Gmünd, who in 1353 started work in the capital, was permitted to place his own bust in the triforium gallery of St Veit's Cathedral alongside those of the imperial family and of the most distinguished men in Bohemia. The protractor on his cap indicates his profession as an architect; that he excelled equally as a sculptor is proved by this bust. In this we see, moreover, a decisive step along the road to realism, a quality quite foreign to the earlier fourteenth century – though in Prague, of course, it was in part a matter of the *genius loci*; in the seventeenth century the realistic portraiture of Karel Škréta stands supreme in Central Europe. The combination of architect and sculptor is also fully in keeping with the Baroque, as in the case of such eminent artists as Fischer von Erlach and Schlüter. The

I

importance of individualism and the liberation of forces latent in the middle class were not lost during the Baroque period, in spite of its feudal character. The artist who had sprung from the artisan class was drawn into the aristocratic sphere.

Another Baroque heritage from the Renaissance is the profound love of nature, a quality which always belongs to the last phases of epochs. It can indeed be considered a general law of art that severe, abstract forms develop into more relaxed, livelier, softer, and more picturesque ones, that is forms as nature offers them. And it is in late phases only that the specific artistic genius of Central European countries finds its fullest expression. One such climax is reached in the Baroque from the eighties of the seventeenth century onwards, another in the Rococo of the mid eighteenth century. This love of nature, however, must not be confounded with naturalism. Nature is allowed entry into artistic creation – that is all; just as vegetation is allowed entry even into the most formal layout of a garden. It is most conspicuous in the interiors of hall-churches with their piers and rib-vaulting, which give you the impression of finding yourself in a forest (Plate 1). That such an effect was really aimed at is shown by the type of decoration used at church festivals, when whole wagon-loads of greenery were brought to adorn the churches, and indeed the taste for it was so strong that around 1500 the ribs were transformed to look like branches of trees. The same was done in the following centuries in the realm of plaster decoration. Such feeling for nature is also met in other north European countries, especially in England and France; but to begin with it was Germany that took the lead. Concurrently, that is also in the first half of the sixteenth century, Albrecht Altdorfer, working in the Danube area, was the first to paint forests without any mythological or religious context.

The love of nature was closely allied to a trend towards motion. Under Benedikt Ried (d. 1534) the principle of double-curved ribs was established. This resulted in an interlacing in the vaults almost as of living and moving organisms. Here, too, the flow of light enhances the spatial effect. Ried completed St Barbara at Kutná Hora (Kuttenberg) in 1481–1548.[1] On the outside are three concave-sided pyramid roofs in a row. Standing as they do in a mining district, their shapes recall the forms of dumps or charcoal kilns. Wide, light galleries in the interior increase the alternating effect of space. Without capitals, the ribs spring directly from the piers and start intersecting at the springing-line. They have lost all functional purpose: some are cut into by the shafts attached to the piers and project at the bottom like the severed branches of a tree; others are completely detached from the vaults. There can be no doubt that in the seventeenth century they served as the model for the Bohemian–Gothic Revival of Santin Aichl. Master Benedikt was regarded as an authority also in Saxony and Silesia; in 1519 he was chairman of the masons' conference in Annaberg.

The achievements of the first two decades of the sixteenth century could be regarded with pride. In Saxony the discovery of silver in the Erzgebirge brought a new impetus to a country long stagnant in architecture. The finest church of this fresh start was erected at Annaberg,[2] close to the summit of the Erzgebirge. As in Bohemia, the piers support undulating rib-vaults that form large rosettes over each bay. The octagonal piers themselves, with their concave surfaces, resemble the stems of plants. A broad belt between two tiers of windows runs round the interior to form a strong horizontal, as the Renaissance was to demand it. This time it is in the shape of a wall-passage that runs very beautifully round the internal buttress-piers. On the hundred panels of its balustrade is depicted a continuous series of biblical scenes, a motif which continued in country churches into the eighteenth century. It was taken over from Franconia, which, with Swabia, is the true source of the Late Gothic style.

Nuremberg occupied the leading place. A strongly developed civic sense had gradually raised the city to an importance beyond that of the electoral and ecclesiastical capitals. The people of Nuremberg were prepared to recognize no one but the emperor as their overlord, and the emperors always favoured the city. Charles IV had intervened personally from Prague in the struggle between the patricians and the artisans, and had reintroduced the rule of the old-established families. In this way a more aristocratic, less narrow spirit prevailed among the Nuremberg bourgeoisie than in any other city at the time, and the petty self-interest of the guild was not dominant. Every artist was free to work as a painter or sculptor. The Emperor Maximilian was the great patron of the artists of Nuremberg and Augsburg, and he fully recognized the value of their work; the relationship with the Hohenzollern, however, who as imperial burgraves dominated the town from their castle, was not friendly. Helped by trade with Venice, the power of the city increased. Knowledge of Italian art came through the merchants, who inspired the artists – one example is the relation of Willibald Pirkheimer to Dürer – and encouraged them to travel to the south and to purchase some of its treasures through them. Of the many qualities attributed at that time to the Franconians, wit – which was synonymous with ability, intelligence, insight – was the one most highly prized. This is strikingly evident in the work of Dürer. He developed a close understanding of nature, and in this respect, too, stands on the threshold of the new age. In addition, a feeling for robust three-dimensionality and incisive line are Franconian traits. Nuremberg, side by side with Lübeck and Ulm, was the leading centre for wood-carving – the finest achievements in this field were the carved altarpieces. The town was also a great centre of wood-block printing, which began to flourish in the fifteenth century.

In the seventeenth and eighteenth centuries, however, Nuremberg lost her cultural supremacy. Her citizens ceased to be patrons of art, and the patronage passed partly to the margraves of Ansbach and Bayreuth and partly to the bishops of Bamberg and Würzburg. As a result of the stagnation that followed, the city retained her splendid early buildings, and until the destruction caused by the Second World War an incredible amount of Gothic art survived amidst the dense conglomeration of houses. There was so much, in fact, that it had been impossible to inventorize and record it fully, which means that a large proportion has been lost without even a drawing or photograph, though the rich treasures of the churches and the collections of the Germanisches Nationalmuseum were saved. In reconstructing the town after the war, the problem of harmonizing a modern way of building with the spirit of the medieval town has not, unfortunately, been successfully solved, except for the excellent way in which the rebuilding of the churches has been handled: the newly built ashlar rib-vaults in St Lorenz, for instance, are masterly.

A comparison between the choirs of St Sebaldus and St Lorenz shows the tenacity of the tradition of the hall-church. They are almost identical in form. Their steep roofs rise high above the older basilican western limbs, harmonizing fully with the roofs of the private houses around.[3] St Sebaldus, built in 1360–79, shows the Nuremberg style in the sculptural effect of the semicircular shafts. The windows are not yet divided horizontally, and Gothic verticalism is still fully preserved. St Lorenz on the other hand, built eighty years later, between 1439 and 1477, shows the transition to the Late Gothic style completed. The sculptural articulation is replaced by a linear network which is further accentuated in the furnishings, for instance in the tabernacle by Adam Kraft (Plate 1). Through two rows of wide windows light falls into the radiating chapels. The horizontal division is emphasized by the wall passages running round the internal buttresses. The carving of the panels of the balustrade is in ever-varied mouchette forms. Nor is the lierne-vaulting evenly distributed: it is massed at individual points into a tight network, leaving other surfaces comparatively free. Originally the effects were certainly further enhanced by painting; the ribs, for example, were frequently painted red, and this made them look like arteries in the body of the building.

The public buildings were in no way inferior to the churches – in their impressive strength they even surpassed them. For example, a combination of high, steep roofs with sturdy compact towers forms the most effective motif of the Imperial Stables (1494–5). They flank the elongated structure of the Burg, situated on the ridge of the hills to form a crown above the roofs of the houses in the town below. As a matter of fact, the commission came from the civic authorities, and their master mason Hans Behaim the Elder built a whole series of similar, vigorous buildings such as the customs house, the weigh-house, parts of the town hall, and the Hospital of the Holy Ghost.[4] Care for old people and for the sick and the poor was quite in keeping with the attitude of the middle classes in medieval times. The finest works of art were donated for the decoration of such buildings; Dürer's *Allerheiligenbild* ('All Saints'), for instance, was given to the Zwölfbrüderhaus (House of the Twelve Brothers), an almshouse for twelve decrepit old men.

All building was centralized under local authority, another development pointing into the future. In the fifteenth century, the administrative head was called master of the works and was drawn from the families who were eligible as councillors.[5] The immediate subordinate of the master of the works was a technician, the *Schaffe* (steward), also called the *Anschicker* ('disposer'), who supervised the workmen. The growing importance of this job is revealed in the changing status of the Behaim family. The son of Hans Behaim, mason and *Schaffer*, achieved the position and title of master mason to the City and Country of Nuremberg, a direct forerunner of the municipal architects of the future.

The homogeneous picture presented by Nuremberg at that time was not attained in other cities. The Gothic tendency to stress the structural members, as seen in the corners of the oriel window of the town hall of Sterzing (Vipiteno; completed in 1524; Plate 4A), was in striking contrast to the later trend, when decoration was lavished over festoons and all kinds of pediments, gables, and similar crowning motifs. In the castles

4

the stress on structural members is more and more combined with rich interlacing. The Albrechtsburg above Meissen is a good example. It was built from 1470 onwards by Arnold von Westfalen for the brothers Elector Ernst and Duke Albrecht of Saxony, and in it practical needs were subordinated to the representational function of the building. The old system of a two-naved hall was retained. Following the French pattern, the stone masons concentrated mainly on the decoration of the newel staircase in front of the façade. Inside the rooms, the eye is immediately caught by the varied forms of the rib-vaulting (Plate 2A). Piers and columns have no place intthis system – the ribs rise directly from the floor in concave curves. Ornament is incompatible with such a style. The taste of the time is expressed in the pendant arches of the tracery, which emphasize the con-cave as opposed to the convex shape favoured in early periods; but in the fully developed Baroque there was to be the same interest in elaborate interlacing. It reflects that fascina-tion with an unreal dream-world which is a basic feature of German art.

The popularity of large glazed surfaces in the western areas was shared in north Germany. This gave its character to the most beautiful secular building of the Rhine-land, the Gürzenich at Cologne (Plate 2B), the old 'Tanzhaus', built in 1437–44 for the wealthy Cologne families. Originally the ground floor was more closed and thus effectively contrasted with the upper floor, where the high windows with stone mul-lions and transoms are inserted into a system of shafts, battlements, and corner turrets. The proud character of the medieval Rhineland is well expressed in the severity of the groundwork, but it is given a finely articulated vivacity by the elegant polished forms of the diagonally set coats-of-arms and the double mouldings of the panels. Formerly two separate roofs were visible behind the battlements. Their shapes were less obtrusive than the more recent, higher roof. Each of the two floors contained a two-naved hall about 180 by 70 feet in size, rising to a height of over 20 feet. The wealth of the western towns is also shown in their town halls. The one at Brunswick rivals the churches in its profusion of tracery work and its crowning pinnacles.

Lübeck was the artistic centre of the northern brick area, and it was also of importance for Scandinavian art. Here, too, the middle-class spirit was the driving force. Through the Hanseatic League, an international note of civic pride was given to the buildings. At the same time, builders were interested also in a world that was really quite foreign to the Hanseatic world, that of the Teutonic Order. The struggle for supremacy in the Baltic had taught even the merchants to be fighters. The town halls vied with the churches, and their imposing fronts express the bold, independent spirit of the middle classes. The councillors' order of the day, which began with Mass, made it convenient that the town hall should lie close to the church. Moreover, special meetings were held in the church. Thus it was customary to place two elongated one-room buildings, town hall and market hall, side by side, separated by a narrow court. Since the need for structural honesty was not yet felt, high show walls were erected which concealed the roof. Blind arcades with pointed arches shaped like windows, and circular openings are among the chief beauties of the Lübeck Town Hall,[6] built in 1315. The front terminated with a strong horizontal. This stern simplicity did not satisfy the Late Gothic taste, how-ever, and in 1435 three perky little turrets with tall spires were added. The Christian humility of an age of religion had been replaced by worldly pride in the achievement of international status.

In the brick area the houses are resplendent with stepped gables (Plate 3). The verticalism characteristic of the Gothic spirit suited brick, and it enabled the architect to give free rein to his imagination. The elevation of a gable was one of the main examination tests for masons. The hall, which ran the whole length of the house, with a little parlour built at half-height into part of it and spiral staircases, were the core of the house, and their popularity continued undiminished into the Baroque. The hall was taken over from the Lower Saxon farmhouse, the primitive germ of all north German housing.

★

Gothic art is related to the art of the seventeenth and eighteenth centuries only in as far as they both participate in certain general characteristics of Central European art, which, at the end of the Middle Ages, was largely determined by the development in Germany. The art of the Renaissance on the other hand is the direct forerunner of Baroque and Rococo and forms one continuous sequence with them. The idea of a new beginning characterizes the early sixteenth century. For this renewal, the age returned to two sources of culture common to all Europe: classical antiquity and the Early Christian period, combining these with the study of nature. Man now considered himself the centre of the world. His physical being was the measure of all things and even of architecture. It gave optimism and sensuous awareness to the age, especially in Central Europe. The tragic note, also an aspect of the time, which was struck in Italy by Michelangelo and in England by Shakespeare, is found in Central Europe only in the art of Schlüter, in spite of the succession of tragedies which befell these countries. In the seventeenth century Leibniz defined the two forces that dominated humanity as nature and grace: man's intimate link with nature was recognized, and his salvation seen by Protestants and Catholics alike as an act of divine mercy. Thus, beginning with the work of Dürer, although German art continued to produce the finest representations of nature, it could also create images of divine mercy, for instance Petel's figure of the Redeemer at Augsburg (Plate 19B). Leibniz's view of a pre-established harmony is that of the Renaissance – here lies the origin of the *Gesamtkunstwerk* of the Baroque. With all the power of his intellect, Leibniz had forced the concept of world unity on an age that was for ever threatened with disruption. In doing so, he continued to envisage humanity as a whole, with its needs and essential desires, but he never in all his intellectual efforts abandoned irrational values.

A second basic principle of his philosophy can also already be found in the Renaissance, above all in Michelangelo. In his chief architectural work in Rome, the centrally planned church of St Peter's, Michelangelo infused dynamic energy into all the individual parts. This was continued to a very much greater degree in the Baroque: Leibniz regarded the ultimate particles of the body as formative atoms containing energy; Böhme speaks of a power in struggle. This dynamic character of Baroque art is most clearly revealed in the atlantes figures. Gothic art, too, had had its own dynamism; but the quality became progressively weaker and only re-emerged in the transition to the Baroque.

A further fundamental feature of the Renaissance was an early form of scepticism, which dominated the thought first of Descartes and later of Bayle. The idea of faith as truth was not, generally speaking, attacked, but for all its activity, religion had been forced on to the defensive. As a result, especially during the Counter Reformation, this activity frequently assumed the guise of propaganda. Once again religion won, thanks in no small measure to the aid of art: but it was forced to adopt many worldly elements.

In the field of architecture, greater importance came to be attached to the building of palaces than had been the case in medieval times; but religious buildings were still required, and church architecture remained equally valid and is just as fruitful as secular architecture.

The impulse to revive forms of classical antiquity came from Italy. Since, however, Late Gothic art retained its vitality in Central Europe, the Renaissance acted only as a stimulus to such painters as Dürer and Grünewald, without tearing up their roots in the native soil. The principle of clarity and harmony of proportions was not accepted, for the Germans loved variety to the point of tangled confusion. For that reason they began by adopting Renaissance ornament derived from wood-engravings. Italian masters who laid claim to higher achievements only penetrated to any extent into Germany in the second half of the sixteenth century.

The doors were opened to them earlier in the eastern lands, as far as the Russian borders. The first country to receive them was Hungary, whose court was closely linked with Italy. Even in the fifteenth century the houses in Buda (Ofen) were laid out 'ad italicorum aedificiorum symmetriam'. Many Italian artists were appointed under Matthias Corvinus, and his architect Chimenti Camiccio lived in Hungary for fourteen years, from 1480 to 1494. Unfortunately only a few fragments of the royal palace in Buda, the chief work of the Hungarian Renaissance, remain. The chapel of Archbishop Thomas of Bakócz in the cathedral of Esztergom (Gran),[7] built in 1507 in the form of a Greek cross, is the first surviving building to bear witness to the complete adoption of the Florentine Renaissance. The example was also followed farther afield, in Poland. The king, when he was still Prince Sigismund, had spent eight years in the castle of Buda, and at the beginning of the sixteenth century the first arcaded court north of the Alps was built on the Wawel in Cracow.[8] In the upper gallery tall, mast-shaped supports carry the overhanging roof – a Gothic element. From 1518 on, after King Sigismund's marriage to Bona Sforza of Milan, the ties with Italy became closer, and the king commissioned Bartolomeo Berecci to build the Sigismund Chapel in the cathedral (1519– 33),[9] where, probably to suit the queen's taste, Lombard ornament covered the elegant pilaster shafts; but at Esztergom the broad, fluted Corinthian pilasters that filled the interior followed the classic norm. Evidently the Renaissance ideal was not so firmly rooted in Poland as it was in Hungary.

Silesia was the earliest of the German–Slavonic countries to adopt the forms of the Renaissance – in the portal to the vestry at Wrocław (Breslau), a town which had begun to flourish through a widely spread carrying-trade. In 1547 the master mason Jacob Parler from Milan began a magnificent Renaissance palace at Brzeg (Brieg), where a profusion of the richest decoration covers the portal, in effective contrast to the jointed ashlar wall.

South Germany accepted the Renaissance only with hesitation, owing to the fact that around 1520 Gothic art and architecture, especially in Nuremberg, was still vigorous. Even after the middle of the century the Emperor Ferdinand I (1556–64) still granted the Germans a fuller understanding of church building than the Italians. On the other hand classical Roman forms found their way into painting and the graphic arts as early as the beginning of the century. They came via Augsburg, a city that had chosen Venice as her model, and one which, through her maritime trade and her warehouses, was in close contact with the great cultural centres of the day. Among artists, Hans Holbein the Elder and Hans Burgkmair had introduced Renaissance buildings into their pictures already in the first decade of the sixteenth century; but for Hans Holbein the Younger it was from the beginning a matter of course that he could draw the nude, produce balanced compositions, and was familiar with linear perspective as demanded by the Renaissance. As for architecture, the first Renaissance building in Germany, the Fugger Chapel in the church of St Anne at Augsburg,[10] was built in 1509–18. An order of pilasters in Venetian forms, placed in front of the walls at the west end of the Gothic basilica below the organ gallery, served as frames for four relief panels. The way in which two orders were superimposed, however, betrays the fact that their true purpose had not yet been grasped. Indeed, initially the Renaissance forms served purely decorative purposes, and the lierne-vaulting is far more characteristic of the interior effect than are the pilasters.

Not until the 1530s was it possible for Italians under the patronage of the princes seriously to compete with the local masons. But in 1537 the dukes of Wittelsbach invited a colony of masons to Landshut, where they built their Residenz[11] as an Italian Renaissance palace, and the German masons were forced to conform to the Italian High Renaissance style in the parts that they built.

Even more outstanding is the Belvedere in Prague (Plate 5). In 1534 the Emperor Ferdinand I invited Italian masons to his court, including the sculptor Paolo della Stella, and in collaboration with German masters such as Bonifacius Wolmuet, they built the Belvedere (1535–60), a banqueting house surrounded by an arcade, in the gardens of the Hradschin. The influence of buildings such as the Palazzo della Ragione in Padua is obvious. For the details, such as the windows, the wood-cuts from Serlio's *Architettura* (1537), the first illustrated treatise on Italian architecture, must have been used as models. The slender arcade recalls the Tuscan Early Renaissance of a hundred years earlier. The articulation of the upper storey is also of great beauty, with niches inserted between the windows and harmonizing with the windows because of their aedicular frames. The elegance of the elevation is continued in the S-shaped outline of the roof. The delicate rhythms of the building had a considerable effect on the pavilion motif in German architecture, and it had worthy successors in the new buildings of Dresden. On the whole, however, heavy, block-like shapes were more in keeping with Bohemian taste, as they can be seen in the Schwarzenberg Palace[12] on the Hradschin. The diamond ashlaring imitated in sgraffito work, and the strongly projecting cornice with its concave moulding, give the appearance of an Italian cloak thrown round the Nordic body. A contrast to this Italism is formed by the gay, dynamic gables with their superstructures, which recall the popularity in the east of the so-called Polish Parapet with its up-curving skyline.

The Renaissance also penetrated into Saxony during the thirties; but the Wettins gave preference to German stone masons and sculptors over the Italians, so that the St George's Gate of the Dresden Schloss,[13] begun in 1530, shows all the characteristics of a German Renaissance. The portal itself, it is true, is a piece of Milanese decorative sculpture, but on the inside the branches of a tree emerge, while on the outside the gate and oriel window are placed asymmetrically. These features show the ease of the German Early Renaissance, which would not be bound by rigid rules. The stepped gables, too, are derived from the Gothic house. The gate, which unfortunately survives only as a fragment, once had brilliant decoration in the form of a frieze of the Dance of Death. George the Bearded, who commissioned the gatehouse and championed the Old Faith to the last in the Lutheranized country, here wanted to see represented in relief on the outside the consequences of the Fall of Man, and on the inside Redemption through Christ. St Michael, chosen by the Catholics as their champion, appeared at the top of the gable.

Even more important architecturally was the hall range of Schloss Hartenfels near Torgau (1532–44; Plate 4B), built by Konrad Krebs for the Protestant branch of the Wettin family. Here the functional character of the Gothic style is much more in evidence than in the St George's Gate. The vertical thrust of the slender stair-tower opening between pillars creates a dramatic tension in its relationship to the long horizontal lines of the cornices and of the upper gallery. Such tensions are unusual in the German Renaissance. In this, the spiral staircase at Torgau differs also from the earlier staircase in the château of Blois (1515–19), which makes a much heavier impression. Unfortunately the dormer windows of the roofs, a favourite motif in the central German Renaissance, have not survived, and as a result the compactness of the elevation has been lost. Immediately afterwards, Krebs was employed by Joachim II, elector of Brandenburg, to work with Kaspar Theiss on the Berlin Schloss, where at the request of the elector he built a stair-turret similar to the one at Torgau (1537–40). At that time the territories belonging to the House of Wettin were culturally ahead of Brandenburg.

Gradually the Renaissance principle of symmetry began to dominate the remodelling of medieval castles. In the middle of the sixteenth century Duke Moritz had a comprehensive enlargement carried out at the Dresden Schloss[14] consisting of a square court with stair-towers in the angles. The medieval corner tower came to stand in the centre of the front facing the Elbe and received a projection on the court side with three-storeyed arcades. The innate German love of decoration, which is the expression of a powerful urge to play, can be seen not only in the sculpture, but also in the sgraffito ornament which covered all the surfaces. Italian masons were called in for the sgraffito work, as they were most familiar with this form of art, but the work was controlled by Germans: Hans Dehn-Rothfelser was the Surveyor General and Caspar Vogt of Wierandt, fortifications engineer and director of the arsenal, the architect.

Far-reaching changes in the whole organization of building were already beginning to appear. During the Middle Ages the lodges of the cathedrals had dominated. They were religious in character, and accordingly bishops frequently designed buildings, fully conscious of the power of art for purely ecclesiastical purposes. Now, with the dawn of the Age of Absolutism, noblemen were beginning to regard the designing of buildings as an employment suitable to their rank. In Dresden this view was held by Count Rochus von Linar (1525–96), a native of Tuscany and a representative of the Italian art of fortification. When criticized by his peers for being something like a master mason, he replied: 'Certainly, not only do I profess to be one, but I regard it as a great honour and distinction and cannot give sufficient thanks to Our Lord for such grace considering how rare are such gifts and skill, yet how highly necessary in war and peace, and also so honourable and praiseworthy in a knight and soldier that in Italy not only the nobility but also the most distinguished princes and gentlemen study them and willingly offer their services in them to their own glory.'

These examples proved fruitful, especially in Central Europe. They also explain the fact that, mainly in Protestant countries, church building was sponsored by the princes. Accordingly, their development was dependent on the palace chapels. For the Augustus-burg[15] (1568–73, by Hieronymus Lotter of Leipzig), which was built for the Elector Augustus with an eye to defence on the summit of a hill, Erhard van der Meer built a chapel with three tiers of galleries and attached demi-columns. Acoustic rather than optical considerations were the main concern of the interior. Outwardly the chapel is no longer recognizable as such. The age of Church government by the lay ruler had dawned, by no means to the advantage of the Church; for she tended to lose sight of her social responsibilities. A further disadvantage lay in the fact that, with the growth of schools, divine service, too, acquired a school-like character. Faith was demonstrated in a rational way – a contradiction of its very essence. In the palace chapel of Schmal-kalden[16] the pulpit and organ were built above the altar, thus expressing the unity of the whole service. The fabric of the chapel was completed in 1586. This arrangement was advantageous for symmetry in the layout of the interior and for that reason was retained until the eighteenth century.

Among the Catholics, the plan of a church with galleries was frequently adopted by the Jesuits, for instance in the university church at Würzburg (1582–91),[17] which was meant to represent the Catholic as against the Protestant ideal: yet it, too, has galleries in three tiers, and the influence of the Roman humanist school can only be seen in the strict application of orders of demi-columns, and in the existence of an apse. Only very rarely did the Catholics adopt the pulpit–altar combination.

From a national point of view the best results were to be expected where the new forms could mingle with a Late Gothic art of still recent vitality so as to achieve a German transformation of the Renaissance. This is true of Dürer. Subsequently it applies to Franconia, where the middle classes frequently retained political supremacy. The town hall at Rothenburg on the Tauber is the finest product of the period around 1570 in Franconia (Plate 6A). It already contains one fundamental feature of the Baroque: the desire for all-embracing unity. So the town hall was built in such a way as to harmonize with the general plan of the town. The dual problem arising from the corner site at Rothenburg – the need for a gabled front and that for an elongated body – was solved by linking the two by an oriel window at the corner. The contrast between the high gabled front and the turreted front of the old town hall close by is counteracted by the monumental arrangement of the long façade, with a centrally placed stair-tower and attached arcades. The common centre for both parts, the corner oriel is further stressed by the steps. Inside, it also forms the real centre. The assembly hall lies immediately behind the oriel, and only the windows adjacent to the oriel are grouped in threes and fours. This arrangement of the gabled front was carried through with complete disregard for the central axis; the corner is the focal point of the building, though it does not disturb the rhythm as a whole. The spectator may be only subconsciously aware of this, but he will certainly select a spot opposite the corner, with the view in all directions on to the town, from which to take photographs. All details are powerfully articulated. One senses the approach of the heroic age, when Central Europe was preparing to plunge into the Thirty Years War. Nowhere do we find mere imitation of the classical canons, but the horizontal axes are vigorously stressed in the cornices. Leonhard Weidmann, later master mason to the city of Rothenburg, who submitted a plan in 1568 and worked as a stone mason on the building, is regarded as the real creator of the town hall.

The growing interest in town planning led to a series of beautifully laid out towns the fame of which (apart from Rothenburg, Dinkelsbühl for example) spread beyond the boundaries of Germany. Photographs showing Queen Victoria driving in a carriage drawn by four horses through these towns are still preserved in the local inns. To be successful many qualities were necessary: understanding of the peculiarities and beauty of the landscape; the retention of native types, whose charm afforded a certain variety; particular viewpoints, which have to appear at the right distances; and, more than anything else, the art of organizing space, for which there were no valid rules of relationships, but only individual intuition, which changed from place to place. Above all, in Alpine districts, it produced most beautiful arcaded courts, e.g. in Schloss Porcia near Spittal in Carinthia. Often, a poetic mood seems to be expressed. In the town of Sterzing (Vipiteno) on the Brenner, for example, this creates an ideal setting for Goethe's Faust. Dr Faustus was still alive when the town hall of Sterzing was built (Plate 4A).

The Schloss of Heidelberg is the most popular building of the German Renaissance and the chief source of the layman's ideas of it, although so many varied influences met there that the achievement is less well defined than in civic buildings. These latter are more firmly rooted in tradition, and therefore the new orientation could prevail less than in the palaces, sponsored by the courts. The Glass Hall Range, begun in 1544, is the earliest Renaissance part of the Schloss of Heidelberg, with its plain surfaces and the clear-cut motif of a three-storeyed arcaded hall of sturdy Romanesque proportions, inserted as a quiet zone between the lively façades of the neighbouring buildings. There are other occasions, too, when the appearance of classical forms was intended to evoke memories of their first penetration north of the Alps. In popular art especially, the experience of the Renaissance was reflected in an imitation of Romanesque forms. The principle of planning in fixed units was another feature that was bound to lead back to the Romanesque foundations of Central European art. Planning by triangulation and quadrangulation had been the tradition in the Gothic lodges. Beginning with the triangle and the square, the plans were usually developed diagonally across the corners, while the principle 'unitas in pluralitate' was decisive. But there was no conscious effort to make these basic rules obvious. The Gothic builder wanted to convey that feeling of mystery which he himself felt in the presence of the works of the Creator. The Renaissance, on the other hand, like the Romanesque, allowed the carefully calculated proportions to be clearly revealed. Moreover, the mythological world in which they lived was expressed in the decoration. The Elector Ottheinrich, who, during the four years of his reign (1556–9), built the range of the castle that bears his name, made great efforts to spread humanist scholarship by enlarging the university, the schools in his country, and his own library. So the façade of his new range of the palace, with its figures of deities in the niches, its caryatids and termini, victories, naiads, and putti, was also meant to conjure up the world of the south (Plate 6B).[18] It goes further in this than any other façade of the period. Everywhere north Italian influence is in evidence, but it is always turned in the northern manner. Decoration later allowed the welcome introduction of humour and satire, features that were only permitted to a very restricted degree in Christian art, because they were (among other objections) in conflict with its educational mission. Satire was, however, a basic aspect of the Renaissance, which had witnessed the collapse of so many apparently permanent human standards; and as for the Baroque, its very name suggests such a basis as its starting point. This trait is scarcely perceptible in the Schloss at Heidelberg, which was built at a time when admiration for the newly discovered world of Antiquity was just at its height. The outlook of the Mannerists was needed before a sense of contrasts, often unconsciously exaggerated, could evoke the satirical spirit.

The façade of the Ottheinrichsbau was determined by the sculptor rather than by the architect. Although the proportions are obviously balanced, there is no consideration of strictly architectural demands. The large portal with its rich composition as a triumphal arch was compressed into an area the same size as the lateral twin panels. Nor is there a vestibule behind the portal to respond to the breadth of the façade. Similarly the lower windows are unduly elongated, to suit the excessive height of the ground floor. In comparison their pediments are over-heavy. Pilasters alternate with niches for statues. Above these are brackets to indicate that for functional reasons here also there should be pilasters. The sculptural details, however, are extremely fine, so that the façade as a whole is of great beauty. It is the expression of an age with strong aesthetic leanings but as yet no Renaissance tradition of its own. Characteristically enough there does not seem to have been any clear idea about the upper termination of the façade. A high double gable was added in the following period, which must have looked extremely incongruous.

Among the artists working on the building the name of the sculptor Alexander Colin of Malines is recorded. During the succeeding period, Netherlandish artists working in the Mannerist style evolved capricious forms of ornament; this is inaugurated by Colin on the Ottheinrich Range, where it appears, however, only in the strapwork flanking the sculptured top of the portal. It is not known who did the designs for the front from which Colin worked. Likely candidates are the architects Kaspar Fischer and Jacob Leyder, who were both present when the contract was signed.

The Friedrich Range, dating from the early seventeenth century, shows how the same problems were solved with greater dynamic consistency but less artistry during the heroic age (Plate 15B).[19] Yet the influence of the Ottheinrich Range continued, as can be seen in the impressive Haus zum Ritter at Heidelberg.[20] On the other hand the work done in 1561–9 on the Plassenburg near Kulmbach by the same Fischer for the Hohen-zollern was fundamentally different and much more German in character.[21] Arcades on short sturdy pillars open in the two upper storeys. All the surfaces are completely covered with relief. Fischer showed excellent judgement in treating the pillars as decorated strips rather than as attached orders – a study of the orders was fortunately at his time not yet part of the architect's compulsory equipment. But buildings that followed Italian patterns accurately were also built during the same years; for instance the porch of Cologne Town Hall,[22] erected in 1569–73 by Wilhelm Vernucken, which shows the influence of Cornelis Floris, architect of the town hall at Antwerp.

In addition to these there are also such fantastic and thoroughly German buildings as the façade of the Hexenburgermeisterhaus at Lemgo of 1571.[23] The two lower floors have bay windows on the left and the right, yet the entrance and archway is not in the middle. Furthermore, in the four upper floors the windows with their framing half-columns are not axially placed but all out of line, so that on each floor one half-column always stands below the central axis of the window above. The gable is higher than the whole underneath part and its steps are framed by large volutes. The architect was evidently determined to keep his independence and resist the tyranny of rules.

In the north half-timber work continued to flourish, as it did in Westphalia and Hesse. The structural character of the building was retained and the world of antiquity only represented in popular form in the carvings.

In the political field the experience of the first half of the sixteenth century was ignored. The attitudes of the Catholics and Protestants hardened, and moreover the ruling classes as a whole turned a blind eye to social problems. However, Bishop Julius Echter von Mespelbrunn's achievements during the forty-four years of his reign at Würzburg, from 1573 to 1617, form an exception. He invited the Jesuits to Würzburg, founded the university there in 1582, and between 1576 and 1585 built a large hospital as well as many similar institutions throughout his diocese. His work was continued later by the Schönborn family. Himself one of the most militant supporters of the Counter Reformation, he was fully aware of the greatness of the artistic achievements of the old Church. As a result, the first Gothic Revival is associated with his buildings, and the Julius Style retained its importance even into the later seventeenth century, which was due to the vigorous way in which Antonio Petrini adapted its forms to the Baroque. This was in direct opposition to Renaissance theory, which was based on a passionate rejection of the Gothic; but people had by now grown accustomed to being involved in conflicts of ideas. Michelangelo was the first out-and-out secessionist. After him much lesser personalities, for instance Wendel Dietterlin, dared to work out conflicting systems of their own, although not with the urgency that impelled Michel-angelo. Opposition led to sharply divided camps. The effects of this situation were felt even into the twentieth century, and the unity underlying Renaissance, Mannerism, and Baroque was overlooked. Mannerism and the Baroque both developed out of the Renaissance, working to a different set of rules but retaining the basic principles. There is nothing inconsistent in extending, as the nineteenth century did, the stylistic concept of the Renaissance to cover the whole of the three hundred years from the sixteenth to the eighteenth centuries, and in placing the end of the Gothic at about 1500 and of the Renaissance at about 1780 and the outbreak of the French Revolution; for Mannerism and Baroque had the same aims as the Renaissance, though they used different means and also differed in mood. Both forms were necessary within their respective circles in order to achieve a final unity of style common to all. The Renaissance could not have achieved it alone, because its artistic endeavours were individual in character.

The subsequent unity of form was the concomitant of a renewal of feudalism, as it came about during the sixteenth century and as it repelled the middle classes, especially in central Germany. Artificial ceremonial, subservience to etiquette, affectation, un-natural proportions dictated by convention became the rule in a hidebound way of life. Attitudes and actions were lifted out of the realm of everyday life into a world of theatre and opera, and it is characteristic that e.g. in Vienna the passion for the theatre even exceeded the passion to build. It was not, however, a question of pure formalism as opposed to spiritual content, even though with the rise of Mannerism among Michel-angelo's followers preliminary signs of a spiritual impoverishment did appear. Reacting against the unique nature of his genius, they turned his highly personal means of expression into baser coin so as to be able to appear like Michelangelo without actually being like him, and primarily to establish their membership of an inner circle. But the moment genuine artists appeared once more, they infused a new spirit into these school recipes. Tintoretto and El Greco, whose elongated figures with small heads betray their Mannerist origin, could successfully interpret in ever new and convincing ways the old established biblical scenes. Artists on the other hand who turned again to nature, as they did in the Netherlands, had to abandon the Mannerist idiom.

In spite of this, Mannerist supremacy, especially in Central Europe, was by no means confined to the second half of the sixteenth century, but continued into the third quarter of the seventeenth century. For Mannerism, which was fundamentally anthro-pocentric, figural representations were of primary importance, but ornament, too, offered a fruitful field (cf. p. 32). Owing to its self-imposed restrictions Mannerism could only share to a limited degree the full-blooded vitality that was the mainspring of the Baroque. Baroque differs from Mannerism in the way that Rubens differs from Tintoretto. But the deeper justification of Mannerism lay in its awareness of the tragic aspect of life. In addition, its love of the unexpected, of paradox and surprise, made it the chief vehicle for satire. The tendency of Mannerism to intensify forms was further increased in the Baroque, whose dynamic character in fact made this a necessity. In architecture, such elements as columns and pillars were continued by projecting pieces of entablature, the pediments were broken, and the fragments of pediments rolled inward. Something similar had been attempted in Late Antiquity, and so Baroque architects could refer to that period in order to refute classicist critics. Impelled by this dynamic energy, the walls of Baroque buildings curved outwards or inwards. The favourite plan was the oval, because it always implies movement. Giant orders were used to unite several storeys and so to unify the body of the building. The prototypes were the buildings of Rome, especially those of Michelangelo, which could be studied in countless engravings. As opposed to the Italian Baroque, however, which frequently appears uncouth and shows unmistakable evidence of decline when compared with the styles of the preceding centuries, the Central European Baroque retains greater freshness, is less inclined to exaggerate, and often seems to be so obvious an expression of national character that it could be appreciated by all and even merge with folk art: farmhouses for instance preserved elements of the Baroque style until far into the nineteenth century. Moreover, liberty to develop the most diverse forms allowed architecture to compete with sculpture and painting in evoking particular moods that can move us like music. The aim was to achieve complete unity, the closest harmony between all the parts, no one of which was conceivable as an isolated thing. Thus the Baroque even embraced the layout of gardens and the planning of towns. But the aim of the Baroque, as has been said, could perhaps be best realized in the world of theatre and opera, a world in which men move on a loftier plane, directed only by the dictates of art. There everything that was dear to the Baroque could be cultivated: masquerade, surprise, mime, fantastic disguise, symbolism, allegory. In such an atmosphere the imagination was bound to be stimulated, as it always is when things are merely suggested or have double or hidden meanings. Similar stimuli were offered to the imagination in the fleeting sketch as against the finished picture. In sketching and designing for theatrical sets, the Italians were the undisputed masters.

The libraries of the period offer the best examples of the unifying, all-embracing principle of the Baroque. The idea of a cosmos comprised in the range of books was at the back of the minds of designers. It was expressed in the compact shape of the rooms, the centralizing effect of vaults and domes, and the ceiling paintings interpreting symbolically the forces of nature and of the spiritual world. The duality in all education which tries to be both Christian and humanist was revealed in the unconcerned juxtaposition of mythological and biblical figures and scenes. The same principles governed the arrangement of the books according to subject. With their fine leather bindings and gold lettering, they seem to be the walls of the rooms, while the shelves on which they stand tend to recede and disappear. In this way the Baroque library symbolizes in the highest sense the world of the intellect. Also the room had to be serene and lively, so as to rouse in the reader the heightened, optimistic mood which belongs to the Baroque and even more to the Rococo. This world was expressed in shining, light colours and subtle nuances of tone, flowing smoothly into each other, without hard contrasts and not in monochrome. The pattern of this character of colours and light was France.

The sensuous richness and warmth of the Baroque caused it to flourish first and foremost in Catholic countries, but the Protestant contribution, too, was considerable. It was more sober in work for churches – this hardly needs saying – but it exhibits the same quality, especially when the religious element is absent, as for instance in the decoration of palaces. Yet it is never dull. During the later seventeenth and eighteenth centuries religious differences had lessened progressively. Surviving descriptions show that when, for instance, the Protestant margrave of Bayreuth visited his Catholic neighbour, the bishop of Bamberg, he felt quite at home. In middle-class society the differences were more marked, especially in Huguenot circles; for the Huguenots never forgot their French culture and were fully conscious of its superiority.

It cannot be denied that, with the exception of the south, Central European Baroque and Rococo painting never produced anything to compare with the western achievements. In the field of architecture, on the other hand, they maintained an independent position, and their sculpture was at least equal to that of France. This suggests that the Central European artist could express himself most perfectly in sculpture. Architecture too was approached in the spirit of the sculptor, and because they also were first and foremost sculptors he was ready to accept the architecture of Michelangelo and his followers down to Bernini and Borromini. The supreme results were obtained in Central Europe by the collaboration of sculptor and architect: one example is the Dresden Zwinger.

During the Rococo French influence increased. In France the disposition and decoration of the interiors was dictated by *convenance* and strict aesthetic principles, and also the correspondence between the decoration and the function of a room. Central European art, which tended to be heavy, accepted to its advantage the lighter and more graceful forms of France, but, free from the French pressure of theory, Rococo art in Central Europe could acquire a much more universal validity and, instead of being exclusively subservient to court circles, could flourish also in churches and among the people. In addition the eighteenth century saw a great flowering of poetry and music in Central European countries. Further, the destructive tendencies that led to the revolution in France were less at work. The bourgeoisie, which had been kept down for so long, resumed its cultural responsibilities, and this led for instance to an increase in the importance of the graphic arts. It is a curious fact that, whereas at the beginning of the sixteenth century German prints had been the best in Europe, very little was achieved in this field during the Baroque. Austrian and south German painters found tremendous scope for their talent in the decoration of ceilings and vaults, but there were no similar opportunities for graphic artists. This was probably due to the architectural and sculptural character of the Baroque. On the other hand, there were exceptional possibilities in the field of interior decoration; for instance Abraham Röntgen and his son David, cabinet makers from Herrnhut, the centre of Pietism, influenced by the Chippendale style, acquired an international reputation during the eighteenth century as makers of furniture. This is all the more remarkable in view of their Herrnhut piety – which is difficult to reconcile with the luxury of costly dressing tables. And Germany invented and developed porcelain and in this field succeeded in establishing leadership for the whole of Europe.

Seen as a whole, the Central European Baroque remained in a sense fragmentary. This is due partly to the premature deaths of some of the greatest artists, such as Elsheimer and Liss, who would have been able to hold their own with the best of the Dutch and Flemish painters; more damaging, however, was the oppressed state of the middle classes, due to unfortunate political circumstances, which made it very rare for artists to enjoy the proud security of life in a flourishing community.

Criticism of Mannerism and the Baroque was directed at first against the use of ornament on façades. As early as 1615, under the influence of his visit to Italy, Inigo Jones wrote in his sketch book the famous passage: 'And to saie trew the composed ornaments the wch Proceed out of ye aboundance of dessigners and wear brought in by Michill Angell and his followers in my oppignion do not well in sollid Architecture and ye fasciati of houses, but in gardens logis stucco or ornaments of chimnies peeces or in the inner parts of houses thos compositiones are of necessity to be yoused. For as outwarly every wyse man carrieth a graviti in Publicke Places, whear ther is nothing els looked for, yet inwardly hath his imaginacy set on fire, and sumtimes licenciously flying out, as nature his sealf doeth often tymes stravagantly, to dellight, amase us sumtimes mouf us to laughter, sumtimes to contemplation and horror, so in architecture ye outward ornaments oft [ought] to be sollid, proporsionable according to the rulles, masculine and unaffected.'[24] This opposition was not directed against forms that attempt to interpret a state of mind, but only against their use in the wrong place. In Germany Elias Holl's buildings at Augsburg suggest that he held similar views at the same time.

Over and above this, however, two further ideas are implicit in Inigo Jones's words: the importance that ornament had acquired, and the increased desire to express by means of architecture individual feeling. Both aims were well established in the tendencies that led to the Baroque, particularly in Mannerism. Following the urge for unity, during the Early Baroque architecture and ornament link up and interpenetrate; on the other hand the opposition to the Baroque made use of the principle of *convenance*, a basic principle of French architectural theory, and divided the spheres of competence, allotting to each its proper place. Two poles were thus established: unification and division. As for the Baroque, its anthropocentric credo could not admit as objectionable even the interpretation of a window as the wide-open jaws of a hideous monster; the passer-by saw the eyes of the monster leering at him above the window, and in this way felt himself drawn into the world of fantasy by which he liked to be surrounded. In respect of such effects, Germany did not lag behind Italy or the Netherlands. Würzburg buildings of the seventeenth century are a veritable mine of grotesque masks, particularly the bosses of the Marienberg fortifications. Baroque art shared with Mannerism the aim of infusing human emotions into architecture, but rose from mere satire into the realms of tragedy and mythology.

In France and England scarcely any interest was aroused by the German versions of the Renaissance. The only exception is the work of the eccentric Wendel Dietterlin, who occasionally seems to have fascinated English architects. Moreover Elsheimer was admired and appreciated by the Flemish, Liss by the Italians. But the fact that French and Netherlandish architects were widely employed to build in Central Europe, whereas the great German architects, such as Fischer von Erlach and Neumann, were not employed for buildings abroad, clearly shows the verdict passed on them.

The activity of Italian architects in southern Central Europe and of Netherlandish architects in the north was often the result of family relationships, for instance those between the House of Hohenzollern and the House of Orange. Whereas the Italians were the recognized authorities on palace and church architecture, the Netherlanders were regarded as experts on middle-class domestic building. It was they who introduced to the north houses with plain brick walls and garlands beneath the windows, but with sandstone cornices and shallow pilasters. Their unbroken gables weigh heavily on the façades, but the roofs still rise steeply above them. Netherlandish classicism also found its way into German theory, the connecting link here being Sturm's books (cf. p. 226).

French eighteenth-century styles were almost without exception transformed in Central Europe; only in the Rhineland were French buildings erected by architects from France called in by the various rulers. But the effects of French models were profound and stimulating and made themselves felt over the whole country. Proof of this is the popularity of the mansard roof (which derives its name from François Mansart). In the middle of the seventeenth century the municipal authorities had begun to ban high, steep roofs.

As frequently happens, condemnation by the theorists was not borne out in practice. The French would never have obtained their dominant position if they had not also undergone the influence of the Baroque. Indeed in his article in the *Mercure de France* of 1754/5, Cochin praises the Baroque architects for introducing a freer, more serene style of architecture. Even behind his criticisms, admiration can be felt. Cochin says of Meissonier that he was the first to destroy the old-established use of straight lines, that everywhere he twisted and inflated the cornices and bent them up and down in all directions, that he was brilliantly successful in turning the hardest of marble cornices to accord gracefully with the bizarre subtlety of cartouches, and that he introduced the charming S-forms used everywhere so that his drawings were in effect only one vast combination of this form in every possible way. Nevertheless in another essay in which he expresses his own academic point of view, Cochin concludes: 'Il n'y a que l'angle droit qui puisse faire un bon effet.'

French criticism of German buildings even extended to the palaces of kings themselves steeped in French culture: thus Voltaire said of Sanssouci that it was built fifty years too late. In Germany, too, critical voices were raised as early as the beginning of the eighteenth century. When Joseph Emanuel Fischer von Erlach was given his appointment, the Lord Chamberlain stated in the decree of 19 June 1722 that the architecture of the day had deviated all too much from the Roman way of building.[25] In the 1740s, as a result of the hostile criticism of local architects expressed in an anonymous pamphlet, the Roman architect Gaetano Chiaveri had to ensure the support of the Saxon royal family in order to be justified in employing his fully Baroque style. The anonymous writer stressed the fact that Baroque forms were in contradiction to the nature of things, and gave as an example columns merging with the pilasters into the wall behind and cornices jutting out to top them. His ideas were clearly based on French principles. First and foremost he condemned the diagonal placing of the church, because it was the negation of the principle of symmetry.

Strangely enough the new ideas were even spread by architects who had not abandoned the Rococo style in their own work. An example is the Dresden architect Friedrich August Krubsacius. In his *Betrachtungen über den wahren Geschmack der Alten in der Baukunst* ('Reflections on the true taste of the Ancients in the art of Building'), published in 1747, Krubsacius says: 'The noblest structure, man, the perfect proportions and graceful symmetry of his figure, were the first standard for architectural inventions.' He considered clear articulation of the members to be the one essential and proper decoration for buildings and called the intrusion of shell-work and other freaks illogical. He condemned curved gables, projections, corner pilasters, blind arcades, and broken rooflines. Yet, however greatly he was influenced by French theory, he did not accept the 'architecture françoise' as his rule, but regarded Italian architecture as the only one to be taken wholly seriously. Even Cuvilliés's Residenz Theatre in Munich, the greatest masterpiece of the Bavarian Rococo, was condemned immediately after its erection in 1751–3. When in 1753 Cuvilliés sought an increase in salary on the strength of his many years' successful service the reply was: 'Nothing is known of Herr Cuvilliés's "Meritten" (merits), apart from a mannered opera house.'[26]

The very term Baroque is a derogatory one. Presumably it derives from the Portuguese word *barroco*, meaning irregularly rounded, and applied to pearls of imperfect shape. As early as 1570 the term was used in Italian burlesque and satire to designate strange, bizarre, or ridiculous ideas. Then, as the political hostility to feudalism increased during the second half of the eighteenth century, the character of moral depravity, attributed to anything that is against nature, came to be associated with the word. This interpretation was familiarized by Winckelmann (1717–68). Even in his very first essay, the *Reflections on the Imitation of the Works of the Greeks*, he had laid down the direction to be followed in future. In Dresden in 1748 Winckelmann met Adam Friedrich Oeser, who had even earlier been inspired by the new ideas of classicism when he studied under Georg Raphael Donner in Vienna. Imitation of the Greeks and their 'noble simplicity and calm greatness' was Winckelmann's message. Naturally this changed outlook brought about a reduction in the formal repertoire that had been evolved during the Baroque. Something new arose, but as it was not directly descended from the national tradition, it lacked creative power. It is true that the styles derived from the Renaissance were not evolved in Central Europe either; they were, however, introduced by Romance nations in which something of the civilization of antiquity had survived and which at the same time were akin to the Central Europeans and kept up continuous contact with them. Nothing of this sort applied to Greek culture. It was put across purely by native poets and scholars. Its supreme values made it part of the patrimony of the educated but never part of everybody's life – as the Renaissance must have been, or else it could not have retained its vitality for more than three centuries. In his excellent interpretation of the Baroque Benz writes: 'These qualities of inexplicably rich creative impetus yet utter remoteness as a style of life must seem a lost paradise to us who come later.'[27]

So the derogatory attitude to Baroque and Rococo could not last. The rehabilitation began in France, i.e. in the country where opposition had been strongest. Once again, as in the seventeenth century, it was the attractive personality of Rubens that paved the way for an understanding of the Baroque. Delacroix was the pioneer. But the Neo-Baroque of the nineteenth century, which was the art of the Second Empire, was never really sincere and remained superficial and imitative. No matter how hard we may try to be fair to this nineteenth-century revival, there is little chance that it will ever again be appreciated – the note of insincerity is too obvious. Successful as were the efforts of individual artists such as Menzel to revitalize the world of the Baroque and of the Rococo, we cannot but regret that Menzel in particular did not apply his genius more exclusively to the great tasks of his own day. The attempts of scholars and collectors to appreciate the inherent values of the Baroque were on the other hand more justified. In 1887 Cornelius Gurlitt began his series of studies of Baroque architecture with a history of the Baroque in Italy. This was followed in 1888 by his history of the Baroque and Rococo in France and in 1889 by the history of the Baroque and Rococo in Germany. The Baroque, not even now by any means exhaustively studied, has remained a favourite topic for German art historians.

Yet it remains in the end unlikely that the English will ever be able to appreciate the Central European Baroque, as long as they keep to books alone. Its striving for unity links it so closely with the character of the peoples and with the scenery of the countries that a direct and intensive study on the spot is necessary fully to experience it. One single subject of universal applicability would be enough, provided it is studied sufficiently intensely, never for instance forgetting music as an art, whether the subject be Austrian ceiling paintings of the eighteenth century or upper Bavarian churches and abbeys or country houses and their gardens in the Main area or the Baroque art of Prague or the work of Andreas Schlüter.

CHAPTER 2

SPECIAL CONDITIONS

Historical Background

IT has already been said that the seventeenth and eighteenth centuries are an age of monarchies growing in power and importance. The focal point of this development, into which Central European art and architecture were of course drawn, was Paris. Here, Richelieu had laid the foundation for the absolute monarchy of Louis XIV by ceasing to summon the *états généraux*; the comparable step in the cultural field was the institution of the Académie Française in 1635. But Central Europe could not develop such a cultural centre on account of the never-ending dissensions among the various states. These were the outcome of its geographical position. During the Middle Ages the antagonism between Germans and Czechs prevented Prague from becoming a centre capable of setting a standard for the whole Empire; and in the seventeenth and eighteenth centuries the influence of Vienna, the centre of Catholic power, could reach only to the Prussian frontier, for the expansion of the Counter Reformation had been limited by Swedish support for Protestantism, which had thus been able to maintain its leading position in the north. This being so, there were, apart from Paris, three more magnets attracting Central European patrons and artists: Rome, Antwerp, and Amsterdam, according to whether an area was Catholic or Protestant. However, a clear division into Catholic and Protestant countries was impossible – there were far too many sovereign states, down to the free imperial cities. It is true that Leibniz, who strongly believed in unity, had been able in 1700 to achieve the establishment of the Academy of Science in Berlin; but his efforts to found academies in other capitals as well had remained vain. So the importance of Paris as the prime educational centre continued to grow. In the second half of the eighteenth century England, with London, also exerted a strong cultural attraction, and the work of Shakespeare became a powerful stimulus; French art and literature on the other hand was considered too formal, and French influence suffered a decline. In the eighteenth century, universal agreement existed only in admiration for Greek art, and in the field of architecture Palladio's work was equally universally accepted as the supreme model.

During the seventeenth century, owing to this passion for foreign art, Central Europe experienced a veritable invasion of artists and architects from Italy and the Netherlands. In the eighteenth century the same applied to France. Yet national styles did develop in Central Europe, in spite of all the perilous effects of political disruption and the predominance of foreign ways. This was not only due to native talent; the existence of innumerable small centres also favoured the cultivation of regional individuality, just as had been the case in Italy, and this regionalism helped to counterbalance convention and uniformity. The wealth of artistic expression thus developed makes compression into one volume a hazardous task. What can have been the sources of such abundance? The simplest answer is the most probable one: an all-pervading love of art.

Around the year 1600 the Empire, in contrast to France and England, was politically disabled by the fact that no ruler appeared of the calibre of Henri IV in France and Elizabeth I in England to reconcile the conflicting parties and at the same time increase the authority of the Crown. The power of the emperor was strictly limited by its commitment to the diet which from 1663 onwards sat permanently at Regensburg. This might have had a beneficial effect, if the diet had been governed by common national ideals; as it was, the rupture between a Catholic and a Protestant Germany likewise split the three councils of the diet: the electors, the princes, and the free cities. Among the larger countries within the Empire, Austria and Bavaria were on the Catholic side, as of course were also the bishops with, at their head, the electors of Mainz, Trier, and Cologne, the archbishop of Salzburg, and the bishops of Würzburg, Bamberg, Hildesheim, and Münster. The Protestant side was represented by the electors of Saxony and Prussia, the dukes of Württemberg, Brunswick-Lüneburg and Wolfenbüttel, Hanover, Mecklenburg, and Oldenburg, the Palatinate, and the landgravate of Hesse; but even within the Protestant ranks the Lutherans and the Calvinists fought one another passionately. Although the Emperor Rudolph II (1576–1612) wanted a reconciliation and made an attempt to unite the opposing powers by means of the common cause of a war against the Turks, he was unable to concentrate on this political aim, for his cultural and artistic interests absorbed too much of his time and energy. These interests of course benefited his own capital, Prague, enormously.

The imperial power – which had fallen to the house of Habsburg in the sixteenth century – had as its foundation a large area comprising not only the alpine territories but in addition Bohemia, Moravia, Silesia, and much of south-western Germany, e.g. the Breisgau. However, here, too, the religious differences had disastrous consequences. The most threatening elements of conflict developed under the emperor's own jurisdiction, in Bohemia. In 1609 the 'States', that is the Bohemian parliament, had extorted from him a charter conceding religious freedom to both confessions; yet the struggle continued, and under his successor, the Emperor Matthias, came out into the open. The immediate cause of the outbreak of the Thirty Years War was the brutal act of the Protestant rebels in hurling two Catholic councillors, Martiniz and Slawata, out of the windows of the Hradschin, the imperial castle. Of the champions of Catholicism, the two most determined, the Emperor Ferdinand II and Maximilian, duke of Bavaria, made common cause. Their army under the command of Johann Count Tilly won the battle of the White Mountain on 8 November 1620, against the Protestant troops of Frederick, Elector Palatine. Neither could Christian IV, King of Denmark, and now the head of the Protestants, resist the conquering imperial generals Tilly, Wallenstein, and Pappenheim. It was not until the Swedish king, Gustavus II Adolphus, intervened in 1630 that the northern countries began to get the upper hand, and luck then remained with the Protestants until Gustavus Adolphus died in the battle of Lützen. As the war dragged on, and especially after the entry of France into the combat, its aim shifted more and more towards the acquisition of new territories. Finally, after prolonged and terrible devastations of the German lands, the Peace of Westphalia was signed at Münster in 1648. It favoured to a substantial degree the expansion of France and Sweden, that is the foreign powers; the concept of a superterritorial Germany did not regain importance until after the imperial general Montecucculi had defeated the Turks at St Gotthard on the Raab and then after the heroic defence of Vienna against the Turks and the relief of the city by a German–Polish army in 1683.

It was in consequence of these events that the arts began to revive. Only now could the Baroque style evolve fully, almost a hundred years later than in Italy and Flanders. The feeling of elation was heightened by the victories of Prince Eugene of Savoy, especially the conquest of Belgrade in 1717. However, at the same time Austria's leading position in the Empire began to be impaired by the development of Prussia towards absolutism. In 1675 Frederick William, the so-called Great Elector, had triumphed at Fehrbellin over the Swedes, who, as allies of Louis XIV, had invaded Germany. The imperial army on the other hand was not able to prevent French conquests and devastations on the Rhine, such as the destruction of Heidelberg, Mannheim, Speyer, and Worms. The decisive rise of Prussia took place somewhat later, however, at the time of Frederick II, who reigned from 1740 to 1786 and who wrested Silesia from the Empire. He maintained its possession in three wars against Austria, France, and Russia and crushed the hegemony of Saxony, who had sided with Austria. In 1697 Augustus the Strong of Saxony had won the Polish crown; the most brilliant period of Saxony ensued and continued under his son Augustus III. However, in the military defeat inflicted by Frederick II Saxony lost Poland and with it her wealth and glamour. Austria on the other hand, by means of a settlement with Hungary, preserved her powerful position in spite of the defeat of the Empress Maria Theresa (1740–80) by the Prussians, and the ensuing reforms in all fields of administration, of finance, and of education helped her to recover. Her fame was not built on conquests, like that of Frederick II, but on the well-being of her subjects.[1] The settlement with Hungary and the loss of Silesia, however, were bound to lead to a shift of the centre of gravity of the Habsburg Empire to the south-east.

Economics, Arts, and Letters

A long period of peace before the outbreak of the Thirty Years War had allowed the Central European countries to grow strong economically and administratively. Under the leadership of Augsburg and the Fuggers and Welsers, south German trade formed part of that growing European capitalism which had come into being in the fifteenth and sixteenth centuries. In other parts of Germany trading companies sprang up too, e.g. at Nuremberg, Frankfurt, Hamburg, Danzig, and Breslau, and the Leipzig Fair became the most famous in Germany because of its relations with Silesia and Poland. The governments of the many states within the Empire fostered mining, agriculture, fruit-growing, mill-building, and the textile industry; at the head of this movement was Saxony, under the exemplary administration of the Elector Augustus, known as 'Father

Augustus' (1526–86). On the other hand, in the decades immediately before the Thirty Years War a certain decline set in, caused by the Dutch and English East Indian trade, by the incipient colonial power of these two countries, and by their industrial development. As a result, the Hanseatic League lost its importance; as a league of mere towns, it could not maintain its status against whole countries and the increasing power of their rulers.

As wealth grew, luxury spread and morality declined, as in the Renaissance. Italo-Netherlandish Mannerism with its excessive eroticism offered it a rich soil in art, especially at the German courts. Drinking, the great vice of the time, possessed all classes down to the servants. As a sense of national unity was lacking, the affectation of foreign ways spread far and wide. On the other hand, criticism also made itself heard almost at once, and to re-establish faith in the 'mother-tongue of German heroes', Ludwig of Anhalt founded in 1617 at Weimar the 'Fruchtbringende Gesellschaft des edlen Palmen-ordens' (Fruit-bearing Society of the Noble Order of the Palm Tree), in imitation of the Florentine Accademia della Crusca of 1582. The situation was, however, aggravated by the Thirty Years War, and in his great novel *The Adventurous Simplicissimus*, Hans Jacob Christoffel von Grimmelshausen (1625–76) held up a mirror to his nation. As a result of the terrible devastation of the country prosperity gave way to extreme poverty, especially in the countryside, exposed defenceless to a dissolute soldiery. However, industry, the quality which, according to Leibniz, predominates in the German character, will never be defeated, and so Germany put her hand to the task of reconstruction, in spite of economic collapse, the unlimited egoism of the governments and all classes of society, and the immense loss of moral and cultural values. The sufferings of the war brought out a depth of feeling in the best of the nation such as had hardly ever appeared before. The songs of the 'Trutznachtigal' (The Defiant Nightingale) by Friedrich von Spee s.j. (1591–1635) and the hymns of the Lutheran minister Paul Gerhardt (1607–76) in their fervour and depth have never been surpassed and rarely equalled in German religious poetry. The music of Heinrich Schütz, too, Bach's great precursor, who had been appointed Kapellmeister to the court at Dresden in 1618, matured during the decades of the war.

The great rise which set in after the war had its roots in this period of introspection. Finally, at the end of the century, the sense of national unity emerged, and this at last furnished the prerequisite for the flourishing of the Central European Baroque. Admittedly this sense of national unity could as yet only work within the compass of a culture centred in courts and the nobility. Absolutism proper prevailed only in Prussia and a certain influence of the 'States' was retained in the other regions. The most unpleasant aspect of this outwardly brilliant world was the arrogant behaviour of the nobility towards the townsmen, who submitted with servility, and the oppression and exploitation of the peasants, who sank into hereditary serfdom, especially in the east. In the south, class distinctions were less marked: among the religious orders, for instance, which were of outstanding importance for the unfolding of the Baroque, the middle class predominated.

Mercantilism, taken over from France, now flourished. By the systematic exploitation of mineral resources and protective tariffs the governments of the different countries tried to increase exports and restrict imports. The formation of standing armies helped to rationalize military affairs, too, and in this Prussia took the lead. Meanwhile the political rulers sought to justify their increased power by cultivating music, the arts, and architecture, and in 1667 one of the first opera houses built in Germany, and certainly up to that time the most beautiful, was inaugurated at Dresden. At the time all opera was Italian, but long experience of it provided a firm basis when German opera flowered during the eighteenth century. However, music dependent on courts has its limitations, and the greatest German music, that of Bach, belongs to the middle-class Leipzig milieu. Nor were the encouragement of science, letters, and poetry the concern of the courts during the Baroque proper. This began to change, however, with Sophia Charlotte of Brunswick, later Queen of Prussia. She was the protectress of Leibniz, who said of her that she wanted to fathom the 'why of the why'. After her death Leibniz found a new patron in Prince Eugene, whose wonderful library was purchased by the Emperor Charles VI; the magnificent architecture of the Imperial Library in Vienna, which forms part of the palace, symbolizes an Austrian culture grounded in spiritual and intellectual forces (Plates 50B and 51). We find this same trait in Frederick II of Prussia, even if it has to be admitted that the only culture that he acknowledged was French. The French reciprocated his admiration and were the first to bestow upon him the title 'the Great'. Voltaire was his friend for a time. But Frederick did not appreciate German poetry, which was then beginning to flourish, and treated the members of his Academy in just as arbitrary a manner as he did the artists whom he employed.

The Religious Foundations

In the seventeenth century the religious foundations of culture were still intact. Catholicism reached its zenith in France as an outcome of the Counter Reformation, and the Catholic countries in Central Europe followed. The Jesuits fought for papal authority and were at pains to catch up with the Protestants in the field of learning. Lutheranism had grown torpid at the universities of Leipzig and Wittenberg; but Pietism led to a re-birth by its fervent introspection and its faith in practising Christianity. A centre arose at Halle through the activities of August Hermann Francke and the institutions founded by him. In the Brunswick area a union between Catholics and Protestants was striven for, notably by the theologian Calixtus (1586–1656) at the University of Helmstedt, and Leibniz, who lived in Hanover from 1676 to 1716. This attitude is clearly expressed in the medievalism of Paul Francke's church of St Mary at Wolfenbüttel. On the other hand the Pietists of Herrnhut expressed their ideal of brotherhood in simple churches, simple cemeteries, and estates of small houses. The mystic revival among both Protestants and Catholics is reflected in the inspired paintings of Willmann and Škréta in Silesian and Bohemian abbeys.

That the Catholic Church consciously used the arts to make converts was an outcome of her inherent need of a tangible form that could be apprehended by the senses. In Germany she accepted the optimistic, joyous attitude of a Rubens. The degree to which the faithful were willing to accept the sensuous beauty of form as representing a religious meaning is evident in the angels painted and carved by Baroque artists. They often re-call ballet-dancers more than anything. In this connexion three factors must be borne in mind. Firstly, ecclesiastical Baroque was closely related to humanism and the spirit of antiquity, and so pagan deities could be favourite subjects in the decoration of monastic libraries and bishops' palaces. Secondly, life itself was permeated by a theatrical spirit. And thirdly, the will of the artists was decisive, and they refused to renounce their favourite themes. We know that theologians did occasionally object. When commis-sioning sculpture for the garden of his abbey the abbot of Admont wrote to Marx Schokotnigg that they were to be 'nit viel blos am Leib' (i.e. the nude body should not be too much exposed). The representation of the Holy Ghost as a beautiful youth, follow-ing the revelations of the Blessed Crescentia of Kaufbeuren (1682–1744), was forbidden by the pope in 1745 at the instigation of the bishops.

Protestants for whom the bible was the only source expressed their faith in altar-structures on which they depicted the Life of Christ with parallels to the Old Testament and symbolic allusions. The rulers of the established Church, or alternatively the feudal patrons, were often prominently shown as donors.[2] It was only natural that the principle 'Cuius regio, eius religio' should lead on the one hand to a secularization of the Church and on the other to an unjust severity on the part of the rulers; that such intolerance frequently had a paralysing effect on the best artists is shown by the life of Elias Holl, the eminent master-mason of Augsburg. In 1630, in the very middle of the Thirty Years War, an entry in his diary reads: 'I should have dearly loved to continue this building, but owing to the unfortunate [Counter] Reformation and our resulting dis-missal from office I have had to let another take over the building, although I was master mason to the city until now, and, as was required of me, erected many fine buildings in my country. Patientia!' When Gustavus Adolphus captured the town in 1632, Holl was reinstated; but only three years later, when the Swedes were forced to withdraw, he lost his job again and finally, because he was unwilling to return to the Catholic Church. He died in 1646.

A still greater evil of misguided fanaticism was witch-hunting. It was indeed with funds derived from the confiscated property of witches who had been burnt to death that the magnificent palace at Aschaffenburg (Plate 13B) was built by the archbishop of Mainz. Often Protestant theologians were even worse than Catholic ones. A shining counter-example was given, however, by the Jesuit poet Friedrich von Spee (cf. p. 24), who, following experience gained as a confessor of reputed witches, started a passionate crusade against the attitude of the jurists, which involved him in bitter contention.

Intolerance came to a head in Louis XIV's fateful repeal of the Edict of Nantes in 1685. France herself and the whole Catholic Church suffered heavily through the result-ing emigration of the Huguenots and the embittered reaction of the Protestants. In Austria too the expulsion of the Protestants seriously undermined the strength of the country. Certain Lutheran countries were also affected, for instance Saxony, where the Huguenots fleeing from France after the repeal of the Edict of Nantes were not accepted, because they belonged to the Reformed Church. Thanks to the intelligent policy of the

Great Elector their emigration to Prussia was encouraged, however, and they proved of considerable assistance in the rise of the country to power. This intolerance of the seventeenth century made it easy for the rationalists of the later eighteenth century to undermine the foundations of religion. In the opinion of Lessing, an unbiased witness (writing in 1769), what the so-called 'Freedom of Berlin' amounted to was the liberty for all and sundry to express openly as many anti-religious stupidities as they pleased. In this respect, too, incidentally, the devout Empress Maria Theresa was the opposite of the Prussian king.

Ecclesiastical architecture not only showed an astonishing power of resistance, but indeed round about 1750 reached a climax in the magnificent works of Balthasar Neumann, Dominikus Zimmermann, and Johann Michael Fischer. Nor did the Church renounce its claim to universal validity, as is testified by the libraries of the Austrian and south German abbeys which, with the range of their books, co-ordinate all branches of learning in one grand system. Similarly also, it was not until the eighteenth century that the Protestants found a perfect architectural solution for their basic idea of 'Soli Deo' in the Frauenkirche in Dresden, in which the concepts of the central plan, the hall-church, and the church with tiers of galleries are fused.

Artists – Guilds – Academies

In contrast to conditions in France and England, the Baroque artist in Central Europe, to his own advantage, still had his roots in the crafts. He was apprenticed to a master for three to six years. A minimum age of twelve or in some cases of fourteen years and a proof of legitimacy were required for admission. At the end of his apprenticeship he became a journeyman, and remained in that position for many years. To become a master, the works he submitted had to be approved by the guild. Often he could only establish himself by marrying into an extant workshop. Many artists worked first in sculpture and then moved into architecture, a combination that was to prove a great asset in the formation of the Baroque; Fischer von Erlach, as mentioned before, was trained as a sculptor in his father's workshop at Graz. Schlüter, like Bernini, was equally eminent as a sculptor and as an architect. There were also other combinations: the painter–architect is represented by Longuelune, the painter–sculptor by Wenzinger.

Since the Baroque was based entirely on the Italian Renaissance, the artist was compelled to master mythology as well as Christian iconography: he had to understand the southern interest in the nude as well as the northern passion for expressive drapery, the Romance structural articulation as well as the freer, less rational approach of his native tradition. As a result prolonged visits to Italy became necessary. For example, during a ten years' stay Furttenbach (1591–1667) acquired a thorough knowledge of Italian architectural theory; Rottmayr worked from 1675 to 1688 in the workshop of Loth in Venice. At the same time Permoser spent fourteen years as a sculptor mainly in Florence. Others, such as Elsheimer and Liss, settled permanently in Italy. On occasion, however, artists such as Willmann would, like Rembrandt, confine their studies to journeys in the north in order to escape Romanist influence. During the Early Baroque, knowledge of

Italian art was spread by artists from the Netherlands, while travelling Italians diffused throughout Central Europe their art of casting in bronze, their stucco work, and their faith in symmetry in architecture. Frequently too Italian teams dominated artistic enterprises, until finally, at the end of the seventeenth century, a swing of the pendulum brought a revival of a German national art. When, in the eighteenth century, French art became the standard, Frenchmen and Belgians such as Longuelune, Silvestre, Pesne, and Cuvilliés found an outlet for many-sided activities at Central European courts.

During the seventeenth and eighteenth centuries the guilds were pushed more and more into the background, mainly through the growing influence of the academies. In addition, even more than the guilds, the cathedral lodges declined in importance, and in 1671 they were deprived of their jurisdiction over members. Earlier, many artists had tried to break away from the tyranny of the guilds by entering the service of a court. A career as gun-founder or officer in the Engineers, whether in connexion with road and bridge building or with fortification,[3] provided an opening for free artistic work, and princes, for instance Max Emanuel of Bavaria, sent their artists to Paris for long periods of study. Furthermore, the rank of officer raised the social standing of the artist. Some were even ennobled – this was especially frequent in Vienna. As a result, an artist or an architect could assume the way of life of the gentry – and this in its turn gave him a deeper understanding of his patron's commissions.

The academies, which provided a modern form of art education, had begun as private institutions, for instance in Nuremberg in 1662 and in Vienna in 1692. The first official academy in Germany was founded in 1699 in Berlin, on the example of Paris (1648) and Rome (1666). The Elector Frederick III appointed Schlüter as one of the directors. The Municipal Academy at Augsburg was declared a public institution in 1710, and under the joint direction of a Catholic and a Protestant grew to be a centre of art for Bavaria and Swabia. The Vienna Academy of Fine Arts, established in 1725, obtained a position of importance for the whole of Germany under the leadership of Donner and Moll. The guilds, however, though only temporarily, succeeded in the teeth of strong opposition in retaining the monopoly for the teaching of painting. Finally, in 1764, under its principal Christian Ludwig von Hagedorn, the newly created academy at Dresden became famous, and painting came to dominate the curriculum.

The Execution of Works of Art

The establishment of academies raised the study of art to university level. Entrance examinations were required. Drawing from plaster-casts from the antique and the live model was to equip the student to represent the nude (Plate 42). Theory was taught in courses of lectures on anatomy, perspective, geometry, and civil and military architecture. Joachim von Sandrart's *Teutsche Akademie der Bau, Bild und Mahlerey Künste* ('German Academy of the Arts of Building, Sculpture, and Painting') of 1675 and Andrea Pozzo's *Perspectivae Pictorum atque Architectorum* of 1706 formed the basis. At the same time the aim of the academies was to cultivate a truly classical taste, and this meant that they turned against the Baroque, which had been thriving in the workshops.

The guilds limited the number of apprentices if possible to one or two, of journeymen to two or three.[4] Considerable specialization often necessitated the co-operation of different workshops and artists for individual enterprises, e.g. the large altarpieces and the superstructures of funeral monuments.[5] Working hours varied between twelve and fifteen hours a day. During the building of the palace at Kempten, for instance, thirteen hours were prescribed by their guild for the teams of masons and decorators from the Vorarlberg. The hours were spread out as follows: 4 a.m. to 7, 8 to 12, 1 p.m. to 7. However the regulations and customs of the guilds, which were observed minutely, did offer a certain protection, though wages were relatively lower than they are today, and were sharply graded according to ability: for instance the masons building the Catholic church for the elector at Dresden, which was begun in 1738, received six Groschen (about sixpence) daily, the carpenters five, the hodmen three;[6] but for carving a capital in the same building the sculptor earned one hundred Taler (about £5), and Lorenzo Mattielli was paid 500 Taler for each of the double life-size figures of saints on the roof. In addition, this pampered artist received from the elector a yearly salary of 560 Taler (about £28), free quarters, stabling, 100 Taler for firewood, and 300 Taler for two horses. Mattielli was soon able to purchase a valuable estate at Pillnitz, near Dresden.[7]

Gradually increasing control enabled the state to exploit artistic production systematically and profitably. Clerks of work checked delivery, execution, and expenses for royal or municipal buildings and audited all the accounts. The Office of Works also checked up on private building enterprise. This led to an official architecture on an organized basis. The brilliant architectural output in the ecclesiastical principalities in the Rhine and Main areas was in the hands of one man, an outstanding architect, as it happened: Balthasar Neumann. Contracts for individual buildings were signed on the strength of drawings and models submitted, and for statues on that of models made in clay, plaster, wax, or wood. For frescoes, oil-sketches gave an idea of the colour scheme. Since the artist wished to stimulate the patron's appetite he generally took great pains with these sketches, which often surpassed the finished work.[8]

Materials were extremely important in Baroque art. Not only was the country ransacked and exploited for materials hitherto unused or found only in poor quality, but precious materials such as ivory were imported. The effect of plain stone was not always regarded as satisfactory, and it was whitewashed or painted over: the statues in the gardens of Veitshöchheim for instance were painted white with a small amount of gold, which gave them the appearance of large porcelain figures.

For Baroque art, linked so closely to the theatre, that is a world of make-believe, stucco, a cheap material that could be worked easily and at low cost, was an ideal medium for achieving rich decorative effects. Stucco work, at first an Italian speciality, later became very popular in upper Bavaria, and there was one particular place, Wessobrunn, where at times up to six hundred plasterers were living. According to what the architect required, the plasterers either followed his designs or made their own. Stucco marble also, which is what the Italians in England called *scagliola*, became indispensable, chiefly owing to its colour.

When, following the French example, building enterprises assumed a vast scale, the execution often proved to be slipshod. Also, inferior material was used to ape solid stone. Thus Duke Anton-Ulrich of Brunswick-Lüneburg commissioned the architect Hermann Korb to build the palace at Salzdahlum in half-timber work, imitating stone; but by the beginning of the nineteenth century this remarkable building was in ruins and had to be taken down. Towers, too, often collapsed, and of this the fate of Schlüter's Münzturm of the Royal Palace in Berlin (1702–6) provides a classic example. Then, from about the middle of the eighteenth century, mathematics was called in to help. In 1743 three Italian mathematicians tried to find by calculation the causes of some damage discovered in the dome of St Peter's in Rome and the measures necessary to redress it; and it was again an Italian, Gaetano Chiaveri, who estimated accurately the stability of the dome of the Frauenkirche at Dresden.[9]

What is especially admirable in Baroque artists is their skill in execution. In fresco-painting and stucco work in particular we find an admirable sureness of hand, inventiveness, and powers of improvisation; for the rapidly drying materials demanded a swift and faultless touch. Yet in spite of this and other signs of personal initiative, the works of the Baroque were based on rational numerical relations, just as those of the Italian Renaissance had been. The proportions were derived from what was known as the Orders of columns: the radius of the shaft of the columns at the bottom served as the module, and with the aid of quadrangulation and triangulation harmonious proportions were fixed. Nevertheless, both here and in the Orders there was a departure from Renaissance rules in so far as the single measurements were related less to the Orders than to the dimensions of the whole building. This was in keeping with the Baroque ideal of unity.[10]

The Patrons

The patron exerted a far-reaching influence on German art in the seventeenth and eighteenth centuries. This meant that art tended to have an aristocratic bias, and not until the end of the century was there any inclination to depict bourgeois life and the life of ordinary folk. During the Rococo, the nobleman still sought refuge in a mythological world that resembled a ballet, and this courtly and somewhat operatic attitude affected even religious subjects. Fortunately in the south German and Alpine abbeys the monks were mainly of peasant or bourgeois stock and so kept art close to native handicraft and popular feeling; but even so, during Mannerism and Baroque it was only in exceptional cases, Elsheimer's for instance, that the interpretation of ordinary life was imbued with that popular spirit which began to pervade contemporary German poetry. Before the Thirty Years War, it was only in the free imperial cities that it was possible for the bourgeoisie to rise to a position of influence on the arts. This was especially so in Augsburg and Nuremberg. In the capitals of the many large and small states, on the other hand, even a municipal building such as the Frauenkirche in Dresden had to be submitted to, and approved by, the Governor – whose good advice in the case in question added considerably to the success of the project (Plate 121, A and B).

From the time of the Renaissance even the practice of architecture had been regarded as 'honourable and glorious' for a member of the gentry or the army (cf. Count

Rochus of Linar, p. 10), and also a liberal education prepared aristocratic patrons for giving advice to artists and architects. An example of such a patron is Prince Karl Eusebius of Liechtenstein, who on 25 June 1681 wrote to his son John Adam Andreas:[11] 'You ought to become a perfect architect surpassing Michael Angello Buonarota, Jacomo Baroccio Daviniola [Vignola], who is our esteemed master, from whom we learned and accepted the system of the five Orders, Bernin, and others.' In his book on architecture, surviving in manuscript, he shows himself fully conversant with the current problems of Baroque building. A palace, he said, should be placed on an eminence 'so that, as soon as you open a window, you may enjoy the prospect of a wide landscape stretching in front of you'. His interest was focused entirely on Italian architecture: 'Welschlandt in denen Gebeun ubertrift die ganze Welt' (Italy surpasses the whole world in its buildings). Our people should not imitate the French pavilion system with its *corps de logis* and galleries, but the Italian 'Palatio in quadro'. He demands emphasis on axiality, an ample use of columns, and two projecting windows on every façade. In his opinion staircases with a continuous flight of stairs are superior to those with three intermediate landings, such as were usual in France. Churches were to have detached columns on the façades and also along the sides, chapels should be oval in shape and well lit. He even considered the necessity of the bases of domes over cruciform plans over-lapping into the arms of the cross, as was actually done later by Balthasar Neumann in the Schönborn Chapel at Würzburg. Often a relationship of mutual confidence was established between patron and architect, and occasionally this even developed into friendship. Thus on 7 February 1696 the Bohemian Count Andreas of Kaunitz wrote: 'We mourn with all our hearts the honourable Mr Matthieu; God rest his soul. It will be some time before we again have such a man in Prague. I could wish that the above mentioned Martinelli be given substantial employment or benefices so that he may remain permanently in Vienna or elsewhere in the Crown Lands. Otherwise it is to be feared that we may lose him too.'[12]

It is an established fact that Augustus the Strong and Frederick II played an active part in the planning of their buildings and made their own sketches.[13] But whereas the Saxon elector and Polish king yielded to the superior genius of his artists, the Prussian monarch persisted in his ideas, so that he was continually involved in conflicts with his architects (p. 271).

Ornament

In the following chapters we shall study the highest achievements of German art during the seventeenth and eighteenth centuries – though the highest achievements are not necessarily those most fully revealing the character of an age; for the great artist often finds himself in opposition to the trends of his period and to those who swim with the tide. They represent the age as it is; the solitary genius shows what it could be. Some preliminary remarks may therefore be helpful for an understanding of the background against which such great achievements stand out; and they are to deal with ornament, because the changing ornamental forms of a period express the general character even down to changes of mere fashions.

Towards the end of the sixteenth century ornament began to acquire an ever-increasing importance in the development of European art as a whole. Not the least of the reasons for this was the development of strapwork, in which the leading part was played by the Netherlands. Later, following the general tendency towards a more 'painterly' taste, came the soft *Ohrmuschel* or auricular style of about 1620 and after, characterized by forms like parts of conch shells or the gristle of the ear. Introduced by Cornelis Floris and Vredeman de Vries, trained at Antwerp, strapwork came to Germany about 1580. South German fresco-painting, which had flourished since the days of Holbein, provided an uninhibited playground for a freely roving artistic fantasy; and a climax was reached in the startling inventions of the painter Wendel Dietterlin of Strasbourg (1550/1–99) as seen in his collection of prints *Architectura und Austheilung der V Seulen*, published in 1593, 1594, and 1595. Significantly enough, in accordance with the title of his book, Dietterlin always took the canon of the five Orders as his starting point; but he then interpreted the individual Orders – even in windows, portals, fireplaces, fountains, and funeral monuments – in a florid, tempestuous, and eclectic manner, thereby, as he writes, 'revealing the usefulness and entertainment of such an art' (Plate 7).

Later on Augsburg again took the lead in the person of Lucas Kilian (1579–1637), a friend of Elias Holl (pp. 36-8), whose *Neues Gradesca Büchlein* and *Schildbüchlein* were published in 1607 and 1610. The 'grotesques' of Late Roman art offered unlimited scope for capricious and exuberant invention, and Kilian's cartouches, impelled by some inner force, curve out, split, and then roll up again. This style, descended from the craft of the Augsburg goldsmiths, was expressed in small-scale works such as Kilian's 'A B C Büchlein' (1627) (see initial letter S). In 1619 Kilian applied *Ohrmuschel* forms, used by Dietterlin in 1598, to the frame of Holl's portrait (Plate 8). The inherited nordic love of abstract lavishly interlaced decoration, the underlying significance of which could only be felt, not analysed, found free expression in the doughy twists of this ornamentation. It frequently led also to a revival of Late Gothic non-structural forms. These irrational, grotesque forms were an expression of the Mannerist style that dominated Germany until the middle of the seventeenth century, that is to say during a strained and troubled period. The decorated frame of Elias Holl's portrait, with its freely developing, supple *Ohrmuschel* ornament, is in sharp contrast to the severe architecture of Holl's town hall, the design of which he holds in his hand; and indeed, a kind of tension between law and licence dominated the age, just as evident in the conflicts of professed faith and the political conflicts as it is in art.

With the rise of the Baroque the contrasts lessened and a greater unity appeared. *Ohrmuschel* ornament had followed its own criteria, which seem to be an imaginative paraphrase of nature (Plate 7); but during the second half of the seventeenth century foliage reappeared, representing natural forms, and especially the acanthus leaf, as had been the rule in ancient Roman art. Italy once more furnished the models. The introduction of figures into foliage was due to Stefano della Bella (1610–64). This new type appeared for the first time fully developed in the *Raccolta di varij capprici et nove inventionij di fogliami romane* published in Graz in 1679 by Matthias Echter, a painter.

Kilian's friendship with Holl incidentally has a parallel in Echter's with Fischer von Erlach who, in an early work, the stucco decoration of the oval dome in the Mausoleum at Graz, succeeded in infusing into palm-leaves and acanthus scrolls a new explosive energy.

The craving of the late seventeenth century for unity and also for a renewed understanding of nature as the source of life is recognizable not merely in the homogeneity of ornament but also in the fields of jurisprudence, philosophy, and religion. In 1672, for example, Samuel Pufendorf published his *De iure naturae et gentium*, and in 1689 John Locke in his *Two Treatises of Government* started from the concept of a natural order, basing the rights of the people on the laws of nature.

This sympathy with nature gained increasing momentum during the eighteenth century, and it brought about, among other things, a refinement in ornament. The creative quality of the age lay both in its recognition of the abundance of nature, and in its ability to reduce it to unity. Leibniz summed it up: 'Utique delectat nos varietas, sed reducta in unitatem'. An all-round scholar of the very highest distinction, Leibniz's most obvious title to fame is his invention of infinitesimal calculus. This is symptomatic in that mathematics supplied the clarifying and regulating principle of the age. Though ornament had reverted to the intricate forms of arabesque, grotesque, and Netherlandish scrollwork, ribbonwork, introduced in France at the beginning of the eighteenth century, insisted on simpler geometrical relations on the surface. Its curves support an architectural frame to which the acanthus foliage is subordinated, in the early eighteenth century threaded through with ribbons. For this type of ornament, Germany selected as her model the work of the great innovator Jean Bérain, whose *Ornaments de peinture et de sculpture qui sont dans la galérie d'Apollon* appeared in 1710, a year before his death. The boldly flowing curves of the ribbonwork appear in the plaster ceilings of Andreas Schlüter's Alte Post in Berlin as early as 1704,[14] and through the engravings of his pupil, Paul Decker, in the *Fürstlicher Baumeister* of 1711 it became known throughout Central Europe.

At this point German art began to develop away from that of Italy, which had been the example for two hundred years, and came under French influence. The rapprochement with France had become possible as soon as France accepted Rubens and certain Flemish–Italian elements of the Baroque in the work of Oppenordt, Watteau, Meissonnier, and others, and thereafter, as a result of the reaction against Baroque exuberance, the influence of French standards increased from decade to decade. The acceptance took place in two phases. First, ribbonwork dominated from 1715 to 1740, even overflowing into purely architectural elements such as the balustrades of Hildebrandt's Daun-Kinsky Palace in Vienna (*c.* 1715; Plate 53A) and Schloss Mirabell near Salzburg (1722). Secondly, about 1740, the year of the accession to the throne of both Maria Theresa and Frederick II, the transition to the Rococo style began, with its naturalistic renderings of plants and shells. It appeared first in 1729–37 in Cuvilliés's work in the Reichen Zimmer of the Residenz at Munich and then set out on its all-conquering course, spreading to the Franconian centres along the Main and to Berlin and Potsdam. Close to nature and yet subordinated to an aesthetic principle, free of exacting symmetry yet controlled by its architectural setting, German Rococo corresponds to a conception of life which, while retaining the existing social standards, strove for greater liberty, ease, and grace. Outside the Bavarian and Prussian courts, however, *rocaille* was by no means so popular. This was the case where a close contact with Italy existed, as in Vienna, or where Italians were at work, as with Chiaveri in Dresden: for the Italians were unwilling to exchange wind-swept palm trees, naturalistic flower sprays, bouquets, and flower garlands for their acanthus scrolls and festoons. However, this Italian tradition did not prevent Germany from developing *rocaille* to its utmost refinement, not only in the art of the courts, especially at Potsdam and Charlottenburg, but later also in popular art, particularly in upper Bavaria. It acquired a significance of its own more marked than in France, where it was always subordinated to an architectural order. Most important of all, it appears in Germany on façades too, whereas in the French view *rocaille* is exclusively an element of interior decoration.

PART TWO

THE HEROIC AGE 1600–39

CHAPTER 3

ARCHITECTURE

Swabia

B Y the beginning of the seventeenth century the time was ripe in southern Germany for attempts to adapt the style of the Italian High Renaissance to the national character. This period is here called the Heroic Age, because the term was coined at the time to express adherence to the classical ideal. The fact that it was coined primarily at Augsburg can be explained by the *genius loci*. From early times, *Augusta Vindelicorum* had had close commercial ties with Venice, and Renaissance forms had been used as early as 1509–18 in the chapel of the Fuggers, the great merchant family, in St Anne. The art of Augsburg became known far and wide, not only in Germany but also in England, through the Augsburg goldsmiths and printers and through the painters, headed by Hans Holbein. There was also the added prestige of a town hall built by Elias Holl in a well-balanced Renaissance style, springing from an understanding of Italian forms gained at first hand. The ground had been prepared, however, by Heinrich Schickhardt (1558–1634), also of Swabia, who, as architect to the duke, had supervised all building in Württemberg from 1590 onwards; that is, he occupied a position equivalent to the later *Oberlandbaumeister* or the English Surveyors General. He had been well trained by Georg Beer of Stuttgart, also an architect attached to a court, and had had a part in Beer's Banqueting House[1] erected in 1581–93 (unfortunately demolished in the nineteenth century). With its high roof, richly articulated pediments, round corner towers, and two two-armed external staircases, it formed a northern counterpart to Palladio's Basilica, but was directly related to it only in as far as it was a hall reaching up through two storeys. The German climate alone sufficed to prevent the elaboration of the surrounding arcades into an imposing monumental motif, as had been done by Palladio. In 1598, as companion to Duke Frederick, Schickhardt visited Lombardy and the Veneto, and in 1599/1600 the two reached Rome.

Schickhardt's was in fact a journey undertaken for a specific architectural task: the Neue Bau at Stuttgart[2] (1599–1609), which was to be added to the old Schloss. Extant diaries and sketch-books testify to the thoroughness of his studies.[3] While Beer in the Banqueting House had kept his round towers low and detached them from the corners, Schickhardt merged his corner towers into the building and even raised them above the four storeys. The emphasis on height is a northern feature, and the north at that time, owing to strangely conflicting tensions, again approached the Gothic style; but the uniform symmetry of the body of the building and the harmonious articulation of the façades show that Schickhardt had assimilated the Italian rules of proportion. The lower storey was intended for the royal stud. The two-storeyed great hall was above and the armoury at the top. Orders appear only on the corner projections and on the central parts of the long sides. The storeys, recessed upwards, were articulated by string-courses, and the two rows of windows, one above the other, of the great hall were divided by a cornice so that the full height of the hall behind was to some extent concealed. Typically German and in the manner of his teacher was Schickhardt's treatment of the high hipped roof. Unfortunately the building was taken down in 1777.

The square plan for the small town of Freudenstadt shows Schickhardt closer to Italian patterns. The church, the town hall, the market hall, and the hospital were inserted as angles in the closed corners of the arcaded central square.[4] An unexecuted design shows that Schickhardt meant to set the castle diagonally into the square, touching the sides of the larger square at their centres, and that the strongly fortified corners were to stand on the axis of the main streets: thus the medieval custom of setting out by means of squares placed diagonally within squares reappears here in an unexpected way.[5]

However, it was not until the following generation, the generation of Rubens and Elsheimer, that perfectly clear and homogeneous solutions for almost all the architectural problems of the time were found – by the great town-architect Elias Holl (1573-1646) (Plate 10). He was descended from a family of masons that can be traced back at Augsburg to the fifteenth century and had risen to prominence in the service of the Fuggers, the great patrons of art. In 1600/1 a short journey had taken him to Venice and northern Italy. Although the good citizens of Augsburg, largely owing to lack of suitable building stone, allowed the painters free scope for their rich inventions on the exteriors of their houses, the interiors of the great pillared and groin-vaulted halls, used as warehouses in the south, and the arcades surrounding the courtyards did offer suitable surfaces for architecture proper. One has to look to them for Holl's examples. Holl believed in symmetry and tried to impose it even on his domestic buildings. In place of Gothic spiral staircases he incorporated into his plans flights of straight stairs which were broken at right angles and approached by vestibules, as at St Anne's School.[6] In the arsenal[7] as well as the Hospital of the Holy Ghost, groin-vaulted halls take up the entire depth of the long wings. Holl exploited the Renaissance motif of high arcades encircling a court when he rebuilt the Willibaldsburg of Eichstätt[8] in 1609-19, and to an even greater extent in the Hospital of the Holy Ghost, just mentioned, which occupied him from 1626 to 1630.[9]

In addition to the quest for symmetry, a practical approach is discernible in his considerations of the complex problems of planning as they arose both where he had to cope with old buildings and where he designed new ones representative of the economic developments and cultural requirements that had come with the Renaissance. Holl was responsible for the entire building programme of Augsburg during his working years, including houses, warehouses, guildhalls, and in particular market halls for the various trades: butchers, bakers, and weavers. The municipal authorities commissioned him, as we have seen, to rebuild the town hall, the arsenal, and the hospital. They also asked him to provide the city walls with new gates and towers. In St Anne's School, the classrooms were sensibly arranged so that they received light from both sides, and the needs of the headmaster and the boarders were also considered. On both sides of the Barfüsser Bridge, inspired by the Rialto Bridge in Venice, he placed booths with, in the centre, a *Gewölblein* (miniature vault) 'so that you can look down into the Fischgraben'. The Italian motif blends most successfully with the Renaissance gate-tower rising behind it and the Gothic Greyfriars church soaring up.

Holl's first civic building, the arsenal,[10] five storeys high, with powerfully projecting and receding cornices, was probably built to a design by Joseph Heintz.[11] Holl began it in 1602, upon his nomination as master mason to the town. Hans Reichle's dynamic bronze group of *St Michael fighting the Dragon*, which was placed above the central portal in 1607, intensified the Baroque character in a way that Holl could scarcely have been capable of; his essentially different conception of architecture, closer to the Renaissance, can be seen in the façade of St Anne's School[12] (1613; Plate 9A), where the horizontals are emphasized consistently in the hoods of the windows on all three floors and in the top cornice.

After these trials Holl was ready to embark on the most important work of his life, which he appropriated to himself, the new town hall (Plate 10). However, it was not until the belfry of the old town hall had been installed in the Perlach Tower,[13] the height of which had been raised by Holl for this purpose (1614–16), that the aldermen permitted him to turn to the designs for a new building (1615–20). The first plans show all the *gravitas* of a Roman palace (Plate 9B), but the block with its uniform sequence of windows did not correspond to the interior, which in addition to low rooms had to contain a high assembly hall. Augsburg, where the emperor was a frequent guest, surpassed all other German towns in luxury and glamour; so Holl designed the Golden Hall in the centre of his building, taking up three full storeys, raised in height externally and running through its full depth,[14] and with vestibules in the two lower storeys. In the centre of the long sides are staircases. Two towers added by Holl in 1618 round off the whole most successfully. His aim was, as he puts it in his diary, 'to obtain a bolder, more heroic appearance'. The towers are crowned by the bulbous domes of the 'Welsche Hauben' (Italian bonnets), characteristic of the Bavarian and Swabian foothills of the Alps, and first used in 1524/5 for the towers of the Frauenkirche in Munich.[15]

Holl was fully justified in claiming that his building was 'well proportioned'. The two main cornices emphasize one block. Above this and corresponding to it is a second block of the same proportions. In order to achieve this effect, Holl carried the top cornice of the corner pavilions across the centre, although by doing so the connexion of the upper row of windows of the Golden Hall with the two lower ones is severed. Even though the full height of the hall is thus not recognizable from outside, it is emphasized sufficiently by the contrast of the higher windows with the lower ones in the side parts. Behind these lie the smaller public rooms and the offices. Not only does the town hall represent the culmination of Holl's own work, but, over and above this, it is a magnificent witness in the field of architecture to the humanism and classical orientation of this great age of bourgeois culture.

The endeavour to attain the utmost clarity of form by studying Italian architecture continued in the following generation and is represented in the same upper Swabian circle by Joseph Furttenbach of Ulm (1591–1667). He published the results of a ten years' stay in Italy in his *Newes Itinerarium Italiae* (1627) and in his *Architectura Civilis* (1628). In these works he appears as the first exponent in Germany of the principle, so important for Baroque palace design, of the *enfilade*: that is, the arrangement in line of all the doors of a suite of state rooms. He also believed in long corridors and in ample staircases with two arms that lead up on both sides of the entrance hall behind the portico. Even U-shaped plans with three ranges along a courtyard occur in Furttenbach's work.

Bavaria

In the adjoining duchy of Bavaria Italian influence was even stronger and, owing to Bavaria's fervent championship of the Roman Catholic cause, assumed a distinctly Roman character: Roman, however, in this case does not mean classicism in façades, but inspiration from ancient Roman internal planning. Wilhelm Egkl in Munich, for instance, used the Roman type of tunnel-vaulting with large penetrations for the Antiquarium in the Ducal Palace, one of the first rooms in Germany built specially to be a museum (1569–71).[16]

The interior of St Michael, the Jesuit church of Munich, is similar in character (1583–97).[17] Here the tunnel-vault, with a span of about 60 feet, not broken into by penetrations for windows, rests evenly on the broad piers and the lateral transverse tunnel-vaults of the side chapels. Galleries were inserted in the chapels. Similar effects had already been produced in Gothic buildings in Germany and other countries, when buttresses had been inside and not outside churches, and chapels had been placed between them.[18] The system of St Michael, i.e. massive piers attached to the walls and an absence of clerestory lighting, was to become typical for southern Germany (Plate 11). The gabled façade is only loosely related to the interior and gives no hint of the splendour within. The building of the church and its college was paid for by the pious Duke William V (1576–97), a determined champion of the Counter Reformation. He favoured the Jesuits, and thus a dome, a Jesuit motif familiar from the recently built Gesù in Rome, was indeed to be added to the east of the nave, where the duke's funeral monument was to be placed. Instead, after the collapse of the tower, a chancel and transept, without a dome, were added in 1592. These were designed by Friedrich Sustris, a native of Flanders, trained in Italy and architect to the duke at the time. It is not known who designed the nave.

The Protestants, for their new church in the Palatinate at Neuburg on the Danube,[19] built in 1607–16 as a *Trutz-Michael* (Counter-Michael), chose a basilica with three aisles, free-standing piers, groin-vaults, and galleries in the tradition of the Gothic hall-churches, because for their tastes the scheme of St Michael smacked too strongly of Rome. But the Jesuits themselves also favoured the native type of hall-church, and in their church at Dillingen (1610–17)[20] they discarded the galleries and the transept, deviating in this from the Munich pattern. The lateral chapels rise without interruption between the internal buttresses and cut into the main tunnel-vault with their transverse tunnels. In the chancel, galleries with piers rising above them detached from the walls create a more sacred setting. The architect, Hans Alberthaler from the Grisons, had been architect to the bishop of Eichstätt from 1609 and probably also built the Jesuit church there[21] (1617–20). Here, the internal buttresses rise unimpeded, as the gallery is reduced to a narrow balcony along the walls.

The role of Bavaria as the foremost defender of Roman Catholicism in Germany was strengthened under Maximilian I (1598–1651), who was created an elector when he acquired the upper Palatinate in 1623. He enlarged the old castle in Munich, turning it into the most magnificent palace of his day in Germany.[22] In 1581 Sustris (d. 1599) had begun the Grotto Court for Maximilian's father. This is a secluded courtyard, adapted to the contemplative character of the duke, and designed in the Florentine manner. Its centre is the Perseus Fountain by Hubert Gerhard. To this Maximilian added the Grotto Hall with a shell-fountain. Then, between 1612 and 1618, he created out of older irregular wings the diagonally set octagonal Fountain Court, the large square new building of the Imperial Court, and the adjoining Kitchen Court, a vast symmetrical layout with long regular fronts. There was as yet no interest in Germany in accentuation by pavilions, and a majestic effect was obtained in the Bavarian and Swabian manner by a painted-on order of two storeys. Stone was confined to the two portals of red marble and the middle niche with the bronze statue of the *Patrona Bavariae* by Hans Krumper (1616; Plate 19A). A son-in-law of Sustris, Krumper had succeeded him as Superintendent of Works and must also have had a say in determining the plans for the palace. In the richly appointed interior the Imperial Staircase had already been designed in conjunction with vast vestibules. Coupled columns support the vaults, which are covered by fine decoration in the antique taste set with small paintings by Peter Candid. Heinrich Schön the Elder designed the Hofgarten with the rotunda in 1613. The former Residenzgarten directly adjoined the Grotto Court and the Antiquarium on the south side, and for this Hubert Gerhard destined his beautiful bronze figure of *Bavaria*,[23] which was later placed on the rotunda in the Hofgarten.

Austria

East of Bavaria Italian influence was yet stronger. In the archiepiscopal province of Salzburg this was due to the Archbishop Wolf Dietrich von Raitenau (1587–1612), who was a great-nephew of the Medici pope Pius IV, had studied at Pavia and Rome, and at the early age of twenty-eight became archbishop of Salzburg. In 1602, a fire destroyed the lead roof of the old Romanesque cathedral; the archbishop then proceeded to demolish it entirely, including even its interior fittings, regardless of its great historical value – in this surpassing the example set by the popes when they pulled down old St Peter's. A plan for a great new cathedral was then furnished by Vincenzo Scamozzi of Vicenza, Palladio's principal follower. As was often the case with Italians working in foreign countries, Scamozzi had acquired an eye for native characteristics. Accordingly his design for a three-aisled basilican church on a Latin cross plan with a semicircular termination to the transepts, a dome over the crossing and another over the choir, and two west towers is half Italian Renaissance, half German Romanesque in derivation. The radical clearance of the site corresponded to the ideas of Italian town-planning and at the same time supplied space for a new bishop's palace. The building was not actually begun, however, until 1614, in the reign of the following archbishop, Marx Sittich, Count Hohenems, and Marx Sittich's successor, Paris, Count Lodron, consecrated the cathedral in 1628. The plan finally adopted was not Scamozzi's, however, but one by Santino Solari from Verna in Val Intelvi. Solari abandoned the idea of aisles and limited himself to chapels and galleries between internal buttress piers, and this resulted in a grand unity of space which comprises nave, chancel, and transepts with three terminal apses. The link with German Romanesque churches such as St Mary-in-Capitol in Cologne was thus preserved, in spite of the general Italian character. This also applied to the well-knit square in front of the cathedral which, with the marble façade and towers of the church (Plate 12), forms a *Paradisus*, i.e. a medieval feature in an Early Baroque disguise. Here, in this 'northern Rome', amidst the unparalleled beauty of the Alpine scenery, the happiest blend of north with south has been achieved, even down to the houses with their parapets concealing gabled roofs behind.

The archbishops were also eager to transplant the Italian *villa suburbana* to Salzburg, and Marx Sittich therefore commissioned Solari to build Hellbrunn (1613–14), a summer villa with numerous fountains and grottoes in the grounds. The hall is here on the west, i.e. a narrow side, and set asymmetrically, with a projecting octagonal closet. Both rooms are decorated with illusionistic frescoes.

Styria, which had only after a prolonged struggle been recovered from Protestantism by the forces of the Counter Reformation, now also came to the fore. Here the idea, current at the time, of paying heroic tribute to the dead in special mausolea was realized twice. For Ruprecht von Eggenberg, the victor over the Turks, Hans Walther of Plauen in the Saxon Vogtland, a Protestant architect, erected a central building at Ehrenhausen (1609–14), flanked by two colossal statues of antique warriors.[24] The decoration shows the influence of Dietterlin's fantastic ornamentation. In contrast to this Pietro de Pomis, a native of Lodi (1569–1633), built the mausoleum of the Emperor Ferdinand II at Graz (1614–38) in the heavy Roman Baroque style.[25] A particular significance attaches to the adjoining oval funeral chapel, for this is the first appearance in the north of this typical Baroque form.

Schloss Eggenberg (Plate 13A, Figure 1) on the other hand has a northern appearance. It was begun in 1623 by Laurenz van der Sype (d. 1634 at Graz) for Johann Ulrich of Eggenberg, Governor General of Inner Austria, during the ten years following his nomination as prince of the Holy Roman Empire. Framed by four corner towers, on the model of the palace of Aschaffenburg, the plan includes a large arcaded central court, followed by two smaller ones. In the middle of the inner cross wing a fifth, higher tower

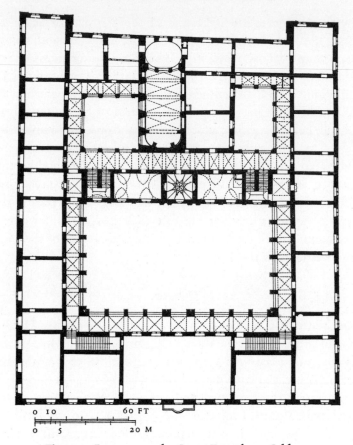

Figure 1. Laurenz van der Sype: Eggenberg, Schloss,
begun 1623. Plan

rises over a square chapel with a Gothic rib-vault – evidently such a vault had sacred
connotations. Otherwise a desire for simplicity reigns, as shown by the horizontal
cornices of the windows and by the restriction of pilasters to the angles. The great hall
on the third floor is emphasized solely by higher, grouped windows. A pleasing symmetry prevails everywhere, even in the stairs, which lead off the vestibule on both sides.
The three-storeyed arcades of the courts, with Tuscan three-quarter columns, show the
same simple yet heroic style. The chapel at the rear was not built until the middle of
the eighteenth century.

Bohemia

Owing to the pressure of the Thirty Years War nothing of importance was built in
Vienna, but in Prague the all-powerful position of Albrecht von Waldstein, the great
general, was expressed in the grandeur of his palace. To make room for an extensive
layout with gardens and outbuildings numerous houses in the Old Town (Malá Strana)
had to be pulled down. The palace, begun in 1623 by Andrea Spezza, contains a well-
lit two-storeyed hall which on both long sides opens in two rows of windows. The

upper windows break into the entablature of the gigantic order of the interior, a typically Baroque motif. In contrast to this the garden loggia, with its three enormous arcades resting on coupled Tuscan columns, is built in a pure Renaissance style. Only the roof with its dormer windows is an un-Italian feature, characteristic of Prague. Waldstein, in his ambition to rival the emperor, attached great importance to winning the population over to his side and thus gaining control of them. He gave his extensive possessions a capital, Jičín (Gitschin), which he enlarged on a grand scale. The big marketplace is surrounded by houses with arcades. On one side stands the castle, with its several courts enclosed by arcaded walks and its adjacent park. The architecture here is still entirely Renaissance, as it is in the Chapel of the Assumption of 1590 in sv. Kliment (St Clemens) in Prague. S. Anna dei Palafrenieri in Rome is the prototype for the oval ground plan, which appears here for the first time in Central Europe. However the Counter Reformation, which set in after the victorious Battle of the White Mountain in 1620, had not yet taken a real hold.

Hungary

Owing to King Matthias Corvinus and his Italian wife Beatrice, Hungary, at a very early date, became familiar with the Italian Quattrocento. This had great future repercussions; for it meant that Baroque in the strict sense of the term could evolve only to a limited degree. However, the Baroque style received the support of the Habsburgs, who occupied the Hungarian throne from 1526 onwards, of the Roman Catholic Church, and of the feudal lords. But the evolution of Hungary was greatly limited by the power of the Turks, which menaced the country for a hundred and fifty years. The narrow northern and eastern strip alone remained free; that is, the small centres of upper Hungary and Transylvania. The Turks did not, however, confine themselves to erecting fortifications in Hungary. Solyman the Magnificent was there for a considerable period in the sixteenth century, and Szokoli Mustafa Pasha set up three dome-shaped Turkish baths. The precise Turkish ashlar work can be traced in many places even today, and indeed some minarets have survived, for example in Eger (Erlau).

In the west, where the nobles adhered to the Roman Catholic Church and to the house of Habsburg, the Baroque of the Counter Reformation was taken over at the beginning of the seventeenth century. In consequence, some of the towns in ancient north and west Hungary received a Baroque character as early as the seventeenth century. At Nagyszombat (Trnava, Tirnau) the Italian Pietro Spazzo erected the university church in 1628, and at Győr (Raab) the Baroque church of St Ignatius was built in 1635-41, both on the pattern of St Michael in Munich. At that time Baroque forms were also introduced at Bratislava.[26] On the other hand, among the Protestants in the 'Zips', where the towns had been mostly settled by Germans, the Renaissance style was preserved, owing to the presence of Italian and partly of Polish artists. Sgraffito friezes and crowning pinnacles are typical of the façades of the manor houses. The Protestant churches, too, accepted the Renaissance, and its characteristic forms appear especially in the towers and façades: an example is the Reformed church at Košice

(Kaschau). In Transylvania Renaissance motifs occur on the ceilings of the Calvinistic churches, decorated with painted flowers, and in the arcaded courts of the farmhouses. Here the Baroque style had only slight influence. The Renaissance dominated right down to the beginning of the neo-classical movement – a state of affairs frequent in areas which had been separated from the German mother-country, and which thus had no further share in its development.

Franconia and Alsace

The Late Renaissance version of the northern castle found its most perfect manifestation in Franconia. In 1605–14 George Ridinger of Strasbourg (1568–after 1616) built for the archbishop of Mainz the palace of Aschaffenburg as – to put it in his own words – an 'heroic opus of his Grace the Prince' (Plate 13B). The square structure with its four wings and corner towers was modelled on French châteaux – an inspiration which had in fact been at work even earlier, in Westphalia, at the noble country house of Horst (1559).[27] At Aschaffenburg the heroic character is conveyed by the elevated site, the high, powerful towers, and the gables over the centres of the fronts. Articulation is achieved not by orders, but by strongly projecting string-courses, the diminishing height of the storeys, and the wider spacing of the windows towards the centre. The ornamental taste of the time is revealed only in the strapwork of the gables. In the courtyard, which has staircases in the four angles, a medieval tower was retained, and this permitted a freer arrangement. The chapel with its higher windows is attached to the tower. The arcades built on the south side and in the north-west corner of the court, unlike those in the second large Late Renaissance palace of Franconia, the Plassenburg near Kulmbach (1560 ff.), had little effect on the design (cf. p. 13).

Alongside Mainz the bishoprics of Würzburg and of Bamberg gained architectural importance. Julius Echter von Mespelbrunn, who has been mentioned before, became bishop of Würzburg at the age of twenty-eight in 1573 and died in 1617. He erected a number of monumental buildings at Würzburg in the spirit of the Counter Reformation. The first of these was the Julius Hospital of 1576–85. This was followed between 1582 and 1591 by the university, with its church.[28] On the other hand, in his efforts to restore the old faith, Echter often preferred the Gothic style – so much so that the name 'Julius Style' has been given to this form of Gothic Revival. Born in 1545 in the beautiful medieval moated castle of Mespelbrunn,[29] Echter lavished special care on the enlargement of another old castle, that of Rimpar, where he added two round towers as companions to the medieval round belfry. On the Marienberg, above Würzburg, he connected the wings of the castle to form a vast elongated rectangle (1600–7). Red sandstone doorways and gabled dormer windows are the only ornament.

The architect was Jakob Wolff the Elder (c. 1546–1612), master mason to the city of Nuremberg and a renowned architect. Even when the age of the burghers was drawing to an end in Germany, this old metropolis of art still maintained its hegemony, and this is most forcibly expressed in the high-gabled house, the 'überherrliche' (super-magnificent) house, which was built for Martin Peller in 1602–7 by Wolff and Peter Carl

(Plate 14). The house was a victim of the Second World War. To begin with, the owner, a former consul at the Fondaco dei Tedeschi in Venice and son-in-law of the Venetian Bartolo Viatis, wanted a design in the Italian taste with round-arched windows and half-columns,[30] but the architects succeeded in imposing their German style. In their impressive simplicity the three lower storeys of the building with their rusticated walls were truly in the heroic style. Above, a vigorous note was struck by a typical German gable, also three-storeyed. It was framed by volutes and obelisks. The quiet majesty of the whole composition was primarily due to carefully balanced proportions.

Jakob Wolff the Younger (1571-1620), the son of the great Nuremberg master, successfully developed the Late Renaissance style of his father in the enlargement of the town hall (Plate 15A). The Nuremberg Council had sent him at the beginning of the seventeenth century to Italy, where he learnt above all the art of restraint, which would allow the principal features of a composition to dominate. He thus designed the ground floor of the town hall (1616-22) as a simple base, to set off the three-dimensional values of the three portals with their framing columns. Above it the closely set windows are attached to simple string-courses, but the third floor with the rooms for public occasions is imposingly crowned by gables above every second window, linked with the parapet, and by the three superstructures typical of Nuremberg. The town hall is situated in an ascending narrow street, and so the long, horizontal, strongly foreshortened lines are most effective. The roof is of no importance – which was an innovation by comparison not only with the older civic buildings of Nuremberg, but also with the Franconian town hall type, of which the one at Rothenburg on the Tauber has been discussed earlier.

How this late phase of the Renaissance differed from the preceding one and paved the way for the Baroque is apparent in Franconia in the Friedrichsbau of the Schloss of Heidelberg (1601-7; Plate 15B), which has already been referred to. The Friedrichsbau continued the system of the older Ottheinrichsbau (1556-9; Plate 6B), which, as we have seen, had been the first fully mature Early Renaissance building in Germany; but in contrast to the composition of the Ottheinrichsbau, the architect of the Friedrichsbau, Johannes Schoch of Strasbourg, arranged his doorway laterally and developed the middle axis evenly, with powerful pilasters and mouldings. In place of the overlong pilasters on the ground floor of the Ottheinrichsbau, Schoch designed pilasters with sturdier proportions and set them on bases. Everywhere the architectural elements are more closely knit and more vigorously moulded. In the tracery of the lower windows of the chapel Schoch appears as an exponent of the Gothic style and its functional structural articulation. The lavish decoration, in Heidelberg unlike Nuremberg a feature of the town itself (as seen for instance in the Haus zum Ritter of 1592),[31] betrays the vicinity of the Netherlands.

The same situation as at Heidelberg is to be found in the upper Rhenish area, where Schoch's native town Strasbourg was the centre. Here, as has already been noticed (p. 32), the fantastic inventions of Hans Vredeman de Vries of Antwerp were outstripped by the amazing conceits of Wendel Dietterlin's *Architectura* (1593, 1594, and 1598), in which Gothic naturalism and Netherlandish strapwork form the strangest of alliances (Plate 7). Strasbourg, however, remained impervious to such incredible ornament, thanks to the Gothic tradition of its minster and to the half-timber work of the houses. This even affected architecture in stone, as can be seen in the Neuer Bau (1582–5), designed allegedly by Schoch.[32]

Upper Saxony

In general the construction of new churches had been given up by the Protestants in the sixteenth century, and they restricted themselves to the building of castle chapels. The first was that of Schloss Hartenfels at Torgau, erected by Nickel Grohmann in 1543–4 and dedicated by Martin Luther himself. It is a hall with double galleries in a still half Gothic style. The altar is placed in the centre of one of the longitudinal walls, opposite the rulers' pew. This architectural type was developed still further in the chapel of the Augustusburg [33] and that of the Wilhelmsburg near Schmalkalden (1584–90),[34] where the centralizing tendency is even more evident in that altar, pulpit, and organ are arranged along the middle axis. This arrangement was so much in keeping with Lutheran requirements that it was retained until well into the nineteenth century, especially for the combination of pulpit and altar. The credit for the design of the Schmalkalden chapel must be given to Landgrave William IV of Hessen himself and to the masons Christoph and Hans Müller, who executed it. The delicate and well preserved strapwork and scrollwork decoration in stucco is by Wilhelm Vernucken, an artist from the lower Rhine. The enormous hall in the Wilhelmsburg is only about fifteen feet high against a length of eighty-two feet and a width of forty feet; it thus reveals the curious spatial extremism typical of Mannerism in Germany, and particularly southern Germany.

In Dresden the Surveyor of the Electoral Works was Paul Buchner (1531–1607), Master of the Ordnance. During his term of office the arsenal with its four wings, staircase towers, and a tall gabled dormer was built, and also the new city wall with its mighty rusticated gateways. Of this work, the doorway to the Schloss in the Schlossstrasse,[35] built in 1589, has survived – a fine example of the current popularity of architectural sculpture, one of whose leading exponents was Andreas Walther. The lions' heads in the metopes of the doorway also illustrate the general taste for the grotesque and the entertaining.

About this time the Electoral Stables with their courtyard were built to the east of the Schloss, the masterpiece of Dresden architecture in the latter part of the sixteenth century.[36] Their long arcades with groined vaults resting on Tuscan columns[37] open spaciously and majestically towards the tiltyard. The architect may have been Buchner, or perhaps Hans Irmisch; it is in any case probable that Giovanni Maria Nosseni from Lugano (1544–1620) collaborated. This versatile and imaginative artist had entered the service of the Elector Augustus in 1575. Later, under the latter's son, Christian I (1586–91), who had a passion for building, Nosseni transformed the Gothic choir of Freiberg Cathedral into a princely mausoleum in the Late Renaissance style of northern Italy. The rich sculptural decoration was entrusted by Nosseni to Carlo de Cesare (1590–3). This awkward task of conversion prevented Nosseni from displaying his talent to the full; he was more successful with the heptagon which he began in 1606 at Stadthagen as a mausoleum for Count Ernst of Schaumburg-Lippe, another connoisseur of art. The bronze group of the *Resurrection* by Adriaen de Vries (1618) forms a magnificent centre-piece to this work.[38] In Dresden in 1589 Nosseni began the three-storeyed banqueting house on the Jungfer, a charmingly situated bastion above the Elbe. This, with its pro-fuse decoration and curving roofs, has special significance as a precursor of the Zwinger. It was, however destroyed in 1747 by an explosion of gunpowder, and Knöffel's Belvedere rose in its place.

Lower Saxony

Interest in the colourful, vivid play of light on surfaces distinguishes north German buildings from the disciplined three-dimensional Italianate architecture of the Saxon electorate. It is true that the tradition of timber-framing, particularly characteristic of Westphalia, kept alive an interest in structure, but the Renaissance orders were regarded in north Germany as an ornament, which could be easily reproduced in timber to cover the frame with a brilliant decorative cloak. After 1560 this richness was further augmented by ribbon- and strapwork, unfolding particularly luxuriously over the high gables. Such decoration was frequently repeated on oriels and dormers built behind and above one another, their outlines manifoldly curved. A specially good example of the variety which could thus be achieved is the town hall at Paderborn (1613–20).[39] That a half-timbered house stood model for this is evident from the windows, stretched be-tween continuous horizontals and projecting oriels. It is kin also to the lower Saxon farmhouse, as is proved by the many wide-arched entrances.

The particular preference for dormers in lower Saxony can be seen in the country houses too. Frequently they transmitted the forms of the French château to central Ger-many, as we have seen to have been the case at Schloss Horst with its four wings and corner towers (p. 43). The Hämelschenburg (1588–1618)[40] has wings along three sides of an oblong courtyard, a form that was later of considerable significance in the north-west. The alternation between smooth and patterned blocks on pilaster-strips, quoins, and horizontal courses also served to enliven the surface. Owing to their innate con-servatism, the Westphalians, even in the sixteenth and seventeenth centuries, retained moats and round corner towers in building their country houses; but as symmetry was now an additional interest, they sometimes, in enlarging houses, added new round towers to correspond to the old ones. In the Siegerland the composition with the court-yard open on one side occurs as early as the middle of the sixteenth century. Crottorf, a house of the Hatzfeld family, was built at that time. It has three ranges, four corner towers, an outer bailey also with three ranges, and two low battery towers at the corners on either side of the main entrance.

In the duchy of Brunswick-Wolfenbüttel Paul Francke (1538–1615) emerged as the great architect. His two most conspicuous works, Helmstedt University and the church of St Mary at Wolfenbüttel, were the fruits of his successful collaboration with a highly gifted patron, Duke Julius Heinrich, famous as the author of the first German comedies.

He reigned from 1589 to 1613 and is said to have himself made designs for his buildings. At Würzburg the Roman Catholics had planned their university as a building with four ranges round a courtyard containing on the ground floor the church and gymnasia which opened on to the court. Helmstedt, built between 1592 and 1613, is, in contrast to this, a truly northern block, two-storeyed, and designed to represent the spirit of a tolerant conciliatory humanism.[41] Northern Renaissance ideals are revealed in the high rooms, a lively roof-line, and a stair-tower in the middle of the main front. Orders were only permitted in the gables. They are painterly in conception, as are all Francke's own decorative forms, in conscious contrast to antique ones; there is not even any consistency in the arrangement of the windows. St Mary at Wolfenbüttel shows a similar independent yet conservative style. The choir destined to become the prince's mausoleum, medieval in its depth, was built by Francke between 1604 and 1615; the rest – partly altered – was the work of his successors Johann Meyer and Claus Müller (completed 1626; Plate 16B). The ideal here was not the Protestant preaching church with galleries round the nave but, owing to the Hanoverian high-church attitude, the medieval Westphalian hall-church with rib-vaults, buttresses, a single tower in front of the church, and cross-gables over the aisles. The decoration used by Francke consists of scrolls and strapwork. Where the Ohrmuschelstil occurs, as in the cross gables, it indicates the work of his successors.

Another important hall-church with rib-vaults was built in 1611–15 at Bückeburg,[42] the town which became a flourishing centre of art under Count Ernst von Schaumburg-Lippe (1601–22). The principal sculptors he employed were Adriaen de Vries and Ebert Wolf and his sons (p. 55). The great columns in the interior of this Lutheran parish church are most impressive. The narrow galleries do not touch them. Nave and aisles lead into a three-sided eastern apse, following the Protestant type, as distinct from the deep choir of the church at Wolfenbüttel. In spite of its rich Late Renaissance decoration, the gabled façade succeeds in appearing monumental.

Rhineland

Gothic traditions were even more decisive for the Jesuit buildings of the Rhineland. The Jesuits regarded the Gothic Revival as a means of restoring the link with the medieval Church and, through this, with the rich Late Gothic past that was still a potent factor along the Rhine. At the same time, with the system of galleries established by the Protestants in the chapel of Schloss Hartenfels at Torgau (1543–4; see p. 45) and much developed since, the Jesuits adopted the modern ideal of the preaching church. Both aims were realized in St Achatius in Cologne (1582–3), a Gothic church with galleries, and further in St Peter at Münster, built by Johann Rosskott in 1590–7.[43] The crowning achievements are the churches by Christoph Wamser: Holy Trinity at Molsheim in Lower Alsace (1615–17) and the church of the Assumption in Cologne (1618–27). It is important to note that all these churches are of the basilican type and that the galleries are carried forward to touch the slender columns;[44] the arcades below and the balustrades above thus lie between the columns. The disadvantage of this arrangement was that the parapet of the gallery ran against the curving columns, and in south Germany

47

the Jesuits found a better solution by using piers with attached pilasters instead of columns.

In spite of these difficulties, Wamser produced in the Assumption at Cologne a well proportioned and harmonious interior. In the broad nave the columns are set close together. The rib-vaulting was moulded in an especially rich way. The church was burnt out in the Second World War, so that we can no longer appreciate the harmony which existed between the Gothic architecture and the Late Renaissance furnishings, the latter supplied by the workshop of the Jesuit college. In this, as in the details, particularly of the façade, the Jesuits very reasonably kept in touch with the living art of their day. The same thing can be seen in the way the profusion of light increases towards the choir and also in the generous breadth of space.

The North

The same harmony as in the Jesuit church of the Assumption at Cologne was achieved farther north at Bremen, when the Gothic town hall was altered in 1608–13 (Plate 16A). Here Lüder von Bentheim's gabled middle projection and smaller lateral gables emphasize symmetry in the Renaissance sense. The architect also converted the pointed arches of the front arcade into Renaissance arches. He did, however, retain the Gothic body of the hall with its high windows and steep hipped roof, although he toned down the effects of the verticals, and deprived the building of its fortified character by eliminating the battlements and corner turrets. The conception throughout is painterly in its emphasis on flat surfaces. The Renaissance spirit is undoubtedly there, in the horizontals of the entablatures and balustrades, however much the scenic reliefs play around them. In the interior the Great Hall occupies the entire length of the building, and this on the other hand testifies to the pertinacity of the age-old tradition of northern halls. The same situation is evident in the town houses, for instance the Essighaus of 1618.[45] Here, wide halls two floors high with tall windows run through the entire depth of the building, and the rich decoration culminates in the carved staircases.

At this time influence from the Netherlands was particularly strong in Danzig. It was noticeable even fifty years before, at the very time when Hans Kramer, former mason to the city of Dresden, erected a number of important buildings in the upper Saxon Renaissance style (1565–77). Immediately afterwards, under the leadership of Hans Vredeman de Vries and Antoni van Obbergen, Dutch architecture eclipsed all the rest. Brick with stone dressings was the characteristic feature. The outstanding building is the arsenal[46] (1600–5), with its high rectangular windows, ornamented gables framed by curving bands of stone, octagonal corner staircase-towers, and a hall with three rows of columns on the ground floor.

The design of the west wing of the castle at Königsberg in East Prussia was of considerable importance for later Protestant ecclesiastical architecture. The chapel[47] had originally been built by Blasius Berwart of Stuttgart in 1584–92. Between 1602 and 1608 Timotheus Just, an architect from Elbing, provided lierne-vaulting on slender granite piers modelled on the medieval ones of the Marienburg – another example of the progress made by the forces of the Gothic Revival. It is possible that the arrangement of pulpit and altar in the middle of the long sides, where the transept branches off, as it was later built (see p. 226), was conceived already at this time. Its pattern in this case would be the chapel of 1560 in the castle at Stuttgart.

Poland

Under King Sigismund III (1587–1632), himself versed in painting, sculpture, and metalwork, there was a great increase of building activity in Poland.[48] The nobility, gentry, and wealthy citizens competed with the court. After it had been selected as the seat of the Diet in 1569, Warsaw became the model for the whole of the country. Though he was a grandson of King Gustavus Vasa of Sweden, the king was a determined supporter of the Counter Reformation. The Sigismund Chapel[49] on the Wawel at Cracow, built, as we have seen, by Bartolomeo Berecci as early as 1517–33 in a pure north Italian Renaissance style, established Italy as the source of inspiration for Poland.[50] Its square design was repeated frequently, elaborated according to Polish ideas by curving the outlines of dome and lantern; for instance in the Tęczyński Chapel of the parish church at Staszów[51] (1613–25), in the chapel of St Anne at Pińczów, in the Firlei Chapel by the church of Lublin, and others. These buildings were frequently associated with a large masons' yard at Pińczów which had been founded by the Myszkowski family around 1600. The sculptor Santi Succi of Florence and his workshop played an important part. In the seventeenth century the return to the Roman Catholic Church strengthened the Italian influence so much that it became possible to build a Jesuit church in a genuine Roman Baroque, as is the case at St Peter and St Paul at Cracow (1605–9)[52] by Giovanni Trevano. It was at this time that Vilna acquired its conspicuously southern character.

In many cases, however, Polish ecclesiastical architecture adopted the Central European type of a façade with two towers. The height of naves was often greater than in Italy – this is particularly noticeable at Vilna. As a result the façades had to be several storeys high. Even an architect recorded as Paolo Romano was ready to combine the most heterogeneous elements, and in the end succeeded in achieving a new unity, in the abbey church of the Bernardine Fathers at Lvov (Lemberg) built in 1600–30. Here, the varied silhouette determines the effect (Plate 17A). Below, the façade is severe, with a system of Tuscan pilasters, but the gable above is very free, with its forms derived from Germany and the Netherlands under the influence of Vredeman de Vries. The connecting link was Danzig, which belonged to the Polish kingdom. Italian Renaissance motifs were borrowed for the plaster decoration of the vaults, which consisted of geometrically arranged nets often with inserted figures. The church at Zamość,[53] built by Bernardo Morando at the end of the sixteenth century, and St Bernard at Lublin[54] (1602–7) were the models. The motifs thus received were everywhere transformed into a richly decorative style, particularly in town houses, which now changed from timber-framing to stone. Reliefs of stone or stucco with many small figures characterize the façades, and especially the door and window surrounds. The skylines were made interesting by the so-called Polish Parapet, for which the parapet of the cloth hall at Cracow of 1555 was the example,[55] as were also those of the imposing town halls of Poznań (Posen) built c. 1550–60,[56] Calm (1567–97),[57] and Sandomierz[58] and Tarnow[59] (both of the second half of the sixteenth century). The sunken roofs disappear behind the parapets with their blind arcades and crowning tabernacles and pyramids. At Kazimierz, an industrial town, founded about 1350 by Casimir the Great, there remain examples of richly decorated houses with parapets and symmetrically disposed windows and portals dating from the first third of the seventeenth century[60] (Plate 17B). The Polish Parapet is also found outside the borders of Poland, for example in Transylvania, northern Hungary, Moravia, lower Austria, Russia, and Sweden. The windows, set close together, are typical too. They sometimes have columns set into the deep jambs inside. That there were originally arcades of wood in front of the houses is proved by the decree issued at Lemberg in 1600 prohibiting their erection for the future. They were replaced, especially in the market-places, by stone colonnades. Elsewhere in Poland, however, the log house remained predominant. There was no need to economize with space in Poland; this is evident in market-places as well as farm buildings and country houses. During the course of the seventeenth century the latter lost their fortified character, but the flanking corner towers were retained.

In 1597–1619 Sigismund III and his architect Giovanni Trevano converted the palace of Warsaw into a pentagon which incorporated part of the medieval building.[61] The great court was surrounded by long, plain wings and animated by the vertical accent of the high western gate-tower. The vast senate and council halls give the palace a republican rather than a monarchical character.

Three entrances are a constantly recurring distinctive feature in buildings of the period in Poland. The palace above the Vistula later known as the Kasimir Palace was also built for Sigismund III.[62] With its loggias and square towers it was to become a model for Late Renaissance palaces in Poland. The royal palace at Ujazdów near Warsaw,[63] reconstructed in 1630, is also associated with Giovanni Trevano, the builder of the Warsaw palace. The rectangular building has a small courtyard, a six-sided tower, and a high-pitched roof.

Among the fortified palaces of the Vasa period in Poland the castles of the nobles formed a special group. They had to withstand Tartar attacks, which came mainly from the south-eastern borders, and to help in suppressing the revolts of the native peasants. Most important were the castles of Wiśnicz,[64] Łancut,[65] and Połonne, built in this style for Stanislas Lubomirski, Woywode of Cracow, by his court architect. A fortified house at Podhorce[66] was built for the Hetman Koniecpolski by Andreas dell'Aqua of Venice, architect to the king, after the pattern of the 'palazzo in fortezze'. It consisted of a rectangular bastion protected on three sides by moats with the palace rising inside and a garden laid out below. The palace itself had an octagonal centre and two corner pavilions. As late as the second half of the seventeenth century Tylman van Gameren followed this pattern when he built the house for the Rey family at Przecław.

CHAPTER 4

SCULPTURE

In sculpture, as in architecture, the lead was taken by Augsburg, thanks to its whole-hearted acceptance of the classical ideal, its choice of suitably distinguished artists, and the nature of the commissions it gave them.[1] At the time we are concerned with, Giovanni da Bologna's interpretation of the nude, of spiral movement, of the *figura serpentina* with interesting aspects from all sides had been widely disseminated by Netherlandish artists of his school. Hubert Gerhard from Hertogenbosch, an extremely capable sculptor in bronze who worked in this manner, was taken into their service by the Fuggers as early as 1581. It was Gerhard who, between 1587 and 1594, created the Augustusbrunnen,[2] with its figure of the emperor in full Roman dignity, intended as a reference to the foundation of the town. The architect Wenzel Dietrich was consulted about the carefully chosen site near the town hall and about the size of the fountain. Two other fountains in the Maximilianstrasse with bronze figures, one with a Hermes, the other with a Hercules,[3] were the work of Adriaen de Vries of The Hague; these form no part of German art, but had an important bearing on its development. The influence of the allegories on the rim of the Augustusbrunnen can even be seen in Raphael Donner's equally supple figures on his fountain of 1737–9 in Vienna (Plate 63, A and B).

Gerhard's art radiated even more strongly from Munich than from Augsburg. There, working at St Michael for the Roman Catholic Church, he designed the bronze statue of *St Michael*[4] on the façade (1588) and that of the Virgin as *Patrona Bavariae* on the high altar (1613). In 1638 the noble figure of the Virgin was removed from the church and set up on a column in front of the town hall, a sign of triumph to commemorate the victory over the Protestant armies at the White Mountain (Plate 18b). This Munich precedent was followed in 1603–6 by Hans Reichle's *St Michael* in front of the Augsburg Arsenal[5] and in 1616 by Hans Krumper's *Patrona Bavariae* in front of the Residenz at Munich (Plate 19a). They are both further removed from classical models, less beautiful, but of stronger individuality and expression. Reichle's figure shows a touch of Mannerism in its exaggerated movement and disrupted outline. Compared to the figure by the Dutchman, Krumper's *Patrona* is more popular, warmer, and more natural, but on the other hand weightier and less suitable to crown a column.

Krumper can be traced in Munich from 1587 onwards, where he was a pupil of Gerhard. In 1596 he went to Italy at the expense of Duke Maximilian. Then, until his death in 1634, he worked for the court of Munich. He achieved greatness in his portrait statues of bronze, for example those of the robust Wittelsbach family by the tomb of Emperor Ludwig the Bavarian in the Frauenkirche (1622), excellent in their lifelike characterization of the individual figures.[6]

Hans Reichle, a native of Schongau, was equally independent of the Netherlandish masters. He, too, was trained by Giovanni da Bologna and worked as his assistant in

F

Florence from 1588 to 1593. The bronze statue of the *Magdalen*[7] of 1595 in St Michael, Munich, is his work. Immediately after completing it he went to Brixen (Bressanone) in the Tyrol, where he modelled for the episcopal palace forty-four terracotta statues of members of the house of Habsburg.[8] From 1602 to 1607 he was at Augsburg, occupied with his two main works: the *St Michael* already mentioned, and the four bronze figures of 1605 for the altar of the Holy Cross in St Ulrich. In 1607 he returned to Brixen, where he died in 1642. His fame had spread as far as Danzig, where he modelled the *Neptune* for the fountain on the Lange Markt in 1620.

The powerful Italo-Netherlandish influence was mainly confined to work in bronze; the Bavarian and Swabian masters – even if they had passed through this school – reverted to tradition as soon as they started to carve in wood. This applies especially to Hans Degler, trained in Munich under Krumper, who from 1591 worked at Weilheim, an important provincial centre of the popular art of wood carving. He completed the pulpit and three high openwork retables for the church of St Ulrich at Augsburg in 1664 and 1667.[9] In spite of a very personal mixture of Renaissance and Baroque forms, they combine with the Late Gothic architecture to form an organic and impressive whole; indeed they have the appearance of a teeming stage, a feature derived from medieval retables.

Georg Petel (*c.* 1591–1633), like Degler, came from Weilheim. Mainly through his friendship with Rubens, he acquired in Rome and Antwerp an understanding of the great achievements of Flemish art. He avoided the Mannerism of the German carvers and turned direct to nature, though at the same time preserving an ideal style. This was a course frequently adopted later, during the realistic phase of the seventeenth century, even in German art, wherever it was not thwarted by the Thirty Years War or led astray by false values. In his powerfully expressive figures of Christ, for example that of the ivory Crucifix in the Reiche Kapelle of the Palace in Munich and the *Salvator Mundi* in St Moritz at Augsburg (Plate 19B), Petel endowed the grandiose ideal of the heroic age with true feeling. This earned him a great reputation, particularly as an ivory carver, a reputation that went far beyond the bounds of Germany. At that time the minor arts regained once more the importance which they had had during the Renaissance.

The activity at Constance of Hans Morinck (d. 1616), a native of Holland, established a link with Venice and Jacopo Sansovino. However, in striking contrast to this style, which was essentially Renaissance in character, the true German art of wood carving found a home at nearby Überlingen, thanks to the activity of Jörg Zürn (d. before 1635). His high altar of 1613–19 in the minster shows evidence of Italian models only in the striving for greater monumentality, while his personal manner emerges in a rugged, exceedingly dynamic style with jagged drapery folds, deep wrinkles, unruly curls, and swelling veins (Plates 20 and 21A). The art of the Zürn family and that round Lake Constance as a whole later acquired importance for the 'Innviertel' (i.e. the region of the upper Inn) and Austria (p. 106), for the upheavals caused by the Thirty Years War resulted in a migration to the less harassed south-east of Europe. Martin Zürn, Jörg Zürn's brother, worked at Wasserburg from 1636 onwards. To him are ascribed the figures of *St Florian* and *St Sebastian* (now in the museum at Berlin-Charlottenburg), as having come from the high altar of St Jacob in Wasserburg.[10] But Swabian wood carving was transplanted even to the north-west, in spite of the Netherlandish hegemony there. About 1630, for example, Jeremias Geisselbrunner of Augsburg modelled the figures of the apostles for the Jesuit church in Cologne,[11] to the building of which Elector Maximilian had contributed. This Augsburg artist lost some of his austerity in the climate of Cologne, and his art gained in suppleness and beauty.

In Franconia sculpture did not occupy the leading position that it had in the south. There the Kern family was prominent. They were from Swabia too, domiciled at Forchtenberg on the Kocher in Württemberg. Michael (1580–1649), who worked chiefly at Würzburg as a sculptor in stone, was less important than Leonhard (1588–1662), who enlarged his knowledge by anatomical and architectural studies made during a visit to Italy between 1609 and 1614. After 1620 he lived at Schwäbisch Hall, where, like Petel, he became famous for small sculpture. His best known large works are the figures on the two outer portals of the Nuremberg Town Hall (1617). The reclining figures, personifications of the four empires, are Michelangelesque in their imposing earthbound heaviness, and they are all the more effective as the façade itself is unadorned. Leonhard Kern, again like Petel, was a keen student of nature. In 1626 he writes in a letter that he 'was modelling a crucifixus from a fine-looking, well proportioned live model whom he had hung up and bound to a cross'.

The work of Johann Junker, which can be traced from 1598 to 1623, reflects the culture of the bishoprics on the Franconian Main in all its lavish colourfulness. He was active at Würzburg, Mainz, and Aschaffenburg, and was most successful as a figure sculptor. He worked in particular for Johannes Schweickardt of Kronberg, elector of Mainz, for whom the Schloss at Aschaffenburg was being built. In his altar for the chapel in the Schloss (1613) the white, partially gilded alabaster figures[12] stand out against the black and red marble of the shrine, their precious beauty enhanced by Junker's virtuosity in the treatment of his materials. But he was at his best in works such as the altar of the Magdalen in the Stiftskirche at Aschaffenburg, in the representation of exquisite, ecstatically spiritualized saints and charming putti. His training in Italy and Munich proved of fundamental importance for his art, as it was for that of Sebastian Götz, creator of the statues of the Friedrichsbau at Heidelberg (1604–7).[13]

During the last quarter of the sixteenth century – this has already been reported – the overwhelming impact of Giovanni da Bologna's Mannerism made itself felt in the electorate of Saxony. It was evident in the work of Giovanni Maria Nosseni of Lugano (1544–1620), an artist of universal talents whom we have met as an architectural designer, commissioned by the elector to work on the mausoleum at Freiberg (1588–93). In 1590 he was joined as modeller and bronze caster by Carlo de Cesare from Florence. The ingenious Nosseni had been appointed in 1575 by a document characteristic of the organization of art in Saxony: 'He shall accept employment for all kinds of artistic work, as sculpture, painting and portraiture, stone tables, alabaster sideboards, the devising of buildings, the invention of triumphal entries, mummeries, and the like.' It was due to his influence that, especially in the new fields of bronze-casting and stucco work, a more monumental, more strictly architectural conception prevailed. At the same time however the link was maintained with the solid tradition of the stone-masons of Dresden and Pirna and the wood-carvers of Freiberg and Schneeberg.

Italo-Netherlandish influences also reached Dresden by way of Prague, where Adriaen de Vries was at work. Sebastian Walther (1576-1645), the most prominent Saxon sculptor of the first half of the seventeenth century and a member of an old Dresden family of sculptors, was inspired by this style, especially in the altars of the Sophienkirche at Dresden (1606)[14] and the chapel of Schloss Lichtenburg (c. 1611-13). At the same time his interest in small forms and restless movement, in jagged drapery and in detailed modelling continued (Plate 21B) – a case similar to that of his collaborator Zacharias Hegewald (Plate 22). But the style as a whole became broader, fuller, and more painterly. Dignity began to look convincing, and a certain continuity of rhythm heralds the Early Baroque.

Next to Dresden, Pirna, situated at the edge of the sandstone area along the upper Elbe, was the centre of stone carving in the electorate of Saxony. Its most important monument, the retable in the parish church,[15] was done by the brothers Schwenke in 1610-12. To David Schwenke, who was an architect, we owe the broad surround, still imbued with the spirit of the Renaissance; to Michael Schwenke (1563-1610), the most prominent Pirna master, the sculpture. In his *Vision of Ezekiel*, Michael Schwenke achieved a style in which the movement flows boldly in continuous waves throughout the relief; and by this means, like Walther, he arrived at an Early Baroque style.

More indigenous, closer to nature, and more wilful is the Mannerism of the Freiberg and Schneeberg school, which expresses the delight in fancy dress and the bold, reckless spirit which prevailed before the Thirty Years War. The audacity of the idiom that runs riot in the scrollwork provided an artistic freedom which formed a preliminary condition for the Baroque.

How a style like this can be modified on the one hand by the reawakened interest in Gothic art and on the other by court influence, becomes clearer if we compare two altar-pieces by the father and son Franz and Bernhard Ditterich. Franz Ditterich in his altar at Strehla (1605; Plate 23A)[16] retains a horizontalism of shape and a fantastic richness of form; but the lofty retable by Bernhard in the church of St Mary at Wolfenbüttel is in a refined Mannerist style. Commissioned by Heinrich Julius duke of Brunswick-Wolfenbüttel for a Protestant church in Prague, Bernhard's design was submitted in 1612 to Nosseni for his opinion. The outbreak of the war prevented its execution in Prague, and it was not set up at Wolfenbüttel until 1623, after it had been recast and adapted to Francke's Gothic Revivalism.[17]

Generally speaking, sculpture in the Protestant north was inspired by Holland, and it was by no means inferior. Wall-tablets and retables were richly adorned in a similar way to those farther south. The *Ohrmuschel* style, with its soft, doughy forms, appeared already by the second decade. In contrast to the south, figure sculpture was intended to have the effect of a sermon with plenty of symbolic references, whereas for Roman Catholic art a sacred object was the starting point and as such called for an artistic form; for example the relics of saints were represented by the statues above them. From the end of the sixteenth century until its destruction in 1631, Magdeburg was an important northern centre. Here, after a long period of stagnation, a revival had been inaugurated by Sebastian Ertle from Überlingen. The outstanding master was Christoph Dehne, who developed a highly personal style, gradually relinquishing the impressions received during his Italian training.[18] This led him from the nude to the draped figure, from architecture to the new gristly ornament, now become independent, that is, from Italian to northern abstract expression.

In lower Saxony, at Bückeburg, the arts flourished under Count Ernst of Schaumburg (1601–22), proving that where there was a patron the newly awakened talents could reach considerable achievements. From 1608 onwards the count enlisted the services of Nosseni of Dresden and Adriaen de Vries of Prague for the execution of his mausoleum at Stadthagen[19] (cf. p. 46), and from 1603 employed the brothers Ebert the Younger, Jonas, and Hans Wolf of Hildesheim for the magnificent wood carvings for his palace. These carvings, in the chapel and the Golden Hall, are the chief products of the highly inventive Mannerist style made popular by Dietterlin, and they vie with Dietterlin's etchings in their fantastic strapwork and their penetration of forms. The climax is the altar in the chapel, carved by Ebert Wolf the Younger about 1608 (Plate 23B). Its top, following the tradition of the altar at Hartenfels, is carried by angels, who have been swept to their knees.[20]

Gerhard Gröninger (1582–1652), who was born at Paderborn and became a citizen of Münster in 1609, was the most distinguished sculptor in Westphalia. He worked for the Roman Catholic Church, to which the country had reverted through the zeal of Prince-Bishop Diedrich of Fürstenberg (1546–1618) and of the Jesuits, who began to be active at Paderborn in 1580. Passionate by temperament, Gröninger found an expressive interpretation of the suffering Christ[21] that was to influence Westphalian sculpture for a long time to come.

As we proceed northwards, we find an ever-increasing tendency to throw aside all restraint in favour of heightened expression. This applies particularly to the work of Ludwig Münstermann (Plate 24).[22] He became a master in the wood-turning trade at Hamburg in 1599. As a sculptor he supplied the decoration during the first third of the century for new churches in the wealthy villages and small towns of Oldenburg, which, thanks to the efforts of Count Anton Günther, an enlightened patron of the arts, was spared the ravages of the Thirty Years War. Working in wood or alabaster, Münstermann more than any other German sculptor succeeded in infusing a passionate, flaming intensity into figures which are forceful though ugly (Plate 24). He broke away from all architectural discipline and all attempt at solid construction, developing his forms out of his ornament and giving his retables extremely jagged outlines; at the same time he pierced the back wall of the shrine so as to endow the light and dark shadows in the background behind the figures with a spiritual meaning too. Although Münstermann had studied nature, nature never took command in his work, and in this respect it is still fully in keeping with the spiritualism of the Mannerists. A comparison between his *St Luke* of the Blexen altar (1637/8) and Franz Ditterich's *Christ Appearing to the Magdalen* of the Strehla altar (1605; Plate 23A) reveals the contrast between the heroic but theatrical attitude of the Early Baroque of the beginning of the seventeenth century, and the deep sincerity of the mid century, which arose from the experiences of the war and is expressed in the compelling gesture of Münstermann's Evangelist.

Wherever Catholic and Protestant lands adjoined, both denominations demanded large, richly carved altarpieces. This was for instance the case in East Prussia, where the duchy of Ermland had remained true to the old faith after its subjection by the 'German Order'. The standard here was high. The two outstanding retables of this time, those of the Altstädtische Evangelical Church in Königsberg[23] and of the Lutheran parish church at Insterburg (c. 1623; Plate 25), still adhered to the medieval type of the shrine with wings, and at Insterburg the ornament, under Netherlandish influence, already shows the new gristly style. Figures and composition are conservative in their treatment and exhibit Renaissance, i.e. not yet Manneristic, features.

North Germany, with Hamburg as its centre, was the first to concern itself with the Baroque organ. In the wake of the musical efflorescence of the seventeenth century, richly carved organ cases began to be made which represent fundamentally Baroque sentiments, common to music and art: a feeling for polyphony, an upward surge, and an irresistible flow. However, in contrast to the 'elegant' cases of the eighteenth century (p. 198), those of the seventeenth are comparatively simple in the arrangement of the pipes. An example is the organ of St Aegidius at Lübeck of 1626,[24] which has a central round tower, lateral turrets projecting triangularly, and flanking towers for the tall bass pipes.

Whereas the Italians dominated architecture in Poland, German artists were conspicuous as sculptors. But they adjusted themselves to Polish taste and its fondness for covering the entire surface with sculptural ornament, as can be seen for example in the cathedral and in the mausolea of Kampian and Boimów (1609–17; Plate 18A) at Lvov. The most prominent sculptor was Johann Pfister, a native of Breslau (1573–c. 1640). He also designed monuments in the cathedral of Tarnow (1621) and in the palace-chapel of Brzeżany.

PAINTING

The revival of German art about 1600 did not restore to Germany the leading position which, alongside Italy, she had held in European painting during the early sixteenth century. Only the work of one painter, Adam Elsheimer, attracted the notice of the whole of Europe. His small pictures, painted mostly on copper, contributed substantially to the development of Netherlandish art and influenced Italian painters too.

Born in 1578 at Frankfurt on the Main, he had enjoyed from his youth the advantage of a local tradition that included works by Dürer as well as Grünewald; and, furthermore, Frankfurt brought him in contact with Netherlandish art. Sandrart describes Elsheimer's master, Philipp Uffenbach, as 'a great lover of all works of art, especially of the old German masters';[1] but first and foremost it must have been in Altdorfer's small landscapes that Elsheimer discovered something congenial to his own aims. What Elsheimer has in common with Altdorfer is a feeling for the unity of man with the nature that surrounds him – nature in the work of both artists reflects the character of man and even of the events which had such deep significance in these heroic years. Accordingly Elsheimer's landscapes (Plate 27B) are boldly conceived, especially the mighty trees, the dead branches of which bear witness to the tragedies that have passed over them. In his representations of the mysterious life of the forest – for instance in the subject and setting of such an early painting as *The Sermon of St John the Baptist* (Munich, Pinakothek)[2] – he shows an affinity with Gillis van Coninxloo. In the Munich picture the Baptist stands in the centre, where light falls on him, surrounded by a circle of listeners. In the version in the Hamburg Kunsthalle[3] Elsheimer goes even further in subordinating action to setting. St John, pushed towards the left into the background, is hardly visible, and the strong appeal emanating from him is apparent only in the attentive attitudes of his audience in the foreground. Nor did Elsheimer stop here. His ardent wish was to revive the romantic atmosphere of the Danube School of the Renaissance and to evoke a sense of poetry; for this, he perceived, was the special task of German art.

The *Rest on the Flight into Egypt*[4] in Berlin (c. 1600) is the first painting in which he arrives at that dreamlike atmosphere which we regard as most typical of Elsheimer and which appeals to us by its simplicity and lack of affectation. The tender embracing of the Christ Child by an angel is a specially characteristic gesture. Here Elsheimer considered the landscape as a mere setting not sufficient. The entire space is enlivened by figures, right up to the chain of angelic putti winding heavenwards. Elsheimer was particularly interested in the rendering of luminous shadows, as can be seen also in the *Baptism of Christ* of the same years (London, National Gallery).[5] The flesh colour, with its brownish tints, and the softening of all harsh colours, such as the Turkey red of Joseph's mantle, is in keeping with this. Elsheimer delighted in the interplay of yellow with red and blue, and he used it to brilliant effect in the robe of yellow silk with a red and blue pattern of the tall angel kneeling at the Virgin's right.

His indebtedness to the Venetian school is proved by numerous reminiscences in the pictures of his early period. Travelling as a journeyman, he had reached Venice in 1599, where he allegedly entered the workshop of Rottenhammer. At that time the problem that chiefly engaged his attention was to find a better, more impressive way of rendering the nude; the *Deluge*[6] in the Städel Institute at Frankfurt clearly reveals the influence of Tintoretto. Elsheimer's dramatic vitality is, however, intensified yet further when he can display his narrative sense, as in the stream of human beings swept along with their animals. At the same time he likes to draw attention to touching minor episodes, such as the little child floating in its crib on the water or the boy coming up behind, clinging to his father's hand yet reluctant to abandon his lamb. Elsheimer's gift for representing a dramatic event with a large number of figures and many details is again displayed in the *Burning of Troy*[7] at Munich, where the effect is heightened by the myriad flames, throwing a gruesome light on the scene of destruction. Outstanding is the group in the left-hand corner with Aeneas, his father, and his little son led by Creusa, who has raised her hand in a prophetic gesture – an unforgettable figure.

Elsheimer reached Rome in 1600, and there became acquainted with the art of Caravaggio. This increased his interest in realism and his concentration on character, but his inborn sense of the poetic kept his art from degenerating into insipid naturalism. An example of the new influence can be seen in the so-called *Small Tobias* (Plate 26A), a masterpiece which reveals to the full the originality of his art. Sandrart gives a vivid interpretation of what his contemporaries felt: 'a small sheet of copper *einer Spannen lang* [i.e. which a man's hand can span], wherein the angel assists young Tobias to cross a shallow stream and the little dog jumps from one stone to the next, determined not to be left behind. The rising sun shines brightly into the faces of both. The landscape is of such beauty, the reflection of the sky in the water so natural, the travellers and the animals so well portrayed that until now nobody had ever seen a manner so true to nature. Therefore in the whole of Rome the talk was all of Elsheimer's new inventions in painting.' The picture in the collection of Lady Martin in London is regarded by Weizsäcker as the original.[8] Elsheimer himself made an etching after it and varied the theme in the so-called *Large Tobias*, but without achieving the same degree of concentration.[9] Both the distant view and the way in which the boy, a somewhat prettified figure, looks out of the picture divert the eye. In contrast to this, the *Small Tobias* impresses us by its spiritualized realism, which at first glance shows nothing but the haste of the boy wading through the water, the completely natural manner of the helping angel, and the anxious efforts of the little dog to keep up with both. This truth wins over the spectator, who finds himself fully prepared by it to believe in the supernatural events, indicated from the outset by the wings of the angel.

Elsheimer also retains this spiritualized realism where his subjects are symbolic, as in the central panel, showing the *Glorification of the Cross*,[10] of a small altar at the Städel Institute at Frankfurt, painted probably for a private house. The vertical axis of the great cross contrasts with the processions of saints and angels sweeping diagonally along the paths of light and shade and merging into the infinite heavens above, and this endows the work (which is evidently inspired by Venetian art) with the monumentality and dynamic vitality that is the hallmark of great art. In addition, Elsheimer has his own inimitable way of giving to all his figures a lively, varied characterization. In the opinion of a contemporary Roman authority nothing could possibly be painted that would in any way be better than this picture.[11]

A beautiful late painting, the *Flight into Egypt* in the Munich Pinakothek (Plate 26B), shows a leisurely progress through a peaceful landscape, a favourite subject of Elsheimer's. As in the *Small Tobias*,[12] the group is enclosed in a ring of dark trees with ball-shaped tops, while at the same time the movement is carried forward. Contrary to his usual custom, Elsheimer has placed the figures in the middle. The dark shade enveloping them, which is lightened a little by Joseph's torch, gives a deeper significance to the landscape on the right, with the moon reflected in the water, the dark-blue sky, crossed on the left by the milky way, and the shepherds' fire, promising warmth and shelter, towards which the travellers are making their way. In the metaphysical sense Elsheimer's romanticism reaches its culmination here.

The small picture (6½ by 9 ins) in the Dresden Gallery of *Jupiter and Mercury visiting Philemon and Baucis*[13] reflects once again Elsheimer's state of mind during the last years of his short life, his desperate longing for a peace that was not to be. The farmhouse interior, with its timber ceiling, the semi-darkness only dimly lit by a single oil lamp and two candles, is portrayed with real devotion, and the entire scene breathes the happy security of the two travellers who have survived the storm and the kind hospitality they are enjoying (Plate 27A; the size of the plate is almost exactly half that of the original). Rembrandt, stimulated by Elsheimer, took up the theme in an etching, adding his sense of mythological greatness in particular to the figure of Jupiter; but Elsheimer does not lose in the comparison, thanks to the truly human quality of his painting.

The profound appeal of Elsheimer's art, the sensation which it created by its originality, can be explained primarily by the fact that he was neither a Mannerist nor a classicist nor a pioneer of the Baroque. He was too unaffected to accept Mannerist forms as constituent elements of his style; where they occur, they seem alien. Nor can we link up Elsheimer with the Baroque in so far as it was the art of the Counter Reformation, aimed at spreading the Roman Catholic faith. Elsheimer's pictures do not plead for any cause: they are the creations of an artist absorbed in his own world. He was, however, a religious man and a true believer, converted in Rome to the Roman Catholic faith, and he painted his religious pictures in the spirit of this faith (notably the *Glorification of the Cross* in the Städel Institute at Frankfurt). The devotion which is expressed in the pure and humble figure of his St Laurence in the picture in the National Gallery embodied his own religious ideal. Describing this figure, Sandrart says that 'he turns devoutly to heaven with ineffable feeling'. In his representation of *The Slaying of Holofernes by Judith*,[14] in the collection of the Duke of Wellington (London, Apsley House), his art is clearly distinct from the Baroque of Rubens. The painting by Rubens, reproduced by Galle in an engraving, is packed with a seething mass of figures, and the background is not even indicated. Elsheimer on the other hand depicts the event in the semi-darkness of an interior, suggesting the sinister mood of the feast and its bloody end. In contrast to the full-blown figure of Rubens's Judith, Elsheimer's Jewish heroine retains a certain maidenly delicacy.

A consideration of what Elsheimer did not choose to paint can also help us to understand his character. He avoided subjects which called for a purely objective interpretation of reality – that is, the very subjects that appealed to Dutch artists. For Elsheimer it was the human experience that counted, however closely he might associate it with nature. His religious pictures were intended to stimulate quiet meditation in the privacy of the home. The danger that threatened later German romantics, the danger of becoming too abstract, too simple, too purely linear and perhaps anaemic, did not exist for Elsheimer. He was far too intent on painting as such. As an artist who in the force of his sensuous perception was not inferior to Rembrandt, he did not avoid erotic subjects, and was attracted to them particularly after 1606, the year when his short married life, to an Englishwoman, started. The beauty to which he attains in the representation of the nude female body can be seen in the gouache study of *Bathsheba* in the Berlin Print Room, which immediately recalls Rembrandt (Plate 28A).

When Elsheimer died in 1610, only in his thirty-third year,[15] Rubens wrote to Dr Faber, a friend of both, in Rome that the death of his beloved Adam had hit him hard. 'After such a loss our entire guild should be plunged in deep mourning. It will be no easy task to replace him. In my opinion he never had an equal in the field of small figures, landscapes, and many other subjects. He died in full possession of his powers, and his harvest was only just beginning to ripen; we could have hoped for things from him that now will never exist. Fate has shown him but in his beginnings.' The work of Rembrandt more than compensates for Elsheimer's loss; yet how much of the warmth of feeling, of the deep sincerity and true insight into the real value of life does the greater, more comprehensive art of Rembrandt owe to the new range of ideas for which Elsheimer had blazed the trail!

If Elsheimer contributed substantially to the rise of Dutch art, without himself forming part of it, the second great German painter of the day, Johann Liss, a 'Holstein man', as he called himself, made it his goal to develop the world of Rubens and Frans Hals in a Venetian way. He was probably the son of a painter-couple, Johann and Anna Liss, who had come from Oldenburg. Born at Schleswig about 1597, he must have received some stimulus from the teaching of his parents and also from the court of the duke of Schleswig-Holstein at Gottorp Castle. About 1616 he probably went to Amsterdam and Harlem for further training, and there, according to Sandrart, followed the manner of Goltzius. He was extremely susceptible to the new *joie-de-vivre* that swept the country as soon as the fight for freedom was over, and by studying the art of Frans Hals and Rubens and getting to know the Dutch way of life, he learnt how to express exuberance and animal pleasure. A few years later he went to Venice. He stopped in Paris on the way and must have reached Venice by 1621 at the latest, as his presence is recorded in that year. About 1622 he continued his journey to Rome and there became a member of the Netherlandish 'Schilderbent' (painters' club). An allegorical drawing now at Brno of a voluptuous woman looking upwards and wearing a crown which is beginning to fall off is inscribed: 'All art and cunning are but dust. High wisdom is to believe in Christ. Johann Liss painter from Holstein. Rome, 19 March A° 16..' Probably this is the date of his conversion.

Liss's life, according to Sandrart, was spent in a perpetual alternation between intense concentration on his work, even through the night, and equally long periods of wandering about. Similarly, his range extends from the world of the senses to the heights of tragedy. Examples of the latter are *The Mourning over the dead Abel*[16] in the Accademia at Venice and *The Cursing of Cain*,[17] formerly in Berlin. He was in his element in Venice – more so than in Rome – and gives a brilliant portrayal of the splendour of her citizens at this period. Sandrart, who was a personal witness, wrote of him: 'He drew much in our academy in Venice from the nude, and he knew how to endow the models with a special grace and with something as it were more than natural, but he did not pay much attention to classical art and the serious antique schools, saying that though he valued them very highly, if he attempted to adopt a manner so opposed to his own, he would have to start again at the beginning. He was more attracted to the manner of Titian, Tintoretto, Paolo Veronese, Feti, and other Venetian artists, but especially to that of the last-named.' In the opinion of Italian scholars,[18] he greatly influenced the much debased Venetian school of painting of the seventeenth century: 'He was bound to give to the academic and manneristic Venetian circle of that time an impetus that helped to lift it out of its groove. He set before the Venetians the best elements of their own art united to a sensible, moderate eclecticism made up of Caravaggist, Flemish, and Dutch elements, that is to say of elements from the schools then most vitally alive. In the eighteenth century Bencovich attached himself to the manner of Liss, and even Piazzetta and Tiepolo owe him something.' Compared with Rubens, he seems less dominated by the antique ideal of beauty. In his *Toilet of Venus* at Pommersfelden (Plate 29), for instance, the nude is close to nature and not affected by the heaviness of the Early Baroque. For Venetian art, his great skill in lightening his colours and making them translucent was of special importance. In this Liss revived the great Venetian traditions. On the other hand he also liked figures emerging with sudden highlights from deep shade. An example is his *Soldiers' Camp* in the Germanisches National museum at Nuremberg (Plate 28B).[19] All too early, in 1629, Liss died in Venice of the plague.

In Germany itself Mannerism, in its Netherlandish form, dominated and often chilled the art of painting. Friedrich Sustris (*c.* 1540–99) and Peter de Witte, called Candid (*c.* 1548–1628), are the best exponents of this style. They both worked in Munich on the decoration of the Residenz. At the court of Vienna and Prague, that is the court of that remarkable collector, Emperor Rudolph II, an immensely skilful and highly artificial art was introduced by Bartholomäus Spranger (1546–1611), whose Mannerism shows in a hard, metallic modelling, stone-grey flesh tints, and an affected eroticism. In Prague his manner was taken over by Hans von Aachen of Cologne (1552–1615) and Joseph Heintz of Basel (1564–1609). The Munich painter Hans Rottenhammer (1564–1625) came under the influence of Tintoretto during a visit to Venice in 1600. From 1606 onward he found ample scope for his work at Augsburg and occasionally, in certain idyllic moods, comes very close to Elsheimer.

PART THREE

THE YEARS OF RECOVERY AFTER THE THIRTY YEARS WAR 1640–82

CHAPTER 6

ARCHITECTURE

THE early part of the period between 1640 and 1682 was overshadowed by the consequences of what had been in effect a civil war. This is why a feeling of national unity
could not at once emerge, and why foreign influences throve and, at least in architecture, led to complete subordination, especially to Italian culture. The scene was dominated by the Maestri Comacini and masons from the Grisons. And yet in painting the
seeds of future growth were sown: Mannerism was slowly being discarded in favour
of adherence to nature, and portraiture, in particular, displayed a healthy realism. In
the field of architecture the Jesuits continued their consistent building programme and
were gradually followed by the older orders. The Protestants, however, from whose
ranks so many eminent artists had come during the preceding period, for a time fell
back.

Austria

Immediately after the conclusion of the peace treaty, Austria once again took the lead
in the development of the Baroque style. One motif of future importance already
heralded was the central plan for churches. At Innsbruck, in fulfilment of a vow made
by the Tyrolese nobles to avert the impending danger of war and in gratitude for their
liberation, Christoph Gumpp, architect to the emperor, erected the Mariahilfkirche[1] as
a domed circular building (1647). The beautiful interior opens in six arches to the vestibule, the choir, and the chapels, probably inspired by Serlio's plan for a temple in the
third volume of his *Opere d'architettura*. The choir, with its three-quarter apse for the
high altar, is more spacious than the semicircular lateral chapels. The oval shape, too,
which had appeared in the north even before the war, in the Graz Mausoleum, was used
again by Carlo Canevale for the church of the Servites in Vienna (1651–77).[2] As was
also to be done later in Holy Trinity at Salzburg and the churches of St Peter and St
Charles in Vienna, the oval is placed longitudinally, not transversely. In addition, a cross
shape is indicated by larger transeptal chapels. Thus the form which was to be decisive
for the eighteenth century had here already been found; only the addition of a dome on
a drum was still lacking. For the church façade, a novel and fully Baroque solution was

introduced by Carlo Antonio Carlone at the church of the Jesuits in Vienna, dedicated to the Nine Angelic Choirs (Plate 30A). This was built in 1662. In order to provide sufficient space for the front, which faces a large square, Am Hof, the two upper storeys recede, whereas the ground floor with the two framing wings of the Casa Professa keeps flush with the neighbouring houses. The wings with their giant pilasters correspond to the then current type of palace façade. The window-bays, joined together in vertical bands, introduce a motif which was to become characteristic of Viennese palaces.

Side by side with the monasteries, the court made important contributions during these years. The Emperor Leopold I (1658–1705) had a new façade erected for the Hofburg, the Imperial Palace (1661–8; Plate 30B), the entire range being thenceforth known as the Leopold Range. In the even sequence of the vertically joined windows – originally numbering forty-four – and in the absence of projections or eminences, the front recalls those of the Munich Residenz, though the Viennese did not imitate the Bavarian fashion of external fresco decoration. The articulation indicated in the pilastering is kept very shallow. The architect, Philiberto Luchese, admitted a three-dimensional accent only just below the eaves in the grotesque faces on the brackets. The Starhemberg Palace, presumably erected in 1661, shows a similar restraint in the vertical articulation (Plate 31B), though window pediments and putti carrying the upper brackets furnish a vigorous three-dimensional contrast.

In upper Austria large-scale activity in the monasteries began with the Benedictine abbey of Garsten[3] (1677–85) and the Cistercian abbey of Schlierbach[4] (1679–85). They were built by the Carlone, conspicuous among them Carlo Antonio, who was to become the greatest of them. The architects retained the internal buttress piers and galleries of the older churches, but discarded transept and dome. The main effect is produced by the sumptuous, heavy stucco decoration and the frescoes framed like easel pictures. Giovanni Battista Carlone was the most outstanding of the plasterers. He later worked at Passau and Waldsassen.

Related to these upper Austrian churches is the new church of the Augustinian Canons at Vorau in Styria (1660–2).[5] The interior decoration was not done until after 1700, when the period of excessive plasterwork was over, so that the impression produced by the painted interior and the superb high altar by Matthias Steinl (1700–4), with its curving transparent groups of columns, is one of far greater harmony.

Hungary

During the seventeenth century the possibilities for the expansion of Hungarian art were limited to a few areas; for until the termination of the wars of liberation (1683–99) the entire Hungarian lowland was occupied by the Turks. Nevertheless Hungary did contribute a number of important buildings to the brilliant development of European palace architecture. In 1632–49, under Count Paul Pálffy, the rebuilding of the royal castle at Bratislava (Pozsony; Pressburg),[6] probably begun from a design by Elias Holl, was completed. The medieval citadel, rising about 250 feet above the Danube and dominating the city in which the Hungarian kings had been crowned for centuries past, now acquired a more regular shape. The four wings form a huge square, similar to the Willibaldenburg at Eichstätt, which had also been enlarged by Holl. The main building was raised by one storey, the towers by two, and the roof itself was also raised. Those parts of the towers which appear above the roofs are octagonal. The work was executed by Hans Alberthaler. The castle was burnt in 1811, and has since remained a ruin. Červeny (Biberburg), not far away, originates in the same sphere. It was built by the Fuggers in the sixteenth century as a fortress, and also as a wine store; the enormous fortified cellars testify to this.

At Eisenstadt (Kismarton) under Count Paul Esterházy the medieval castle[7] was refaced from designs of Carlo Martino Carlone in 1663-72. The fronts display the then popular motif of giant Tuscan pilasters beneath projecting eaves carried on brackets. The side towards the courtyard is decorated with stucco. As was usual in Bohemia, expressive masks appear on the string-courses above the ground floor and on brackets below the eaves. The skyline of the castle lost its original, characteristically Baroque form when the bulbous domes of the four corner towers were replaced by roofs of low pitch. Here, and also in Schloss Esterháza at Fertöd,[8] much of Haydn's music was heard for the first time; for during the main part of his life, from 1761 to 1790, Haydn was the conductor of Prince Nicholas Esterházy's orchestra. Indeed, the Hungarian nobility in general took a keen interest in the golden age of Viennese music. The compositions dedicated by Beethoven to the Brunszvik family of Martonvasar, to whom he was devoted, bear further witness to this.

In the seventeenth century the religious plays of the Jesuits and the Piarists had inspired the Hungarians with heroic ideals and national feeling. A hundred years later Donner expressed this in a most characteristic manner in his equestrian statue of *St Martin* in Bratislava Cathedral, represented not as a Roman soldier, but in the costume of a Hungarian officer of the hussars (Plate 64).[9]

Bohemia and Moravia

In Bohemia the vast estates accumulated after the Thirty Years War by those members of the high nobility who had supported the emperor's cause offered a unique opportunity for the building of new palaces. The inducement was further increased by the claims to sovereignty staked even against the emperor (though of course not openly) by families such as the Lobkowicz, the Piccolomini, and the Černín. The swelling pride that had inspired Waldstein, the eminent general, too, was later the cause of his secret rivalry to the imperial enterprises. In Bohemia, Italian architects and plasterers dominated the scene more than in any other imperial province,[10] grouping themselves in co-operative associations with the necessary trained craftsmen available. At Prague Carlo Lurago's team reigned supreme. Even in the German towns of western Bohemia, the teams of the 'Welsch', i.e. Italian, masons dominated; at Pilsen for instance, as a speculation, they built houses for the merchant class around the Ringplatz.

The Bohemian variety of Mannerism had first been developed by the Jesuits in the Clementinum[11] of Prague University, built by Carlo Lurago in 1654-8. The Bohemian preference for heavy, massive forms can be seen in the banded giant composite pilasters, whose tops are decorated with the grotesque heads popular in the architectural sculpture of the day. The entablature is split up by inserted windows.

The first palace of note to be built after the war was that of Roudnice (Raudnitz) [12] above the Elbe, begun in 1652 by Prince Wenzel Eusebius of Lobkowicz to replace the medieval castle. It was intended to be a large oblong with an inner courtyard. By 1665 Francesco Caratti of Bissone on Lake Lugano had built the two lower storeys of the east wing, and the palace was completed in 1668–97 by Antonio Porta, whose design of 1672 determined the final form. The ashlar-faced base contained two mezzanine floors, and the two floors above are linked together by giant Doric pilasters. The vertical accent was stressed further by raised panels in the sill-zone of the windows. The main entrance is in the south façade, which is terminated towards the court by a colonnade with a high tower above the gateway and lateral flights of stairs. Originally the colonnade had a terrace on top adorned by statues in the Italian fashion. Two spacious staircases were placed in the angles of the southern wing. The saloon, rising through two storeys, is in the western wing, i.e. not yet on the main axis; the chapel, also two storeys high, is in the south-east corner. The doors are already arranged according to the system which the French call *enfilade*, that is, they are all aligned and placed close to the window wall. Contrary to the express wishes of the client, a corridor exists only in the south wing. Prince Lobkowicz was on the other hand responsible for the raising of the tower in order to provide a stronger vertical emphasis to counteract the even flow of the horizontal lines of the roof. The tradition of a triclinium and a giant order of pilasters, initiated by Waldstein in his palaces of Jičín (Gitschin) and Żagań (Sagan) in 1626 and 1627, is carried on at Roudnice and resulted in a building of far-reaching significance.

Only by exchanging pilasters for demi-columns could the exteriors be made yet more monumental, and this step was taken, on the authority of Palladio, in the façade of the Černín Palace in Prague. From the time of his third visit to Rome in 1662 the client, Count Humprecht Hermann Černín, had been obsessed by the idea of erecting a vast palace in Prague in the Italian style. The opportunity came in 1666, after he had acquired a building site in the vast Loretto Square on the Hradčany (Hradschin). The site was of considerable width, though shallow in depth, and this width made it possible for Černín to outrival the fronts of the nearby imperial castle. After a prolonged search, he discovered a suitable architect in Francesco Caratti, whose work at Roudnice had prepared him for this new tremendous undertaking. He was the chief architect of the Černín Palace from 1668 until his death in 1677.

The façade is of twenty-nine bays and c. 465 feet long (Plate 31A). Above the basement with its diamond-rustication giant three-quarter columns rise to the height of two storeys. As in the Clementinum, the entablature is interrupted by mezzanine windows. Following the pattern familiar in Vienna and Prague, the fantastic capitals are composed of grimacing heads between Ionic volutes. The start of building operations coincided with the termination of the Leopold Range of the Vienna Hofburg, whose long, even, regular fenestration had served as a model. According to an old tradition, the emperor, when examining the unfinished building, was unable to conceal his annoyance at the fact that the Bohemian count, whose political career had been anything but brilliant, should in the majesty of his palace have surpassed his own. The splendid monotony was certainly intentional on the part of Černín. It is Mannerist, not only in the details such as the grimacing heads, but also in the way in which the vertical thrust, starting right down in the mouldings of the basement, terminates abruptly in the roof zone. Later, in 1747-50, Anselmo Lurago enlivened the rigidity of the façade as far as possible by introducing three portals with balconies. The height of the staircase hall, criticized as insufficient, was increased by Franz Maximilian Kanka in 1717. Towering above it in mighty masses, the ceiling fresco by Wenzel Lorenz Reiner spreads in a majestic composition.

This grandiose building, where the initiative of the patron is everywhere discernible,[13] has a further surprise in store for us in the long, luxuriously equipped stables at the back and the picture-gallery above them. The relatively narrow garden front on the north side has two arcades, like the Villa Medici in Rome, arranged on the principle of the so-called Venetian or Palladio motif.[14] The large saloon behind the middle of the main front is seven windows wide and two and a half storeys high. It never received any decoration, although Domenico Egidio Rossi in 1696 supplied brilliant sketches of architectural perspectives. Owing to its extravagant size, the palace was never an economic proposition, and inevitably it became an increasing burden for the family. At the end of the eighteenth century it was criticized as a 'tasteless mass of stone',[15] and in 1851 it was sold to the state and adapted as a barracks.

In Moravia, the example of the Leopold Range of the Vienna Hofburg influenced the Archbishop's Palace at Kroměříž (Kremsier),[16] built in 1679. At Plumlov (Plumenau),[17] the learned dilettante-architect Prince Karl Eusebius of Liechtenstein retained control, in contrast to the situation at the Černín Palace, where the client, despite his wish to design himself, had yielded to the genius of his architect. Following Prince Karl Eusebius's advice, Caratti's son, in 1680-5, piled three orders of columns projecting one above the other, a unique testimony to the presumption of a princely client.

Moravia's contribution to the developing Baroque style in ecclesiastical architecture lies in two significant buildings at Olomouc (Olmütz). The first of them is the church on the Holy Mountain,[18] the earliest of the series of Moravian pilgrimage-churches. The building dates from 1669-79 and was designed by Baldassare Fontana. Seen from a distance, the façade with its twin towers flanked by the two symmetrical wings of the monastery is highly impressive. The long, low wings, with their giant pilasters, not yet set on bases, and their attic crowned by statues, form a prelude and an effective contrast to the verticalism of the towering church façade. An arcaded ambulatory with a central chapel rounds off the back. The second church, St Michael,[19] of 1676-1703, marks an important advance. With its three domed compartments in a row, it offers a motif which was welcomed in the Slavonic east (cf. p. 308).

The decided preference for Italian architecture among such members of the Bohemian and Moravian high aristocracy as Prince Liechtenstein and Count Černín was shaken when Johann Friedrich, count of Waldstein, archbishop of Prague, brought with him in 1675 as his personal architect the Frenchman Jean Baptist Mathey. Mathey, who probably came from Dijon, was originally a painter. In Prague, the Frenchman suffered from the hostility of the local guild, which forbade its members to work for him, and it was only through the emperor's support that he was able to maintain his position. The guild, in attacking Mathey, defended the north-Italian–Bohemian Baroque against the invasion of French early classicism. Yet from 1679 to 1694 Mathey was able to design noteworthy buildings in Prague which can indeed be regarded as a criticism of the customary type of Bohemian architecture. At Troja, a country house near Prague[20] (1679–96), he introduced a grouped composition with a raised centre and lateral wings surmounted by towers. The introduction of an outside staircase on the garden side whose flights, adorned by sculpture, encircle an elliptical grotto also affords a new motif. His ideal of a town house was realized in the Toscana Palace,[21] built in 1689–90. It forms the greatest conceivable contrast to the Černín Palace. A shallow articulation by lesenes or pilaster strips flanks every window, and pavilion roofs rise above two lateral bays with balconies supported by coupled columns.

Mathey's sv. František (Kreuzherrnkirche) in Prague[22] of 1679–88 is a remarkable piece of ecclesiastical architecture. Here, four arms extend from an elliptical central space that rises evenly over pendentives and drum into a dome. In his abbey church of St Josef Malá Strana (Kleinseite), on the other hand, Mathey followed a Roman model. The elliptical ground plan opens on each of the two longitudinal sides in three niches set between coupled Corinthian columns. The effect of these buildings was felt less in Prague itself than in Fischer von Erlach's Holy Trinity in Salzburg and St Charles in Vienna. He had retained his Prague impressions in some sketches. In Prague, indeed, the opposition against the tendencies propagated by Mathey had won a decisive victory in the very year 1679 in which Mathey had arrived: this was the acceptance of Guarino Guarini's design for the church of the Virgin of Alt-Ötting, a victory without doubt, although the building was never executed. His bold constructions with their reciprocal penetration of space by diagonally placed pilasters, making a sequence of central spaces, made a deep impression on Christoph and Johann Dientzenhofer, the most prominent members of the family which was going to build the leading churches of Prague in the next generation and who started to work at about that time (see p. 127).[23]

Prague was bound to have the greatest influence in those parts of southern Germany which lay close to the Bohemian border, for instance at Passau, where the nave of the cathedral was rebuilt after 1668 by Carlo Lurago of Prague (c. 1618–84). He introduced here at a remarkably early date transverse elliptical saucer-domes on pendentives between the transverse arches of the nave (Plate 32), a form of vault which was developed at Schlierbach eight years later and which had an important bearing on the development of ceiling painting and on the tendency to introduce centralized elements into longitudinal churches. Passau Cathedral is a basilican building the aisles of which are lined with chapels between internal buttressing walls, a motif known from Kempten. The sumptuous stucco decoration by Giovanni Battista Carlone (begun in 1677) introduced an important innovation in the use of human figures projecting into the architectural framework. In the choir of Passau Cathedral yet another innovation appears: Carpoforo Tencalla's frescoes of 1678 conceal all divisions between the bays, forming a homogeneous decoration of the vault.

Franconia

The Bohemian Baroque also reached Franconia, where, in the nave of the newly constructed Cistercian abbey at Waldsassen[24] (1681–1704), Abraham Leuthner of Prague, aided by his foreman Georg Dientzenhofer, introduced elliptical saucer-domes on pendentives similar to those at Passau. The lateral chapels received shallow oval domes pierced at their apex and with these openings surrounded by balustrades. Such interpenetration of space is typically Baroque. The same motif was repeated in the chapels of the collegiate church of Dürnstein in upper Austria. The hemispherical dome rising without a drum over the crossing is also a motif which was to be of importance later.

At Würzburg the buildings of Bishop Julius Echter von Mespelbrunn stand at the beginning of a policy of grandiose building which, under the Schönborns, was to go from strength to strength. The first of the three great prince-bishops of the Schönborn family, Johann Philipp (1642–73), had a substantial share in bringing about the Peace of Westphalia. The loyalty towards the emperor which was to be characteristic of the Schönborns shows itself already at this early date. During the period of Italian ascendancy, from 1651 until his death in 1701, the architect of the prince-bishop of Würzburg and also of the elector of Mainz, Antonio Petrini from Trento, remained unchallenged. He reached the height of his powers with the huge Benedictine abbey church of Haug at Würzburg (1670–91), which combines Italian with northern elements (Plate 33A). The transept is shifted to a position midway between west and east, a motif that was going to be of great importance later. The façade with its two towers and the great octagonal dome create a unified, demonstratively vertical, and picturesquely varied silhouette. The transepts project far, and the chancel ends in five sides of a dodecagon, a northern and Gothic motif.

Silesia

Silesia, the battlefield between the Catholic south and the Protestant north, could not produce anything as homogeneous as the Baroque of Austria, Bohemia, and Moravia. On the one hand the Austrian authorities tried by every means in their power to reconvert the country to the old faith, and this expressed itself in its buildings; on the other the Protestants, aided by Sweden, gave expression to their religious mood in architectural forms of their own. By the Peace of Westphalia the Swedes succeeded in obtaining sanction for the Silesian Protestants to build three timber-framed churches, and in 1651, 1654, and 1656 these three 'peace-churches', at Głogów (Glogau), Jawor (Jauer), and Swidnica (Schweidnitz),[25] were erected. Even their interiors were monuments to northern carpentry, in so far as the necessity of accommodating great numbers in a limited space resulted in several tiers of wooden galleries. This motif points to the west, while the log construction of other Silesian churches displays an affinity with the Slav east. Only there did the log house with its horizontal logs survive, although it had once, many centuries earlier, been customary in all districts where the German tongue was spoken.

Poland

Poland in the middle of the seventeenth century suffered from the consequences of the double war with Sweden and Russia and from perpetual party strife. In contrast to the French principle of absolutism, which was victorious in Central Europe, the Polish aristocracy kept its *Liberum Veto*, so that a single individual could enforce his will when votes were taken at the diet. This had its dangers, as bribery by foreign potentates was rife; but the courage of the Poles and their love of liberty could also sometimes assert itself with the aid of the same law. When in 1672 King Michael (1669–73) concluded an ignominious peace with the Turks, the diet repudiated it and ordered Marshal John Sobieski to renew the struggle. In 1673 Sobieski gained the brilliant victory of Chozim over an enemy vastly superior in numbers and was elected king in the following year. By a second victory over the Turks he rescued Lemberg (Lvov) in 1675, and finally, in 1683, saved the Empire when, as general in command of the allied forces, he relieved Vienna – in opposition to the wishes of the court, which sided with France in the hope that Turkish dominion would weaken Germany. German historians agree that the relief of Vienna would have been impossible without Sobieski.

During the early years of this period, that is the forties and fifties, Poland produced buildings full of character; for example much of the episcopal palace of Kielce (Plate 33B, Figure 2).[26] The central part of the building dates from the second half of the sixteenth century: this is proved by the doorcases of the great hall on the east side and the painted beamed ceiling of the Episcopal Hall on the garden side. The rest of the palace was erected mainly in 1638 by Thomas Poncini at the order of Bishop Jacob Zadzik (d. 1642). It is placed on the axis of the cathedral, but about six feet out. The centre of the façade was emphasized by three arches on the ground floor and three large windows above, each subdivided into three. The four hexagonal towers were detached from the square block, to create a building well articulated in the sense of the Renaissance. The square was surrounded by arcades.

Another contribution to Polish town-planning is the Ringplatz at Zamość,[27] also with arcades on all sides. The piers here are strongly battered. Between and below the windows of the façades the stucco decoration includes ample strapwork. There is one house with a giant order of pilasters, niches, and busts. (The attics were replaced by prosaic parapet walls in the nineteenth century.) The square is dominated by the town hall, whose high tower with its mighty buttresses forcibly emphasizes the vertical in bold contrast to the horizontal cornices (Plate 34). Only the flight of stairs in front with its curving arms brought a contrast in the eighteenth century. Similarly the Sigismund Column in front of Warsaw Castle,[28] erected in 1644 by the architect Constante Tencalla and the sculptor Clemente Molli, is derived from the Column of the Virgin in front of S. Maria Maggiore in Rome. In ecclesiastical architecture the Gothic style was generally retained for the body of the building, the Renaissance appearing only in the details. An example is the church at Rydzyna, built in 1641.

The wars in Poland caused extensive devastation. In 1655 the Swedes laid waste Poznań, Warsaw, and Cracow, the Russians Vilna, Grodno, and Kovno. The plucky

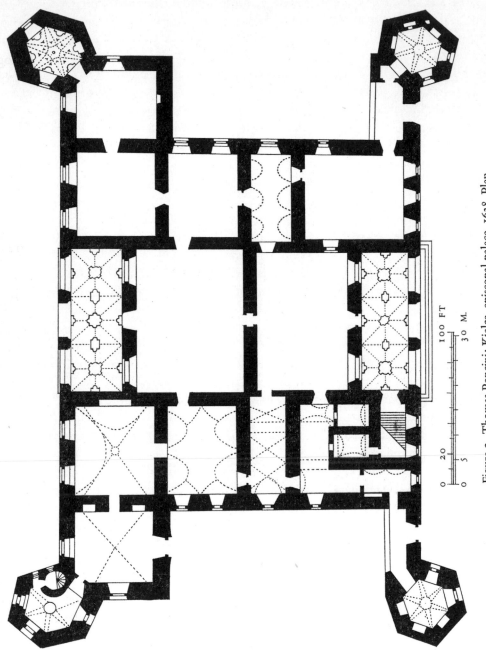

Figure 2. Thomas Poncini: Kielce, episcopal palace, 1638. Plan

inhabitants of Lemberg were the only ones to offer resistance. As soon as times became more peaceful, the will to reconstruction made itself felt. The Dominican church at Vilna,[29] burnt down by the Russians in 1655, rose again in 1688 with a mighty dome. The extremely lively Baroque fittings belong to the eighteenth century. The church of St Peter and St Paul in the suburb of Antokol, built in 1668–84 by Jan Zaor from Cracow for the Lithuanian *hetman* Michael Pac, has excellent stucco work. Zaor is said to have engaged for the work three hundred plasterers from Warsaw, who, under the direction of the two Milanese Giovanni Galli and Pietro Peretti, produced about two thousand figures. They are based on an accurate study of nature, and some of the saints are evidently portraits.

The earliest and most magnificent central building of the second half of the seventeenth century is the Camaldolensian church at Pozajście near Kovno.[30] It was built by Lodovico Fredo in 1667–96, its models being S. Agnese in Piazza Navona in Rome and S. Maria della Salute in Venice. The latter church was also the inspiration for Pompeo Ferrari when, at the beginning of the eighteenth century, he completed on an altered plan the Philippine church at Gostyń[31] begun by Jan Catenacci in 1675. Drum as well as dome are octagonal.

The ancient wooden churches also rose again in the countryside, with their shingled exteriors (Plate 35A) and richly painted interiors,[32] and in the Cracow region the Jews erected profusely decorated wooden synagogues.

Upper Saxony

The third quarter of the seventeenth century was bound to be an unproductive period in the electorate of Saxony; for the country wavered between support of the Catholics and of the Protestant powers, and was therefore deeply involved in the vicissitudes of the war. In spite of this, the delight in court displays kindled by Nosseni flared up ever anew, and in addition good artists like Wilhelm Dilich (1571/2–1650) were quietly at work. Dilich had been in the service of Johann Georg I as Electoral Inspector of Works since 1625, and as such provided the Hall of the Giants[33] of the palace at Dresden with a segmental wooden vault, furnishing also rough drafts for about forty-six views of Saxon towns to be fitted as panels into the walls and the ceiling. Being less intent on gain than Merian, he was not only a conscientious topographer, but in addition a better artist, especially by virtue of his vivid, sketchy draughtsmanship. He proved his wealth of ideas by more than four hundred ideal plans of fortified towns, which were published at Frankfurt in 1640 under the title *Peribologia oder Bericht von Wilhelmi Dilichii von Vestungs-Gebeven*, an important contribution to the transformation of the fortified town, which became a fully planned, aesthetically considered unit. In general he used the Italian radial system with a polygonal square, the form given to Palma Nuova by the Venetians in 1593. By means of sheets of water Dilich also arrived at more individual solutions. A plan showing the larger part of a town in a grid of oblong blocks, and the smaller one on the opposite bank with streets radiating towards an open space near the bend of the river, calls Dresden to mind.

After the fire which destroyed the Dresden Neustadt (p. 190), his successor, Wolf Caspar von Klengel (1630–91), partly utilized Dilich's plan in his project for the reconstruction of the town. He too started as a fortification engineer, but he was not a topographer, but an officer in the artillery. The architectural tradition of Dresden had been handed down to him through his mother's family. His grandfather, Paul Buchner, had built the fine Stallhof and the arsenal in a Late Renaissance style, and sympathy with their compact, vigorous forms is occasionally apparent in Klengel. In addition he had studied the Baroque style in every way in Italy from 1651 to 1655 and also on subsequent journeys, in spite of being in military service most of the time.[34] In 1655, at the age of twenty-five, he was called to Dresden from the Turkish front in Dalmatia to become Inspector General of Works. However, his desire to erect a mausoleum at Dresden for the Wettin dynasty, as Nosseni had done fifty years before for the Schaumburg-Lippes at Stadthagen, was not to be fulfilled: the Elector Johann Georg II, who was well disposed towards him, commanded in 1658 that a number of houses on the Seegasse should be bought for the mausoleum, but more than that did not happen. Klengel would have enlarged Nosseni's octagon by four arms of equal length; he would also have replaced the pilasters at the portal by columns and changed the pyramid roof with its lantern to an upper storey with the ogee outline of a big bulbous dome. As a kind of compensation, Klengel was commissioned to build an annex to the chapel of the Castle of Moritzburg (1661–72). Here, by means of the high arched windows which he also used in the room for ball games next to the castle at Dresden (1668), he succeeded effectively and monumentally in linking the new work to the old moated castle of the sixteenth century, with its round towers.

This sympathy with the German past should be specially appreciated in an architect who lived so much in the artistic atmosphere of the south that he provided his Dresden sketches and plans with explanatory remarks in Italian. Even his looks were foreign, in spite of his pure German extraction (Plate 44A). Inspiration from the south was an inner necessity to him, as was later the case with Goethe; there was therefore nothing negative in their attitude. In the Saxony of those days the partiality of artists for Italy had its nobler counterpart in the musicians, and music meant a great deal more to the artistically minded public than the fine arts. For the chorales of Bach's great precursor, Heinrich Schütz, Klengel installed curved galleries in the chapels of the castle of Moritzburg[35] and the palace at Dresden. Further, in 1664–7 he erected an opera house next to the palace (Plate 35B). The building, which unfortunately stood only for a short while, was far in advance of its time in the spaciousness of the interior, with its fully detached columns and pillars. Even the stairs contributed to this sense of space, as they wound up round the front columns of the auditorium and led in broken flights to the top gallery, the whole culminating in the ceiling fresco by Johann Oswald Harms which showed the chariot of Apollo ascending into the skies – the first great achievement of ceiling painting in the north.

During the following decade Klengel's duties as chief inspector of civic and military buildings and his work for the artillery corps frequently interfered with his architectural tasks. In 1693–6 however he built the upper part of the tower of the palace, a completely

German design. Klengel was a man of wide cultural interests, which would itself be sufficient to establish him as the founder of the Dresden Baroque. This is confirmed by his output during the last decade of his life (cf. p. 190).

Second to Klengel and, in 1672, his successor as Inspector General of Works, was the rather younger Johann Georg Starcke (c. 1640–95). His patron Johann Georg III, then still crown prince, and later to be famous for his victory over the Turks, commissioned him to build an important palace in the Grosser Garten at Dresden. This park was made at that time and the palace was to be at the crossing of the two principal avenues. It was built in 1679–83 (Plate 36A). The idea of an H-shaped plan with a large transverse central hall and exterior flights of stairs on both sides can probably be traced back to a drawing by the crown prince, inspired by a similar project of Klengel.[36] The exterior however, in contrast to Klengel's buildings, shows French influence, and the rich decoration is not yet organically integrated into the whole.

Whereas thus no large-scale building took place in the electorate of Saxony, where a considerable number of castles already existed, the position was different in Thuringia, where in the smaller principalities of Gotha, Zeitz, and Weissenfels new buildings went up to realize a new ideal. After the fire of 1618 the palace at Weimar had been reconstructed by Giovanni Bonalino of Milan. Here, in the system of the façades towards the courtyard with rusticated ground floor surmounted by an order of pilasters, he introduced an Italian model, the beauty of which lay in proportions, not in decoration. It made a suitable starting-point for new developments after the war. In Thuringia, as in Saxony, German architects now began to replace the Italians. Andreas Rudolff, an engineer, who specialized in fortification and had like Klengel been trained in Holland, erected the simple but impressive Friedenstein Palace above Gotha in 1643–54.[37] He worked in collaboration with the architect Caspar Vogel. In accordance with a tradition of French châteaux, the elongated rectangle of the courtyard, surrounded by arcades, is closed on one side by a low range. This is occupied by the riding-school. The principal range, crowned by a turret, contains the saloon, and to its left and right, in the corner towers, the private apartments. The two symmetrically arranged staircases lie in the corners between the principal range and the wings.

The same tendency appears in the palaces designed by Johann Moritz Richter. He built the palace of Zeitz[38] in 1657–78, the Moritzburg, and the palace of Weissenfels[39] in 1660–93. They consist again of three ranges with a tower dominating the centre of the main range and a low fourth range. At Zeitz Richter introduced a type of staircase that was very progressive for the Germany of his day. On either side of the gateway below the central tower two flights lead up to an intermediate landing, where they turn back in one flight over the gateway. Following the French system, the New Augustenburg at Weissenfels terminates the two lateral wings in domed pavilions. The north wing contained a gallery leading to the chapel, the south wing probably the saloon. The lack of exterior articulation, apart from plain lesenes, is striking. The palace depends for its effect exclusively on its block-like shape.

Lower Saxony

In Westphalia also, at the end of the Thirty Years War, *cours d'honneur* and pavilions were introduced. The architect responsible was Peter Pictorius, a Dane who had been trained in Holland. For the prince-bishop of Münster he erected the Luidgerusburg near Coesfeld[40] in 1655-9, in which the corner-pavilions with high pitched roofs and the central block of the *corps de logis* projected far forward. (This was destroyed in 1688.) A giant order of Corinthian pilasters rose on low bases. Thirteen years later, in the palace at Osnabrück,[41] the Baroque character is even more pronounced. The means employed here are the difference in the importance of the storeys and heavy hoods above the windows. The position of the staircase in the centre is of considerable interest too.

In the Protestant north, architecture is well represented in the large church of St Michael in Hamburg, built by Christoph Corbinus in 1649-61. It was a hall-church with wide galleries over the aisles, set between the columns in the usual inorganic manner. A tower with a high cap was built in front of the west façade in 1663-8, by Peter Marquardt. The church did not, however, lose its Catholic character until it was reconstructed in the middle of the eighteenth century.

Brandenburg

In the north, Brandenburg, which even in the sixteenth century had still lagged behind the Saxon lands of the Wettin princes, began to give proof of its rising power as an absolute monarchy. Frederick William, the Great Elector (1640-88), was one of the strongest personalities of the age. His predecessors had already built large palaces to emphasize their power, in frank contrast to the wretched houses in the smaller places. The sandy soil of the Mark offered little hope of prosperity to the population, especially as the state drew heavily on the nobility and the merchant class for military and civil tasks.

The palace in Berlin had already at that time achieved its final size, with two large internal courtyards. The south wing of the smaller one had been constructed in 1538-40 for Joachim II, elector of Brandenburg, by Konrad Krebs, architect of Schloss Hartenfels near Torgau, and he repeated here his famous Hartenfels spiral stair. But by the seventeenth century the fine, gracefully decorated building was in a bad state of repair. The Great Elector, being a thrifty man, did not envisage comprehensive rebuilding; he did, however, make some well thought out alterations, arranging his private apartments in the wing alongside the Spree, and building the Alabaster Hall in the court opposite (1681-5). He had a special affection for the newly laid-out 'pleasure garden' facing the north front, and here Johann Gregor Memhardt, born at Linz and trained in Holland, began his activity in 1650 by building a summer house. Four octagonal rooms were set round a small square hall, and there were two towers in front and a dome. In the much elongated giant pilasters of the façade, the high windows and heavy garlands, and the brick walls with ashlar dressings the Dutch style is apparent; it was popular at the court owing to family ties with the House of Orange. Louise Henriette of Orange, the wife of the Great Elector, in fact formed a Dutch colony on the banks of the Havel, with the hunting-lodge of Oranienburg. The link with Memhardt can still be seen in the orphanage there (1650–60), a plain, long brick building with a high hipped roof and quoined projections (Plate 36B), admirably suited to the simple disciplined character of the inhabitants of the Mark.

At Potsdam the Walloon architect Philipp de Chieze erected the Stadtschloss[42] between 1660 and 1675. This was later rebuilt by Frederick II and has recently been demolished. The *corps de logis* consisted of a central range and two corner pavilions, all three heightened by towers. The forecourt facing the town was surrounded by one-storeyed wings, also with corner pavilions. Here, too, simplicity was retained; orders of pilasters, for instance, were lacking completely. Especially characteristic of the Great Elector was the laying out in 1647 of an avenue of 1,000 lime-trees and 1,000 walnut-trees, planted in six rows, and running due west from near the palace. This was the avenue later known as 'Unter den Linden', so that in fact, with brilliant foresight, the Great Elector had established a main axis for Berlin, an axis which under his successor, Frederick III, later King Frederick I, was lengthened to cut through the Tiergarten as far as Charlottenburg. Alongside 'Unter den Linden' Memhardt also planned a new quarter, the Dorotheenstadt, in a series of oblong blocks. The westerly direction was dictated by the course of the Spree. The fact that the axis was not in line with the Lustgarten front of the palace was to prove fortunate; for the long façade, the result of later additions, thus appeared to the eye foreshortened and thereby formed an effective termination. In 1678 Memhardt died, and for the completion of the palace at Potsdam an agreement was signed in 1679 with the contractor Michael Matthias Smids, a native of Breda. In 1683 Smids was succeeded in his turn by the engineer Johann Arnold Nering, who extended the wings and shut off the enlarged court by a curved gallery in the shape of an omega, the front portal of which was surmounted by a tower with a bulbous top.

In Nering the Great Elector had found the right man to inaugurate a development of architecture in the Hohenzollern state which was to continue in uninterrupted progress to the very time of Schinkel. Just as Klengel laid the foundation for the Baroque of Dresden, so Nering did for Prussian classicism. Like Klengel, Nering was a military man, suited to his great task by having equal talents as an architect, city-planner, and engineer. Born in 1659 at Wesel, in 1676 Nering received a government scholarship to study the science of fortification, and then in 1677 a grant of 300 Thaler, for three years in succession, for his 'good inclination to the study of mathematics' – quite in keeping with the spirit of the Cartesian century. A compulsory journey to Italy was included in the scholarship. In 1680 Nering was made Oberingenieur, in 1685 a colonel in the Brandenburg general staff, and in 1691 Surveyor General of Works. As such, at the early age of thirty-two, he was head of the entire state building department: the rising state of Brandenburg was as quick as any other German land to recognize and further outstanding talent.

South Germany

We have already seen that one of the consequences of the Thirty Years War was the preponderance of foreigners. Because of their proximity to Italy, this was felt particularly in Bavaria and the region of the Austrian Alps. In Bavaria, moreover, the attitude of Henriette Adelaide of Savoy (1652–76), wife of the Elector Ferdinand Maria, was strongly anti-German. She considered the natives 'troppo idioti dell'edificare' (too stupid for architecture). The extent of her ambition is evident in her expressed aim of making the church of the Theatines, which was to be erected as a thanksgiving after the eagerly awaited birth of an heir to the throne, the most beautiful and costly in the city; and for this enterprise she attempted to enlist the services of Guarino Guarini, the most celebrated architect of the Theatine order. Had she succeeded, a novel situation would have arisen for the whole of southern Germany. That the Bavarians would have eagerly accepted Guarini's ideas of the interpenetration of space is proved by the Dientzenhofers, who just at that time left their upper Bavarian home and put Guarini's ideas into practice in Prague, where they had first encountered them. In the event, however, Agostino Barelli, called to Munich by Ferdinand Maria in Guarini's stead, in accordance with the wishes of the electress modelled the Theatine Church on S. Andrea della Valle in Rome. In addition, Barelli looked to Salzburg Cathedral; for this must be the source of his twin west towers. Furthermore he replaced the pilasters by demi-columns in order to produce a richer relief. The building took from 1663 to 1671, but all decoration came after that year, when Barelli had been replaced – a characteristic move – by a master from the Grisons, Enrico Zuccalli. Generally speaking the *muratori* of the Italo-Swiss alpine districts soon acclimatized themselves to Bavaria, learning German and making their permanent homes there; and thus it was in the case of Enrico Zuccalli (1642–1724), from Roveredo. He became architect to the elector in 1672, and dominated building in Munich until 1715. For technical reasons he reduced the size of the dome of the Theatine Church, disregarding all previous models in the curious volutes which project from the highest octagonal storey of the towers (completed in 1690).

In the event, Adelaide's ambition did the country more harm than good. The church of the Theatines had a retarding effect on the development of Bavarian art, although the luscious acanthus decoration of their Italian colleagues proved an education for the famous native Wessobrunn school of plasterers.

In a remote part arose a centralized structure of great originality, the pilgrimage church of Maria Birnbaum (1661–5),[43] situated near Aichach, in the heart of the country. The building, by Konstantin Pader, the most talented Bavarian mason–architect of the sixties, was to be an affair of the Bavarian people. It is reported that, because the site was unsuitable and very hilly, many strangers from distant villages offered to work for four, five, six, and eight days to help in the levelling of the ground. The rotunda, with two trefoil-shaped annexes, has a large circular opening at the apex of the dome, and in this was intended to recall the Pantheon in Rome. An earlier attempt at a centralized structure had been begun, in 1620, in the abbey church of Volders[44] near Hall in the Tyrol (completed 1654); Maria Birnbaum takes the conception further and enriches it by the bulbous domes, which evoke the ideals of the Eastern Church. Twelve years later, Zuccalli revived this Bavarian conceit in his splendid design for Altötting,[45] the most famous pilgrimage church of Bavaria. He wished to incorporate the circular chapel, probably dating from the eighth century, in the ambulatory of his large rotunda so that the pilgrims could both look into it from the large rotunda, and walk round it as they prayed. The galleries of the two-storeyed interior were to have formed a second ambulatory. Finally an outer enclosure would have been formed by placing the church in the middle of a wide seven-sided precinct with detached houses connected by arcades. However, only the houses for the canons were built, and of the church no more than the foundations.

Barelli's palace at Nymphenburg, begun in 1663 for Ferdinand Maria and Henriette Adelaide, is virtually no more than the plain central block of the present palace (Plate 112A), which was altered in the eighteenth century by extending the great hall and the façade.

The new electoral opera house on the Salvator Platz was the first detached theatre built in Germany. Marx Schinnegl, cabinet-maker and deputy architect to the elector, directed the building operations from 1651 to 1654. After 1662 the Venetian carpenter–architect and theatre-engineer Francesco Santurini completed it, certainly with a better understanding of Adelaide's taste. In 1665–8 he also built the Bucentauro, the electoral pleasure-boat on the Lake of Starnberg.

In Swabia after the war the great abbey church of Kempten was erected by masters from the Vorarlberg (1652–66; Plate 37). This inaugurated a long series of triumphs for the builders from the heart of the Bregenzer Wald. Linked closely together in guilds and by family ties, they not only worked as travelling craftsmen, but also achieved a high reputation as architects, primarily for the great Benedictine monasteries in the south-west. Their triumph in works of between 1670 and 1682 was the triumph of the German element over the Italian. What the Baroque church wished to achieve, namely the fusion of the longitudinal and the centralized types of building, the re-establishment of the hall type with free-standing piers, and an organic incorporation of galleries into the interior, was already being tackled here at Kempten. Low galleries are placed in the aisles of a basilica. A curious self-contained octagon with two-storeyed ambulatories and four central piers to carry a dome is inserted between nave and chancel, but the domed space does not yet affect the spatial character of the nave. Similarly in the exterior an attempt was made to apply the new north Italian forms organically to the whole mass of the façade, at the same time retaining the two towers. The design was probably made by Michael Beer of Au near Bregenz (d. 1666), who worked on the building until 1654. It was completed by Johannes Serro from Neuburg on the Danube, who heightened the nave by about five feet and enlarged the windows.

Switzerland

As representatives of an Italian Baroque adapted to German Alpine ideas, the Vorarlberg men assumed a special importance for Switzerland. There the Gothic style had prevailed in ecclesiastical architecture until the middle of the seventeenth century: the change-over began with the Jesuits, in whose churches the standard Vorarlberg plan was gradu-ally perfected during the course of the seventeenth century. In addition to the Jesuit church at Dillingen[46] of 1610, which has already been mentioned, considerable impor-tance attaches to the newly built Jesuit church in Innsbruck[47] (1627–35), the work of P. Karl Fontaner. There we find the narrow gallery-bridges at the ends of the transverse arms, as they were to be characteristic later for Vorarlberg buildings. On the other hand the basilican scheme, revived in the Jesuit church at Lucerne[48] in 1666–73, did not con-stitute progress in the Vorarlberg sense. This was achieved first in the Jesuit church at Solothurn (1680–8; Plate 38). Its significant features were internal buttress-piers, a tunnel-vault above the nave extending into the chancel, thus eliminating a domed crossing, transverse tunnel-vaults above the galleries, and narrow gallery-bridges in the transepts. Since the galleries were no longer separated from the nave by arcades and an entablature above, as they are at Lucerne, the width is increased in the manner of the ancient hall-churches. The choir is slightly narrowed, thus lending prominence to the chancel arch with its Corinthian pilasters. Moreover the upper windows in the chancel walls allow a greater influx of direct light. As opposed to the interior, the façade reveals French influence. According to the inscription it was 'a monument to the generosity of the most Christian king, Louis the Great [Louis XIV of France]'. At that time buildings of the upper German province of the Jesuit order were under the general supervision of Brother Heinrich Mayer, who worked as an architect and plasterer; nevertheless it seems probable that the Solothurn church was the work of a more distinguished master, perhaps Hans Georg Kuen.

CHAPTER 7

SCULPTURE

THE German contribution to the leading trends of European art in the middle of the seventeenth century was only sporadic, the work of individual artists who had escaped the tragedy of the war and had been in the great cultural centres in Italy and the Netherlands. In the field of sculpture, this applies to Justus Glesskher (1613–81), who was the son of a Hameln family and had settled at Frankfurt about 1648. Sandrart calls him 'a born sculptor', and mentions his journeys to the Netherlands and Italy, where 'especially in Rome he very wisely drew great profit from the antique statues and other works of art' and thus became 'an artist of unusual quality, particularly in ivory'. The group of the *Crucifixion* in Bamberg Cathedral (1648–53), attributed to him, reveals a style modelled on that of François Duquesnoy, in which the pathos rings true as a direct expression of the tragic events of the time, without any trace of Mannerism.

As a result of the strange situation in Germany during the seventeenth century even the most gifted artists lacked a definite direction; on the other hand, they remained capable of assimilating new and unexpected experiences, and in this way avoided the rigidity of a style that had hardened to a routine. Matthias Rauchmiller from Radolfzell (1645–86) was endowed in full measure with the mental equipment required. He probably visited Antwerp workshops during his years as a journeyman and came in contact with the art of the elder and younger Artus Quellinus, an art which was inspired by a deep feeling for nature. He is recorded at Mainz between 1669 and 1671, and the Crucifix in the cathedral is probably one of the things he did at that time.[1] The tomb in the Liebfrauenkirche at Trier of Bishop Karl von Metternich (d. 1636) of *c.* 1675 is also assigned to him, on stylistic grounds (Plate 39A). In the modelling both works reveal an artist trained as an ivory carver, and a powerful dynamism is expressed in the drapery. This quality recurs in the representation of the Rape of the Sabine Women on his ivory tankard,[2] dated 1676, formerly in the Liechtenstein Collection, which recalls the work of Rubens.

An opportunity arose in the following year, 1677, for Rauchmiller to show his skill as architect, painter, and sculptor in the new Mausoleum for the Piast dynasty at Legnica (Liegnitz) in Silesia.[3] In the oval interior, articulated by eight giant Corinthian columns, Baroque forms are present only in the mighty volutes of the brackets supporting the four statues; the *Ohrmuschel* ornament of the frescoes on the wall panels and on the medallions of the dome is not obtrusive. Below, the eye is drawn to the alabaster figures of the duke and his wife, their daughter Charlotte, and their son Georg Wilhelm, the last of the Piast family. Here, too, the Baroque style is subdued, and there is a marked contrast between the ceremonial attitude and the emphatic naturalism of the figures, which are intended to be portraits. The same tendency is noticeable in the exceedingly skilful handling of the rich costumes. Rauchmiller's abiding interest in the Antique is apparent in the round fresco above, representing Apollo in his chariot drawn by four horses. The horses are shying back, as it were shocked by the tragic death of the young duke. The artist has certainly succeeded in giving a sensitive interpretation of the emotions of the mother and at the same time of the Protestant community, which felt itself threatened by the extinction of the Piasts. It is evident, too, that the spirit of Silesian poetry had gripped Rauchmiller. Indeed, Kaspar von Lohenstein had written a poem in praise of Rauchmiller's ivory tankard and had been instrumental in having him called to Liegnitz; and the tomb of the child Oktavius Pestaluzzi[4] (d. 1677) at Wrocław (Breslau) is a further example of the literary element in Rauchmiller's art. In 1676 he moved to Vienna (cf. pp. 104–5).

Not until forty years after the destruction of Magdeburg in 1631 could the city reconstruct its churches and, in connexion with this, re-establish its once flourishing sculptural workshops. In Tobias Wilhelmi of Brandenburg, who became a citizen of Magdeburg in 1663, the services of a distinguished sculptor were secured. He was obviously personally acquainted with the art of Flanders. His first known work, the altar in the church of St John,[5] dates from 1669/70. With its smooth, slender Corinthian columns, it is more architectural in character than is the general run of Baroque altars of the period with their twisted columns and garlands. Wilhelmi substituted foliage scrollwork for *Ohrmuschel* decoration. In the angel figure supporting the pulpit in the church of St Peter,[6] a late work of 1685, he found an important new solution for one of the principal sculptural problems of the time, namely the figural support for the pulpit. The new solution differed considerably from his earlier one of 1674–6 in St John;[7] instead of a figure with billowing drapery folds turning on its own axis, the later figure is simpler, more natural, and more harmonious, but also grander, in accordance with a new, more remarkable period.

In upper Saxony the main centres were Dresden, Freiberg, and Schneeberg. At Schneeberg three generations of the Böhme family produced outstanding works, especially funerary tablets. Being only moderately classicist, they already paved the way for the Baroque. Johann Böhme the Elder was the most noteworthy. He was sculptor to the electoral court from 1636 to 1680.

In Dresden the alabaster relief of the *Annunciation to the Shepherds* (1640; Plate 21B), a late work, testifies to the admirable craftsmanship of Sebastian Walther, which still has its roots in the Late Renaissance. It is a highly sensitive interpretation of what Christmas meant to a sculptor who was personally affected by the miseries of war. That the shepherds must also be portraits of real people is evident even if one looks only at the two women who appear among them (cf. p. 54). The plunge into Baroque was made here by George Heermann (cf. p. 200) and Jeremias Süssner (1653–90).

The retable in a Protestant church represents the Theologia Crucis in its biblical and theological context, whereas in a Catholic church it is associated with the consecration of the altar. Thus the retables of the Meissen sculptor Valentin Otte and of the painter Johann Richter represent a climax in Protestant work. The former developed a type corresponding to the Gothic altar shrine in four altars done for the churches of Mittweida[8] in 1661, Leisnig (Plate 40B) in 1664, St Afra at Meissen[9] c. 1665, and Sitten in

1669. In each case the traditional wide central panel has been replaced by the figure of the *Ecce Homo*.

A work of equal quality in the north was the retable of the Protestant parish church at Bartenstein in East Prussia of about 1655, presumably by Joachim Pfaff.[10] Here the composition is held together by the lively *Ohrmuschel* frame. The figure of Christ on the Cross is effectively emphasized by the columnar architecture surrounding it, and the Baroque character further increased by inserting it between the fragments of a broken pediment.

Alongside decadent works which reflect excessive foreign influence, there are others in the north that show a more independent spirit. The new freedom of the Baroque enabled the inborn delight of the country in imaginative ornament to emerge once more in a revival of the very characteristic *Ohrmuschel* work. This applies especially to Hans Gudewerth (*c.* 1600–71), who ran a workshop at Eckernförde in Schleswig. There the dukes, Frederick III in particular, had been chiefly responsible for making Schloss Gottorp a centre of culture that attracted personalities such as the poet Paul Fleming and the scholar Adam Olearius, who at the duke's instigation visited Persia and Russia. The interior decoration of the palace gave ample opportunity for the craftsmanship of the celebrated *Snitker* (carvers).[11] The aristocracy were incidentally the chief patrons for carved altarpieces in the churches too. Gudewerth detached the tendrils from the structural members, so that they seem to float freely in the air (Plate 40A). But his real aim was to infuse the maximum vitality into his altars, and in the dynamic twirls of the scrolls sweeping round the figures we sense a direct reflection of the stormy times. This is further enhanced by the artists's inherent feeling for symbolism. Yet nowhere does the ornament swamp the figures; on the contrary, in avoiding this, his style is most his own, though also directly informed by the spirit of the age. His finest work, the altarpiece at Eckernförde of 1640, contains very natural figures, such as the putti acting as caryatids (Plate 41A) or the St Mark (Plate 39B). Basically Gudewerth is a realist rather than a materialist.[12] In his carvings the oak is not polychromed, though originally certain parts were probably heightened with gold. In some works, for example the Bornsen Monument of 1661 at Eckernförde,[13] the outlines are so delicately drawn as to give an almost Rococo-like lightness.

In every respect a complete contrast is the work of Charles Philippe Dieussart of Mecklenburg (cf. p. 149). The kneeling figure on a sarcophagus of the Privy Councillor Günther von Passow in Güstrow Cathedral[14] (1657–8) is a distinguished example of Netherlandish portraiture, concealing an inner intensity beneath outward reserve.

CHAPTER 8

PAINTING

AFTER the devastating storms of the Thirty Years War, German painting revived. To begin with it developed almost exclusively within the orbit of Netherlandish art, then at the very height of its fame. It was thus only natural that the German trading centres, in close touch with the culture of the Netherlands, should supply the artists who in the first place drew their knowledge of painting from Netherlandish sources. In view of the widespread imitation of foreign ways, however, few only achieved complete independence of style. An outstanding example was Michael Willmann (1630–1706). Born in East Prussia, he displayed the characteristics of his race, which could at times be coarse and violent, but to which Germany is indebted for so many great artists down to Lovis Corinth and Käthe Kollwitz. Sandrart, possibly relying on information given him by Willmann himself, says that at the age of twenty he already excelled the artists of his home town of Königsberg.[1] His contacts with artists in Holland, more especially in Amsterdam, so Sandrart says, and to an even greater degree his concentrated study of many celebrated works of art had helped him to develop his own passionate temperament – 'insignia ibidem ferroris sui incrementa persensit non visitatis tantum illius loci Artificibus sed et perlustratis operibus in eadem Urbe celeberrimis variis'. Sandrart goes on to tell us that after an initial training under Jacob Adriaensz Backer,[2] following the example of Rembrandt and others, he earned his living by working day and night. He continued his intensive studies in Poland and Germany, and, with outstanding success, in the Imperial Collection at Prague. The fact that he owed his training not to a single master but to the study of Netherlandish painting as a whole is reflected in his work. To begin with, Rembrandt, Rubens, Ruysdael, and van Dyck were his models. Sandrart, who held quite different views, could nevertheless write of Willmann, perhaps quoting the painter's own words: 'The artist is formed not by long journeys, but by his own genius and by nature.' After travelling around for ten years he gained a footing in Silesia. In Breslau, however, painters, cabinet-makers, gold-beaters, and glaziers forbade him to work on his own, especially as a portrait painter, because he had refused to join their guilds; such independence was characteristic of the artist of the seventeenth century. But fortunately, in Arnold Freiberger, abbot of the Cistercian abbey of Lubiąż (Leubus), he found a patron who was not bound by the guild regulations. Among other things Willmann painted the *Landscape with John the Baptist* for him (1656; formerly Breslau gallery),[3] a work which already reveals his distinctive style. Even though Ruysdael's influence can be seen in the huge gnarled trees, the importance attached to the small idyllic scene of the reclining St John with the lamb reveals his interest in figure scenes and also a poetic, mystic strain alien to the Dutch, but near to the style of Altdorfer. The somewhat later *Landscape with the Flight into Egypt*[4] shows how greatly this quality developed. Sandrart is fully justified in stressing that he is 'historiarum et

Poematum lectioni deditissimus'. In the seventeenth century the poetic atmosphere in Silesia was emotionally overcharged; but during his work on the Stations of the Cross at Krzeszów (Grüssau) Willmann also came in personal contact with a truly great poet: Angelus Silesius.[5] Throughout his life the high religious seriousness of the Silesian Cistercian abbeys enthralled Willmann, and the Great Elector did not succeed in attaching him permanently to his court. From 1657 to 1660 he worked in Berlin, where he was nominated 'pictor aulicus Electoris'. In 1660 he decided to settle at Lubiąż, entered the Catholic Church, and worked 'ultra quadraginta annos'. He was held in high esteem there and dined every day at the abbot's table.

The subject matter favoured at that time by the Catholics, especially scenes of martyrdom, encouraged Willmann in his efforts to infuse dynamic vitality into all parts of his pictures. He did twelve oil paintings (each 10 by 13 feet) for the upper part of the walls of the nave in the collegiate church at Lubiąż (Plate 43B),[6] a task that occupied him between 1661 and 1700; but in his sketches for the Krzeszów Book of the Passion he penetrated still further into the mystery of triumphant suffering. Even idyllic scenes, to which the poetic strain in his nature drew him, were charged with emotion, for instance the *Creation*[7] of 1668 in the Wrocław (Breslau) gallery and *Orpheus among the Animals*,[8] formerly owned by the Countess Maltzan-Militsch. Nature in such scenes has mysticism, but while Willmann appeals to the emotions he yet retains a firm grip on reality and guards against sentimentality. In his *Kiss of the Virgin* of 1682 in the Wrocław gallery (Plate 41B) he attained his classic style, partly owing to the fact that he, like so many others, was profoundly influenced by the new spirit of the eighties (cf. p. 146).

In the north, artists with less individuality than Willmann surrendered to Rembrandt's art. This is true for instance of Christoph Paudiss of Hamburg (c. 1625–66), who was probably a pupil of Rembrandt about 1648.[9] After that he went by way of Dresden to Vienna and Freising, where he found a patron in Prince-Bishop Albrecht Sigismund. He now began to lighten his palette and to find his real strength in the study of nature. He was, however, defeated in a competition at Nuremberg, the subject of which was a wolf devouring a lamb, and this defeat so upset him that he died a few days later. Sandrart rightly praises the sculptural quality of this work. Matthias Scheits,[10] Willmann's exact contemporary (c. 1625–1700), also belonged to the Dutch school, but in his genre pieces he used broader, more fluent brushwork.

The prevailing passion for hunting is well expressed in the excellent work of Carl Ruthard of Danzig (c. 1630–after 1703). His animals, generally either fleeing or fighting, are suitably set in wildernesses. He is recorded in the Antwerp guild in 1663/4, and in the following years in Vienna and at Graz. From 1672 to the end of his life he lived and painted in the monastery of S. Maria di Collemaggio at Aquila in the Abruzzi, where he was known as Father Andrea. The attraction of Italy for German artists, particularly in the second half of the seventeenth century, was so great that, even in their own country, they were to some extent forced to imagine themselves in the southern climate before they could work creatively.

Joachim von Sandrart (1606–88) was regarded as Germany's greatest painter by his contemporaries, for instance in 1651 by Hoogstraaten. Opinion in our day, hostile to the academic outlook, has been all the more disparaging, and it is not sufficiently appreciated that in his great history of German art, the *Teutsche Akademie* of 1675, he showed himself fully able to recognize and appreciate achievements of genius, even if his judgement was influenced by the academic view that nature should be imitated correctly. He grew up in Frankfurt, and received an excellent education there and also at Nuremberg, Prague, and Utrecht, where he became a pupil of Honthorst whom he accompanied to London in 1627. He lived in Italy from 1628 to 1635 and in Amsterdam from 1637 to 1642, everywhere enjoying the friendship of leading artists and scholars.

In 1662 he realized his lifelong ambition to improve the technical and theoretical instruction of art by founding the Teutsche Akademie in Nuremberg. It was the basis of his literary work. Following the example of Rubens, he led a country life on his estate at Stockau near Ingolstadt, but from 1674 onwards he lived permanently in Nuremberg. Even though his work was influenced by too many models of all kinds, yet, in its sensitive characterization, particularly in portrait and still-life, it remains of interest today (Plate 44B). The same can be said of his large altar-paintings. Though he was in fact somewhat trammelled by the very extent of his learning, yet after the vacuum of the war years it enabled him to supply the basis for a revival of art in Germany, his own country, to which he was truly devoted.

The ability to concentrate on specific subjects, which was a unique achievement of the Dutch painters in the seventeenth century, was lacking in Germany, where there was a tendency to dissipate talent in all directions. Johann Heinrich Schönfeld (1609–82/3), who came from Biberach am Riss and worked in Augsburg, is a case in point. He had all the makings of a great German genre painter, but the wide variety of impressions he absorbed from all sides stifled his creative power. Sandrart wrote of him: 'His agile mind showered, as it were, an abundance of well-ordered ideas into his alert hand.' During his extensive study journeys in Italy 'he gained so much experience by copying the best ancient and modern Roman statues as well as paintings, that these copies seem in all respects to be his own inventions'. When Sandrart adds that 'an uncommon grace was joined to his nimble brush', he adequately defines the charming character of his art. He infused an extraordinary intensity into his picture *Christ with his Disciples on the Lake of Genezareth* (c. 1670–80, Augsburg Museum; Plate 43A), but was equally capable of giving a close interpretation of reality, in a romantic guise, as for instance in his rendering of *The Life-Class in the Augsburg Academy* (after 1660; Plate 42).[11] His characterization of the pupils, e.g. the two on the right, engaged in ceremonious greetings, suggests a veritable Grimmelshausen of painting. His lightly poised figures, the well developed chiaroscuro, the witty, imaginative treatment of mythological scenes, in particular where children can be introduced, and the precise, goldsmith-like technique are all expressive of the true German painter-poet of the seventeenth century. According to Sandrart he also designed 'graceful inventions for the goldsmiths even in his old age'.

Alongside Dilich (cf. p. 71), the most outstanding exponent of central German painting was Johann Oswald Harms (1643–1708). Apart from the decorations for the palace chapel at Weissenfels (1682), only drawings by him have survived, which are in the print room of the Brunswick gallery. He was a native of Hamburg, a pupil of

Salvator Rosa in Rome, but a follower more than of anything else of the ceiling paintings of Pietro da Cortona. From 1675 to 1682, as 'Court and Chief Theatrical Master'
in Dresden, he painted extensive ceiling frescoes with illusionistic architecture for the
palace (Plate 35B). From 1689 on, as court painter to Duke Anton Ulrich, he worked on
the decorations for the Brunswick opera house and for the country palace at Salzdahlum
(cf. p. 220). Immediately afterwards, in the service of Landgrave Charles of Hesse at
Kassel, he began the decorations for the Kunsthaus. Infected by the prevailing passion
for the theatre in Dresden, Brunswick, and Hamburg, he designed many stage sets,
which included romantic landscapes with ruins, grottoes, woods, sea coasts, and banks
of clouds. Evidently inspired by his surroundings, he surpassed mere Baroque routine.

The interior of the palace in the Grosser Garten at Dresden was painted by Samuel
Bottschild (1641–1706) and Heinrich Christoph Fehling (1654–1725). Fehling was later
director of a drawing school in Dresden which became an academy of painting in 1705.
In his fine portrait of Klengel, he succeeds in revealing the latter's sensitive artistic nature
beneath the grand military trappings (Plate 44A).

The growing importance of Bohemia as a centre of Central European culture in the
seventeenth century was considerably strengthened in the field of painting by Karel
Škréta Šotnovoský of Zábořice (c. 1610–74), a remarkable and far too little known
Czech painter. In 1628, after the victory of the Roman Catholic Church, the young
man, who was a member of the Protestant party, fled with his mother to Freiberg in
Saxony. A year or two later he went to Italy and spent several years in Venice, Bologna,
Florence, and Rome (1634), where he acquired a thorough artistic training. Like many
northern artists of the time, he appears to have been so strongly attracted by the Catholic
Church that the idea of a change of faith began to take shape. On leaving Italy he went
first to Freiberg, but after he had finally gone over to Catholicism he settled in Prague,
where he soon occupied a leading position. To regard him merely as a realist in the
following of Caravaggio is quite unjustified and is disproved by his work. He did
indeed, especially in portraiture, come close to nature; but his painting is far too universal in the sense of the high painterly achievements of the mid seventeenth century to
confine it to realism in the narrower sense. Still less can one call it a 'fact that a very
considerable number of his works reflected the standpoint and interests of the progressive sectors of society whose development was forcibly repressed in the process of
feudal reactionary tendencies, but who still found strength to resist the Counter-
Reformatory efforts of the Church'.[12] In reality, an ardent mysticism and reverence for
the saints is reflected just as fervently in his as in Willmann's work, for instance in the
altar panel with the *Holy Family* in the Teyn Church in Prague (1664; Plate 45B). If in
his portraits of the Bohemian nobility and ecclesiastical dignitaries – an example is the
Maltese prior *Bernard de Witte* of 1651 (Plate 45A) – he gives an unflattering representation of their presence, he nevertheless manages to endow them with a sense of magnificence in keeping with the splendour of their lives. They never seem to pose in any way,
but in carriage and bearing their personalities are characterized in an unobtrusive manner. The animation of the faces is due to Škréta's mastery in rendering the eyes. His
portrait of the gem-cutter *Dionisio Miseroni and his Family* (c. 1653, Prague, National

Gallery) is an eminent example of a group portrait, a genre that was at that time highly developed in Holland and Spain and in which individuals are represented in their own environment. The family life of one who was evidently Škréta's friend is characterized discreetly and with a genuine warmth of feeling. In the background we can see the busy workshop. The artist never aimed at achieving complete unity of space. Although many details are taken from nature, the composition is dominated by the desire to emphasize essential ideas. Thus Škréta was fully qualified to interpret religious emotions. His intensity of expression increased as he grew older and culminated in the heart-rending *Scenes from the Passion* of 1670 in St Nicholas in Prague.

The leading figure at this time in the field of ceiling-painting in stucco frames was Carpoforo Tencalla (*c.* 1623–85) from Bissone on Lake Lugano. His famous *Apollo crowning the Genius of the Arts* (1674) on the ceiling of the great hall of the castle at Olomouc (Olmütz) has unfortunately been destroyed, as have his somewhat later frescoes in the castle at Kroměříž (Kremsier) (see p. 113).

PART FOUR

THE BAROQUE PERIOD 1683–1739

CHAPTER 9

AUSTRIA

Architecture

DURING the last quarter of the seventeenth century, under the leadership of Johann Bernhard Fischer von Erlach (1656–1723), Austrian architecture developed more freely than had previously been possible. The victory over the Turks at St Gotthard in 1664 and the relief of Vienna in 1683 stimulated national pride, and the words of Hans Jacob Wagner von Wagenfels in his *Ehrenruf Teutschlands* (Vienna, 1691) testify to the general feeling that 'the cities and buildings of Germany surpass Paris and at least equal their Italian models'. Secondhand imitation of what architects and plasterers from northern Italy had offered as patterns was no longer acceptable, and there was a great desire to study at the source – in Rome itself – and to develop independently what was found there. Thus Fischer von Erlach, the son of a sculptor in Graz, the capital of Styria, left that city, presumably in 1674, and went to Rome and Naples, staying there, as seems likely from a passage in one of his letters, for twelve years. He still remained a sculptor, however, as his father had been. The only works that have been traced from this Roman period are two medals representing Charles II of Spain and his queen Marie Louise (1679 and 1682).[1]

In Rome he must have learned of the change which was taking place in France in the eighties, when the greatness of Rubens was at last acknowledged and the Baroque was beginning to take some hold. He must also have been encouraged to take as his models the work of Bernini and Borromini. This was decisive for the future attitude of German architecture to the Roman Baroque – an attitude which was not at all indiscriminate. What aroused admiration was the audacity and originality of new artistic concepts, the powerful rhythm of architectural masses, and the imposing unity achieved by the complete fusion of every part. Bizarre devices were avoided, as was any exaggerated crescendo in the architectural elements. As in Italy, architecture was closely coupled with sculpture and painting so that each might profit to the utmost from the values of the other two. The figure of Atlas, which appears over and over again at the portals and in the vestibules of Baroque palaces, is highly symbolic of this striving to imbue architecture with the vitality of the sculptured figure and to impart to the latter the completeness and significance of an architectural member joined firmly to the whole system of a given structure. As has already been said, about 1680 the *Ohrmuschel* ornament at last disappeared, and moulded foliage began to predominate. This change is characteristic of the more general change of aims. In place of stilted, exaggerated, grotesque forms large, organically conceived acanthus leaves appeared, once again related to classical art, though now rather freely.

The ceiling fresco formed the link with painting and, as previously in Italy, sought to continue the architecture and connect it with the surrounding sky. Austrian and south German artists succeeded in heightening spatial effects by intensifying the colour and vitalizing the stucco decoration. Naturally, it was in the Catholic countries of Germany that ceiling painting and rich interior decoration were most brilliantly developed, and we sense everywhere the influence of the many superb monasteries and pilgrimage and parish churches. Ecclesiastical architecture, too, once again took the lead in many fields, and if it linked up with secular building, the reason was that both were inspired by the same spirit. There was no predominance of feudalism in the monasteries; for the clergy were mostly simple folk, often peasants. As a result, the Baroque penetrated not only to the monumental buildings but also to the innumerable small chapels and statues throughout the countryside. The tragic mood that Michelangelo had infused into the Baroque was supplanted by the glowing vitality of Rubens, which was welcomed in southern Germany where it found an echo in the sanguine temperament of the people. Whatever was built on a grand scale was eagerly accepted even by the middle classes, whose pleasant dwelling houses were often given gorgeous stucco façades.

The rise of a German Baroque architecture during the eighties of the seventeenth century coincided with the culmination – at the upper Austrian monasteries of Garsten, Schlierbach, and St Florian – of the Italian style of decoration with its heavy plaster-work, acanthus scrolls, and swags of large flowers and fruit. Following the age-old custom, most of the master masons had come from the Italian lake district. Carlo Antonio Carlone, the most distinguished architect of the Carlone family, to whom we owe the monastery church of St Florian, was born at Scaria near Como. At the beginning of the High Baroque in Austria and southern Germany, that is round about 1680, he was the first to introduce the *Platzlgewölbe*, a form of shallow domical vaulting necessary for the development of unified ceiling frescoes. In the abbey church of Schlierbach,[2] begun in 1679, the ceiling panels are still surrounded by individual plaster frames;[3] but at St Florian (Plate 46), built in 1686-1708,[4] the paintings cover the entire area of the *Platzlgewölbe*[5] of the nave bays and reach their culmination in the great drumless dome on pendentives.

This type of dome was to acquire great importance in the future, as it brought the painting closer to the spectator. Such structures, which mark the summit of the work of Italian architects in Germany and Austria, prepared the way for the triumphant rise of the German Baroque. The future indeed belonged to the painted ceiling, not to plaster decoration. It was of the utmost importance for Fischer von Erlach that during his stay in Rome he was able to witness the development of the ceiling fresco in the work of the Jesuit father Andrea Pozzo. The latter, who had been in Rome since 1681, began the ceiling fresco of S. Ignazio in 1685.[6] It marked the dawn of a new epoch in this field.

The walls of the church lead directly into painted architecture and on into the sky above. The nave is like an open court surrounded by columns; architecture, sculpture, and painting combine in a great dynamic impulse. Just as the real architecture passes in masterly foreshortening into the painted forms, so the sculpture seems to come alive in the dynamic figure groups of the fresco and, detaching itself from the structural background, joins the figures soaring upwards on clouds.

During his stay in Italy Fischer certainly saw the completion of two other painted ceilings, both superbly executed, one by G. B. Gaulli in the Gesù in Rome (1668–83),[7] the other by Luca Giordano in the gallery of the Palazzo Medici Riccardi in Florence (1682).[8] These already accomplish what was later aimed at in Austria, namely a more flexible composition, increased transparency, and an abundance of light. At the same time the large architectural perspectives were abandoned.

That Fischer was deeply impressed by the importance of ceiling painting is evident from his designs for the interior decoration of the Mausoleum in Graz,[9] which he made about 1687 after his return from Rome. These included a large fresco for the dome above the elliptical burial chamber that adjoined the chapel proper; however in 1688 this suggestion was criticized by the authorities, who preferred the customary individual paintings in stucco frames. The oval plan chosen for the Mausoleum as early as 1614 by the architect, Pietro da Pomis, suited Fischer admirably. A favourite spatial unit in Roman Baroque architecture, he had encountered it everywhere in Rome, and it was to become a dominant feature of his plans, not with an undulating outline, but as a simple, clear-cut shape. Used in such a way, it enabled him to achieve the balance between dynamic motion and dignified restraint which was evidently his ultimate aim. Schloss Vranov (Frain) in Moravia (1690–4; Plate 47) shows the importance that Fischer attached to the oval, for he not only used it for the great hall, but actually extracted the hall from the body of the building and moved it to the very edge of the rock-face to form the pointed end of the Schloss. That he and his patron were able to attract and influence the leading artists of the day is shown by the fact that, in 1696, Johann Michael Rottmayr painted the ceiling of the great hall.[10] This amounted to providing a piece of freely rising Baroque architecture with a grand painted finale, which was made specially necessary by the presence of deep penetrations into the vaults.

By 1690 Fischer was firmly established in Vienna, where he had designed the triumphal arches[11] commissioned by the civic authorities and the foreign merchants on the occasion of the ceremonial entry into the city of the Emperor Joseph I. Even the accepted ideas on statics were affected by the Baroque, as can be seen from the large columns set above the centres of the lateral arches of the Merchants' Arch. As engineer to the court, Fischer had taught the eleven-year-old Crown Prince Joseph 'to draw an Architecturam civilem'. The boy had a natural bent for art, but unfortunately his reign lasted only from 1705 to 1711. From 1705 until his death in 1723 Fischer held the office of Chief Imperial Inspector of all buildings for Court and Festivities. In 1696 he was ennobled and received the surname of Erlach, probably in memory of his mother's first husband, the sculptor Sebastian Erlacher from Tegernsee in Bavaria.

During the early nineties his designs for banqueting houses and summer houses provided imaginative and varied solutions for the relations of volumes and spaces (Plate 48A). In most cases a central ellipse dominates the wings, which are set obliquely or in a concave curve. The buildings all have a flat terraced roof *à l'italienne*, though later some of them, for instance the great hall at Vranov and the banqueting house of Count Althan at Rossau,[12] were provided with high-pitched roofs. For Fischer as for the French, Bernini's first designs for the Louvre were of decisive importance. Wherever he followed older models – such as Vaux le Vicomte and Le Raincy – with central oval halls projecting from the façades, he modified them accordingly.

Fischer's plan for a new imperial palace at Schönbrunn,[13] which he published later in *Entwurf einer historischen Architektur*, represents the most brilliant architectural scheme of the period. The immense width of the front and the flat roof recall Versailles. Bernini's Louvre plans served as a model for the large concave bay. Typical for Fischer is the choice of rising ground with terraces and a circular forecourt rounded off by a large fountain. In 1704 he drew up a similar plan for King Frederick I of Prussia (Albertina, Codex Montenuovo, fol. 25; Plate 48B). Neither design was executed, however; for in 1696 Joseph I made Fischer follow a new plan[14] for Schönbrunn in which practical considerations triumphed. The building was removed to the foot of the slope and the entire layout changed. Stepped wings took the place of rounded ones. The giant pilasters remained, except on the central projection, where columns were used. The flight of stairs which leads up to the outer terrace conforms to the circular shape of the forecourt with its central fountain. The large hall, the central axis of which extends to the garden front, opens above in five high, arched windows. The centre block was further accentuated by an upper loggia. An equestrian statue of Joseph I was planned for the central arcade. The large court in front, flanked by stable ranges, the attractive motif of two obelisks on either side of the entrance, and a corresponding layout of the garden produced a generous setting of extraordinary beauty which affords some compensation for the great number of alterations made to Fischer's grand design. After the death of Joseph I the palace passed to his widow, the Empress Wilhelmina Amalia, and extensive rebuilding under Maria Theresa further reduced its architectural value (cf. p. 291).

From 1705, inspired by his visit to Rome, Fischer had been working on a remarkable book, *Entwurf einer historischen Architektur in Abbildung unterschiedener berühmter Gebäude des Altertums und fremder Völker.*[15] On the accession of Charles VI to the throne in 1712, Fischer speedily completed it and presented it to the emperor. In 1721 it appeared in print in a somewhat enlarged form. It proves Fischer a pioneer as a historian of architecture; for he tried to be archaeological as far as the limited knowledge of his time permitted (for instance in his description of the Seven Wonders of the World). The fact that in his selection, illustration, and supplementation he should take the standpoint of the self-confident Baroque architect, and even include his own work, is natural. He was not a scholar in the full sense of the term; 'he intended', so he wrote, 'to please the eye of the amateur by some examples of different ways of building and to inspire the artists to inventions rather than to inform the erudite'. The most valuable result of the material in the book was his own building, the Karlskirche in Vienna (Plate 50A).

An important factor for Fischer's success in the nineties was the generous patronage at

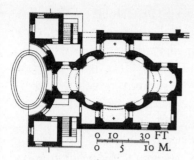

Figure 3. Johann Bernhard Fischer
von Erlach: Salzburg, Dreifaltigkeitskirche, 1694. Plan

Salzburg of Prince-Bishop Ernst Count Thun-Hohen-
stein, who made it possible for him to realize his ideas
on a really big scale. In the Dreifaltigkeitskirche (Holy
Trinity; Plate 49A) he developed further a prototype
by Borromini, S. Agnese in Piazza Navona (1653–7).
There it had been impossible to achieve substantial
depth, but at Salzburg this was managed (Figure 3). The
concave recession of the façade is continued in the longitudinal oval of the interior, and in the adjoining space
containing the high altar. The entablature running
through the whole length was retained, as was also the
drum of the dome. The transverse axis widens into flat
chapels, and the diagonal ones into niches. The monumental character of the façade is
stressed by raising the main storey on a high base; to make it fully effective Fischer
discarded the attic storey and kept the two towers and the drum low. On the other
hand, the dome, drawn forward as in S. Agnese, dominates, or should dominate, the
front; the subsequent heightening of the towers, which were originally lower and
capped by pediments, has had an unfortunate effect. The treatment of the columns as
emblems of ecclesiastical dignity is characteristic of Fischer. They flank the middle
axis in pairs, each one carrying two statues above the protruding entablature. As in
Rome, the site was favourable, and indeed almost demanded a concave façade.

Of still greater importance was Fischer's second commission in Salzburg, which came
in the same year, 1694. It was for the building of the Kollegienkirche (collegiate church)
of the Benedictine University (Plate 49B) which was flourishing at the time as a result of
the excellent instruction it provided in canon law and philosophy. The foundation-stone
of the church was laid in 1696, and it was consecrated in 1707. In the closely built-up

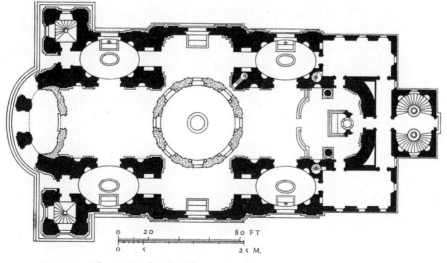

Figure 4. Johann Bernhard Fischer von Erlach: Salzburg, Kollegienkirche,
1696–1707. Plan

centre of the town, it was designed as an annex to the triangular block of the college buildings. Fischer therefore decided to stress the façade towards the narrow University square by giving it a convex centre between sharply outlined, flanking towers (Figure 4). Compared with the Roman Baroque, this trust in sculptural qualities certainly shows the greater vitality of a young, still developing style. The stimulus which the church provided was correspondingly vigorous. The front of the abbey church at Weingarten (Plate 104B), its most important successor, confirms the significance of the convex curve for the German Baroque. As opposed to the massiveness of the body of the building, the broad pilasters appear comparatively flat. The clipped towers and the heavy rounded central attic with its flat gable show that Fischer was claiming architectural licence as much as Borromini and Guarini. In the upper part of the towers the lateral panels with their cornices and balustrades rise like diadems between the diagonally placed volutes. Fischer used a similar solution in later works, for example the Dietrichstein-Lobkowitz Palace[16] in Vienna and the high altar of the Franciscan church at Salzburg[17] of 1709. It was a means of introducing an illusion of three-dimensional space into an essentially flat form. In the Kollegienkirche, planned as a Greek cross extended in depth, with longitudinal oval chapels at the intersecting angles, we can see how Fischer wished to improve on Lemercier's church of the Sorbonne by a more rounded and sculptural moulding of the body of the building. In the elevation he enhances the impressive effect of the Corinthian pilasters and of the two columns at both sides of the high altar by increasing their height.

Twenty-two years later, in Vienna in 1716, Fischer once again had occasion to build a large church, and this enabled him to develop his ideas with greater clarity (Plate 50A). It represented the fulfilment of a vow made by the emperor to St Charles Borromeo in 1713, a thanksgiving for deliverance from the plague. The Knights of the Order of St John of Jerusalem administered the building. Here he was able to emphasize the core of the building even more freely and clearly than at Salzburg through the enormous oval of drum and dome. As at Salzburg, the two towers of the façade were kept relatively low. An innovation were the two immense flanking columns with spiral relief-bands modelled on Roman prototypes, symbolizing the victory of faith over the disease which had threatened.[18] Drawing on his universal knowledge of architecture, he borrowed the idea of the minaret shooting upwards at the side of the mosque to accentuate the vertical thrust of these two columns, and to give the majestic edifice the tension and the dynamism which the Baroque style demanded.[19]

As a whole the Karlskirche is still Baroque,[20] in spite of the greater restraint of the columns of the portico, and what keeps it so is the dominance of a painterly element in its spreading ensemble. Since it was planned for a wide site, the façade, like that of St Peter's in Rome, is very broad. It conceals the body of the building, which has the form of a longitudinal oval intersected by a Greek cross (Figure 5). On entering the church, the clarity of the spatial form is all the more striking. The horizontal accent is retained in the main entablature and in the drum of the dome, while the elliptical shape is echoed in the elevation and in the dome itself, where Rottmayr's fresco continues the upward trend. Compared with the Kreuzherrnkirche in Prague,[21] built by Jean Baptiste Mathey

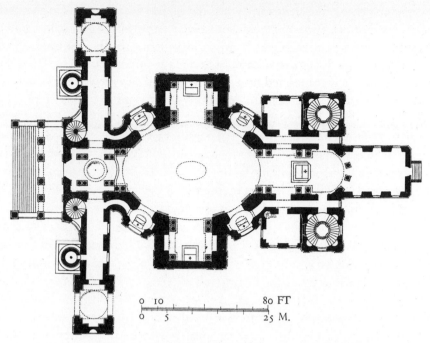

Figure 5. Johann Bernhard Fischer von Erlach: Vienna, Karlskirche,
begun 1716. Plan

thirty-seven years earlier, of which Fischer had made a sketch, the elliptical shape is
much more strongly emphasized, not only by the broad concave diagonal axes, which
open into oval-shaped chapels and galleries, but also by high pilasters rising right up to
the great entablature at the foot of the drum. On the other hand the imposts of the
arches opening in the arms of the cross are in no way emphasized, while in Mathey's
church the main emphasis in the corresponding arms had been on the entablature.
Fischer's giant pilasters testify to his fundamentally Baroque outlook. At his death in
1723 the building was incomplete, and the drum and dome were executed, in a somewhat modified form, in 1723–4 by his son Joseph Emanuel.[22]

In 1716, the year in which the foundation-stone of the Karlskirche was laid, Fischer
began the electoral chapel[23] attached to the cathedral of Breslau. It was built for Franz
Ludwig, count palatine of the Rhine, bishop of Breslau and from 1716 elector of Trier,
who was also the brother of the dowager empress, and dedicated in 1724. This and the
altar of the Franciscan church at Salzburg are regarded by Sedlmayr as the most exquisite
works in Fischer's *œuvre*. Here once again, this time in eastern Germany, where the
Baroque continued longer than in Vienna, Fischer tackled the problem of dynamic
form. The longitudinal oval, frequently broken in the lower orders, dominates in the
entablature at the foot of the drum. The transition from the pilasters to the columns of
the transverse oval chancel is particularly successful.

The new type of Viennese palace with a powerfully projecting centre had been introduced by Domenico Martinelli in the Liechtenstein Palace[24] (1692–1705). In the palace
of Prince Eugene[25] (1695–8), Fischer enlivened the uniform range of the giant pilasters

93

above the two lower mezzanine storeys with a lavish use of sculpture. On the Batthyány Palace, completed about 1700, a Tuscan aedicule in front of the grooved wall encloses the portal surmounted by an arch which curves forward. In the five central bays tapering pilasters with handsome imaginative capitals divide the upper storeys, and the sculptural character of the façade is completed by a sequence of statues above the cornice. For the winter palace of the Bohemian Chancellery[26] (1708–15) and for the Trautson Palace[27] (1700–12), Fischer adopted a new arrangement in which he emphasized the centre with a crowning pediment. This idea was further elaborated in the Clam-Gallas Palace in Prague,[28] for which the foundation-stone was laid in 1707. Here three projections of greater height give increased fluidity to the skyline. The corner projections, with the walls dissolved in large windows above portals, are particularly striking. Schlüter's Royal Palace in Berlin had probably served as a pattern for this. The sculptural element in Fischer's architecture is already evident in the caryatids at the entrance of the Court Stables at Salzburg;[29] it appears further intensified in Giuliani's statues in the vestibule of Prince Eugene's palace, and is at its grandest in the powerful dynamism of Braun's pairs of figures on the portal of the Clam-Gallas Palace in Prague (Plate 79).

In the Imperial Library, begun in 1722, the year before his death, Fischer's art entered its last phase.[30] Rich sculptural decoration was reduced to the attic zone (Plate 50B), and the influence of French classicism imposed greater moderation upon the moulding of the surfaces – with excellent results. The *porte en niche* takes the place of the portal with aedicule, and the window pediments disappear. Again in accordance with French prototypes, banded rustication enlivens the surface. The high ground floor with its batter and giant Ionic pilasters, the cornice, and the attic storey increase the monumental character of the building. At the same time the old ideal of using an oval as the three-dimensional centre of the building is realized in the middle transverse block of the library, although the rounded interior is inscribed externally in an octagon. The structure thus takes the form of a central pavilion with wings and a prominent roof. Gradually the terrace *à l'italienne* is disappearing in favour of northern architectural forms.

The library not only represents the culmination of the brilliant sequence of Austrian libraries: it is the crowning achievement of Austrian Baroque as a whole (Plate 51). As opposed to the longitudinal ovals of his churches, Fischer, in order to emphasize the centre, here pierced the oblong space with an ellipse inserted transversely. In accordance with the exterior, the interior architecture is clearly articulated. Subsequently, between 1763 and 1769, this was further stressed by an enlargement of the piers supporting the great arches of the central hall. The Roman ideal appears in the pairs of Corinthian columns set into the longitudinal wings after the manner of the Palazzo Colonna in Rome. The bookshelves are united yet more firmly to the walls by the dynamic flow of the balustraded gallery, a motif successfully exploited by Daniel Gran in the dome fresco of c. 1730, which foreshadows Rottmayr's fresco in the Jesuit church at Breslau. The big windows cut into this painted world like suns. The library was completed in 1735 by Fischer's son Joseph Emanuel (1693–1742).

Joseph Emanuel was extensively employed for the enlargement of the Hofburg, and during the course of his manifold activities he was able to develop a style of his own in the great court of the wing housing the imperial chancellery,[31] begun in 1729. He lacked his father's richness of imagination and monumental conception of form, but he did bear witness to his excellent architectural training in the concise grouping and careful insertion of the rich ornamentation required in this context. The rows of Corinthian columns supporting the gallery in his Winter Riding School[32] of 1729–35 avoid heavy mouldings or Baroque forms, and characteristics of early classicism are already present in the coffered ceiling. In 1729 too he built the left side of the Michaelertrakt as part of the Winter Riding School. It must be assumed that he used a design of his father's,[33] which may have corresponded to the engraving by Salomon Kleiner. The flat roof is still retained, and is profusely decorated with war trophies. Joseph Emanuel built a dome and an adjoining higher roof on the corner.[34] (In 1774 Frederick II of Prussia ordered G. C. Unger to use the whole remarkable plan with the concave front and convex lateral wings swinging forward for his library in Berlin.) The Michaelertrakt was not completed until 1893, after a wooden model made presumably by Joseph Emanuel. The high central dome was added at the same time.

About 1710 the High Baroque under French influence entered its second phase. That the general feeling of the time was changing is proved by the transition from the heavy acanthus wreaths to lighter formations. Ribbonwork interlaced in various ways made its appearance and remained dominant until 1740. In Austria, Johann Lucas von Hildebrandt (1663–1745) is the main representative of this new style that discards the naturalism of the Antique and favours playful, graceful forms. In his case, however, personal conditions were too complex to make him a direct follower of the French school. German Alpine craftsmanship was the source of Fischer von Erlach's art, but Hildebrandt's must be seen against the much less unified background of the whole Austro-Hungarian monarchy.

He was born and grew up in Genoa, the son of a German captain in the Genoese army. About 1690 he went to Rome where, as a pupil of Carlo Fontana, he was trained in town-planning and as a fortification engineer. As royal military engineer he accompanied Prince Eugene on his campaigns in Piedmont of 1695 and 1696. Immediately afterwards he embarked on his career as an architect in Vienna. As early as 1698 he was given the title of an Imperial Councillor, and in 1700 he became Hofbaumeister (architect to the Court). He was ennobled in 1720 and in 1723, after the death of Fischer von Erlach, he succeeded him as Erster Hofbaumeister (Surveyor General of Imperial Buildings). We find his patrons, not at the Habsburg court, but among the aristocracy. The most important was Friedrich Carl Graf von Schönborn, the Imperial Vice-Chancellor, who had the utmost understanding for Hildebrandt's somewhat erratic genius; the great architectural developments of the Hofburg, Schönbrunn, and Laxenburg were entrusted by the Imperial Court to men of far lesser talent. Impressions received in his youth in northern Italy persisted throughout Hildebrandt's life. One instance of this is his preference for a lavish decoration inspired by sixteenth-century Mannerism; another the way the building is set into the landscape. Moreover, such characteristic Hildebrandt motifs – his signature as it were – as the waist-bands round columns and pilasters are derived from the architecture of Genoa and Turin. Non-structural architectural members

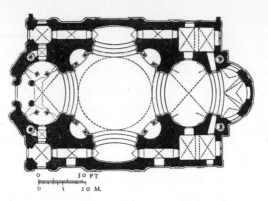

Figure 6. Johann Lucas von Hildebrandt:
Jablonné v Podještědí (Gabel), St Laurence,
1699. Plan

serving as frames are stressed, whereas columns and pilasters lose the importance they enjoy in Fischer's buildings. There is less weight and more fantasy in Hildebrandt's work. The monumental pilaster is replaced by a lighter, tapering form, also adorned with a waist-band. Images of Palladio's villas live on in his designs too.

North Italian also are the sources of St Laurence at Jablonné v Podještědí (Gabel) in northern Bohemia (Figure 6) which dates from as early as 1699. Here, inspired by the architectural ideas of Guarini, Hildebrandt bevels the edges of the dome piers and continues the wavy rhythm vertically through the arches and pendentives to the concave surfaces of the dome vault. The plan for the Piaristenkirche in Vienna[35] of 1698 is similar, and for that reason ascribed to Hildebrandt. An essential difference, however, is the omission of the drum in the interior; as a result of this the dome fresco comes down much lower and can have a stronger effect, especially as the arches cut directly into the vault. In his later churches Hildebrandt abandoned Guarini's ideas, which conflicted too strongly with the Austrian desire for spatial clarity.

The longitudinal ellipse appears once more in one of Hildebrandt's churches – the Priesterseminarkirche at Linz (1717–25). Not until this moment, at the summit of his career, did he develop all the fluency of Austrian Baroque. The type of front which swings forward and recedes in the centre is also used again. However, the broad bay of the central axis dominates, crowned by a pediment. The impetus continues directly in the tower, with its steeply rising cap drawn in tightly halfway up.

Presumably between 1702 and 1707 Hildebrandt amended the designs for the Peterskirche in Vienna.[36] The longitudinal oval plan had been fixed by Gabriele Montani, who began the building in 1702. Here again the omission of the interior drum permits the dome to rise directly on the arches. The façade with projecting centre, receding along the portal axis, resembles that of St Laurence at Jablonné v Podještědí. It is flanked by two low towers set diagonally so as to reflect on the outside the oval shape of the interior. As at Jablonné, the towers remain low. Everywhere Fischer's ideas are the starting-point for Hildebrandt, but he develops them according to contemporary taste to lighter, more fluent, and less monumental forms.

Hildebrandt was primarily a secular architect. For the summer palace of the Schwarzenbergs[37] just outside Inner Vienna, begun in 1697, he adopted Fischer's sculptural style for the flat-roofed drawing-room on the garden side, which projects in a semicircle beyond the front (Plate 52A). On the other hand his personal style can be seen in the organization of the parts and in the flat expanse of the front on the town side. He already related the building to the open space by framing it with curving wings and with tall hedges. Whenever possible he developed his gardens into depth by skilfully designed parts separated by terraces, so that long, narrow sites were welcome.

For the two palaces that he built for Friedrich Carl von Schönborn, the summer palace just outside Inner Vienna[38] (1706–17) and Schloss Göllersdorf[39] (1710–17), Hildebrandt produced designs that Pöppelmann could exploit in the Dresden Zwinger. The straight expanse of the *corps de logis* is like a flat barrier, although thanks to Hildebrandt's preference for a pavilion-shaped centre, the sense of body in the building remains alive too. The mansard roof is furnished with a pediment, usually curved and with small projecting corners. The most outstanding examples are on his Franconian buildings.

Thanks to Prince Eugene's passion for building, Hildebrandt was able to realize his ideas fully in the Vienna Belvedere.[40] As early as the sixteen-nineties he had begun to level the terraces, and by 1714/15 the Lower Belvedere was completed. Like the adjacent Schwarzenberg Palace, the building had to be erected on the low-lying part of the site. It was not until later that the ambitious idea matured of crowning the garden with an Upper Belvedere, whereby one of Fischer's favourite ideas was at last brought to fruition (Plate 53B). The Upper Belvedere was begun in 1721, and by 1722 the rough fabric of the narrow, elongated, beautifully graded building was finished. The four corner pavilions recall the old motif of corner towers. The outline is so distinct that a single glance is enough to reveal the unique grace of the whole structure; the wealth of ornamental detail requires closer study to be appreciated. Hildebrandt's feeling for space, so superbly revealed in the exterior, appears equally strikingly in the interior. In 1711 he had been called to Pommersfelden[41] in upper Franconia by the Elector Lothar Franz, an uncle of Friedrich Carl von Schönborn, to solve the problem of the staircase in his palace; he obtained the 'rechtmässige Proportion' (correct proportion) by inserting a gallery running round the stairs. In the Upper Belvedere he achieved an even more fluent spatial sequence by improving the relationship created by the staircase between the Sala Terrena, the large saloon above facing the garden, and the entrance hall opposite and halfway down.

Hildebrandt's share in designing palaces for the centre of the city was less important. His glamorous style shows to greatest advantage in the Daun-Kinsky Palace in Vienna,[42] built in 1713–16. The use of tapering pilasters and a narrower spacing emphasizes the vertical and gives greater lightness to the whole, which is typically Austrian (Plate 52B). In the interior, Hildebrandt showed once again his mastery in staircase design. The narrowness of the available space in no way cramped his style; in fact it suited him. The intricate stone panels of the staircase balustrades (Plate 53A), here and also in the contemporary Schloss Mirabell in Salzburg and twenty years later in the Harrach Palace in Vienna, are striking examples of his inventive powers.

From 1720 to 1723 and again from 1729 to 1744 he took part in the planning and rebuilding of the Residenz at Würzburg.[43] For the elevation there, thanks to the insight of Friedrich Carl, he was obliged to collaborate with Balthasar Neumann, a man of equal genius but with an essentially different outlook (cf. p. 154). It is noteworthy that for the final plan precisely those parts of Hildebrandt's designs were accepted in which the decoration was most lavish and brilliant, as for instance in the upper part of the central pavilion on the garden side, the interior decoration of the Imperial Hall, the chapel, and the railings of the *cour d'honneur*, 'the greatest adornment of the whole work' – unfortunately demolished in 1821. It revealed more than mere decorative talent. The warmth of an artistic temperament formed under the Mediterranean sun informs all important parts of this great Franconian masterpiece of the central German Baroque.

After Fischer von Erlach's death in 1723 his son managed to oust Hildebrandt and secure the commission for executing the plans of the Hofburg. As a result Hildebrandt was pushed into the background in Austria. In spite of this, however, he was still able to undertake important buildings, although his ambitious plans were only partly executed. In 1719 he began the enlargement of Göttweig,[44] an abbey magnificently sited above the Danube. From 1725 to 1732 he was employed by Prince Eugene for Schlosshof[45] in the Marchfeld, where his main contribution was the great series of terraces leading down to the river March. Finally, from 1727 to 1730 and in 1734–5, he worked for the counts Harrach on the enlargement of their Vienna summer palace.[46]

During his last years he made the plans for the monastery of Louka (Klosterbruck)[47] near Znojmo, which were only partly carried out after his death. As at Göttweig, the idea was to give a residential rather than a monastic character to the whole. The church was to be surrounded by palatial blocks with a majestic centre and dome-capped corner projections. At that time Hildebrandt used a sculptural style recalling that of his early days, which is also in evidence in the parish church of Göllersdorf (1740–1),[48] with its rounded façade, powerful, curved Hildebrandt pediment, and boldly modelled tower cap.

Alongside the German architects, a few Italians were able to obtain leading positions – for instance Donato Felice Allio (1667–1761), a native of Milan or its surroundings. His façade of the Salesianerinnenkirche[49] in Vienna, built in 1717–30, retains the Italian form with two superimposed orders of pilasters, and volutes on both sides. The interior on the other hand has the longitudinal oval shape at that time firmly established in Vienna. However, he divided it into six instead of the usual eight compartments, thus avoiding the Greek cross shape and allowing the spatial recession to proceed all the more freely. His most important commission was for the enlargement of the ancient Augustinian monastery at Klosterneuburg,[50] which was to serve as a retreat for the Emperor Charles VI. The foundation-stone was laid in 1730. Of the four courts originally planned as a symmetrical setting for the church, only the north-eastern one was executed. The residential character is revealed in the oval entrance hall on the southern side, with the library above, and more especially in the elliptical building supporting the imperial crown on the east front facing towards Vienna. Inside, the Marble Hall is built over the Sala Terrena and the oval windows of the hall cut into the dome. Allio's plans were, however, completely remodelled by Joseph Emanuel Fischer of the Imperial Office of

Works, who adapted them to correspond to his own buildings in the Hofburg, increasing the ostentation of the whole.

The third great Austrian architect, Jakob Prandtauer, stands midway in age between Fischer and Hildebrandt. He was born at Stanz in the Tyrol in 1660 and died at St Pölten in lower Austria in 1726. After training as a mason he began to work as a sculptor, and as such became in 1689 a resident of St Pölten. Like Fischer he was one of the Baroque sculptor-architects, and must as such be distinguished from men such as Hildebrandt who had first specialized as fortification engineers. From 1701 onwards, from his headquarters at St Pölten, he directed building operations for the abbeys of Melk, Sonntagberg, Garsten, St Florian, and Kremsmünster. He was in every respect the master mason in the old sense of the term.[51] He did not limit himself, as Hildebrandt did, to the drawing of the plans, but kept close supervision over the building operations until the work was completed down to the last technical detail.

Men working for monasteries did not receive the rewards and honours that fell to those in the service of the court. On the other hand, the master mason was not exposed to the arrogance of aristocratic employers or the intrigues and jealousies of the court. Whereas the court architects tried to imitate as far as possible the way of life of their patrons, monastic builders lived in a less disconcerting atmosphere. Prandtauer belonged to a religious brotherhood, and his son was a canon. He gave 700 florins towards the rebuilding of the church at St Pölten. For all their splendour, his religious buildings display a monastic character which was at times ridiculed by laymen,[52] who missed the elegance and worldliness deriving mainly from the French academic influence on Austria. On the other hand this monastic art was very closely linked with nature and with the people. Its spiritual source was the liturgy, and a learned theology in which the Benedictine fathers of Melk, who were associated with the Congregation of St Maur in St Germain-des-Prés in Paris, reached a high standard of accomplishment.

The extraordinary initiative which made the extensive reconstruction of the abbey possible was mainly due to Abbot Berthold Dietmayr, and was connected with his work at the university of Vienna, as a member of the diet, and in the administration of the conventual estates. He was opposed by the believers in the very strict monastic discipline practised at Melk. Eventually, however, Baroque Catholic ideas triumphed, and it was accepted that a display of splendour serves to glorify God. Even so, after Dietmayr had been in office for twenty years a kind of revolt broke out in the monastery. The abbot, however, was able to prove that everything in the rebuilding had been paid for from the current revenues. Furthermore when the extension of the monastery was begun in 1702, he insisted that Prandtauer retain as far as possible the old site extending along a rocky ledge (Plate 54). The monastic character is mainly visible in the evenly developed southern façade, with no articulation by pilasters, its effectiveness being entirely due to its extreme length. All the more remarkable is the way in which Prandtauer detached the church from the surrounding buildings which had formerly, following the medieval custom, screened it from the outside world; now, crowning the whole group, it was to be a focal point for travellers along the Danube.[53] Previously the west side had been shut off by a plain arcaded court. Prandtauer opened up this court, thus allowing the façade of the church with its twin towers to become visible. The forecourt was enclosed by two magnificent buildings, the Marble Hall and the Library, with a low gallery in front which had a wide opening flanked by columns with the Venetian or Palladio motif in the centre to assure the view. The lateral wings converge forward, their shape recalling the shape of Michelangelo's Capitol in Rome, though in Prandtauer's case the reason for the form is very different: the proximity of the cliff edge. He went even further, indeed, and allowed the form of the cliff to be reflected in the curving lines of the front communication gallery and in the façade of the church. The light undulation and the shadows cast by the profiles are exquisitely attuned to the picturesque character of the landscape. Originally the bulbous caps of the towers had a plainer silhouette; they were not given their present more restless shape until 1738, after Prandtauer's death and after a fire at the monastery had made a rebuilding necessary. They were designed by Prandtauer's successor, Joseph Munggenast, who as his cousin, pupil, and overseer had been very close to him. In the interior the slight undulation of the walls is carried on spatially: whereas the entablature recedes slightly, the graceful, richly decorated galleries, designed by Antonio Beduzzi, a painter and theatrical designer, curve forward. The *Platzlgewölbe* of the nave is a further development of Carlone's model at St Florian. In accordance with Prandtauer's style, the colouring is intense and rich. Pilasters of reddish brown marble are set against a background of rather paler red. The colour only lightens in Rottmayr's fresco above.

Enriched by the experience he had gained at Melk, Prandtauer approached his second great work, the reconstruction of the monastery of St Florian[54] in upper Austria. Here again, in a design the general layout of which was fixed by the west wing erected by Carlo Antonio Carlone, Prandtauer's mature style appears in all its splendour in the staircase block (1706-14) and the Marble Hall (1718-24), which lie at the critical points on the axes of the great court. As always, his ideas are relatively simple and restrained. Arcades between pilasters open on to the staircase that was already built. The motif of the Venetian window conjures up the image of the Basilica at Vicenza, while a vivid Alpine note appears in the decoration of the ascending flight of stairs. The theme of large joined openings is even more successful in the Marble Hall in the south wing, where the superimposed, closely placed windows contrast with the bare wall surfaces of the wings. The sculptured decoration at the level of the capitals is continuous and forms a most attractive crowning garland. The slight accentuation of the three central bays through the projections of the curving mansard roof is barely perceptible; in the interior it is emphasized by columns, beautifully inserted by a true master. How unstereotyped Prandtauer's art was is shown in the mouldings at St Florian, which are fashioned in the sense of the sculptor and show no trace of the linear art of the draughtsman.

The site chosen for the monastery of Melk in the valley of the Danube had proved brilliantly successful. Fifteen years later a similar problem was tackled with more modest means but even greater boldness at Dürnstein,[55] a particularly charming spot in the Wachau. For the rebuilding of this ancient priory of the Augustinian Canons, the energetic Hieronymus Übelbacher was determined to have the best artists (1716-33).

Almost certainly he approached Prandtauer first, for advice and perhaps even for designs. As at Melk, church and towers and a front terrace are set diagonally facing across the Danube, in full view from the river. The connexion with Melk is further demonstrated by the fact that from 1724 onwards Munggenast is documented as one of the masons. Matthias Steinl, the outstanding Viennese sculptor, engineer, and architect, who had worked for the Augustinians at Klosterneuburg, probably also had a major share in the success of the work. He was particularly talented as a decorative artist, and the liturgical vessels and textiles he designed, for example the monstrance of 1714 with the 'Finding of the Veil' for Klosterneuburg, are masterpieces of the minor arts of the Baroque. They formed the basis for his brilliantly designed altarpieces, in which the architectural elements are often replaced by sculpture: an example is the high altar of 1700–4 in the monastery of Vorau,[56] which is crowned by a rhythmic arrangement of an open colonnade allowing a flood of light to fall on it. At Dürnstein, in collaboration with Munggenast, he was probably responsible for the very free disposition of the architectural members, for instance the vigorous, broken lines of the galleries (Plate 57A) with their convex and concave curves leading alternately to elliptical openings above the side altars. The same free handling can be seen on the portals, whose lavish sculpture is inserted with a sure feeling for painterly effect.[57] This modification of the architectural elements to enhance the decorative sculptural character is best seen in the tower. A typical feature is the insertion of large buttress-like brackets, which also occur on the façade of the abbey church at Zwettl,[58] built by the same two men. Obelisks placed in front of the pilasters help to produce a more lively and painterly silhouette.[59] Frequently there are reminiscences of Gothic art, as at Zwettl, where Munggenast replaced the still extant Romanesque basilica by two western bays as a continuation of the Gothic hall-church, using the same type of granite. Baroque forms appear only in details such as the capitals. He used a design by Steinl for the façade (1722–7), with a tower rising to a height of about three hundred feet. Here, too, the vertical lines are accentuated and the outline is enlivened by enormous statues.

The extensive reconstruction of the monastery of Altenburg[60] in 1730–3 afforded Munggenast an opportunity of working independently, bound only by the medieval layout. The contrast between the regular façade, 675 feet long, and the central vertical line of the Gothic choir surviving inside the Baroque casing, and in addition the picturesque site above a narrow densely wooded valley, recall the situation of Melk. In the composition the sculptural element dominates. Above the arch of the gateway leading from the inner court to the church a colossal pilaster serves to enhance the effect of the mighty figure of the Virgin standing on the apex of the pediment. To conceal as far as possible the architectural error, the pilaster is made very flat. Munggenast borrowed Fischer's longitudinal oval for the plan of the church (Plate 56). Like that of the Peterskirche in Vienna, the dome is without a drum, which allowed Troger's frescoes to come low down into the interior. The beautiful colour harmony recalls that of Melk. The reddish-brown of the scagliola pilasters, enhanced by the gold of the capitals, reappears in the painted clouds of the fresco in the dome, and the white of the background and of the plasterwork and the blue, for instance in the mantle of the Virgin, intensify the effect of brilliance. Equally masterly is the sculpture on the altar and the stucco work, carefully executed by Franz Josef Holzinger in 1734–5.

With the library Munggenast, in collaboration with Troger and the plasterer Johann Michael Flor, reached a culmination of Baroque art (Plate 55). The hall, a simple elongated rectangle, is skilfully articulated by three domes divided by barrel-vaults and enlivened by light falling in from both sides. Here again, in his preference for columns, Munggenast appears as a follower of Fischer; but he achieved greater accentuation by placing the columns diagonally in the more colourful manner of Steinl, giving them a bluish white marble graining, and crowning them with dynamic plaster figures, for instance rearing horses.

The art of her Bavarian neighbour left its mark on the artistic circle of Linz in upper Austria. The small centralized type of building, popular in Bavaria, is followed in the pilgrimage church of Christkindl[61] near Steyr. It was begun by Carlo Antonio Carlone in 1706, three years before his death, and finished by Prandtauer after 1708. The central circle opens in four niches. The front consists of two towers flanking the portal. The church at Stadl-Paura[62] near Lambach (1714–24), built by Johann Michael Brunner (1669–1739), municipal architect of Linz, has a much more regular elevation. Like Georg Dientzenhofer's chapel near Waldsassen[63] (Figure 9), the dedication to the Holy Trinity is expressed in a distinct triple division. An inner circular dome-capped drum is enlarged by three apses with towers in front. The result is a triangle, the sides of which open in three doors, and the whole has a compact, elegantly curved silhouette.

With the exception of Schönbrunn, there are few examples of the Rococo in Austria. One such exception is the interior of the abbey church at Wilhering,[64] which has a vivid painterly decoration. The new building, which incorporated part of the Romanesque walls, was begun in 1733 and was probably the joint work of Johann Haslinger of Linz and the Imperial theatre engineer Andreas Altomonte. The far-projecting attached piers and the *Platzlgewölbe* of the bays result in a vigorous articulation of the building. The stucco ornament of the nave was the work of Franz Josef Holzinger; that in the transept and chancel is by Johann Georg Übelherr of Wessobrunn. Bartolomeo Altomonte executed the ceiling frescoes.

After Fischer von Erlach had left Styria for Vienna, architects from the north Italian lakes, the so-called 'Comaskin', were predominant there until about 1720. As a result, when the Augustinian monastery of Pöllau[65] was rebuilt, possibly from designs furnished by Carlo Antonio Carlone in 1689, the model was still Salzburg Cathedral. A more independent development began with the building of the pilgrimage church of Maria Trost near Graz in 1714–24. A site on high ground at the end of an idyllic valley was selected for the building, which was to dominate from afar. The lines of the twin-tower façade blend with the gables of the adjoining monastery to give a graceful undulating contour. The church of the Brethren of Mercy in Graz, built between 1735 and 1740 by Johann Georg Steng (d. 1753), is of the same type, as is also the church of the Cistercian abbey of Rein, rebuilt with some additions between 1737 and 1742 by the same architect. The fashionable *Platzlgewölbe* and convex galleries are included in the interior design.

Greater originality is shown in secular architecture. The Attems Palace in Graz[66] (1702–c. 16) is powerfully articulated by one order of giant pilasters for the two upper main floors and by banded rustication to unite the two lower floors as a single base. Above, the pediments of the high windows together with the capitals form a *mouvementé* sculptural zone. Three hipped roofs give an Alpine character to the whole. The Wildenstein Palace,[67] built at the same time, owes its unusual effect to the elliptical Corinthian columns of its giant order, which are flanked by quarter pilasters.

An independent contribution to the Austrian Baroque was made in the Tyrol, even though most of its talented artists left the country – a fate the Tyrol shared with the Italian Lake District. The Gumpp family were the pioneers of Baroque architecture in northern Tyrol. Johann Martin Gumpp the elder (1643–1729), Hofkammerbaumeister at Innsbruck, was a true Tyrolese. At first sight his style appears serious and rather heavy, but a closer inspection reveals a spirited, robust wit in the decoration. He rebuilt the Fugger-Welsberg Palace in the style of an Italian palazzo in 1679–80, and remodelled the old Government House in 1690–2. Both works show a vigorous sculptural treatment of the masonry but no accentuation of the architectural members. The lively surface effect derives from the coarse foliage design of the window hoods and the gargoyle heads on the cornice. His churches, for instance the Spitalkirche of 1700–1, which is skilfully inserted into the front towards the Maria-Theresienstrasse, follow the south German tradition of hall-like interiors and rich plasterwork.

This connexion, partly a geographical one, with the Swabian and Bavarian foreland of the Alps is even more apparent in the most striking Baroque church in Innsbruck, the parish church of St Jakob. The building was begun in 1717 after a plan of 1712 by Johann Jakob Herkommer of Füssen. On his death in the same year his foreman Johann Georg Fischer completed the work. The church, which has no galleries, is designed with internal buttress piers, *Platzlgewölbe*, and a vigorously moulded cornice curving upwards above the elliptical windows and the tripartite skylight. It bears a striking resemblance to Herkommer's earlier church of St Mang at Füssen, built in 1701–14 (p. 165). Like the contemporary abbey church of Weingarten (1715–22), the third bay is emphasized by transverse niches. As opposed to the dark, hemispherical, drumless dome over the crossing at Füssen, however, there is a light one over the chancel at Innsbruck which heightens the tension in the interior and gives an impressive spatial articulation. Unlike those at Füssen, too, the outer walls do not project beyond the composite pilasters, and the interior acquires the appearance of an aisleless hall.

Georg Anton Gumpp (1682–1754), the third member of his family to be master mason to the Innsbruck court, was evidently critical of the easygoing methods of his father and developed a vigorous, strictly architectural High Baroque based on Roman studies. The full impact of this style is revealed in the splendid façade of the Landhaus at Innsbruck which culminates in the dynamic verticalism of the central projection (Plate 57B), built in 1725–8. The Tyrol was indifferent to classicist criticism, which meant that Gumpp had a free hand to express the independent spirit of the various strata of society which, in addition to the clergy, the aristocracy, and the bourgeoisie, included, as it had even in the feudal age, the peasantry. Powerfully moulded cornices and bands co-ordinate all parts of the structure. In the centre four proud pilasters surge upwards over the giant piers below. Following the tradition of the medieval Tyrolese castle, the great hall, in which the diet met, is placed high up, marked by the large, richly decorated windows of the second and third storeys of the central block. Above the capitals are sculptured groups representing the four estates executed by Alessandro Callegari in 1727. A deeply shadowed pediment bearing the Tyrolese eagle crowns this unique front, which appears as a symbol of the freedom of an Alpine people.

Sculpture

Austrian Baroque sculpture developed in noble competition with architecture. This was assured in the first place by Fischer von Erlach's background as the son of a sculptor and by his general outlook. It was in connexion with his buildings, which owed much to impressions received in Rome, that sculpture began to flourish at Graz, Vienna, and Salzburg. We have already described the beginnings at Graz in the decoration of the Mausoleum, as also Fischer's vain attempt to reserve the dome of the chapel as a field for painting (cf. p. 89); but painting had not yet acquired a dominant position. Although a painterly style characterizes Baroque art as a whole, and informed both architecture and sculpture in Austria at this time, painting itself did not flower until later. When it did, it outlasted the other two arts in Austria by half a century.

In Vienna the trend towards the unity of the arts was very strong, especially in the eighties. An example of its influence is the Pestsäule (1682–94), vowed by the Emperor Leopold I during the terrible plague of 1679 (Plate 58). It was the fruit of a wonderful co-operation between the greatest sculptural talents. The idea of a pyramid, floating on clouds, to be erected in an oblong open space, the so-called 'Graben', evolved gradually, inspired by Bernini's work in the Piazza Navona and the Cathedra in St Peter's. These, however, had still been architectural in style, whereas in Vienna Lodovico Burnacini, architect and theatrical engineer, had had the imaginative idea of setting the monument freely in the spacious street so that, for the passer-by, it seems to materialize out of the sky and the clouds. The column is also a reminder of the important part which theatrical perspective played in the development of the Baroque style. Leopold I was primarily interested in opera, and under Burnacini the Viennese Baroque opera reached its first peak.

The Pestsäule was commissioned first from Matthias Rauchmiller (1645–86). Born at Radolfzell in Baden, he had made his reputation with his works in the Rhineland and Silesia (pp. 79–80), and had been active, with interruptions, in Vienna since 1676. His famous ivory tankard in the Liechtenstein Collection, with the Rape of the Sabine Women,[68] is dynamically conceived in the spirit of the time with soft flowing forms and densely packed figures in abundant relief. It is amazing how far Rauchmiller anticipated the style of the eighteenth century. According to Winckelmann 'he even surpassed the Greeks in tenderness'. His monument for the Graben was in the shape of a column standing on a base with three wings. Owing to his early death in 1686, of the nine figures of angels planned to rise from the base only three, with a trumpet, a lute, and a book, modelled in the delicate manner of his last years, were used. Fischer von Erlach and

Burnacini were commissioned to continue the work. Fischer conceived the idea of a pyramid of clouds on which the angels found their place: a reaction against the excessive use of commemorative columns in the villages. In addition Fischer gave a more architectural shape to the base and modelled the six reliefs of the concave lateral surfaces in which sculpture vies with painting – an express aim of the Baroque sculptor (cf. p. 87). They were executed by Johann Ignaz Bendl. Prominent among the many artists who shared in the work was Paul Strudel (1648–1708), a south Tyrolese, whom therefore his Vienna colleagues called Italian. The model for the bronze Trinity which crowns the pyramid is his, as are also the models for the statues of Leopold I, Faith, and the Plague standing on the pedestal. The type of his figures, which is already classicist, reveals his Venetian training, as does the rather finicky, restless modelling of the drapery, in small folds that have lost their textile character and play about the limbs like waves or clouds.

The sculptural taste of the German Baroque is characterized by the popularity of ivory carving. The smooth, pale glow and softness of the flesh could be as exquisitely expressed in this medium as harsh, jagged, deeply undercut outlines, brittleness, and crispness; in a word everything that appealed to the taste of the time. As far as inventive genius is concerned, the more conventional art of Ignaz Elhafen, who was in Vienna during the last fifteen years of the seventeenth century and who worked after engravings, was far surpassed by that of Rauchmiller and even more by that of the imaginative Matthias Steinl (1644–1727). Steinl's important contribution to the development of Austrian Baroque architecture, especially in its decorative aspect, has already been described (p. 101). From 1688 he was Ivory Carver to the Emperor in Vienna; his superb skill in this field is shown in the three equestrian statuettes of the Emperors Leopold I, Joseph I (Plate 59), and Charles VI in the Kunsthistorisches Museum in Vienna. In spite of the rather ostentatious display of the glory of monarchy, Steinl's skill can be seen in the characterization of the men portrayed. For so independent an artist, the common conventions used to make heroes out of the emperors were not sufficient; evidently he subscribed to no theory but relied exclusively on his inventive genius, which was steeped in the spirit of the Baroque. Thanks to the universal nature of his talents, he was given a teaching post at the Academy. The latter had been founded in 1692 under imperial patronage by Peter Strudel, brother of Paul Strudel, and in 1705 under Joseph I it was publicly recognized and given the title Imperial.

Steinl was obviously most at home in the cultural milieu of the monasteries. There genuine talent was better appreciated than in Vienna, where genius often only aroused jealousy. The extraordinary impetus of his art made a deep impression on his contemporaries.

During the last decade of the seventeenth century another artist, the Venetian Giovanni Giuliani (1663–1744), began his career. For fifty years he worked for the Cistercian abbey of Heiligenkreuz, near Baden, and in addition was employed by Prince Liechtenstein and others. He soon managed to adapt his rather soft, sentimental style to the Austrian spirit, as did Mattielli a little later. As a young man Raphael Donner was apprenticed to Giuliani.

The most influential sculptors during this first great period of the Viennese Baroque came mainly from Swabia, which had political ties with Austria. In the Salzburg area, where there was a decisive break-through of the Baroque, the incentive came from the same direction, in this case carried by artists of the so-called Inn Quarter (Inn Viertel). The originally Swabian families of sculptors, the Zürns and the Schwanthalers, were highly productive there; their work, rooted in the old family traditions, reached its peak during the 1670s and 1680s (cf. p. 52). Thomas Schwanthaler (1634–1705), active at Ried, the author of the double altar at St Wolfgang (1675/6),[69] embodied the family spirit. As a young man he had had to take over his father's workshop, and even though his mother and his wife were both natives of the district, he himself was looked upon as an outsider. As a result he had to face the opposition of a native-born rival. Being first and foremost carvers the country artists were closely connected with the Gothic tradition also by the colouring of their figures.

Schwanthaler excelled in the life-like quality of his work, immediately arresting yet without any exaggerated naturalism. Meinrad Guggenbichler, a direct follower of Schwanthaler, was even more successful. He also came from the south-west, from the Swiss canton of Schwyz. The son of a master builder and stone-mason, he was baptized in the collegiate church of Einsiedeln in 1649. His whole life was spent within the orbit of a specifically monastic culture. In 1670 we find him in Austria for the first time doing work for the monastery of St Florian. From 1672 onwards he was employed by the monastery of Mondsee, where he settled and remained until his death in 1723. Though he adopted certain motifs from Schwanthaler, for example the very fluffy treatment of wind-swept hair, especially in beards – an instance of this is the figure of St Benedict on the Holy Ghost Altar at Mondsee (Plate 60A) – he went far beyond the older artist. By using thinly sawn wood and by deep undercutting he succeeded in projecting gestures and billowing drapery dynamically into space, and thereby, as also by the polychromy of his figures, creating painterly effects. Thanks to this quality. Rottmayr's painting on the high altar of the abbey church of Michaelbeuern seems directly continued in the carved parts of the altar.

How difficult it is to reduce these country artists to any common denominator, how far the personality and the life of the individual set a stamp on his work, is manifest in the art of Michael Zürn the Younger, a native of Wasserburg, and the nephew of the brothers Martin and Michael Zürn. From 1679 to 1681 the highly gifted but erratic artist can be traced at Olomouc (Olmütz). After 1681 he worked in Gmunden. His greatest achievement, sixteen over-life-size figures of angels carved in white Salzburg marble for eight altars in the abbey church of Kremsmünster (1682–6),[70] shows that he had travelled widely. He had obviously come into contact both with the Bernini school and with the ecstatic, unrealistic eastern Baroque of the Slavs, and in the process had lost touch with his own heritage, the native art of upper Austria. The drapery, drained of its textile character, flickers over the bodies in agitated folds, and is reminiscent of that of his contemporary Paul Strudel on the Pestsäule in Vienna. It is characteristic that Zürn chose much quieter, more classicist forms for the eight angels he did last, probably owing to adverse criticism of his Baroque style.

As sculpture became independent, leaving the shrine for the open space, ornament, too, broke loose from architecture. In the last years of the seventeenth century a group of altars have broad acanthus wreaths carved round the paintings. Acanthus interlaced with ribbons made its appearance after 1705, especially in the Salzburg and Inn Quarter regions.

The popular art that flourished in the adjoining areas was in marked contrast to the art of the Salzburg court, where the archbishop reigned also as a secular prince. Here, the ecclesiastical link with Italy was in itself sufficient to increase the influence of the Italian Baroque. As a result, under Johann Ernst Count Thun (1687–1709), the mercurial development inaugurated by Fischer von Erlach paralleled that of Vienna and Graz. The best tradition of the Italian period, represented here by the sculpture for the Residenz Fountain near the cathedral[71] (1658–61), was infused with the new self-confident spirit of a national German art. From the three athletes supporting the basin of the fountain the Salzburg sculptors learnt how to model powerful human bodies, their effect further enhanced by the contrast with the bodies of animals treated in a similar way. Above, three dolphins hold up a smaller basin into which water pours from the shell of a triton. At the foot of the rock-covered base four horses rear up out of the large basin, puffing water from their nostrils. This work by an eminent Italian sculptor – possibly Tommaso Garona[72] – develops the style of Bernini's Roman fountains in an independent way. At Salzburg it kindled the artistic imagination all the more readily as during the Baroque – and in this too it followed the Roman pattern – the city was one of fine horses and ever-playing fountains. Opposite the portal of the Archiepiscopal Stables, designed a year earlier by Fischer von Erlach, Michael Bernhard Mandl (1660–1711) in 1695 executed the Horse Pond Monument, a massive rearing horse and a naked youth leading it by a bridle (Plate 60B). The new ability to depict movement and to fuse parts into a coherent group is displayed in the merging of the two figures. The youth leaps forward, and his back is on the same level as that of the horse. It is in fact a translation into the Baroque language of the two Horse Tamers of Monte Cavallo. The assumption that Fischer von Erlach had a share in the monument is supported by the fact that he had collaborated with Mandl in the building of the church of the Trinity. There the two marble angels who raise the oval frame on the northern side-altar, modelled on Michael Zürn's angels at Kremsmünster, are Mandl's work.[73] Sculpture was now coming to the fore, taking the place of architectural members: that this occurred within the framework of Fischer's art proves the extent to which he was influenced by an inherited instinct for sculpture. For the high altar of the collegiate church[74] he went even further, confining himself to a relatively low semicircle of columns filled with numerous figures while, following Bernini's pattern, the concave wall of the choir is covered with stucco clouds and figures of putti. In the centre, the Virgin of the Immaculate Conception appears on a globe. Further evidence of the new aims which inspired the Salzburg sculptors at that time, in contrast to the preceding generation, is given by Mandl's figures of St Peter and St Paul in front of the cathedral (1697); they are flanked by St Rupert and St Virgil, dating from thirty years earlier.[75] In place of the block-like solidity of the older figures, the later ones are relaxed in body and spirit; in place of an emphasis on line there is now a painterly style, especially obvious in the drapery.

That Guggenbichler 'as a foreigner' was unable to gain a footing in Salzburg was not entirely due to the particularism of Germany: sculptors in stone had better chances at Salzburg. A sculptor of the highest rank was indeed available just then, one whose distinguished talents should certainly have been enlisted and who moreover was deeply attached to his home town, to which he invariably returned from abroad. The artist in question was Balthasar Permoser, born in 1651 in the village of Kammer near Otting in the Chiemgau on a farm that was leased from the abbey of Nonnberg in Salzburg. He thus belonged to the first generation of outstanding Austrian Baroque artists, the generation which comprises Fischer von Erlach, Guggenbichler, Steinl. At Salzburg Permoser was apprenticed about 1663 to Wolfgang Weissenkirchner the Elder (1609-77), who was not able to teach him much. On the other hand the unknown sculptor of the Residenz Fountain seems to have taught him a great deal, and the statues of the Gods and Seasons in the parks of Hellbrunn and Mirabell too must have introduced him into a world which was to be of importance for his later work. Three of the Mirabell figures – *Bacchus* and *Flora*, now in the Lower Belvedere in Vienna, and *Apollo* on the great staircase of the episcopal palace in Salzburg – have been convincingly attributed to Permoser.[76] They appear to presuppose Permoser's traditional fourteen years' stay in Italy,[77] which would thus have fallen between 1671 and 1685. There, in the school of Bernini, Permoser received an impeccable training, including all technical matters. The Florentine works of 'Baldassar Fiammingo' demonstrate this: the coat of arms of 'Religion' and the statue of *St Gaetano* at S. Gaetano in Florence.[78] Permoser here adopted the flowing draperies, the masterly rendering of the texture of materials, and the Italian interpretation of piety to such an extent that the attribution of such works to Permoser would be far from easy, were it not for the testimony of the Florentine topographers.[79] The Mirabell figures, on the other hand, already show the verve characteristic of his Saxon works.

The second phase of Austrian Baroque sculpture, represented by the generation of artists born around 1690, necessarily brought a certain relaxation of tension. The real representatives of the new style which emerged during the Régence were Frenchmen. In Vienna, however, as opposed to other German royal cities, they were not able to gain a footing on account of the hostility arising from the War of the Spanish Succession. Under such conditions it was possible for Lorenzo Mattielli, a native of Vicenza (1688-1748) and a man of wide talents, to satisfy the demand created by the union of Italian genius with the new flowering of Austrian art. Furthermore, Mattielli could adapt himself without losing his own personality and this adaptability made him an ideal sculptor for the decoration of gardens and buildings, a type of work for which there was a great demand at that time especially in Vienna. At the age of thirty-one he began the groups of Rapes and of Seasons for the Schwarzenberg garden (1719-24). The abduction of a woman, a subject frequently treated by Bernini's followers, is presented here with charming lightness (Plate 61B), and the youthful female bodies are most delicately moulded.

Mattielli was endowed in full measure with the typically Italian gift – strengthened by the plays that were then in vogue – for lively characterization of strange grotesque creatures. A good example is the statue of *Winter* as a weird old woman with a pig (Plate 61A). The same sense of humour, which certainly appealed to the Viennese, can also be seen elsewhere, especially in the animals in the Hercules groups for the Imperial Chancellery (1728–9). Another Italian gift, his ability to give convincing human form to the numinous, is revealed most beautifully in the *Archangel Michael* above the entrance to the Michaelerkirche in Vienna (1730), where with irresistible lightness and ease St Michael strikes Lucifer down. Mattielli was able to demonstrate his talents much more extensively and in a more serious context when he was asked much later to do a series of statues for the Roman Catholic Royal Church in Dresden (1740–8), that is a diaspora. In Vienna he was unable to compete with the genius of Donner, especially as the latter was the younger man. Mattielli was defeated by Donner in 1737 in the competition for the fountain on the Mehlmarkt, but his emigration to Dresden, where he appears in 1739 in the service of the court, gave him the chance to occupy for the last nine years of his life the leading position from which he had been debarred in Vienna.

Mattielli seems to have achieved everything that could be achieved by an Italian sculptor working in Vienna during the second period of the Austrian High Baroque. The impetus of comprehensive movement, the dominating, expressive, and pathetic gesture, a beauty appealing to the senses, all this was welcome in Vienna; but it was not entirely in keeping with the very distinctive character of that city. Similarly the artists who came from Alpine and Inner German districts brought with them innate regional traits which prevented them from becoming completely Viennese. A warmth of manner, friendly yet reserved; a shunning of extremes; elegance which in its unaffected simplicity and avoidance of ostentation could achieve real charm; a refinement of taste even pervading fashion; a zest for life that evokes responsiveness to every form of beauty; a lightness that is physical but can also inform the mind and ranges from easy conversation and slightly ironic wit to a shrewd sense of real values that can penetrate and solve the most intricate problems – these and many other qualities in the Viennese character could only be crystallized into art by one who possessed them all.

Such a one was Georg Raphael Donner (1693–1741), born at Esslingen in the March-feld, with his roots in Viennese soil. His achievement, so striking in comparison with all that existed in Vienna, was crowded into two decades, and his real masterpieces were not done until the thirties. Obviously he needed some time to free himself from tradition. His innovations do not lie in classicism as opposed to the Baroque: Donner was still capable of uniting both. He accepted the ideal of ancient art and yet was still able to infuse movement into his figures. Nor did he feel the need for concessions to the light-ness of the Rococo. When he gave up massive, rounded forms he tended, like Hilde-brandt, to Mannerism, to over-long figures with small heads, but he did not achieve the ideal of immaterial form. His aim was to find a more directly effective expression for the beauty of the human figure. He was academic only in his devotion to what was taught at the academies, that is the study of the human body from the antique and from life, intensified by the study of anatomy. His archaeological knowledge, above all of costume, has been emphasized by Goethe's friend and teacher, the painter Oeser, who was first introduced to such things by him. However, no rigid theories cramped his style; he followed his own rules and the instincts of his race. Even in his choice of materials he was opposed to Austrian traditions, restricting himself to stone and metal, and excluding wood. Prior to his apprenticeship to Giuliani at Heiligenkreuz he worked for a goldsmith in Vienna. His preference for metal is recorded, probably by the abbot: 'When Donner was a boy of about thirteen he was taken on by chance by Giuliani. He showed remarkable genius. He stole candles and the lids of pewter jugs and engraved them with his burin at night.'[80] In 1726 he was employed for a time in Salzburg as a medallist. He worked in bronze and also had a particular liking for lead, its softness and dull sheen being well suited to his style.

His career began at Salzburg, where he worked for the archiepiscopal circle and in that respect followed the usual custom of Austrian artists at the time. In 1726–7 he made the sculpture for the great staircase in Schloss Mirabell. Evidence that he regarded the figure of *Paris*[81] as his best work is given by the signature 'G. R. Donner 1726' placed conspicuously on the base. Perhaps he was thinking of Michelangelo, whom he was following here in the heavy crossed limbs and relaxed posture. The firm outline to which his practice in medal cutting had trained him is a characteristic feature of his work, in keeping with his temperament and his deliberate avoidance of all exaggeration. The suavity and the pose of the figure were inherent in the mythological theme; the fact that he paid attention to it is evidence of his archaeological knowledge.

His *St Johannes Nepomuk*[82] in the parish church of Linz, done in the following year, seems in its quiet refinement and relaxed grace like a protest against the usual interpretation of this popular wayside saint, the 'Hansl am Wege'. The two putti at the saint's feet introduce a humorous Viennese note. The curving Baroque pedestal is carefully adjusted to harmonize with the figure. This also applies to the figures in Bratislava (Pozsony, Pressburg) Cathedral, Donner's next great masterpiece. He had been called to Bratislava about 1729 as chief architect and sculptor to the court of the Prince-Bishop Emmerich Count Esterházy. In the same cathedral Donner designed the chapel of St Elemosynarius[83] (consecrated in 1732) as the prince's tomb, and also the high altar,[84] a semicircular colonnade with an equestrian statue of St Martin (consecrated in 1735; Plate 64). Unfortunately the superstructure of the altar was removed during a Neo-Gothic restoration in 1865, but the sculpture has survived. In the elliptical chapel, which is also by Donner, the pilasters and the altar niche have rich ribbonwork decoration. The tabernacle is flanked not by columns but by two marble angels,[85] whose monumental character and heavy contrapposto form a distinct contrast to the usual Baroque treatment of angels (Plate 62); indeed their effect is classical even to the simplified modelling of the powerful limbs. The Baroque reliefs of the altar with scenes of the Passion form close-knit, dynamic groups. The tragic theme is reflected in the almost painful tension between the expanding and contracting forms of the nude figures. The drapery on the other hand seems little more than a low-toned accompaniment; yet Donner, if he deemed it necessary, was perfectly capable of a brilliant rendering of cloth and embroidery, as for example in the statue of the kneeling prince-bishop at the side,[86] a masterly rendering of an aristocratic prelate.

The composition of the high altar was still fully Baroque. This, however, was probably a concession on the part of Donner to the form sanctioned by the ecclesiastical authorities. At any rate the lead group of *St Martin and the Beggar* (Plate 64),[87] with its concentrated energy, shows an essentially different style. It is composed two-dimensionally and circumscribed by a circle. Even more striking is the fact that Donner discarded the usual iconographical interpretation and presented the Hungarian saint, a Roman officer of the patristic period, in the guise of a hussar. This turns out to be in no way detrimental to the religious feeling. Here again, in the two angels kneeling at the sides inner vitality is concentrated within closed contours.

This art, based on rationalism as understood by the eighteenth century, could no longer count on the illusionism of the Baroque. The transcendental expression that Permoser was still able to infuse into his *Apotheosis of Prince Eugene* (cf. p. 201) is no longer convincing in the angel of the corresponding group of 1734, exalting Charles VI in the Lower Belvedere in Vienna.[88] One no longer credits the angel with the capacity to rise, and he seems to adhere so lightly to the emperor that at any moment he may crash down.

In the very last years of his life Donner produced one of his greatest masterpieces: the fountain for the Mehlmarkt in Vienna.[89] It was commissioned by the municipal authorities and executed between 1737 and 1739. In this work Donner seems to anticipate the future in so far as he makes no attempt at a glorification in the Baroque sense of the term, but only tries to represent what was regarded in the Age of Reason as the most vital forces: rational planning for the future and circumspection, expressed in the central figure of *Providentia*, and the rich fruits of nature in lower and upper Austria, expressed in the personification of the rivers Ybbs, Traun, March, and Enns (Plate 63).[90] By entrusting Donner with the commission, originally intended for Mattielli, the counsellors decided in favour of a compatriot, but they also recognized in him 'undoubtedly the superior artist'. Once again he chose lead as his material. Donner has always been admired for the way in which, despite his passion for relief in a single plane, he solved the problem of erecting a monument in an open space by presenting the wonderful figures spirally after the pattern of Giovanni da Bologna, so that the spectator is forced to proceed round the fountain in order to admire them from all sides. Moreover they appear immediately before him on the basin's edge and are arranged in pairs, contrasting male and female, old age and youth and childhood, so that the eye is drawn from one figure to its counterpart in the next. In his sensitive understanding of the individual character of each task, Donner came very close to nature here, especially in the youth personifying the Traun, who bends in a spontaneous movement over the edge of the basin, aiming at a fish he is about to spear.

In 1741, the year of his death, Donner completed the lead *Pietà* for the cathedral at Gurk. Usually so fond of compressing a figure in order to increase inner tension (which shows above all in the treatment of skin), he has here placed the figure of Christ in a long-drawn-out diagonal formed by the angel, the Virgin, and the putto kissing Christ's arm. The deeply moving adagio of the group is brilliantly continued in the relief below, with the dead Christ lying in his tomb.

Donner's work marked a turning-point in Austrian art, though this was more apparent in Vienna than in other parts of Austria, where the Baroque style ruled into the second half of the eighteenth century. This was due to the family relationship between the monasteries and the artists they employed, who were thus able to develop their individual styles unhampered by the exigencies of the day and the changing taste of impersonal patrons. In such an atmosphere Franz Josef Holzinger (1691-1775) executed his vast *œuvre*, especially for St Florian, where he owned a house. He was an important sculptor who worked in stone, wood, and plaster. Throughout his life he remained faithful to ribbonwork ornament, like most Austrian artists rejecting the *rocaille* as a foreign product. He did, however, develop a vivid, fluent, full-blooded and painterly style in a curiously expressive and personal way, as for example in the dancing and whirling figures on the piers in the library of Metten Abbey[91] (1722-4). He had a fundamentally German feeling for form and avoided the use of caryatids, a typically southern motif.

The variety of art in different parts of the country – or rather Alpine valleys – is also amazing. In the hills artists felt closer to nature and were less inclined to indulge in flights of imagination than they were in the wide, flat Danube valley, which tended to inspire romanticism. Characteristic of this is the contrast between two sculptors of the same generation: Holzinger, who worked in the Danube area, and Josef Thaddäus Stammel (1699-1765) from the upper Enns valley. Stammel, a native of Graz, was a pupil of Johann Jakob Schoy (1686-1733), who was responsible for the lively figures on the high altar of Graz Cathedral.[92] As a young man Stammel came as sculptor to the Benedictine monastery of Admont, situated high up in the upper Enns valley, where a fine artistic tradition prevailed, and where he was able to develop his individuality. As the Baroque in Vienna was related to the opera, so was his art to the Passion and Nativity plays of the peasants, which continued a tradition in the Alps that went back to the Middle Ages. His portrayals of the hill people whom he knew so well, with their robust character and rustic humour, are irresistible.

The strength of Stammel's opposition to Viennese art is shown in his altar of St Martin in the church of St Martin near Graz of 1738-40 (Plate 65). He began the work some three years after Donner had completed his St Martin at Bratislava, and it has every appearance of a critical comment made by the man of the Alps on the work of the metropolitan. Like Donner, he claimed the right to characterize his environment in the figure of the horseman: but in the earlier altar we see an aristocratic hussar officer on parade, mounted on a thoroughbred; here he is a young peasant on a stamping stallion, who wears his antique apparel in the natural and unconcerned way in which he would do so in a festive procession. At Bratislava even the beggar, fashioned like a classical river-god, has a touch of refinement; in Stammel's work a true beggar, weakened by disease, lies on the ground as he would in reality, raising himself slightly as he holds out his hand to beg. To Stammel it seemed that the moment when the horseman, touched by the appeal, pulled up his horse and expressed his sympathy was better suited to his theme than the more complicated scene showing the cutting of the coat in two – a further indication that his starting-point was a religious play. Architecture serves as a background. Four putti, in the carving of which Stammel competes with Guggenbichler, surround the group and form its base. The theme is followed up at the sides in two scenes connected with horses: *The Conversion of St Paul* and *St Eligius healing a Horse*. As in the Miracle Plays, there is a lighter note too, introduced here by the delighted farrier and the putto who is dragging St Martin's lance. While Donner's work was suitable for Bratislava, the ancient Hungarian coronation city, Stammel's popular saints were appropriate for the abbey farm with its rural setting.

Stammel endeavoured to depict life in all its manifold aspects in his own personal manner; thus he represented the universe in the shape of a pyramid covered with sculptured groups. The work, done in 1760, stood in the central hall of the library at Admont between the statues of the Four Last Things.[93] It was unhappily destroyed by the great fire of the monastery in 1864.

The Mur Valley in upper Styria, which even in the Middle Ages had produced excellent carvers, retained its sensitive, spiritualized ideal of beauty in the Baroque period. This is proved by a *Mater Dolorosa* in the Bavarian National Museum.

Painting

A conservative attitude stemming from Italian influence, especially Bolognese eclecticism and Venetian art, typifies Austria at this time. In painting there is no Fischer von Erlach. The north Italians held sway, and primarily Carpoforo Tencalla from Bissone on Lake Lugano, whom Sandrart esteemed highly both as a man and as an artist. His paintings frequently took the form of works on canvas in stucco frames; his work at Olomouc (Olmütz) and Kroměříž (Kremsier) has already been referred to (p. 86). In Austria he executed frescoes in the monastery of Lambach, at Heiligenkreuz, in the chapel of the Hofburg in Vienna, and elsewhere.

The transition to High Baroque can clearly be seen in the work of Hanns Adam Weissenkirchner (1646–95), who came of a family of artists in Salzburg. In Rome he came under the influence on the one hand of the Carracci, Guercino, and Guido Reni, and on the other of Poussin, which led him into Baroque classicism. His style is close to that of Murillo. Working in Graz, he endowed his pictures with a robust, rustic quality. His most important creations are the series of paintings in stucco frames in the state room of Schloss Eggenberg, near Graz (1684–5).

But the great period of ceiling painting in Austria began in 1695. That year witnessed the collaboration between Rottmayr and Fischer von Erlach at the castle of Vranov (Frain) in Moravia (Plate 47), where the addition of a painted world to enhance and complete his architecture – denied to the architect seven years earlier for the chapel in the Mausoleum at Graz – was successfully achieved.

Johann Michael Rottmayr (1654–1730), born at Laufen near Salzburg, came from the same area and belonged to the same generation as Permoser. Like him, too, he began his career with a long stay in Italy. In 1675 he went to Venice, where for thirteen years he was employed in the workshop of Karl Loth. He was thus in Italy at the same time as Fischer von Erlach, and was certainly impressed by the superb examples of Italian fresco painting produced at that time (cf. p. 89), although the Venetian development, culminating in Tiepolo, was later than the corresponding one in Rome (Giovanni Antonio Fumiani painted the ceiling of S. Pantaleone in Venice as late as 1700). Indeed Rottmayr's first works at Salzburg, for example the ceiling of the Carabinersaal in the archbishop's palace (1689) with its seething movement and massive figures, give no indication of his future eminence as a painter of ceilings. As has been said, Rottmayr's real talent was first revealed in the great hall at Vranov through his contact with Fischer von Erlach. It was probably Fischer who conceived the idea of accentuating his favourite shape, the large oval, by a powerful frame with transitional groups in the great lunettes. This frame, interrupting the direct transition to the architecture, surrounds the scene in the skies, a glorification of the House of Althan. Feeling that some arresting motif was still needed to form a link, however, Rottmayr draped a huge carpet over the frame.

In 1696 he went to Vienna, where he worked for thirty-four years, until his death, the acknowledged leader of the Viennese school, and where he was entrusted with the most important commissions. The fresco of 1702 in the Great Vestibule at Schönbrunn, the former dining-room, would represent a chief work of his early Vienna period if it could be ascribed to him with certainty.[94] The subject represented is probably Joseph I's expedition to Spain; in any case it mirrors the elation which filled Vienna at the time when Prince Eugene was just starting his brilliant career as commander-in-chief of the imperial armies. The introduction here of a motif that is neither figure nor architecture, namely a layer of cloud extending diagonally across the picture, conspicuous against the throng of men and ships, would be quite consistent with Rottmayr's bold style.

The significance attached to ceiling painting at the imperial court is proved by the fact that Leopold I summoned Andrea Pozzo, the chief artist of the day, to Vienna, where he arrived in 1702 and worked until his death in 1709. In 1705 he painted ceilings in the Jesuit church and in the Liechtenstein Palace.[95] His prestige was considerably increased by his famous text-book, *Perspective Pictorum et Architectorum*, first published in Rome in 1693 and 1700. Rottmayr, however, even at that time, was already beginning to break away from the Italian pattern. The works of Rubens which he could see in the great Vienna collections must have had a tremendous impact on him, as they had on the whole generation of the High Baroque, beginning in France. The art of Rubens also inspired the development of oil painting in this period, as can be seen in the picture of *St Benno*[96] (1702) in the Staatl. Sammlung in Munich. There, an all-pervading golden brown tone is intensified by the addition of pink and contrasted with the pale blue of the sky.

Rottmayr's masterpiece of the first decade of the eighteenth century was, however, painted not in Vienna but in Wrocław (Breslau). This is the ceiling of the Jesuit church of St Matthias (Plate 66A), done in 1704–6, when the Jesuits, despite strong Protestant opposition, had succeeded in founding their university. The fresco in the church represents *The Triumph and Veneration of the Name of Jesus* and *The Expansion of his Church*. Of particular importance was Rottmayr's use of an ellipse for the shape of the ceiling of the nave and, following the Roman pattern, the uniting of the three-bay vaults in one great representation. The throngs of saints and angels on concentric banks of clouds are dominated by the mighty halo round the Name of Christ. At the sides the paladins of the Church on earth appear behind balustrades, among them Prince Eugene, a happy choice of motif as regards both content and form, for it acts as a transition to the celestial spheres.

Between 1710 and 1711 Rottmayr was again at Salzburg, where he painted the ceiling of the Residenz. A little later, in 1715, he produced another of his greatest works, the fresco of the dome of the Peterskirche in Vienna. Here he again used the oval shape, so well suited to the dynamic processions of saints; he also accentuated the direction towards the high altar expressed in the fresco by placing the *Coronation of the Virgin* above the chancel arch. Rottmayr's solution for the problem of a transition to the lantern was to make the fresco progressively lighter in colour in the upper part, while a dark wreath carried by angels lies immediately beneath the opening.

In 1717–18 he came in contact with Hildebrandt, when he painted the ceiling of the Marble Hall at Pommersfelden. In 1719 he was working in the abbey church at Melk, where the division of the nave into bays by broad transverse arches made a special expedient necessary. He solved the problem, not entirely satisfactorily, by painting clouds and angels over them. This must have made all the more welcome the great commission to paint the dome in the Karlskirche in Vienna, an added attraction being that here again he was able to collaborate with Fischer. What the two artists had in common was a High Baroque appreciation of heavy sculpturesque forms. For the Karlskirche[97] Rottmayr could develop the composition which he had worked out at the Peterskirche, completed in 1725, and by increasing the progressive lightening of the colour, he also achieved greater unity of form. Violet, a colour much favoured by the followers of Rubens, dominates the colour scheme. For the rest, the painterly style is subdued by a use of strong contrasts in the modelling. His figures, especially in the frescoes, retain a certain heaviness and down-to-earth robustness. The impetus and dramatic vitality that characterize the art of his successor Troger are not yet apparent.

In many cases Rottmayr had to work alongside Italian artists, who were favoured especially by the nobility. In 1716, for example, Prince Eugene commissioned Martino Altomonte to paint the ceiling of the Marble Hall in the Lower Belvedere,[98] and in 1723 he succeeded in obtaining the services of Francesco Solimena, head of the Neapolitan school, for the fresco in the Upper Belvedere. Altomonte, who also came from Naples, worked in Vienna from 1703 until his death in 1745. As a pupil of Giovanni Battista Gaulli in Rome, he was already aware of the new ideal: less solidity and a greater play of light. His Belvedere fresco, the subject of which was *The Apotheosis of Prince Eugene*, shows a break with Pozzo's architectural schemes in favour of a contrast between the dark painted coffered ceiling and the luminous vision of the celestial scene.

Against the many Italian painters employed in Vienna at that time, only relatively few Germans, apart from Rottmayr, were able to establish themselves. Among them were Anton Faistenberger (1663–1708) and his brother Joseph (1675–1724), who made a name for themselves as landscape painters. They were natives of Salzburg, descended from a well-known Tyrolese family of artists. In their pictures they still followed the Italian pattern of stage-like perspective (i.e. obtaining recession by a kind of painted scenic wings). Christian Hilfgott Brand (1695–after 1756) is more original. He was a native of

Frankfurt, but worked in Vienna from about 1720 until his death. He successfully exploited the Dutch technique of painting, and attained an early romantic style which foreshadows the beginning of a new independent era in German landscape painting. In this he had a successor in his son Christian Brand. As a still-life painter, Franz Werner Tamm (1658-1724) of Hamburg, who was called to Vienna by the Emperor Leopold I, excelled in the sensuous rendering of plumage and fur.

During the entire eighteenth century the influences of France appeared and grew, but despite this Vienna was able to maintain her artistic independence, though with some concessions. The demand for academic training, it is true and has already twice been referred to, caused the painter and sculptor Peter Strudel (1660-1714), brother of Paul Strudel, to found a private institution in 1692. Called the 'Academy of Painting, Sculpture, Fortification, and the Art of Perspective and Architecture', it enjoyed imperial patronage, and in 1705, under the Emperor Joseph I, was established as a public academy. In his capacity as Surveyor General, Strudel was the head of the institution. One of its chief aims was to release its members from the obligation to join a guild, and this meant a break with the artisans, which had both advantages and disadvantages. After Strudel's death the activities of the Academy came to a standstill until 1725, when under the directorship of Jacob van Schuppen, a pupil of Largillière, the spirit of the French Academy began to prevail. The fact that in 1735 Adam Friedrich Oeser, then eighteen years old, was awarded a gold medal by the Academy was of some importance for the history of German art; for by the award the Academy honoured the artist who was to be the future inaugurator of classicism in Germany. The young artist had developed his ideas in friendly intercourse with Donner at the time when the latter was working at Bratislava. In 1739 Oeser went to Dresden, where he formed a close friendship with Winckelmann, and as a result the Austrian conception of art, with its union of Baroque and classicism, gained considerable influence on the development which was then beginning in the heart of Germany.

Daniel Gran (1694-1757) is a typical representative of the Baroque-classicist ideal. Though he retained a painterly conception, he strove to clarify his compositions by emphasizing the individual groups. In doing so the impetus of the preliminary sketches was lost, and sometimes Gran even failed to clarify the meaning, although clarity was regarded as a particular quality of his work. Thus the colour scheme in the design for the dome in the Palais Schwarzenberg in Vienna, a sketch in oils owned by G. Engelhardt (Plate 67), is much better suited to the theme – the struggle between light and darkness – than is the finished fresco.[99] Gran's greatest work, the dome of the Vienna National Library (1726-30)[100] depicting the *Apotheosis of the Emperor Charles VI and the Humanities*, which he patronized, shows how his compositional skill had matured through the study of Rottmayr's art. Fischer von Erlach's architectural device of eight upright oval windows which cut into the lower part of the dome was an excellent preparation for the painting (Plate 51). After the manner of Rottmayr's fresco in St Matthias at Breslau, an illusionistically painted entablature and a gallery with the representatives of the arts and the sciences form the link with the lower arches. Gran's colour, with its dominant brownish tone lightened by gold, is kept dark to harmonize with the bookshelves and architectural members, but the light grey of the columns introduces a special note. The importance of this achievement was later recognized by Winckelmann. In spite of this, however, it was not the style of Gran's followers that led to the full maturity of the Vienna school, but a more fully Baroque trend.

The leader of this movement was Paul Troger, who was born at Welsberg in the Pustertal in 1698 and died in Vienna in 1762. He continued Rottmayr's forceful style and endowed it with a yet stronger impetus, an irresistible movement, a more accomplished mastery of his craft, and indeed greater beauty. His biographer Michailow is therefore justified in saying: 'Strictly speaking it was not until the appearance of Troger that Austrian painting achieved European as well as national significance.' Extensive study in Italy over a period of years enabled him to penetrate to the true sources.

Thanks to the patronage of the Counts Firmian he was able, at the early age of sixteen, to enjoy an Italian training under Giuseppe Alberti of Trento, who had a school of painting at Cavalese. Subsequently he worked in Venice, where he acquired a knowledge of the painterly, excessively expressive style with its dramatic contrasts of light and shade which was favoured by artists such as Piazzetta and Pittoni in Venice and by Solimena in Naples. In Venice, too, he must have become aware of the new trend towards lighter colours and a more subtle rendering of atmospheric effects, which was to lead Venetian art to its climax. Tiepolo was only two years older than Troger and can therefore have been of assistance to him only as a fellow worker with similar aims. Later, in 1722, Troger painted the *Descent from the Cross* for the church of the Holy Cross on the Calvary Hill at Kaltern in the Tyrol,[101] which reveals Venetian influence in the broad drapery folds. The elongated figures with their small heads correspond to the Mannerist tendencies of the period. Afterwards Troger proceeded to Rome, where the most significant ideal of the time was revealed to him. He made friends with Martin van Meytens, later the favourite artist of Maria Theresa, and 'studied with untiring energy the works of the ancients to be found in Rome and its surroundings'. In Rome he had the opportunity of seeing the great achievements of ceiling painting, especially those of Luca Giordano, a kindred spirit. After Rome he went to Naples and Bologna, where he was entrusted with commissions. The idea, held also at that time by Donner, that the first and most important task for the artist is the representation of the human form must have matured in him during the years between 1722 and 1728. In the final analysis his art appears rooted in the Renaissance, and more specifically in the art of Correggio.

After his return to Austria, Troger worked for his patron the prince bishop of Gurk in Carinthia. Next, and this was even more important, in 1728 he painted the elliptical dome of the Kajetanerkirche in Salzburg. Shortly after, he went to Vienna. There he had the full support of Count Gundaker von Althan, Surveyor of the Imperial Works. Troger's association with the Academy provides further evidence of his sympathy with Donner's ideas. In 1751 he received a professorship and from 1754 to 1757 he was President, alternating in this office with his compatriot and fellow student Michelangelo Unterberger. His stability of character is reflected in the even tenor of his work, in which the only evidence of change – and that due to a general change of taste – is in the colour, which passes from a more sombre to a lighter, more brilliant tone. The oil painting of *The Agony in the Garden* in St Peter in Salzburg is characteristic of his early style (Plate 68B). (A replica is in the Barockmuseum in Vienna.) [102] The powerful figure of Christ, in a blue mantle and blood-red dress, emerges in vigorous foreshortening from a darkly shaded zone that occupies two-thirds of the picture. His head is inclined to the right and he is sunk in an agony of prayer. The deep reddish flesh tints of his face contrast with the lighter ones of the angel, who is in a similar posture but pointing upwards so that an S-curve develops along his arm and chest. As we can see from the sketch, the highly expressive blending of the two figures was a successful last-minute solution.

A particular quality of Troger's art lies in his ability to intensify the expression without impairing the realistic nature of the scene. This was probably due to a hereditary Tyrolese acceptance of religion in everyday life. Troger's religious expressions remain convincing even in a period that favoured ecstatic, exaggerated poses.

His collaboration with his compatriot Munggenast at Melk and Altenburg helped Troger towards final maturity. In the interior of the church at Altenburg the cornice, interrupted by the oval windows cutting into it, formed a curving foot line for the frescoes in the dome over the chancel (1732–3) and in the oval nave, which made a peripheral zone of painted architecture superfluous. The spectator is brought into direct contact with the dramatic representation (Plate 66B). Moreover, Troger succeeded in focusing the attention on essential details, as for instance on the apocalyptic woman clad in the sun fleeing from the dragon (Plate 68A), whose defeat at the hands of St Michael she witnesses while she herself is crowned as the Mother of God. Troger always preferred the use of white and blue instead of the usual red and blue for the Virgin's garments, which is in itself an indication of the desire for a lighter and cooler colouring. In addition he enlivens the scene by landscape details, and in this lies the principal difference between the sketch for the *Feeding of the Five Thousand* in the refectory of the monastery of Geras, now in the Vienna Barockmuseum,[103] and the finished work of 1738 (Plate 70), in which he allows tree-tops to rise into the almost empty sky. The figures, moreover, are closely related to the painted architectural border zone. Similarly, in the chapel of Schloss Heiligenkreuz-Gutenbrunn, the vigorous sculpture with its white volutes gives increased transparency and brilliance to the painting in the dome (1739; Plate 69). The idea of a lower zone on earth is stressed by the presentation of the female precursors of Christ against a greenish background, and by the figure of the Church holding the tables of the law and the Holy Scriptures, while above the celestial spheres open to reveal the Coronation of the Virgin, the Triumph of the Church, and a circle of saints. A spiral movement embracing groups that are linked or detached carries the figures of the Virgin, Christ, and God the Father, in robes of blue-white, light red, and pale mauve, upwards to the centre, where the dove of the Holy Spirit floats in a blaze of light.

Troger's brilliant art culminates in his late style, for example in the frescoes at Brixen (Bressanone) of 1748–50[104] (cf. p. 120) and in the dome of the church at Dreieichen[105] of 1752. The dynamic tension is in no way diminished, and cosmic events and atmospheric effects are still vigorously rendered, but the figures, in dense, seething groups or long-drawn-out rows, harmonize better with the clouds and appear to float in eternal movement. In a preliminary drawing for this splendid composition the pen strokes strive to follow and define the movement in all its complexity. There are as well preparatory studies for the transitions from shadow to light as they appear in the finished composition. The bodies are clearly modelled in the details and at the same time the painterly values are indicated, but the drawing is lively and vigorous throughout with no hint of the approaching classicism.

Alongside Troger, smaller artists were at work, satisfied with following their fixed recipes. Among them Bartholomäus Altomonte-Hohenberg (1702–83), the son of Martino, made a great name for himself. Although he had acquired Austrian citizenship he had been trained by his father, and during visits to Italy – to Bologna in 1717, to Rome in 1719, and to Naples in 1721–3 – he had made a careful study of chiaroscuro. His large fresco in the choir chapel of the church at Spital am Pyhrn of 1741, with the Assumption in an open columnar rotunda, is directly dependent on Pozzo's *Theatrum Sacrum* for the Gesù in Rome.

Genre painting of the pre-Rococo period is represented by Johann George Platzer (1702–60), a member of a family of painters domiciled in South Tyrol.[106] From 1721 onwards he worked principally in Vienna, where his small pictures, frequently done on copper in gay, lively colours, often thronged with Mannerist figure groups, appealed to the public taste.

In Styria the Festenburg was redecorated and adapted as a church between 1710 and 1723 by the Tyrolese artist Johann Cyriak Hackhofer (1675–1731),[107] and here the Baroque and romantic joy in nature had a chance of expressing itself. Hackhofer, who had worked in Rome around 1700, where he was known as a man of wide interests, was called to Vorau in 1708 by Johann Philipp Leisl, the prior of the monastery. At Vorau he was extensively employed in both the monastery and the parish, but his most important work was the decoration in 1715–16 of the sacristy of the priory church. He made use of the natural lighting of the large room to suit his subjects, contrasting the Kingdom of Christ on the well-lit eastern half of the ceiling with the representation of Hell on the dark western wall. On the whole, he followed Rottmayr's early style.

During the last two decades of the seventeenth century the Baroque style of ceiling painting was introduced into the Tyrol by Egidius Schor (1627–1701), one of a family of painters. By the middle of the seventeenth century he had established a reputation in Rome, especially as a decorative artist. Accordingly, at the expense of the figure scenes he painted broad decorative frames with lively architectural motifs round his ceiling frescoes. Johann Josef Waldmann, who was born in Innsbruck in 1676 and died in 1712, also belonged to a family of Tyrolese painters. He, too, set his ceiling frescoes in rich painted or plaster frames. The dome in the Servitenkirche at Rattenberg (1709–11)[108] is the first work in which he covers the entire surface with a figural composition. The figures themselves are massed together on concentric banks of clouds with a minimum of foreshortening. The outmoded character of such works was especially obvious because the country was exposed to the influence of Pozzo, who was a master of the art of perspective. Pozzo was born at Trento, where he spent his early years, and he later worked in the Tyrol. In the northern Tyrol his influence was supplemented by that of Piazzetta and Tiepolo.

Owing to the emigration of her most gifted artists the Tyrol was at that time unable to compete with her more progressive neighbour, Bavaria. Until the middle of the eighteenth century, the major commissions were entrusted to two outstanding Bavarians, Cosmas Damian Asam and his pupil Matthäus Günther. The reconstruction of the parish church of St Jakob at Innsbruck marked the decisive step. As early as 1712 the task had been allotted to Johann Jakob Herkommer of Füssen (cf. p. 103) by the municipal authorities of Innsbruck, who had thus established a link with the Bavarian and Swabian borderland. The church, like the one at Weingarten, had a flat *Platzlgewölbe* set transversely, and also a circular dome over the chancel, and these offered convenient surfaces for fresco and plasterwork. In 1720, after they had completed their work at Weingarten, Cosmas Damian Asam (1686-1739) and his brother Egid Quirin (1692-1750)[109] began the decoration of the Innsbruck church with the frescoes and the stucco work above the organ gallery. The same was carried out at great speed inside the other domes in 1723, as the brothers were called away to continue their work for Freising Cathedral, and for the monastery church at Fürstenfeld. The importance they attached to painted architecture betrays their Roman training, although the boldly pierced painted domes are separated from the real architecture by a wide ornamental frame. The freer distribution of groups, the greater abundance of light, the substitution of paler, cooler colours for the usual sombre browns – all this impressed the Tyrolese as the manifestation of a new and superior art.

Asam's pupil Matthäus Günther (1705-88) further increased the prestige of Bavarian art in the Tyrol. His home was Augsburg, but during the course of his life he painted many churches in the Tyrol, often in collaboration with Franz Xaver Feuchtmayer, the head of the famous Wessobrunn school of plasterers. Following the Venetian pattern, he included popular types, often in fantastic attire, in his groups. The figures stand on the inner edge of the dome, while painted architectural motifs, for instance rotundas opening on to other structures, are massed behind them. In the abbey church at Neustift (Novacella) near Brixen[110] the painted surfaces of the frescoes are frequently invaded and enlivened by *rocaille* motifs from the ornamental surrounds. Gradually, however, the function of the painted architecture changed, until it became a mere setting for a stage-like scene, as for instance in the parish church at Wilten[111] (1754), where the painted fortifications of the besieged town form a kind of backdrop for the fresco of *Judith and Holofernes*. The influence of Tiepolo is dominant in such works – not only his glamour but also his worldliness.

There is, however, one example in which the more serious, more deeply religious side of the Tyrolese character is revealed, namely the magnificent fresco by Paul Troger in the cathedral of Brixen[112] (1748-50) to which reference has already been made. Unfortunately, the painting has not survived in its entirety. In place of the customary stucco frames he had carried the wall paintings right up to the figure scenes above. Further, following the example of Pozzo in the Vienna Jesuit church, he had painted a feigned dome above the crossing. In 1894-6 the ceiling paintings were set in frames, the other surfaces covered with plasterwork, and the painted dome replaced. Troger's ability to subordinate endless throngs of figures to a central theme was again revealed here. In the choir the eye is led directly to the dominant figure of Christ who, with arms out-stretched, approaches the kneeling figure of the Virgin. In the nave the central figure of the Lamb appears on a hill in a halo of light surrounded by triumphant angels. The elect below turn towards the symbol of the Saviour in an elongated curve which dies away deep down.

CHAPTER 10

HUNGARY

Architecture

THE reconstruction of Hungary after her liberation from the Turks was effected during the eighteenth century. A charter of Leopold I granted autonomy to the expanding capital of Buda, including the Castle Hill, though it remained separated from Pest. But in 1723 the town was the victim of a great fire, which only the town hall survived. Pest was then able to develop faster than Buda, and Anton Erhard Martinelli was commissioned by Charles VI to build, in the Viennese style, the large hospital for disabled soldiers (now the city hall; 1728–37). For the rest, members of the imperial family were less prominent as patrons than were the Hungarian nobility and the citizens. Their way of life found expression in pleasant, low buildings of an unpretentious character. Country houses frequently retained the four corner towers which had been an obligatory feature until then.

Italian architecture ruled supreme during the seventeenth century, though at the same time, in accordance with the growing prestige of the Austro-German Baroque, then at its peak, German artists – for example the Bavarian Johann Höbling – began to establish themselves. The graceful style of Hildebrandt made a deep impression on the people, and he received from Prince Eugene of Savoy the commission to build Schloss Ráckeve on the island of Csepel in 1701–21[1] (Figure 7). Here he combined the French ideal of a wide, one-storeyed structure with north Italian details. In spite of this, the composition as a whole, with the central octagonal saloon, curving-out diagonals, square rooms, a vestibule keeping close to the saloon, and roofs of the pavilion type is entirely Hildebrandt's. Ten years later Hildebrandt began to rebuild the former imperial hunting lodge Halbthurn (Féltorony) as a palace for Count Aloisius von Harrach. After a further ten years, when the palace had reverted to the crown, he added the buildings along the courtyard. Finally, in the second half of the eighteenth century alterations were again made, mainly to the interior. At that time, 1765, Maulbertsch painted the beautiful fresco of *Aurora* and *Apollo* on the ceiling of the central hall. The façades are composed in characteristic fashion, with a central projection crowned by a curved pediment, and with lateral corner pavilions. Unfortunately here, as at Ráckeve, the broken roof line of the pavilions has been replaced by a straight one.

The country house built about 1730 for Count l'Huilier at Edelény shows French influence in the flat, finely proportioned fronts and brilliant Rococo decoration. This style re-appears in a less pure form in Schloss Cseklész, built for Count Joseph Eszterházy in 1711–23.[2] The style was skilfully continued in the wings added in 1756 by Jakob Fellner (Plate 71).

In ecclesiastical architecture the link with Austria and Silesia was even closer. There is,

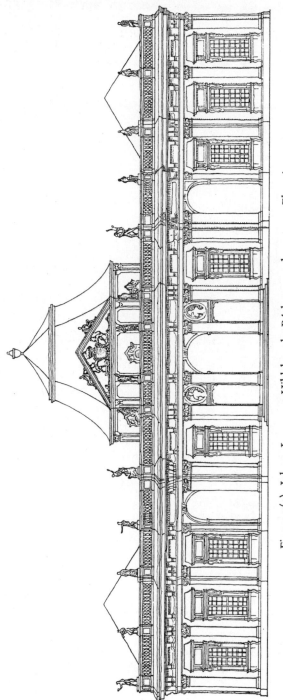

Figure 7(A). Johann Lucas von Hildebrandt: Ráckeve, castle, 1701–2. Elevation

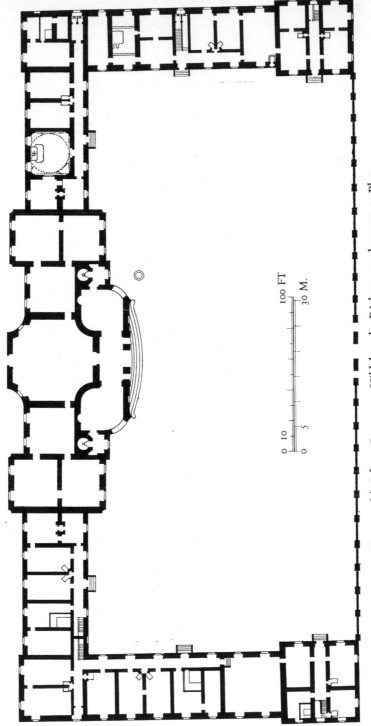

100 FT

30 M.

0 10

0 5

Figure 7 (B). Johann Lucas von Hildebrandt: Ráckeve, castle, 1701–2. Plan

for example, a close resemblance between Holy Trinity at Bratislava (Pozsony, Press-burg) with its oval interior of 1717–25, and Hildebrandt's Peterskirche in Vienna. In the church at Esztergom (Gran) in the Viziváros[3] the new ideal of lighter forms is realized in the façade, curving forward and flanked by two slender towers. The same vertical tendency characterizes the university church at Pest, built in 1730–42, which is very similar to the Silesian type (Plate 72B). Andreas Mayerhoffer was entrusted with the execution of the building, which was probably designed by another hand. Mayer-hoffer had come to Hungary from Salzburg in 1720, and after his appointment as Sur-veyor of Buildings at Ráckeve became a citizen of Pest in 1724. Many Baroque palaces in which the castellated character with four corners has been dropped, can be ascribed to him. He also probably designed the rotunda representing the Hill of Calvary (endowed in 1739), now in the garden of the Academy of Art. The stairs have a flowing move-ment and are richly ornamented.

Painting

In Hungary, a profuse flowering of Greek Orthodox ecclesiastical painting occurred in the east. The greatest Hungarian Baroque painter, particularly of portraits, is Adam von Mányoki (1673–1757), who worked for many courts but mainly the Saxon ones, in Dresden (1713–23) and in Warsaw (1731–56).[4] He was trained by Andreas Scheits at Lüneburg, and northern simplicity and warmth of feeling are expressed in his art. He absorbed French influence while copying the pictures of Largillière in the gallery of Salzdahlum. Contact with his own country was established in 1707, in 1711–12, when he was painter to Franz Rakoczy II, prince of Transylvania, and again during a long visit to that country between 1724 and 1731. His talent and his attractive personality are best revealed in his informal portraits.

CHAPTER II

BOHEMIA AND MORAVIA

Architecture

THE great flowering of the Austrian Baroque, which began in the eighties, had repercussions only a few years later in Bohemia and Moravia, although the hegemony of
Italian architects was particularly well established there. About 1680 in Prague seven
northern architects faced twenty-eight Italian ones; ten years later the Italians had been
so far ousted that the numbers were about equal, and a further ten years turned the scales
in favour of the northerners. Among the joiners and carpenters, it is true, the German
element from the Bohemian Forest border land with its early German settlers had always
predominated, and among masons in Prague the Czechs were in the majority. Accordingly, the building daybooks were kept in Czech. The immigration of German architects, to whom Prague owes its finest Baroque buildings, occurred mainly during the
decisive last decade of the seventeenth century. The first important master, Abraham
Leuthner, came from Wildstein in upper Austria. He became a citizen of the Nové Město
of Prague in 1665 and rose from an artisan in the building trade to the rank of Ober-
baumeister (Surveyor of Imperial Works) in Bohemia. His book on the orders of
columns, published in Prague in 1677, shows that he wanted to be more than an artisan.
He died in Prague in 1700.

Leuthner's followers were the younger members of the Dientzenhofer family, architects from the district of Aibling in upper Bavaria. They can first be traced in Prague in
1678, significantly enough through marriage into the Leuthner family. Georg (born
1614) and his sons, who all followed their father's profession, had settled in the
rapidly expanding city of Prague. They were destined not only to give its particular
character to the Bohemian Baroque but also, when their activity spread to Franconia
with the subsequent diffusion of their forms throughout Germany, to play a decisive
role in the whole development of the German Baroque.

Christoph Dientzenhofer (1655–1722) was the most outstanding architect in Bohemia.
As early as 1679 he was able to continue the construction of the Dominican church of
Mary Magdalen in Prague, begun by Francesco Caratti, the architect of the Černín
Palace. His desire to blend central elements with a longitudinal plan is apparent in the
shifting of the domed crossing towards the centre. As an independent architect in
Leuthner's employ, he supervised the building of the monastery of Teplá (Tepl), after
1689. 'Artem suam belle intelligens, multisque in locis practicans, tametsi quidem legere
et scribere absolute nesciverit' ('He understood his art very well, working in many
fields, though he was quite ignorant of reading and writing'):[1] thus did the *Annales
Teplenses* characterize the brilliant master mason in 1699. Here, as we have seen more
than once before, it was on Slav soil and at a propitious moment that the German

architect was given the opportunity of developing his ideas and the freedom to work them out which would not have been accorded to him in Germany.

Actually the spark that fired the Bohemian Baroque was not struck by a German but by an Italian, Guarino Guarini, the architect of the Theatine Order. Guarini composes with circular shapes which intersect and interpenetrate, proceeding always from diagonally placed pilasters. He stayed in Prague presumably to design the church of St Mary of Alt-Ötting (1679). The plans were never executed, but they evidently made a deep impression on Christoph and Johann, the most distinguished members of the Dientzenhofer family. Guarini's influence was further increased when the rest of his designs became known after the publication of his *Architectura civile* in 1686. The warm response denied him in Paris, where he had built the Theatine church in 1662, was accorded him in the much less theory-conscious Bohemia.[2] In spite of this, French early classicism appeared there at the same time, represented by Jean Baptiste Mathey (cf. pp. 66–7), a painter-architect, probably from Dijon, who during his stay in Prague from 1675 to 1694 enjoyed the patronage of Johann Friedrich Count Waldstein, archbishop of Prague. In 1679–88 Mathey built sv. František (the Kreuzherrnkirche) in Prague,[3] a structure in which the transverse arms project from an elliptical central space that rises evenly embracing pendentives, drum, and dome, an example of considerable importance for Fischer von Erlach's Dreifaltigkeitskirche in Salzburg and more especially his Karlskirche in Vienna. In 1682–92 Mathey built the church of St Josef on the Prague Malá Strana (Kleinseite), modelled on Flemish and Roman patterns. Its elliptical plan opens on each longitudinal side in three niches between coupled Corinthian columns. This building, too, was recorded by Fischer in sketches. In addition to the longitudinal churches, however, centralized buildings acquired a new importance in Bohemia. Prior to 1679 we find them only on a small scale, for instance the oval cemetery church at Bechyně (Bechin) of 1667–70.

In his palaces too Mathey replaced the usual sequence of evenly spaced bays by a grouping of projections and superstructures. Examples are the façades of the archbishop's palace in Prague of 1675–9, rebuilt in 1764–5, of the Toscana Palace, and of the country house at Troja outside Prague of 1679–96.[4] Here we find the French arrangement of three wings with a raised central section and an external staircase built round an oval grotto. The rhythmic articulation of Mathey's palaces was certainly exploited by Fischer von Erlach and also in Bohemia, but the classicism underlying it was not adopted. Bohemia and the towns to the east as far as Vilna, St Petersburg, and Lvov (Lemberg) were only too willing to accept the more elaborate forms of the Italo-German Baroque, which suited their temperament and their innate preference for painterly qualities. They also provided the enthusiasm necessary for artists and architects to express themselves fully. Guarini's style is one example of such full expression. To appreciate it one must be able to feel the latent dynamism in a static building.

About 1700 the effects of these daring ideas began to make themselves felt in Prague. In 1699 Hildebrandt had begun the first building of this kind, the church at Jablonné v Podještědí (Gabel) in northern Bohemia (Figure 6). Almost simultaneously similar ideas appeared in the work of a Bohemian architect, in the Pauline abbey church at Obořiště

(Woborischt).[5] The plan was accepted as early as 1702, and must accordingly have been worked out still earlier. The church was consecrated in 1712. It is presumably the work of Christoph Dientzenhofer. The longitudinal walls curve inwards three times, as a result of which the pillars form angles into which pilasters are inserted diagonally on both sides. As against later buildings, the entablature continues without a break so that there is no direct transition to the vaulting and a baldacchino shape has not yet developed. Two transverse ovals are overlapped in the centre by a third, narrower one, which expands above into the circle of a pseudo dome. Correspondingly, the walls form three concave curves. The metamorphosis of form is considerably strengthened by the frescoes, which depict a sham cupola on the central vault. In this way a motif was found which was to lead to the most splendid spatial creations and to radiate even to Franconia, in the abbey church of Banz.

There was no tendency towards the true central plan; the development was rather towards the Bohemian hall-church, of two or three bays, with internal buttresses. Walls undulate in graduated curves, resulting in a dynamic rhythmical articulation.

Whereas the abbey church of Obořiště is still inscribed in a rectangle, the entire wall, inside and out, is built in undulating curves in the Schlosskirche at Smiřice (Smirschitz; Figure 8). The result is a longitudinal oval with the long sides curving inward in the centre so that the pilasters can gain the desired oblique position. In addition there are smaller transverse ovals at the west and east ends. The Schlosskirche was dedicated to the Three Magi by Count Johann Joseph von Sternberk and his wife in 1699 but was probably not built until the first years of the

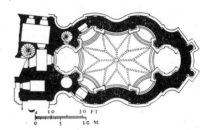

Figure 8. Christoph Dientzenhofer (?) and Johann Santin-Aichel (?): Smiřice (Smirschitz), Schlosskirche, begun *c.* 1700. Plan

eighteenth century. In 1707 Santin-Aichel received payment as a stone-mason for work on the church. The stellar vaulting corresponds to his style, and the rigidity of its forms is not in harmony with the undulating form of the lower part, which presumably goes back to Christoph Dientzenhofer. Here, the continuity of the entablature is interrupted.

At the same time Dientzenhofer was able to realize in a great work the ideas inspired by Guarini. In 1703-11 he built the nave of sv. Mikuláš Malá Strana (St Niklas on the Kleinseite) in Prague for the Jesuits, adjoining their monastery, which had been begun in 1665. The walls of the church with their concave niches and upper galleries seem caught in a flowing, undulating movement (Plate 72A). The corner piers with attached pilasters are set at an angle with the edges facing the nave, like the cutwaters of a bridge, and thus continue the undulating movement of the galleries. The entablature is split up into single pieces above the capitals so as not to impede the upward thrust to the vaults. Re-entrant angles facing the nave are formed between the obliquely set pilasters, which serve as bases for statues. In the colour scheme the reddish-grey of the grained marbling predominates. The profusion of light increases in the upper galleries, where pediments over the windows and over the openings between the piers transmit the movement. A sequence of three ovals results from the diagonal arrangement of the nave piers; their continuation by means of groins touching one another crosswise at the apex, as planned by Dientzenhofer, is no longer visible, as the vaults were painted over in 1760. Following the general development of ceiling painting, the fresco dominates the entire surface. The motif underneath is repeated in the painted architecture, but only in the border zone, where the upper cornice projects powerfully; elsewhere the illusionistic vision into the heavenly sphere dominates the painted surface. The domed crossing and the chancel were added in 1737–52 by Christoph's son Kilian Ignaz Dientzenhofer. In his work there is neither a clear-cut interior design nor well balanced illumination, the effect being sought through a massive and ostentatious display.

The motif of the continuous curve also dominates in the three-storeyed façade (Plate 73, A and B). The German–Bohemian architect surpassed his Italian models by including the entire block in the flowing rhythm, and the convex and concave pediments underline the effect. The individual architectural elements seem to float on rippling waters, an impression produced not only by the diagonal position of the pilasters but also by their delicate flat moulding, which contrasts with the heavy pediments. The same contrast appears on the portal. Columns are detached from the pilasters, and the forward-curving projection of the middle axis is interrupted by a recession in the centre. A contemporary description of 1711 speaks of a 'latomia', a quarry.

Six years later, in sv. Markéta (St Margaret), the church of the Benedictine monastery of Břevnov (Breunau) near Prague (1708–21), now definitely ascribed to him, Dientzenhofer clarified his ideas still further. Here, too, the ceiling is painted to correspond with the basic plan (Plate 74B). Four ovals intersect, and the transverse arches have disappeared, giving way to vaulted surfaces with curving edges which are emphasized by the figural fresco as vantage points for a view into the heavens beyond. This gives rise to a remarkable inversion of top and bottom of this world and the next. The oval space below is granted above only one ornamental vault with a painted medallion on each side. The movement, barely perceptible in the diagonally placed pilasters below, splits the vaults open above to reveal the sky. Only a year later, at Banz, Johann Dientzenhofer made a similar use of this symbolic interpretation of the Baroque metamorphosis of form (Plate 92A, Figure 10) – a sign of how close was the link between Bohemia and Franconia. At Břevnov the slight broadening of the two middle bays and the addition of pilasters to the corner piers shows a definite tendency towards centralization. Along the side walls the pilasters push forward with blunt corners, rounded off in front, towards the choir and the entrance they swing out with the edges of the pilasters facing the middle axis. The elements are characteristically veiled in the Baroque manner so as to allow the imagination more margin.

The originality and force of Christoph's ideas are also apparent on the exterior, where, more even than on sv. Mikuláš, he defies all rules and transcends all boundaries (Plate 74A). The façade, with its Ionic pilasters and columns, curves round the corners. This motif is repeated on the lateral fronts by the central projection of the nave itself which, in fact, consists of two bays. The dynamic quality is emphatically accentuated by the broken pediment at the top. Here a basic characteristic of eastern architecture survives, which had persisted through the centuries. In an earlier period it had found expression in the Polish Parapet (see p. 50), during the Baroque in the vigorous curving of roofs and dormer windows.

Even more remarkable, and only conceivable in Bohemia and Moravia, is the great work of Johann Santin-Aichel, who was born in Prague in 1667 and died there in 1723. He belonged to a family of stone-masons who had emigrated from northern Italy and had been domiciled in Bohemia for three generations. That he had assumed the German name Aichel and that he wrote his letters in German prove that he had become a German Bohemian. He was, however, trained in Italy, as a painter and architect. Study journeys to England and Holland followed. His buildings reveal the eye of a painter, especially in the varied lighting he uses, an essential feature of the Italian Baroque. His Gothicism, too, is a picturesque Baroque affair which completely ignores the structural character of the medieval style (Plate 75A). His only interest was to achieve lively, jagged contours. The surfaces are seldom ornamented, the windows usually without tracery, and the main emphasis laid upon a kind of decorative stellar strapwork executed in stucco. He works towards a climax of light in the cupolas, chancels, and ambulatories. As we know with what ease he could build in the Baroque style, it is doubtful whether he would have gone in for such a curious Gothicism if this had not been suggested to him by certain designs seen in England, or by his employers.

Enthusiasm for Bohemian achievements during the Middle Ages had been awakened by the writings of the Czech Jesuit Bohuslaus Balbin, the most distinguished historian of the Bohemian Baroque and an admirer of German scholarship, and the Church was thus able to link up with a great native tradition. The abbots insisted that their architects should study the ancient buildings and often restore them in the spirit in which they were originally conceived, and characteristically enough it was to the Gothic style that they turned. They even rebuilt churches originally Romanesque, for instance the one at Kladruby (Kladrau), in the Gothic style. In 1703 Santin began the restoration and enlargement of the church of the Cistercian abbey at Sedlec (Sedletz), in 1712 that of the Benedictine abbey at Kladruby (Plate 76) and in the same year that of the Premonstratensians at Želiv (Seelau). The effect is much purer when, as in the collegiate church at Rajhrad (Raigern) near Brno (Brünn; 1722-4), he was allowed to dispense with the medieval trappings.[6] Here he aligned three elliptical spaces each with a dome not set on a drum. They are lit alternately. The arches separating them stand on demi-columns and seem to push into the interior. The arches are stilted, and windows are cut into the domes. The frescoes with their painted skies seem to transcend the material barriers. Small unostentatious chapels offered even greater scope for his ideas, as for instance the chapel at Mladotice (Mlatz; 1708-10), a hexagon with concave walls, or the St Bernard Chapel at Plasy (Plass; 1711), where a lightly undulating outer wall surrounds the inner oval. Here, too, the sequence of curves does not allow any sense of solid piers and solid walls to form. As in the compositions of Christoph Dientzenhofer, the pilasters seem to float in the waves of the concave walls.

The impact of this new style and its association with popular art brought an urgent need for new types of architectural expression, as is especially evident in the many pil-

grimage churches on mountain-tops in Bohemia and Moravia, which show rich imagination. Generally they are enclosed by columnar or pillared arcades, rectangular at first,
later oval or circular, often joined directly to the body of the building so that they
could be used by the pilgrims for processional purposes. The Kappel near Waldsassen
has already found mention (Figure 9). It was begun in 1685 by Christoph Dientzenhofer's
eldest brother Georg and completed in 1689, the year of his death. It was a pioneer
building. The trefoil plan, with circular towers rising at the angles, symbolizes the
Trinity. The whole is surrounded by arcading. The sequence of bulbous domes is
characteristic and points to the East. The chapel at Lomec (Lometz) near Prachatice
marks a step forward which is quite significant. It was built in 1692–1702, perhaps
from the designs of Santin-Aichel, by the mason Mathias Tischler of Roženberk
(Rosenberg; Plate 78A). Professor Frank supposes that Buquoy was only the owner, and
Santin the real architect. The architecture is amazingly light, and the elements thrust
vigorously upwards. The quatrefoil plan with projecting corners develops round a
central canopied altar, and the four sharp corners themselves express an ideal that is
already closely related to Santin's: five sharp corners e.g. project like rays from the
silhouette of Santin's St Johannes Nepomuk on the Green Mountain (1719–22) in
Moravia near the Cistercian abbey of Žd'ár nad Sázavou (Saar).[7] In the plan five oval
chapels are inserted between the points, and the space in the centre is circular. The outer
colonnade was shaped like a ten-pointed star, and five additional pentagonal chapels,
each with one corner projecting outwards, filled in the recesses. Everywhere the pil-
grim is to be reminded of the five stars which, according to the legend, appeared above
the martyr as the waters of the Moldau engulfed him. Santin clearly reverted to the
Gothic style here in order to break right away from the domination of the Antique.
His Gothic is not a copy, and the building calls to mind the *Jugendstil*.

Santin may also have been the architect of the Premonstratensian church at Křtiny
(Kiritein) near Brno, built from before 1712 to 1735 (Plate 75B), the finest of the whole
series of pilgrimage churches in the Bohemian hills. The central space, inscribed in a
quatrefoil, acquires circular shape by the hollowing out of the massive, diagonally set
piers. The arms of the cross terminate in three-quarter circles whereby the laterally
coupled pilasters also come to stand diagonally. In the interior the cylindrical shape is
continued above the entablature and leads into the drumless dome with its gigantic
frescoes, recalling up to a point the Baroque of Vienna. The galleries on the longitudinal
axis are carried round the sanctuary and the organ loft, which heightens the feeling of a
steady spatial expansion. Finally the treatment of the lighting suggests the master hand
of Santin the painter-architect. Upper oval windows rising over lower ones cut into
the foot of the dome. Most impressive of all is the indirect lighting falling in through the
gallery arches at the organ end, which bathes the forms in a shimmering tone into
which architecture, painting, and the carving of the organ screen all blend harmoni-
ously.[8] It is characteristic of the eighteenth century that architects designed the organ
cases (Plate 77). Santin inserted his organ gallery into the surrounding curving walls
and pierced openings in it to correspond with the windows.

The important role played by Fischer von Erlach and Hildebrandt in spreading the

Viennese Baroque to the Austrian crown-lands Bohemia and Moravia has already been described. In addition Domenico Martinelli, himself a member of the Vienna school, made important contributions through his designs for the Sternberk (Sternberg) Palace on the castle hill at Prague of 1698 and for the Schloss at Slavkov (Austerlitz),[9] near Brno, built shortly after in 1700. Fischer's basic form – a high oval central block with wings – was the prototype followed also in other Bohemian country houses, for instance Liblice (Liblitz) near Mělník, erected by Giovanni Battista Alliprandi from 1699, plagiarizing a design for a summer house by Fischer, Buchlovice (Buchlowitz)[10] in Moravia from 1700, and Karlov (Karlshof) near Písek. The original design of 1706 of the Lobkowicz Palace in Prague was also based on this popular type.

It is quite evident that the Baroque was eminently suited both to the German and to the Slav temperaments. Accordingly, it penetrated deep in both countries and stamped its characteristics not only on palaces but also on private houses and even farms.[11] Moreover, the Baroque was retained over an uncommonly long period, whereas the Rococo was hardly known. Christoph Dientzenhofer's son, Kilian Ignaz Dientzenhofer, was the most important architect during the late phase of the Baroque, and in his capacity of court and fortifications architect he supervised all important building schemes in the second quarter of the eighteenth century. He did not follow the tendency of the time towards greater lightness, but on the contrary increased the sculpturesque massiveness of form.

Towards the middle of the century in other areas too a counter-attack was launched by the Baroque on the classical opposition. It is true that in his early work, the charming Villa Amerika in Prague, which he built in 1720 for Count Johann Wenzel Michna, Kilian Ignaz Dientzenhofer, under the influence of Hildebrandt in whose Vienna school he had been trained, modified the dynamism of massive walls. The harmonious proportions here are in striking contrast to the discordant rhythm in which he delighted in his later work. Typical of Prague is the broken roof line with the sculpturally moulded dormer windows and chimneys. But the architect did not continue to develop this feeling for suppleness: Prague required a more robust language. The Sylva Tarouca Palace in Na Přékopel (the Graben) in Prague,[12] built almost thirty years later, about 1749, shows increased vitality in the zones of entablature and pediments, and there is a bold rhythmical articulation in the central, projecting, pavilion-like block and flanking wings.

For his church designs Kilian Ignaz Dientzenhofer had recourse to a great variety of Baroque plans. He used a pure oval for Nǎmecké-Verneřovice (Deutsch-Wernersdorf)[13] (1719), a circle for Nicov (Nitzau), an elongated octagon with straight sides for Ruprechtice (Ruppersdorf), and one with concave outer and convex inner sides for Heřmanice (Hermsdorf) near Halbstadt. This latter form was first developed by Santin-Aichel and recurs in several churches, for instance Počaply (Potschapl) near Litoměřice built in 1724–5 (Plate 78B), Dobrá Voda (Gutwasser) near Budějovice built in 1733–9, and sv. Janna Skalce (St Johannes Nepomuk on the Rock) in the New Town in Prague, begun in 1730, which belonged to the Břevnov Benedictines. At Vižňov (Wiesen) Kilian Ignaz used the oval plan, which his father had used at Smiřice (Smirschitz), but in a simplified form with niches on the longitudinal sides. Frequently, following the example of Hildebrandt, he added two diagonally placed towers to the façade.

Specifically Bohemian, however, is the star-shaped ground-plan of the chapel of St Mary of the Morning Star above Křinice (Wockersdorf) in the Falkengebirge. In the Benedictine abbey church of sv. Mikuláš Staré Město (St Niklas in the Altstadt) of 1732–7, elliptical chapels with upper galleries lead diagonally towards the domed centre. This corresponds to Fischer's Karlskirche in Vienna. Otherwise the two buildings form the greatest possible contrast. Fischer's Baroque is essentially noble and serene; but in the Bohemian church there is a veritable riot of forms. The exterior is more successful than the interior. Despite the coupled columns, the isolated pediments, the deep gaps between the central block, and the flanking towers, which lay an exaggerated stress on the grouping, the building remains just within the limits of what can be tolerated. The same applies to sv. Mikuláš Malá Strana (St Niklas on the Kleinseite), built in 1737–52. Here the association of the rather oppressive dome with the more sveltely upsurging tower is of advantage in the skyline of the town (Plate 73A). In the Church of the Magdalen at Karlovy Vary (Karlsbad) of 1732–6 Dientzenhofer combines a transversely set elongated octagon with concave sides and an oval domed central bay with a choir and transverse elliptical bays at the organ end. Two towers were added to the convex centre of the façade. The undisciplined exaggeration and crowding of forms struck a false note: for all his varied inventions, Kilian Ignaz could not conceal the fact that he never achieved the true Baroque aim of perfect unity. Unlike his father, he failed to find a concise and logically developed style, and so on occasion produced chaotic forms which reveal the dangers of Baroque licence.

Some parts of Slavonia produced buildings of a more conservative character. The Eszterházy Palace, about ten miles east of Bratislava (Pressburg; 1714–22) has three slender towers in front of the centre of the *corps-de-logis* and the ends of the two wings. It was burned down in 1911, but restored in the same year, in accordance with photographs and drawings. The architect is unknown. Presumably he came from Vienna, and was connected with Fischer von Erlach.

Sculpture

Everywhere it was the intimate association between architecture, sculpture, and painting that led to the full flowering of the Baroque. Bohemia and Moravia were no exception. Baroque sculpture developed along the same lines as it did in Austria, striving for a popular form that would appeal spontaneously to the heart of even the simplest spectator. There can be no doubt that the highly emotional Slav temperament – so fond of colour and of music – responded to the style of the German artists and inspired them to greater independence and to ever bolder inventions. This certainly applies to Mathias Bernhard Braun von Braun (1684–1738), the greatest Bohemian sculptor of the Baroque, who was born at Mühlau near Oetz in the Oetz Valley in north Tyrol. He belonged to the same generation as Mattielli who was his junior by only four years. They were thus both at about the same stage when sculpture became lighter at the beginning of the eighteenth century.

Presumably Braun received an Italian training in the Bernini tradition. In 1709/10 he came to Prague where, largely owing to the enlightened patronage of the highly cultured Count Franz von Sporck, he enjoyed much greater freedom and independence than did Mattielli in Vienna and in Dresden, where more conventional ideas prevailed. Sporck was interested in what seemed to him the most significant values and strongly influenced the members of his circle, which included Braun. Among his interests was religious folk songs, which a priest named Bózau collected and Sporck had printed in 1719 at Hradec Králové (Königgrätz). Enriched by simple chords, they were sung as part songs in the churches, accompanied by violin, clarinet, and trumpet. In this way popular music rose into classical music and in this new form reacted back on the people. Sporck, of course, like the Buquoys, the Kinskys, and the Lobkowicz, had his personal orchestra. In Paris he had had the opportunity of hearing the French horn, and so sent two of his musicians there to learn how to play it; as a result the French horn was introduced into Bohemia, where it soon acquired great popularity. He built a large room for opera performances in his palace in Prague – where a performance was given of *Orlando Furioso* by Antonio Denzio and his Italian company – and finally he even built a proper theatre, leaving the management to Denzio.

He was equally interested in sculpture, on which his views were no less original. A rebel all his life, he joined the Jansenists of Port Royal in Paris, despite his upbringing in the Jesuit College of Hüttenberg. At Kuks (Kukus) he set up a printing press, where French books translated by his daughter were excellently printed. He also championed the poor against feudal exploitation. On one occasion, at a big ball in Prague, he was discovered by his daughter at half past three in the morning deep in a discussion on social abuses in Bohemia. For Kuks, the spa he had built on his estate at Gradlič, he commissioned from Braun a series of statues of the virtues, the vices, and the beatitudes. The subjects are characteristic of his search for a deeper moral foundation of life with which to oppose the conditions and abuses of his time. The visitors to his spa were to find at Kuks physical, moral, and spiritual comfort. For the statues, Sporck could not have found an artist better suited than Braun.

Braun's first masterpiece had been his group of *The Vision of St Luitgard*,[14] commissioned in 1710 by the Cistercian nuns at Plasy (Plass) to adorn the Prague bridge. It was far superior to the usual statuary for bridges. The tradition that it was based on a design by Peter Brandl seems very plausible in view of its painterly conception; but there are other examples, too, in which Braun himself approached his work in a painterly spirit. For all its vitality in the details, his sculpture as a whole is conceived two-dimensionally. Braun was able in every respect to satisfy the popular ideals of the day, providing strong emotion, compelling dynamism, painterly approach, and realism. The Tyrolese was obviously stimulated by his new surroundings, where he found on the one hand a craving for realism, on the other great musicality. Bohemia helped him to develop his special talent for expressive drapery, a Tyrolese heritage from Pacher times.

Indeed, Braun was successful all along the line. In 1711 he was given the freedom of the Nové Město at Prague, and in the same year he carved the statue of St Ivo for the Charles Bridge. Through his association with Sporck he got interested in allegorical figures, a theme for which there was little precedent. In 1712/13, for the terrace in front of the Hospital Church at Kuks, he made six models of the beatitudes, to which he later added a further eight, which were all executed in his workshop. For them he retained the current symbols, such as the Heart and the Cross, symbols to which a definite meaning is attached and which stand for something that cannot be directly expressed in an artistic form. The statue of *Meekness* is a good example of Braun's ability to interpret an attitude of mind less by the features than by the general appearance and by the formal rhythm of curls and drapery. The soft curve formed by the head, inclined low towards the right shoulder, and the uplifted arms, are instinct with meaning. The curve is accompanied throughout by the horizontals of drapery and hair. The figures of genii representing peaceful and violent death followed before 1718. The statue of *Faith* in front of the entrance to the church is an autograph work. Braun could not avoid an overloading with symbols, but he successfully counteracted this by the quiet assurance and serenity of the figure itself, and also by the sweeping dynamism of the mighty wings, a motif he had already used to good purpose on the two angels of death.

He was even more successful in the *Virtues* and *Vices* of 1719, certainly entirely by his own hand. Here he was slightly less tied down by symbolism, and the characteristics which he strove to interpret were reflected in the accompanying animals. How great his inventive powers were can be seen in the figure of *Calumny*, who puts out her tongue, 'the root of evil', while the cynical face reappears everywhere in the agitated drapery intended to illustrate the widespread effects of slander, as destructive as the firebrand that is also shown. Highly expressive too is the figure of *Envy*, an emaciated old woman with an unpleasant leer, chewing a piece of meat. The barking dog between her legs reflects her attitude. But the wildly billowing drapery folds are more telling even than the figure. A subject that was well suited to his art was *Lightheartedness*, which he interpreted as a dancing woman enveloped in flame-like drapery which catches the rhythm of her movement (Plate 80B). The Vices have mask-like faces (Plate 80A), whereas the Virtues have eloquently human expressions. The figure of *Chastity* veiling her head is less successful, but *Charity* (Plate 81A) on the other hand is a very sensitive interpretation of maternal and filial love, and equally fine are the figures of *Faith* and *Patience*. On the whole Braun evidently preferred female to male figures.

In the years in which he worked at Kuks he was extensively employed in Prague. In 1715 he made statues and confessionals for the church of sv. Kliment (St Clemens) there. Even more famous, however, was his portal sculpture, and he gave a very forceful and unconventional interpretation of the time-honoured caryatids for Fischer von Erlach's Clam-Gallas Palace (Plate 79). An entirely original invention is the powerful eagles with uplifted wings spanning the portal of the Thun Kolowrat Palace: not many sculptors would have been bold enough to attempt it, nor is it likely that a patron in Vienna would have accepted it.

Between 1729 and 1735 Braun paid frequent visits to Sporck's estates. The count was always full of new ideas. A passionate huntsman, he conceived the idea of setting sculpture in the forests, and for this purpose Braun carved religious scenes. These were most successful when the subject matter was suitable for an outdoor setting: for example the *Magdalen* in the desert, the hermits *Onufrius* and *Garinus*, *St Francis* receiving the stigmata, *St Jerome* with his lion in a rocky cave absorbed in the contemplation of a skull. The sculpture was cut out of the rocks and was originally polychrome.

Braun's monumental achievement also provides an excellent example of the successful blending of a diversity of forces: an inherited talent; support and stimulus in a foreign country which welcomed him warmly and where the high standard of culture sharpened his artistic faculties; and finally the inspiration given by a cultured patron. The Sporcks came from Westphalia, a rich and fertile land; his father had earned fame, fortune, and nobility as a general in the Austrian cavalry. The count's association with an artist who came from the most southerly province of the Teutonic world proved just as successful as did the association during the same period of the Westphalian architect Pöppelmann with the Salzburg sculptor Permoser on the Dresden Zwinger. The result, however, is completely different. In Dresden Permoser, who had been given little scope in religious art, had recourse to classical mythology; in Bohemia on the estates of a nobleman both devout and progressive, Braun not only had every opportunity to discover new means of expression, but also his imagination was further stimulated by the patronage of a born rebel who consistently attempted to probe the realities of this world, and above all of human nature.

Next to Braun, Johann and Ferdinand Maximilian Brokoff, father and son, were the most noteworthy Baroque sculptors in Bohemia. Johann, who was born in 1652 in St Georgenberg in northern Hungary and died in 1718 in Prague, began as a wood-carver. He went to Prague as a journeyman in 1675. In 1682 he made a full-scale model for the statue of St Johannes Nepomuk for the Charles Bridge in Prague after a small bozzetto by Matthias Rauchmiller.[15] It was cast in Nuremberg. This beautiful and unpretentious work, with its lightly swaying pose and genuine warmth of feeling, set an example not only for later statues of the saint, which were legion, but also for Bohemian Baroque sculpture as a whole. Throughout the entire Austro-Hungarian monarchy the 'Hansl am Weg' (wayside St Johannes Nepomuks), especially on the bridges, came to symbolize bygone times. The simplicity of Rauchmiller's work, however, soon gave way to a more dynamic conception. Johann Brokoff made further statues for the bridge, sometimes whole groups, as for example the *Pietà* of 1695, now re-erected in a garden belonging to the Sisters of Mercy. Indeed, more than half the statues for the bridge came from his workshop (but cf. Plate 81B). He was assisted by his son Ferdinand Maximilian (1688–1731), who soon surpassed his father. The figures give the impression of saints reciting the litany. In the groups of the *Baptism of Christ* (1706) and of *St Adalbert* (1709), *St Cajetanus* (1709), *St Francis Borgia* (1710), *St Francis Xavier* (1711), *St Vincent*, and *St Procopius*, Ferdinand Maximilian produced massive, many-figured compositions, often loosely composed and without organic articulation. They lack the inner life which Braun infused into his statues, but their expressive if slightly theatrical gestures enable them to dominate the place where they stand. Fischer von Erlach admired Brokoff's art, and in

1722 called him to Breslau to decorate the electoral chapel in the cathedral. He also designed the high altar for the Vienna Karlskirche in 1728 and worked for the abbey church at Krzeszów (Grüssau) in 1729–30 (cf. p. 145).

Painting

Whereas Karel Škréta, the eminent Czech painter (p. 85), had beeen able to develop a personal style, Bohemian painting around 1700 fell under the influence of the expanding Austrian Baroque. This expansion was greatly helped by the new techniques and new artistic devices for ceiling painting. As has already been said, the decisive step was taken in 1698 in Moravia, when Rottmayr painted the great hall of Schloss Vranov (Frain). His successors were Troger, at Olomouc (Olmütz) in 1729–33 and at Hradiško (Radisch) in 1739, and above all Maulbertsch at Kroměříž (Kremsier) in 1758–60, at Znojmo (Znaim) in 1768, Hradiště (Pöltenberg) in 1768, Dyje (Mühlfraun) in 1775 etc., Louka (Klosterbruck) in 1778, and Strahov (Strahow) near Prague up to 1794. Furthermore Cosmas Damian Asam introduced Bavarian fresco painting at Břevnov in 1727 and at Kladruby (Kladrau) in 1734.

The native artists generally studied fresco painting at its source in Rome and under Pozzo in Vienna. They were headed by Franz Gregor Eckstein (1666–1736). In 1700 Eckstein was one of the signatories to the articles of the Brotherhood of St Luke in Brno, and in 1732 he painted the rooms of the Landhaus there. Other important works by him are the ceiling frescoes of the church of Velehrad (Welherad) of 1730 and the Jesuit and the Dominican churches at Opava (Troppau) of 1732. At the end of his life he went farther east, as far as Lvov (Lemberg), where he painted the interior of the Jesuit church in 1734–6. Though Eckstein was well trained in the tricks of illusionism, his excessive use of decorative and architectural motifs prevented him from achieving well-grouped, close-knit compositions.

Johann Peter Brandl (1668–1735) of Prague enjoyed the favour of Count Sporck, the great Bohemian patron, and occasionally collaborated with Braun. From his teacher Christian Schröter, court painter and keeper of the gallery on the Burg in Prague, Brandl can only have learnt the technique of painting. On the other hand the imperial collection, which remained in Prague until it was transferred to Vienna in 1720, offered him a substitute for foreign travel. His impetuous, unbridled temperament is revealed in his portraits.[16] He combined a broad brush-stroke with a highly expressive interpretation. His altarpieces are painted in the bold, intensely dynamic spirit of the Prague Baroque, with a lively interplay of light and shade.

Close to Brandl was Wenzel Lorenz Reiner (1683–1743) of Prague. The debt he owed to Pozzo is shown by his adaption of the *Theatrum Sacrum* for his composition of *The Feeding of the Hungry*, which he painted on a wall of the refectory in the Clementinum in Prague. Reiner, too, favoured the pictorial realism and sombre tones characteristic of Bohemian painting.

Johann Hiebel of Swabia was also primarily a fresco painter. He was born in 1681 at Ottobeuren in the Allgäu and trained at Wangen and in Munich. He came to Vienna in

1706, where he worked for three years as a pupil of Pozzo. After Pozzo's death in 1709 he moved to Prague, and in 1716 painted the frescoes in the Jesuit church of Klatovy (Klattau). Both the feigned dome painted on the vault of the crossing and the figure scenes are brilliant examples of how he could cope with vast surfaces. His talent is still too little known, even today. His chief work, the fresco in the interior of the church of the Premonstratensian nunnery at Doksany (Doxan) (signed and dated 1722), shows his mastery of perspective. The many paintings are all centred on one viewpoint below the dome over the crossing. In Prague he decorated the interior of sv. Kliment (St Clemens in the Altstadt) and that of the Clementium library.

Johann Kupecký (1667–1740) must also be included in any account of Czecho-slovakian painting, in spite of the fact that he was neither trained nor did he practise in his own country. He did, however, even abroad, remain true to his own people and to the religious beliefs of the Moravian Brethren, and he developed a style that testified to an innate liking for realism. He was born in Prague but was forced to emigrate with his parents, who were Protestants, to Pezinok in the Slovakian part of Hungary. At the age of fifteen he ran away from home to avoid being apprenticed to a weaver. He entered the workshop of Benedikt Klaus in Vienna, remained there from 1684 to 1686, and then went to Italy. There, after years of hardship, he was able at last, about 1700, to estab-lish a workshop of his own in Rome. In 1729, after a twenty-two years' stay in Italy, he accepted an invitation from Prince Adam von Liechtenstein to go to Vienna. His steadily growing reputation caused several princes to seek his services, but he resolutely refused all offers of court service or titles. The most eminent among his sitters – Prince Eugene and Peter the Great – were precisely the ones who had an understanding for the artist, in spite of his unprepossessing ways. In 1723 he moved to Protestant Nuremberg where, as a sectarian, he felt safer.

Kupecký's realism was a powerful stimulus for portrait painters at the end of the eighteenth century, who wanted to get away from the Rococo. Anton Graff remarked that 'In Kupetzký's pictures you find true nature, life itself. Compared with them all other painting seems superficial.' His friend Johann Caspar Füssli characterized him as follows: 'Fate gave to Kupezki a more humble, less sensitive spirit [than it gave to van Dyck]. In his paintings there is no idealism, except perhaps in the colour. On the other hand he seized on all excellent points in nature wherever he found them with an inimit-able appreciation of shadow and light. And his jealous eye penetrated even to the minor beauties and blemishes in nature. To gain a correct idea of Kupezki's heads you must imagine the power of Rubens, the delicacy and the spirituality of van Dyck, the sombre-ness and magic of Rembrandt.' What he had in common with Rembrandt was not only his technical ability, but also his sense of truth, his independence, and his psychological interest. He liked to portray his sitters engaged in some kind of activity, preferably making music. He was perfectly capable of depicting the lightness and grace of the eighteenth century – provided the sitter appealed to him; this can be seen in the portraits of the miniature painter *Karl Bruni*[17] (1709) and of *Franziska Wussin* (c. 1716; Plate 82A), both now in the Prague National Gallery and both painted in Vienna. On the other hand his *Self Portrait* in the gallery of the Prague Hradshin, done at the end of his life, expresses a depth of feeling that is curiously reminiscent of Rembrandt – the work of a great artist matured by suffering (Plate 82B).

The vitality of Bohemian and Moravian Baroque painting did not diminish during the second half of the eighteenth century, and in the eastern districts, especially in Hungary, there was still considerable demand for it. The distinguished Moravian painter Johann Lucas Kracker for example found a fruitful field in Hungary. He was born in 1717, probably at Znaim, and spent eleven years as *civis academicus* of the Vienna Academy, where he was influenced chiefly by Troger. In 1760/1, after his removal to Prague, he painted one of his most important works, the fresco in the nave of the church of sv. Mikuláš Malá Strana (St Niklas on the Kleinseite) (Plate 83, A and B). He gave a brilliant new interpretation of the old idea of blending the architecture with the painted world, with less emphasis on the figures below and more on the scene in the skies. Furthermore, by a skilful exploitation of Christoph Dientzenhofer's architecture he increased the dramatic tension. From 1764 until his death in 1779 he worked extensively in Hungary. Troger's influence lives on in his figure scenes, which culminate in one significant gesture. Kracker blended such composition with landscape settings.

Franz Xaver Karl Palko was born at Breslau in 1727 and died in Prague in 1767. In his paintings, frescoes or panels, he intensified the expressive quality and the painterly effect of a deeply shadowed background flecked with light. His art radiated beyond the frontiers of Bohemia to Kremsier (Kroměříž), Brünn (Brno), Dresden,[18] and Munich.

The Rococo achieved only a limited hold in Prague. Norbert Grund (1717–61) painted popular subjects on small-size panels in which he showed little imagination:[19] their value lies in the purely painterly quality of the light colours laid on with a broad brush. The easy, flowing rhythm of his pictures has a musical quality which came as naturally to the Grund family as it suited the Bohemian character.

CHAPTER 12

POLAND

DURING the last two decades of the seventeenth century a new flowering of the Polish Baroque was inspired by the powerful personality of King John Sobieski (1674–96). Tylman van Gameren, a native of Holland (before 1630–1706), had already had experience as an academic teacher when he came to Poland in 1665.[1] In 1672 he was appointed military engineer in the royal army, and at the same time his title of nobility was confirmed. He worked especially for Queen Maria Kasimira. His centralized churches at Warsaw – the church of the Holy Sacrament,[2] Vienna (1688), St Casimir (1688–9), and St Bonifaz[3] in the Czerniaków quarter (1690–2) – are finely proportioned and restrained in their articulation, in a Baroque style with classicist elements, which is what one would expect from a Dutchman. The church of St Anne at Cracow[4] (1689–1705), however, based on a design by Tylman, has powerful projections and recessions that are much more Baroque in character, probably as a result of Baldassare Fontana's collaboration. The two pierced tabernacle-like storeys of the tower herald the style of the eighteenth century.

Tylman's Castle Nieborów[5] (1680–3) is adapted to the new taste by the introduction of a pedimented central projection, arched windows, lower, broader flanking towers, and sculptural ornament in place of window pediments. A magnificent relief fills the large central pediment. This latter motif was also the dominant feature of the Krasiński Palace in Warsaw of 1682–94. For this, the distinguished Prussian sculptor Andreas Schlüter executed the sculptural decoration during his early Warsaw period.[6] The building itself was begun by Giuseppe Belotti but completed by Tylman, and the original, typically Polish plan with corner pavilions was modified in the process. The suggestion that Schlüter may also have had a say in the architecture is very plausible in view of the magnificence and unusual character of the palace: it is quite possible that it was Schlüter's idea to intensify the vertical accent by pilaster strips attached to the square pillars of the upper storeys and to place in the central projection large, arched, originally unglazed window openings. The monumental and painterly decoration of the interior is the work of Michel Angelo Palloni of Florence, an outstanding painter of the Polish Baroque.[7] Schlüter, too, was employed at Żółkiev, where he did the alabaster monuments for John III Sobieski, the uncle of King Stanisłav Daniłłowicz, and for Marek Sobieski, the king's brother.

Wilanów, eight miles south of Warsaw, originally an ancient Polish manor house with four corner pavilions and soon to become the king's favourite palace, was attractively altered for him by Agostino Locci, the royal architect and adviser on art, in 1677–96. Following the local custom, it was richly decorated with sculpture (Plate 85A) – Schlüter and Szwaner worked there. To suit the contemporary taste for long low wings, Locci added galleries with flanking towers to both sides, and in 1692, perhaps with the collaboration of Schlüter, built an additional storey in the Baroque manner on to the central block and gave caps to the towers. Lateral wings were begun too. They were completed in 1730–3, with a different distribution of rooms, by Augustus the Strong. The central portals, the façades, and the White Saloon with its composite pilasters are good examples of the Saxon Baroque of the thirties. In the bay directly adjoining the White Saloon, in front of the tower, the king had a monument erected to his predecessor John Sobieski, modelled on Bernini's equestrian figure of Constantine.

Pompeo Ferrari (1660–1736) of Rome was one of the most outstanding architects not connected with the court of Augustus II. He was called to Poland in 1696 by Stanislas Leszczyński, the future king of Poland, then Woywode of Posen, to build the Leszczyński Palace for him. Unfortunately it was burnt down by the supporters of Augustus II in 1707. His patron's political setback prevented Ferrari from obtaining more important commissions, and he had to confine himself to building churches, for example the parish church of Wschowa, the chapel of Archbishop Teodor Potocki, the cathedral of Gniezno,[8] and the Cistercian abbey church at Ląd on the Warte. He was strongly influenced by Borromini, and favoured centralized churches with elliptical domes. The Polish architect Kasper Barzanka (1680–1726) had a similar outlook. The interior of the missionary church at Cracow[9] (1719–28) was evidently modelled on Borromini's church of the Collegio di Propaganda Fide, while the exterior reveals the influence of Bernini's S. Andrea al Quirinale.

The Saxon elector Frederick Augustus I (1694–1733), from 1697 King Augustus II of Poland, who has just been mentioned, owed his election to the Polish throne to the support of Austria and Russia and, even more, to Saxon money. Dresden artists, whom he regarded as indispensable, were called in by the king and the pomp and luxury of their style were greatly approved of in Poland. The king, who was keenly interested in the enlargement of Warsaw, founded an 'Oberlandbauamt' (Supreme Building Commission) to which competent men were appointed. In addition, whenever necessary, he sought the advice of Dresden architects. Thus in 1699, three months after his entry into Warsaw, he sent for Johann Friedrich Karcher (1656–1726), who was to bring books on architecture, and nominated him chief architect of Poland and Saxony. Karcher's style, which originated in garden architecture, appears in the design for an enlargement of the royal palace at Warsaw, ascribed by Gurlitt to Pöppelmann.[10] In 1703 the king appointed the highly gifted Marcus Conrad Dietze as 'Konducteur' (Comptroller) for Poland; but Dietze unfortunately died in a fire in Pietrowia in 1704. The outbreak of the Northern War of 1702–9 put an end to all projects.

Extensive plans for a large-scale reconstruction of the Saxon Palace in Warsaw were not developed until after 1726, when sufficient land had at last been purchased to offer a big enough site. Starting from the Cracow suburb, this site covered an area of 950 by 460 yards, proportions that approximate those of half the Grosser Garten in Dresden, which had an overall size of 2,200 by 1,100 yards. In this way the city received a monumental new centre which has survived down to our own times as the great Saxon Square and Saxon Garden.

In 1728 two leading Saxon architects, Pöppelmann and Longuelune, who for the last ten years had been fully conversant with the site, were appointed, receiving equal salaries. During the last years of Augustus the Strong's reign Pöppelmann's son, Carl Friedrich Pöppelmann (d. 1750), must have had a decisive say in the development of the plans. He was permanently attached to the king, 'having been accorded the high favour of entertaining his majesty by reading aloud to him, by explaining his ideas, projects, and designs until the illustrious monarch's death'. Presumably he had a share in the building of the Blue Palace in Warsaw, situated alongside the Saxon Gardens.[11] This was built between 1717 and 1726 for Countess Anna Orszelska, an illegitimate daughter of the king. The style is dependent on that of Pöppelmann the Elder. To him is to be retraced the fine plan for the Saxon Palace, in which his son probably participated (Plate 85B). It consists of long, low structures surrounding vast courts. The alternation between tall, multiple-curved crowning gables and the termination in horizontal balustrades and attics containing statues gives a lively silhouette. But during the twenty years that intervened between the design and its execution a reaction had set in against overornate Baroque forms, which caused Mathaes Pöppelmann, in collaboration with his son, to restrict the profusion of sculpture to the central section.

It was due to the lasting impression that Versailles made on the king that the garden front in this design unfolds without any breaks and that *cours d'honneur* with stepped sides open to the west. Two further courts opening to the north and south are enclosed by passages only. The inner court is nearly square, bounded by oblong pavilions with roofs of concave-sided pyramid shape. The main range is displaced by the width of one window to the east, and this results in a stepped garden front which makes the corners of the pavilions visible. Four larger rooms are inserted in the wings of the lateral courts. Only the central part was eventually built. It dates from shortly before 1730, and is known as the 'Grand Salon' of the palace garden. The real value of the king's work for Warsaw lay not so much in the finished building as in his town-planning and in the idea of adding imposing fronts to the large houses lining the terrace overlooking the Vistula.

Hermann Weidhaas has pointed out in a review that 'the history of Polish art ought not to be treated as a parallel to that of western Europe'. Popular art which still exists in the villages and is subsidized methodically by the government reaches a high standard, even nowadays. In many cases it can be retraced to an ancient tradition, going back to remote antiquity. This popular art would perish if it had to compete with industrial products. The government buys up the genuine ware at adequate prices, selling it, in Warsaw somewhat cheaper, in a big shop. Travelling in Czechoslovakia and Hungary, I constantly admired this popular art without having leisure to study it; I can therefore only allude to it. Art imported from the west does not represent the east.

From Poland the Saxon Baroque radiated to the north in so far as the Danish architect Nils Eigtved (1701–59) was employed by Karl Friedrich von Pöppelmann in 1725–33. The latter's influence is apparent in the layout in front of Christiansborg in Copenhagen, which was designed by Eigtved in 1733–45.

CHAPTER 13

SILESIA

Architecture

AFTER a period of stagnation, Silesian architecture received fresh impetus from the programmatic activity of the Roman Catholic Church, especially that of the Cistercian, Premonstratensian, and Jesuit orders. Thus, thanks to her close association, as a Habsburg dominion, with Bohemia and Austria, Silesia was enabled to have a direct share in the great flowering of the 1680s. The individual mainly responsible for the high quality of the Silesian Baroque was Franz Ludwig, count palatine and bishop of Breslau (1683– 1732), a great connoisseur of art.

Visiting Italian artists frequently attempted to combine the naturalism of stucco garlands and cartouches with the classical demand for giant orders, and the façades of Pietrowice Wielkie (Gross-Peterwitz) Castle of 1693/4[1] offer a curious example of what such architects deemed permissible in the east, far away from their own country. On the other hand a very rigorous discipline prevailed in the façades of the Premonstratensian abbey of Breslau,[2] with their regular sequences of Corinthian pilasters, begun as early as 1682 by Hans Fröhlich of Troppau (Opava). The Cistercians too, the second old-established monastic order in Silesia, were caught up in the general building fervour. The monasteries of Henryków (Heinrichau), Krzeszów (Grüssau), and Lubiąż (Leubus) were partly rebuilt at the end of the seventeenth century and formed a prelude to the far more magnificent schemes of the eighteenth century.

Finally, the consistent development of Jesuit church and college architecture led to energetic achievements that rivalled the Austrian Baroque. In spite of official support, the Jesuits could only establish themselves with difficulty against the Protestant opposition, and they were not to build their first church until 1688 – at Nysa (Neisse), consecrated on the feast of the Assumption of the Virgin.[3] The plan was basilican with two towers, galleries, and an apse. However, only a year later the Jesuits built a much more modern church at Breslau, dedicated to the Name of Jesus but later known as St Mathias or the Universitätskirche.[4] The plans were first sent to Rome, where they were approved in 1688. As was frequently the case, the square east end facilitated the erection of a large reredos. Despite the fact that wide openings existed on all sides, the massiveness of the walls, which were much thinner than at Nysa, is reduced. Between 1704 and 1706 Rottmayr painted the magnificent ceiling fresco representing *The Veneration of the Sacred Name* (Plate 66A). By 1722, however, the Jesuits had already embarked on a great re-decoration. This was executed by the lay brother Christoph Tausch, a pupil of Pozzo.

If the first step in the development of Silesian Jesuit architecture had been the change from a basilican to a hall-church still with galleries, the second was taken in 1714, when the Johanniterkirche at Legnica (Liegnitz)[5] was begun. Here the relationship to the

Baroque of Christoph Dientzenhofer is evident. As in sv. Mikuláš Malá Strana, there is an undulating front broken by the convex centre; in the interior the piers are set diagonally, the galleries curve in and out, and the capitals of the piers project freely. The massiveness of the walls is still further reduced. The vaults, probably inadequately supported, collapsed before the end of the eighteenth century;[6] possibly they were of the Bohemian type with 'three-dimensional' arches across. Here again the architect is unknown; this is characteristic of the Jesuits, who did not care for recording personal achievements. The influence of Fischer von Erlach makes itself felt in the articulation of the façade of the neighbouring Jesuit college. Finally at Legnica, in 1705, Martin Frantz the Younger (1679-1742), a native of Reval, at that time a Swedish town, was appointed architect in charge of the Jesuit buildings.[7] Circumstances forced the 'Swedish' architect to familiarize himself with the Silesian type of architecture, influenced by the Austro-Hungarian Baroque; his Protestant employers on the other hand wanted the emphasis to be on the traditional northern style.

The Protestants themselves were able, to a limited degree, to compete with the Catholics, and were as ready to take advantage of a good opportunity as were their opponents. In 1707 at the Altranstadt Convention Charles XII of Sweden obtained from the emperor permission for the Silesian Protestants to build six 'Gnadenkirchen' (Grace and Favour Churches). As opposed to the Jesuits, who preferred the Roman longitudinal plan with numerous altars in the side chapels, dedicated to saints, the Protestants, who wished to stress that the church's one foundation was Christ, favoured a Greek cross, i.e. a central, plan. The most important church is that at Jelenia Góra (Hirschberg),[8] built in 1709-18 by Martin Frantz (Plate 87). It was modelled on St Catherine in Stockholm. The Swedish church, with its octagonal towers flanking the central dome, had been built by Johan de la Vallée in 1656-76, under the influence of Dutch architecture. A successful grouping of the galleries and the walls, such as we find later in Bähr's Frauenkirche in Dresden, was not yet achieved at Hirschberg. The need for the sermon to be audible to a large congregation outweighed all other considerations. How wide the gap was between the two faiths can be seen by comparing the Swedish church with Catholic centralized buildings, such as the Electoral Chapel of Wrocław Cathedral, built by Fischer von Erlach (p. 93), or the Benedictine church of St Hedwig at Legnickie Pole (Wahlstadt), built by Kilian Ignaz Dientzenhofer in 1727-31, where the forms flow rhythmically, curving and interlocking in all directions.

The native character is more pronounced in the monastic architecture of the Cistercians, the finest examples of which are at Lubiąż,[9] Henryków,[10] and Krzeszów.[11] The abbey church at Krzeszów was erected in 1728-35 by the Hirschberg architect Anton Jentsch (1699-1757). For the interior, it is true, the plan of sv. Mikuláš in the Prague Altstadt was used again, after an interval of twenty-five years; but the galleries are lowered, thus allowing the piers to rise more majestically than was the case either at Prague or at Legnica. It is almost a hall interior. The front with its two towers is entirely original and represents the greatest achievement of the Silesian Baroque (Plate 86). The irrational, emotional quality of eastern art is expressed in the treatment of the individual architectural members. The massive forms rise weightily, and their intense dynamism produces small waves, concentrated round the entablature, which ripple across the façades.

The fervour with which the Jesuits pursued their educational policy is expressed in the immense plans for Breslau University.[12] The one wing which was actually built represents in itself a peak of their Silesian college architecture. Owing to the opposition of the overwhelmingly Protestant population, the foundation stone was not laid until 1728, and the building was erected within the precincts of the imperial castle. The designs were perhaps furnished by Christoph Hackner (1663–1741), the municipal architect of Breslau. He was a widely employed Silesian master of conservative character. The long, narrow building takes full advantage of the site on the banks of the Oder. The high hipped roof was crowned by an observatory. To correspond with this, a slender tower, twice as high, above the imperial gate, and another one above the unfinished wing upstream were planned. Notwithstanding certain advanced features, Breslau University is still conceived in the spirit of the seventeenth century. The slightly projecting pavilions with their pilasters are barely noticeable and do not interfere with the even rhythm of the great front. Nor do the low rooms, for the most part in a heavy Baroque style, give any hint of the grace of the approaching Rococo. When Frederick II seized Silesia, in 1740–1, building operations came to a standstill.

On the whole, Silesian Baroque palaces are simpler than those of Bohemia and Austria. The majority are elongated buildings with high, broken hipped roofs and straight fronts. They have single *cours d'honneur* and are surrounded by living quarters for the members of the household and for employers. Schloss Chocianów (Klein-Kotzenau)[13] is an exception in that it has a certain monumentality. It was built by Martin Frantz the Elder in 1728–32 as a massive stepped cube with a dominant tower, obviously a development of the Friedenskirche at Jelenia Góra. As a counterpart to this building with its northern flavour, Lucas von Hildebrandt introduced the softer, less sculptural Viennese note into his contemporaneous Schloss Kunewald of 1726–30.

Twenty years earlier, in 1705, the same architect had begun the Schreyvogelhaus in Breslau as a model of a wealthy town house.[14] This elegant building, unfortunately demolished, had a central projection with four Corinthian pilasters. The balcony supported by columns over the entrance and the statue on the pediment presented the only Baroque feature. On the other hand – to judge from the design by Christoph Hackner – the former Hatzfeld Palace in Breslau of 1723–5 was built in the heavier, more dynamic Silesian Baroque.[15]

Sculpture

Silesian sculpture was dominated by artists who had emigrated from Bohemia. Grüssau, where high standards of taste prevailed, was the first to open its doors to the invaders. Johann Ferdinand and Ferdinand Maximilian Brokoff, Anton Dorasil, and Matthias Braun all found employment there. Ferdinand Maximilian Brokoff's most outstanding work in Silesia is the bust for Johann Georg von Wolff's monument in the church of St Elizabeth in Breslau (1721),[16] which has the powerful realism of Prague portraiture.

The distinctive sculptural style of Thomas Weissfeld (1670–1720), a Norwegian by birth, was affected by the peculiar position of Silesia between the south and the north. In his statues in the Stiftskirche at Kamienec Ząbkowicki (Kamenz), the drapery is carved in parallel folds with heavily undercut, bunched-up pleats that play across them. The figures themselves have a similar rhythm; their transcendental, visionary expressions are conceived in a Mannerist spirit.[17]

Painting

Willmann (p. 82), whose mature art had gained him a leading position in Silesia, further consolidated it when he turned to fresco painting in the eighties. This brought him into contact with the Italo-south German style, and in 1689 he went to Prague, accompanied by his Italian-trained stepson Johann Christoph Lischka, where the latter painted the ceiling of sv. Frantisek. In the large ceiling fresco of the refectory of Lubiąż Abbey representing the Triumph of Virtue (100 by 33 feet in diameter) which he painted in 1691/2, he strove to outdo even the Flemish artists in his forceful representation of the vices. But the frescoes in St Joseph at Krzeszów, begun in 1692, were to prove his masterpiece.[18] He followed the ideas of the abbot Bernhard Rosa, and the result brought out all the best qualities of his art. The frescoes are natural in style, and show a dynamic vitality of all the parts within a unified composition; the brushwork is broad but the modelling sensitive; powerful deep shadows contrast with light areas. In the oil paintings of this late period, too, there is a corresponding increase in brilliance. The *Landscape with Jacob's Dream*,[19] for instance, shows the full effect of his poetic imagination in the vision of the ladder (Plate 89). The *Pietà*[20] formerly in the Dr Bernt Collection at Kaaden is a forceful High Baroque composition with sweeping lines. As for his portraits, that of his great patron *Abbot Rosa* of Krzeszów,[21] painted shortly before the latter's death in 1696, is rightly described by Kloss as the best German portrait of the seventeenth century (Plate 88B). Here, at the end of the century, in the lifelike interpretation and in the virtuosity of the powerful, dense brushwork in which each stroke is applied individually, Willmann does indeed reach the high standard of Netherlandish portraiture.

The style of Bavarian fresco painting was introduced into Silesia by Cosmas Damian Asam's ceilings in the former abbey church of Legnickie Pole, painted in 1731.[22] Willmann's art, however, which had taken root in Silesia, was continued by his pupil Georg Wilhelm Neunhertz (1689–1750) in the frescoes of Lubomierz (Liebenthal) Abbey (1735 etc.), and at Krzeszów (1734). Franz Palko (1723–67), a native of Breslau, carried Silesian art into Bohemia, Moravia, and Saxony[23] (cf. p. 139).

CHAPTER 14

FRANCONIA AND THE MIDDLE RHINE

Architecture

FRANCONIA, with its alert and receptive people, became the leader in making the Baroque a specifically German style. Two hundred years earlier it had done the same for the Renaissance, when Dürer was the innovator. Now it was Balthasar Neumann who, during the brilliant third decade of the eighteenth century, in a series of superb buildings, put Franconia in the front rank of German art. In a surprising number of ways, including the universal nature of his talents, Neumann can be regarded as the heir of Fischer von Erlach, who had died in 1723.

The Franconians had managed to keep in touch with the rest of Central Europe and remain loyal to the Empire without sacrificing any of their individuality or becoming in the slightest degree less German. The distinguished Schönborn family took the lead in this respect. Lothar Franz, Count Schönborn (bishop of Bamberg from 1693, elector of Mainz from 1695), was in fact the propagator of 'Germanism' (*Theutscher Gusto*, as he called it). He and his nephew Friedrich Carl, who was made Imperial Chancellor in Vienna in 1705, were in close contact, both politically and culturally, with Austria. Their ambition was to continue and perfect the imperial style, and to resist the increasing tendency towards the imitation of French art. They were thus ideal patrons for Neumann.

Franconia was furthermore drawn away from French and under Central European influence by its close links with Bohemia. The Bohemian Baroque had been introduced by the three Dientzenhofers, Georg, Leonhard, and Johann. Neumann was their immediate follower. His abbey church at Neresheim, built in the middle of the eighteenth century, marks, as we shall see, the final and complete consummation of the style.

The fact that the rulers of other German states in the Main area held very different ideas did nothing to impede the progress of Franconia. The Protestant margraves of Ansbach and Bayreuth, for instance, were far more sympathetic to France and the north than the Catholic bishops of Würzburg and Bamberg. Religious ties with French refugees of their own denomination led to their sharing the same architectural theories. In 1691 Philipp Dieussart, a Huguenot and an exponent of Dutch classicism, left Berlin for the court of Christian Ernst of Bayreuth. His *Theatrum architecturae civilis* (first edition 1679) even had its effect in Bamberg. Later the Margravine Wilhelmine, sister of Frederick II, helped to introduce the Rococo there. The bishops of the Rhine were only partly culturally more inclined towards France, as was Maximilian von Welsch, the favourite architect of Lothar Franz, elector of Mainz.

We must now fill in some of the background to this great mid-eighteenth-century flowering in Franconia. It was, in the first place, well supplied with conveniently sited

quarries yielding white, yellow, greenish, and red sandstone: these give their characteristic colours to the Main towns.[1] The history of its Baroque era begins in 1651, when
Antonio Petrini (p. 68) of Trento, the representative of the Italo-Alpine Baroque,
settled at Würzburg, where he remained for fifty years, making it his second homeland.
In 1687 Petrini began work on the Marquardsburg for Prince-Bishop Marquard
Sebastian Schenk von Stauffenberg, on a site to the east of Bamberg. His design was
based – possibly to please his patron – on Schloss Aschaffenburg, built nearly a hundred
years earlier. Apparently he considered this medieval, fortress-like building, with its four
corner towers and four wings round a central courtyard, to be a suitable model for a
Franconian bishop's palace, and he seemed unaware of the fact that at the end of the
seventeenth century palaces everywhere, including Germany, had open courts and were
related to the surrounding landscape. The heavy, massive window pediments and balustrades were taken from Italian models.

Petrini continued to build important works in the same vigorous style until the end
of his life. In 1696 he began the completion of the façade and tower of the Universitätskirche (finished 1703; Plate 90) and in 1699 the court wing of the Julius Hospital (Plate
84), both in Würzburg. His additions to the Universitätskirche bore no relation to the
Gothic Survival motifs of the lower storey, but kept to their Late Renaissance rhythm,
though in an architecturally more serious way. The Julius Hospital, too, followed the
pattern of what already existed, though Petrini tended to use bolder architectural members; for instance he placed rectangular panels into giant pilasters (where engaged
columns would have been more Baroque). His alternating segment- and triangle-
headed windows are also a rather dry, unimaginative motif.

The more monumental style of the next generation is shown in Georg Dientzenhofer's façade of St Martin at Bamberg, built in 1681–91 (Plate 91). Here the arcading
is carried across the whole front, resulting in six niches progressively increasing in
height, which gives the upper storey the look of a classical triumphal arch.

The Kappel near Waldsassen of 1685–9 (Figure 9), a pilgrimage church, is another
example of Georg Dientzenhofer's inventive genius.[2] It was also due to Georg Dientzenhofer that the transverse oval saucer domes of
Waldsassen (which derived in turn from Passau)
were used in the Oberpfalz and from there spread
to the adjacent bishoprics of Franconia – he had
worked as foreman for Abraham Leuthner, the
builder of Waldsassen, from 1682 until the latter's
death in 1689.

Another member of the Vorarlberg school was
the master-carpenter Joseph Greising of Bregenz
(1664–1721). In his domestic architecture, e.g. the
Rückermainhof in Würzburg of 1715–23,[3] he
combined a Late Renaissance style with motifs
derived from timber-framed work. The orders
were attached to the front like wooden panels, the

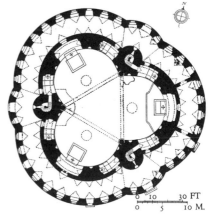

Figure 9. Georg Dientzenhofer: Waldsassen, Kappel, 1685–9. Plan

proportions developed horizontally, and empty spaces covered with boldly conceived ornament. But Greising's greatest success was as a church architect, a fact which is perhaps best explained by his Vorarlberg origin. His work on the Neumünster at Würzburg[4] is a good example. In 1711 a huge octagonal domed building, in the tradition of the Haug church, was started in front of the old Romanesque nave. That Greising was alone responsible for everything, especially the façade, appears unlikely. Possibly Johann Dientzenhofer supplied a design, and he could well be the 'Bamberg architect' who, according to the documents, was consulted in 1711. The whole was completed in 1716. Following the Roman–Franconian Baroque style, the mighty façade projects forward on both sides in two great curves with superimposed orders.

The arrival of the French Huguenot Charles Philipp Dieussart at Bayreuth has already been mentioned. In 1691, while he was working at Schloss Seehof, he rebuilt the old Schloss at Bayreuth, in a modern form, with a street front open above the ground floor. He avoided Petrini's rather crude methods and in his role of 'Architectus Romanus' introduced classicist motifs such as roundels with busts of Roman emperors between the rusticated pilasters of the ground floor.

In 1696 Leonhard Dientzenhofer (d. 1707) also came to Bayreuth. Since 1690 he had been at Bamberg, and in fact he forms a sort of connecting link between the two courts, in spite of the fact that he could hardly draw or write. His earlier appointment at Bamberg was doubtless due to his brother Georg's recommendation. Leonhard's style can be traced back to various influences. His designs of 1687–98 for the monastery of Ebrach have a great deal of Leuthner in the long façade and the sequence of giant pilasters. On the other hand the influence of Dieussart (of whose *Theatrum Architecturae* he had published the third edition) predominates in his enlargement of the Bamberg Residenz (1695–1704);[5] although he uses superimposed orders he does not succeed in avoiding a tedious uniformity.

But in his rebuilding of the Cistercian monastery of Schöntal in Württemberg[6] between 1700 and 1717 he achieved a brilliant success (Plate 88A). There had been a medieval building on the site and this possibly led him to decide in favour of a church with free-standing pillars. (Near by, at Grosskomburg,[7] and practically simultaneously (1707–15), Josef Greising was also achieving an impressive interior by adapting a medieval site.) These orders of powerful pillars of Leonhard's, faced with pilaster strips, were to have considerable repercussions in Swabia. In deference to the prevailing taste for centralized buildings, he inserted a transept with domed crossing between the four nave and the three chancel bays. One of Leonhard's great talents was his ability to plan large monastic layouts on hilly sites, as for example his Benedictine abbey of St Michael at Bamberg, built between 1696 and 1702.

The youngest of the Dientzenhofer brothers – Johann (1663–1726) – was also the most distinguished. In a letter to the Elector Lothar Franz he writes that he learned the basic rules of architecture from two experienced architects at Prague and had also travelled in Italy between 1699 and 1700. He was certainly familiar with Roman Baroque: that is evident in his rebuilding of the cathedral of Fulda[8] (1704–12), where he follows the model of Borromini's S. Giovanni in Laterano and carries through a rhythmical alternation of narrower and wider bays. Later, however, in the first decades of the eighteenth century the Roman impressions were superseded by the impact of Christoph Dientzenhofer's buildings in Bohemia. For the Benedictine church of Banz of 1710-18, rising above the banks of the Main and sited according to Benedictine custom on the summit of a hill, Johann Dientzenhofer conceived a bold plan with an interpenetration of forms and changing shapes. The nave suggests two transverse ovals. The diagonal positions of the pilasters are continued in the concave sweep of the lateral altar niches and their galleries (Plate 92A). The two transverse ovals are interlaced by a central one inserted between them and continued by two half ovals at the two ends of the nave (Figure 10). At the bottom these transverse ovals are formed by hollowing out the masonry of the zone of the pilasters. Above they are more clearly defined, and thrust the arches aside to form domical vaults. These are covered by frescoes in which great religious sequences unfold in symbolical representations: *Melchisedek*, the precursor of

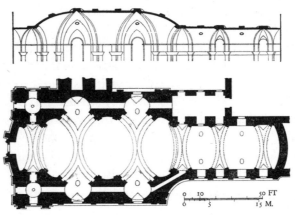

Figure 10. Johann Dientzenhofer: Banz, abbey church, 1710-18. Section and plan (1 : 1100)

Christ, blessing Abraham; *The Last Supper*, immediately above the Eucharist table; *The Descent of the Holy Ghost*; and finally *The Conversion of St Paul*. The idea is that just as the future apostle was flung from his horse, so the works of man, the arches supporting the vaults, must move aside. These three-dimensional arches touch as if they belonged to a rib-vault, but do not belong together. The spectator is always aware of the conflicting forces of the higher and lower spheres. This interpenetration above of forms merely suggested below has religious implications that were quite in keeping with the symbolic conceptions of Bohemian architecture.

A year after he had begun the church at Banz, Johann Dientzenhofer started his second great masterpiece, Schloss Pommersfelden, which he built in 1711-18. The owner, the Elector Lothar Franz von Schönborn, was a past master in the traditional family policy of enlisting the services of several eminent architects to compete with one another and criticize each other's plans: thus for Pommersfelden he called Hildebrandt from Vienna and Welsch from Mainz. In spite of this, however, Dientzenhofer's sculpturesque Franconio-Bohemian Baroque style predominated: the general layout of the monumental winged building with its boldly projecting central pavilion decorated with coupled columns, and the simple alternation of segmental and triangular pediments over the windows in the wings, are a proof of this (Plate 93). On the other hand the gently curving lines of the staircase are reminiscent of Hildebrandt, who had been called in to solve a problem that had arisen: the elector had allotted too large a space to his staircase, on the design of which he prided himself. Hildebrandt, who was to find later a much more supple solution for the sequence of a Sala Terrena, a Staircase, and a Saloon at the Upper Belvedere in Vienna, corrected this mistake by building a three-storeyed gallery round the staircase. An elliptical part inserted into the gallery leads to the Marble Saloon (Plate 92B). Like the Sala Terrena below, this is characteristic of Dientzenhofer. He also stressed the verticals in the columns and pilasters of the hall, rising on their high pedestals in the Franconian Baroque manner. Oval windows and paintings are inserted between the capitals and the separate pieces of entablature, and corresponding arches lead up to the vault. The Electoral Stables, which close the court in a quadrant, were built by Maximilian von Welsch between 1714 and 1717, in the style of his orangeries.

Von Welsch (1671–1745) had begun his career as an officer and fortifications engineer, and it was primarily as an engineer that he was employed by the Schönborn family. He entered the service of the prince bishop of Mainz in 1704. The belt of fortifications that he built round the fortress of Mainz was a model of its kind. His first orangery, the so-called 'Favorite',[9] was begun in 1700; the influence of Marly was to be seen in the pavilions, set like the 'wings' of a theatre at each side, but in other respects the building followed the robust Franconian Baroque. It was all destroyed later by the French. Welsch's later work, e.g. the Fulda orangery of 1722–4,[10] and his designs for the Schloss-kirche at Würzburg and for Vierzehnheiligen, show him breaking away from the Franconian influence. But he was never able to compete with Neumann; even his plans for the Schönborn chapel at Würzburg Cathedral were altered by Neumann to give them greater unity.

The Franconian branch of the Margraves of Brandenburg could not hope to rival the spectacular achievements of the Schönborns: the two principalities that they owned were too isolated from the north and the means at their disposal too severely limited. Nevertheless they were ambitious, and the results, though erratic, were considerable. Their chief architect was the south Tyrolese Gabriel de Gabrieli (1671–1747) who before he came to Ansbach had, in the early 1690s, been in the service of Prince Johann Adam von Liechtenstein at Vienna. He now became Surveyor General to the Margrave Wilhelm Friedrich, and in 1713–14 rebuilt Schloss Ansbach for him after its destruction by fire.[11] His adaptation of the Venetian-window motif to the arcades of a courtyard inserted between giant pilasters was original and impressive. The outer façade towards the south-east, with its tapering pilasters and refined articulation, recalls his Vienna period. He left Ansbach in 1714 and in 1716 settled at Eichstätt. There he remained for thirty years, giving that little town its peculiarly aristocratic stamp. Eichstätt seems indeed to have been specially attractive to Italian architects: Jakob Angelini ('Engel', active in Eichstätt 1670–1714) had preceded him and Moritz Pedetti (1719–99) was to follow him. The Austrian quality of Gabrielis's Baroque is well shown in the cathedral façade, with its diadem-like arch, and in the side pavilions.[12]

The margravine of Ansbach, Luise Frederike, was another sister of Frederick II, and this close political connexion between Prussia and Ansbach is reflected in its architecture. The decoration of Schloss Ansbach in the thirties by Leopoldo Retti was done in an Early Rococo style that bears comparison with the later work at Würzburg and Munich. Similarly, when Erlangen was enlarged after 1686 for the margraves of Bayreuth, it was by the addition of a rectangular network of streets designed by the architect Johann Moritz Richter of Thuringia. The houses are all uniform, with mansard roofs, and two storeys high, only the ones at the corners having an additional third storey.

Protestant church architecture at this time was chiefly dominated by a desire to be different from the Catholic: sometimes sobriety goes almost too far. Two examples may be mentioned. The church of St Georgen am See, near Bayreuth,[13] was an entirely new foundation of 1702. The Sophienkirche at Bayreuth of 1705–11 was built by the Prussian engineer Gottfried von Gedeler; here a new (Protestant) solution was found for the exterior, with large arched windows that foreshadow the Frauenkirche in Dresden.

In 1712 Prince Georg Wilhelm succeeded to the margravate of Bayreuth. He and his wife Sophia (known as 'the Franconian Lais') had a taste for parties, whose moral tone was very frivolous, at which the members of the court dressed up as hermits. This was Georg Wilhelm's excuse for commissioning Johann David Ränz to build him a 'Hermitage'.[14] It was put up in 1715–18, and consisted of a 'refectory', 'cells', and, not quite consistently, a 'grotto', all one-storeyed buildings, grouped round a cloister. The final result was less like a monastery than a pretty *maison de plaisance*. Presumably Ränz derived certain elements from Paul Decker, who in 1712 was called to Bayreuth from Berlin where he had spent two years in Schlüter's house. His talents lay not so much in architecture proper as in his skill as a draughtsman and in his stimulating and imaginative assimilation of ideas. His conception of an exuberant, fantastical Baroque is shown in the engravings of his book *Fürstlicher Baumeister* of 1711.

Ränz also rebuilt the Schloss at St Georgen for Georg Wilhelm between 1725 and 1727.[15] It served as a chapter-house for the order 'De la sincérité', founded by the apparently monastically minded prince. In the central block the Baroque idea of mounting tension is intensified by the excellent sculpture, probably the work of Johann Gabriel Ränz, the architect's brother.

In spite of all the works that have been described, Baroque architecture in the second decade of the eighteenth century had still not reached the standard that it had attained in southern Germany and Austria: at Pommersfelden, for instance, Hildebrandt's intervention was necessary before the building could be successfully completed. But with the advent of Balthasar Neumann in the third decade all was changed. Neumann, like the Dientzenhofers, forms a vital link in the artistic current that flowed from east to west, and Franconia could now stand comparison with any other centre in Germany.

Neumann was born at Eger (Erlau) in 1687. His family were clothiers, but he was trained as a cannon- and bell-founder. Evidently he showed remarkable ability even before he left his home town; three times the municipal council of Eger – who must have hoped that he would return when he had completed his studies – sent him sums of money when he was away. In 1711, thanks to the patronage of Andreas Müller, a captain in the engineers, he was enabled to begin studying geometry, surveying, and civil and military engineering at Würzburg, in addition to his work in the foundry. In 1714 he enlisted in the palace guards as a 'Stückjunker' (lieutenant of artillery). He took part in the Belgrade campaign of 1717 as an engineer, and in the following year visited Milan and Vienna. On his return to Würzburg in 1720 he and Johann Dientzenhofer were appointed surveyors of the future episcopal palace, the gigantic project of the prince bishop Philip Franz von Schönborn.

At about that time Neumann began to take an interest in town planning too. He compiled a treatise, illustrated with many plans, for the enlargement of Würzburg, and when in 1722 the prince bishop established a municipal commission for the supervision of all civic building in Würzburg, Neumann was put in charge. But it was not until 1729, after Friedrich Carl von Schönborn had become prince bishop, that he was really given a free hand. He was appointed superintendent of all military, ecclesiastical, and civil building operations in the two bishoprics of Würzburg and Bamberg, a post which included responsibility for the bishop's private palaces. After 1733 he held the same position in the electorate of Trier. There, too, his patron was a Schönborn: Franz Georg, elector of Trier. In addition he was appointed architect to yet another Schönborn, also in a territory in the Rhine: Damian Hugo, bishop of Speyer.

Neumann was also interested in practical engineering. In 1730 he laid on a fresh-water supply for Würzburg, and in 1733 he set up a glass-works in the Steigerwald and a mirror factory in Würzburg. Furthermore he took pleasure in teaching, instructing his pupils in his own two large houses in the Franziskanergasse[16] where he had installed models in rooms on the upper floors. He made a great point of the fact that his method of teaching included working from proper models and from nature and was not confined to the usual theoretical instruction from books. His models included fortifications, civil buildings, draught-machinery, wells, and mills and further, objects (such as a globe) to illustrate geography and even a piece of land. In 1731 Friedrich Carl appointed him lecturer on military and civil architecture at Würzburg University. Like most architects of the Baroque, he was very prosperous. He could afford to buy Edelhof, a country house at Randersacker, together with vineyards in the 'Teufelskeller', where he built a fine pavilion in the village street.[17] At the end of his life – he died in 1753 – Neumann's fame had spread far beyond the boundaries of the bishoprics which employed him: he alone had been able to solve the problems of the staircases in the palaces at Bruchsal and Brühl, and the grandiose plans for the royal palaces at Stuttgart, Karlsruhe, and Vienna show the extent of his influence (Figures 29 and 30). Until the end, however, he retained the status of an officer, and he is no doubt one of the most brilliant and many-sided representatives of the type of the officer-architect. In 1741 he was appointed colonel in the Franconian artillery.

Neumann remained faithful to the Baroque, at a time when the architects of Munich, Berlin, and Bayreuth were succumbing to the charm of the Rococo. His first major commission was the Würzburg Residenz. The patron now was prince bishop Johann

Philipp Franz Schönborn, who lacked the sure judgement of his uncle Lothar Franz and his cousin Friedrich Carl, but who had a veritable passion for building. He sought advice from all sides – from Mainz, from Vienna, from Paris – from Hildebrandt, von Welsch, de Cotte, and Boffrand. During the first four years of the work, from 1719 to 1722, Neumann was dependent on all these various advisers, and the history of the design is therefore complicated and uncertain.

The original inspiration seems to have come from a project drawn up twenty-three years earlier by the Venetian superintendent Count Matteo Alberti for a palace near Heidelberg.[18] This had envisaged a vast group of buildings with a *cour d'honneur* surrounded on three sides by wings with inner courts, an Italianate roof-terrace, far-projecting pavilions, and rounded corners in the courtyard. This was soon modified at Würzburg. Instead of dynamic façades, co-ordinated by long horizontal lines at the top, a pavilion system was introduced, with pediments and roofs curving at the corners and in the centre, following the northern tradition (Plate 94). The basic design, with its corner pavilions, large octagonal central room on the garden side, and oval rooms in the centres of the north and south fronts, was probably the work of Maximilian von Welsch. But the two superimposed orders of the façade, each of them covering main floor and mezzanine, show the influence of Hildebrandt.

Neumann only gradually gained the confidence of his patron. In 1723, when the northern block was already begun, he was sent to Paris with the plans, and there the royal architects Robert de Cotte and Germain Boffrand went over them again. Next year Boffrand came personally to Würzburg. The suggestions of these two Frenchmen had important results: the principle of the enfilade was introduced – the placing of all the doors of a suite of rooms on one axis (Figure 11); large arched windows and balconies supported on columns were inserted wherever possible; and the central projections of the *cour d'honneur* with their metope friezes were built. Finally, they decisively influenced the design of the staircase. In place of the duplication of stairs on both sides of the vestibule, which the bishop wanted, they advocated a single flight, on one side only, five bays long, and with windows towards both the *cour d'honneur* and the inner court. This suggestion led to the magnificent staircase that was finally built and which in the end took in all the space of the original inner court (Plate 96).

After the death of the prince bishop in 1724, the work was halted under his economical successor Christoph Franz von Hutten, and it was not until the reign of Friedrich Carl von Schönborn (1729–46) that the building was completed, under the increased influence of Hildebrandt. In 1729 and 1730 Neumann was sent to Vienna with fresh plans. An important change proposed by Hildebrandt was the introduction of a mezzanine floor on the garden side to raise the central pavilion above the Kaisersaal (Plate 95A). The light yet vigorous forms of the large pediments above the projections, with their characteristic 'Hildebrandt' break and the curving window-pediments and roofs, add a touch of Viennese lightness and charm to the otherwise severe building. This was even more pronounced as long as the original colour, silver-grey offset against a yellow ochre ground, remained. The statues were painted, porcelain-like, in white, and the coats of arms and the symbols were gilded. Today the greenish-yellow sandstone and the grey

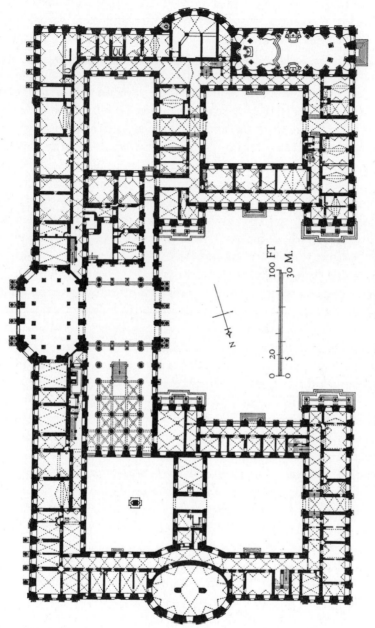

Figure 11. Balthasar Neumann: Würzburg, Residenz, begun 1719. Plan

limestone of the façades make a rather drab impression. Similarly the splendour of the whole has been impaired by the loss of the rich iron grille from the *cour d'honneur*, a famous work by the Tyrolese artist Johann Georg Oegg which was sold to England in the nineteenth century.

Welsch's plan for a centralized oval church in the middle of the south front was abandoned and the chapel (Hofkirche) was placed at the western end. At a meeting in Vienna on 25 September 1730 it was agreed that Neumann should do the architecture and Hildebrandt the decoration. Neumann's design was typically Franconio-Bohemian. Not having to conform to the articulation of a façade, it seems to be in deliberate opposition to the severity of the exterior. A central elongated oval is preceded and followed by two transverse ovals, to which are appended the space for the altar with a bishop's gallery above it and an anteroom with corresponding organ-galleries.[19] Following the pattern of Banz, the arches meet above the transverse ovals like the ribs of cross-vaults. The division into two storeys, required in a palace chapel, accentuates the contrast between the upper and lower zones. Below, the effect is determined by the marble columns supporting the gallery. They are set according to the curves of the plan. Above, the delicate, flowing Hildebrandtesque forms, the plasterwork of Antonio Bossi, and the paintings of Johann Rudolf Byss dominate.

Neumann was able to develop his ideas of dynamic space even more freely for the staircase. After the design had been finally approved in 1735, he commenced building in 1737. Unlike Pommersfelden, a central flight of stairs leads up to the landing, turns through 180 degrees, and returns in two flights, so that the impression of the vastness of the hall develops only gradually. On the first floor a balcony or gallery runs all the way round and the vast vault, with a span of *c.* 62 by 107 feet, was not carried by any intermediate columns such as that of Pommersfelden. Originally the two upper arms ascended along arcaded walls towards the passage encircling the great well of the staircase. Thus at one time Neumann's ideal of a tremendous spatial impact was even more fully realized than it is now. The vault offered a unique opportunity for ceiling painting. Following the custom of the Würzburg bishops, who were satisfied only with the best judged by European standards, the successor of the Schönborns, Karl Philipp of Greiffenklau, enlisted the services of the greatest fresco painter of the mid eighteenth century, Giovanni Battista Tiepolo, who was commissioned in 1750. His representation of the *Four Continents* bathes the whole interior in the warm glow and brilliant colouring of the south.

The impression is all the stronger since the entrance hall, though wide, is low. It leads straight on to the entrance hall on the garden side, a great octagonal room with twelve marble columns supporting a vault which contains a fresco by Johann Zick representing the Olympian Gods.[20] Here, too, Neumann's elevation and Bossi's plasterwork supply a brilliant setting for the fresco. Still more effective is the Kaisersaal on the floor above. Here Hildebrandt's alteration permitted the raising of the vaults and the introduction of penetrations. The effect of the giant red marble columns and pilasters combined with Tiepolo's painting and Antonio Bossi's plasterwork is one of unforgettable splendour (Plate 95B). Such an enhancement was certainly necessary to prevent a feeling of anticlimax after the staircase. Fortunately these main rooms of the Residenz escaped serious damage in the Second World War, whereas the famous sequence of state apartments with the Mirror Closet were entirely destroyed.

The enforced collaboration between Neumann and Hildebrandt on the Residenz, which had after all proved advantageous, lasted nearly ten years, from 1729 to 1738. It continued for the building of Schloss Werneck (1734–45; Plate 98A). There, however, it was Neumann's Franconian Baroque that predominated. Built as a country-seat for Friedrich Carl, the extensive group of buildings with projecting pavilions and curving roofs is more vigorously articulated than is the Würzburg Residenz, where the front had been kept flat in the French manner. At Werneck Neumann would have liked to go even further, by bevelling the edges of the pavilions, but his idea was not accepted at the conference held in Vienna in 1733 to discuss the plans. On the other hand his plan for a chapel consisting of a circle with ten niches and convex galleries *was* accepted, and this created a thrilling spatial movement (Plate 97).

Neumann was more successful in imposing his ideas for private houses than for palaces, where he was compelled to compromise with colleagues of his own standing. These houses formed part of his carefully worked-out town planning schemes in which whole rows of streets, for instance the present Theaterstrasse in Würzburg, were laid out in a uniform manner.[21] In the house at 7 Kapuzinergasse which he originally built for himself in 1723/4, the windows, doors, and cornices form continuous horizontal lines related to the line of the street. Only the huge pilasters at the corners introduce a vertical accent in the Baroque sense. The beauty lies in the proportions. The eye is not diverted by details but sees the entire house spanned by curving roofs, as one complete whole. With an artist of this kind, who subordinated everything to the architectural idea, even the *rocaille* ornament had to conform to the clearly defined lines of the composition, as can be seen in the beautiful Hof Rombach, 23 Eichhornstrasse.[22] The former Priesterhaus in Bamberg, today the town hall, with its ashlar façades and curving window pediments, may serve to illustrate the type of town house as it appeared between 1732 and 1737[23] (Plate 99).

The chapels of Würzburg and Werneck described above have already introduced us to Neumann's most special field of interest, the designing of church interiors. His first important work of this kind, the Schönborn Chapel attached to Würzburg Cathedral,[24] was a small domed centralized structure executed between 1723 and 1736. As we have seen, this was a revision of plans by von Welsch. Neumann's chief innovation was to increase the size of the dome to the maximum possible extent, in order to harmonize with the cylindrical shape of the central space. The dome also covers kidney-shaped side rooms, so that outward-curving, three-dimensional arches are formed. This gives greater unity to the spatial composition. The pendentives of the dome rest on pairs of columns, an early indication of Neumann's preference for columns over pilasters.

The great Benedictine abbey church of Münsterschwarzach[25] on the Main, built in 1727–42, had a basilican plan of slender proportions, a two-tower façade, and a dome, without a proper drum, over the crossing: another tower was built over the choir, containing the high altar. Here, as in the Schönborn Chapel, pairs of columns were set in the oblique angles of the crossing to support the pendentives and allow the ribs of the arches to swing into the transepts so that similar curves were formed. The magnificent building was unfortunately demolished in 1821–37.

In the pilgrimage church of Gössweinstein[26] in Upper Franconia, too, Neumann sought to fuse the space over the crossing beneath a flat elliptical dome with the tunnel-vaulted transepts by building the latter not rectangular, but over three sides of the octagon. As in all his buildings, he laid great stress on the use of local stone, and the yellowish sandstone, quarried in the neighbourhood, gives a warm tone to the building, which is also beautifully sited.[27]

For the abbey church of St Paulinus at Trier,[28] begun in 1734, Neumann used a specific Würzburg motif – and also a Gothic one – namely a powerful west tower with emphasized verticals. The task was to rebuild a Romanesque church destroyed by the French in 1689. In the interior, Neumann's influence is most marked in the fluid transition from the nave to the only slightly narrower choir.

Two further commissions during these years, one in 1738 for the church of St Peter in Bruchsal and the other for the Dominican church in Würzburg in 1741, again brought him into touch with the Gothic style, for which he evidently had a certain sympathy. At Bruchsal the five-sided Gothic termination of the choir suggested a form that could be repeated in the transepts. For the Würzburg church he adapted the newly built nave to the tall fourteenth-century choir.

In the church of Heusenstamm near Offenbach,[29] too (1739–40), he established a close harmony between the shallow vault of the crossing and the arms of the transept by terminating the latter in three sides of an octagon. Four columns are placed in the angles of the crossing to support the elliptical arches of the vault.

The invitation extended to Neumann in the thirties to intervene in the building of Schloss Bruchsal marked the change from local to universal renown. It was probably Welsch who had furnished the first design for the palace in 1720 for Damian Hugo von Schönborn, prince bishop of Speyer. Unlike the rest of his family, Damian Hugo wished to economize in his architect and soon replaced Welsch, whom he described as too 'precious', by the foreman Johann Georg Seitz, and in 1723 called in Michael Rohrer, a master mason from Rastatt. Dissatisfied with the latter, in 1725 he appointed Anselm Franz Freiherr von Ritter zu Grünsteyn 'Hofrat' (privy counsellor) and architect in Mainz. Ritter designed the *corps de logis* with four wings and a central staircase inserted as a transverse oval between two small courts.[30] He resigned the following year, however, on discovering that his patron had had a mezzanine inserted above the first floor, which ruined the proportions of the central block and made the roof appear too flat, although as a result the wings containing the chapel and the chancellery acquired increased architectural prominence. Giovanni Francesco Marcini's frescoes on the façade were highly successful, and added a gay note.

Neumann began to take a hand at Bruchsal only in 1728. His main task was the staircase (1731–2) which had to be built between the two smaller courts. He enlarged the upper landing connecting the two state rooms on the court and garden sides, forming a transverse oval shape that was encircled by the ascending stairs. The vast staircase itself, the two adjoining state rooms, the Rococo plasterwork by Johann Michael Feuchtmayer, and the frescoes of Johann Zick formed together a magnificent composition, spatially exciting and glowing with colour. It was all completely destroyed in the Second World War. But this was still not the culmination of Neumann's work. That had to wait until the forties (pp. 251ff.).

In Mainz, as in the Rhine area everywhere, a forceful Baroque style remained dominant. A typical example of this is the Dalberger Hof of 1715-18 with its coupled giant columns set diagonally and its recklessly indented pediments.[31] On the other hand the aristocratic court architects of the Italian school who were trained in Paris – Anselm Franz von Ritter zu Grünsteyn (1701-65) is an example – favoured greater moderation. Ritter's part in the design of Bruchsal has just been mentioned. He also designed the Deutsch-Ordens-Kommende[32] built in 1730-7 which, in spite of its classicistic pedimented central projection, is a comfortable German affair with its great mansard roof.

The French architect Robert de Cotte has already been mentioned in connexion with the Würzburg Residenz. Some eight years before that, however, in 1715, he had been appointed Surveyor General in Bonn, where he carried on with the work Zuccalli had begun at the palace.[33] His refined, harmonious style can be better appreciated, however, at Schloss Poppelsdorf,[34] with its one-storeyed wings and higher pavilions. It was begun from his plans in 1715-16 and completed by Guillaume d'Haubérat in 1730-40. The Palais Thurn und Taxis at Frankfurt,[35] a typical Parisian *hôtel*, built by d'Haubérat in 1732-41 after de Cotte's design of 1727, appeared before its destruction in the last war as a foreign element in Germany.

Mannheim was the next city to become a cultural centre of international importance, under the electors Karl Philipp (1716-42) and Karl Theodor (1743-99). Karl Philipp transferred the capital of the Palatinate there from Heidelberg in 1720. The town had already been laid out as a rectangular network of streets in the seventeenth century. When it became the capital, a vast new palace about 2,000 feet long was begun on the side facing the Rhine.[36] The original plans were by Louis Remy de la Fosse, but they may well have been altered during the actual building by Johann Kaspar Herwarthel of Mainz (d. 1720) and Johann Clemens Froimont. It culminated in the latter's great hall, with its beautiful plaster relief by Egell. After 1726 Guillaume d'Haubérat directed the work. Although French architects were so largely concerned with it, it remains characteristically German, chiefly because of its strongly projecting angles and tower-like pavilions. It was destroyed during the war but has been substantially rebuilt.

In 1737 the Mannheim opera house (celebrated in musical history) was designed by Alessandro Galli da Bibiena, son of the more famous theatre architect Ferdinando. It was burnt down as early as 1795. Bibiena stayed to do further work – the façade of a store on the Paradeplatz, with a tall impressive central tower, and the adjoining Jesuit church (1738-56),[37] which after his death in 1748 was continued by Franz Wilhelm Rabaliatti. The Gesù is again the model, although that was by no means the standard type for Jesuit churches in Germany. There is an effective contrast between the height of the nave – approximately 100 feet – and the width, which is little more than half that, while the dome is some 90 feet high inside. In accordance with the taste of the time, the interior is strongly lit by tall, wide windows.

It is interesting to note that the Jesuit church at Heidelberg, the Ignatiuskirche (designed in 1712 by the Franconian architect Johann Adam Breunig and completed in 1759),[38] is modelled on the German Romanesque, and has free-standing piers. It serves to mark the contrast between the old and the new capital of the electors.

The fact that communities of different religious denominations lived side by side determined the cultural development of the areas north of the Main and the Rhine just as it did in central Germany. As early as 1597 the Neustadt at Hanau in the county of Nassau, founded for Protestant refugees from Wallonia and the Netherlands, had established the type of settlement that was later used over and over again. It consisted of a rectangular network of streets of simple, uniform houses, with a church in the middle of a square. The most successful realization of it was at Kassel,[39] where from 1688 onwards the Oberneustadt was built for the Huguenots by the refugee architect Paul du Ry (1640–1714) (Plate 98B). The flowering of the arts in Kassel, which lasted for about a hundred years, was certainly in large part due to the keen interest and understanding of the Landgraves Charles (1670–1730) and Frederick II (1760–85), and it was their influence that assured a continued and varied development. With the appointment of Giovanni Francesco Guerniero in 1701 the influence of the Italian Baroque increased. For Schloss Wilhelmshöhe he designed a magnificent garden laid out down a steep hillside in the Italian Baroque manner with terraces and cascading fountains. The Italian note was further emphasized by the crowning octagon built in 1718. At the top rises a pyramid surmounted by a copper statue of the Farnese Hercules. In the Orangery on the other hand, built in the Karlsau in 1703–11, French influence prevailed.

Sculpture

The decisive personality in the development of sculpture in Franconia and in the Palatinate was Paul Egell (1691–1752) of Mannheim.[40] His influence even radiated into southern Germany. He had been a pupil of Permoser in Dresden, so that his art had been formed on the sculpture of the Zwinger during the second decade of the eighteenth century. However, particularly in his drawings, he transformed the bold Alpine–Roman Baroque character of Permoser into a kind of Mannerism with elongated figures. In 1715–16 he furnished a crucifix for the monastery of St Michael at Bamberg. In 1721 the Elector Karl Philipp appointed him sculptor to the court at Mannheim, and there he worked for thirty-one years, until his death. There, too, he met the elector's French architects Froimont and Haubérat, and was thus introduced to French artistic theories, which, however, made but little impression on his Baroque ideas: the *rocaille* was the only form of French art that he accepted, since it was related to his own. On the high altar of the Unterpfarrkirche in Mannheim of *c.* 1735 (now in the Berlin museum), instead of the customary columnar aedicule he framed the Crucifixion group with palm trees, the branches of which turn outwards and lead to a shell-shaped crown at the top. We find similar altar superstructures in Joseph Anton Feuchtmayer's designs during the forties.

When Ignaz Günther was in Mannheim in 1751 he was greatly impressed by Egell's style (p. 238), and Johann Peter Wagner, who also visited Egell a year or two before the latter's death, was impressed too (p. 259). Indeed the impact of Egell's Baroque on both was so great that the influence of the Donner school of Vienna was pushed into the background. For Egell the expression still lies less in the body than in the drapery with its heavily massed folds, and in the careful characterization of face and hands (Plate 101B). His figure of *St Francis Xavier* in the Stadtgeschichtliches Museum in Mannheim (Plate 101A) and his *St Anne* on the altar of the Immaculate Conception in Hildesheim Cathedral (Plate 100B) emphasize the spiritual significance in a way that recalls Permoser's *St Augustine*. Yet here, as opposed to the Bavarian manner with its sturdy Alpine flavour, the style is more sophisticated, more intellectual, and we sense the closeness to the French border. Yet for all that, Egell's figures do not lack vitality, as can be seen for example in the *Adoring Angel* from the high altar of the Unterpfarrkirche in Mannheim (Plate 100A). The sincerity of the figures kneeling in fervent prayer before the Holy Sacrament could never, as do Ignaz Günther's figures, suggest ballet dancers, nor do the bare arms and legs arouse any erotic feelings; they serve only to emphasize the power of the angels.

During the twenties and thirties Egell was chiefly concerned with architectural sculpture. Examples are the decoration of the Neckar Gate (1724), crowned like the Zwinger pavilions by a figure of Atlas, the plasterwork for the staircase and the great hall of the Schloss done in 1729, and the reliefs of the Trinity for the pediment of the Schlosskirche and for the Jesuit church done in 1731 and 1749 respectively. Unfortunately little of his work survives, owing to the destruction of Mannheim and the loss of the pieces in the Berlin Museum.

Painting

There was no independent development of painting in Franconia. Even the Schönborns were compelled to draw their painters and sculptors from the great art centres of southern Germany and Bohemia. In this their ties with Austria stood them in good stead. In 1707 the Elector Lothar Franz commissioned the Tyrolese artist Melchior Steidl (d. 1727) to paint the Kaisersaal of the Residenz at Bamberg.[41] Steidl had established his reputation with his frescoes for the abbey churches of St Florian (1690–5) and Lambach (1698), and for the Kaisersaal at Kremsmünster (1696). The elector had, in the first place, approached Andrea Pozzo and Andrea Lanzani, but both had been put off by the low hall, which would impair the effect of perspective painting. The elector for his part considered the fees they asked, 7,500 and 14,000 fls., respectively, as too high. Steidl had to be satisfied with 1,000 fl. The growing importance attached to wall painting at that time can be judged from the fact that Lothar Franz had the walls kept flat so as to leave the entire surface free for the paintings. His choice of subject was 'romanische Historia oder sonsten etwas von seiner intention, so in das Moralische einläufet' ('Roman history or something connected with it that has moral implications'). Steidl gave vivid representations of Roman emperors, their German successors, and finally, on the ceiling, 'das Moralische', an allegory of good government. He was still very dependent on the style of Pozzo, which in view of the proportions of the hall was not altogether a good thing.

In 1713 Lothar Franz called the Swiss-born Johann Rudolf Byss (1660–1738) to decorate Schloss Pommersfelden.[42] Byss had already had considerable professional experience. He had visited England, Holland, and Italy, worked in Prague in 1694, and settled in Vienna in 1704. From 1713 to 1718 he painted the frescoes for the staircase at Pommersfelden, in 1732–3, at the end of his life, the ceiling of the Schönborn Chapel attached to the cathedral, and in 1735 the ceiling of the chapel in the Residenz. Byss, who was interested in details and still-life, lacked boldness of execution, but his decorative talent was a great asset in the furnishing of the Residenz.

CHAPTER 15

VORARLBERG, SWITZERLAND, AND SWABIA

Architecture

WHEREAS the taste for Italian architecture was so strong in Bavaria that it could, on occasion, lead to actual copying as for instance in the interior of the Theatinerkirche in Munich, in Swabia, bound to the empire by manifold ties, it was the German Alpine character introduced by Vorarlberg architects that predominated.[1] Zuccalli and Viscardi, the leading masters during the first period of the Bavarian Baroque (1683–1714), were Italians from the Grisons. The Vorarlberg artists on the other hand came from the heart of the Bregenzer Wald. They worked in families, headed by the Beers, the Thumbs, and the Mosbruggers, and were employed chiefly by the monasteries, especially the Benedictines and Premonstratensians. The Swabian monasteries, as free imperial foundations, occupied a prominent political and economic position without forming a direct part of the court circles.[2] In Switzerland conditions were similar: the predominance of the nobility was confined to the royal monastery of St Lorenz at Kempten, while elsewhere the abbots, drawn from the ranks of the peasantry, were the principal employers. The bishops, on the other hand, as opposed to their colleagues in Franconia, had but little influence on the arts.

Beginning as simple craftsmen, the Vorarlberg masons threw off the yoke of the guilds and started to become free architects. But the stages of this process are difficult to trace. Possibly the individual sequence was as follows: Michael Beer (d. 1666) who began the abbey church at Kempten; Michael Thumb (d. 1690) who built the abbey church of Obermarchthal; then Franz Beer (1659–1726), one of the architects of Weingarten, followed by Caspar Mosbrugger (1656–1723), the art-loving monk of Einsiedeln, and finally Peter Thumb (1681–1766), architect of St Gallen and Birnau.[3] Since, however, other architects participated everywhere it is hardly possible to ascribe the creative achievements to a single architect.

Michael and Peter Thumb were father and son, both from Bezau. Michael built the pilgrimage church high up on the Schönenberg near Ellwangen, begun in 1682. The façade, visible from afar, shows an early attempt to stress the vertical lines by fusing the towers with the body of the church (Plate 105B).[4] In the interior the tunnel-vault is still stilted by an attic storey, so that more light is gained. Semicircular arches carry the galleries inserted between the wall-piers. Michael Thumb stressed the Vorarlberg type ('Vorarlberger Münsterschema') still further in the Premonstratensian abbey church of Obermarchthal on the upper Danube, built in 1686–92.[5] Here, the galleries and the transept are only faintly reminiscent of St Michael, and in his use of detached piers for the choir, Michael Thumb conforms more to the Jesuit church at Dillingen of 1610–17. The narrow bridges of the galleries and of the transepts are characteristic features of the Vorarlberg pillared hall-churches. The nave remains dominant, its tunnel-vault with deep-set lunettes stretching to the beginning of the choir. The transept, of little importance in itself, has only a preparatory function. The individual elements, for instance the powerfully projecting upper members of the entablature, are more clearly enunciated. It was still possible in 1689–92 for Johann Schmutzer of Wessobrunn to cover the vault panels with foliage decoration in plasterwork to the exclusion of all ceiling painting.

The church of Obermarchthal was the immediate starting point for Franz Beer, who was to become one of the leading architects. After the death of Michael Thumb in 1690 he undertook to continue the work together with Christian Thumb. Fourteen years later his abbey church at Rheinau in Switzerland (1704–11; Plate 102) marked a decisive achievement in the development of the Vorarlberg type. By setting the galleries farther back, he reduced the effect of their horizontal lines and obtained a much stronger accent on the upright fluted Corinthian pilasters, especially as these lie not only along the front but also along the sides of the internal buttresses. They are further emphasized by the entablature, which is not continued along the lateral walls but reduced to the fragments above the pillars. Unfortunately the architectural effect is spoilt by the altarpieces in front of them. Strangely enough Beer placed the transept so far east that it opens from the monks' choir. As opposed to the tunnel-vault of the nave, he used a saucer dome in the choir.

Beer went even further in the Cistercian abbey church of St Urban in the canton of Lucerne, built in 1711–15 (Plate 103). Monks' choir and nave are of equal length. The latter has two bays with chapels and a transept. The former also has two bays and a transept; the dimensions, it is true, are smaller, but the choir is lengthened by a square recess for the high altar. The galleries are not set back as far as at Rheinau, but they are kept narrow; in this way the light can fall more directly into the nave. The chapels have segmental terminations and this makes it possible for the altars to be placed more favour-ably than at Rheinau. Although coupled pilasters are used they look like detached pillars, since the interior buttresses do not project so far into the nave, and the galleries are more clearly visible. The increased light in the niche with the high altar, obtained by the addition of two lateral windows, is the result of careful planning. Beer brings a variation to the Vorarlberg two-tower façade by using the Gothic Survival tower of the former west front of 1572–8 as the south tower of the new front and copying it exactly in the north tower, built between 1706 and 1711.

New ideas, which were, like those of Beer, in the end to culminate in the Benedictine abbey of Weingarten, were contributed by Johann Jakob Herkommer (1648–1717) and Caspar Mosbrugger (1656–1723). All three belonged to the generation after the Thirty Years War, and were only a few years younger than the Grisons architects Zuccalli, born in 1642, and Viscardi, born in 1647, who, as will be remembered, were the leading architects in Bavaria. Herkommer, who was a native of Sameister near Rosshaupten, thus did not belong to the Vorarlberg school. Moreover as an architect, painter, and plasterer he was closer to the universal type of Italian artist and as such occupied the position of Kunstintendant (Surveyor) to the Benedictine monastery of St Mang at Füssen in the Allgäu. A stay in Venice which lasted until 1685 and a further visit in 1694 made him familiar with Italian art.

On his return from Venice in 1685–6 Herkommer built a chapel in his native village, Sameister, founded by his brother. It has a cruciform plan with a drumless dome and a lantern. Domed buildings were rare in Swabia, for the one at Kempten had not proved a success. Herkommer's great objective was to develop the longitudinal plan with centralizing elements. When he reconstructed the church of St Mang at Füssen between 1701 and 1715 he was restricted by the necessity of building over Romanesque foundations. Significantly enough he replaced the usual tunnel-vault by a series of saucer domes, probably on the Austro-Bohemian pattern, and pierced the walls with the internal buttresses. A semicircular dome was built over the crossing. As we have already seen (p. 103), in 1712 – i.e. three years before Weingarten was begun – Herkommer in his parish church of St Jakob at Innsbruck[6] allowed a fully lit dome on a drum to follow the saucer domes and formed the transept by extending the lateral sides of the crossing in conch-shaped niches. To judge from the description of Weingarten in 1724, the analogous form there may be traced in part to Herkommer's plan. He even managed to insert his favourite feature, a dome crowned by a lantern over the choir, when he rebuilt the Late Gothic hall-church of Heiligkreuz at Augsburg in 1716–19. The spacious hall, the ideal of the age, was given a Baroque veneer by transforming the circular piers into Corinthian columns with correspondingly high bases and imposts.

Of greater significance than Herkommer was Caspar Mosbrugger,[7] a lay-brother in the monastery of Einsiedeln. He was born in 1656 at Au in the Bregenzer Wald, the headquarters of the Vorarlberg masons' guild, and from 1670 to 1673 was apprenticed to a stone-cutter. In 1682, when he was twenty-five, he became a novice at Einsiedeln, where he worked until his death in 1723, frequently travelling around in connexion with his work.[8] By 1684 he had acquired such prestige that Willibald Koboldt, abbot of Weingarten, sought his services as consulting architect for the renovation of his church.

It is difficult to estimate the effects, if any, of Mosbrugger's proposals for Weingarten, seeing that the church was not begun until 1715, after an interval of twenty years. Furthermore Sebastian Hyller, who was then abbot, was in close touch with the Benedictine abbey at Salzburg and would hardly have been disposed to accept outmoded plans. The fact that Mosbrugger's name is not once mentioned during the building operations also speaks against his participation. Moreover, Mosbrugger's great work, the abbey church at Einsiedeln, despite certain similarities to Weingarten, reveals a fundamentally different conception. Even the convex front, which the two churches have in common, is treated in a different way.

At the time of its completion a description of Weingarten was published, naming Beer as the architect and mentioning a plan by Herkommer. Other reports limit Beer's share in the work. The foundation stone of the new church was laid in 1715. The very next year Beer turned down the commission to undertake the building, when the collegiate church refused to agree to the contract stipulating 27,000 gulden, and moreover demanded caution-money from the architect. This must have resulted in an increase in the influence of Andreas Schreck, lay-brother and 'murarius' at Weingarten, who was supervising the work. Schreck was a native of the Vorarlberg, a friend of Mosbrugger's and confidential adviser and deputy for the abbot in all building matters. He was fully capable of drafting plans and from 9 to 21 February 1715 in the priory of Hofen he drew the 'ideam novi templi Weingartensis'.[9] The aged Christian Thumb also had a share in the work.

In 1717 Donato Giuseppe Frisoni, Surveyor to the Duke of Württemberg, sent sketches for the upper storeys of the towers and for the gable of the façade. In 1718 he sent additional drawings for the dome and for the decoration of the nave, and in the same year contracts were successfully concluded with Franz Xaver Schmutzer the Elder of Wessobrunn for the plasterwork and pulpit and with Cosmas Damian Asam for the frescoes.

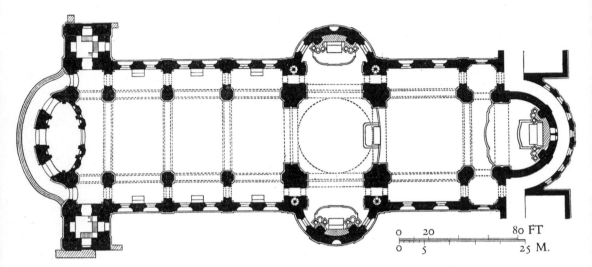

Figure 12. Weingarten, abbey church, begun 1715. Plan

Weingarten (Figure 12), with its total length of 378 feet, is the longest Baroque church in Germany. But it is more than that. It places the Vorarlberg school in the very front rank of German ecclesiastical architecture of the High Baroque, in a position it shares only with the contemporaneous Karlskirche by Fischer von Erlach in Vienna. The abbot's interest in Fischer's Salzburg churches proved fruitful, and he insisted that the façade and dome of his church should be a counterpart to Fischer's Kollegienkirche at Salzburg. At Weingarten, as at Salzburg, the concave recession of the side bays brings the convex centre of the façade in line with the flanking towers (Plate 104B). A uniform three-storeyed front results, which sets off to great advantage the distant view of the abbey, rising impressively above the town. A high basement forms the plinth for the giant order, so that the main entablature develops above the third storey. Frisoni's pediment, however, for all its restless energy, can in no way compare with Fischer's powerful attic.

The great beauty of Weingarten lies in the interior (Plate 104A), where the master builders from the Vorarlberg could give free rein to their native style. Internal buttresses were retained, but they were detached from the walls by galleries receding in curves and

by large passages, so that they resemble free-standing pillars. Their size and heavy mouldings make them suitable supports for the mighty arches and saucer domes. Following the
Italian pattern, the dome and drum now appear in their correct place over the crossing.
The transept arms terminate in apses. The design of the east end, with a square choir bay
followed by a narrow bay leading to the high altar in the apse, represents the classic
solution to the Vorarlberg plan. The opportunities for the development of ceiling painting at Weingarten were of the utmost importance. Here for the first time, in the Haug
Chapel (1716), Cosmas Damian Asam was able to demonstrate his outstanding ability
for covering vaulted surfaces with extensive and dominating frescoes.

The achievement at Weingarten can scarcely be attributed to a single artist. If the
opinion held by a number of scholars,[10] that the real credit goes to Caspar Mosbrugger,
were correct, it would be inconceivable that his name should not occur in the building
documents. That Herkommer contributed certain ideas – probably the insertion of
saucer domes and the dome on a drum and also the apses of the transept – can be inferred,
as has already been pointed out, from his earlier plan for the Jacobskirche in Innsbruck.
For the rest, the emphasis on the detached piers is entirely in keeping with the ideas of
Beer. Related features which occur in Mosbrugger's church at Einsiedeln, for instance
the convex centre of the façade, the details of the piers, and the curving galleries, cannot
have had any importance for Weingarten, seeing that they were later additions at Einsiedeln. However, close relations certainly did exist between Weingarten and Einsiedeln,
and they included architectural ones, as is proved by the plans of Weingarten preserved
at Einsiedeln such as a sketch of the Romanesque church and a cross-section of the new
building. On the actual construction Mosbrugger must have exerted some influence,
even if only in the capacity of adviser to Andreas Schreck, the resident clerk of works.

Further evidence that Weingarten is the fruit of an extensive collaboration can be
obtained by comparing it with the Premonstratensian abbey church at Weissenau near
Ravensburg. The reconstruction of this church was begun in 1717 by Franz Beer a year
after he had refused to direct the building operations at Weingarten. Beer's style is
clearly demonstrated in the internal buttresses that are so far detached from the walls as
to resemble piers, and in the middle bay of the nave, enlarged, as at St Urban, by niches.
As a result, the rhythmic articulation begins in the nave even before the transept is reached,
and it is accentuated by columns set at the angles of the crossing. Unfortunately Beer
was compelled to retain the old narrow choir, which was out of proportion with the
rest of the building. He had intended an oval with six piers to carry a dome with a lantern; it cannot have been a mere coincidence that in 1727, three years after the completion at Weissenau, Zimmerman used a similar plan for the near-by pilgrimage church
at Steinhausen. Two plans for Einsiedeln, which have been attributed to Beer, show the
same oval design for the choir.

The idea of inserting centralized units into a longitudinal building was developed most
consistently by Mosbrugger (p. 43). It was probably from his plans that the Ticinese
plasterer Giovanni Betini rebuilt the church of the former royal Benedictine abbey of
Muri in the canton of Aargau (1695–8). The changed mood of the time, expressing
itself in the demand for light and airy rooms, was no longer compatible with the old

Romanesque building. The sense of wide space, felt as one stands in the open below the infinite dome of the sky, was to be reflected in the interior. Of the old building the two Romanesque towers and the choir were retained. The narrow Romanesque nave and aisles were replaced by an octagon. The four corners at the west and east ends of the former aisles, which were superfluous as being outside the octagon, became galleries. The eight arches are of equal height. The imposts of the narrower arches in the diagonal axes are placed at a higher level than those of the longitudinal and transverse ones; it had not yet occurred to the architect to stilt the arches on the diagonals so that they could be set on the same capitals as the larger ones, an idea introduced five years later by Viscardi in Mariahilf at Freystadt. The idea at Muri was a large saucer dome with penetrations. In these are large semicircular windows. The haunches in the diagonals are stilted. The result is an interior flooded with light. Inside, the windows rest on a slightly curving entablature on pilasters broken round the corners. The abundance of light is further increased by the great windows of the chapels on the transverse axis. Unfortunately the rich interior decoration is of lower quality than the architecture.

The particular attraction of Mosbrugger's greatest work, the rebuilding of the Benedictine abbey and pilgrimage church of Einsiedeln,[11] is also due to the interior lighting, which was made even more colourful during the eighteenth century. Work began with the rebuilding of the choir between 1674 and 1676, followed in 1679–84 by the confessional chapel on the left terminating in the chapel of the Magdalen, with an originally octagonal choir crowned by a dome. As early as 1681 Caspar Mosbrugger had worked as stone-mason under the architect Hans Georg Kuen of Bregenz, and the abbey was built, with the exception of the north-western half of one wing, between 1704 and 1717, from Kuen's plan and model of 1703. It formed a gigantic rectangle. The symmetrical plan with its elongated church along the central axis and the transverse axis of two ranges starting in front of the choir and running north and south to form four courts represents the ideal of a Baroque monastery. On the sloping ground Mosbrugger built the church in 1719–23. The long façade is in complete harmony with the beautiful wooded landscape (Plate 106). For the centre he planned originally a straight church front with two towers, similar to the one at St Urban; not until after the building was under way did he choose a more Baroque, convex form modelled on Weingarten. However, probably out of consideration for the plain fronts of the monastery, he restrained the details, giving some of them a Renaissance character; for instance the twin windows. The old church consisted of the upper and the lower minster, separated by a pair of towers. A division in two was also essential for the new building, where the Chapel of Mercy, an older little 'Casa Santa' and the goal of the pilgrimage, formed a centre immediately east of the west front in opposition to the normal centre of the whole church farther east (Figure 13). The Chapel of Mercy was built on the site on which the cell of St Meinrad had stood originally, 'in a dark forest'. The saint was murdered in 861.

When Mosbrugger died in 1723 the brickwork of the octagon was complete. The two next bays to the east were begun from his plans. Both are square in plan. The first received a saucer dome. Mosbrugger had planned a dome on a drum for the second, but

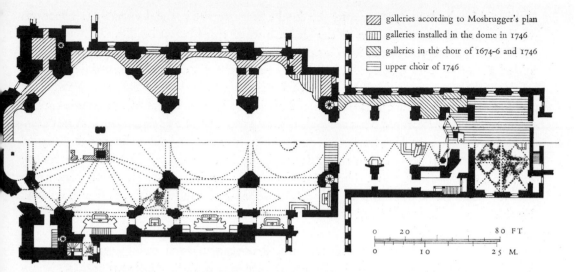

galleries according to Mosbrugger's plan
galleries installed in the dome in 1746
galleries in the choir of 1674-6 and 1746
upper choir of 1746

Figure 13. Hans Georg Kuen and Caspar Mosbrugger: Einsiedeln, abbey church,
designed 1703. Plan

only a few weeks before his death it was decided at a church council to substitute a drumless dome with a lantern, for reasons of economy. Thus the intended accentuation of the
entrance to the choir was not achieved. Nevertheless the alignment of the two magnificent ceiling frescoes is most effective. Work was begun in 1724 by Cosmas Damian
and Egid Quirin Asam, who almost certainly owed the commission to Cosmas Damian's
success at Weingarten. At Einsiedeln, too, the quiet white colour of the wall panels and
pilasters enhanced the architectural effect. Unfortunately in 1909–10 additional ornamentation was applied to the walls, and the interior now appears over-ornate. The choir
in its present form was not built until 1746–51. It is the work of Franz Kraus from
designs of Egid Quirin Asam.

In combining three different centralized units to increase the transparency of the building, Mosbrugger had gone much beyond what had been done at Weingarten. The wide
dome over the old Chapel of Mercy rests on eight attached corner piers and two free-
standing ones at the back of the chapel. An ambulatory which is carried behind the
corner piers also links the side chapels with the two succeeding bays to the east. A corresponding passage joins the galleries above. The diagonals open aisle-like in two large
superimposed arches (Plate 105A). The ones in the galleries lift up the entablature. The
flow of light is increased by the ring of windows in the vaults. As at Weingarten, the
galleries of the lateral chapels sweep back to the outer walls. This motif, essential for a
more satisfactory effect in the galleries, first occurs here. A few years later we find it
also in Protestant church architecture, for example in Bähr's Frauenkirche in Dresden.
The two nave bays that follow have similar wide openings. The corner piers round the
area dominated by the pulpit are set at a sharp angle. Egid Quirin Asam made this more
effective by crowning the piers with fragments of pediments. Organ galleries with

169

sloping sides, built in 1746, occupy the dead eastern angles in the domed part. There are wall piers in the first two bays of the choir, but the third bay is basilican.

The colour scheme in the interior consists of white in the lower zones, to which is added the greyish pink of the foliage. In the vaults the colour passes from the red inlays of the arches, interrupted by the green of the rosettes and considerably heightened with gold, to the deeper shades of the painted ceiling. The superb art of the Asams on the ceiling, where the painted parts seem almost to grow out of the plasterwork, is not continued in the choir; it does, however, re-appear in the curving, broken lines of the chancel arch, which are reflected even more dynamically in the painting above to express the crescendo of Christmas joy. The decoration of the ceiling above the choir returns to the older scheme of the framed picture. The necessary intensification of effect is secured by the greater use of gold and dark colours and in no small measure also by the seventeenth-century screen.

Compared to the Catholic achievements, Protestant church architecture in Switzerland lagged far behind. Not a single new church was built in Basel at that time. Many Protestants certainly rejected the Baroque as a Roman Catholic product. As a result classicism was adopted early, for example already in the interior of the Heiliggeistkirche in Bern built in 1726–9. In the elongated octagon the mighty entablature is supported by tall Corinthian columns, and the galleries are inserted between the columns. The exterior on the other hand is still Baroque. Generally speaking, the Baroque style was also not adopted for secular architecture; the Zürich Town Hall, built between 1694 and 1698, with its rusticated pilasters on every floor, retains the character of the Renaissance.

The Bavaro-Swabian Baroque libraries [12] reveal a certain measure of independence in as far as, initially, there was no attempt made to follow the Austrian style and place the balconies as close as possible to the walls. The architects made the most of the opportunity to display the scagliola columns; there are thirty-two of them at Wiblingen and as many as forty-four at Ottobeuren. The Ottobeuren library was built in 1721–4, and here it was probably Johann Michael Fischer who insisted on a severer, straighter form for the balconies. Enrichment is restricted to the projecting entablatures of the columns. On the other hand the balcony of the library in the former Benedictine monastery of Wiblingen runs diagonally at the corners and curves outwards on the central axis, giving an impression of great mobility. The painting dates from 1744. In both libraries the light falls in from the two long sides, and there are two doors on each narrow side. In 1739, for the library of St Peter in the Black Forest, Peter Thumb followed the Vorarlberg type using internal buttresses without columns and a balcony undulating round them.

In the Alemannian and Lower Swabian towns of Rastatt, Karlsruhe, and Stuttgart, the political centres of Württemberg and Baden, the commissions were more for palaces than for churches or monasteries – especially as the population was not entirely Catholic. The proximity to France brought an increasing influence from French art; but on the other hand the political and cultural relations with Austria made themselves felt too. Margrave Ludwig Wilhelm of Baden, who had fought victoriously against the Turks and the French on the side of the Austrians, called Domenico Egidio Rossi from the service of Count Hermann Jakob Černín in Bohemia to build his hunting palace at

Rastatt.[13] Begun in 1698, it had an oval staircase, a portico with columns, giant corner pilasters, a flat roof with balustrades, and three raised pavilions, the design following in all this the Italo-Austrian pattern. Only two years later, however, the newly built walls were pulled down, because the margrave had decided to turn Rastatt into a fortress and to include the new building in an extensive system of fortifications as a protection against renewed French invasions. A city was laid out systematically, probably from plans by Rossi, on the slope descending to a bend of the river Murg. The burghers were forced to build their houses according to prescribed models. Three radiating streets cut through the rectangular blocks, the middle one running through the park as far as the *cour d'honneur* of the palace. The horizontality of the long front of the palace is anticipated in the town below in the transversely placed, elongated market-place. The fabric of the palace was completed by 1702, and in 1705, only two years before his death, the margrave and his family moved in.

Rossi, though he retained a basically Italian style, borrowed various elements from Versailles. Thus when developing his plans he transferred the banqueting-hall from a longitudinal position on the main axis to a transverse position on the garden side. Two symmetrical double-flight staircases rise from the vestibule. The dome that the margrave wanted over the staircase was never executed – two curved skylights had to suffice. After her husband's death the Margravine Auguste Sybille appointed Michael Ludwig Rohrer,[14] whose father was a hydraulics expert in her service, to replace the Italian architect. As early as 1705 the margrave had ordered Rohrer's father 'to set his sons to work exclusively in the art of building, most graciously informing him that owing to all kinds of mistakes and intrigues noticed by His Highness the same did not desire to employ foreign architects in the future, but to use his own men'. For the margravine Rohrer built the Hofpfarrkirche on the south side of the lateral wing of the palace (1720–5). It is a structure with internal buttresses. On the narrow sides, by means of an ingenious arrangement of them and of the arches, a three-sided composition is achieved. The choir is raised after the medieval pattern, and two curving flights of stairs connect it with the nave. Later Franz Ignaz Krohmer built the theatre in the northern wing of the palace as a companion piece to the church.[15]

Four years later another important palace was begun, at Ludwigsburg in Württemberg.[16] Duke Eberhard Ludwig chose for his architect a young theologian, Philipp Joseph Jenisch of Marburg (1671–1736), whose architectural studies he had financed. Jenisch began the rectangular *corps de logis*, the so-called Fürstenbau, in 1704, but only the ground floor was actually built, with a vestibule divided into three parts by six columns and set in the Italian manner on the central axis. In 1707 Jenisch was replaced by Johann Friedrich Nette, a better architect. He was a north German and an officer in the engineers in the duke's service. He gave the façade a simple but effective articulation, enlivened by undulating window pediments. The two wings projecting laterally were made into powerful self-contained blocks rising boldly upwards. The central Fürstenbau was flanked on either side by galleries, and one axis of these, facing the court and containing a passage on the ground floor, was used as a communicating link to the laterally projecting wings. This made a very satisfactory arrangement (Plate 107). The galleries lead into two square pavilions, the hunting pavilion on the west, begun before 1714, and the games pavilion on the east, begun in 1715. The decoration, especially in the galleries, with mirrors, statuary, stucco, and painted ceilings, is extremely beautiful. Frederick II of Prussia, then crown prince, stayed with his father at Ludwigsburg when he was eighteen, and it was probably from here that he derived the idea for the galleries in his own palace.

From 1709 Donato Frisoni (1683–1735) had a share in the plasterwork, and he proved so excellent that after Nette's death in 1714 the duke appointed him his successor. The fact that the plasterer, a native of Laino between Lakes Como and Lugano, successfully mastered the difficulties of completing the unfinished work as a unified composition shows the ever-growing importance that was attached to stucco in the Baroque period: as the task of relating ornament to architectural space devolved increasingly on the plasterer, he finally became himself an architect. Moreover the Italians had an innate feeling for the *genius loci*, even in the north. Thus Frisoni hit on the excellent idea of adding a mezzanine floor to the five central bays of the Fürstenbau and a double-curving hipped roof and turret: this not only served to lead to the central block dominating the court, but also added a homely Swabian note. Thus the building as a whole represents the work of a Comacino artist completing an Italianate building designed by two German architects. Frisoni enlarged the court to a length of some 530 feet by the addition of apartments for the courtiers, by adding galleries to the wings, and by closing the narrow side by a southern block, built in 1724–33. In the centre of this the great elliptical marble hall jutted out towards the park in a flat segmental arch articulated by giant pilasters. This part of the palace, too, was under construction during the visit of the Prussian crown prince, and it must have aroused his interest: the memory of it lived on at Sanssouci. As at Rastatt, single buildings, for example the chapel (1715–23), the Ordenskapelle (c. 1725), and the theatre (1724), were attached to the main group.

Frisoni showed a similar skill in the grouping of parts in the small banqueting-house called Favorite, situated opposite the palace and built in 1718 etc. by Paolo Retti from his design. The outside staircase, the low lateral wings, and the higher recessed central block with four pavilion-like corner structures on the roof produce a lively yet finely co-ordinated outline.

Frisoni was also entrusted with the planning of the newly created town of Ludwigsburg. He showed his independence of the Versailles model by not subordinating the town to the palace but developing it alongside, with streets running parallel. The same tolerance appears in the market-place, where the Protestant church occupies the centre of one side and the Catholic church the centre of the other.

In Karlsruhe on the other hand, under Margrave Karl Wilhelm of Baden-Durlach, the idea of absolute monarchy was much more forcibly expressed in the town plan of 1715–19. The military engineer Jakob Friedrich von Betzendorf was the margrave's architect. Thirty-two avenues radiate in all directions from the octagonal tower attached to the palace; to the south they cut across the town, to the north across the forest.[17] The wings of the palace, by projecting obliquely, are likewise incorporated in this radial system. The plan for the remodelling of the palace which was executed between 1749 and 1771 by Albrecht Friedrich von Kesslau was based on a large number of competitive plans – three of them by Balthasar Neumann – but retained the basic idea of thirty years before in all essentials. It can be traced right back to the town-planning ideas of the Italian Renaissance.

Sculpture

Bavaria had provided the impulse behind Swabian painting when Cosmas Damian Asam went to Weingarten, and much the same thing happened in sculpture. In 1706 the Bavarian sculptor Franz Joseph Feuchtmayer of Wessobrunn, a member of a well-known family of stucco-artists, arrived at Salem on Lake Constance where work was available on the reconstruction of the Cistercian monastery, burnt down nine years before. With him he took his ten-year-old son, Joseph Anton Feuchtmayer (1696–1770).[18] They settled in the neighbouring village of Mimmenhausen. Franz Joseph bought a house there and some land on an idyllic island called Killenberg, in the Killenweiher. Years later, in 1727, Joseph Anton was still called 'the plasterer and stucco-artist of Salem'. But although life under the rule of the abbot and the tuition of his rather ordinary father was pleasant enough, he could not have learned more than the rudiments of his profession there: his real teacher, especially in the technique of applying the armature, was undoubtedly Diego Francesco Carlone (1674–1750), with whom he worked at Weingarten in 1718–25.

At Weingarten Feuchtmayer did not only stucco work but also sculpture in stone and wood, in which he soon gained a reputation. In the figures of the angels for the stall backs for the abbey church (1720 ff.), his interest in powerfully projecting forms is already apparent. But he still keeps close to nature. In the Weingarten *Crucifixus* he stresses the realism of the details of the tortured body. The famous *Immaculate Conception* (Berlin Museum) and *Angel playing a Lute* (Karlsruhe, Landesmuseum) – Feuchtmayer's by attribution only – probably belong to this early period and already show a capricious style, the attraction lying as much in the scintillating vitality as in the rich sensuousness. This comes out even more in his stucco works, where the technique of applying the plaster lends a quality of extemporization to his art: in the figures in the abbey church of St Peter in the Black Forest, done in 1724–7, this is obvious in the deeply undercut rounded drapery and almost kneaded-looking shapes of the limbs. It was, however, in the figures of the donors of the house of Zähringen that the artist most successfully exploited the technique, breaking away completely from the traditional statuesque solidity. These figures resemble dressed-up dolls in violently gesticulating attitudes, and their weirdness is enhanced by their monumental setting in front of the pilasters of the nave. Evidently the artist was carried away by a love of startling, inventive masquerade. Such caricatures of donors would not have been possible in the electorate of Bavaria, where popular art was influenced by the style of the court; but in the Swabian monasteries the artist was able to indulge a spirit of mockery more freely. A kind of Mannerism underlies Feuchtmayer's style: it is even apparent when he obviously did not wish to belittle his subject. This is true of the figures of the devout Emperor Henry II and the

Empress Kunigunde at Merdingen im Breisgau (1740–1), where the forms are fantastically distorted and even the greaves have small shields with comic masks.

Painting

The centre of Bavaro-Swabian painting was Augsburg. The character of its people and its status as an ancient imperial city gave Augsburg a character entirely different from that of Munich, capital of the electorate of Bavaria and barely forty miles distant. Like the western Swabians, the people of Augsburg cultivated the long-standing relations with Austria. The remarkable flowering of painting round about 1730 can be traced to two principal factors: first, the position of Augsburg as the centre in Germany for goldsmiths and engravers, and its proximity to such artistically flourishing places as Landsberg and Wessobrunn; and secondly the foundation in 1710 of the municipal academy, with its Catholic and Protestant directors.

The first director was a Protestant, Georg Philipp Rugendas (1666–1742), a painter and engraver who, after visits to Vienna, Venice, and Rome in 1690–5, became the leading painter and engraver of battle scenes in Germany. According to his biographer Füssli,[19] the siege of Augsburg in 1703 gave him the opportunity 'of seeing with his own eyes what until then had been merely an idea in his mind'. He was excellent at portraying horses in movement, and also possessed both the right temperament for making the events of a battle dramatic and the ability to harmonize the action with the setting in a classical landscape, as can be seen for instance in his picture *The Pillage after a Battle* in the Brunswick Gallery, painted before 1737.

In 1730 a suitable Catholic director for the academy was found in Johann Georg Bergmüller (1688–1762).[20] He was a native of upper Alsace, born at Türkheim, and had studied first at Munich and then in Rome under Carlo Maratta. In 1712, at the age of twenty-four, he settled at Augsburg. The ceiling frescoes at Diessen of 1736 and at Steingaden of 1751 are among the best of his many works. Like Johann Baptist Zimmermann, his senior by eight years, he achieved a close relationship between the ceiling fresco and the plaster frame round it. At Diessen the central painting is still framed by a curving balustrade; but at Steingaden the flame-like *rocaille* penetrates the picture. Also, the representations become increasingly realistic. At Diessen the eye is drawn upwards to the solemn procession presenting the charter of endowment to the pope; but it is even more forcibly attracted by a barking dog on the bottom step. At Steingaden stonemasons are shown in the foreground building the church. Bergmüller, with his simple, direct approach to art, remained untouched by academic rhetoric. His solid talent attracted many pupils, among whom Holzer, Göz, Zeiller, Günther, Kuen, and Zick are the best.

Johann Evangelist Holzer (1709–40) of Burgeis in southern Tyrol, a pupil of Bergmüller in 1731, was an artist of unusual freshness and originality. During a creative period of only ten years he produced an *œuvre* of outstanding quality (Plates 108–9). He was certainly the most distinguished artist of the Augsburg circle. Unfortunately the greater part of his work has disappeared – for instance the painted façades of Augsburg houses, of which only studies and later engravings by Johann Esaias Nilson have survived. That these perishable works made a deep impression even on a generation with a different outlook is proved by the letters of S. E. Bianconi describing the most remarkable curiosities of the electoral capital of Munich (Munich and Leipzig, 1771). The Italian admired south German wall-painting: 'This custom of painting houses that are suitable for it *al fresco* is in my opinion very beautiful. You will be convinced that it is so if you take note of the charm and gaiety that it lends to a town. We Italians, especially in Bologna, have given it up, using in its place pure white fronts which we now prefer even on the most miserable huts; these, especially in some of the newly whitewashed lanes, remind me of the whited sepulchres of the gospels. Is it not true that in spring men, like quails and cranes, descend from the Lombard lakes on the whole of Italy armed with terrible brushes and pails full of whitewash and, accompanied by numerous children and apprentices, run around defiling the fairest buildings of our most beautiful regions in a truly barbaric manner? . . .' Holzer aroused his especial admiration: 'Observe in the first place the façades by Holzer, who died young, fifty years ago, and who even at that time accomplished miracles. Among other things note the front of the house of Pföffel, the engraver, on which the story of Castor and Pollux is splendidly painted *al fresco*, in the most elevated taste. Likewise the paintings on the inn called the Bunch of Grapes, which has tall caryatid figures and gods of the boundaries and roads that are in very truth worthy of the Carracci school. On another inn Holzer depicted a life-size dance of peasants, also *al fresco*, which shows the ingenious inventiveness of this artist and what talent he possessed [Plate 109]. I do not believe that human imagination can depict beautiful nature in a more understanding way. Here you can see some dancing peasant women dressed in Swabian attire capering about, kicking up their legs, and they seem truly to be alive and detached from the wall. Some lads are dancing with them, and their faces express in an inimitable way their delight and pride in their inns and the happy thoughts that fill them on such occasions . . . Count Algarotti, assuredly one who could appreciate the fine arts, could not take his eyes away when we were looking at them together one day.'

Whereas Bergmüller never went beyond a generalized conception of the life of the people, Holzer grasped its peculiar character. His peasant boy in St Anton at Partenkirchen, who hangs up his crutch as a votive gift, is a true south Tyrolese boy, just as the praying child has the attitude and expression of a little peasant child from the same countryside. They also show the amazing sculpturesque quality of his figures which, as the Italian observed so correctly, seem to detach themselves from the walls. The explanation lies in the extraordinary virtuosity of Holzer's treatment of light and shade. He never undertook the customary grand tour, but he made the most of the opportunities afforded in Augsburg, the engravers' town, of studying Rembrandt and Wattcau. According to Nagler he did fourteen etchings in the manner of Rembrandt; that he studied Watteau's work is proved by three charming designs for fans in the Karlsruhe Kunsthalle (1734). They are not, however, really characteristic of his style: his dramatic sense was far too strongly developed for him to be content with an idyllic interpretation of the world.

The ceiling fresco in the former summer palace at Eichstätt, an allegory of spring, shows the triumph of the world of light over the world of darkness. Particularly characteristic is the slight yet vigorous curve that flows through the whole composition. The movement is even more turbulent in the oil sketch for the *Fall of Phaeton* (Munich, private collection). The fresco in the dome of St Anton above Partenkirchen, dating from 1739, is painted in powerful chiaroscuro[21] (Plate 108B). A rotunda of columns stands out darkly against a lighter ambulatory. Light and shade play over the figures of the sick seeking health, and the energetic curves of the outlines rival the contrast of lighting. In spite of the academic pathos of conventional attitudes, they are real people like those Holzer had seen in the miracle plays of his Alpine home. The fact that the dome has no lantern is a great advantage; evidently the architect had the frescoes in mind when he designed it, not long before they were painted.

Holzer's monumental art culminated in the ceiling frescoes of 1737–40 for the abbey church at Münsterschwarzach which, as we have seen, was later demolished. Their quality can be judged from the sketches preserved in the Augsburg and Nuremberg museums (Plate 108A). The colours are attuned to a dominant grey, and all the parts, even the framing architecture, are absorbed into the vibrant light encompassing the figure of St Benedict in glory. The saints of the order, individually characterized, are placed as near the edge as possible and, to prevent overcrowding, submerged in darkness that is strongly interwoven with light. As a result the legs, which are so often a disturbing element in such frescoes in vaults, are half-hidden. The oil sketch for the ceiling of the gallery in the Würzburg Residenz (now in the Germanisches Museum in Nuremberg) is also a work of inspired grandeur. Here, with amazing virtuosity, Holzer groups the figures of the Seven Arts, taken direct from life, to harmonize with the strong foreshortening of the gallery. In many respects his art recalls the art of Schönfeld, his predecessor in Augsburg. Had he been granted a longer life, Holzer would certainly have been the equal of Maulbertsch.

CHAPTER 16

BAVARIA

Architecture

AT a time when Baroque art in Austria, Prussia, and Saxony was approaching its climax, Bavaria lagged behind. The blame, if it is to be visited upon anybody, must go to the Elector Max Emanuel, and the disastrous instability of his policy. He had succeeded to the electorate in 1679, at the age of seventeen. As the son-in-law of the emperor he took part, with Prince Eugene, in the successful war against the Turks of 1685–90. In 1691 he was appointed Regent of the Spanish Netherlands, but in 1701, with the outbreak of the War of the Spanish Succession, he switched from the Austrian to the French side. The Bavarians and French were defeated at Blenheim in 1704. Max Emanuel was placed under the ban of the empire and deprived of his electorate (1706). He spent the years of his exile in Paris, and was re-instated only after the Peace of Rastatt (1714), returning to Munich in 1715.

Now, however, during the last ten years of his life (he died in 1726), Max Emanuel was able to indulge his passion for building to the full. In these ten years he spent 7,776,989 florins on his palaces. One result was that the Bavarian national debt rose to more than 30 million. His artistic taste, like his politics, shows a switch from imperial to French loyalties. His mother Adelaide had always loved Italian and French art, and considered her German subjects to be totally lacking in appreciation. We find her son likewise complaining, on his return from exile: 'Je peus imiter le goût de la France en bâtiments et jardins, mais les habitants ne se changent pas.' The conservative character of the Bavarians made them suspicious of foreign innovations, and it was not until the younger generation had been trained in France that the elector succeeded, at the end of his reign, in imposing the Regency style on his country. The architectural revival in Bavaria did not really begin until Max Emanuel's appointment of Effner as architect to the electoral palaces.

That was in 1715. But first we should go back to the beginning of his reign and then trace developments during the troubled interval. At the turn of the century Bavaria was dominated by Italians – the two Grison architects Enrico Zuccalli and Giovanni Antonio Viscardi. They would both probably have been even more influential had they not been on bad terms with one another, a frequent state of affairs among Italian artists in the north. Zuccalli was excessively domineering and also excessively violent when defending his own interests.[1] Though as an artist Viscardi was in every way his equal, Zuccalli always referred to him as a 'mere master mason', and prevented his advancement at court by every means in his power. In most cases the elector, who all his life held Zuccalli in high esteem, supported him. But public sympathy was more on Viscardi's side, which, as we shall see, helped him during the period of Austrian rule.

Before that time, during Max Emanuel's first spell of effective power, most of the work was in Zuccalli's hands: he supervised the beginning of Schleissheim and the decoration of the Residenz (Imperial Suite, 1680–1701; Alexander and Summer Suites, 1680–5). Wherever possible he engaged Italians to work for him, partly because he preferred speaking that language. When the well-known Bavarian sculptor Balthasar Ableithner was replaced by the Tyrolese artist Andreas Faistenberger (a follower of Bernini) there was an outcry from the local chamber of trade, but as usual Zuccalli had his way.

The remodelling of Schleissheim began about 1684, with the approaching marriage of the elector to the emperor's daughter, Maria Antonia. Max Emanuel no longer felt satisfied with the country house built by Maximilian I, and envisaged something far grander based on Versailles, with far-flung wings, extensive park, fountains, and long ornamental canals and lakes. The flat country north of Munich, where Schleissheim lies, was extremely suitable for this treatment. When building was about to begin, Max Emanuel sent Zuccalli to Paris, but he seems to have been less impressed by the French style (although he did adopt the idea of articulating the palace by pavilions) than by Italian Baroque designs, for instance Bernini's plan for the Louvre.

His immediate task at Schleissheim was to build the small banqueting house called Lustheim, in which the desired festive setting could be more rapidly achieved than in the great palace (Plate 110A). Lustheim was to be situated on the middle axis of the garden, and the idea was to approach it by gondola down a wide waterway. In fact, however, only the house itself was completed – between 1684 and 1689. Everything is Italian-style except the French corner-pavilions. The saloon, although it rises through two storeys, is less dominant externally than the two angle pavilions, but a giant order, projecting cornices, a higher roof, and a belvedere restore the required emphasis. Before the balustrades were removed from the roof, the Italian character of the building was yet more pronounced. The frescoes with powerful atlantes by Giovanni Trubiglio lend an Italian Baroque note to the interior.

During the nineties, Zuccalli made numerous designs for the main palace itself. Following Bernini's plan for the Louvre, most of them show a square, with inner courtyard, flanking pavilions, and staircases in the inner angles, though, in accordance with modern ideas on palace architecture, the west wing assumed the shape of a low colonnade closing the court. The wide outer court in front of the colonnade was to be surrounded by enormously long stables in the favourite form of an omega. To begin with, possibly inspired by the contemporaneous plans of Fischer von Erlach, an oval hall was projected as a centrepiece to link two quadrangles.[2] Later, however, the example of country houses built by Daniel Marot in the Spanish Netherlands, for example Ryswyck, was followed, and the east front was extended by one-storeyed galleries terminating in pavilions. Accordingly, of the building with four wings originally planned, Zuccalli built only the long east wing, completing it between 1701 and 1704.

From the battlefields of the War of the Spanish Succession Max Emanuel urged on the building of Schleissheim with the same impatience that was later shown by Frederick II, during the Silesian wars, over the building of Sanssouci. Owing to the excessive haste with which the building was done, part of the arcades of the vestibule collapsed, and further time was lost when the two staircases already completed were pulled down and replaced by one large central one. Of this early plan the giant order of the central pavilion with the high round-headed windows of the piano nobile, the great vestibule with its columns, the lateral position of the staircase, the saloon, and, in part, the arrangement of the rooms were retained or completed later, after 1715.[3] On the other hand Effner did not keep Zuccalli's rather unprepossessing central tower.

Zuccalli was also unlucky in his rebuilding of the palace at Bonn, begun in 1695, for Max Emanuel's brother, the Elector Joseph Clemens, archbishop of Cologne. Here again he was not able to give architectural unity to the monumental building: the lateral pavilions are not powerful enough to articulate the vast monotonous front. In 1702 the allies captured Bonn, and Robert de Cotte undertook its completion (see p. 159).

When the Austrians took over the administration of Bavaria (1704–14), Zuccalli lost his official post, but he still received private commissions. In 1709 he was given the important task of reconstructing the dodecagonal Gothic abbey church of Ettal. Zuccalli designed an oval nave crowned by a dome, and a smaller oval chancel. As in the Kollegienkirche at Salzburg, and later at the abbey church at Weingarten, the undulating façade projected convexly between receding towers (Plate 110B). The towers are set farther apart to harmonize better with the site, i.e. the adjoining monastery and the wide valley between the mountains. The façade was begun in 1711, but the work was greatly hampered by lack of funds, and the chancel and the high altar were consecrated only in 1726. On the death in 1736 of Abbot Placidus Seiz, who had been the heart and soul of the whole undertaking, the two lateral towers were incomplete and the dome not even begun. Finally, a disastrous fire in 1742 made rebuilding necessary. For this Zuccalli's plans were largely retained, though the height of the towers was reduced.

It was a real tragedy that Zuccalli, who never came to appreciate the French style, should have been tied to a prince who admired it so immensely. Where, as in the Porcia Palace in Munich of 1694, he was not forced to adopt the French style and could remain faithful to the architectural language of northern Italy, his genuine talent is clearly revealed, in the expressive sculptural articulation of the façade.

The work of Viscardi was perhaps even more influential than that of Zuccalli, although both are key figures first in the transmission of Italian Baroque to Bavaria and then in the initiation of a specifically *German* baroque. They lead directly to Fischer von Erlach (born 1656) and then to Schlüter and Pöppelmann. Viscardi was born at San Vittore, in the Grisons, in 1647, five years after Zuccalli, and died eleven years before him in 1713. In 1678 he succeeded Kaspar Zuccalli as master-mason to the court, and in 1685 became chief architect. During the next four years, until 1689, he had a hand in most of the important building projects, sometimes employing as many as 150 apprentices. But he was perpetually at loggerheads both with the Bavarian masons' guild and, as we have seen, with Zuccalli, and in 1689 was ousted most unfairly from his court post, to be replaced by a friend of Zuccalli, Giovanni Andreas Trubiglio.

From now on he relied more and more on church designing. In 1692–5 he was architect to the Theatine Fathers, and with the beginning of the new century he was at last able to develop his talents freely and independently. His first important job was given him by Count Franz Xaver Tilly, who commissioned him to build the pilgrimage church of Mariahilf at Freystadt in the Oberpfalz (1700–8). The plan, with a dome and eight arches opening out in the interior, was to have a great future even outside Bavaria (Figure 14). In 1708 it was published in an engraving, and George Bähr used it as a model for his Frauenkirche in Dresden, the outstanding example of Protestant church architecture. Equally outstanding is Viscardi's exterior, built of red sandstone ashlar with a dome of curved outline placed on a low drum, and with four towers (Plate 111); at Rott am Inn in southern Germany Johann Michael Fischer from the Oberpfalz developed this octagonal form into a perfect type of Baroque church. Viscardi's idea of

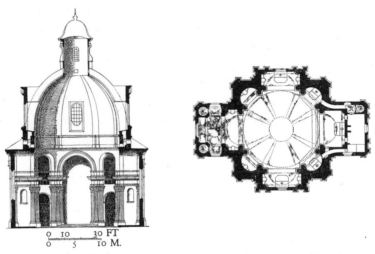

Figure 14. Giovanni Antonio Viscardi: Freystadt, Mariahilfkirche,
1700–8. Section and plan

giving the arches in the main directions and in the diagonals the same height proved to be an innovation of deep significance. Admittedly the diagonals could be made only about half as wide, and contain oratories over niches to counteract the vertical emphasis of the narrow arches. And they had to be considerably stilted to raise them to the required height. But the important feature is that the dome can rest on eight arches, which is most effective. The plasterwork by Francesco Appiani framing the small frescoes by Cosmas Damian Asam gives a rich beauty to the whole interior.

An important contribution to the evolution of the church with internal buttresses was made by Viscardi in the Cistercian church of Fürstenfeld.[4] The foundation stone was laid in 1701, but in 1705 building came to a halt owing to the War of the Spanish Succession. It was completed between 1718 and 1736, except for the façade, which was not erected until 1747. Viscardi's plans were retained in spite of the fact that taste had changed meanwhile. In his efforts to obtain a church with free-standing piers and to discard the basilican plan, Viscardi raised the lateral walls to such an extent that the transverse tunnel-vaults of the galleries above the chapels are almost as high as the crown of the nave vault, and the latter begin to assume the form of saucer domes. The nave is still emphasized by broad piers with pairs of engaged columns and coupled transverse arches, but it opens on all sides in arches and windows, especially as the lower gallery is no more than a passageway between the two tiers of windows. The façade is vigorously articulated by rows of superimposed columns with heavily projecting entablatures.

Zuccalli's rivalry interfered with Viscardi's work for Max Emanuel's palaces. Nevertheless in 1702, when the elector returned to Munich from the Netherlands, Viscardi was entrusted with the enlargement of Nymphenburg, for which Zuccalli had already furnished the plans (Plate 112A). To harmonize with the French idea of detached pavilions as demonstrated at Marly and Bouchefort, he extended the block-shaped casino by two-storeyed galleries leading to lower side pavilions, which have a similar form. Two more pavilions are added in front of these. The northern one contained the chapel. Furthermore it was Viscardi who began to build the saloon, with arched windows on all sides, into the old casino, so as to adapt it as far as possible to Baroque requirements. In 1704, the defeat at Blenheim brought building operations here, as at Schleissheim, to a standstill. Under the imperial administration that followed, Viscardi, it is true, became chief architect and held the job for seven years, from 1706 until his death in 1713; but there was then a dearth of important commissions, and the only ones he received were for the Jesuit assembly hall in Munich, the so-called 'Bürgersaal' (1709–10), and the church of the Holy Trinity (1711–14).

Contemporary Bavarian architects never reached the standard of Zuccalli and Viscardi. They did, however, prepare the way for the great achievements of the following generation.

Wessobrunn in upper Bavaria, the creative centre of the plasterers, was the home of Johann Schmutzer (1642–1701). Both he and his son Joseph Schmutzer were masons to the monasteries in that area, and worked throughout their lives as plasterers and architects. Johann Schmutzer was famous among the Wessobrunn masters during the eighties and nineties for his boldly conceived naturalistic acanthus scrolls and other foliage work, culminating in 1698 in the rich profusion of the ornament for the Schlosskirche at Friedrichshafen. The north Italian plan of a square inscribed in a quatrefoil appears in his pilgrimage church of Vilgertshofen of 1687–92, but in a Bavarian version with tunnel-vaults and no dome. The chancel, narrower than the body of the church, has a two-storeyed ambulatory with windows on the upper floor, an arrangement which foreshadows Zimmermann – who was presumably a pupil of Schmutzer.

In Bavaria as in Franconia it was the generation of Bach and Handel (both born in 1685) who first reaped the harvest. The leading artists were born about 1690: Cosmas Damian Asam in 1686, Effner in 1687, Johann Michael Fischer and Egid Quirin Asam in 1692, Cuvilliés in 1695. The climax thus came rather later than in Austria, Prussia, and Saxony. On the other hand, when it came to introducing the Rococo, the Bavarians under Cuvilliés were about a decade ahead of the Prussians. Max Emanuel still held the centre of the stage. After returning from exile he succeeded in awakening the artistic genius of his people. During the ten years he spent as governor of the Netherlands, from

1691 to 1700, followed by a stay in Brussels in 1704–6 and finally by his ten years exile in France from 1706 to 1715, he had – this has already been said – become increasingly absorbed in French art. Fully realizing the importance of good craftsmanship, he called French artists to Munich and placed them at the head of the newly founded court workshops: blacksmiths, turners, upholsterers, silk embroiderers, goldsmiths, and tapestry weavers. Wood carving and plastering were carried out in four workshops. Even more successful was his idea of employing German artists trained in France and in the Netherlands; for instance he sent Adam Pichler, a wood carver, probably a Tyrolese, to study in Paris from 1709 to 1715, and when he returned Pichler was made director of the court cabinet-making shop in Munich, where at times up to eighty craftsmen and a few sculptors were employed.

Max Emanuel's most outstanding successes were the training in France of Joseph Effner (1687–1745), the son of the Dachau court gardener, and of François Cuvilliés (1695–1768), a dwarf, who belonged in this capacity to Max Emanuel's household.[5] It was in 1706 that Effner, then nineteen years old, was sent to Paris to be trained first as a garden architect and later, after 1708, as an architect in the full sense. Quite evidently he studied under Germain Boffrand. In 1713 the elector appointed him to direct the building of his house at St Cloud, and on his return to Munich in 1715 he made him architect to the court and put him in charge of all work on palaces. This meant in fact that Zuccalli, then seventy-three years old, became redundant. The elector, however, successfully avoided an open break by honouring the older artist in every way.

One of Effner's earliest works in Munich was the rebuilding of Schloss Dachau (1715–17). Here he was already able to carry out the programme later demonstrated at Schleissheim, i.e. multiple rows of superimposed round-arched windows, the centre emphasized by giant pilasters, and a large, well-proportioned, well-lit staircase. At Nymphenburg Effner continued Viscardi's work on the saloon of the main palace (Plate 112A). He was responsible for the great pilasters on the garden front, which co-ordinate the two rows of large round-arched windows, three in each row, for the oval niches for busts, and for the upper windows. Through this co-ordination, the building, which had preserved a Renaissance flavour, acquired a dominant centre in the Baroque sense, and from it the great axis spread east and west leading, as at Schleissheim and following the Versailles pattern, to the long ornamental lake. Even more significant, however, was the interior decoration, which Effner executed entirely in the French Regency style. During the course of the work he showed great talent as an organizer, training the best carvers and plasterers to work from his drawings. The wooden panelling with thin, delicate relief was commissioned from Adam Pichler and his workshop. Most of the stucco was done by Johann Baptist Zimmermann of Wessobrunn, who later worked equally successfully in Cuvilliés's style.

Between 1716 and 1719, following an idea of Max Emanuel, Effner built the Pagodenburg in the Nymphenburg gardens as a small, intimate octagonal building enlarged to a cross-shape, thereby allowing the rooms to flow smoothly into one another. The Chinese fashion is noticeable only in the interior. Immediately afterwards Effner built the Badenburg (1718–21), one of his most successful works. Following his usual custom, he gave the large front room a regular arrangement of semicircular windows with oval ones above, which also break through the rounded corners. Three French windows lead to the wide platform above the front steps. The articulation is restricted to Tuscan pilasters. The bath lies to the right of the two back rooms. Its size, 29 by 20 feet, and height, two storeys with a gallery running round, surpass those of Louis XIV's baths.

In 1718 Effner paid a short visit to Italy, and in the following year he resumed the building of Schleissheim. The plan with four wings was abandoned, and as a result the west front was unusually long (Plate 112B). In order to give its centre the necessary emphasis, Effner added an upper storey over the middle eleven bays. He also altered Zuccalli's elevation (which comprised a distracting variety of forms) and at this point provided three even rows of arches, thus giving the centre of the long front the prominence that it needed. The window-surrounds were modelled on those of Bernini's Palazzo Barberini in Rome, which Effner probably saw on his Italian journey. Unfortunately the pediments over the central bays, which helped to articulate the façade, were removed at the beginning of the nineteenth century.

The approaching marriage of the prince, fixed for 1722, led Effner to concentrate mainly on the interior decoration. In 1720 he engaged Johann Zimmermann, the plasterer, to do the entire stucco work for the main staircase in accordance with drawings and a model. It created a sensation. Starting from the comparatively low vestibule, with its many columns, the triple flight of stairs led like an outside staircase to the saloon. Light pours in from the many windows all the way up to those of the lantern. The stairs at that time were only of wood; they did not receive their marble facing until the nineteenth century. The saloon is lit by the upper row of windows along its two long sides. The stucco decoration here, probably also the work of Zimmermann, was executed about 1723/5. The two vast paintings on the narrow sides of the room are by Joachim Beich to commemorate Max Emanuel's victory over the Turks, and the ceiling fresco is by Amigoni. Stylistically the transition from the staircase to the saloon shows Effner's growing independence of French models. For the ornament, in which he was particularly interested, he adopted the late phase of the French Regency style in the freer version introduced by Oppenord. The plasterwork, which he considered more important than a rigid architectural system, developed into ever richer and more dynamic forms.

He boldly displayed these ideas on decoration, in defiance of French theory, on the actual façade of Count Preysing's palace opposite the Residenz, under the very eyes of Max Emanuel. A comparison with Hildebrandt's Daun-Kinsky Palace in Vienna (Plate 52B), built ten years earlier, shows how ornamental Effner's style had become. Instead of pilaster strips he used ornamental bands, and he reduced the entablature to a minimum. A love of ornament was common to both men – both liked, for example, to use termini pilasters – but their approach was clearly different.

Max Emanuel died in 1726, to be succeeded by Karl Albrecht (1726–45). Effner, at the early age of forty-three, was deprived of his post and replaced by Cuvilliés. Possibly, after fifteen prolific years, he had gone too far and left the taste of the court behind. Two further important commissions were, however, given him shortly before and shortly after Max Emanuel's death in 1726. One was the interior decoration of the Reiche Zimmer in the Munich Residenz, the other the treatment of the semicircle east of the façade of Nymphenburg. Four rooms of the Reiche Zimmer, begun in 1726, survived the fire of 1729; the redecorating of the others was given by the new elector to Cuvilliés. At Nymphenburg, following the French fashion, Effner placed single pavilions along the semicircle. On the central axis, the great fountain in front of the palace was continued by the long canal. This was bordered on both sides by double rows of trees and by roads with small houses and gardens in which artisans and tradesmen lived under court patronage. The 'Karlstadt', as it was called, was planned as a whole little town, but the influx of settlers had ceased by the forties. Effner received no further important commissions, and his last fifteen frustrated years – he died in 1745 – were spent doing administrative work for the court and as superintendent of the gardens.

The flowering of secular architecture was matched in church building too, but with one important difference. Religious art in southern Germany was centred on the monasteries, and they naturally turned for their artistic inspiration not to France but to Italy. It was thus quite a normal thing for the brothers Cosmas Damian and Egid Quirin Asam to be sent in 1711 to Rome instead of to Paris. Their patron was Abbot Quirin Millon of Tegernsee, where their father, the painter Hans Georg Asam, had been working since 1689. It was a Benedictine abbey with great educational and cultural traditions. Two hundred and fifty years before, in conjunction with the theologian, philosopher, and mathematician Nikolaus Cusanus, it had been one of the most eminent champions of a reform within the Church in face of the then threatening schism. Also, as we have already seen in the case of Swabia and Switzerland, the monasteries had remained more closely in touch with the peasantry and bourgeoisie than the court had, and more independent of foreign influences in the arts.

It would, in fact, be a mistake to think of the flowering of court architecture as coming before that in church building. In 1716, the year in which Effner started to build the Pagodenburg, the foundation stone was laid for Cosmas Damian Asam's abbey church at Weltenburg on the Danube. These two buildings, each in its own atmosphere, inaugurated the great period of Bavarian Baroque art. There was a give and take that was highly profitable to both sides: on the one hand the running of the workshops on a French basis, organized by Max Emanuel, raised the quality of the workmanship; and on the other the more popular religious art introduced more Baroque freedom into the rigidly disciplined French style, with its classicist tendencies. Religious art was firmly and permanently rooted in the Bavarian tradition, and academic rules were often ignored – especially in the interest of a vivid interpretation of reality. Painting and sculpture played the chief roles, being the arts closest to nature.

Cosmas Damian Asam was a painter, Egid Quirin a sculptor. That Cosmas Damian chose the caricaturist Pierleone Ghezzi as his teacher in Rome should not surprise us in view of his keen, typically Bavarian sense of humour. His art thrived in the atmosphere of Baroque Rome. In 1713 he won a prize at the Accademia di San Luca. Egid Quirin completed his training under Andreas Faistenberger in Munich in 1716. He was a confirmed bachelor, bought four houses in the Sendlinger Strasse in Munich, and, at his own expense, built the church of St Johannes Nepomuk and a house for the priest adjoining his own house, so that he could live in congenial religious surroundings. Cosmas Damian on the other hand settled with his family outside the city, at Thalkirchen. He painted his house with architectural motifs, religious scenes, and allegories of the three muses favoured by the brothers: Architectura – Scenografia – Decus.

As for architecture, both brothers practised it. Their aim was to build a church interior as close to real life as the scenery on a stage – a scenografia. The decoration – decus – was to reveal all the splendour that an age of decoration could devise. Their work was overwhelmingly successful. No Bavarian court artist achieved anything comparable. The Asams carried their art to Swabia, the Tyrol, the upper Rhineland, Franconia, Bohemia, and Silesia, and it had an immediate and overwhelming impact. Into richly varied compositions they infused a unity that can be felt but not reasoned. Light and colour were exploited to a hitherto unknown degree.

Scarcely had Cosmas Damian completed his first frescoes, in 1714, when he received the commission from Abbot Maurus Bächl of the Benedictine abbey of Weltenburg, west of Regensburg, to rebuild the church on a large scale. The foundation stone was laid in 1718. In 1721 he painted the main ceiling fresco, while Egid Quirin carved the statuary of the high altar. At the same time Patricius II von Heyden, an Augustinian priest of almost seventy, entrusted Egid Quirin with the reconstruction of the near-by monastery church of Rohr, and this was executed in 1717–25. The two most important works inside Weltenburg are spectacular indeed: St George on horseback, appearing out of the depths as on to a stage and illuminated by concealed lighting; and the ceiling fresco, also by Cosmas Damian, which is painted on a flat surface visible through the central oval-shaped opening of the dome below, the edge of which hides the upper circle of windows. At Rohr on the other hand, in the figure of the Virgin carried upward by angels behind the high altar, Egid Quirin tackled the problem of relating a large, apparently freely floating group to the entire interior space of the church. The architecture of both buildings, the elliptical plan with the shallow wall chapels at Weltenburg and the basilican plan at Rohr with its powerful mouldings, shows Roman influence, especially Weltenburg. There is also a recognizable link with Viscardi's Holy Trinity in Munich, the interior of which had been painted by Cosmas Damian immediately before.

The earlier achievements of the brothers were surpassed, however, in St Johannes Nepomuk in Munich, a mature work of 1733–46. Endowed as it was by Egid Quirin, it could bear an entirely personal stamp. The front with its mightily writhing pediment lies between the priest's house and Egid Quirin's house (Plate 113). The plaster decoration playing freely over the surface vies with what is usually reserved to painting, even in subject matter. The theme is a symbol of artistic creation. It is alluded to even in the figure of the Virgin Mary, which bears the inscription 'Pulchra es Maria'. The composition culminates in the representation of Apollo playing the lyre. Then there is a group which at first sight seems to be a guardian angel with a boy, but is really a full-blooded Minerva indicating the angelic choir and the rearing Pegasus above to a youth who follows her eagerly.

In the interior the hand of the sculptor is everywhere apparent – in the rhythmic articulation of the walls, the rounded corners, the perspective foreshortenings, the inserted balcony modelled on those of contemporary libraries, and above all in the way in which everything is attuned to the glorious drama of the figures (Plate 115). It is most regrettable that in the nineteenth century the open space between the twisted columns above the high altar was closed by a wall and a painting. Originally this space had been occupied by a statue of St Johannes Nepomuk, on which the light fell from a room at the back. The highly individual Asam style pervades the entire church down to the last detail, so that later alterations and war damage, especially to the ceiling fresco, have not been able to rob the whole of its magic.

Sculpture

The name of Faistenberger has already been mentioned as the teacher of Egid Quirin Asam. From him in fact came the initial stimulus that led to the whole full development of Bavarian Baroque sculpture – a movement whose peak is Egid Quirin's *Assumption of the Virgin* at Rohr (1718-22; Plate 114) and whose high quality was maintained for half a century until the death of Ignaz Günther in 1775.

Andreas Faistenberger (1647-1736) belonged to a family of artists from Hall, in the Austrian Tyrol, so he was not a Bavarian.[6] In 1674, at the age of twenty-seven, he came to Munich, probably after spending some years as a journeyman in Italy. In 1676 he was appointed sculptor to the Bavarian court. He was extensively employed for the leading works of the time: in 1681-91 he did the pulpits for the Theatinerkirche and the chapel of the Residenz. His *Annunciation* in the Munich Bürgersaal of 1710/11 and his *St Sebastian* from the Frauenkirche, now in the Bavarian National Museum, display his mastery in the modelling of the human form and at the same time reveal the religious fervour typical of the Tyrolese.

From Joseph Emanuel's workshops with their Paris-trained craftsmen came a refining influence. Among the outstanding carvers who worked from the designs of Cuvilliés for Nymphenburg and the Residenz mention must be made of Joachim Dietrich (1690-1753). The majestic figures of the *Fathers of the Church* on the high altar at Diessen are ascribed to him by a doubtful monastic tradition. The framework is by Cuvilliés. Probably the statues are not entirely Dietrich's work. The noble composition suggests Flemish influence, presumably introduced by Cuvilliés.[7] The same can be said of Wilhelm de Groff (c. 1680-1742) of Antwerp, who had been in the service of Louis XIV and was enlisted by Max Emanuel in 1714. His life-like silver statue in the pilgrimage chapel of Altötting of the Electoral Prince Maximilian kneeling before the image of the Virgin is exceedingly naturalistic.[8]

A specifically Bavarian note was first introduced into Munich sculpture by Egid Quirin Asam, whose development has already been described (p. 184). The character of the Asam style, in which sculpture forms an indivisible whole with architecture and painting, even to the character of light and colour, is due to the multiple talents of the two brothers; but nevertheless Cosmas Damian was first and foremost a painter, Egid Quirin a sculptor, mainly in plaster but also in wood. Unity is the aim even of the models of Asam buildings. They show the essential furnishing and architecture together. When the job was the remodelling of an older church, such harmony could only be obtained by a complete transformation in the Baroque sense. The innate consciousness of what it was capable of encouraged the time in these undertakings. On the other hand the Asams revealed a subtle understanding of the medieval attitude to space, for example in the Heiligengeistkirche in Munich (1724–30). The striving for illusion also forms part of the desire for universality. Egid Quirin Asam's sculpture, set in architectural surroundings resembling the stage in the theatre, had to be realistic to the point of deception. The figures emerge from the architectural frame and act their parts freely in space. In *The Assumption of the Virgin* at Rohr (1718–22), the apostles crowd round the open sarcophagus with passionate, excited gestures. The glorious figure of the Virgin, carried by angels, soars above, visible between the altar columns. Even the movement of her arms is imbued with such compelling, expressive force that all logical considerations about sculpture without any visible support are silenced (Plate 114). A Bavarian characteristic which survives down to the present day is expressed here, which shows itself in the talent for religious drama and the art of miming which is an integral part of it.

In addition the art of the Asams has an element of gaiety and a typically upper Bavarian element of wit. At Weltenburg the heroic appearance of St George and the horrified gestures of St Margaret seem a suitable finale for an effective popular play in which an undercurrent of mischief brings a twinkle to the eye of the spectator. If the art of the Asams remains permanently convincing, this is due to a personal stamp directly expressive of the genius of the Bavarian people.

The decoration of the former Premonstratensian abbey church of Osterhofen (c. 1730–5), south of the Danube near Vilshofen, shows the collaboration of the two brothers at its best. As has already been explained, Johann Michael Fischer was in charge of the reconstruction from 1726 onwards. The feeling of continuous swaying movement in the architectural parts is intensified by the plasterwork and culminates in the superstructures of the altars, which are caught up in the powerful general rhythm. Here, too, as on a stage, the figures seem alive and participating in real action. Egid Quirin's most individual work, St Johannes Nepomuk in Munich, which has already been described, immediately followed Osterhofen.

Painting

The development of fresco painting in Bavaria is summed up in the career of Cosmas Damian Asam. His success is the more remarkable since he had no forerunners there – indeed to find one at all we have to go back twenty years to Rottmayr and his work in Schloss Vranov (Frain) in Moravia (1696).[9] Asam continued Rottmayr's style in many ways, but made it softer and more painterly, and more inventive in composition (Plate 116B).[10]

The ceiling fresco at Weingarten (begun in 1718) established his reputation beyond the then Bavarian frontier. The space required to achieve the ideal form of a large uniform fresco, such as Rottmayr had executed above the nave of the Matthiaskirche at Breslau, was not available here; but the large surfaces offered by the saucer domes, introduced by the architects with an eye to painting, offered suitable areas for Asam to develop a sequence of scenes with the required increase of emphasis. He still followed Pozzo in the use of architectural perspectives seen from below, but exploited them fully only in two scenes: the first, the *Vision of St Benedict* in the third bay, is set between four considerably foreshortened piers, giving a view into the dome of heaven which the real dome represents; the second is in the chancel dome, where Asam gives free rein to his sense of humour in the brackets supporting the columns, which project beyond the pendentives and by means of perspective seem enormously large. Anyone looking upward has the terrifying impression that the colossal blocks of stone and the columns will collapse at any moment. In the representation of the *Descent of the Holy Spirit* the figures are completely subordinated to the painted architecture of the dome. The Virgin and the apostles appear in the narrow zone behind the columns of the drum, and it requires the full force of Asam's mastery of gesture to draw the spectators' attention to them at all. In the upper part of the fresco the Holy Spirit appears in the lantern, bathed in light. Tongues of flame shoot out, and on three ledges of cloud the Holy Spirit is represented in action: awakening the dead by two angels blowing trumpets, punishing the damned by arrows of fire, saving the redeemed by angels making music and swaying in a rhythmic dance. In its imaginative power, technical ability, and beauty of form, the work is supreme.

Despite the extensive demands made on the brothers during the seventeen-twenties and thirties, the quality of their work remains outstanding down to the smallest detail. Probably, as his sketches suggest, Cosmas Damian had acquired such skill that he could work without a cartoon. The sketches also show his interest in effects of light and shade, which were heightened by careful lighting of the interior. In this respect Weltenburg is Cosmas Damian's crowning achievement. The flat painted oval dome is illuminated by a row of concealed windows placed behind the lower cove of the inner dome, an arrangement that occurs elsewhere as well.[11] The areas to be covered with fresco and plasterwork were frequently enormous and yet were completed by the Asams in an astonishingly short time, as for instance at Freising Cathedral and the pilgrimage church of Einsiedeln in Switzerland, both of 1723–4; but their inventive power never failed. Often, as in the *Nativity* at Einsiedeln, an atmosphere of intimacy and happiness reigns.

The greater the freedom permitted them, the more the Asams' Bavarian exuberance triumphed; hence Cosmas Damian's secular frescoes at Mannheim (1729–30) and Alteglofsheim (1730) are so outstandingly successful. He recounts the love stories of ancient mythology with inimitable verve. The customary use of architectural motifs as a transition from real architecture to painting is abandoned in the frescoes for the Rittersaal at Mannheim (destroyed by bombs in 1944), and the mythological subjects – *The Marriage of Peleus and Thetis, The Procession of the Gods, The Hunt of Diana*, and a *Bacchanalian Dance* – are all swept together in Elysian ecstasy. Asam drew from two different sources, the Italian tradition of Correggio and Pietro da Cortona and the Flemish of Rubens; Pozzo's mathematical constructions are at last discarded.

The frescoes in the Benedictine church of Kladruby (Kladrau) in Bohemia were completed in 1726. Further cycles were painted for the Benedictines in the saloon of Břevnov

Abbey near Prague in 1731 and, in 1733, in the church of Legnickie Pole (Wahlstadt) in Silesia, more to the north-east. Though Cosmas Damian no longer continued the real architecture in his ceiling frescoes, he did introduce buildings which suited the subject matter: at Legnickie Pole for example he used buildings of Jerusalem as a setting for *The Finding of the True Cross* (Plate 116A), and on the ceiling of St Johannes Nepomuk in Munich he painted Prague Cathedral, in powerful foreshortening. This compromise was then adopted by many others. The frescoes at Osterhofen, painted in 1733, the same year as the beautiful work at Weltenburg, represented St Norbert, the founder of the Premonstratensian Order, as a youth of almost girlish beauty and charm. Perhaps, in this tenderness, we can recognize Cosmas Damian's character. Füssli Senior called him 'a man of impeccable manners, courteous and sociable'.[12]

CHAPTER 17

UPPER SAXONY

Architecture

DURING the critical sixteen-eighties three distinguished artists arrived in Dresden, and there laid the foundations of the outstanding achievements of Saxon architecture in the first half of the eighteenth century. The first of them, Marcus Conrad Dietze, a sculptor and architect and a native of Ulm, settled at Dresden in 1680. Then in 1689, after a long stay in Italy, Balthasar Permoser (cf. p. 201) arrived, and in 1691 Mathaes Daniel Pöppelmann (1662–1736), who was appointed Konducteur (Inspector) in the Landesbauamt (Surveyor's Office). A spirit of optimism had been awakened in Dresden too by the relief of Vienna, in which Johann Georg III, the 'Saxon Mars', had taken part.

Activity began after the great fire of 1685 in Alten-Dresden, when Klengel put forward a project for a monumental rebuilding of this old part of the town, which henceforth became known rather confusingly as the Neustadt. The plan is in the Roman manner, with streets radiating from the bridgehead and a broad avenue as their central axis. The frontages of the houses were deflected towards the Elbe from c. 125 to c. 190 feet, and a guard-post beside the bridgehead was to form the focal point. In this plan, the Italo-German Baroque introduced by Klengel and reinforced by the younger architects triumphed over Starcke's style with its French orientation: the extent to which the two styles differed can be appreciated in a comparison of the Englisches Tor (1682; Plate 117A), done in the Starcke style, with the Grünes Tor (Plate 117B), the upper part of which was designed by Dietze in a robust and vigorous Italo-German manner in 1692–3.[1]

When Augustus the Strong came to the throne in 1694 he appointed Dietze the architect to carry out his own ideas. In 1703, despite the threat to his Polish throne resulting from the victories of Charles XII of Sweden, he was thinking up magnificent projects for the rebuilding of the royal palace at Dresden, and these were realized on paper by Dietze.[2] Schlüter's recent designs for the Berlin Schloss were also consulted. At the same time the king commissioned Permoser to begin work on an equestrian statue to his own majesty. Meanwhile Starcke, who had succeeded Klengel in 1691 as Superintendent, had died (1697), and was in turn succeeded by August Christoph, Count Wackerbarth, who kept the job until 1728. He had been attached to the electoral court since 1685, and under Klengel's supervision had received a thorough training in architecture which included study abroad. Although he never became an architect like Klengel, he is known to have had very good judgement and thereby to have helped the sudden flowering of architectural achievement in Saxony.

The plans for a new residence were designed without at first paying any attention to the old Schloss at its side with its irregular additions. Instead, the new buildings were to develop westwards from the Schlosstrasse, in a system of courts centred on large open squares. The king, who loved an outdoor life, attached great importance to the exteriors, as the German Baroque did in general. Dietze's plan provided for a square forecourt on the east side surrounded by low galleries with arcaded inner passages. In the middle of the four sides were to be magnificent portals. The palace itself was to be joined to it by a smaller outer court, and visitors to be received by a sumptuous staircase of two arms, the flights interrupted by landings. Further courts with adjoining apartments for court celebrations were envisaged, already heralding the future Zwinger; the Zwinger seems foreshadowed too in the horseshoe-shaped orangery planned by the king and his architect to adjoin the palace in the Grosser Garten. The crowning of the central entrance pavilion by trophies recalls the sculptural decoration of Dietze's Grünes Tor, while the rows of statues on the flat roofs in the designs for the palace also reveal the incipient Zwinger style. Unfortunately, in the very next year, 1704, Dietze's promising career was cut short by his death in Poland, when a barn was burnt down. Had he lived, he might well have ranked as a sculptor-architect alongside Bernini, Fischer von Erlach, and Schlüter.

Dietze's successors, Pöppelmann and Permoser, were masters in their arts and worked in most successful collaboration. Although the reverses of the northern wars prevented the realization of the over-ambitious projects then conceived, they are known to us in a series of drawings by Pöppelmann who, though he lacked the dynamic temperament of Dietze, infused them with the harmony and the poise that characterize all his finished buildings.[3] Proportions are taken rigorously into account. The eaves are all at the same level, and the mansard roofs form a happy conclusion to the vertical articulation below. The majestic façades were presumably inspired by Schlüter's plans for Berlin. They have giant vertical openings on the central axes and a regular sequence of courts, more loosely grouped round the far court, which is flanked by wings for the chapel, for the theatre, and for additional rooms, while the central axis is continued in the long riding-school. The proposed towers along the central axis follow the tradition of the old 'Hausmannsturm'. The same sense of continuity dictated the use of the spiral stairs, as they existed in the Renaissance court of the old Schloss. Once again the Zwinger style is foreshadowed in the richer decoration, in the statues on the lower roofs, and in the wide openings between the clusters of columns.

In 1705, a year after Dietze's death, Pöppelmann was appointed Landbaumeister. The commission for the Taschenberg-Palais, built in 1705–15 for the king's mistress Countess Cosel, provided him with the opportunity of designing a larger building in which he could blend Starcke's decorative style – e.g. single, isolated garlands – with a lighter, more supple elevation. According to Marperger, Johann Friedrich Karcher, from 1684 head gardener of the Grosser Garten and known as an architect from his plans for Schloss Weissenfels and Wilhelmshöhe, also had a share in the design; the complicated, rather confused layout of the staircase might be ascribed to him.

At the end of the first decade of the eighteenth century, after Peter the Great's victory at Pultava in 1709, the king's passion for building re-emerged. In 1710, the year of his appointment as 'Geheim Cämmeriere' (Privy Counsellor), Pöppelmann was sent to

Vienna and Rome to study palaces and gardens and to seek expert opinion and advice for the designs of the Dresden Palace. The impressions received during this journey, particularly from Lucas von Hildebrandt's palaces for Friedrich Carl von Schönborn and Carlo Fontana's buildings for the Vatican, are reflected in the Zwinger (Plates 118 and 119A), the only part of the palace that actually went up. It consists of a court built into the walls of a bastion. The arcades and pavilions were to serve as an orangery and a grandstand from which to watch tournaments and similar performances. Pöppelmann called it a 'römische Schauburg' (Roman theatre), and indeed the rectangular shape, enlarged at the far end to the shape of an omega, does resemble an arena. The north-western part was built between 1709 and 1717, and in 1718 the idea was conceived of enlarging the south-eastern half symmetrically by adding an opera house and an assembly-room. In 1719 the building, still in a half finished state, was used for the festivities on the occasion of the marriage of the prince-elector to the emperor's daughter Maria Josefa. Finally, in 1847-9, the north-eastern side was closed by Semper's rather ponderous Picture Gallery.

Semper's original intention had been quite different: he had wanted to follow the old designs and add a second court adjoining the first on the Elbe side, in order to connect the group of buildings with the river. Pöppelmann, in a brilliant plan, had conceived the idea of two series of adjacent courts on the west side.[4] Like the Zwinger itself, they were to have long wings rising to towering pavilions, and to extend yet farther in depth. The bastions were to be turned to aesthetic account by the addition of a richly star-shaped platform surrounded by a moat. On the central transverse axis of the palace a long ornamental canal spanned by five bridges would have served to enliven the scene. The end courts on the west side were to open in arcades. In the centre, the Schlosskirche would have had a dominant position, and its rounded, projecting façade would have been visible from the Elbe. The library, picture-gallery, hall for ball-games, theatre, and assembly-room were to be built at the sides. The block with the festival hall at the end of the great court next to the Zwinger could then be seen from a distance. The carriage ramp, vestibule, and staircase were all of moderate size. Here, too, the architecture was to be a richly dynamic frame for the large, beautifully articulated courts.

The perfection of the Zwinger results from the co-operation of two men of genius and represents a fusion of southern and northern Germany. The man from Salzburg with his inborn sculptural sense and the Westphalian with his feeling for architecture complement one another, and the dynamic vitality of Permoser's mythological figures was kept under control by the restraint of Pöppelmann's architecture. Elongated one-storeyed galleries accentuating the horizontal form the chief motif of the Zwinger; only in the foliage hanging from the capitals and in the swags, shells, and palm-leaves is the abundance heralded which, increasing in the four two-storeyed corner pavilions, culminates in the higher pavilions at the intersection of the two axes. They are carried in lower passages, in the Wallpavillon, up steps, and round fountains to the rampart. The southern gate, the Kronentor (Plate 118), was built in 1713, the Wallpavillon, the climax of the whole composition (Plate 119A), in 1716. The eastern gate was not finished until 1780-4.

For all its rich Baroque quality, Pöppelmann's architecture is never violent or exaggerated in form or movement. In the Wallpavillon the axes taper slightly, and the lower pilasters are replaced by satyr terms. Above them are stone vases behind which rise the upper pilasters. At the critical points of transition sculpture takes over. The use of arches to pierce the entablature, an old-established feature of Baroque architecture, gave Permoser's genius full play. In close co-operation with Pöppelmann, he provided the strongest sculptural accentuation in this zone so that the crowning statue of Hercules carrying the globe was a symbol both of architectural power and of sculptural vitality. It is Permoser's entirely, and bore his signature. The Greek hero was a symbol of the king's physical strength and also of the burden he had assumed as king of Poland and deputy head of the empire. As a further happy thought, the small intimate Nymphenbad was added to the north corner of the Zwinger, and here, too, as in the large court, rippling water was to play everywhere. Finally, colour was essential to give full effect to the Zwinger, and one must try to visualize the vivacity of the clothes worn by the various groups in pageants and tournaments.[5]

The idea of a court surrounded by architecture as by a frame to connect it with space beyond also determined the composition of Schloss Pillnitz on the Elbe (1720–3). The Wasserpalais range, which stretches along the river bank (Plate 120A), was built by Pöppelmann. The universal China fashion, intensified in Augustus the Strong with his collection and his manufactory of porcelain, is reflected in the shapes of the roofs and in the painting of the façades. Unfortunately, owing to the later addition of communicating links, the pavilions are no longer clearly distinguishable. In 1724 Pöppelmann built the Bergpalais as a companion piece to the Wasserpalais, higher up. It closes the elongated court for tournaments and pageants on the side along the hill. Permoser had no part at Pillnitz, and one senses his absence. Eleven years older than Pöppelmann, he had matured under the influence of the Italian Baroque which he revived so successfully in the Zwinger. Pöppelmann loved Baroque exuberance too, but the difference lies in his need for moderation, for a harmonious balance in the French sense.

In 1723, immediately after the completion of Pillnitz, Moritzburg was begun. The old Renaissance hunting-lodge, built in 1542–6 as a rectangle flanked by four round towers, was now remodelled in the Baroque style. The outer walls were pulled down, but the round towers were retained and their height increased, while the transverse axis was developed, including the old palace. Klengel had already taken this course when he added the chapel on the west side; now a festival hall was added on the east side as a companion piece. The demolition of the old outer walls enabled the once closed building to be opened on the south and north sides by forecourts. Pöppelmann was responsible for the basic idea of the remodelling but Longuelune directed the job, and he enlarged the four main rooms.

A third monumental task was the extension of the Holländisches Palais (renamed Japanisches Palais) on the Neustadt side of the city. In connexion with the rebuilding of this part of the town, which was given the name Neue Königstadt, Augustus the Strong had a new axial street laid out leading northward to the Schwarzen Tor. The arrangement of the palace as a building with four ranges round an inner court was a favourite idea of the king; it occurs often in his designs, generally in connexion with a central building. Once again Pöppelmann was chiefly responsible for the construction, his superior from 1728 being Jean de Bodt. The latter, as Wackerbarth's successor, had been appointed Superintendent of all civil and military buildings, and had completed the Arsenal in Berlin and the Stadtschloss in Potsdam. Presumably the details of the Japanisches Palais were due to his influence, though his chief contribution was certainly the classicism of the central pavilion to the north. The rest of the front with its pilaster strips was probably designed by Longuelune and the undulating roofs by Pöppelmann.[6] The original purpose of the building as a 'trianon de porcelaine' can still be seen in the Japanese termini in the courtyard, and indeed the decoration of the whole interior was to be of porcelain, the intention of the king being no doubt spectacular propaganda for the Meissen factory, the first western establishment where porcelain was produced.

The Augustus Bridge, rebuilt by Pöppelmann in 1728, also made an effective contribution to the river front. The king, who had a flair for picking the best models, began by ascertaining the exact measurements of the Karlsbrücke in Prague. Like its model, the bridge across the Elbe was to be enlivened by statues on the breakwaters; according to an engraving by M. Bodenehr, done in 1733, they were to represent Saxon princes belonging to both the Ernestine and Albertine lines. Pöppelmann widened the bridge by providing pavements for pedestrians, the paving stones resting on pairs of superimposed projecting stone corbels. The tops of the breakwaters were raised to allow small platforms to be constructed above them. The bridge rose vigorously towards the centre, where a crucifix was set up; otherwise the decoration was confined to ornamental lanterns above each arch.

From 1715 onwards Zacharias Longuelune (1669–1748) was associated with Pöppelmann. Probably born in Paris, he had first worked in Berlin. He was a painter-architect, and his influence lay less in his buildings than in his numerous beautifully drawn designs, which embodied French classicist theory. On the other hand his genuine feeling for Baroque sculpture was quite in keeping with the development in Dresden, though he moderated the character of his façades in accordance with the principle of noble *simplicité*. Of an unassuming disposition, he nevertheless affected the architecture of Saxony more than would appear at first sight. As a teacher he laid considerable emphasis on the principles of architectural articulation.

Longuelune's numerous plans for an extension of Pillnitz were never executed. Similar designs followed for the palace of Gross-Sedlitz, where he worked together with Pöppelmann and Knöffel. The king's favourite plan, a building with four wings and a domed central hall, appears over and over again in his sketches; also in his plans for Pillnitz, for a new arsenal, and for Schloss Ujazdov in Warsaw. The great scheme for the garden of Gross-Sedlitz was probably designed at the king's suggestion in 1726.[7] The obtuse angle of the transverse axis is replaced by a symmetrical arrangement with a central axis on which were cascades and two U-shaped parterres. Its particular beauty lay in the initial downward slope of the garden and subsequent rise on the opposite side. This made it easy to grasp the composition of the whole. A number of sketches for fountains by Longuelune show that, where no strictly architectural principles were involved, he tended to develop the Baroque towards an all too dominant naturalism.

His work reached its peak in 1731 in his plans for the termination of the Hauptstrasse in the Dresden Neustadt towards the Elbe. From the Baroque point of view, which is to let *points-de-vue* appear one after the other, the fact that the bridge was not in line with the Hauptstrasse was an advantage. Adjoining the bridgehead Longuelune built the 'Blockhaus' (guard-post) as one *point-de-vue*. In his drawings he crowned this either with an equestrian statue of the king or with an obelisk – a very successful idea. He also designed a companion piece to flank the bridge symmetrically on the opposite side, but this was never executed. Unfortunately the addition of two floors with living quarters in place of the pyramid with the crowning statue, which was not executed, robbed the 'Blockhaus' of its monumental character.

The porcelain decoration of the Japanisches Palais gave Longuelune the opportunity to display his decorative talents. The addition to the palace, begun in 1729, served primarily to exhibit the china. It followed a system as carefully worked out intellectually as visually.

The influence of the Saxon Baroque was felt not only in Poland but also in Denmark. Nils Eigtved (1701–54), the most important Danish architect of his day, had joined the Saxon Engineers under Mathaes Pöppelmann in 1725. Presumably he had a share in the planning of the Saxon Palace. In addition to the works of Pöppelmann he must have been influenced by those of Longuelune and de Bodt; for his four palaces facing the square in front of the Amalienborg in Copenhagen reproduce the façade of the Japanisches Palais. The execution too of this fine octagonal square reflects Saxon training in the rhythmical alternation of palaces and pavilions with connecting links. Eigtved remained in Saxon service for eight years.

How deep the impression was which Longuelune's quiet activities had made is proved by the work of Johann Christoph Knöffel (1686–1752). The Wackerbarth Palace of 1723–8, which served the purpose of an academy for noblemen, and the Kurländer Palais of 1728–9 are both masterpieces of restrained pilastered architecture (Plate 177A). Scarcely a decade had elapsed since the Zwinger had received its elaborate sculptural decoration, and already the French school represented by Longuelune and de Bodt was beginning to triumph. The ornamentation of the buildings was limited to pilaster strips and a few areas in the centre. Unfortunately both buildings were destroyed in 1945 when Dresden was bombed. After Wackerbarth's death in 1734 – Augustus the Strong had died in the preceding year – Knöffel entered the service of Heinrich Count Brühl, who was soon to control – not to its advantage – the destinies of Saxony. In 1737 Knöffel began to build Brühl's palace in the Augustus-Strasse. Longuelune's influence can be seen in the plan, and it had indeed been Longuelune who furnished the first design. This provided for a simple articulation with pilaster strips. Knöffel adhered to this, and allowed a pediment only over the central projection. A limited addition of architectural sculpture and grilles produced a warmer, more decorative effect, however. The large festival hall in the interior was the most brilliant example of the Dresden Rococo as Knöffel developed it around 1740. When the palace was pulled down in 1899 the hall was transferred to the Kunstgewerbemuseum, and it was destroyed therein 1945.

The development of middle-class building was in no way stifled by the brilliant production for the court: on the contrary, it roused a competitive spirit, as was made explicitly clear by the town council when the Frauenkirche was built. The pietist views of a man like Philipp Jakob Spener, who was Chaplain to the Court in Dresden from 1686 to 1691, were not held by many. Spener condemned both the life at the court of Augustus the Strong and all ostentation in church architecture – 'the money spent on it would be better used to help the poor'; but in the country which has been called the cradle of the Reformation, where Bach and Handel were both born in the same year, 1685, it was no longer possible to repress the genuine desire to uplift the heart by giving artistic expression to the divine. From 1690 to 1694 Leonhard Christoph Sturm made a close study of the writings of Nikolaus Goldmann in an attempt to understand the problems of Protestant church architecture. Some years previously, in 1684–8, the joiner Hans Georg Roth had built a small square central church with chamfered corners on the heights of the Erzgebirge at Carlsfeld (Plate 120B). It was allegedly taken from an Italian design. The curved roof with its crowning tower and the galleries in the interior, which leave the windows free, are an expression of the flourishing carpentry in the rich timber area.

The same forms recur forty years later on the most monumental scale in the Frauenkirche. The architect, George Bähr, was born in 1666 at Fürstenwalde near Lauenstein in the Erzgebirge. Like Roth, he rose from the ranks of the artisans. Even as a journeyman he had shown a desire to improve his mind: when in 1705 he was nominated Ratszimmermeister (master carpenter to the city) in Dresden, the records mention that he had learnt carpentry, had worked as a journeyman for several years, and had then turned his attention quite successfully to various branches of mechanics. His general interest in many arts was noted, and the fact that he had invented a camera obscura and a mechanical organ. He called himself an artist – later an architect – and disliked being treated by the council as a master carpenter.

The basis of Bähr's early plans was the Greek cross, which was popular on account of its symbolism. He used it in two churches in the Erzgebirge, one at Schmiedeberg (1713–16), the other at Forchheim (1719–26), as well as in his first project for the Dresden Frauenkirche. By shortening the arms and arranging the galleries octagonally he met an objection raised in his books by Sturm, i.e. he avoided confusion and cut costs. The Erzgebirge churches with their tower-capped roofs display a closed silhouette that seems to reflect their mountain setting. Much earlier, between 1705 and 1708, Bähr had designed the parish church of Loschwitz as an elongated octagon to harmonize with the narrow terrace above the road to Pillnitz, with the many wealthy country houses strung along it. The nave of the church of Hohnstein, which was begun the year before the foundation stone of the Frauenkirche was laid, has a rectangular plan with chamfered corners and is joined to a relatively long chancel which is crowned by a tower. The foundation walls of its Gothic predecessor were retained, which meant that a medieval arrangement was re-asserted; this was also done in the Frauenkirche, where there was no necessity for it.

The plans for the Frauenkirche, which were begun as early as 1722, passed through many stages – to its final advantage. It was commissioned by the civic authorities, who wished to have a building 'that could vie with those of the king', whereas the church authorities considered the expense too great. During an inspection Valentin Ernst Löscher, the rector of the Kreuzkirche, declared that the size and the splendour displeased him. On the other hand the king was quite willing to give financial support in spite of the fact that, in 1725, Wackerbarth insisted that a competitive plan be submitted by Knöffel. This plan was not accepted in its entirety, but certain valuable suggestions it offered caused Bähr to revise and improve his own design.

The initial plan, a Greek cross with octagonal galleries, had already provided for eight arches in regular sequence, following the pattern of Viscardi's pilgrimage church of Freystadt which was begun in 1700.[8] Furthermore the dome rested on a concave base, which gave an undulating rhythm to the outline; but the idea of setting a Baroque belfry over the chancel was an unfortunate one. Knöffel's plan led Bähr to choose a square ground plan and a circular arrangement of the piers, to do away with the belfry, and to introduce angle turrets. Knöffel had suggested two flanking ones for the west façade; at the important conference held on 18 March 1726, at which Wackerbarth presided, the number was increased to four in order to flank the dome on all sides. Bähr set them diagonally as stair-towers, thus obtaining the square shape with obtuse angles which was wanted, and the transition to the circular dome, originally stepped back twice, was now achieved in one concave curve. This made the building more homogeneous, inside and out. Wackerbarth's other objection – that the dome was too flat – was also accepted and led ultimately to the outstanding success of the final solution: for Bähr increased the height and pitch of the dome and of the turrets and so achieved a unique and mighty upsurge (Plate 121A). The larger windows, not obstructed by small oratories, which he had been asked to use were also a success. Bähr furthermore raised the choir so that it had to be entered by two curved flights of steps, thus following the arrangement of the Roman Catholic Schlosspfarrkirche at Rastatt built shortly before. From Rastatt he also derived the idea of a termination in three arches. At first the pulpit was placed in the centre of the chancel balustrade; but this concentration of pulpit, font, and altar along the middle axis was later abandoned, and the main pulpit was placed in front of the left-hand pier.

By 1726 preparations were sufficiently advanced for the foundation stone to be laid, and by 1729 the walls had reached the height of the main cornice. Bähr insisted on using stone as his building material; statically speaking a wooden dome would have been the right thing, but the desire for the exterior to look of stone won the day. Wood was prominent in the interior, however, owing to the variety of elaborately curved galleries (Plate 121B). These were no longer obstructive and gloomy, as at Jelenia Góra and Waltershausen, but clearly defined architectural members, receding at the main windows and at the entrance to the choir.[9] The same basic S-form that dominated the exterior silhouette of the dome also dominated the contour of the galleries. The eight slender supporting piers stood out freely. Following Balthasar Neumann's churches in Franconia, the interior was to have an openwork appearance; but Bähr went beyond what could be risked – as a result of which intensive protective measures became necessary during the twentieth century.[10]

The growing importance of church music at the time of Bach was in itself a sufficient reason for arranging the interior along the lines of a theatre, with the organ, not the pulpit, as the dominant feature. The organ was built by the famous Gottfried Silbermann in 1732–6 and placed above the mighty superstructure of the altar. The deep and lofty choir was eminently suitable to house it. Singing tribunes were built on either side of the altar superstructure, and on high feast days, when there was a very full choir, the members could spread round the great circular opening of the inner dome, which came down very low. The dome itself consisted of an inner and an outer shell with a ramp rising in a spiral between.

When Bähr died in 1738 the church was standing as far as the top of the dome, but the not unfounded suspicions as to the stability of the piers caused considerable delay before it was finally completed. The large and dominant lantern was erected in 1740–3 from Bähr's plan by his cousin and successor Johann Georg Schmidt.

The Frauenkirche was the culmination of Protestant church architecture in Germany. The starting-point had been the Katharinakyrka in Stockholm;[11] the Gnadenkirche at Jelenia Góra (Hirschberg), with its drumless dome rising out of the undulating roof between four stair-turrets, was a further step towards it. The preliminary stages in central Germany had been the churches at Carlsfeld and Waltershausen in Thuringia. They have in common with the Frauenkirche an octagonal plan and an undulating roof crowned with a turret. At Waltershausen (1718–23) an oval gallery runs round the interior.[12] Baldassare Longhena's church of S. Maria della Salute in Venice (1630–56), with its octagonal plan and volutes forming the transition to the circular dome, must have been the southern prototype. In a rather later building, the Radcliffe Camera at Oxford (1739–49), a vast circular dome with coupled columns and an unbroken main cornice rises from a similar octagonal base. Concave buttresses lead up to the dome. The architect, James Gibbs, stressed the articulation of this splendid building in the spirit of antique columnar architecture, whereas the Frauenkirche seems the outcome of organic growth. Bähr was not interested in the individual parts as such; what he wanted was to extract the maximum effect from the mass and upward thrust of the building as a whole, with the dome as the dominant feature. For that reason the Frauenkirche was of the greatest significance for the skyline of Dresden, and its loss is all the more terrible (Plate 119B).

The laying out of the Hauptstrasse in the Neustadt gave rise to a second important task in the field of church architecture. The provisional building erected after the destruction of the Gothic Dreikönigskirche was in the way, and it was pulled down in 1731. For the new church, inserted into the west side of the Hauptstrasse, Pöppelmann had planned a hall church with lateral galleries and groin-vaults. It was built between 1732 and 1739, but unfortunately the tower was not placed on the Hauptstrasse side, as the king had wanted. After the death of Augustus the Strong in 1733 Bähr was entrusted with the supervision of the building. Characteristically enough he widened the interior by placing the central three piers on either side farther back towards the wall, so that an almost oval nave resulted, with a trough-shaped vault. This shape and the absence of a separate chancel were of decisive importance for the Catholic Hofkirche and for the Kreuzkirche.

The Hofkirche is the most important building in Dresden after the Frauenkirche; in 1738, when the Baroque was almost at an end, the Hofkirche successfully revived it in Dresden, thanks to its Roman architect Gaetano Chiaveri (1689–1770).[13] Chiaveri had taken part in the construction of St Petersburg from 1717 to 1727, and so had gained experience of the particular problems involved in building on the banks of a river. In Dresden his task was to give a characteristic expression of the Roman Catholic faith to rival the Frauenkirche. The driving mind which evolved the bold idea of erecting such a mighty Roman Catholic church in the heart of a Protestant country was really Queen Maria Josefa's. She was the daughter of the Empress Anna Amalie, who had been converted to Roman Catholicism when she was still princess of Brunswick. The queen of Saxony followed in the footsteps of her pious mother. She found full support in the person of Pater Ignaz Guarini, the king's adviser, who, unlike the over-subtle diplomat Count Brühl, was appreciated at both the Vienna and the Berlin courts: Frederick II sent greetings 'to the Jesuit who would be a charming man if he were not a churchman and who possesses enough qualities to make him a heathen like ourselves'.

The plans show the Italian's sensitive understanding of the character of a particular landscape – it is interesting that at the precise moment that Chiaveri was beginning the building Bernardo Belotto, called Canaletto, was doing his beautiful views of Dresden, which for sheer artistic quality had no precedent (p. 288). Chiaveri chose an excellent position for his church, setting it diagonally to the bridge and to the Schloss, approximately on the transverse axis of the Zwinger and the projected buildings for the palace. Not only did he take advantage of the bend in the river, but also he placed his tower at the correct distance from the tower of the Schloss as a *point-de-vue* for the Schlosstrasse. Since it stood at the intersection of many axes, the tower had to be as transparent as possible, a feature that had in any case been popular since Bernini had designed the campanili for St Peter's in Rome. Chiaveri's work in St Petersburg and Warsaw had familiarized him with the northern tradition of a single west tower, and he used it for his otherwise Roman plan for the Dresden church, which foresaw a basilica with the east and west ends rounded off in the then customary manner. An ambulatory for processions was carried right round the nave with a high gallery above for members of the court, modelled on the palace chapel at Versailles. On the outside Chiaveri added a ring of chapels. Typically Roman is the treatment of the exterior with numerous projections and recessions that give a delightful play of light and shade. The roofs are kept flat to allow Lorenzo Mattielli's agitated statues of saints, standing on the top balustrade, to be fully effective. The mighty dome of the Frauenkirche symbolized the Lutheran faith, in which human merit is not recognized, but only the grace of God; the Catholic Hofkirche on the other hand, with its numerous altars and statues, conveyed the idea of the communion of saints.

The Hofkirche had been planned as part of great schemes for a new palace – as we can see from the series of designs by Chiaveri – and had finally emerged as an independent building. On the plan he drew up immediately after his arrival in Dresden, around 1737, the future site of the Hofkirche is already determined, but the church remains integrated in the palace. The gallery which was to house the king's collections is very advanced for its time. The subsequent plans follow the Roman ideal and detach the palace from the church, making it a mighty, independent block which was to continue the Zwinger along the Elbe front.

The buildings in Dresden became the prototypes for the whole of upper Saxony, although the country had also contributed to the formation of the Zwinger style. The Dresden influence can be seen in the work of Johann Georg Fuchs (1650–1715), master mason to the city of Leipzig, in the house he built for the ambitious Mayor Franz Conrad Romanus (1701–4). In Leipzig this was the signal for a change from individual architectural ornaments derived from Holland to sculptural forms penetrating the entire body of the building. The Baroque flung aside all restraint; it grew softer, more personal, but also less harmonious. Bay windows and courts crossed by carriageways became characteristic for the town. The style culminated in Fuchs's Ackerleins Hof, 11 Markt (1708–19), in which the type of the many-storeyed block of flats is already fully developed.

Like Fuchs, David Schatz (1667–1750) was called to Leipzig from Dresden. Schloss Burgscheidungen on the Unstrut, built in 1724–32, is his most important work, showing the manner in which the Zwinger style worked itself out.

The extent to which the artistic efflorescence in Saxony was indebted to the enlightened patronage of the king is clearly revealed by comparison with neighbouring Thuringia. Thuringia was ruled by the unpredictable Duke Ernest August I of Saxe-Weimar, who had little understanding of the arts. Moreover his capable Surveyor General, Gottfried Heinrich Krohne (1703–56), was unable, in his many plans and false starts of buildings, to express the lively, decorative, and personal style developed in his youth in Dresden and during a visit to Vienna in 1726. The only exception is the Dornburg, which Goethe called 'super-lovely'. Situated on a steep cliff above the river Saale, this beautifully modulated yet powerfully compact block rises on a rectangular plan pierced by the arms of a cross.

Sculpture

The flowering of Saxon sculpture in the eighteenth century was not brought about by Permoser alone. The way had been paved by numerous native artists, among them George Heermann (c. 1645–1700), court sculptor at Dresden. Thirty years before, he had reached a stage preceding the Zwinger statues with his giants on the staircase outside Troja, near Prague (1685).[14] His figures are indeed too heavy, especially in the drapery folds, but the step towards greater organic unity had nevertheless been taken. Other excellent artists at this time were the brothers Jeremias (1653–90) and Conrad Max Süssner,[15] who also were court sculptors at Dresden. Jeremias, like George Heermann, worked on the figures in the palace in the Grosser Garten. The Süssners also made the statues in sv. Frantisek in Prague (1689–90). Jeremias was a classicist, the presumably younger Conrad a genuine Baroque master, superior to his brother in his lifelike modelling.

However, notwithstanding the available competent men, Johann Georg III, victor over the Turks, did well in 1689 to enlist an artist who surpassed them all, Balthasar Permoser (1651–1732) from Salzburg, at that time in Florence. He remained in Dresden for forty-three years and was responsible not only for the Zwinger sculpture (Plate 123A) but also for the training of numerous pupils and collaborators.[16] His outstanding skill, acquired during fourteen years' activity in Italy, and his strong, typically Bavarian character made him the dominant figure in Dresden in the field of sculpture during the great first third of the eighteenth century – to the exclusion of any other independent sculptor.

In a competition between Permoser and two French sculptors for the figure of a young woman, no decision could be reached; but in a second round it was won by Permoser for his figure of an old woman. For the extensive teamwork on the Zwinger his collaborators obviously subordinated themselves to his superior genius, so that it is difficult to distinguish between the various hands. Permoser attracted many pupils to Dresden. After the *Apotheosis of Prince Eugene* in Vienna was finished, Joseph Winterhalter and Donner, who were deeply impressed by Permoser's technique, went to Dresden to study under him.

Permoser derived his painterly conception of sculpture, and his virtuosity in the rendering of light and shade and the texture of materials, from Bernini. He was less extreme than Bernini in that he never sought to startle by effects such as the sheen of silk, but, like Bernini, he endeavoured to replace the hard and isolating quality of sculpture by the softness and continuity of painting (Plate 123A). He gave a symbolic interpretation of the ultimate aim of his art in a group – unfortunately long since destroyed – for the Grosser Garten in Dresden: it represented Painting embracing Sculpture, and he also added his own portrait. Winterhalter said of him: 'No one could rival him in his understanding of the principle that a good painter must also be versed in sculpture, and a good sculptor in painting.'

Permoser, as has just been observed, was less interested in reproducing in stone the particular characteristics of any given matter than in extracting painterly effects from the material itself. He did this mainly through the use of coloured marble from the quarries of his native Salzburg, a town to which he continued to pay regular visits. His *Scourging of Christ* for Moritzburg and the Hofkirche in Dresden are outstanding examples of this technique, as is also the head of one of the damned in the Leipzig Museum (Plate 122). The grey, white, and flaming red graining of the marble in the latter work gives a gruesome intensity to the man's expression of screaming agony.

The deliberate posing in the sculpture of his Italian period disappeared completely in Dresden, where the prevailing atmosphere seems to have favoured the free unfolding of Permoser's individual manner. Not that there were no critics in the name of classicism: but during the first third of the eighteenth century they were unable to exert any influence. Furthermore, the king was far too much of a connoisseur not to recognize Permoser's value. He expressed what he felt about the personality of his royal patron with particular force in two *Apotheoses*, which perished in 1945. The only remaining monument immortalizing the king is the equestrian statue of copper in the Hauptstrasse of the Dresden Neustadt, made by Ludwig Wiedemann in 1733 from a model by an unknown artist. Its dramatic, victorious gesture embodies the spirit of this great patron of the arts.

Permoser died in 1732, a year before his royal patron. He was an eccentric and a man of strong views – for example he referred habitually to marriage, anger, and strong drink as the three-headed murderer of human life – and as an eccentric was certainly a misfit at the volatile court of Augustus the Strong. Moreover it seems a pity that, court life being what it was, the bulk of the commissions he received was either for satyrs and nymphs to gratify the delight in all kinds of masquerade or else for official pieces to enhance royal prestige. But his *St Augustine* (Plate 123B) and *St Ambrose* show how eminently fitted he was to interpret qualities of the spirit. In these statues he revived the medieval Alpine tradition of carving, as did at the same time his contemporary Guggenbichler. On the other hand his particular, somewhat coarse Bavarian humour found an outlet in the bucolic world he had to represent. As a matter of fact he was out of sympathy with his own oppressed age, as he called it. He never even considered adapting his way of life to the court manners of this age of the late years of Louis XIV; on the contrary, he provoked ridicule, for instance by going about with a beard, a leather jerkin, a dagger, and a red coat, like some figure from the heroic age of the seventeenth century. He also despised the fashion of carrying a cane. Whereas most court artists liked to keep their own carriages, Permoser as a young man had gone on foot from Salzburg to Rome. Nor did he permit himself the luxury of a country house, the dream of so many artists; but with his savings he founded a school in Otting, the village next to his own – probably because he knew from experience what was most needed at that time for a talented village boy.

Two artists come close to Permoser through their documented work at the Zwinger: Johann Christian Kirchner (1691-1732) and Benjamin Thomae (1682-1751). Kirchner's qualities can be recognized in his Rococo-like statues in the castle and park of Joachimstein, which are effective, though somewhat theatrical (1728),[17] and those of Thomae in his rather heavier figures in Dresden churches. They already verge on classicism.

Contact with the Heermann family of sculptors was brought about primarily by Paul Heermann, who also participated in the work on the sculpture of the Zwinger.[18] His greatest achievement arose from his collaboration on the staircase outside Troja (1705), the altar of the parish church of Lommatzsch (1714), and the model for the equestrian statue of Augustus the Strong. His was not the equal of Permoser's fiery temperament, which is obvious especially in the rendering of the horse. However, occasionally he was stimulated by the task allotted to him, as in the head of the king, which shows considerable verve.

The powerful influence of Permoser persisted even after his death in 1732, and is particularly striking in the field of porcelain, the new material that played such a considerable part in forming the style of the eighteenth century. After many futile attempts in Italy, France, and England, Johann Friedrich Böttger (1682-1719) was finally successful, at the beginning of the eighteenth century, in producing the true porcelain that had been known in China a thousand years earlier. He had a predecessor in the person of Ehrenfried Walther von Tschirnhausen, a mathematician and physicist working in Saxony, as did Böttger. Tschirnhausen, according to the principles of Mercantilism, searched the country for precious stones and set up mills for grinding and polishing them. He also founded three glass works and made experiments to improve the dye-works, producing the blue dye which was of such importance for ceramics. He used large burning-glasses to smelt the various materials and claimed that he had produced porcelain – though this cannot be substantiated. However that may be, the credit for stimulating the discovery of porcelain must go to him.

Böttger, as an apprentice to an apothecary in Berlin, had attracted the attention first of the Prussian and then of the Saxon king by his known alchemistic searches for the philosopher's stone and by rumours that he had in fact succeeded in making gold. Augustus the Strong ordered him to be brought to Dresden under military escort in 1701 and established him there in a laboratory under the solid vaults of the Lusthaus, on the Jungfern-Bastei. As a result of his collaboration with Tschirnhausen, Böttger's interest was deflected from his futile alchemy and focused on the study of various materials, particularly coloured earths, with an eye to their industrial exploitation; and at last, in 1709, after years of research, Böttger succeeded in producing porcelain. As a result, he was able to put red stone into production, and by 1713 white porcelain equal in quality to the Chinese. At first objects were being made in red earthenware that were later to become typical porcelain products – for instance tea-, coffee-, and dinner-services, toilet-sets, apothecary's jars, vases, epergnes of various kinds, heads and figures, reliefs, crucifixes, etc. Grinding and glazing improved the quality, and decoration in shallow relief was applied. To prevent competition the greatest care was taken to keep the process secret. To begin with, the goods were sold at the Leipzig Fair, which was held three times a year. Success, which was slow in coming, was due to the support given to the brilliant inventor by the king, who helped the factory in every possible way.

Böttger's earthenware, which obtains its colour from the iron content in the minerals used, has powerful sharp-edged outlines and often resembles turned wood or metal. The forms were either based on Chinese and Japanese porcelain or designed by the goldsmith Johann Jakob Irminger, with increasing understanding for natural ceramic shapes. It was not, however, until the production of porcelain was begun in the factory – which incidentally was (and is) at Meissen, not in Dresden – and after a kaolin deposit had been discovered at Aue near Schneeberg that the way was open to world-wide success.

In view of the king's particular liking for Chinese underglaze blue and of the wealth of cobalt ores in Saxony, great efforts were directed towards the production of blue and white ware. This, however, was not achieved until 1719, i.e. after Böttger's death. Nor was Böttger successful in producing pure white porcelain: his always had a warm yellowish tone. To begin with the forms developed for red earthenware were adopted, although porcelain in itself is not as suitable as earthenware for moulding into sharply defined shapes. Once the difficulties of the first decade had been overcome, however, full technical, artistic, and economic success was achieved, particularly after more attention began to be devoted to colours. Johann Gregorius Hörold was the first professional painter to be employed at the factory. He worked from 1720 to 1765, and it was he who really established the artistic character of Dresden china. He evolved the characteristic bright colour scheme of blue, lemon yellow, iron red, purple, green, and brown. From that time on it became possible to comply with the king's request and adopt Far Eastern prototypes, rivalling them freely with new inventions.

The painterly phase of Dresden china was replaced during the thirties by a sculptural one, and with the appointment in 1727 of Gottlieb Kirchner the high standard of Saxon sculpture began to make itself felt. But the real impetus came in 1731 under Johann Joachim Kändler (Plate 124). Kändler was born at Fischbach-Seeligstadt near Bischofswerda in 1706, and from 1723 he worked on the interior decoration of the Grünes Gewölbe in the Dresden Palace, under Benjamin Thomae, who was a collaborator of Permoser. The king recognized his great talent, and shortly before his own death rendered a final service to his favourite enterprise by appointing Kändler to the Meissen factory. Furthermore he set him the important task of decorating the Japanese Palace entirely with porcelain. For this purpose 25,215 pieces were envisaged, and they included much on a large scale, for instance the throne for the audience chamber, the animals for the long gallery, and the decoration of the chapel with an altar, a pulpit, and life-size figures of the apostles. Sketches and models were sent from Dresden to Meissen. Kändler's interest in animals led him to produce the famous series comprising a sea hawk, an osprey, a white eagle, an owl, a falcon, water fowl, etc. They are mostly represented in action; for instance the white eagle tearing a carp to pieces, the peacock spreading its tail, or the bison fighting a wild boar. The movements are obviously studied from nature. It is, moreover, certain that the king insisted on interpretations of the characteristic attitudes and the nature of the animals. For months on end Kändler made sketches from life in the menagerie belonging to the Moritzburg and in the Dresden lion- and bear-houses, and also from stuffed animals in the Kunstkammer. His interest in the animal world, stimulated by hunting and by watching animals fighting, found novel means of expression in the new medium. The fact that he never sought colour effects brought him into permanent conflict with Hörold.

Religious scenes conceived in the spirit of the Catholic Church also offered a new field in Saxony, and Kändler, who had been brought up in a Protestant parsonage, entered fully into a religious outlook that was new to him. He also increased the size of the figures, up to as much as 7 feet. In 1735 he produced his celebrated series of apostles, in which the figures were 16½ inches high. They were followed by groups, for instance *The Death of St Francis Xavier* and the *Madonna and Child on the Globe with a Dragon*, both of 1738. Portrait commissions followed.

Even in tableware Kändler found an outlet for his joy in modelling in the round: for the handles, curved rims, and legs of the dishes could be suitably shaped to harmonize with the curved outlines and the reeding of the flat surfaces. Nude women and children, and dolphins and other animals, were among the most popular themes. Colour was added only sparingly, to give a little pointed enrichment to the white which was Kändler's favourite. He produced his masterpieces, the table sets for the ministers Sulkowski and Brühl, in less than five years. For the famous Swan Set (1737–41) he made two thousand two hundred pieces, which in itself gives some idea of the magnitude of the undertaking (Plate 124A). The sets included the most precious epergnes. Here the full effects of the Baroque of the Zwinger are first seen: everything is translated into rhythmic movement, and despite the variety of form a harmonious unity is achieved. A similar excellence distinguishes the popular small figures and groups, taken usually from the world of the theatre and of fancy-dress balls. Brühl's taste was certainly decisive, however; in certain pieces, for instance the celebrated chandeliers and the snowball vases, his delight in technical achievement led to an overloading with ornament (cf. also p. 287).

In many ways the development in gold- and silver-smithing paralleled that of Dresden china. The forms used in compliance with the king's wishes by Johann Melchior Dinglinger (1664–1731) are very similar. For cabinet pieces – such as the large *Chemistry Parnassus, The Household of the Grand Mogul of Delhi* (Plate 125A), *The Obeliscus Augustalis, The Temple of Apis* – familiarity with a wide variety of arts and crafts was essential: sculpture for the many figures, enamelling for the coloured settings, the goldsmith's craft proper, skill in gem cutting, and the carving of fine woods, bone, ivory, and stone. Characteristically enough Dinglinger's sculptural talent, fired by Permoser's example and stimulated by his delight in unusual arrangements of deep colours, appears at its most brilliant in the representation of negroes; an example is the negress term carved in rhinoceros bone, holding a cup above her head.

Dinglinger's sumptuous dinner sets rival Kändler's. Frequently, following the encyclopaedic interests of the eighteenth century, the epergnes are overloaded with symbolic figures or allusions – but all the same the graceful structures retain their aesthetic unity. Where the subject matter is suitable, for instance the *Bath of Diana* (Plate 125B), Dinglinger is remarkably successful, despite the combination of the most diverse materials: the oval chalcedony bowl which serves as a bath for the ivory figure of the goddess rests on the antlers of a newly killed stag, with the dogs still burying their teeth in its head. Dinglinger's art is certainly a particularly impressive example of the inventive spirit of the Dresden Baroque, which succeeded in creating diverse modes of expression in a variety of fields.

Painting

It was only for painting that the hour of greatness had not yet struck. Efforts to transplant the flourishing south German wall and ceiling painting to Dresden proved abortive, and the most important contributions in the seventeenth century were made by Harms, whose lost paintings in the palace have already been discussed (pp. 72, 85). The ceiling frescoes in the central room of the palace in the Grosser Garten (after 1693) by his successor Samuel Bottschild do not reach the same standard. His nephew Christoph Fehling (cf. p. 85), who painted the ceiling in the French Pavilion of the Zwinger, was more progressive. In 1697 he founded a school where students drew from life, thus giving the first impetus to a development that a hundred years later was to lead to a flowering of German painting in Dresden. His portrait of *Wolf Caspar von Klengel* (Plate 44A) is a good example of his mature style in portraiture. Later, at the close of the

Baroque, the landscape painter Alexander Thiele (1685–1752), who as painter to Augustus III had worked in Dresden from 1738, sought a monumental fantastic style, but never achieved unity of form.

Owing to the lack of significant native painters, foreign artists came to the fore. Louis de Silvestre occupied the leading position as court painter from 1716 to 1748. Instrumental in bringing him to Dresden was his countryman, the interior decorator Raymond Leplat, who had been working for Augustus the Strong on the alterations to the interior of the palace since 1698. Now that the palace has been destroyed, Leplat's style is best represented in the interior decorations of Moritzburg. Here the king had wanted to imitate the rich and massive style of Versailles, which he had visited when still crown prince, and he had to be convinced that taste had since changed and that lighter forms were more fashionable.

CHAPTER 18

PRUSSIA

By issuing the Edict of Potsdam in 1685 as a counterstroke to the Edict of Nantes, the Great Elector of Brandenburg had done his country a great service. Twenty thousand French émigrés were admitted to Prussia, and they made up forty-five per cent of the population of Berlin. Through their industry, skill, and artistic talents the Huguenots soon formed an élite, and their descendants were among the most faithful servants of the state.

Under the elector's successor Frederick III – after becoming king he called himself Frederick I – the settlement policy was continued by the vigorous Superintendent of the Royal Works (Oberbaudirektor) Johann Arnold Nering (cf. p. 75). In 1688 he and Michael Matthias Smids were commissioned to build the Friedrichstadt as a southern extension of the Dorotheenstadt, on a similar rectangular plan. Nering himself commissioned and supervised the building of three hundred similar two-storeyed houses, which were based on his designs. His ability as a town planner is further demonstrated by the building of the Leipziger Tor (1683) and of a covered arcade with shops on the Mühlendamm to replace the old shambles. He had already done the same thing in the

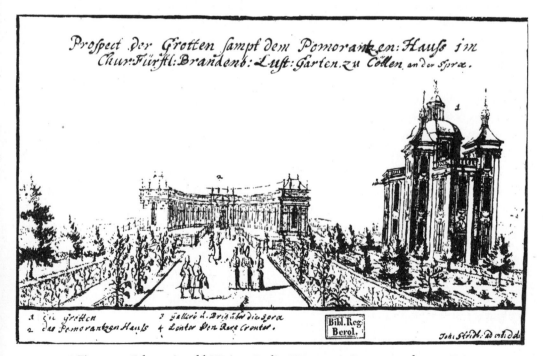

Figure 15. Johann Arnold Nering: Berlin, Hetzgarten, Pomeranzenhaus, 1685.
Engraving by Johann Stridbeck

tiltyard of the palace in 1681. The idea of inserting single structures of curved shape into the angles of the bastions proved most successful, and he adopted it for the Pomeranzen-haus in the Hetzgarten (Figure 15) and made a design of the same kind for the north side of the Arsenal. This, however, was not executed.

From the splendour-loving Frederick III he received more monumental commissions: first, the palace of Oranienburg, which acquired its present form during the reconstruction of 1689–95. The two main floors are linked by pilasters, and a tall attic stands in front of the broken roof. There are courts in front of the *corps de logis* on both sides. Then, shortly before Nering's premature death in 1695, three more important buildings were begun. For Queen Sophie Charlotte, who with the help of Leibniz had succeeded in making Berlin an intellectual centre, he began the Royal Palace of Charlottenburg with an oval room projecting on the garden side in the French manner. This was re-tained in the later reconstruction. At the same time, probably using a design of François Blondel's, he began work on the mighty block of the Arsenal, standing at the beginning of Unter den Linden (Plate 126). Finally, he laid the foundations for his most original building, 'a religious haven for all émigrés', the Reformed Parochialkirche. It consisted of a central square with four apses formed of five sides of a twelve-sided polygon, the sides being concave (Figure 16). A central tower was to rise above four semi-domed roofs, but Nering's successors, Martin Grünberg and Philipp Gerlach, confined them-selves to sloping roofs and a tower in front of the façade.

Nering was not a great architect in the Baroque sense. During a visit to Berlin in 1688 Nicodemus Tessin the Younger, the Stockholm court architect, described the plan for the Arsenal that had just been commissioned as rather 'extérieur'. Nering, he said, was 'excessively simple as regards the drawing and planning'.[1] It was, however, this very simplicity that saved the best buildings in Berlin from excesses. Nering, moreover, had sensible ideas, which were to prove fruitful later, and he was energetic enough to carry them through. He was by no means only at the receiving end in his relationship to the expanding Saxon Baroque. Near Dresden, the suburb of Leubnitz-Neuostra, with four main streets and rectangular blocks of houses, had already been begun in 1670; in 1728 it was given the name of Friedrichstadt. But the idea of settling a large colony of artisans there did not materialize. In Berlin the building commission headed by Nering had far-reaching powers and was able to call in troops to force reluctant building patrons to conform to the general scheme. Further, Nering's insertion of curved build-ings in the angles of bastions was an idea that was taken over splendidly in the Zwinger, where the Wallpavillon has concave intercolumniations similar to those on the exterior of the oval hall at the palace of Charlottenburg. The 'simple' manner, in as far as it was adhered to, formed a sound basis for the Prussian style. Nering was unequivocally a follower of Palladio, a result of his Dutch extraction. The addition of a high dome to the Charlottenburg Palace by Eosander von Göthe certainly added to the grandeur of the building, but it deprived it of the sturdy vigour characteristic of the Mark of Brandenburg.

A year before Nering's death, in 1694, Andreas Schlüter came to Berlin from War-saw. Schlüter was destined not only to succeed Nering, but in the fullness of his genius to outclass him entirely. However, despite the heights to which he rose and despite the

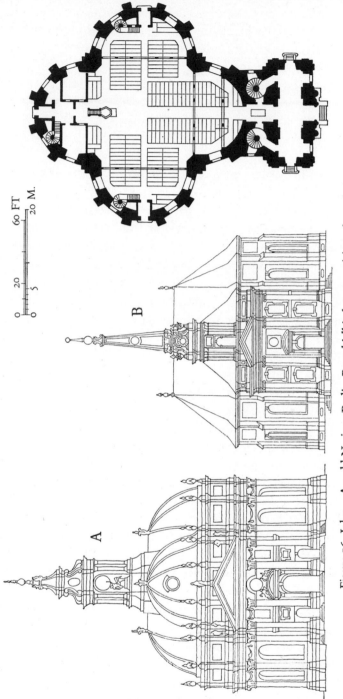

Figure 16. Johann Arnold Nering: Berlin, Parochialkirche, 1695. (A) as planned; (B) as executed

fact that his achievements really established Prussia's claim to leadership both in architecture and sculpture, he was relentlessly dogged by ill-fortune, and in a tragically complex way himself partly to blame for his failures. Even though he had the collaboration of a large workshop, his work bears the imprint of a strong personality. His early years are wrapped in darkness, and even the date of his birth is not known. As his birthplace Abraham Humbert suggests Danzig, Friedrich Nicolai Hamburg.[2] The former says that he was born in 1662 or 1663, the latter in 1669. All are agreed that he was trained in Danzig. But we have no information on the details, nor do we know anything about the journeys that, in view of his comprehensive education, he must have undertaken.

He is first heard of in 1689–93 in connexion with payments made for the pediments and the stone coat-of-arms for the palace of Jan Dobrogost Krasiński in Warsaw. These do not yet show his later style, which first appears on the monument of Jakob Sobieski, father of King John Sobieski of Poland, in the parish church of Żółkiev (1692–4). The female genii already have something of the grace and softness that characterize Schlüter's statues of women, and the putti are amusing and charming in the same way as his later figures of children, but the compelling rhythm is missing. Schlüter must evidently have developed this first in Berlin, after he had come in contact with the dynamic vitality that even at that time characterized the future capital of Germany. Nor can his presumed share in the decoration of Wilanów, near Warsaw, a royal country house, under the architect Agostino Locci, be fully substantiated by stylistic criteria. Indeed Schlüter does not appear to have worked as an architect in Poland at all. Marperger's assertion to the contrary is not borne out by the document of appointment at Berlin, where only Schlüter's ability as a sculptor is extolled.

His prestige is further confirmed by his election to a chair at the projected Academy of Sculpture and by the important commission of 1696 for more than a hundred keystones for the windows and doors of the ground floor of the Arsenal. Presumably he himself was partly responsible for the introduction of so much sculptural work. In any case it already fully reveals his personal genius. The cartouches on the outside are decorated with helmets, on the north front with pairs of Medusa heads (Plate 128B) and a harpy shield, in the courtyard with heads of dying warriors (Plate 128A), and on the gates with a soaring eagle and a bundle of twigs. The simplicity of the ground floor, which is articulated only by means of pilasters and slight projections, and the sculpture, stretched by the joints as in a net, have their fullest effect. Keystones were popular with sculptors even in the sixteenth century, for on them they could express the Mannerist delight in grotesque forms. Those on the Arsenal retain a fantastic, fabulous feeling in the helmets, but in the heads the expression is raised in the Michelangelesque sense to the heights of tragedy; and indeed Schlüter's depth and sincerity are closer to Michelangelo than to the more superficial virtuosity of Bernini. Schlüter's conception, like Michelangelo's, was rooted in Late Antique art. This can be seen not only in the adoption of motifs such as the Medusa Head, or the Barbarian who, like the Dying Gaul on the Capitol,[3] remains dignified despite his suffering, or the Laocoon as the symbol of heroic death, but also in his ability to give spiritual expression to physical pain. The destruction of youthful, vigorous life, and all the other tragedies which the Thirty Years War had brought to Germany, found a timeless, monumental expression in Schlüter's art. In this respect it is unique. The full extent of his genius could only be appreciated today if the fragmentary remains of his work were to be assembled in a museum.[4]

In view of his Roman-Baroque sympathies Schlüter will certainly have opposed the plans for the Arsenal, the first building in Berlin to show the effects of French influence.[5] His ideal was to give more and more importance to sculpture in architecture. This aim had already been apparent in the Krasiński Palace in Warsaw, for the centre of which he had done a cartouche with a coat-of-arms supported by genii. This was removed in the nineteenth century, but is known from a painting by Canaletto. He also did sculpture for the pediment. In the same year he was appointed to conduct the building of the Arsenal, and for it he designed a cartouche with a coat-of-arms that was even larger than that at Warsaw. It soon became apparent, however, that Schlüter was insufficiently prepared to assume responsibility for a building, for a pier collapsed, proving that what had been erected was not secure – a mishap that was to be repeated three times during Schlüter's Berlin years. The investigating commission did not confirm his opinion that the mason was to blame. We must, however, bear in mind that the standard of the Berlin building trade was very low at that time, as is proved by quite a series of disasters, demolitions, and collapses in the eighteenth century. In 1699 Schlüter was replaced at the Arsenal by Jean de Bodt, who discarded the heavy attic, presumably designed by Nering, and used instead a lighter balustrade and a slight middle projection with a pediment on four columns, in the style of Louis XIV (Plate 126). The figures he designed for the balustrade were executed by Guillaume Hulot.

In 1696, while he was working on the keystones, Schlüter also began the bronze statues of the Great Elector and his son. The statue of Frederick III was intended to stand in the centre of the court of the Arsenal, but after considerable journeyings it finally came to rest at Königsberg, where it was erected to commemorate the coronation of the elector. The equestrian statue of the Great Elector on the other hand (Plate 131) was placed on the Lange Brücke near the Schloss. It was cast in 1700, the group of four slaves belonging to it in 1708. Here, too, Schlüter used a Late Antique piece as his model – the statue of Marcus Aurelius on the Capitol in Rome. The philosopher emperor with his tranquil attitude, however, can only be considered a prototype in as far as Schlüter – just like the French sculptors – took over his imperial costume and the forward position of his thighs. Marcus Aurelius's fiery, prancing steed on the other hand, ready at any moment to break into a canter, was a much more acceptable model for Schlüter, especially the proudly poised head and windswept mane. Girardon's contemporary equestrian statue of Louis XIV in the Place Vendôme in Paris, dating from 1699, does not achieve the same degree of tempestuous vitality either in horse or horseman. Schlüter's group, once the symbol of the rising Prussian state, now stands in front of Schloss Charlottenburg.

The admiration aroused by Schlüter's sculptural achievements made the court overlook his failure with the Arsenal. After the dismissal of the all-powerful minister Eberhard von Danckelmann in 1697, his successor Johann Kasimir von Kolbe, Count of Wartenberg, favoured Schlüter. Moreover the new minister proved the right man to carry out the elector's magnificent projects. A few days after his appointment he was made 'Protector' of the Academy of Fine Arts, and a few days later Superintendent of the Electoral Pleasure-Seats. In this way he also became Schlüter's immediate superior at the Academy, which Schlüter directed from 1702 to 1704. In 1744 and again in 1768 Humbert stressed the inventiveness of his mind and his assiduity.

In 1701 Schlüter was also elected a member of the Academy of Science 'on account of his great gifts, his intellect and excellent understanding of the art of building and the related arts of mathematics and mechanics of which he had given laudable and concrete proof'. His appointment to the Academy was the result of Leibniz's efforts to bring that body into contact with practical achievements. For his part Schlüter, like so many other important architects of his day, for example George Bähr, wanted to give scientific perfection to the technical side of building, among other things by the use of iron. In this he was well in advance of his age; for it was not until the middle of the eighteenth century that the time was ripe for this and for applying to architecture calculations based on mathematics and statics.[6] However, his calculations and experiments, for instance his attempts to invent a perpetuum mobile, were frequently Utopian rather than practical: in the opinion of Sturm, the architectural theorist, mathematician, and architect whom we have met before and who was working in Berlin at that time, Schlüter was a good sculptor and could draw neat perspectives, but had not sufficient knowledge of mathematics for the erection of a building.

Schlüter's powers were strained to the utmost during the few years in which he received his greatest commissions. The elector, who was making every effort to be raised to royal rank, wished to surround himself with the appropriate splendour, especially through the reconstruction and enlargement of his palace. In 1698, therefore, he entrusted Schlüter with its supervision and the following year made him Surveyor General of the palace. In this capacity Schlüter's working powers proved truly prodigious. He was not only expected to direct the planning and execution of the work, and this included the interior decoration, but also had to engage suitable craftsmen and supervise their work, procure the materials, and control the accounts. How seriously he took his duties can be seen from the report that he sometimes examined a piece of work twelve times, helping with it and making alterations, which meant that he had to pay as many as thirty or forty visits in one day to workmen and artists. He also had to plan the programme of the interior decoration down to the individual subjects and the size of the ceiling paintings. His sketches were examined by the Academy and also had to have the king's approval.

Schlüter no doubt made his plans in full awareness of the plans for the princely palaces at Vienna, Dresden, and Stockholm. Fischer von Erlach's designs for Schönbrunn developed during the nineties, which envisaged a long building with wings in the shape of an omega, dominating the surroundings, were brought to the notice of the Prussian court during Fischer's visit in 1704 and by a similar design made by him for Berlin. But the hilly site was lacking in Berlin. That conversely Schlüter's building made a deep impression on Fischer von Erlach can be seen from his corner pavilions of the Palais Clam-Gallas.

In Berlin the basic shape of the old Schloss, hallowed by tradition, was retained, and the side facing the river Spree, closely associated with the Great Elector and his wife, was left in its original form. Thus the chapel of the pious Electress Louise Henriette remained intact until 1945, just as her hymn 'Jesus, meine Zuversicht' (Jesus, my trust is in Thee) has retained its popularity throughout Protestant Germany down to the present day. The position in Dresden was similar, owing to the existence of the old Renaissance Schloss. But at Dresden the first plans for new buildings were made only after the fire of 1701. They were inspired and influenced by Berlin. Schlüter was in Dresden in 1702, and in 1703, as already mentioned, he sent designs to Augustus the Strong. The Swedish court on the other hand was a little in advance of the Prussian; for the plans of Nicodemus Tessin the Younger for the new palace for Stockholm were made in 1697, after a fire. The Swedish architect had been in Berlin in 1688, where he had asked to see Nering's plans for the Arsenal (p. 208). At that time he submitted a plan in the Roman style for the restoration of the medieval castle at Stettin, which was not executed.

This cubical form of building, thus already outmoded, was taken from Bernini's design for the Louvre. A similar influence is also perceptible in the Schloss in Berlin. However, Tessin, whose taste tended towards classicism, was closer to Bernini than was Schlüter. The latter, driven by his fiery temperament, used projections with giant columns to obtain an increased vertical thrust as a contrast to the static mass of the palace. Relations between the Swedish and the Berlin courts were kept up during the period of the rebuilding of the Berlin palace, and in 1699 a request was sent by the electoral court of Brandenburg to Sweden, possibly an appeal for advice. In any case the Stockholm palace itself, a mighty flat-roofed building with four wings and giant pilasters in the centre linking the two upper floors, is sufficient proof of the contact that existed and of the influence exerted by the Swedish building.

Schlüter, however, with his more dynamic temperament, sought a greater contrast between the vertical thrust and the static mass by the employment of a large columned projection. Following Tessin, he did not insert a pediment above the four columns as a transition to the roof, and this omission was intended at once to demonstrate how different his building was from the Arsenal. In his book on Schlüter, written in 1891, Cornelius Gurlitt suggests that for the palace with its three and a half floors and its windows resting on string courses, plans by an earlier Roman architect may already have existed, so that Schlüter himself was responsible only for the central projection. There is, however, no evidence for this in the documents. Moreover the contrast between the centre and the rest of the façade appears perfectly in keeping with Schlüter's character. The columnar centrepiece was intended to ring out in the palace square like a fanfare of trumpets.

Furthermore, on the garden side Schlüter did omit the giant order and introduced richer architectural sculpture in order to lead from the colossal to something lighter and more vivacious (Plate 127). In the courtyard he carried on the motif of two storeys of arcades inserted by Nering about 1690 into the south-east corner, but he only used giant orders for the middle projections of the south, east, and north wings, not in the corners.

The orders are of Corinthian columns. The powerfully projecting entablature, a profession of faith in the Roman Baroque, supports statues placed in front of the pilasters. The wide opening of the bays by means of windows was an idea that roused the particular interest of Fischer von Erlach (p. 94).

Inside, the columns and atlantes in front of the walls round the great staircase bear witness to the same emphasis on three-dimensionality, but they also serve to mollify the harsh clashes between the architectural members (Plate 130). In addition to the termini, recumbent figures were also used to symbolize the carrying of the weight of the room. The conceit behind all this is a dramatic one, the Battle of the Giants. On 11 December 1700 a royal command was issued to Schlüter urging him to carry on the work in the rooms of the palace with the utmost despatch and to complete the ceilings. Schlüter's own part in the interior decoration was best seen in the figural sculpture. In the Elizabeth Hall and in the Baronial Hall for instance he placed agitated figures on the cornice of the walls at the height of the door pediments; these, in the contrapposto of the limbs, and particularly the bent legs, show him developing Michelangelesque motifs. In the sense of Michelangelo the essential expression lies in the figure sculpture, not in painterly effects as with Bernini and his followers. It was entirely due to Schlüter's inspiration that the plasterers – among whom Giovanni Simonetti appears as a recognizable personality – achieved such a high standard. Schlüter himself no doubt only prepared the models.

The palace was hit by bombs in 1945, but the essential parts remained undamaged, notably the sculpture on the Lustgarten façade, on the great staircase, in the Baronial Hall, and elsewhere. Indeed the architectural details had survived better than in the majority of German palaces; but for political reasons, the Schloss was demolished in 1950, though the sculpture was first removed.

During the years between 1700 and 1705, when he was ceaselessly busy, Schlüter was responsible for four other important works. In 1700 he did the monument to the court goldsmith David Männlich in the church of St Nicholas, borrowing the idea of a doorway from Bernini's monument to Alexander VII in St Peter's. Schlüter's youngest son Gotthard had died in the same year, a tragic blow for the artist who, as his art shows, must have loved children. It was this that gave such terrible immediacy to the experience of losing a child. Death is seen clutching the boy, who struggles helplessly (Plate 129). His elder brother, who watches the scene in frozen horror, is a figure of supreme beauty. Happily the monument has survived, though the bronze plaque with the two children represented as they looked in life is lost. The grief-stricken angels at the sides hiding their faces in the shroud should be looked at specially.

In 1701–4 Schlüter built a new Post Office (later to be known as the 'Old Post Office') at the east end of the Lange Brücke near the monument of the Great Elector. Count Wartenberg's official residence was on the main floor. Here, too, there was a wealth of architectural sculpture, strictly organized by a framework of fluted pilasters. The building terminated in an attic which concealed the roof and in an unbroken main entablature of austere monumentality. Unfortunately the building was demolished in 1889, although the architect Schinkel had restored it in a remarkably appreciative way.

In 1703 Schlüter designed the pulpit for the church of St Mary in Berlin. This is specially important because it represents an example of his work for churches, which is otherwise known only from an altar at St Nicholas, Stralsund, badly executed from his design.

Schlüter's fourth masterpiece of the first years of the eighteenth century is the bronze sarcophagus in Berlin Cathedral of Queen Sophie Charlotte, who died in 1705. In the heavily draped coffin surrounded by mourning figures the danger of excessive natural-ism inherent in his art has not been quite avoided; he was therefore wise, both on this sarcophagus and on the later one of 1713 for the king, not to represent the deceased as living people, as Moll had done on the sarcophagus of Maria Theresa in Vienna. Schlüter shows the deceased in portrait medallions. The profile of this highly intelligent queen, done at a happier moment in the artist's life than that of the king, is sculpturally far better. The chief artistic emphasis, however, lies not on the portraits but on the large allegorical figures, for instance Death writing Sophie Charlotte's name in the book of eternity, a figure of haunting vitality, and the weeping figure at the feet of the king, of timeless beauty and moving truth.

In his supervision of the royal buildings, damage through faulty building occurred several more times; for instance a great crack opened on the Lustgarten façade of the palace. These did not cost Schlüter his position at court, but Nemesis finally overtook him over the Münzturm (Figure 17). In 1702 he had undertaken to build a new and more attractive water tower at the north-west corner of the palace, to be called the Münzturm after the near-by mint. The ideal he envisaged was a transparent columned tower based on Bernini's campanili of St Peter's and Wren's towers on the west front of St Paul's. He hoped that by following Nering's idea for the tower he would be able to combine a compact lower half with two open columnar storeys above to form a campanile of the slenderest proportions, tapering only slightly, the light soaring outline of which would appear to even greater advantage by contrast with the heavy massive palace. The two belfry storeys rose from a square lower platform over a cruciform plan. The superimposed coupled columns were set well away from the walls, which increased in thickness towards the top. The crowning, stepped-back top terminated in a fantastic-ally shaped spirelet.

Two years later, however, in 1704, increasing structural difficulties forced Schlüter to work out a new plan in which the lower part was enlarged by piers and wings. Artistic-ally this design was an improvement – in the first place because the pairs of columns were set diagonally on the upper floors. Instead of the original eight pairs he now placed twelve on every floor, though he still allowed the columns to stand almost directly one above the other in order to give the upper part the effect of rising almost weightlessly. In 1706, however, when work was complete as far as the lower columnar storey, the west side of the tower began to give way. In desperation he made a design reducing the superstructure, so that a bell-stage with pillars instead of columns would have to sup-port only a light four-columned tabernacle. But it was too late even to carry out this idea. Without waiting for orders he had the tower, which was near collapse, pulled down. The findings of a commission composed of Schlüter's rivals Eosander von Göthe, Sturm, and Grünberg were as follows: that the errors lay in using the old tower,

Figure 17. Andreas Schlüter: Berlin, Münzturm, plan of 1704, elevation (1 : 1100)

overloading it, providing insufficient foundations by driving only single posts into the swampy ground, attaching the wall casing round it by means of an iron construction that dragged it down instead of supporting it, and finally allowing the pressure of the walls which widened towards the top. In 1708, in a letter to the Electress Sophie of Hanover, the king angrily referred to Schlüter as 'the rogue who built the tower so badly'. At the beginning of the same year Schlüter had lost the office of surveyor of the palace. His successor Eosander, when he had to enlarge the great court, was wise enough to repeat Schlüter's façade; his own bombastic manner appears for the first time on the triumphal arch of the gateway on the west front facing the Schlossfreiheit, which was completed in 1716. The royal chapel, with its elliptical dome over the west portal, was built by August Stüler between 1845 and 1852.

In spite of these devastating blows, Schlüter's creative powers appeared undiminished once again in the house he built in the Dorotheenstadt for Ernst Bogislav von Kamecke (1711–12; Plate 132). It has now been entirely destroyed by bombs, except for four of the statues on the upper cornice. Even before that, however, the wings had lost their original roofing and their dormer windows, which had been replaced by an attic storey, though the central block and the original plasterwork with the *Four Continents* inside had survived intact. Schlüter was able to devote more time to this building, and as a result achieved a superb unity of all the parts, culminating in the sculptured figures (Plate 133, A and B); indeed it seems as if the undulating façade with its convex ends and concave centre rotating in undulating lines were set in motion by the pairs of figures: Apollo and Daphne, Poseidon and Amphitrite. The sinuous movements of their bodies and their raised feet turn as if about to dance. Streaming hair and billowing drapery folds enliven the contours. In the modelling, for instance the deep-set eyes and the protuberant bridge of the nose, they exaggerate natural forms. Once again, then, the entire building was conceived in a sculptural spirit. There were no carved capitals to rival the statues, and the articulation was confined to wall strips, a feature that was soon to become fashionable. They are set as far apart as possible, the intervening spaces opening in windows. The central axis alone is more powerfully emphasized by the two Baroque pediments, but they do not detract from the dominance of the cornice with the statues.

The king died in 1713 and, as we have seen, Schlüter made his bronze sarcophagus in that year. Under his thrifty successor Frederick William I many artists left Berlin. Schlüter's services were enlisted by the ambassador Jacob Bruce for Russia, and he moved in 1714 to St Petersburg, where he died in the same year. The exact date of his death is not known, nor do we know where he was buried, and no portrait of the great artist has survived.

Next to Schlüter General Jean de Bodt (1670–1745) was without doubt the most important architect in Berlin. He left his native France as a refugee in 1685, was trained as an architect for a time in Holland, then worked in England, and finally, in 1698, came to Berlin. Both in his completion of the Arsenal and in his work on the tower of the Parochialkirche he shows himself to be Schlüter's successor in as far as he realized the latter's ideal of a pierced columnar bell-stage, based on Borromini's campanili of S.

Agnese in Piazza Navona, but crowned by a pyramidal spire. The gatehouse of the Potsdam Stadtschloss, which he built in 1701, shows that, although he really favoured a
severe classicism, he was able skilfully to adapt himself. In 1728 he left Berlin and went
to Dresden, where he occupied an important position, succeeding Wackerbarth as
Superintendent (p. 194). As was so frequently the case at that time among architects, he
was able to realize his boldest ideas only in drawings. This is the case both with his plans
for a vast project embracing the cathedral and the hospital for disabled soldiers, and
later with the Dresden palace.

Schlüter's real successor, the Swede Johann Friedrich Eosander von Göthe, a pupil of
Tessin, who continued the influence of Swedish architecture which Tessin had started,
came to Berlin in 1699 and enjoyed in the first place the patronage of the queen. He was
thus extensively employed in 1704-5 for her Charlottenburg palace and for its interior
decoration. After the queen's death in 1705 work continued with equal vigour, spurred
on by the king's passion for building. It was probably at the king's instigation that
Eosander built the domed tower, a feature that is appropriate for religious architecture
but not suitable for a palace. Eosander surpassed the buildings that inspired him in that
he attached much greater importance to the tower, as its height alone shows. The west
wing of the Berlin palace was also intended to be crowned by a three-hundred-foot-high
tower, to proclaim the king's newly acquired status, but only the portal designed like a
triumphal arch, to which reference has already been made, was actually built. In 1722
Eosander, too, went to Dresden. Here he built the small palace of Übigau on the Elbe
(1724-6). He died in 1729, with the rank of a Saxon Lieutenant General.

Martin Grünberg (1655-1706) was of still less importance artistically compared with
Schlüter. From 1695 to 1699 he was court architect in charge of the royal palaces and
from 1699 to 1706 Director of the Royal Works in Town and Country, in accordance
with the centralization of the administration of buildings that was just beginning.

Grünberg was succeeded by Philipp Gerlach (1679-1748), who in 1720, under
Frederick William I, became Director General of the Royal Palaces. In this capacity he
had to submit designs to the king, which the latter then usually modified for reasons of
economy. The king's desire to create order everywhere, if necessary by enforcing it,
made him remodel the by-laws which were administered in Berlin by the so-called
Building Commission. They carried out their work with severity, but the reduction of
taxes and cheap or free delivery of materials favoured building as a whole. Under
Frederick William I, the soldier king, Gerlach continued Nering's work by building the
Friedrichstadt and the Dorotheenstadt as far as the Pariser Platz and the Wilhelmstrasse –
the population, between 1680 and 1740, had increased from 9,800 to 90,000. The Wilhelmstrasse was the most westerly of three radial roads which, following the model of
the Piazza del Popolo in Rome, started from the Belle-Alliance-Platz at the Halle Gate,
also built at that time.

Though very different from his lavish father, Frederick William I was not entirely
without artistic interests, especially when they served educational or propaganda purposes. He had a particular liking for high church towers, and the tower he wanted for
St Peter in Berlin would have surpassed that of the cathedral of Strasbourg; its collapse

when half-finished, however, put an end to an ambition almost reminiscent of the building of the Tower of Babel. On the other hand, Gerlach, as Schlüter's successor, built a tower for the Garnisonkirche in Potsdam (1730–5), and this stood firm.

Gerlach belonged to the academic school of Goldmann and Sturm. Following their ideas, several Berlin churches were built on circular plans, or like the Garnisonkirche in Potsdam, with an altar and pulpit in the middle of one of the two long sides opposite the royal pew.

The credit for building the finest church towers in the Mark of Brandenburg must go in the event to Johann Friedrich Grael (1708–40). The tower of the Sophienkirche in Berlin was erected by him in 1729–35, and, in 1732–4, that of the Heiliggeistkirche in Potsdam. The proportions are beautifully balanced. That the arrangement of the upper columns in the Sophienkirche is so effective is largely due to their uniform repetition on two floors. In the Heiliggeistkirche the attractive site on the river Havel and the layout of the streets on the town side have been skilfully exploited for the tower. There can be no doubt at all that the most perfect German columnar tower of the period, the one on the Catholic Hofkirche in Dresden, was inspired by the Berlin school.

Grael had a great deal to suffer from his master's capricious and tyrannical treatment. He built the tower of the Petrikirche much too slowly for the king – though it was obviously for reasons of security – and so was dismissed and replaced by Gerlach. When the disaster occurred the king blamed Grael and had him arrested. Later he was banished. He died at the early age of thirty-two, in the service of the margrave of Bayreuth.

CHAPTER 19

LOWER SAXONY AND THE LOWER RHINE

Architecture

GENERALLY speaking the high cultural standards of the lower Saxon courts at Hanover, Celle, Wolfenbüttel, and Brunswick, ruled by the various branches of the Welfen, were intellectual rather than artistic. Under Duke Anton Ulrich of Brunswick-Wolfenbüttel, who reigned from 1685 to 1714, however, art too acquired considerable importance, though even here the emphasis was laid on architectural theory. Anton Ulrich was born in 1633. At a comparatively early age, in 1654–6, he was able to study French architecture in Paris, and it is quite clear that Salomon de Brosse's Luxembourg Palace served as the model for the forecourt and the colonnades of his palace at Salzdahlum (1688–94). Nevertheless the personal contributions, not only of the patron himself, but also of the competent architects he employed, dominate throughout. For reasons of economy the building was timber framed, the traditional building method of the country, but adapted on the exterior to look like stone.

In 1687, a year before building started, Johann Balthasar Lauterbach (1660–94) came to Wolfenbüttel. He was a native of Ulm and had studied at the university of Jena in 1680. The duke appointed him professor of mathematics at the newly founded Academy for Young Noblemen in Wolfenbüttel, and court architect. With the duke he most probably played an influential part in the planning of Salzdahlum. This means that, contrary to previous opinion, it is not entirely the work of Hermann Korb, a cabinet-maker promoted by the duke to be his architect. Korb was in Italy when building operations began and did not return until about 1691.[1] In 1692 he was given the post of comptroller of buildings, and in 1694 was put in charge of all matters pertaining to building in the duchy of Brunswick. In spite of this, however, he was not appointed to the professorship which became vacant on Lauterbach's early death, because he was regarded as a mere practitioner. The successful candidate was Leonhard Christoph Sturm, who had had an academic training and whom we have met more than once before. As a result, from the very outset, conflicts arose between the architect with theoretical leanings and the practical builder.

For Schloss Salzdahlum Lauterbach had designed two flights of stairs up to the left and right of one flight leading down to a lower room called the grotto (Figure 18). Twenty-two years later this idea was revived by Johann Dientzenhofer at Pommersfelden, and thirty-three years later by Lukas von Hildebrandt for the Upper Belvedere in Vienna, in order to connect the sala terrena with the vestibule and staircase. In the same way the idea of piercing the staircase walls by arcades to allow a view of the rising stairs was also revived, at a much later date, by Prandtauer at Melk. A design, known from an engraving, is superior to the finished work in that it has a rusticated base and the giant

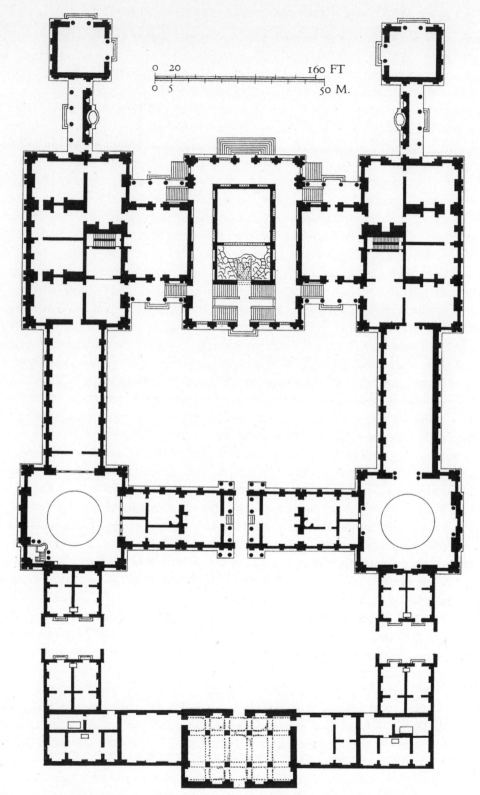

Figure 18. Johann Balthasar Lauterbach: Salzdahlum, Schloss, *c.* 1690. Plan

pilasters appear not only in the centre but also on the corner pavilions. Later, in an engraving in his book *Architektonische Reiseanmerkungen* (1719), Sturm expressed his criticism by altering the fronts and adapting them to those of the Luxembourg Palace – not at all to their advantage. Other changes he made were the discarding of the attractive motif of the two-storeyed arcades and the contrasting giant pilasters. Following the Luxembourg Palace, the wings of the courtyard had galleries.

In order to house his large collection, the duke instructed Korb to build the Long Gallery, which was lit by upper windows placed above the sixteen feet of wall space reserved for the pictures. Furthermore, in 1708 the Small Gallery turning off at right angles was made and the Porcelain Gallery, again at right angles to it, was added. In this way the duke's privy garden was surrounded by galleries on three sides. Small cabinets for the smaller paintings were built on to the galleries. In this respect, too, Salzdahlum was afterwards imitated. Unfortunately, during the later eighteenth century it did not receive the proper care needed for half-timber work, and so it was demolished as dangerous in 1813.

The contrast between Lauterbach, the trained architect, and Korb, the assured practitioner with little interest in proportions, can be seen again in the church of the Holy Trinity at Wolfenbüttel. The flanking stone towers survive from the building of 1693-9, designed probably by Lauterbach. After a fire in 1705 Korb brought the receding front forward in line with the tower fronts and, as opposed to Lauterbach's rhythm, allowed the pilasters on the centre to rise from the ground. As in the majority of his churches, he put an octagonal gallery inside, supported on powerful free-standing columns each with the fragment of an architrave, making them as conspicuous as possible and thus combining the idea of the hall church with that of a building with galleries (Plate 134B). In his church at Hehlen (1697-9), the outer walls form an octagon. Of his numerous palaces Hundisburg, built in 1694-1702, survived until 1945 (Plate 134A). There he enlarged the medieval castle into a symmetrical Baroque palace by repeating the extant tower, a motif characteristic of lower Saxony. The simple central Dutch gable, the two-storeyed arcades linking the corner pavilions, and the vast, lofty vestibule, staircase, and upper saloon in the centre foreshadow his future style.

Korb's inventive mind is most brilliantly displayed in the free-standing library (1706-10), put up to house the enormous number of books at Wolfenbüttel (Plate 135A). It was built, on the advice of Leibniz, as a central structure. The oval interior surrounded by galleries and lit by windows in the dome can be compared to those of Protestant churches (Plate 135B). The building, unfortunately also mainly of half-timber work, was demolished in 1887.

In Hanover the younger branch of the Welfen, though politically more successful, was less active in the field of architecture. Sophie von der Pfalz, wife of Duke Ernst August (1680-98), was the only one to make an important contribution, by enlarging the Grosse Garten of the summer palace of Herrenhausen near Hanover (mainly 1692-1710). The close ties with the court of Orange meant that inspiration came from Dutch rather than French architecture. The originally square plan was transformed into a rectangle. It is unique in that Early Baroque parts were preserved. The duchess was a great garden enthusiast, and the hedges, extending for thirteen miles, are characteristic of Herrenhausen. Here her daughter Sophie Charlotte had her conversations with Leibniz. In 1696–1700 a gallery was built by Johann Peter Wachter, architect to the Count-Palatine, containing frescoes with subjects from the *Aeneid* by Tommaso Giusti. The palace was altered several times, given its final classicist form in 1820–1 by the Surveyor General Georg Ludwig Laves, and finally destroyed by bombs in 1943.

Dutch and Flemish prototypes were even more decisive in Westphalia, as can be seen among other things in the use of brick alternating with ashlar in the pilasters, cornices, and festoons below the windows. Nevertheless conservative native characteristics found expression also, e.g. in the retention of the castle type and of the massive shapes with high hipped roofs, a type going right back to the lower Saxon farmhouse. The initiative for increased building activity came from the bishops of Münster and Paderborn. The vast palace of Ahaus (1690–2) was commissioned by Prince Bishop Friedrich Christian von Plettenberg (1688–1706). Built by Johann Quincken (d. 1712), it is a fortress-like structure with curving roofs on the corner pavilions. Friedrich Christian also commissioned Nordkirchen, built in 1703–12 by Gottfried Laurenz Pictorius (d. 1725), the son of Peter Pictorius. In his work, the rise of Westphalian architecture begins which was to culminate in the work of Schlaun. At Nordkirchen, the Westphalian Versailles, the plan of the forecourt with its stepped wings shows the new grandeur of the High Baroque; yet simplicity is preserved too – for instance in the absence of window pediments. In the disposition and decoration of the rooms as well Pictorius, under western influence, remained moderate. His buildings at Münster also bear witness to this: the Bevenförder Hof (1699–1702), the Merveldter Hof (*c.* 1702), and the Schmiesinger Hof (*c.* 1716). They have forecourts, shallow Dutch gables over the central projections, and stone dressings.

The same desire for simplicity, often satisfied with pilaster strips instead of pilasters or columns, determined the early work of Johann Conrad Schlaun (1695–1773), especially as it was his job to build quite simple churches for the Capuchin friars. That at Brakel dates from 1715–18, that at Münster from 1724–9 (Plate 136). For the Jesuit college at Büren (1716–20) he was in competition with Pictorius. The latter's design, aiming at a simple massive effect, was accepted in preference to Schlaun's, who had wanted a centrally planned church. The patronage of Franz Arnold von Wolff Metternich, Prince Bishop of Paderborn and Münster, enabled the young Schlaun to broaden his outlook by travel abroad, undertaken even before 1715. He was especially anxious to establish contact with the south.

Still greater opportunities were offered him by Metternich's successor, Clemens August of Bavaria, who ruled from 1719 to 1761, and in his passion for building and love of ostentation followed in the footsteps of his father the Elector Max Emanuel. The fact that Clemens August's background was south German meant that the earlier influence of Dutch classicism on Westphalia was considerably weakened. This must have made Schlaun all the more anxious to enlarge his knowledge of south Germany. No place was more suitable for this than Würzburg, and accordingly he spent the period from 1720 to 1721 there, studying under Balthasar Neumann, who was eight years his senior. At that time the fierce controversy over the plans for the Residenz had just broken out. In 1722 Schlaun went on to Rome, where his interest in the buildings of Bernini and Borromini is attested by careful drawings. He returned to Münster via France in 1723, and in 1724 undertook a further journey, this time to Munich. In Munich it was only natural that he should be particularly interested in the palaces of Nymphenburg and Schleissheim built for Clemens August's father.

The first major success of his career came in 1725. In that year he was appointed Chief Architect and Engineer to the elector of Cologne and given the rank of Captain. The elector entrusted him with the enlargement of Schloss Brühl, and Count Ferdinand von Plettenberg, the all-powerful minister, commissioned him to build the country house of Oranienburg at Nordhausen. For Schloss Brühl Schlaun kept to the Westphalian tradition in as far as he repeated the old round tower in the south-west corner, built a moat round the U-shaped building with its small courtyard, and articulated the central projection by giant pilasters. On the other hand he turned to the Austrian Baroque with his semicircular windows flanked by columns, his pilasters standing against demi-pilasters, his piercing of the main entablature on the central axes, and his rounded corners. However, in 1725 Clemens August attended the wedding of Louis XV in Versailles, and on the strength of this visit switched his interest to the most recent Franco-Bavarian manner. As a result, when the brickwork of the building was completed in 1728 he dismissed Schlaun and replaced him by François Cuvilliés. The latter eliminated all traces of the Westphalian moated castle from the building. Both the round towers were removed in 1735–6 (p. 229).

Schlaun's activities were henceforth restricted to Westphalia, where he developed a native Baroque style of remarkable consistency. From 1725 he erected various buildings in the park of Nordkirchen for Count von Plettenberg – the Oranienburg and the new orangery, in which he showed all his old skill in the disposition of the parts. The brick surfaces with their unpretentious articulation by means of wall strips and rounded corners are attractive in their simplicity. His prison (1732–4), now unfortunately demolished, showed the complete independence of his approach. He used the corner formed by the two wings of the building which met at an obtuse angle as a central projection, rounded it off, set the two doors in the curve thus obtained, and crowned it with a gable.

Between 1736 and 1750 Schlaun built the hunting-lodge of Clemenswerth near Sögel (Plate 137A) for Clemens August. It was probably at the latter's instigation that he tried to compete with the Pagodenburg of Nymphenburg, with Marly-le-Roy, and with the hunting-lodge of Bouchefort near Brussels, built by Boffrand for Max Emanuel of Bavaria. Eight pavilions, all built of brick and articulated with wall strips, are grouped round a central block, which has rich sculptural decoration, in the form of garlands.

At the beginning of the eighteenth century the Jesuit Gothic Revival came to an end. Anton Hülse (1637–1712), a lay brother and a competent architect of the Order, had carried on the tradition in the church of St Francis Xavier at Paderborn (1682–6). In accordance with the development of the Baroque he increased the force of his architecture by using powerful columns, but the building as a whole lacked the subtlety of its Cologne model. A new departure came with the Church of the Sacred Name of Jesus at Bonn, built in 1686–98. Here the hall-church scheme was introduced and the nave galleries were discarded. Remaining Gothic features such as the octagonal piers, and especially certain elements of the façade, were considerably modified, presumably under the influence of Jakob de Candrea, who executed the building. He was an engineer and also master mason to the elector.

Sculpture

Once again it was a member of the Gröninger family who became the most distinguished Westphalian sculptor of the High Baroque. Johann Mauritz Gröninger presumably came from Paderborn. In 1674 he was appointed sculptor to the court at Münster by Prince Bishop Christoph Bernhard von Galen 'because of his much praised art', and he remained at Münster until his death in 1707. Presumably he studied under a Belgian sculptor, most likely Artus Quellinus the Elder. His first work at Münster, the monument of his patron in the cathedral, which was completed before the latter's death in 1678, is rather clumsy and uncoordinated in the composition. The aged soldier in Gröninger's representation has lost all fire. Gröninger's weakness of composition is also revealed by the six large alabaster reliefs that once adorned the choir stalls in the cathedral of Münster (1705). This weakness led him to imitate Belgian and French models. His real strength came out only when he could work direct from nature. In addition, like Gerhard Gröninger before him he was successful in expressing pain and suffering, for example in the representation of the death of the Ewaldi Brothers.

His work was continued by his son Johann Wilhelm Gröninger, who was born in 1676, completed his journeyman years in 1701, and became a citizen of Münster. He was presumably the author of the monument of Prince Bishop Friedrich Christian von Plettenberg (d. 1706) in the cathedral of Münster. In the general arrangement he followed Girardon's tomb of Richelieu in the church of the Sorbonne in Paris (unveiled in 1694). There is nothing awkward in Gröninger's composition. The figure of the peacefully reclining prelate engaged in theological discussion is a fine piece of spontaneous characterization. The various figures, including saints, are of white alabaster and stand out against the black marble setting. The tomb of Canon Ferdinand von Plettenberg (d. 1712) in the same cathedral was probably also done by Gröninger. It represents Christ on the Mount of Olives and has the typical Gröninger expressiveness, but now combined with greater grace.

CHAPTER 20

THE NORTHERN COAST

Architecture

WITH one or two exceptions, the coastal areas of Germany remained on the fringe of the architectural efflorescence of the Baroque. Holland was the model for Protestant churches, as indeed for all other types of architecture. J. A. Nering's enlargement of the Burgkirche at Königsberg, carried out between 1687 and 1701, was modelled on the Nieuwe Kerk in The Hague.[1] Two short transepts, both ending to the north as well as the south in five-eighths of an octagon, were added to the nave, and a similar apsidal extension was built on the east side. The result of this composition was that the pulpit and altar could be placed centrally between the two transepts in the middle of the south side.

The Schlosskirche at Königsberg, on the other hand, represents the German Protestant type.[2] Joachim Ludwig Schultheiss von Unfriedt retained the neo-Gothic stellar vaulting and adapted it in 1705–10 as the Prussian coronation church by inserting Baroque galleries on three sides and placing the pulpit and altar in the centre of the side left without galleries. They came thus to stand opposite the royal pew, an arrangement that may have corresponded to the original plan of the building. This transverse orientation was found so practical that it was taken over in the Garnisonkirche at Potsdam and in Berlin Cathedral.

When Leonhard Christoph Sturm (1669–1719) was called to Schwerin in 1710 and made Superintendent of the buildings there, his influence in the north, already considerable throughout Protestant Germany on account of his many publications, was further increased. The publication and exploitation of the manuscript *Civil Architecture* by Nikolaus Goldmann (1611–65), one-time teacher of mathematics and architecture at Leiden, was of less importance than were his actual designs for Protestant churches. These were first published in 1712 in *Architektonischen Bedencken von Protestantischen kleinen Kirchen und Einrichtung* and again in 1718 in an improved edition: *Vollständigen Anweisung, alle Arten von Kirchen wohl anzugeben*. He was opposed to the cruciform plan and recommended churches with transverse orientation like the Schlosskirche at Königsberg, with pulpit and altar in the centre of one long side facing the ruler's pew, while the congregation were accommodated in the nave facing, wherever they sat, towards pulpit and altar. He also published a plan and elevation for a church on a square ground plan, which he preferred to cruciform, round, or triangular plans. As for style, he was a champion of classicism partly in its Dutch and partly in its French form, as opposed to the Baroque, which he rejected, condemning 'the thousand crooked lines, the thousand curved projections and recessions favoured by our worthy architects today'. Perrault's east façade of the Louvre was his ideal, 'which in execution and correctness can scarcely be equalled anywhere'. Unfortunately his ingenious remodelling of the chancel in the church of St Nikolai has not survived.[3] The church itself had been begun in 1708 by the engineer-architect Jakob Reutz on a Greek-cross plan, as part of the newly laid out Schelfstadt of Schwerin, and after Reutz's death Sturm completed it (1711–19). He placed pulpit and altar in the centre of a two-storeyed transparent columnar structure that extended as far as the beginning of the eastern limb. Singing tribunes were added over the orders.

In the north of Germany Catholic church architecture appeared only in one part of Ermland which temporarily belonged to Poland. The new pilgrimage church of Swięta Lipka (Heiligelinde) in East Prussia (1687–1730), built for the Jesuits by one Ertly, a mason of Vilna, was well adapted to the surrounding scenery.[4] The basilican plan with galleries and long choir is characteristic of the Order. On the two-tower façade is an impressive relief with the sacred lime-tree (Heiligelinde) and the figure of the Virgin and Child framed by coupled columns. It is probably the work of Matthias Poertzel of Königsberg, executed about 1730. The curving wooden caps of the towers give a northern note to the fine structure. Following the eastern type of fortified pilgrimage church, it is surrounded by an outer colonnade with corner chapels.

The domestic architecture of the Hanseatic towns continued to exploit the old form of a two-storeyed hall with built-in internal oriels and galleries. In Lübeck and Bremen the halls grew in size, giving ample scope for staircases with richly carved banisters. In Hamburg and Danzig on the other hand the narrow medieval frontage and the considerable depth of the plot were usually retained.

Excellent sandstone ornament decorates the façades of the houses at Bremen, culminating until after the middle of the seventeenth century in the fantastic decoration of the gable contours. About 1670 Dutch influence caused a reduction of the many steps of the gables to two. In Lübeck the gable was generally framed simply by two elongated volute bands. Stone was frequently replaced by brick. The wall was reduced to slender piers with attached orders of columns between high windows. The motif of superimposed orders was generally abandoned during the course of the late seventeenth century, but at the end of the century giant orders came into fashion. Baroque feeling found expression in the large volutes of the gables, which were retained. In the eighteenth century brick façades were articulated simply by wall strips or blind arcading. The windows were flush with the walls, and had white casements subdivided like English Georgian sashes. The economic decline of Danzig during the Baroque period led to a general use of plaster or brick instead of stone; in Bremen, on the other hand, the traditional art of decoration by sandstone ornament enjoyed a final efflorescence during the first half of the eighteenth century, with curving entablatures over doors and windows. In Bremen oriel windows were often added even to the older façades. The gables facing the streets were gradually abandoned during the course of the eighteenth century. In Danzig the middle class built little raised terraces, so-called 'Beischläge', in front of their houses, and here much of the day-to-day life of the family took place. During the seventeenth and eighteenth centuries they were given rich architectural ornamentation.

In 1733 the Duke of Mecklenburg-Neustrelitz began close to his palace at Neustrelitz a suburb planned on Renaissance principles with a square, centrally placed market and eight radiating streets.

Painting

The most famous north German painter of the day, Balthasar Denner of Hamburg (1685–1749), dazzled his contemporaries by the detailed naturalism of his heads, which were executed in a porcelain-like way. His real talent, which is reminiscent of Hogarth's, can be seen in the portrait heads of forty-six members of the court, including secretaries and footmen (Schwerin Museum), which he painted hastily, shortly before his death. His approaching end prevented him from giving them the usual miniature-like, exaggerated finish.

PART FIVE

ROCOCO AND ITS END 1740–80

CHAPTER 21

BAVARIA

Architecture

At this time, the political ties that linked the Elector Max Emanuel with the lower Rhine and France were once more a great cultural asset. The extent to which Bavaria profited can be seen from the dates: the first work of the Rococo in Germany, the Reichen Zimmer[1] of the Munich Residenz, was built in 1730–7; but it was not until ten years later that comparable work was done at Charlottenburg, under Frederick II. The chief credit for giving Bavaria her ten years' start goes to Max Emanuel personally; for it was he who, while Stadholder of the Spanish Netherlands, recognized the genius of a boy, of dwarfish body, and had him trained.

The boy was François de Cuvilliés, born at Soignies in Hainaut in 1695. He was about thirteen years of age when Max Emanuel appointed him a court dwarf, but had him educated with the sons of the aristocracy. Cuvilliés accompanied his patron to Munich and worked there as a draughtsman for the Generalbaudirektor (the Inspectorate of the Works). For further training the elector sent him to Paris, where he remained from 1720 to 1724 under the personal supervision of François Blondel the Younger. On his return to Munich in 1725 he was appointed Architect to the Court alongside Effner, and when Max Emanuel's son Karl Albert succeeded in 1726 he chose Cuvilliés to carry out his building projects. From 1728 Cuvilliés was also employed by Karl Albert's brother, Clemens August, elector of Cologne, for his palace at Brühl, between Cologne and Bonn – Schlaun, as we have seen, had been dismissed, because his Germano-Roman Baroque was no longer fashionable. In collaboration with the garden architect Dominique Girard, who had also come from Munich, Cuvilliés linked the palace more coherently with the surrounding squares and gardens. Various alterations to the façades, for instance a judicious distribution of segmental and semicircular window-heads, gave them a more elegant look. Cuvilliés's ideas can also be seen in the interior, which was not in fact decorated until some years later. His influence in later years was largely transmitted by his volume of engravings. The hunting lodge, Falkenlust (1729–40), built on the east side of the park, testifies to Cuvilliés's skill in the organization of space. The interior spaces also determine the shape of the exterior. Falkenlust foreshadows the more important later Amalienburg.

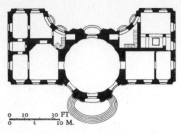

Figure 19. François de Cuvilliés:
Nymphenburg, Amalienburg,
1734–9. Plan

In Munich Cuvilliés's fame was established by the decoration in 1730–7 of the Reichen Zimmer of the Residenz. Natural forms make their first appearance there: flowers, branches, tendrils, and palm-leaves replace the usual ribbonwork, and their growth gives the whole scheme an increased verticalism. The strict division in panels, characteristic of the French Regency, is gradually relaxed as more dynamic forms are introduced. The upper cornice especially is often set in motion, and issues naturalistic windswept foliage that curves into the ceiling. Owing to their size and the emphasis given to every one, the individual motifs are far more impressive than those of Effner. Trelliswork with curves and branches is the most significant, more certainly than the shell. All the figurework is exceptionally fine. An essential part of the credit for the work goes to the craftsmen, to the plasterer Johann Baptist Zimmermann and to the wood-carvers Joachim Dietrich and Wenzeslaus Mirofsky.

The Amalienburg, part of Nymphenburg, built in 1734–9 for the Electress Maria Amalia (Plates 137B and 138 and Figure 19), represents the culmination of Cuvilliés's art. Adjoining the central circular saloon are two rooms on either side, scaled in proportion. The *enfilade* lies along the central axis and ends in either direction with a window. The harmony of the whole is enhanced by the colour, an alternation of blues and yellows, with silver for the decoration shedding a radiance over everything. Externally the central room projects in an undulating curve, and at the back the façade recedes concavely. Originally the balustrade carried vases. The dome served as a platform to shoot pheasants from. In the eighteenth century the axes of the Amalienburg were continued in avenues of the French type.

When Cuvilliés was working in the city, he must have had closer contacts with the German Baroque. The façades of the Munich palaces adjoined the fronts of the homely middle-class houses, and this in itself must have linked the two approaches to architec-

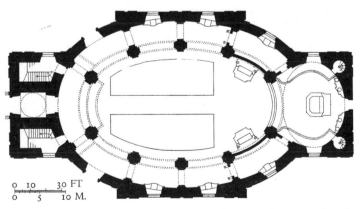

Figure 20. Dominikus Zimmermann: Steinhausen, pilgrimage church,
1728–31. Plan

ture. On the other hand, the Palais Piosasque de Non in the Theatinerstrasse (1726) has Ionic columns left and right of the portal and details in the central projection which are clearly French. The abundance and gaiety of the ornament, however, are equally clearly Bavarian. The same applies to the Preysing Palace in the Prannerstrasse (c. 1740). Between 1733 and 1737 Cuvilliés designed a thoroughly Baroque façade, surging upwards in a giant order of columns, for the Palais Holnstein, later the episcopal palace. In his most beautiful late work, the Residenz Theatre in Munich, built in 1751–3, he paid tribute to the Rococo. Here again, inside, instead of columns he used palm-trees that seem to sway in the breeze.

In 1763 Cuvilliés was finally appointed Oberhofbaumeister (Chief Architect to the Court). During his last years, from 1765 to 1768, he made a model for a remodelling of the Residenz and for the façade of the Theatinerkirche in which he reduced the high relief of Zuccalli's design. Until his death in 1768 he continued to work on a volume of engravings for ornament and architecture which he had begun in 1738; it was this book that gave the German Rococo its particular character.[2]

While architecture at the court was receiving its ultimate refinement at the hands of Cuvilliés, rustic upper Bavarian as well as upper Swabian architecture was flourishing in the idyllic Pfaffenwinkel east of the upper Lech. Its roots were entirely different; its brilliance of colour and light revealed the unspoilt freshness and purity of the foothills of the Alps. The genius in this area was Dominikus Zimmermann,[3] a simple master mason. His most appreciative patrons were the Premonstratensians of Schussenried and Steingaden. Born at Wessobrunn in 1685, Zimmermann, following local custom, was first trained as a plasterer. In 1716 he moved to Landsberg, where he worked as an architect. As such he developed the conceit first realized by Viscardi and later by Fischer of an elongated oval nave surrounded by arcades with an ambulatory and a transverse oval for the chancel. An example is the pilgrimage church of Steinhausen near Schussenried, built by Zimmermann in 1728–31 (Plate 139 and Figure 20). Though he had not invented this scheme, it brought out his creative powers to the full; he accepted inspiration from others, but he recognized the specific problems involved in his tasks, and in the end he always produced original solutions.

An essential factor in Dominikus's success was his collaboration with his brother Johann Baptist Zimmermann, who had acquired a big reputation as a painter and plasterer through his work for the Residenz and the Amalienburg. The composition of Steinhausen, with a narrow ambulatory and high lower and broad upper windows, was calculated to assure the greatest influx of light at the top so as to give full effect to the painting in the vault (Plate 148B). This composition is even more successful in the Wieskirche, where the wooden construction permitted a shallower vault built into the rafters of the roof. Zimmermann's pleasure in graceful nimble forms derives from the French Rococo; the delight in natural forms, however, is not French. The curving outlines of his windows are entirely his own, and, as soon as one arrives, proclaim his authorship. Such irrational, abstract motifs are on the other hand typically German. At Steinhausen his passion for irrational curves is visible not only in the windows of the gables of the front and the straight centres of the sides, but also in those set transversely, left and right

of the transept-like centre, and rising with their curved sides into the roof (Plate 140).
Just as the interior recalls Late Gothic hall churches, so these features of the exterior
recall the gables of the German Renaissance. The slender tower rising above the porches
is also a German motif, whereas the subtle harmony of the light colour scheme of the
interior is Rococo. Favourite colours were a delicate pale blue and pink for the capitals,
and for the rest white, gold, and yellow set on a green ground, or an interplay of blue,
yellow, and white. The so-called 'Bavarian Manner' consists of white or coloured
stucco, with only the most important points heightened with gold; the 'French Manner', used exclusively by the court, preferred gilded or silvered sculpture and plasterwork set on a white ground. At Steinhausen the polychrome interior forms an introduction to the magic of Johann Baptist Zimmermann's frescoes, with their dominant
radiant blue. They were painted in 1730–1 (Plate 148B).

The ideas only in bud, as it were, at Steinhausen appear in full flower seventeen years
later at the Church in the Wies, built in 1745–54 (Plate 141A and Figure 21). Here,

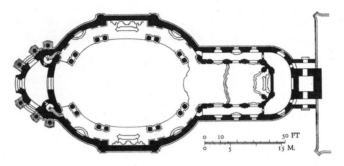

Figure 21. Dominikus Zimmermann: Die Wies, church,
1745–54. Plan

between the oval nave and the ambulatory, instead of single pillars and an even spacing
Zimmermann used coupled columns and an alternately wide and narrow spacing. The
result is a more vigorous rhythm. The increased width of the arches on the longitudinal
axis is repeated on the transverse axis. The wooden construction, in which horizontal
beams span the interstices between the columns, permitted the arches – being no more
than an infilling – to be erected regardless of static limitations. The enchantment of the
colour is even greater than at Steinhausen. Pink and green combined with gold and the
bluish white of the shells that dominate the ornament merge into the deeper blue and
red of the chancel columns and lead up to the pale blue of Johann Baptist Zimmermann's great ceiling fresco. The *stucco lustro*, with its transparent, shimmering tones and
increased luminosity, was an ideal material for an art that was at once unreal and earthbound. Equally new and happy ideas appear in the details, for instance in the columns,
which consist in section of four sharp edges of an imaginary square inner pier set diagonally and the curving surfaces between. Thanks to the wooden construction, Zimmermann was able to keep the arches quite flat and scroll them up and, in the choir,
even scroll them down with *rocaille* forms.

This climax of the German Rococo was reached in the middle of the eighteenth century, at a moment when classicism was just round the corner, and when most of the men whose taste counted no longer had any patience with this kind of work. The abbots of Steinhausen and Schussenried were dismissed because of the high cost of their buildings. But among ordinary folk and those artists who were close to them the Baroque was so firmly rooted that there was agreement in its favour even where no outstanding architect was at hand. This was the case with the rebuilding of the Benedictine pilgrimage church of Andechs on the Ammersee (1746–59). Here we find a characteristic group of men: the abbot Bernhard Schütz of Wessobrunn, almost certainly belonging to a local family of masons and plasterers, Lorenz Sappel of Munich, the master mason, Ignatius Merani, a lay brother in the Jesuit seminary of Landsberg on the Lech, Johann Baptist Zimmermann, the plasterer and painter, and Johann Baptist Straub and Franz Xaver Schmaedl, the sculptors. The basic idea was a brilliant one: to remove the easternmost pair of free-standing piers of the medieval church, to build a polygonal gallery round the enlarged interior, and to clothe the whole in Bavarian Rococo ornament.

Without renouncing its essential native qualities, the architects and artists of the Bavarian Rococo were still able to express the new ideals. This applies in particular to Johann Michael Fischer. He was born in the Oberpfalz in 1692, the son of Johann Michael Fischer, municipal master mason of Burglengenfeld. The pilgrimage church of Mariahilf at Freystadt near by, built by Viscardi, was an example of a centralized building with the dome supported by eight pillars, and this plan was to be varied and further developed throughout the younger Fischer's work. He could also have been in contact with the Dientzenhofer circle without leaving the Oberpfalz. Then, working as a foreman in Brno and other parts of Moravia about 1715–16, he got to know the Austrian style. Round about 1717–18 he was certainly in Munich working as a foreman for Johann Mayr, mason to the city. In 1722 he became master mason himself. He died in 1766. The inscription on his monument in the Frauenkirche in Munich records that he built thirty-two churches, twenty-three monasteries, and very many palaces, and adds that he also edified many hundreds of souls by his ancient German honesty and sincerity.

Compared with Zimmermann's, Fischer's style is less rustic and has less popular appeal, and accordingly is less closely linked with the Gothic traditions of the hall church. Indeed, the feeling for clarity and harmony which was characteristic of the age became more and more pronounced in his work as he grew older. In the early church of St Anna am Lehel in Munich (1727–39; Figure 22),[4] which is equal in quality to the contemporary Steinhausen, he comes very close to Zimmermann. Here, too, the plan consists of an elongated oval with a transverse oval chancel. The eight pillars, on the other hand, are not free-standing but attached to the walls. The chapels do not open from an ambulatory but project directly from the oval nave, and the centralized effect is emphasized by the framed oval fresco of the vault. As in Zimmermann's work, the flow of light is carefully calculated – in this case it is determined by the large upper windows. The dynamic verve demanded by the Baroque is secured by the upward thrust of the slender piers with their high fragments of entablature and the curving transverse arches. Above, bands of plasterwork shaped like volutes form the transition to the frame of the

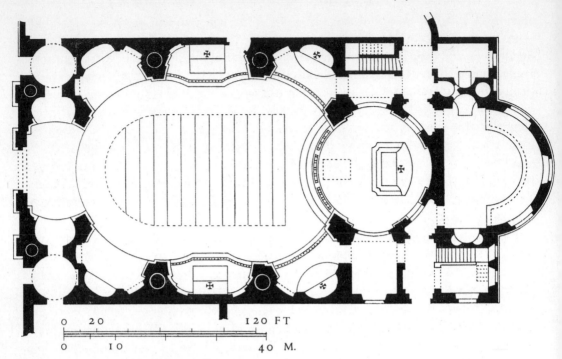

0   20   120 FT

0   10   40 M.

Figure 22. Johann Michael Fischer: Munich, St Anna am Lehel, 1727–39. Plan

painting in the vault, which is also curving. The composition is already based on calculated geometrical relationships.

The pilgrimage church of Maria Schnee at Aufhausen near Regensburg, built immediately after, from 1736 to 1751, has Fischer's favourite plan, an octagon with unequal sides, in the severe form developed from circle and square. Even so, the square anteroom and chancel produce an elongated rectangular shape for the whole building. However, the central octagon with its eight coupled pilasters dominates unmistakably. The span of the arches opening into the chancel and the anteroom is far wider than at St Anna. Furthermore, the arches into the two chapels on the transverse axis are given the same span. The resulting contrast with the diagonal chapels, the spacing of which is only half as wide, creates a strong rhythmic articulation. Galleries are inserted above the chapels to prevent the arches from appearing too high and too narrow. This, too, follows Viscardi's model. The coupled pilasters, broken across the corners, have strongly dominant capitals and fragments of entablature, secured as they are by the galleries which act as a kind of bracing. The galleries are continued on either side of the chancel along the main line of vision. The link between the arches and the great central round of the fresco in the vault is successfully established by three-dimensional arches ('diadem arches') which reach into the base of the dome. Here again the vertical thrust is clearly emphasized in the eight main supports, but at the same time movement radiates from them in all directions. The balustrades of the small galleries curve forward too.

The blending of clear composition with delight in movement, added to gay colours and a great influx of light, is one of the chief beauties of Fischer's interiors. An excellent

234

example of this was the pilgrimage church of St Mary at Ingolstadt (Plate 141B and Figure 23), built by Augustinians in 1736–9 and now destroyed. The general elevation was similar to Maria Schnee, but the octagon and the radiating chapels were more compact. The oval diagonal chapels curved forward into the interior, and the outer walls of the chapels bulged outward along the transverse axis. The adjoining square choir was surrounded on either side by galleries

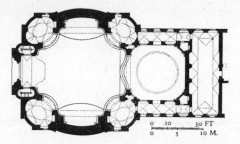

Figure 23. Johann Michael Fischer: Ingolstadt, St Mary, 1736–9. Plan

and passages. Light poured into the church from all sides, and the indirect lighting of the galleries produced the effect of a brilliantly lit ambulatory.

Whereas the church at Ingolstadt had a comparatively pure central plan, the plan of the church of the Fraternity of St Michael at Berg-am-Laim near Munich (1737–43) developed during the course of the building into a series of four rooms scaled in proportion. By following a first octagon by a second on a smaller scale and with three-quarter columns to heighten the sculptural effect, Fischer created a crescendo towards the high altar. The lower zone of the vault that leads the eye to the fresco higher up is again enlivened by 'diadem' arches. Small independent cupolas crown the side penetrations. The reflection of the great central area in miniature in the smaller vaults is typical of Fischer and expresses his sense of the unity of a building. This unity, it is true, could not embrace plasterwork, painting, and sculpture quite so successfully as it does in the work of the Zimmermann brothers, since Fischer was forced to collaborate with a variety of painters and sculptors. For a year during the course of building Jacob Kögelsberger of Munich succeeded in ousting Fischer from the direction, and it was he who was responsible for the two-tower façade.

The interior decoration of St Anna am Lehel and of the church of the Premonstratensian abbey at Osterhofen (1726–31), also an early work, was carried out by the brothers Asam, and their brilliance and gaiety dominates the whole in both cases. Osterhofen is Fischer's first important building designed on a longitudinal plan. He enlivened the system of internal buttresses and galleries by making the pilasters recede in concave curves, chamfering the edges of the piers and bringing the arches forward in a corresponding convex curve. There can be no doubt that the building shows signs of his contact with the Dientzenhofer circle; as opposed, however, to the church at Krzeszów, built two years later and also influenced by the Dientzenhofers (Plate 86), Fischer gives a smoother, more even flow to the wavy lines of his composition.

In his next work, the church of the Augustinian Canons at Diessen on the Ammersee (1731–9), Bohemian features tend to give way to a more Bavarian character. The galleries are discarded, so that the internal buttresses project more vigorously into the interior. They are oblong in section, and this gives all the more monumentality to the forward-sweeping curves of the ribs above.

Compared with the interiors, the exteriors of Bavarian churches are often of little importance. Certain of Fischer's façades do, however, form an exception, and Diessen is an example. Fischer's personal style can be seen in the architectural articulation in which, for all its disciplined severity, there is a supple vitality. While here, however, the wall still remains flat, in the façade of the Benedictine abbey church of Zwiefalten in Swabia, built later, from 1741 to 1765, the soft curves have a much more three-dimensional effect. In the centre Fischer replaces the pilasters by pairs of columns with a broken pediment above them. In the interior, too, the accent is on the coupled demi-columns set in front of the internal buttresses. The effect is further intensified by the dominant pink and pale blue-grey of the scagliola in the lowest zone, and by the continuation of the rounded forms of the plan in the forward curve of the galleries. Moreover Fischer surpassed himself in providing ample vaulted areas for the frescoes.

With Zwiefalten Fischer established his reputation in Swabia too, and as a result he was commissioned in 1748 to complete the rebuilding of the imperial Benedictine abbey of Ottobeuren near Memmingen. This great task occupied him throughout the 1750s. He was tied to a plan of the 1730s, but the imprint of his personal, more advanced style gave an overall unity to the whole structure. The building history is somewhat complicated. In 1732 Dominikus Zimmermann had submitted a plan for a longitudinal building with a large oval central space surrounded by a narrow ambulatory in the manner of Steinhausen. Owing to the important nature of the commission, however, more monumental forms were required, and these had been introduced by Zimmermann in his plan in the design of two front towers. In 1736 the abbot decided to call in Simpert Kramer, a mason from the Allgäu, experienced in work for monasteries. He replaced Zimmermann's elongated oval by a central transept, the arms terminating in apses, widened the ambulatory, and, following Weingarten, changed the front between the

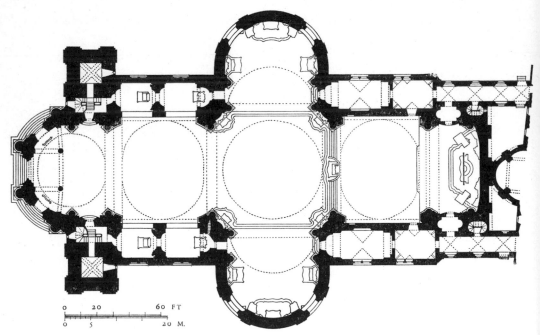

Figure 24. Johann Michael Fischer and others: Ottobeuren, Benedictine abbey church, begun 1737. Plan

towers from a concave to a convex curve. The foundation stone was laid in 1737. But it was not until 1748, after Fischer with his greater capacity for work had been called in, that the building really got under way. By giving a more pronounced chamfering to the crossing piers and adding demi-columns, Fischer gave the transept a centralized appearance (Figure 24). He also obtained the kind of sequence he favoured by placing a hemispherical vault without a drum over the crossing and by adding transversely oval saucer domes over nave and choir (Plate 142).

During the last years of his life Fischer worked for the Benedictine abbey of Rott am Inn near Wasserburg (1759–63; Plate 143 and Figure 25). Here he was again able to

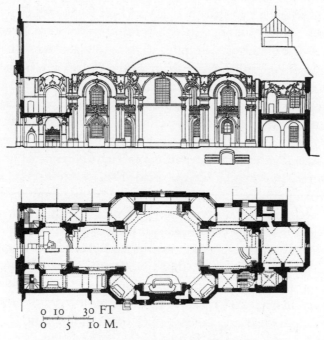

Figure 25. Johann Michael Fischer: Rott am Inn,
abbey church, 1759–63. Section and plan

provide an octagon formed by piers as the centre of a longitudinal building. This central area is the dominant element. Tangential octagonal chapels lie on the diagonal axes. Smaller squares are added, in front of and behind the centre, and all three areas are covered with flat domes containing paintings by Matthäus Günther of Augsburg. The building is less dynamic, but lighter and more transparent. This effect is produced mainly by large upper windows and galleries which also flank the two squares. In spite of the impressive length of the church, the idea of a centralized building is never lost. The three circular domes emphasize it successively. In his preference for circular plans and for plans where an octagon is developed from a square, Fischer was more up-to-date than Zimmermann, who retained the oval plan.

Sculpture

In the field of sculpture Faistenberger and Egid Quirin Asam had established a firm tradition in Munich. This was carried on by Straub, and culminated in the art of Ignaz Günther. Unlike the older generation, the younger artists born in the eighteenth century were attracted less to Rome and Antwerp than to Vienna, the imperial capital.

Johann Baptist Straub (1704–84) was born at Wiesensteig near Geislingen, at that time part of the Bavarian electorate. He was trained in Munich, and during his subsequent journeyman years visited Vienna, where he worked for six years, until 1734, with Christoph Mader, who was engaged on the reliefs for the columns of the Karlskirche. He was recalled to Munich by Faistenberger, and here from 1735 to 1784 he ran a large workshop for ecclesiastical sculpture in which many artists were trained.

The importance of sculpture at that time can be appreciated from the extent to which sculptured altarpieces determine the rhythm of the church interior. At Ettal on each side of the rotunda are three altars by Straub done in 1757–65. The asymmetrical forms of the Rococo retables become part of a harmonious whole by means of an ingenious system of counterbalancing adjacent as well as opposite altars. Moreover, as became customary after the middle of the eighteenth century, the figures were painted white and gold and thus at once catch the eye of the spectator. Straub achieved a similar harmony in the altarpieces and pulpits that he made for Diessen (*c.* 1739) and for the abbey church of Schäftlarn (1755–64). His work is less sensitive and individual than is the work of his pupil Ignaz Günther. Straub never lost a Viennese touch, which can be seen in the realistic attitudes and the complete absence of any Mannerism; his figure of *Raphael* from the abbey church at Schäftlarn (*c.* 1760; now in the Bayerische Nationalmuseum; Plate 144A) once ascribed to him, is presumably a work of Günther. Compared with it, his *David* in the church of Rott am Inn is more emotional. He is represented not as a beautiful youth but as an old man, his left hand expressively outstretched. On occasion Straub could come very close to nature, as can be seen in his *St Catherine of Siena* for the high altar of the church of Altomünster (*c.*1760; now in the Bayerische Nationalmuseum; Plate 144B). It is a splendid piece of work, presenting the great Dominican saint in the character and quality of a noble Bavarian nun. Faced with the same task, Günther would have been much more personal in his style; Straub was still bound by the older tradition which made the artist subordinate his own style to the service of the Church.

Ignaz Günther (1725–75) was born at Altmannstein near Ingolstadt in the valley of the Danube, the son of a joiner. He was apprenticed to Straub, and remained with him for seven years (1743–50). As can be seen from his early drawings, he studied, among other things, bronze sculpture of about 1600 in Munich. It suited his innate sympathy with Mannerism, which emerged fully in his later work. His architectural designs show an understanding of the spatial problems of church architecture that goes beyond the realm of sculpture.

His subsequent journeyman years took him first to Salzburg and then to Mannheim, where the Mannerist quality of Paul Egell's Baroque made a deep impression on him. In addition Egell's interest in nature, and the dynamic character and strong emotions of his figures, intensified Günther's dislike of cold classicism.[5] But Günther developed his style more in a Mannerist than in a Baroque direction. With such ideas he found little to stimulate him in Vienna, where he went after Egell's death in 1752. He studied at the Vienna Academy for six months and won a first prize. The wooden statuettes of the *Borghese Gladiator* and the *Medici Venus* carved at that time show the nature of academic tasks.

Immediately afterwards he returned to Munich, where he set up on his own, and during the last two decades of his life worked with ever-increasing fervour. The commission for the altarpieces of the church of Rott am Inn (1760–2; Plates 145A and 146), where he collaborated with Johann Michael Fischer and the painter Matthäus Günther, gave Ignaz Günther a share in one of the greatest tasks of the Bavarian Rococo. Günther's Mannerism, it is true, with his preference for over-slim figures in angular postures, drapery billowing sideways, and small heads on long bent necks never attained the over-all unity that had characterized the Baroque some twenty years before. The high altar at Diessen with its many figures and flowing movement shows that clearly. On the other hand the spectator looking at an altar by Günther is inescapably arrested by the individual figure, not so much by a general theatrical pose as by the virtuosity of a vivid naturalism heightened by polychromy. So one has to go near a figure by Günther to receive its full impact. The spectator feels these figures may at any moment move and speak. Only an artist steeped in native tradition could grasp the essential character of a personage and interpret it in such an original and personal way. All the native characteristics of the Bavarians are concentrated in his art: sensuous warmth, fun, and coarse vitality. Even when he accepts the aristocratic culture of the court he never loses these qualities.

It might be asked how far an art that can present the angel in the celebrated group of the *Annunciation* at Weyarn (1764; Plate 147) in the guise of a ballerina with low décolleté can be called religious. The answer is that such a figure expresses popular piety – the people regarded it as beautiful and willingly gave it a place in their heaven. The same applies to the *St Joachim* represented as a slender dancer who seems to have stepped straight out of the world of Italian Comedy. In many respects Günther's art seems to have drawn the ultimate possibilities from that of the Asam brothers. He expressed his admiration for the 'artistry' of Egid Quirin Asam both in writing and in his sculpture: the *Minerva* on the façade of the Asam House, who is drawing the attention of the 'Münchner Kindl' to art, lives on in Günther's even more Bavarian *Guardian Angel* of 1763 in the Munich Bürgersaal (Plate 145B). Among his favourite subjects are putti with little button noses, chubby cheeks, and slanting eyes, and he introduces them in every possible mood. Always the curly hair forms a rippling Rococo frame for the face.

Church art had established a link with the court, if only by adopting elegant poses from it and applying them to religious figures. Ladies and gentlemen had their place even in the most edifying religious scenes. Sculpture in porcelain supplied the common ground. The success of this form, and the great reputation of the Nymphenburg porcelain manufactory, had been made by the southern Swiss Francesco Antonio Bustelli (1723–63), whose Mannerist style, wit, and realism were akin to Günther and very different from Kändler. Bustelli's aristocratic dancing couples are an illustration of the eighteenth century's love of music. His famous bust of *Count Sigismund Haimhausen* of 1761 is the most outstanding work of Bavarian Rococo portraiture; the vivid expression and at the same time the monumentality of form rival French art of the period.

Painting

After the death of the Asam brothers the centre of south German painting shifted from Munich to Augsburg in Swabia (p. 247). The fame of its academies attracted artists whose home was in Bavarian territory, among them the brothers Thomas and Felix Anton Scheffler of lower Bavaria, pupils of Cosmas Damian Asam (see p. 247). In Munich the mantle of the Asams fell on Johann Baptist Zimmermann (1680-1758), who from 1721 was employed frequently by the court. Working under the direction of Cuvilliés, he accepted the Rococo to a much greater degree than did the Asams. His experience as a plasterer led him to use plaster motifs and landscape elements as a transition to the ceiling frescoes instead of the customary architectural members (Plate 148B). The typically Bavarian–Swabian church interior, resplendent with light colours, is largely Zimmermann's creation.

How vital this style was is proved by the length of time it endured in Bavaria – a parallel to the situation in the Tyrol of which mention has been made earlier. Christian Wink (1738-97) retained it until the end of the eighteenth century, his greater sense of realism adding a new note. Moreover he remained a master in the art of grouping in continuous lines of composition and in achieving the illusion of space by a broad painterly technique and chiaroscuro effects. He became the most sought-after painter for small village churches; examples are Lohe near Deggendorf (1768) and St Leonhard at Dietramszell (1769; Plate 149). At the very end of the eighteenth century frescoes of this kind were still painted for peasants on the walls of their houses, which shows how deeply attached the entire population was to these vivid representations (Plate 148A).

The leading portrait painter of his day was George de Marées (1697-1766). He was born in Sweden and studied painting under his great-uncle Martin Mytens the Elder in Stockholm. In 1724 he went to Nuremberg via Amsterdam, where he met the aged Kupecký. His journeys took him to Venice in 1725, where he visited Piazzetta, back to Nuremberg in 1728, and to Munich in 1731, where he remained for the rest of his life, one of the favourite portrait painters of the court. His *Self-Portrait* of 1728 in the Germanisches Nationalmuseum at Nuremberg reveals both French influence and the somewhat limp effeminacy of his own style. The portrait of the painter *J. F. Beich* of 1743 in the same museum is more vigorous, somewhat in the manner of Kupecký. Under the influence of the Rococo Marées's art became lighter and more varied in colour, and he paid more attention to costume, as can be seen in the portrait of *Count Max of Preysing-Hohenaschau*. In other works, for instance the portrait of *Countess Holnstein* in Munich (Plate 150A) or that of *Elector Max III Joseph of Bavaria with his Intendant Count Seau*, he appears more personal (Plate 151B). There is more than a touch of decadence in this latter portrait. The elector's crown lies beside him, and a barely visible canopy rises above him; in his hand, instead of the sceptre, he holds a cup of chocolate, and his lap-dog is on his knees. It is left to the Intendant at his side to make the commanding gesture.

Marées's brilliant but superficial art is in complete contrast to that of his successor, Johann Georg Edlinger (1741–1819). The latter, the son of a gardener from Graz, settled permanently at Munich in 1771. The difference between the two artists is due basically to the times in which they lived and to the social strata to which they belonged. Marées was the painter of the court, Edlinger of the middle classes. Edlinger was in no way conventional; he consistently followed his sense of reality, something which did not appear in Munich again until a hundred years later. He ought really to be understood as belonging to 'Sturm and Drang' – more so than Graff. Also, his preference for brown tones and his broad, fluffy, painterly technique link him more closely to the Baroque than to classicism (Plate 150B).

CHAPTER 22

SWABIA AND SWITZERLAND

Architecture

DURING the Rococo period Swabia and Switzerland fell more and more under the influence of Bavarian art, especially as transmitted by way of Zwiefalten and Otto-beuren. Swabia in particular appreciated its painterly qualities; as early as 1727 the brilliant work of the brothers Zimmermann at Steinhausen, with its combination of Bavarian and Swabian characteristics, had gained them tremendous prestige. The hold of Bavarian art was strengthened at Zwiefalten, where the scagliola of the coupled columns shimmers on the white wall and passes from brown to blue and gold in the capitals. The plan with internal buttresses was kept, but the emphasis is on the decoration. The buttresses are pierced by arches only at the top; the real attraction for the eye is the side altars below.

The masters from the Vorarlberg too were aware of the Bavarian successes, for they invited the Asams to work for them at Weingarten in 1718–20 and at Einsiedeln in 1724–6. The Vorarlberg style, with its robust, solid forms, did not take easily to the Rococo spirit; but Peter Thumb (1681–1766) did succeed in creating something new out of the traditional elements of the internal-buttress plan in the pilgrimage church of Birnau on Lake Constance (1746–58). Indeed, Birnau rivals Wies, begun in the same year, in the dynamic beauty of its interior, flooded with light (Plate 153). Thumb was encouraged here by the understanding of his patrons, the Cistercians of Salem, who chose the splendid site by the lake, and by the skill of his collaborators, the sculptor and plasterer Joseph Anton Feuchtmayer and the painter Gottfried Bernhard Göz of Augsburg, both outstanding artists.

Peter Thumb was born in 1681 at Bezau in the Vorarlberg, the son of Michael Thumb, a master mason of Schönenberg and Obermarchthal. From 1704 he worked as foreman for Franz Beer, whose eldest daughter he married. Subsequently he occupied an influential position at Constance, and in 1738 built the library of the monastery of St Peter in the Black Forest (see p. 170). Several features of the library he used again at Birnau: the plan with a narrow balcony; the undulating balustrade of the balcony, formed by introducing segmental curves in the long sides, a kind of rudimentary transepts, and by rounding the corners between nave and first piers of the receding chancel; the vault with penetrations; and the division into two parts with a central axis. The curves of the ribbonwork on the balcony balustrade seem to reflect Hildebrandt. A wealth of light floods in through the double ring of windows, illuminating the very shallow vaults, whose large, unbroken expanse presents a fine surface for the painter, and the whole of the delicate, pale colouring of the interior. At the front a slender, vigorous tower rises high between two flanking priests' houses with hipped roofs, and the resulting compact group stands splendidly above the lake.

For the final building of the Benedictine abbey church of St Gallen, the old type of a hall plan with internal buttresses was combined with the later type of a central rotunda with piers. Peter Thumb was employed for eleven years on this building, from 1748 to 1758; his contribution is not at all clear, however, because, besides him, seven others had furnished projects, all of which had influence, such as those of Giovanni Gaspare Bagnato of Como, master mason to the Works of the Teutonic Order on Lake Constance, whose co-operation was enlisted in 1749. The result was the design of the great rotunda with six chapels in the form of fragmentary ovals. In addition, he probably influenced the design of the splended two-towered east front (Plate 152B). The old nave was pulled down in 1755; by 1760 the new building, including its decoration, was complete. The new east front, erected by Johann Michael Beer of Bildstein between 1761 and 1768, is a magnificent finale to the Baroque age. Interestingly enough, the abbot noted in his diary that Beer was incapable of inventing or drawing a competent plan.

To pay tribute to the importance of the historic site, the medieval plan with an apse at either end was retained for the new building. Chancel and nave are of equal length, and each has a system of internal buttresses, thus carrying on the tradition of the Vorarlberg cathedrals – but there are no galleries. The sense of unity of the Baroque is thus no longer fully appreciated. Both the sculptured reliefs and the painted vault begin to stress the isolation of each individual figure. The *rocaille* ornament becomes detached from the architecture, over which it hangs like a cobweb. On the other hand the old unity is still fully preserved in the east front. The idea of a rounded central projection between two towers, developed at Weingarten and Einsiedeln, is adopted, and the upward thrust is even more emphatic. Baroque dynamism sets all parts of the façade in motion, even to the pilasters of the towers.

For the library of St Gallen, built in 1758–67 (Plate 152A), Peter Thumb employed the system of internal buttresses that he had already used for the library of St Peter in the Black Forest. Indeed he actually improved on it by using three-quarter columns instead of brackets to support the gallery curving round the buttresses, thus giving a sharper articulation.

Another important library was built slightly earlier, for the abbey of Schussenried. This was probably designed by Dominikus Zimmermann, and was completed c. 1757. It has a gallery supported by free-standing columns and bookshelves that line the walls. In its all-embracing yet restrained rhythm, it comes much closer to the Rococo ideal of grace than does the library of St Gallen.

The persistent vitality of the Vorarlberg-Swabian Baroque is proved by the fact that one of its most important works, the rebuilding of the Benedictine abbey church of Wiblingen, was begun as late as 1772. Once again the St Gallen design of a central rotunda and a convex front flanked by towers was adopted. The architect, Johann Georg Specht (1720–1803), Imperial Oberamtsbaumeister in the counties of Bregenz and Hohenegg, obviously belongs to the school of Peter Thumb.

At the very same time, after a fire in 1768, the Benedictine abbey of St Blasien in the Black Forest was under construction. With its central plan (in imitation of the Parthenon) and heavy dome, it is decidedly classicist. It was built by the French architect Michel d'Ixnard of Strasbourg, and consecrated in 1783.

In Württemberg the new palace at Stuttgart, begun in 1744, succeeded the one at Ludwigsburg as the most outstanding work of palace architecture. It was Duke Karl Eugen's wish that his palace should be built in the 'neuen Goût der Architektur'. The architects, Leopoldo Retti, who was in charge until his death in 1751, and his successor till 1768, Pierre-Louis-Philippe de la Guêpière, clearly followed French principles. The extent to which their classicist horizontalism differs from the Baroque verticalism of Neumann, who also submitted plans in 1747, is strikingly shown in the latter's suggestion for alterations. Retti's plan allotted an order of pilasters to each floor and allowed the central block with rounded corners to project. Neumann on the other hand, his senior by seventeen years, kept the centre block flush with the *corps de logis* but stressed it by an order of giant demi-columns, by omitting the cornice above the main floor, and by increasing the height of the pediment and roof.

Guêpière also built two charming country houses: Solitude near Stuttgart (1763 etc.) and Monrepos near Ludwigsburg (1764–7). Solitude has the Baroque theme (p. 94) of a central oval room with lower wings and adjoining end pavilions with terraces and a staircase on each side; Monrepos has a similar oval room but with a vestibule in front. The projecting oval on the garden side is counterbalanced, as at Amalienburg, by a concave centre on the entrance side. On all four sides curving stairs lead to what was to have been a series of stepped terraces descending to the lake. Basically the art of laying out a series of interpenetrating rooms is still preserved; but the ornament closely adhering to the surfaces is in the French classicist style.

Sculpture

The plasterers, whose art, similarly to that of the fresco painter, takes easily to improvisation, adopted *rocaille* ornament all the more readily as it gave them a determining part in the Rococo ensemble. The plasterer could emulate such natural forms as shells, corals, sponges, bark with curling ends, palm-fronds, flowering branches, since anything asymmetrical, vaguely floating, or broken was in demand, provided it was vivid enough and fitted in with the whole. The design was left to intuition; it was impossible to make preliminary drawings or models. Wessobrunn experienced a great boom. More and more, plasterers encroached on the domain of the sculptor. In 1724 the Augsburg sculptors sent a long statement to the council complaining of the illegal competition of the plasterers who, as members of the stone-masons' guild, were only entitled to do work connected with masonry. An agreement was reached in 1725 whereby it was ruled that all independent sculpture such as reliefs, statues, coats-of-arms, and shields was to be reserved for the sculptor. It was laid down in paragraph two that masons and plasterers were only permitted to do such work if they called in a sculptor. However the imperial abbeys, who were the chief patrons, paid little attention to such regulations. Johann Georg Übelherr (1700–63) of Wessobrunn, plasterer to the Prince Abbot Anselm of Kempten, was called a specialist in 'large pieces'. Between 1730 and 1733 he collaborated with Johann Baptist Zimmermann on the Reichen Zimmer of the Munich Residenz, where he adopted the Rococo of Cuvilliés. Between 1734 and 1746 the brio and the undertones of melodrama which characterize his style reached a first peak at the former Residenz at Kempten (Plate 151A). From 1741 to 1746 he collaborated with Johann Michael Feuchtmayer on the decoration of the Cistercian abbey church of Wilhering near Linz, and this was followed in 1742–9 by the Benedictine abbey church of Münsterschwarzach and in 1744 etc. by that of the church at Amorbach for the same order.

There was a similar collaboration between artists at the Benedictine abbey church of Zwiefalten. There, for Johann Michael Fischer's church, Johann Joseph Christian (1706–77) did the sculpture, while Feuchtmayer undertook the decorative plasterwork (1744–56). Feuchtmayer generally used models by Christian for his figures. Until a short time ago Christian's importance as a sculptor was not properly recognized.[1] He is something of a lone figure in Swabian art, coming very near to classicism in his reliefs for the choir stalls at Zwiefalten, even though he does allow the rhythm of the *rocaille* to set his frames in motion. Moreover, the choir stalls themselves, carved by the carpenter Martin Hermann of Villingen, are still fully Baroque in the passionate curves of the cornice and the superstructures. In contrast to this, the majestic figures from the New and Old Testaments on the main altar and the stone statue of *St Benedict* over the porch show the noble restraint of which Christian was capable. Even they, however, retain the abundance of the Baroque. In the plaster figures of *St Gertrude* and *St Scholastica* on another altar, modelled by Christian's son Franz Joseph (1739–98), Baroque dynamism is restricted to the broken lines of the otherwise quietly falling drapery folds, and the ecstasy of the saints is but subtly suggested.

The successful collaboration thus established between the architect Fischer, the sculptor Christian, the plasterer Feuchtmayer, and the carpenter Hermann was continued between 1757 and 1766 at Ottobeuren. There, the choir stalls are less exuberant. The larger reliefs and the use of atlantes instead of putti on the backs are evidence of Christian's increased participation in the work. Presumably he had paid a visit to Vienna, where Donner's art must have come as a revelation. Here lies the source of the increased monumentality of his style. Under the influence of works by Donner and Mattielli, he stressed the nude form in the atlantes; clearly he must have made studies from life for them. His interest in psychology, too, was increased by observing living models. The result is masterpieces such as the *St Conrad*, the ideal of the spiritualized bishop (Plate 154B). Indeed, spiritualization is altogether characteristic of his art.

If we turn from Christian's gravity, which was in accord with the new European ideal of the third quarter of the century, to the work of the thoroughly Swabian Joseph Anton Feuchtmayer (see p. 173), we find plenty of signs of the general greater vivacity which belongs to the middle of the century. A comparison between the donor figures of St Peter's and those of about 1742 on the stables of the abbey of Salem shows how Feuchtmayer has now learnt to master the grotesque (Plate 154A). Humour and compelling vitality, of course, went specially well with the *rocaille*. On the other hand it must be admitted that Feuchtmayer had a passion for being original at any price. Collaboration with other artists – as for instance at the Cistercian pilgrimage church at Birnau – had a salutary effect on his brilliant but undisciplined art.

The man who more than any other achieved a unity at Birnau, reflecting the bright serene beauty of the landscape (Plates 153 and 155A), was the abbot, Anselm II. The foundation stone of the church was laid in 1746 and Feuchtmayer, Gottfried Bernhard Göz the painter, and Peter Thumb the master mason started work. At the consecration in 1750 all the altars were complete, but the sculptor continued to work with the ut-most devotion on the furnishings. In 1753, he carved the Stations of the Cross, obviously inspired by faith in what he had to represent. These reliefs show how forcefully the *rocaille* could inform the figures. Feuchtmayer's workshop was responsible not only for all the figures in the church but also for the entire decoration (Plate 153). The celebrated honey-licking putto is in its bubbling-over vitality and its enchanting humour a master-piece among the many representations of children in the German Baroque (Plate 155A).

Feuchtmayer's art was nurtured and remained in the religious climate of Lake Con-stance, to which it owes its healthy robustness. His Mannerism may be gnarled, as it were, but it is never artificial. However, he lacks the sense of profounder significance, the grandeur, and the wide range that contact with the Rhine valley, that great interna-tional highway, allowed to develop in Christian Wenzinger (1710-97), a native of the Breisgau. For more than sixty years Wenzinger worked within the shadow of the cathe-dral of Freiburg in the stately house 'Zum schönen Eck', on the balcony of which he placed his highly individual self-portrait in lead (now in the Augustiner-Museum). Its rendering of animated conversation is a sign of the new age. For his training he went to Rome in 1731, and to Paris in 1737, where he received an award at the Académie de Peinture et de Sculpture. He said himself that he had seen many foreign kingdoms, countries, and academies. The high quality of his art is well shown in the twelve poly-chrome terracotta figures of 1743 belonging to a group of the *Agony in the Garden*, which he did for Staufen (now Frankfurt, Liebig-Haus). The powerfully expressive figures, with their soft modelling and beauty of form, are good examples of his mature style. The influence of antique art is already perceptible, but the power and solidity of the Baroque are still well to the fore. Wenzinger liked to conceal the bodies of his figures almost entirely beneath billowing drapery with broad, softly modelled folds (Plate 155B).

Painting

We can best judge the importance of the *rocaille* for all the arts from the ceiling frescoes. Their light, vivaciously vibrating tone is reflected in all the decoration. Fresco-painting became in the whole of southern Germany the climax of artistic achievement. Even a minor artist such as Franz Joseph Spiegler (1691-1757), whose centres of activity were Riedlingen on the Danube and Constance, was inspired at the end of his life, in his work of between 1747 and 1753 at the abbey church of Zwiefalten, to a quality of performance and a mastery of the Rococo which far exceeds anything he had previously accom-plished (Plate 156). The incentive for this great work came from the architect Johann Michael Fischer, from the sculptor Christian, and from the plasterer Feuchtmayer.

Spiegler's *Adoration of the Virgin* of 1751 dominates the vast expanse of the ceiling. By composing the outer groups of the many-figured scene in broad, sweeping, receding rows, he established a harmonious transition from the exuberantly dynamic *rocaille* to the painting. The strips of cloud with their shadowed, deep-brown linings add powerful accents and co-ordinate the seething throngs into groups.

The brothers Thomas Christian Scheffler (1699–1756) and Felix Anton Scheffler (1701–60) were also stimulated by the Rococo. Thomas Christian, a former Jesuit, applied *rocaille* formations to clouds and rocks in his fresco of 1745–7 in the nave of St Paulinus at Trier, with scenes from the life of the patron saint. Trained in the school of Cosmas Damian Asam and associated with Augsburg, the two brothers transported Bavarian and Swabian art to the Rhine, to Bohemia, and to Silesia. The greater heaviness of the ceiling painting in St Paulinus is evidently an acquired Bohemian feature; it enhances the solemnity and deep piety of this work for a Jesuit church.

The migration of artists to the south-east was paralleled by one in the opposite direction. Thus Gottfried Bernhard Göz (1708–74) of Velehrad in Moravia went to Augsburg, where he worked as an apprentice in 1730 and from 1733 as a master. He was soon recognized as an important painter alongside Matthäus Günther, and he also made a name for himself as a graphic artist, especially through his coloured engravings. Something of Holzer's spirit is apparent in the daring and jubilant vitality of his compositions – Holzer's short career indeed lay in the years 1730–40. Göz's principal work was the vault of Birnau (1749–50; Plate 157A), for which he obviously discussed the colour scheme with Feuchtmayer.[2] In the church a warm white dominates at the bottom. The pilasters have a very light marble graining, and only the busts and angels are heightened with gold. To correspond with this, Göz used light colours above a brownish zone. The architectural perspectives in pink and white fade away into the cloudy skies. Dark colours are only used in the figure groups, among which the pale blue of the Virgin's mantle stands out.

Matthäus Günther (1705–88) was an upper Bavarian who was trained in the school of Cosmas Damian Asam but was attracted to Augsburg during the decisive fourth decade of the century. In 1731 he became a master there, after having contracted a convenient marriage. He was Holzer's successor in as far as he purchased drawings from Holzer's widow and made use of them in his own compositions. His wide activity took him from Amorbach to Rott am Inn, and especially to the Tyrol. In 1726 he succeeded Bergmüller as Catholic director of the Augsburg Academy. He did not possess Holzer's sense of beauty, and his compositions are frequently restless and overcrowded, but he did develop Augsburg fresco-painting further along the lines of the Rococo. In addition he was an expert at extracting the essence of his subject. Even in a late work such as the fresco in the vault at Götzens in the Tyrol, painted in 1774, the drama of the sorcerer Simon Magus's fall is impressively brought out. Günther could tell a story succinctly, drawing the eye by skilfully selected compositional means to the decisive gestures and actions.

His work shows that a more spiritualized approach to ceiling painting had been worked out which was based on close contact between artist and theologian. With so much work going on they were all permanently busy on such programmes, and had thus acquired the status of specialists in this extremely complex subject. Church interiors were most suitable for a systematic development of the kind of subject matter they wanted to represent. Important scenes, calculated to intensify devotion, were placed at critical points along the line of vision. Where the eye was drawn upwards to the dome, it was customary to show the heavenly spheres culminating in the haloes surrounding the divine figures. The language of allegory became more and more significant. Prophetic passages and events of the Old Testament were referred to, though less in the medieval sense of types and anti-types than as insertions in a unified programme. Biblical subject matter was enlarged, for instance by the addition of such a scene as the four Continents worshipping the Virgin. Miracles connected with food found their place in the refectories, the juxtaposition of faith and learning in the libraries.

The outstanding importance of the church frescoes remained undisputed. The specific problems of the artist, for instance the representation of light and the introduction of landscape, were in keeping with the yearning of the age for cosmic unity. Landscapes had their place both in biblical scenes and in allegorical themes such as that of the Virgin in the *hortus conclusus*. Church architecture was itself a paean of light, calculated throughout to serve the art of the ceiling painter. What sculpture and altar panels presented at close quarters, the fresco presented from a distance. The worshipper was to feel himself uplifted into the spiritual world and yet remain earthbound, even bound to his particular locality. Sympathy with the earth, the native soil that accepts sensuous delight as a gift of God, gave an enduring freshness to this art.

The Catholic art of the south-west of Swabia and of Switzerland, despite its rich variety and the vigour with which it persisted into the second half of the eighteenth century, represents the close of a great epoch, with scarcely any elements pointing towards new beginnings. In Protestant Switzerland on the other hand, in the work of Salomon Gessner of Zürich (1733–88), the Romantic landscape painting of the nineteenth century is already foreshadowed. Characteristically enough, Gessner began as a poet, and during the first ten years of his activity wrote *Daphnis* (1754), the *Idylls* (1756), and *The Death of Abel* (1758). Not until 1762 did he turn to the fine arts, as a result of his interest in etching. He is thus the first of the German poet–painters. Literature at this moment in German history assumed greater importance than art, and so art could not escape its influence. In Gessner's work, both reflected the longing of the time for a return to 'the most beautiful nature and to the most innocent ages' (Hagedorn) (Plate 157B).

Gessner, who had never had proper training, was in reality a dilettante throughout his life, and was perhaps too exclusively dedicated to his feelings. This remained the same after he gave up engraving in 1780 and turned to painting. In his memoirs, Ludwig Richter, who followed in his footsteps, pointed out how much these small, often childlike etchings meant to the nineteenth century: 'It was precisely these landscapes that brought us in word and picture such a wealth of sensitive, charming traits; the secret beauties of nature had unfolded so freely for him at every step in a way that seemed to me unparalleled in any older master. There was never a trace of manner;

nothing was imitation except for his tragic human beings who, it must be admitted, smack of the plaster model, whereas in landscape he always expressed what he had seen and experienced himself.' Characteristically enough Gessner's best works were vignettes in which poetry and the fine arts could be most easily combined. More readily than in large pictures, which were anyway influenced by Netherlandish painters, he could in such intimate works capture the living spirit of a fragment of nature. Sometimes a child, represented with great tenderness, appears in the midst of all the vegetable growth (Figure 26); and if he excelled in such figures, we must not forget how much of his classicist art was still secretly informed by the Baroque.

Figure 26. Salomon Gessner: Children among Rushes, 1770/80.
Munich, Staatliche Graphische Sammlung

CHAPTER 23

FRANCONIA

Architecture

IT has already been said that the Rococo appeared very early in Franconia. The first work in the new style was the decoration of Schloss Ansbach, begun in 1735. Through Margravine Christine Charlotte of Ansbach, a daughter of Duke Friedrich Karl of Württemberg and from 1723 acting regent, contact had been established with the Württemberg court and with the building under way at Ludwigsburg. Her son Carl Wilhelm Friedrich called Leopoldo Retti (1705–51) to Ansbach in 1731 and appointed him Baudirektor in 1732.[1] Retti's predecessor, Oberbaudirektor Carl Friedrich von Zocha, who had visited France and England, represented French influence. It must, however, have been the Margravine Wilhelmine of Bayreuth, sister of Frederick II, who was largely responsible for the introduction of the Rococo. Unfortunately it is not possible to say who made the designs for the decoration of the margrave's apartments at Ansbach. The themes were inspired by the prevailing passion for hunting. The originality and freshness in the invention of new ornamental motifs, which, though they are subordinated to the wall panels, transform the architecture, endowing it with animation and organic life, can best be seen in the long-necked herons that blend with the rhythm of the contours of the panels and in the arches that are wreathed in foliage. The delight in Rococo ornament is also reflected in the richly carved portals of the houses in the new part of the town, laid out by the margrave.

In Bayreuth Margrave Friedrich (1735–63) and his wife Wilhelmine, both lovers of art, inaugurated a similar, but a much more enduring florescence. The whole capital was systematically organized as a centre of the arts. The stately houses with their sandstone masonry and mansard roofs are of a uniform character; no building could be erected until its plan had been approved. The ties with Berlin and Paris grew closer. In 1736 the margrave called an excellent architect, Johann Friedrich Grael, from Berlin and appointed him Hofbaudirektor (p. 219). Owing to his premature death in 1740, however, Grael never gained any real influence. His successor, Joseph St Pierre, was a Frenchman. He probably built the exterior of the theatre (1745–9) which, with its four Corinthian columns and the heavy attic decorated with figures, has a distinctly classicist character. The interior offers an amazing contrast: it was designed in 1748 by Giuseppe Galli Bibiena and is pure Italian Baroque. Performances of Italian opera were given there by Italian singers, and French comedies acted by Parisian players.

In 1735, the margravine had been presented with the Hermitage, a country house outside Bayreuth, and she devoted herself with the utmost enthusiasm to its alteration. The old house was extended and received some new interior decoration in the Early Rococo style. Then, in 1749–53, a new house was built adjoining it, consisting of a single-storeyed semicircular range with an octagonal central pavilion (this was damaged by bombs). Compared with her adored brother's Sanssouci, begun four years earlier, Wilhelmine's building, Gloriette, has a more Italian character. It is possible that Karl Philipp Gontard (1731–91), who had returned in 1752 from visits to Paris and Holland, had a part in the designing of the beautiful central pavilion, called the 'Temple of the Sun'.

The Neue Schloss at Bayreuth, too (1753–4), shows the capricious spirit of Wilhelmine. Frederick II described it – in spite of its many charming details not quite untruthfully – as a sheep pen. Although St Pierre was presumably the designer of the Neue Schloss, Gontard was the more important figure. He accompanied the margrave and margravine to Italy in 1754, and in 1756 was appointed teacher of architecture and perspective at the newly founded academy of art at Bayreuth, where tuition was given free of charge to everyone. What was later admired in him, the results of an independent study of antiquity, could already be seen in the house he built for himself. He remained free throughout of the dry classicism of the classroom.

Wilhelmine died in 1758, during the Seven Years War, a period of especial difficulty for Bayreuth. Her husband continued to patronize the arts until his death in 1763. In 1761 he took over himself the protectorate of his academy. He attended classes almost daily, and even gave lessons in drawing and watercolour painting to the students. He was always present on prize-giving day. After his death the carefully selected group of artists scattered in all directions. Frederick II was successful in attracting many of the best of them to Berlin, and some of them, for instance Gontard and Georg Christian Unger (1743–c. 1808), became leading lights in the later Friderician Age.

The real centre of the development that was rapidly approaching its climax in Franconia was not, however, in the Protestant territories but in the Catholic bishoprics. Here traditions of the Baroque were so strong that a late flowering became possible, superior to anything that had gone before. For this to come about it was essential that one great genius should appear, and that he should find a worthy patron fully appreciating him and authoritative enough to allow him the development of his powers to the full. Both conditions were realized to a rare extent in the bishoprics of Würzburg and Bamberg in the persons of Balthasar Neumann (pp. 152ff.) and Prince Bishop Friedrich Carl von Schönborn. As a result, their influence spread far beyond the boundaries of the bishopric. Neumann even gained a footing in the Rhineland, in places such as the palace at Brühl, where Cuvilliés's Rococo held sway; for it was Neumann who in 1740 found the solution to the problem of the staircase at Brühl. He transferred the stairs to the north side of the vestibule and pierced the closed walls of the lower flight by arches supported by columns and caryatids. Because of this enlarging of the lower level to the full width of the west wing, it was necessary to retain the two upper corridors flanking the staircase, as they were essential for communication with the north wing. To achieve this, Neumann resorted to the bold measure of setting their inner walls on the crown of the rising tunnel-vaults of the two upper flights, thus overcoming the limited proportions and achieving a magnificent spaciousness. The whole was then crowned by an oval dome with a wreath of windows.

In 1741, in the parish church of Etwashausen near Kitzingen, Neumann once again took up the idea of a central space which is surrounded by columns and opens on to an ambulatory (Plate 158B). Diagonally set pairs of columns support the shallow dome, into which the tunnel-vaults of the short transverse arms penetrate deeply. Transparency and unity of space are both achieved, especially as the motif of the free-standing columns is repeated in the three arches at the end of the chancel. The exterior, too, is beautifully unified. The west tower rises from the convex façade and ends in a sharply pulled-in cap characteristic of Neumann's powerful, expressive modelling.

The penetration of the crossing vault into the vaults of the arms, another favourite motif of Neumann's, appears in a classically simple form in the church of Gaibach near Volkach on the Main (1742–5). Four narrow ellipses are attached to the transverse oval of the crossing, as a result of which the three-dimensional transverse arches touch almost as in a quadripartite rib-vault.

How far Neumann had progressed beyond the Dientzenhofer style can be seen in the pilgrimage church of Vierzehnheiligen, built in 1743–72 (Figure 27). The church stands above the valley of the river Main, facing Banz on the opposite bank and proclaiming the ancient contrast between the Benedictines of Banz and the Cistercians of the monastery of Langheim, to which Vierzehnheiligen belonged. In 1739 Stephan Mösinger, the abbot of Langheim, commissioned Gottfried Heinrich Krohne, the Protestant architect in the service of the Duke of Weimar-Eisenach whom we have met before, to design a centralized building with galleries. This was more in the nature of parish churches such as the Frauenkirche in Dresden than in the style of a pilgrimage church, whose centre must be the miracle-working image or altar. The aged Maximilian von Welsch also submitted a plan, which followed the outmoded style of the Gesù. Most suitable for the particular character of Vierzehnheiligen was the plan designed by Jakob Michael Küchel, who had worked under Neumann as a court architect at Bamberg. It was he who conceived the idea of placing the altar to the fourteen Helpers in Need in the middle of an oval central space with a dome on a drum above.

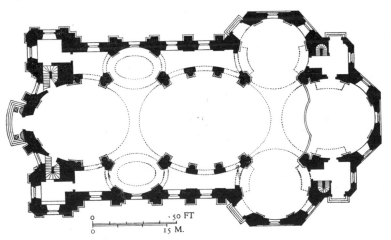

Figure 27. Balthasar Neumann: Vierzehnheiligen, pilgrimage church, 1743–72. Plan

In contrast to all these plans, Neumann designed a basilica on a Latin cross plan. The drumless dome was to be supported by three columns at each corner of the crossing. Although this plan was accepted, the abbot left the execution to Krohne. He began with the choir and at once deviated from Neumann's design, which drew a sharp protest from Prince Bishop Friedrich Carl. As a result, Neumann was able to produce a new plan in which he incorporated Krohne's chancel, and to harmonize with it adopted Küchel's idea of placing the altar in the centre (Plate 158A). In the influx of light through a triple row of windows, in the spaciousness of aisles, transept, nave, and galleries, and finally in the graceful lines of the elevation Neumann went far beyond what had been achieved at Banz thirty-three years earlier. A comparison between the two-tower façades of the two churches confirms this. The dramatic verticalism of the elevation at Vierzehnheiligen, underlined by the slender proportions of the pilasters and columns rising from high bases, is a brilliant example of Würzburg traditions. The glow of the yellowish brown sandstone enhances the life of this superb building in its lovely setting.

Inside, Neumann was not able to use free-standing columns as he would have wished to; he compromised by setting the demi-columns and three-quarter columns against shallow piers (Plate 159). Thus the idea of a reversal was retained. The plan consists of three longitudinal ovals interrupted by two transverse ovals, one representing the crossing, the other marking the bay immediately west of the central longitudinal oval. The latter is enlarged at the bottom by altar niches, the former by intersecting oval transverse arms. In the zone of the vaults, the transverse arches are driven together by the expanding oval fields with their large paintings. The transverse ovals counteract the thrust into depth and the upward thrust. On the other hand the longitudinal ovals strengthen the impression of depth, and the columns and galleries, the organ, the central altar, and the high altar draw the eye up to the frescoes with the Annunciation to the Shepherds, the Holy Trinity, the Virgin, the Fourteen Helpers in Need, and the Miraculous Vision. The superb, delicate, and restrained plaster decoration, grey against a white ground, by Johann Michael Feuchtmayer and Johann Georg Übelherr, the frescoes by Giuseppe

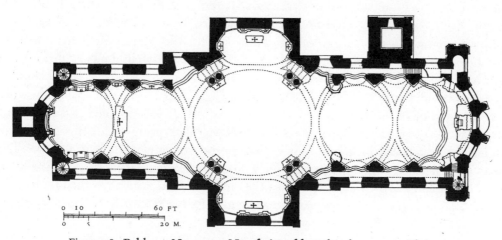

Figure 28. Balthasar Neumann: Neresheim, abbey church, 1747–92. Plan

Appiani, court painter to the elector of Mainz, the altars, especially the central altar, and the pulpit, both designed by Jakob Michael Küchel, were all completed after Neumann's death in 1753. But Küchel, who supervised the work, was fully conversant with Neumann's ideas and followed them closely, though giving greater emphasis to decoration than Neumann would have done.

In the Benedictine abbey church of Neresheim in the Swabian Alps Neumann was able at the end of his life to realize completely his grand Late Baroque vision of a central rotunda within a nave (1747-92; Plate 160 and Figure 28). The growing trend of the times towards classicism expresses itself in the monumentality of the pilasters and columns set on high bases, to which the low-lying galleries correspond. In spite of this, however, Neumann's dynamics of space persist. The central longitudinal oval develops out of the longitudinal ovals of the transepts and the pairs of transverse ovals which represent nave and equally deep chancel. Narrow ambulatories and galleries surround the central space. These two shallow layers of space are like the ground behind the raised parts of a relief. The diagonally placed massive pillars in the nave and chancel and the pairs of columns of the crossing seem to detach themselves from this foil. In Neumann's hands this drama is translated into a harmonious flow of lines with a mastery that could only be acquired at the end of a life-time. Once again the vaults are separated by three-dimensional transverse arches rising from comparatively narrowly spaced pillars. The arches seem to yield to the pressure of the domes, so that each pair is always pressed together to touch at the apex. Neumann's plan, it is true, was modified after his death, and the vaulting was done in wood and shallower than intended; but this resulted in surfaces for Martin Knoller's frescoes which made it easy for the eye to read them.

In other respects these years were not favourable for Neumann. Owing to the attitude of Friedrich Carl's successor, Prince Bishop Count Anselm Franz von Ingelheim, he was cold-shouldered at Würzburg between 1746 and 1749. He switched his energies to making vast projects for palaces, for Vienna in 1747 (Figure 29), for Stuttgart in the same year and in 1749 and 1750 (Figure 30), and for Karlsruhe in 1749. If for church building his chief concern was always with the solution of the crossing, for palace architecture the centre of his thoughts was the symmetrical arrangement of vast staircases placed in depth, between two large rooms and laterally between two courts, the latter as the source of light. His most magnificent design was for the Vienna Hofburg. Here the flights of stairs were doubled and interlocked so that from each of the two vestibules, at the front and at the back of the building, two flights mounted, met at a central landing, and then divided again, each leading to a great hall. The staircase hall rose to the same height as the other halls and was given huge windows. It was enclosed at the top by a colonnade. But Frederick II of Prussia saw to it that such plans could, after a lost war, no longer be realized in Vienna – it is characteristic of him and of his post-Baroque tastes that he disliked great staircases. In Franconia and in the Rhineland on the other hand Neumann's death was by no means the end of the Baroque, even though, by calling Nicolas de Pigage (1723-96) to Mannheim in 1749, the Elector Karl Theodor opened the door to French influence (p. 257).

During these last decades Mainz received its most outstanding Baroque building, the

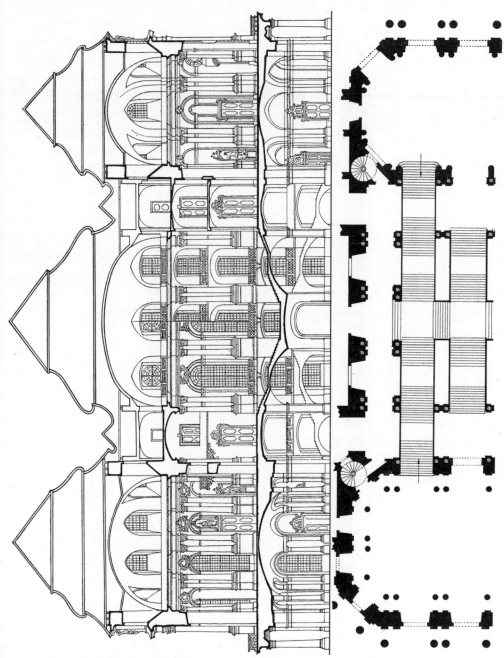

Figure 29. Balthasar Neumann: Project for the staircase in the Hofburg, Vienna, 1747. Elevation and plan

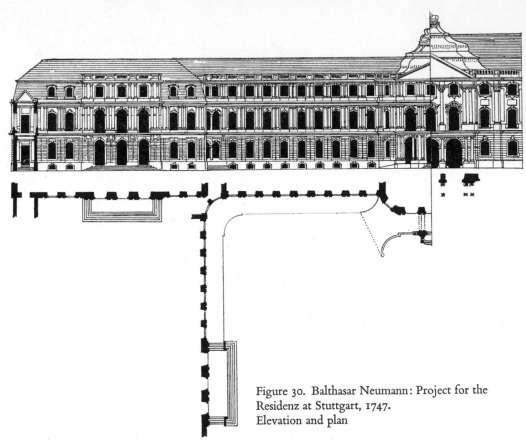

Figure 30. Balthasar Neumann: Project for the
Residenz at Stuttgart, 1747.
Elevation and plan

Jesuit church, which was erected between 1742 and 1746 facing the university. It was
based on plans by Neumann which represent a preliminary stage for Neresheim. Unfortunately the church was burnt by the French in 1793 during the period of the Revolution, but one fine late work in the Borromini style survives: the portal of the house
of the Augustinian Hermits of 1753.

At Trier, close to the French frontier, the emphasis on the German character is perhaps even more remarkable. There the buildings by the Saxon architect Christian
Kretschmar (d. 1768), who had ties with the Saxon and Silesian Baroque, and the court
architect Johannes Seiz (1717–79), who was responsible for the rather turbulent Rococo
of the archbishop's palace (1756–68), are entirely un-French. The same applies to the
Palais Kesselstadt at Trier, built in 1740–5 by Valentin Thoman (1695–1777), which has
a concave front and a central undulating projection, and to the simpler but equally
forceful house at No. 39 Krahnenstrasse (Plate 161B), both of which are in the succession
of Neumann.

Saarbrücken on the other hand, thanks to Duke Wilhelm Heinrich von Nassau and
his architect Friedrich Joachim Stengel (1694–1787), progressed into the vanguard of
Rhenish Protestant architecture. Stengel was born at Zerbst and trained in Berlin; thus
the northern Baroque was his starting point. In 1708, when he was only fourteen years

old, he went to the Berlin Academy and studied under Jean de Bodt and Jean-Baptiste Broebes. In 1712 he served in a regiment of the House of Gotha in Italy. His collaboration with Welsch on the Orangery in Fulda brought him into contact with the Franconian Baroque. After his appointment as Surveyor to the duke at Saarbrücken he was able to model the rising town according to his ideas. His fine late work, the church of St Ludwig (1762–75), has a Greek cross plan with emphasis on the transverse axis. Despite its late date, this Protestant church with its richly framed windows, the statues that crown the balustrade of the roof, and the caryatid figures of the galleries that recall garden statuary bears the imprint of the courtly Rococo (Plate 161A). Furthermore, the site selected by Stengel in the centre of a square, with a street leading to it on the middle axis flanked by wealthy houses with elegant façades and adjoining gardens, was in harmony with the general planning of the town, which had started from the gardens of the palace.

A new centre of European culture was created at Mannheim when the Elector Karl Theodor von Pfalz-Sulzbach took over the government in 1742. Voltaire, Mozart, Lessing, Goethe, and Schiller were all in contact with Mannheim – Schiller spoke of the 'Greek climate in the electorate'. The first performance of Schiller's *Räuber* was the gateway to a new age. Under Karl Theodor's regime public welfare began to be considered – another sign of the times. In 1749 the elector appointed Nicolas de Pigage, an architect from Lorraine, who built the east wing of the palace with the fine library and the gallery and stables adjoining it. Next, in 1752, came the appointment of the sculptor and architect Peter Anton Verschaffelt, who came from Rome. The foundation of the Mannheim Cabinet of Antiquities was yet another pointer to the approach of a new age. In spite of this, however, Pigage's style still echoed the French Rococo, Verschaffelt's the Roman Baroque.

On the other hand, in the grounds of the country palace of Schwetzingen and at Schloss Benrath near Düsseldorf (1755–69) Pigage gave an example of what refinement the French preoccupation with *maisons de plaisance* had led to. The elegant little summer palace of Benrath has a simple exterior, the ground floor with its high windows being in exquisite harmony with the convex curve of the roof, in which the vertically placed oval dormers repeat the verticals of the windows. A German and Baroque note in this typically French ensemble is Verschaffelt's sculpture, especially the group of the Hunt of Diana above the forward-curving front of the circular garden hall. Inside, the one-storeyed building which seems so simple from the outside turns out to be a complex arrangement of eighty rooms, seven staircases, and two courts with four storeys.

In his late period, in his designs for Schloss Bretzenheim (1771–88) and the Mannheim Arsenal (1777–8), Verschaffelt was able to show himself as an architect as well. Here, too, he appears inspired by the Late Roman Baroque as well as by the style of Louis XVI.

Cuvilliés's plans for Wilhelmsthal near Kassel were presumably begun in 1743. The house, based on Jacques-François Blondel's ideas for *maisons de plaisance*, was begun in 1753. Cuvilliés himself had no part in its execution, which was undertaken by Simon Louis du Ry (1726–99), a nephew of Paul du Ry, who built the two lodges (1756–8). Simon Louis produced extraordinarily fine work of the greatest simplicity in and around

Kassel. At Kassel itself, in addition to elaborate façades with Rococo plaster decoration, there were equally attractive ones built in his simpler manner. In 1771 the great sculptor Johann August Nahl, who had escaped from the fetters of the Prussian court, produced a veritable masterpiece in the sculpture of his own house (Plate 162A and B); it is integrated perfectly with the architecture.

Paul du Ry's town-planning was continued by Simon Louis. With increased understanding for the relation of town to open country, he laid out the magnificent rectangular Friedrichsplatz as a link between the Oberneustadt and the low-lying river meadows. In the centre of the north-eastern side of the square he built the large Museum Fridericianum (1769–79), and north-west of this and on the same axis a house for the cabinet minister von Jungken, at the corner of the Königsstrasse (1767–9). For this he used a similar pediment in the middle but placed it on pilasters instead of columns to tone down the effect. To the church of St Elizabeth at the south-eastern end of the same side of the square he gave the same front with pilasters (1770–6). The spaces between the three buildings, which were planted with trees, were unfortunately built up in 1820. Du Ry also left the narrow side of the square with the view down to the meadows open, apart from the provision of a gate.

Sculpture

Although Franconian sculpture had flourished before the Thirty Years War, nearly a hundred years were to elapse before larger workshops run by important sculptors could be re-established. The initiative came from the Schönborns. From 1735 Antonio Bossi of Porto near Lugano was the leading plasterer for the Würzburg Residenz. The statues of the Kaisersaal of 1751 reveal his brilliance as a figure sculptor; but his real genius lay in the power to make *rocaille* a vehicle of passionate movement. The White Salon, lying between the staircase and the Kaisersaal, is entirely decorated by his plasterwork (Plate 95B). Bossi was highly sensitive, and must have been straining his imagination and skill to excess; for in 1757 his brain gave way.

It was his genius that inspired Johann Wolfgang van der Auvera (1708–56), his young collaborator in the Mirror Room, to produce brilliant designs for the wall decoration. Auvera, the son of Jakob van der Auvera who had come to Würzburg from Malines in 1706, had studied at the Vienna Academy at the expense of the Schönborns. On his return to Würzburg in 1736 he was entrusted with sculptural tasks for the Residenz, including the decoration of the gates leading to the *cour d'honneur*, the garden front, and the doorway of the royal chapel. The 'distinguished Statuarius Auvera' was more successful in currying favour than was the far more talented and original Ferdinand Tietz (1708–77). On the other hand Auvera had an excellent understanding of Neumann's ideas, and so it was understandable that he was entrusted in 1741 with the sculpture for the high altar in the cathedral of Worms and in 1745 for that of the Franciscan church in Brühl, both of which were erected to Neumann's designs as lofty canopied structures.

As for Tietz,[2] his style was once again inspired by the Bohemian Baroque; only the heightened dynamism and greater naturalism belong to the Rococo. Tietz, who was born at Holzschitz near Eisenberg in Bohemia, had therefore had the opportunity of seeing Braun's late works. Obviously he learnt a great deal from Braun's expressive, imaginative art and from his vivid naturalism. On Tietz's arrival in Würzburg in 1736 he was given a part in the sculptural decoration of the Residenz, especially the garden front. It was soon appreciated that his wit, his love of grotesque and paradox, and his ability to give warm life to the most fantastic creations made him the ideal garden sculptor. He was therefore commissioned to do the sculpture for the gardens of Schloss Seehof (1747–52), and for the Orangery of Schönbornlust (1754–7).

Adam Friedrich von Seinsheim, who became prince bishop of Würzburg in 1755 and bishop of Bamberg in 1759, took a particular liking to Tietz's bizarre style. He gave Tietz the title of court sculptor, and moved him to Bamberg in 1760, where he continued work for Seehof until 1765. After that he was put on to his most spectacular achievement, the decoration of the gardens of the episcopal country house of Veitshöchheim near Würzburg (1765–8). The individual figures are brilliantly done and give continual surprise and pleasure; but the real genius lies in the sculptural conception of the whole, in the linking by broad gestures of one group to another. This effort to achieve unity was of course typical of the Rococo garden. The rearing figure of *Pegasus*, about to rise into the air, on the large fountain above the Hill of the Muses, strives with even greater vigour than does his model the *Parnasse François* at Versailles (Plate 163). The lively Baroque beast is the most fitting prelude to the transformation of the park into a realm of magic and poetry. Tietz detested anything conventional. Though he seemed to live in a mythological world, his forceful figures, for all their fantasy, are real enough to give them an air of mocking classical ideals: their eyes are slanting, their bulbous noses end in long-drawn-out points, the corners of the mouth and thick lips curl upward. If the figures are not actually dancing, most of them seem about to do so, to join in the compelling rumbustious gaiety of a Bambocciata (Plate 164A). Cleverly thought-out programmes must not be expected; the sculptor selected the usual themes – allegories, the Four Seasons and the Four Continents, types from Italian Comedy, the antique world of the Gods, dancing gentlemen, ladies, and children – and produced something new out of them, evidently a sympathetic caricature of society of his day.

As opposed to the positive, unambiguous style of Auvera and Tietz, the art of their successor Johann Peter Wagner (1730–1809) seems to mirror the most varying influences (Plate 164B).[3] He was the son of Thomas Wagner, a sculptor working at Obertheres, and grew up in the Franconian tradition, beginning his journeyman years when he was seventeen. In Vienna he studied under Balthasar Moll at the Academy, without, to begin with, feeling any particular interest in the Donner style. On the other hand, after continuing his studies in south-western Germany, at Mannheim, he eagerly absorbed the influence of Paul Egell, and with it the Baroque traditions of Permoser. In 1757 he entered the large Auvera workshop, obtaining control of it in 1759 when he married Johann Wolfgang Auvera's widow. His extensive activity was characterized by the bon mot 'the whole of Franconia was becoming wagnerized'. Soon he began to turn increasingly to Louis XVI classicism. The gently undulating contours became firmer, Tietz's bravura disappeared, and a gentler mood prevailed. French models in the manner

T

of Falconet became important, although Wagner still retained much of his original freshness, as can be seen in the putti in the gardens of the Residenz at Würzburg.

In the Palatinate, the work of Peter Anton Verschaffelt (1710-93),[4] whom we have already met, could well be compared with that of Wagner. Actually he was twenty years older, and thus a contemporary of Auvera and Tietz. This seeming contradiction can, however, be explained by the fact that he was born in Ghent and trained there and that, from 1732 to 1737, he worked in Brussels and Paris as a pupil of Verberckt and Bouchardon, through whom he came into direct contact with the French Rococo. After working as a distinguished sculptor for fourteen years in Rome, where he did the bronze angel for the Castello Sant'Angelo, he went to London at the end of 1751 with a letter of recommendation from Cardinal Albani to George Bubb Dodington. He remained in London for a year. In this way he was able to study Roman Late Baroque and English classicism at the sources. Then, in 1752, the Elector Karl Theodor von der Pfalz, the great lover of the arts, called him to Mannheim, where he collaborated with Nicolas de Pigage, mainly at Schwetzingen and Benrath (p. 257).

Even though Verschaffelt's Roman impressions were revived through journeys undertaken in 1754 and 1767, the influence of the French Academy of Architecture gradually gained supremacy, especially over his architectural style. Admittedly in Mannheim, as everywhere in Germany at the time, opinions were sharply divided. In his figures for the Jesuit church, his first important commission at Mannheim – the façade dates from 1756, the high altar from 1758 – Verschaffelt had to adapt his style to the Baroque of Alessandro Galli da Bibiena, the architect of the church; but at the same time, between 1755 and 1757, he was executing the pediment for the electoral library, a Late Rococo building by Pigage (p. 257).

For the park at Schwetzingen the large roundel behind the house was a Baroque idea of Galli Bibiena's, but Pigage enlarged the composition without paying much attention to Galli Bibiena's conceit, especially by developing the main axis from the Stag Fountain to the Great Lake. Finally, from 1776, after a journey to England, Friedrich Ludwig von Sckell began the partial transformation of the park into an English garden. Verschaffelt, and with him Franz Konrad Linck, worked on the decoration of the Temple of Apollo from 1766 to 1773, and of the indoor Tennis Court c. 1772, and they also did individual statues. The beautiful figures of the *Four Seasons* in the oval room of the Bath House are carefully worked from life, as Verschaffelt had specifically demanded. As regards style, Bouchardon was again followed. Verschaffelt's most successful work in the gardens is the two groups of stags and the Four Elements for the Stag Fountain. Work on them began in 1766. The decline of the Baroque style that set in here was accompanied by a new feeling for nature, and this was preserved from getting aesthetically out of hand by being tied to the discipline of garden art.

Painting

Before he died, Prince Bishop Friedrich Karl had taken steps to appoint Johann Zick (1702-62) for the Würzburg Residenz. Zick came from upper Swabia – he was born at

Lachen, near Ottobeuren – had been a pupil of Karl Stauder the Younger at Constance, had spent three years in Italy, and then settled in Munich at the end of the 1720s. From there he went to Würzburg in 1749 to paint the ceiling of the Garden Hall.[5] The fact that the room was a low one led him to arrange his mythological groups, representing the pleasures of country life, at the extreme edge of the vault, linking them to the wavy lines of Bossi's Rococo plasterwork. In this he was certainly right. The work was in the nature of a trial piece, to find out whether 'he had all the necessary ability to be entrusted with the frescoes in the saloon above'. The figures, however, were too heavy, in consequence of which Zick was not further employed for the Residenz.

Friedrich Karl's successor, Karl Philipp von Greifenklau, aimed far higher. In 1750 he gave Giovanni Battista Tiepolo of Venice a contract for 10,000 Rhenish florins to paint the Kaisersaal.[6] He forbade his horrified treasury to attempt any bargaining. Tiepolo and his two sons Domenico and Lorenzo arrived in Würzburg in December 1750, and by July 1752 had completed the frescoes of the vault of the Kaisersaal. They represent in the centre *The Arrival of the Emperor Barbarossa's Bride Beatrix in the Sun Chariot of Apollo* and between the penetrations at the foot of the vault *The Marriage Ceremony at Würzburg* and *The Ratification of the Title of Duke of Franconia to the Bishop of Würzburg*. Highly satisfied with the result, the elector then entrusted Tiepolo with the fresco over the great staircase. This gigantic work, representing Apollo in his sun chariot and the Planets in the centre and the Four Continents at the sides, was completed in little more than a year. Tiepolo left Würzburg with his sons in November 1753, having received the princely sum of 30,000 florins as his payment. This sum, when contrasted with the 1,000 florins allotted to Steidl and Zick for their work, expresses the admiration felt at Würzburg for Tiepolo as a superb artist. The frescoes form a chapter of Italian art history, influenced by Germany only in as far as Neumann's magnificent interiors obviously inspired the Venetian painter. The magic of his light colours, the originality, the stimulus to imagination, the brio, the seeming effortlessness with which large areas were composed and painted, the touches of realism, and the whole sensuous warmth were all elements of the final flowering of Venetian art inaugurated two hundred years before by Veronese, but they were not adopted by German painters, although they gave indirect inspiration to the further development of German fresco-painting.

Strangely enough, at the very moment when Tiepolo was producing these masterpieces, the same Johann Zick who had failed with his ceiling in the Garden Hall at Würzburg achieved such high success at the palace of Bruchsal, where between 1751 and 1754 he painted the staircase, Fürstensaal, and Marble Hall, that he found himself in the very top rank of south German painting. Neumann, who recognized his talent despite the fiasco of Würzburg, had evidently recommended him to Cardinal von Hutten – he would never have allowed a painter in whom he had no confidence to do the painting for his most brilliant staircase. Zick very sensibly used Pozzo's idea of architectural perspectives as a framework for his frescoes. In the White Hall he raised a domed building on four corner piers which merged with the open skies above. He had written a poem, 'Flor des Hochstiftes Speyer im Reich des Friedens', as a programme for the frescoes. The painting was articulated to correspond with the division of the poem into verses. As at Würzburg, the allegories were taken not from the Bible but from classical mythology. Zick skilfully placed his groups at the bottom, in front of the base of the structure. At the top they appeared to be floating on clouds. The forceful contrast between the darker zones at the sides and the paler domed building produced a lively rhythm, and this was repeated with added impetus in the oval fresco above the staircase (Plate 165). The figures here are lighter and more graceful, which was probably due to his collaboration with the plasterer Johann Michael Feuchtmayer. The subject matter of the staircase was *The History and the Glorification of the Bishopric of Speyer*. Once again the painted architecture, following Neumann's articulation of the walls, served to support the groups.

In 1754, in his work for the Marble Hall, Zick's painting is in direct contact with Feuchtmayer's *rocaille*, which frames it, and this intensified the dynamic character of his painting. The supporting function of architectural perspectives became less pronounced. From the frothy curving stucco frames darker and lighter areas of the sky seem to rise, creating the fleeting effect of a vision of light. Even in his Munich days Zick, according to Oefele, 'had studied Rembrandt and taken Bergmüller as model for his inventions'.[7] This strange combination could not last, and the greater master was bound to dominate in the end – even in fresco painting. As a result, in Zick's late works in the parish churches of Amorbach (begun in 1753) and Grafenrheinfeld (1757), the dense crowds grow sparser. Individual figures at the sides stand out dark with fantastically jagged outlines against turbulent skies. The clouds, whose contours were once well defined, develop into indistinct undulating masses. His panel paintings illustrate genre scenes after the manner of Teniers and Ostade, but the choice of small formats also reflects Rembrandt.

This Dutch manner, characteristic of the later eighteenth century, was given a classicist note by Zick's son Januarius Zick (1732–97). He had visited Paris in 1757 and Rome in 1758, where for two years he was in contact with Anton Raphael Mengs. Early works, such as *David and Abisai in Saul's Tent* and *Saul and the Witch of Endor* (1752, Würzburg Museum; Plate 166), show a Rembrandtesque treatment of light. The literary note is typical of his own day and lends the small paintings a touch of grandeur. Januarius Zick assisted his father on the great frescoes at Bruchsal, and between 1757 and 1766 painted many overdoors in the same palace. For the panels of 1759 in the so-called Watteau Room the subject matter only was borrowed from Watteau. His personal contribution lay in his close study of nature. This appears in the execution of all his paintings, but especially the portraits. From 1757 he was in the service of the elector of Trier, and in 1762 he settled at Ehrenbreitstein. Superficially his frescoes conform to the Baroque, but the compelling rhythm and convincing movement of earlier decades are lacking, and there is now an empty theatrical quality instead. The ceiling paintings in Schloss Engers of 1760 and in the convent church at Wiblingen of 1778–80 are melodramatic and have fantastic, exaggeratedly sculptured figures. In the frescoes in the church of Roth an der Roth, which were painted in 1784, he moved on into classicism, but even there could not infuse new life into the moribund art of ceiling painting.

Despite the unfavourable conditions of his development, Zick remained a strong personality. The same is by no means true of the numerous Dutch imitators who were centred in Frankfurt. A modest degree of originality can be accorded only to Konrad Seekatz (1719–68), painter to the Darmstadt court, whose 'natural and innocent ideas' were praised by Goethe in *Dichtung und Wahrheit*. The panels commissioned by Count Thorance for his hotel at Garre, as he met Seekatz in the house of Goethe's father, fragments of which survive in the Goethe-Museum at Frankfurt, reveal the German manner of glamorizing everyday life with a Rococo veneer which stands up quite well. More successful examples of the expiring Watteau style in German art can be seen in the seventeen overdoor pieces from Schloss Braunshardt (1765; now Darmstadt Museum).

Characteristic of the change of taste, of the repression of naïve pleasure in the beauty of life, of the emergence of intellectual, psychological interests is the fact that certain other branches of art now gained importance at the expense of wall and ceiling painting. This applies especially to the portrait. An example is the Tischbein family in Hesse, which produced generations of portrait painters who, following the international trend of the times and in step with the intellectual leaders of the day, sought ever wider contacts ever farther afield, giving up their links with home. Johann Heinrich Tischbein the Elder (1722–89; Plate 167A) is still known as the 'Kassel Tischbein'.[8] He was born at Haina, the family birthplace, and spent eight years, from 1744 to 1751, studying in Paris, Venice, and Rome. In France he worked under Carlo van Loo, in Italy under Piazzetta – the two most famous teachers of the day. After his appointment as painter to the court of Kassel he settled there in 1752. One of his first tasks, still fully in the spirit of the Rococo, was the Gallery of Beauties at Schloss Wilhelmsthal.

Johann Heinrich, however, like the other members of the Tischbein family – Friedrich, the 'Leipzig Tischbein' (1750–1812), and Wilhelm, the 'Goethe Tischbein' (1751–1829)[9] – never achieved the psychological understanding, the variety of interpretation, or the German character of Graff's art. In elegance and painterly refinement in the Rococo sense Friedrich Tischbein, the most outstanding member of the family, comes close to the great English portrait painters. In 1800, a year after Oeser's death, he became head of the Leipzig Academy.

Landscape painting, the other most important and characteristic task at the end of the eighteenth century, found a natural source of inspiration in the spacious country of the Rhine and Main. This part of the country was all the more propitious as links with Holland on the one side and with Switzerland on the other, i.e. the principal sources of inspiration of eighteenth-century landscape painting, were a matter of course. Christian Georg Schütze (1718–91) of Frankfurt occupies an intermediary position.[10] In certain pictures, such as *The Weisenau near Mainz* (Munich, Pinakothek), he still uses the Baroque landscape style with its theatrical compositions and sharp contrasts of light and dark; but on occasion, for instance in the *Taunus Landscape*, his style, in spite of the acceptance of the apparatus of heroic landscape – framing trees and passing thunderclouds – comes close to that of nineteenth-century painters such as Moritz von Schwind and Hans Thoma.

Ferdinand Kobell (1744–99) went even farther.[11] He belonged to the Mannheim circle of artists round the Elector Karl Theodor and followed him to Munich, where his pictures formed the starting-point for nineteenth-century Munich landscape painting. Between 1768 and 1770 he received an allowance from Karl Theodor for a stay in Paris, where he learnt more from the art of Ruysdael and Everdingen than from that of Claude Lorrain. In 1775 he was appointed to the Mannheim court, with the characteristic new title of 'Kabinetts-Landschaftsmaler' (landscape painter of cabinet-pieces). His seven landscape panels, six upright ones with a horizontal one in the centre, painted *c.* 1772 for the study in the Bath House in the gardens of Schwetzingen, show a skilful adaptation of the Dutch style to suit his decorative task. During the 1780s, in his six landscapes of Aschaffenburg, he produced direct interpretations of specific views.[12] Finally, in the picture now in the Schwerin Museum, in which the sole theme is a strongly modelled spur of rock falling sharply towards the back and without a frame of any kind, he overcame the theatrical quality of eighteenth-century landscape painting completely (Plate 167B). In 1793 he moved to Munich, where, like his princely patron, he never felt at home.

His younger brother Franz Kobell (1749–1822) was attracted less by the Dutch than by the southern landscape. He was in Italy from 1779 to 1784, and viewed the country through the eyes of Claude Lorrain. On his return he settled, as his brother did later, in Munich. His art retains a stronger Baroque element than does that of Ferdinand, so that he could not contribute as much as his brother to the rising Munich landscape school of the nineteenth century.

CHAPTER 24

PRUSSIA

Architecture

THE imprint of the character of the reigning prince on the art of his principality is more clearly visible in Prussia than in any other part of Germany. This was especially the case under Frederick II, a personality who was as brilliant as he was autocratic and whom the French were the first to call 'the Great'. In his *Histoire de mon temps* Frederick expressed his criticism of the indifference to learning and the arts under his father as follows: 'La jeune noblesse, qui se vouait aux armes, crût dévoyer en étudiant, ils regardèrent l'ignorance comme un titre de mérit et le savoir comme une pédanterie absurde. La même raison fit que les arts libéraux tombèrent en décadence: l'Académie des Peintres cessa; Pesne qui était le directeur quitta les tableaux pour les portraits.' Although his father permitted him to take lessons in drawing, he did not allow him to make the 'grand tour'. Frederick II never saw the Italian palaces that were the prototypes for his own buildings – his notion of them was based on engravings.

When he was crown prince he passed on his ideas to the circle of officers he had gathered around his person. In Georg Wenzeslaus von Knobelsdorff (1699–1754), a member of that Prussian aristocracy which was later to form the centrepiece of his power, he found a man of high artistic gifts whom he could respect. In 1729 Knobelsdorff had resigned his captaincy to train as a painter at the Academy and in the studio of his friend Pesne. Frederick William I is supposed to have intended him to be his son's tutor, and this is by no means impossible in view of the fact that the king himself 'in tormentis pinxit' (he suffered from gout). Friendly relations developed between the two men. Knobelsdorff produced his first work for the garden which Frederick, when he was still crown prince, had laid out in 1733 in his garrison town, Neu-Ruppin. It is characteristic of both men: a small round temple, dedicated to Apollo as a sign of their devotion to antiquity, with eight Tuscan columns grouped in four narrowly spaced pairs.

The crown prince made it possible for his artistic mentor to do what he himself had been unable to do, namely to visit Italy. On his return in 1737 Knobelsdorff was entrusted with the enlargement of Rheinsberg, an old border castle that the king had presented to his son in 1734 after the latter's marriage. Knobelsdorff's teacher Johann Gottfried Kemmeter, inspector of buildings in the electoral council, had already begun to rebuild the irregular remains of the former moated castle on a regular plan with three wings. Knobelsdorff erected the northern wing and closed the court on the side facing the lake by a colonnade of coupled columns. This motif, here of the Ionic order, later became a favourite of Knobelsdorff; he repeated it, with Corinthian columns, at Potsdam, on the front of the Stadtschloss and at Sanssouci. It was at this time, in the happy circle of young men around the crown prince, that the ideas were first formed which were later to be more fully realized by the king. One example is the building of the library into the circular space of the tower. Impressions received by Frederick in Dresden, when he was sixteen years old, will also have played their part: it was probably the memory of Moritzburg near Dresden that led him to order the tower at Rheinsberg to be duplicated, so that the colonnade could be symmetrically flanked by two round towers.

At the same time the idea was conceived of building a Forum Fridericianum at the beginning of Unter den Linden in Berlin. On the site on which the palace of Prince Henry (today the University) was later to be built, a Residenz was planned for Frederick on a much vaster scale, with a forecourt. Facing it, with the narrow side towards Unter den Linden, the opera house dedicated to Apollo was to stand, and this was actually built during the first years of the young king's reign. The Academy of Science and Letters was to form a counterweight farther to the west, with a similar orientation. These buildings constituted the three focal points of the king's personal life; the Baroque palace of his predecessors, with the near-by church, did not appeal to him. But he needed a fourth centre of activity, nature in its beauty, and for that reason only half the original plan for the forum could be actually carried out. He soon decided to live at Charlottenburg, and in 1744 he moved to Potsdam. Voltaire, influenced by Roman ideas, gave a poetic interpretation of this move, saying that Frederick wished to combine the charms of nature with those of art.

On his accession to power in 1740 the king's pent-up energy found an outlet in the First Silesian War. But even from the battlefield he urged Knobelsdorff to carry on with his extensive building schemes. On 15 June 1742 he wrote to his friend Jordan: 'Press Knobelsdorff to complete Charlottenburg. I hope to spend a good part of my time there.' Also Knobelsdorff was to inform him about the progress of his opera house and of his gardens. In preparation for the work he had sent Knobelsdorff to Paris via Dresden in the autumn of 1740. In the Saxon capital, in view of the nature of Frederick's plans, Knobelsdorff must have been particularly interested in the opera house, built between 1718 and 1719, together with the Zwinger which it adjoined – especially as the termini supporting the columns of the proscenium and of the royal boxes were the work of Permoser and his school. In France, according to the king's eulogy read at the Academy on the occasion of the architect's death,[1] Knobelsdorff had been most impressed by Perrault's colonnade of the Louvre and by the palace at Versailles. The flat, elegant architecture at Versailles by Jules Hardouin-Mansart, which harmonizes with the crowning statues, will certainly have aroused his admiration, as will also the long, low proportions of the Grand Trianon. First and foremost, however, the beauty of the Corinthian columns, both on the Louvre and in the Royal Chapel at Versailles, must have struck a responsive chord. The memory of the Grand Trianon, with its round-arched windows framed by numerous coupled columns and by the continuous horizontal line of the attic with its sculptural decoration, was reflected in his two early works in Berlin: the wings that he added to the palaces of Monbijou and Charlottenburg.

At Monbijou the east wing adjoins Eosander's central block with seven windows, built in 1703. The result is a front facing the garden with fifty-two bays. The delicate relief and rounded corners clearly show French influence. The building, which was completed between 1740 and 1742, was destined for the king's mother. She, like her children, had been subjected to the tyranny of her husband, and when Frederick came to power his first task was to make suitable provision for her.

At the same time Knobelsdorff began the wing at Charlottenburg for the king – initially also for his wife[2] – building a range of living rooms and state rooms to suit his taste. This new wing adjoins the *corps de logis* on the east side as a counterpart to the Orangery on the west. From the outside the two-storeyed building is quite simple. The central pavilion alone is stressed by round-arched French windows and coupled Tuscan columns supporting a balcony. Inside, the great dining room lies above the vestibule. It has five windows on each side. The flying spiral staircase adjoining the vestibule on the west side leads up to it by easy steps. The king was proud of the 'beauté' of his staircase, the light scagliola of which harmonized with the gold of the coupled pilasters and the grey of the walls. Obviously it is inspired by the older square staircase hall in the central block. There, the lightness of the freely rising flights and the severe articulation have a French character. The king had always admired it.[3] The forty years that had elapsed between the two staircases are reflected in the verticalism of the intertwined ribbonwork of the wrought-iron balustrade and in the free disposition of the four plaster groups of the Seasons above the cornice – both German rather than French touches. The strict architectural division of the older ceiling has been abandoned in favour of a more painterly treatment, even though the basic oblong form is clearly defined in the frame surrounding the fine ceiling fresco with *Apollo and Prometheus* by Pesne. Forty years earlier figures with garlands had been dominant on the ceiling; in the later work the sky and a natural rendering of trees claim equal importance with human figures.

The dining room, which Frederick called the Salon, was completed in 1742. It is reached directly from the stairs. According to Frederick the 'noblesse' that characterizes it was partly due to the way in which the white scagliola of the coupled Corinthian pilasters stood out against the pink walls, without any further decoration (Plate 168A). The decorative elements first appeared on the door panels, probably carved by Nahl, and on the painted frame of the ceiling fresco with *The Wedding Banquet of Peleus and Thetis*. The heavy, dynamic Baroque cartouches of the frame formed a contrast to the tameness of Pesne's oval painting.

But the king and his artist were able to orchestrate these harmonies even more richly: in the adjoining Gallery a further surprise awaited his guests after dinner. The king chose to describe it as 'élégance' (Plate 168B). There was much to admire: in the first place the gay, lilting quality and insinuating brilliance of gold in front of light green, red, and violet grained scagliola. The forms – flaming *rocailles*, nets spanned over slim bars and volutes, delicate sprays of blossoms, dancing putti and genii – all whirl together, organized with a sparkling vitality that could scarcely be paralleled in any other room in the world. Light poured in through eleven tall French windows on either side and was reflected by the mirrors on the piers. The main cornice is neither curved nor broken, nor do the decorations which replace the pilasters and panels run into one another: their contours strictly follow the vertical articulation. The work, which was carried through with the utmost care, took six years to complete. In 1746, after the first two Silesian wars had been fought, the Golden Gallery was opened. In his 'Éloge' the king gave the credit for all three rooms to Knobelsdorff. That Knobelsdorff also inspired the decoration is proved by drawings of *rocaille* in his hand and by the fact that in the Golden Gallery the architectural forms, and even the details, are dependent on it. In his relationship with his colleagues Knobelsdorff's generous nature was a great asset; this was shown in his friendship with Pesne and in his understanding of the brilliant sculptor Johann August Nahl, who was in charge of the decoration, though with limited powers. All this splendour was destroyed by bombs in 1943.

The king had an apartment fitted up for himself on the upper floor of the western range. It contained, and this was later to become the rule, a music room and a library, the latter a gallery-like room. Similarly the furnishing with antique statues and French pictures had become indispensable for Frederick. At the same time he had an apartment fitted out for himself in the Schloss in Berlin, of which the round tower room facing the river Spree, which was decorated by Johann Michael Hoppenhaupt, has survived.

In 1741 Knobelsdorff was entrusted with the monumental task of building the Berlin Opera House (Plate 170). The theatre, too, had become an essential need for the king. He ordered theatres to be built in the alabaster hall of the old Berlin Schloss and in the Stadtschloss and the Neues Palais at Potsdam. He must have been responsible for the idea that the opera house was to represent a temple. This is still expressed in the inscription on the pediment, which reads: 'Federicus Apollini et Musis'. The sequence of rooms, too, which differed from the norm, was, so it was said, 'designed by his majesty and executed by Knobelsdorff'. The idea was to forge a close link between the court festivities and the opera, in the same way that it was done at Dresden. There, the Zwinger, opera, and assembly rooms were adjacent; in Berlin they were to be united under the same roof. For that reason the Hall of Apollo, which had satyr terms supporting an upper balcony, served as vestibule and dining room, following the pattern of the bastion pavilion of the Zwinger. Adjoining was the auditorium with, as in Dresden, Italian-type four-tiered boxes with rather flat *rocaille* ornament, and finally the stage, with eight Corinthian columns on either side, in front of which the scenery was placed. The floor of the auditorium could be raised to the height of the stage to make a large ballroom.

Following the French custom, Knobelsdorff kept the exterior of the opera house free of all decoration. The entrances to the stalls were from the basement with its exterior of smooth rustication. In accordance with the tradition of Berlin, two flights of stairs led up to the portico on the narrow northern side, which gave access to the Hall of Apollo. This side – which, thanks to its position facing Unter den Linden and the projected royal palace, was the most important – was designed as a temple front. Six Corinthian columns support the simple pediment containing a relief by Nahl. The lateral intercolumniations had a width of only twice the diameter of the columns; the central one, as was customary, was two and a quarter diameters. In Germany the classicism of this front, which was built between 1741 and 1743, was unique for its period. English models were certainly of decisive importance. The work of Inigo Jones and, more especially, of Lord Burlington and William Kent were studied by the king and by Knobelsdorff. Kent was particularly congenial to Knobelsdorff because he too had started as a painter, and was sensitive to the beauties of nature. Thus English Palladianism reached Germany very early. Kent's designs for the Houses of Parliament with the very similar Corinthian portico date from 1739, i.e. a time when the plans for the Berlin opera house were already being prepared at Rheinsberg. Knobelsdorff might have gone on in an Anglo-Palladian way and adapted it to the Rococo, thus becoming a pioneer of classicism in Germany, if the king had not forced him to follow his own direction, an extremely personal and not always a very consistent one.

To begin with, he was not niggardly with his rewards. Knobelsdorff's appointment in 1742 as Surveyor General of all the royal palaces, houses, and gardens and as director-in-chief of all building in the royal provinces marked the peak of his career. How highly Frederick valued him can be seen from the fact that he also appointed him to the Prussian Council of Ministers and the Generaldirektorium.

The first task that faced Knobelsdorff in Potsdam was the rebuilding of the Stadt-schloss (1744). From the old building he retained Jean de Bodt's Fortuna Portal, facing the market square; otherwise, the steep roofs with towers were removed and the side wings of the court raised to the height of the *corps de logis*, but for the rest the walls with the original fenestration were kept. Judging from a sketch by the king for the pavilion on the Lustgarten side, he laid great stress on the monumental articulation of the façades by a giant order. This is emphasized by three-quarter Corinthian columns flanking the five centre bays, increased to pairs of columns for the three middle bays of the court. Pediments are avoided. On the other hand Baroque motifs do occur, for instance the foreshortened masonry of the jambs of the large arched windows of the main pavilion on the court side (Plate 169A). But Knobelsdorff did not approve of the keystones executed by Boumann for the windows because they looked like superficial trimmings. The effectiveness of the whole was enhanced by the colour; the order was yellow against a red ground, the copper roof lacquered blue, the ornament gilded. Despite his fondness for French art, the king showed a growing tendency to follow Italian architecture. He also said of Knobelsdorff in his 'Éloge' that he had preferred the exterior architecture of the Italians and had not followed the French, still less the English.

Knobelsdorff used his favourite motif, a Corinthian colonnade, to link the palace with the stables on the Lustgarten side. The king, who admired it, succeeded in having the same motif used to close the open space on the east side as far as the parapet in front of the bank of the Havel. This reduction of the colonnade to mere decoration went against Knobelsdorff's architectural sense, and for a long time he fought against using 'this noble column as a railing'. To allow a large staircase with two arms to be built in the interior, the central pavilion on the court side was enlarged. The king did not really care for great Baroque staircases because they were draughty and cold, and for his private apartment a special, smaller staircase had to be built. Probably for the sake of the fine view over the Lustgartenfreiheit, which was used as a parade ground, he had his winter apartment built into the south-east corner.

Under Nahl's supervision the decoration that had been so successful at Charlottenburg was developed with even greater freedom at Potsdam. The music room was of special beauty (Plate 169B). The decoration was in gold against a green ground. Bands with wavy lines replaced the pilasters, a motif musical in itself. In the dining room silver was offset against a pale green ground. In the study and the bedroom blue panelling with silver braid covered the walls, and the cedarwood furniture had silver mountings. The panelling of the cabinet was of cedarwood with gilded bronze decorations. No expense was spared for materials. The walls, like the walls in all the king's rooms at that time, were hung with pictures by Lancret and Pesne. Measurements required for pictures in particular rooms were often sent to the buyers in Paris. On the great staircase, listed by Frederick together with the Marble Hall as a work by Knobelsdorff, the walls were covered with silver-grey Silesian marble. The pilasters in front of them were of white marble. In the large Marble Hall, which contained huge paintings of the Dutch and Flemish schools glorifying the deeds of the Great Elector, Knobelsdorff covered the walls with reddish-grey marble. For the plaster decoration of the ceiling, as a transition from the corners to the central oval painting, he designed in his own personal style palm-trees growing out of bundles of arms, an architectural idea which would never have been conceived by a plasterer. The sketch drawing was in fact finer than the finished work. A transverse gallery was inserted between the staircase and the Marble Hall, decorated with grey marble. At Charlottenburg the stairs led direct to the dining room, which was certainly not a correct sequence.

It is safe to assume that the king and his architects studied the younger Blondel's *De la distribution des maisons de plaisance* (Paris 1738), which enjoyed great authority at that time. From the beginning of the century the French theorist Jean-Baptiste-Alexandre Leblond had demanded one-storeyed buildings raised only a few steps above ground level, with low roofs 'à l'italienne'. This enabled the waste of space of the uncomfortable staircases, passages, and anterooms to be avoided. There were no overhead noises, and access to the garden was easier. The kitchens should be built outside the house and care taken to avoid the prying glances of the servants. The king adopted these fundamental rules and had them observed even against the will of his architects. He was able to realize them fully at Sanssouci, the 'palais à l'italienne' crowning the upper terrace of the Potsdam vineyard.

Sanssouci was begun in 1745, in the middle of the Second Silesian War. Later Frederick wrote to d'Alembert: 'May the devil take the glory of war. Burnt villages, towns in ruins, thousands of dead, thousands of unhappy people, fear and misery everywhere – my hair stands on end. Potsdam, that is what I need to be happy. It was a poky little provincial town in my father's day; he would not recognize the place now, I have made it so beautiful. I love building and decorating, but only with my own savings. The state does not suffer through it. I should be ashamed to tell you how much Sanssouci is costing me.' At Sanssouci everything was to remind him of the carefree days at Rheinsberg – the flanking round pavilions with his library on the east and the colonnade on the north side with its lovely view. He wrote at the side of the surviving autograph sketch that was intended for Knobelsdorff: 'Colonnade Canalée Corintienne, mais le reste comme à Rheinsberg'. The termini – personifications of nature deities – supporting the entablature recall the Dresden Zwinger, the oval central room recalls the room built for his grandparents at Charlottenburg (Plate 171A). In this room, which was used as a dining room by Frederick's famous Round Table and was compared by him to the Pantheon, the monumental character was enhanced by coupled Corinthian marble columns carrying the entablature. Its transverse oval shape was better adapted to the *enfilade* and to the façade. Happily the decoration here survived the Second World War, especially the library panelled with cedarwood and with fire-gilt bronze ornament. The decorative scheme was determined by the Roman busts of Apollo, Socrates, and Homer placed at two-thirds the height of the panelling. The eye is drawn through the high French windows, through a clipped arboured walk to a 'Cabinet de Treillage' with the Roman bronze figure of a praying boy. The music room, too, has survived in its original form. It was decorated by Johann Michael Hoppenhaupt, who continued Nahl's work in a freer, more naturalistic manner. He was also responsible for the wall and ceiling decoration of the small Picture Gallery which, like the library at Charlottenburg, formed a corridor running alongside the principal rooms. His carved woodwork for the Voltaire Room is outstanding.

The hand of Knobelsdorff, the good genius of the Friderician Rococo, can be felt at Sanssouci on the north side, the articulation of which recalls the Palais Bourbon in Paris of 1722, the classic prototype for the Rococo. But it was at Sanssouci that a serious rift appeared between the king and Knobelsdorff. In view of the high site and the broad terrace, the architect criticized the lack of a basement – and it is true that, seen from below, the building seems to sag. Then, in 1746, Knobelsdorff was dismissed as personal supervisor of the building, although the interior decoration was still in full swing. In the same year Nahl, too, fled from Berlin. Knobelsdorff withdrew from the court. After the latter's death in 1753 the king, probably knowing that it was he who had been in the wrong, composed the now famous 'Éloge de Knobelsdorff', which was read at the Academy. A reference to their personal relationship is obviously contained in the passage: 'He loved truth and thought it could offend no man. He regarded complaisance as an obstacle and fled from everything that seemed to restrict his freedom.'

After the departure of Knobelsdorff Johann Boumann of Amsterdam (1706–76) was appointed Surveyor at Sanssouci, remaining in office from 1745 to 1747. Generally speaking his simple, solid style, which yet retained much of Knobelsdorff's elegance, is insufficiently appreciated. He had come to Potsdam in 1732, and had built the Dutch quarter there. The houses with their curving gables in the central street, built in 1737–40, continue the Dutch tradition in the Prussian electorate and are among the best examples of town-planning of the period in Germany. Then, between 1747 and 1750, from Frederick's sketches, he built Berlin Cathedral, on the northern side of the palace next to the Lustgarten. Unfortunately Schinkel's alterations robbed it of its Rococo character.

Frederick's nascent interest in Italian art was strengthened by his friendship with the writer and connoisseur Count Francesco Algarotti. In 1753 Algarotti wrote to him from Italy: 'I have been at Vicenza, where I saw what I am hoping to see again soon at Potsdam.' In 1753 Boumann built the Potsdam Town Hall, doing his best, by adding giant columns and a circular superstructure, to satisfy these new ideas without abandoning his personal manner. In this he was more successful with the palace he built in 1748–64 for the king's brother Prince Henry, in which he was able to retain the formal language of Knobelsdorff – probably encouraged by the future owner. On the site of the Forum Fridericianum once selected by the crown prince for his palace, a building thus arose which, with its *cour d'honneur*, high arched windows, detached Corinthian columns in the centre, and restrained touch of the Rococo, reflects the same classical ideal that also informs the opera house which it faces. In the nineteenth century the interior of this palace was reconstructed to serve as a university. It was destroyed in the Second World War but has been rebuilt.

What a Friderician palace looked like without Knobelsdorff's participation can be seen in the Neues Palais in the park of Potsdam. This was designed in 1755 by Johann Gottfried Büring and Heinrich Ludwig Manger, but not built until after the Seven Years War, between 1763 and 1766 (Plate 171B). The gigantic building, with its central projection of five bays, the two lateral parts each of ten bays, and the low one-storeyed wings, was intended to proclaim that Prussia was not yet at the end of her powers. Frederick himself described it as a *fanfaronade*, and indeed the building has a certain showiness. The motif of the giant pilasters was derived from Vanbrugh's Castle Howard, built more than fifty years earlier, which shows that the king was no longer in step with his own age.

In 1755 he paid a short visit to Holland, where he bought numerous Dutch and Italian pictures. As a result of this visit, he had the pilasters in the Neues Palais placed in front of red-brick walls in the Dutch manner. Four architects – Büring, Manger, Legeay, and Gontard – worked on the building and on the *cour d'honneur* on the west side, without satisfying the king. As usual, he refused to allow a basement, ordered columns of the central projection, already in place, to be removed, and, in the interior, would not permit a large Baroque staircase to be built. He moved his own apartment to the low south wing, and it was decorated for him in 1770 in the by then antiquated Rococo.

Frederick's passion for building was also intended to serve his subjects. Thiébault wrote: 'It is difficult to conceive of the number of houses he caused to be built every year, especially in the main streets. He supplied at his own expense the outer walls, the decoration, the roof, and sometimes even the partition walls. His architect Boumann carried out these buildings with such rapidity that we called the houses "Frederick's mushrooms". He did, it is true, order the hovels of his citizens to be pulled down, but within the year they were replaced by fine solid houses which were worth ten times as much. And there were whole streets which he had rebuilt in this way.' Had the king allowed Boumann a free hand, the results, including the actual architecture, would have been impeccable; but unfortunately he ordered that copies of Italian palace façades known to him from engravings should be used. So he laid the foundations for the historicism of the Berlin streets of the nineteenth century with their grotesque contrasts of style. Forms copied from heroic models of an age long past were stamped on to an urban world from which the muses had departed. The sculptor Schadow describes them as follows: 'The two large rows of houses inside the Brandenburg and the Leipzig Gates were now complete. The king had ordered two, or even three short fronts to be combined into one façade so as to obtain long, even lines. The majority of the owners had a greater sense of ownership than of beauty and had their parts painted distinctively green, yellow, and blue, snapping their fingers at the royal *coup d'œil*.'

As late as 1774–80, after Erdmannsdorff had built Schloss Wörlitz in the purest Palladian style, at the express wish of the king Kleiner's engraving of the Baroque range of the Vienna Hofburg, known as the range of St Michael, was used as a model for the Berlin library regardless of the fact that it in no way harmonized with the severe style of the buildings opposite: the opera house and Prince Henry's palace. Berliners mockingly called it the 'Kommode'. Here the king was paying homage to an ideal picture of the Austrian Baroque that had long faded, and had become incomprehensible even to the man-in-the-street. Thus ended the Friderician Rococo. Called into being by the king who championed it passionately, it had refined what already existed and, thanks to the eminent artists whose services were enlisted, had attained a supreme delicacy. In the end, however, the king's craving for fame and self-glorification led to the errors of copying and pretence, and the style deteriorated into a mere shadow existence.

Painting

The art of painting, the purpose of which should be to interpret human beings and nature, was mainly a commodity to be imported by Frederick II. The most important painter at court, Antoine Pesne (1683–1757), had been called to Berlin by Frederick I and remained there for forty-seven years, continuing to be French in intellect and powers of observation. An excellent portrait painter, though not equal to Watteau, who was a year younger, Pesne was capable of satisfying the considerable demands of Frederick II both in portraiture and in the light and gay ceiling-paintings at Rheinsberg, Charlottenburg, and Potsdam. In Berlin the same situation prevailed as at the Saxon court, where Silvestre dominated the field. No change was possible before 1770, when the newly awakened spirit of the middle class needed urgently to express itself. Characteristically enough, the earliest demonstration of this new spirit belongs to Berlin, a town which had never lost its colonial character, and the artist who brought it about was a man of Polish descent on his father's side, whose maternal grandmother was French, and who had married a Frenchwoman. In his art, too, Daniel Nikolaus Chodowiecki owed much to France: striving for a direct understanding of nature without abandoning the charm of the Rococo, he continued along the lines inaugurated by Watteau in his painted shop sign for Gersaint and by Chardin in his scenes from bourgeois life.

Chodowiecki was born at Danzig in 1726 and apprenticed to a shopkeeper. He already showed signs of his mission in a drawing of the grocery where he was apprenticed, with thirteen customers inside. In 1743, when he was seventeen, he went to Berlin as a shop-assistant and saw the finest of the king's buildings being constructed. He soon made a name for himself with his miniatures, especially portraits, and by 1754 was able to become independent and to marry. He took up engraving and oil painting in 1757, but it was not until 1768 that he found his real field, when he painted the twelve pictures of the months for the Berlin Genealogical Calendar. The subject was left to his own discretion, and his choice could not have been better: twelve scenes from Lessing's *Minna von Barnhelm*. This had been performed for the first time in Berlin in that year, and so Chodowiecki was able to select single characteristic scenes which were still fresh in his mind. With masterly restraint, he inserted the various groups in simple interiors enlivened only by light and shade and framed by oval medallions darkly hatched and with a background of rose garlands. The charm of the Rococo is fully retained, but it is closer to life and at the same time true to the artistic form of the play.

Chodowiecki's refined, sober art was unsuitable for the dramatic, historical, mythological, or allegorical scenes that were then in favour; but in his interpretations of everyday life he showed a keen understanding of human idiosyncrasies and characterized them with inspired realism. It is true that, compared with the magnificent achievements of German literature at that time, his illustrations often appear only as reflections, in their middle-class setting; but we must not forget that he was dependent on this middle class. The growing tendency was to replace the royal patron, who, though he might be arbitrary in his choice, was nevertheless carefully educated to appreciate and to devote himself to art, by a class which wished in the first place to be thrilled and touched. Goethe's keen eye detected the artist's tragic position. 'The Chodowiecki whom we admire would be reduced to meagre fare, but Chodowiecki the artisan, whose engravings illustrate the most miserable scribblers, is well paid.' Even highly intellectual patrons, such as Basedow, who employed him to illustrate his *Elementarwerk* in 1768, and Lavater, who actually used him for fifteen years to illustrate his *Physiognomische Fragmente*, did not realize the burden they were imposing on the artist in the interests of their pedagogic and scientific efforts. His sensitive powers of observation did not register what was generalized or typical but responded to the warmth of real life in all its uniqueness (Plates 172 and 173, A and B). Where he could be independent, for example in the sketches he made of his journey to Danzig in 1773, he gave brilliant proof of his ability to explore this new field. He was thus the inaugurator of a realistic school of painting which culminated in the nineteenth century in the art of Adolf Menzel.

Traces of Berlin realism can also be seen in the work of Anna Dorothea von Lisiewska (1721–82).[4] She, too, was of Polish extraction. Her husband E. F. Therbusch was an innkeeper and seems also to have worked as a painter. Anna Dorothea first came into prominence after her appointment to the Stuttgart court in 1761 and to the Mannheim court in 1763. She spent the years from 1765 to 1768 in Paris, where she became a member of the Academy, without, however, escaping the derogatory criticism of Diderot. She began in the manner of Watteau and Pesne, but later developed towards Dutch art, thereby increasing the sincerity and direct realism of her work. This appears in the outstanding self-portrait of 1770, painted on her return to Berlin and now in the museum there. In this, she was able to express her resignation to her personal lot and yet reveal in her refined features and in the white of her satin dress a sense of beauty that is lacking in her earlier self-portraits.

Sculpture

It is characteristic of the Friderician Rococo that sculpture, though essentially its most important component, expressed itself mainly in interior decoration, and was thus intimately linked with interiors. It was in this way that Johann August Nahl (1710–85),[5] the most talented sculptor available, was employed by the king. Nahl's father, Johann Samuel Nahl, allegedly came to Berlin from Bayreuth in 1695, and there found work in the circle round Schlüter. In 1702–9 he collaborated on the slaves for Schlüter's monument of the Great Elector. He became a member of the Academy of Arts and Sciences in 1709, but under the autocratic régime of Frederick William I he, too, was forced to leave Berlin, in 1717. He continued to work for another eleven years in Saxony and Thuringia.

His contact, through his father, with the Schlüter tradition was of decisive importance for the highly gifted Johann August. Moreover, following the fashion of the day, he was trained in the French manner. He can be traced at Strasbourg in 1729, where he worked under Robert de Cotte on the decoration of the Klinglin Palace, and from 1731 on that of the palace of Cardinal Armand-Gaston de Rohan-Soubise. While he was thus employed he came into contact with Robert Le Lorrain, an important representative of the Flemish Baroque. He spent the next four or five years travelling – three of them in Paris and other French towns – and immediately after went to Italy, where he was staying during the competition for the Fontana Trevi.

On his return to Strasbourg in 1736 he acquired French citizenship, and this later afforded him protection against Frederick II. The latter paid a short visit to Strasbourg in 1740, and from the Rohan and Klinglin Palaces the king was able for the first time in his life to gain direct experience of how a French artistic enterprise was run. This certainly made a decisive impression on him. Presumably he got to know Nahl there, for in the following year, 1741, he appointed him for five years, directly under Knobelsdorff, to be responsible for the decoration of the opera house in Berlin, of the wings of his palace at Charlottenburg, of the Stadtschloss at Potsdam, and of Sanssouci. It was thanks to Nahl that the ornament was equal in quality to the architecture. His wall and ceiling decorations have never been surpassed in finesse, lightness, grace, and imaginative variety, and, moreover, their restraint and naturalness wrung admiration even from classicist critics. In 1747 Johann Georg Fünck, his one-time collaborator on the Berlin opera house, wrote in his book *Betrachtungen über den wahren Geschmack* that Nahl's decoration 'always retained a natural impetus and inflexion, so that each part seemed to follow the other easily; like the muscles of the human body, one side stretched up when the other was drawn in, and, instead of wild and shapeless conch shells, he used for his ornament natural foliage and other things wisely selected from nature.' He made the most of very little and successfully combined a serious quality with his ornament, 'so that his taste more than any other deserved to be called the true *goût baroque*'.

His work for the Berlin court, however, like that of Knobelsdorff, was cut short owing to the extreme demands of the king and the pressure he exerted, and in July 1746 Nahl fled to Strasbourg to escape from the intolerable burden.

CHAPTER 25

SILESIA

THE conquest of Silesia by Frederick II in 1741, as a result of which the country was detached from Austrian domination, brought about fundamental changes. The transfer of government from Vienna to Berlin had great repercussions, in the field of building as elsewhere, owing to the fact that during the course of the eighteenth century the architect acquired more and more the character of a civil servant working within the confines of a bureaucracy. Since, however, the Prussian king for all his autocratic leanings possessed considerable connoisseurship, Silesia did not suffer when it was drawn into the circle of the Friderician Rococo. The new style comes out best in interior decoration. The palace at Breslau (Wrocław) (1750–1), built for the king by the Berlin architect Johann Boumann the Elder (1706–70), was the decisive influence. The simple exterior with its high arched windows was fully in keeping with the spirit of the Prussian régime, while the interior, following French principles, was resplendent with gay *rocaille* decoration. On the other hand the comfortable quality of Austrian architecture was not entirely lacking in the country houses of Goszcz (Goschütz) (1750–1) and Minkowskie (Seydlitzruh) (shortly after 1765). The ground plan of Pokój (Carlsruhe), the combined hunting lodge and country house in Upper Silesia, built in 1752–7 shows Swabian characteristics – which is understandable in view of the fact that the patron was Duke Carl Christian Erdmann von Württemberg-Oels. Nevertheless his architect Georg Ludwig Schirmeister of Brandenburg, a one-time building official, introduced Prussian compactness into the elevation.

The decisive swing from the Baroque to classicism came about under Gotthard Langhans (1732–1808). In his early work of 1762–5, Schloss Żmigród (Trachenberg), Langhans still strove for a dynamic articulation of the long ranges, while in the interior the *rocaille* appears in graceful garlands. The transformation was completed in Breslau in 1765 on the Hatzfeld Palace. There the exterior was designed as a severe closed block, a change of style modelled on the Roman palazzo of the seventeenth century. Inside, the Zopf style, the German equivalent of Louis XVI, began to oust the Rococo. Langhans also designed the Brandenburger Tor, and thus holds an important place in the history of Berlin classicism.

The association with Prussia enabled Protestant church architecture to expand. With the Breslau Hofkirche (1747–50), which had a tall slender tower over the entrance and a gallery inside, and the Schlosskirche at Pokój in Silesia, built by Schirmeister in 1765–75 on a basically similar plan, the link was established with the Berlin churches. Rich *rocaille* ornament was often used for the interior decoration. Catholic church architecture on the other hand was of lesser importance, though the abbey church of Trzebnica (Trebnitz), built by Gottlieb Daene in 1780–5 with a power and a plan similar to those of the Protestant churches, was a competent building. However, as was only natural, the Baroque tradition lingered more persistently among the Catholics.

The reconstruction of the country after the ravages of twenty years of warfare was especially remarkable in the rural and in the industrial buildings in upper Silesia, where Martin Pohlmann of Berlin, Surveyor of Buildings, occupied the leading position. The town hall at Jelenia Góra (Hirschberg), built in 1747 by Hedemann, a Berlin-trained Surveyor of Buildings, may serve best to represent this sturdy spirit. It owes its monumental character to the solidity with which the dominant tower rises in massive stages from the mansard roof, not, as formerly, to the articulation of the parts.

CHAPTER 26

WESTPHALIA

Architecture

OWING to her conservative attitude, Westphalia retained her individuality even in this late period. The lower Saxon farmhouse, the pride of the country, with its large hall, laterally attached cattle-sheds, and living rooms well to the back, culminated in the Wehlburg at Wehdel built in 1750 (Plate 174).

The brilliant development of Schlaun (see p. 223) between 1740 and 1773 was due to the fact that he never abandoned his Baroque style in favour of the then prevailing Rococo. For the house of the Brethren of Mercy at Münster (1745–53), Schlaun inserted the church of St Clement with its S-shaped façade into the pointed angle of the site and let it project into the triangular open space in front of it, thus allowing the traffic approaching from the five roads that converged here to pass right round it (Figure 31) – an idea based on his early studies in Rome. The vertical thrust of the tall, slender cylindrical lantern is offset against the broad mass of the church. For the interior Schlaun used Borromini's plan of St Ivo with its two intersecting triangles.

The chapel of St Johannes Nepomuk near Rietberg, built in 1744–8, also represents a

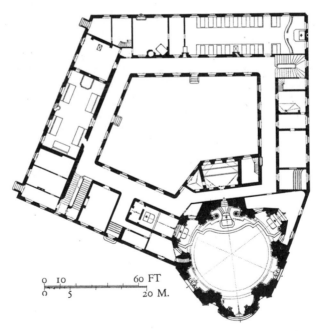

Figure 31. Johann Conrad Schlaun: Münster, House of
the Brethren of Mercy, 1745–53. Plan

development of Borrominesque ideas, and only Schlaun could have designed it. The oval of the small centralized building is pierced by the arms of a cross, forming four projections which curve round the small domed space. Here, as at Clemenswerth, the red-brick walls with their yellow sandstone dressings stand out against the green foliage of the ancient trees.

The Erbdrostenhof in Münster (1754–7) is an even more daring solution of the problem of the corner site than that of the hospital of St Clement. Schlaun partitioned off the right corner of the triangular plot of ground by a railing with curving lines, thus gaining a forecourt at the back of which was the façade. This façade embraces the space, receding both in the middle and at the sides, with a straight section in between. The vigorous concentration towards the centre is heightened by the alternation of brick and ashlar. The lack of depth prevented the building of a large staircase, but the upper ball-room with its two rows of windows, one above the other, occupied the entire centre from front to back. Unfortunately the splendid decoration was destroyed during the Second World War.

There were only two buildings on which Schlaun was able to express his architectural ideas freely: Rüschhaus, his country house near Münster (1745–8; Plate 175A), and his town house at Münster (1753–5). Schlaun's links with the Westphalian rural tradition can be seen at Rüschhaus. This has the lower Saxon plan with a central driveway on the court side and a large hall with lateral stables. On the garden side containing the living rooms the central projection, crowned by a gable, rises between roofs reaching low down (Plate 175B). The incorporation of light, upward-thrusting vertical lines into the heavy, oppressive mass of the building was a favourite trick of Schlaun's. He achieved a similar effect in his town house by means of four horizontal ashlar courses; the middle ones curve round the door opening, which is hollowed out like a niche, and raise the eaves in an arch. The curving flight of wooden stairs on the right of the vestibule inside receives direct light from a window. An oval central room on each floor projects on the garden side to form externally three sides of a polygon.

Schlaun's late work, the Schloss at Münster, built in 1767–73, occupied him during the last six years of his life. Even here he remained true to the Baroque, especially in the pediment of the central pavilion, which curves forward. But the *cour d'honneur* is wider, and the projecting wings do not narrow the space. The impressive effect is rather spoilt here by the restless alternation of brick and ashlar masonry, which is not really necessary; but on the other hand, as in all his buildings, Schlaun's mastery is shown in the way in which the sculpture is used and in the shape and construction of the great mansard roof. The interior, executed after his death, has a sequence of hall, central passageway with adjoining flights of stairs on either side, and oval-shaped large room on the first floor facing the court, which follows the programme of a symmetrical plan built round a central axis – although the staircase does not achieve the magnificent unity of Neumann's.

Painting

It is a tribute to the vitality of the lower Saxon cultural circle that a portrait painter of the distinction of Johann Georg Ziesenis (1716–77), after many changes of residence, was finally able to develop his art to the full at Hanover as painter to the court. He was born at Copenhagen, the son of a painter from Hanover. In 1740 he went to Frankfurt, where he established connexions with Mannheim which in 1750 led him to move there. Study of the art treasures belonging to the elector of the Palatinate, especially those at the Düsseldorf art gallery (which had not yet then been transferred to Munich), helped his further development. He was called to Zweibrücken in 1757, and there in the same year he painted the portrait of *Christian IV, Duke of Pfalz-Zweibrücken* the simple straightforward interpretation of which goes beyond the norm of the formal portrait. His membership of the Moravian Brotherhood obviously influenced Ziesenis.

His art culminated at Hanover in the portraits of *Count Wilhelm zu Schaumburg-Lippe* and of his wife *Maria* (Plate 176B).[1] The count's soldierly bearing reveals the Prussian, but by education and temperament he was English and both traits are expressed in his portrait. He was born in London in 1724 and in 1769, during the campaign against Spain and France, after the liberation of Portugal, he was made a Field Marshal in the British army. He was a friend of Frederick II, but unlike him was opposed to wars of annexation. His small personal army was run along the lines later followed by the German armies against Napoleon.

In a period increasingly interested in human values, the charming, limpid character of his pious young wife could be brought out to perfection in her portrait by Ziesenis, with the help of that most attractive of all styles, the Rococo.

CHAPTER 27

NORTHERN GERMANY

THE building of the great church of St Michael at Hamburg represents an outstanding achievement of this late period in the north. It was begun by Johann Leonhard Prey in 1751 and completed from 1757 by Ernst Georg Sonnin (1713–94). From the older building (p. 74) they retained the five-sided termination of the choir and the western part. The nave and two aisles remained, but the addition of four free-standing pillars and a broad transept, modelled on the Noorder-Kerk in Amsterdam, transformed the interior into a centralized design. The tunnel-vaults of the transept arms remained beneath the line of the eaves, so that the longitudinal axis with its higher trough-shaped vaults is more strongly accentuated. This, together with the curving gallery, produced a spacious interior, similar to that of a theatre. The new tower in front of the west side was not built until 1777–8 and had a height of about 450 feet.

The parish church of Ludwigslust, built by Johann Joachim Busch from 1765 to 1770, has nothing in common with the Late Baroque apart from a theatrical quality; it forms part of the classicist group of buildings designed there from 1764 for Duke Frederick the Pious of Mecklenburg-Schwerin as his residence. Inside, giant Tuscan columns in front of the longitudinal walls support a narrow gallery and a tunnel-vault. The rounded choir niche contains a large painting of the *Annunciation* by Johann Suhrlandt (1742–1827). Beneath it is the raised step on which the altar is placed, and the pulpit stands in front of this semicircle. On either side wide steps lead up to the altar. However problematic the architectural – though not the liturgical – value of the church may be, the planned layout of the Residenz as a whole, with low elongated brick buildings in alternating groupings, is undoubtedly successful.

In Lübeck, too, a considerable number of attractive houses were built during the second half of the eighteenth century. Gabled fronts were retained until the eighties, and the centres emphasized by projections. Usually the windows terminate in segmental arches. The doorways had fanlights, and their curved glazing-bars produced many graceful motifs. The traditional spacious hall was retained in the interior, but the insertion of small lateral rooms above was for the most part discontinued. The house that the widely travelled alderman Heinrich Tesdorf built for himself between 1779 and 1783 at No. 11 Königstrasse, despite its classicist front terminating in a straight balustrade, retained the old Hanseatic motifs of the great hall opening at the back in numerous windows and of a staircase in the hall leading up to an encircling gallery.

An important contribution to Rococo painting was made at the court of the art-loving Duke Frederick of Mecklenburg-Schwerin, where the eminent portrait painter Georg David Matthieu (1737–78) was called in 1764. Matthieu's naturalness and psychological characterization are at their best in the portraits he painted on boards which were probably put up on the backdrops of a stage and intended to compete with the live figures of actors (Plate 176A). He was the son of the Prussian court painter David Matthieu and of Dorothea Elisabeth Lisiewska of Berlin, and it was from his aunt and his step-mother Anna Rosina Lisiewska and from his father that he acquired his technical knowledge and his lively sense of portraiture.

CHAPTER 28

UPPER SAXONY

Architecture

THE last wave of Italian Baroque, which had flowed with Chiaveri, working in Dresden from 1738 to 1748, was already receding during the early forties. As early as 1741 support for the building of the Catholic Hofkirche lessened, and the king transferred his interest to the extensive rebuilding of Hubertusburg, a large hunting lodge. This represented a victory for the French school introduced by Longuelune, and now chiefly represented by Oberlandbaumeister Johann Christoph Knöffel (1686–1752) – although at that time Chiaveri was at the height of his powers. In 1740 Chiaveri made considerable improvements to the large model of the Hofkirche, and in the same year prepared the plans for the river front of the palace at Warsaw (Plate 198B; p. 306). His brilliance was further shown in his engraved work *Ornamenti diversi di porte e finestre* of 1743/4. As he said in the dedication to this book, it was intended to show to all those who, whether from ignorance or lack of imagination, were prejudiced against the *vastità dell'intelletto* and wished to confine it within all too narrow bounds, that the arts and sciences had no limitations and never would have. Such people did an injustice to the minds of those men who sought perfection by following the laws of antiquity, though not without giving thought to a sound foundation in the style of the day. So even Chiaveri, like his predecessor Borromini before him, claimed adherence to classical antiquity – which after all had, at a late period, had its own Baroque.

Shortly before he left Dresden in 1748 Chiaveri once more made a series of magnificent plans for the royal palace. He attempted, within his own style, to satisfy the new demands of the day for monumentality. In doing so, he frequently found himself very close to the theatrical art of Giuseppe Galli Bibiena, who was working in Dresden in 1747–53. Like Galli Bibiena, Chiaveri, for all his fundamental architectural soundness, produced the richest sculptural articulation contrived by means of the careful distribution of light and shade and the skilful use of diagonals. All flat surfaces and purely decorative effects are avoided.

Hubertusburg is in the strongest possible contrast to Chiaveri's style. Between 1743 and 1751 Knöffel completely rebuilt the hunting lodge, which had been constructed only twenty years earlier (from 1721 to 1733) by Johann Christoph Naumann for the then electoral prince. Only sections of the wings were kept. By adding a south-east wing with a chapel, a central oval drawing room and adjoining living rooms, and a northwest wing with a gallery, Knöffel satisfied the demand for 'commodité' to a much greater degree than Naumann had done. He enlivened the building in a masterly way by rounding off the corners, a supple motif that characterizes French designs of the period. The high, wide, arched windows, the projecting oval of the drawing room, and the tower stand out clearly, and the architectural articulation is restrained.

Knöffel's ability can also be seen in his designs for Count Brühl's garden on the terrace above the Elbe, which used to form part of the old walls and bastions of the fortress, especially that for the Belvedere which in 1751 replaced the Banqueting House on the Jungfernbastei, destroyed by a gunpowder explosion in 1747. He combined two large oval rooms with two radially placed smaller ones to form a compact block. In 1759 Frederick II of Prussia ordered the destruction of this fine building, an act of vengeance against the politics of Count Brühl. Brühl's country house of Pförten, near Forst, met with a similar fate in the same year.

The styles of Chiaveri and Knöffel, although diametrically opposed, soon began to be combined in the same buildings. After Chiaveri, angered at the delay in the completion of the Hofkirche, had left for Rome in 1748, Knöffel was entrusted with the continuation of the church. He was responsible for the insertion of the royal pews, which interferes with the transparency of the building at critical points. In Warsaw the two styles appear together in the river front of the royal palace (p. 306).

The tower of the Hofkirche was completed by Julius Heinrich Schwarze (1706-76), who in 1752 became Knöffel's successor as Oberlandbaumeister. He built the two upper floors and the crowning motif. The tower thus became 30 feet higher than originally envisaged on Chiaveri's engraved design. This was an advantage; for it gave the tower the necessary predominance and a greater vertical thrust, and it is likely that Chiaveri, who was again in Dresden in 1752, collaborated on this alteration.

Schwarze was equally successful in following the French Rococo when, from 1742 onwards, he built the house to the south of the Bürgerwiese for Countess F. A. Mosczynska. Unfortunately this, with its beautiful gardens, was pulled down in 1871 when the city was being enlarged.

After Bähr's death, middle-class architecture maintained its link with the Baroque. Johann Georg Schmidt (1707-74), municipal architect from 1764, was the leading personality. He was a cousin and pupil of Bähr and thus very close to him. When Bähr died, Schmidt followed the old guild custom and married his young widow, who had six children, all minors. For his first large building, the church of St Mary at Grossenhain, he retained part of the outer walls of the Gothic church, burnt down in 1744, with their buttresses. He separated the chancel to place his tower into it and enlarged the former chapel of St Elizabeth on the south side to full nave size, thus creating a T-shaped interior. On the north side he placed the group of pulpit and altar in the centre of the wall, and built a gallery with rounded corners to encircle the whole T. In this way he transformed the medieval longitudinal interior with its chapels into a unified preaching hall. Schmidt's plans had to be vetted by Knöffel. The new building was completed in 1748.

When he rebuilt the Kreuzkirche at Dresden, which had been shot to pieces by Frederick II's Prussian troops in 1760, Schmidt again had the problem of creating a centralized space within the framework of a medieval nave. The plans, which included the surviving tower, were begun in 1762 and building started in 1764. As in the case of the Frauenkirche, the town council sponsored the work. Schmidt selected an oblong central space with semicircular terminations. Arcades of ten bays, supported by piers, open into the aisles which contain the galleries. Following the chapel of Versailles, he raised the nave. Schmidt's position was difficult at the outset owing to the criticism of his plans by the classicists. His difficulties were considerably increased in 1765, when the east wall collapsed. Friedrich August Krubsacius (1718–89), royal architect and (from 1764) professor of architecture at the newly founded Academy of Arts, was commissioned by the town council to assess the plans. He condemned the composite order, the half pilasters, the curving of the buttresses on the upper walls, and the winding cornices of the lower windows. In the execution, however, the composite form of the colossal order was retained with the pilasters – the entablature projecting above each – at the back. On the other hand Schmidt's entablatures above the windows were simplified. Most important of all, Christian Friedrich Exner (1718–98) succeeded in imposing less slender proportions.

Exner was made Oberlandbaumeister in 1766 and followed Krubsacius as supervisor of the planning and execution of the church. The tower has four columnar storeys on an elliptical plan. Exner ordered the piers in the interior of the church to be strengthened. The crowns of the arches now lay beneath the architrave, whereas Schmidt in his plans had aimed at a hall-like interior with the arches resting on the pier capitals and supporting a trough-shaped vault cut into by penetrations which let in light from outside. Exner followed the Catholic models of Versailles and Dresden in placing the columns high and developing the interior as a single room with lateral galleries. Nevertheless it was Schmidt's idea of the form of the arcades that was finally adopted almost without change – even though he himself had been forced to relinquish the direction of the building in 1769. Indeed, the tradition of Protestant church architecture as a whole, deriving from the Frauenkirche, persisted with great tenacity. During the final phase of building, from 1777 to 1792, Gottlieb August Hölzer (1744–1814) placed a flat roof over the entire width of the church. This was of advantage for the tower (Plate 177B) in that it could now be reduced to three storeys and thus acquire greater simplicity and monumentality. Hölzer's highly successful design followed the Baroque style in the fluent rhythm of the forms; the classicist spirit can be felt only in a certain sense of restraint. The oblong exterior and the interior, rounded on the narrow sides, with free-standing piers and galleries all round and with high arches, were inspired by Bähr, and were used again by Schmidt for St Anna of 1764–9 and for the Waisenhauskirche (orphanage church), built in 1777–80, after his death.

Andreas Hünigen (1712–81) was the third member of the Bähr school. He, too, was a carpenter. He had erected the Schlosskirche of Weesenstein between 1737 and 1741 from Schmidt's designs, and this was followed by his own designs for the churches at Pulsnitz of 1743–5 and Kittlitz of 1749–55, both in the Lausitz, and St John at Zittau of 1766–1801, which embody variations on basic Bähr ideas. Following the Frauenkirche, the churches of Pulsnitz and Kittlitz have a nave encircled by galleries and a deep choir; at Pulsnitz the shape is nearly oval, at Kittlitz and Zittau the corners are rounded.

Because of the persistence of the Saxon Baroque tradition, it was not until about 1780 that even the classicist architects could escape its influence in their buildings, although Krubsacius attacked it in theory in his *Betrachtungen über den Geschmack der Alten in der Baukunst* as early as 1745. Moreover, the fact that Johann Joachim Winckelmann had moved to Dresden in 1754, where in 1755 he published his *Gedanken über die Nachahmung der griechischen Werke in der Malerey und Bildhauerkunst* which was soon to become famous, placed Dresden in the centre of the classicist movement. In spite of this, Krubsacius remained faithful to the Baroque in his fine Neue Schloss at Neschwitz, built in 1766–75, and now unfortunately destroyed. From a long low orangery with large arched windows rose a central pavilion containing the living rooms. An octagonal vestibule and a double staircase behind it lay on the central axis. The stairs led up to the octagonal ballroom, which was on the transverse axis above the vestibule and was decorated in the purest Rococo style. His Landhaus at Dresden too (1770–6), which was used for meetings of the estates, retains the Baroque features of curving stairs and a vertical articulation of the façade, and only the Tuscan columns supporting the balcony and the large pediment of the central projection are in a pure classicist style. This majestic building was burnt out in 1945.

In Dresden, as everywhere, French classicist theory established itself most firmly in the academy of art, founded in 1763 by Christian Ludwig von Hagedorn, an art critic. He became its Director General, retaining this position until 1780. As a connoisseur of some discrimination, he was able to appoint the right members, for example in 1766 Anton Graff (1736–1813), the eminent portrait painter, and in 1777 Johann Christian Klengel (1751–1824), the founder of the Dresden school of landscape painting which began to flourish at the beginning of the nineteenth century. The same applies to architecture. Krubsacius proved his worth as a professor in the way he trained his pupil Hölzer. In spite of the necessary simplification, he did not renounce the Baroque tradition. Yet Christian Traugott Weinlig (1739–99) in his *Letters on Rome* still attacked the tyranny of classical rules, the timid adherence to symmetry, and the monotony of French architecture, contrasting it with the variety and the painterly charms of Baroque Rome, however much he criticized the buildings individually. Weinlig had gone to Paris and then for the years 1767–9 to Rome.

In Thuringia the fate of Gottfried Heinrich Krohne (1703–56) shows the extent to which the vagaries of a patron, in this case Duke Ernst August I of Saxe-Weimar, could squander an architect's talents. Krohne was mainly a decorator. His best building was the Dornburg (1732–44), a country palace situated high above the river Saale.

Sculpture

The dominant personality in Saxon sculpture was Lorenzo Mattielli (p. 108). He had moved from Vienna to Dresden in 1738, where he received the important commission for the sculptural decoration of the Hofkirche. His statues in the niches and on the balustrades blend in jubilant accord. Today they seem Baroque, but contemporaries, especially Winckelmann, saw in them the embodiment of the new principle of 'the imitation of Greek works', for instance of the three female statues found at Herculaneum and purchased by the Saxon king in 1736 from Prince Eugene in Vienna. Winckelmann said of Mattielli that he was 'filling Dresden with art of timeless value', and praised especially the fact that the three statues from Herculaneum 'formed the basis of his drapery studies'.

The Meissen porcelain factory continued to flourish during the decades before and after 1750. The small figures of lovers, courtiers even when in the guise of shepherds, remained faithful to the Rococo style. In them the spirit of musical reverie is perpetuated. Moreover, this Watteauesque spirit is close to the opposed spirit of the grotesques of Italian comedy. Native Saxon traits were expressed in the pleasant attitudes and friendly mood, and supreme refinement came from an international admixture. This world, which included children and artisans, Chinamen and Japanese, hunting groups and allegories, was conjured up in the first place by Kändler's fertile imagination (p. 204). He collaborated with capable modellers such as Johann Friedrich Eberlein, Friedrich Elias Meyer, and Peter Reinicke, either giving them sketch-models to be worked out in detail, or correcting and finishing their own pieces. A number of larger works, such as the *Crucifixion* of 1743, the copy of Mattielli's fountain in the Friedrichstadt of 1745, the sumptuous mirror presented to Maria Josepha, the king's daughter, on the occasion of her marriage to the Dauphin of France, and, especially, the equestrian statue of Augustus III, commissioned in 1751, increased the prestige of Kändler and the scope of the work required of him.

The execution of the equestrian statue, which was to be over 30 feet high, would have necessitated the preparing of porcelain blocks considerably larger than anything that had so far been made. In 1753 it was carried out small in porcelain; the large model was completed only in plaster, and with the outbreak of the Seven Years War Kändler had to abandon the laborious work. Only the head of the king was made. In this late example of the Baroque equestrian monument there is no longer, as in the Zwinger, a true interplay of architecture and sculpture; in the manner of Longuelune, the high pedestal with the equestrian figure rises on a rocky base surrounded by a ring of allegorical figures. Following the old Baroque pattern, the rearing horse is supported by an allegorical figure – Envy – lying under him. Had it been executed it would have been necessary to set it, not in a square, but in a park, so as to comply with the new relationship between art and nature that was now being sought.

The later eighteenth century could no longer appreciate an artist like Kändler, whose powerful talent was rooted in the Baroque. He himself was quite willing to attempt the reconstruction of the factory, which had been idle during the Seven Years War, and to adapt his style to the new demand for 'smooth' work and for a momentous content; the judgement of Winckelmann, arbiter of neo-classicism, is: 'Most porcelain is in the shape of ludicrous dolls. The childish taste which developed from it has spread everywhere.' The new trend was initiated by a memorandum written by Prince Xavier, the administrator of the manufactory. He demanded 'the re-establishment of good taste', especially in sculpture, and 'correct draughtsmanship'. A school of art was created inside the manufactory, and Dietrich, painter to the king, was made its director. His task was 'to introduce a more correct and better taste than that current hitherto, as until now work has been done merely on the basis of modern fancies, neglecting beauty and antiquity'. Kändler tried as best he could, according to the wishes of his clients, to do mythological subjects in an antique manner, but also asparagus as knife-handles, cabbages as soup-tureens, dolphins as boxes, etc. Winckelmann had denied all value to the happy world of porcelain. He said that 'no worthy and instructive memorial had ever yet been imprinted on such costly work'. But the only effect of such objections was as a rule that wit, humour, and fancy were being ousted by the prose of rationalism and naturalism and the banality of the jokes of philistines proud of the education they had been able to afford. All the same, Kändler himself managed to keep his noble style, but his delicate creations were no longer animated by the flow of a life of which art formed an organic part.

Painting

Under Augustus III Baroque painting, though it retained its colour, produced nothing that could be compared with contemporary architecture or sculpture. Like Silvestre, who remained at the Saxon court until 1748, the painters who produced the altarpieces and ceiling paintings for the Hofkirche – Stefano Torelli, Carl Palko, and Charles Hutin – remained within the framework of their native art. Only Bernardo Belotto (1720–80), nephew of Canaletto and himself known as Canaletto, succeeded in a masterly fashion in giving a local character to his views of Dresden, where he worked in 1746–58 and 1764–8, and to his views of Vienna and Munich and later of Warsaw. In 1776 the famous Maulbertsch painted the ceiling of the Benno Chapel of the Hofkirche (destroyed in 1945). By then, however, Dresden had turned classicist.

Classicist ideas were introduced from Vienna which, thanks to Donner, had become the true centre of the school that turned towards the Greek ideal. Oeser (p. 116), who had come under the influence of Donner, moved to Dresden in 1739, a year later than Mattielli. His attractive art and mental alertness made a considerable contribution to the success of the new movement, especially through the influence he exerted on Winckelmann in Dresden and later, after having become director of the Leipzig academy in 1764, on Goethe. Goethe stressed the grace of his works but could not accept their nebulous character. Owing to the predominance of literature over art, Oeser produced his best work in etchings for book illustration; this he did within the framework of the Rococo. He was not successful when he attempted large-scale work, for instance the theatre curtain of 1766 for Leipzig. He liked intellectual and complicated conceits, but his compositions were only too gentle, and so he never achieved the convincing and compelling quality of Baroque mythology and allegory. Goethe as a young man, for all his sympathy with his mentor, regarded it as strange that, on the curtain mentioned above, Oeser should represent Shakespeare, in a light coat, ignoring the group of muses and poets around and making alone towards the distant temple, which is the symbol of immortality.

The problems involved in the great reorientation of art are even more in evidence in Anton Raphael Mengs (1728–79; Plate 178, A and B), because he was an artist of greater talent and because he was once internationally celebrated. The source of his art was the collection of paintings brought together with fanaticism of acquisition by Augustus III – an eclectic source, not one of the immediately preceding past. It was even in this eclectic sense that his ambitious father Ismael Mengs had given him his Christian names. Raphael and even more Correggio were his guiding lights. His own age saw in him the fulfilment of Winckelmann's demands: 'on him a certain form of Greek genius, from the greatest age of Greece, had descended – so profound were his ideas, so noble his emotions, so artless and innocent his morals.' When he was only thirteen his father took him to Rome, where he forced him to spend all his time drawing and restricted him to the Laocoon, the Belvedere torso, and the frescoes of Michelangelo and Raphael in the Vatican. In doing so Anton Raphael developed a genuinely critical approach to art which later found expression in his writings. But in spite of this, he did not immediately lose the spontaneous naivety of his artistic perception. On his return to Dresden in 1744 he did a series of portraits in crayon which, in their fresh, direct interpretation of personality, in the beauty of their colour, and in their technical perfection are among the best things achieved in Germany before the middle of the eighteenth century.

He then returned to Rome and, during a four years' study, again of antiquity and of the paintings in the Vatican, he strove for a deeper understanding and tried to break away from the Baroque. This was followed by a stay in Dresden lasting from 1749 to 1752, where he received the commission to paint the *Ascension of Christ* for the altar in the Hofkirche. Afterwards he returned to Rome for the third time and stayed there for nine years. His friendly association with Winckelmann strengthened the classicism of his theory. His friend and biographer Prange said of him: 'Mengs was a philosopher and he painted for philosophers.'[1] In his art the result was a certain dualism. His *Parnassus* in the Villa Albani, though it was no longer composed in Baroque foreshortening, was nevertheless still attached to a ceiling, and though he wanted to model it on Raphael, he did not get wholly away from the Rococo. This resulted in a loss of vigour, naturalness, and unity. The *Parnassus* became slightly effeminate; the figures are posturing and the composition is artificial. The same applies to the Dresden *Ascension*, which was modelled on Titian. During the last phase of his career Mengs worked in Rome and, from 1761 to 1768 and again from 1773 to 1777, in Madrid. In spite of being in competition at Madrid with Tiepolo, he now reached the peak of his world-wide fame. His portrait of the *Infanta Maria Theresa* (1772–1807), a late work, is a masterpiece in the psychological interpretation of a child and in painterly refinement (Plate 178B).

During the last third of the century the conflicts that arise in a period of transition were largely resolved. Graff was enabled to produce a consistent *œuvre* as a portrait painter through English influence and the effects of the great intellectual impetus of the age of Goethe and Schiller. The brightly coloured portraits of the Pesne school, with their stereotyped smiles, disappeared, and the colour scheme was now attuned to black and white with some intermediary tones. In the very bearing and expression of his sitters Graff reveals not only their own characters but also the character of the age (Plate 179A); for instance in his portrait in the Leipzig Museum of *Louise Elisabeth von Funcke*, née von Unruh (1763–97), painted during the French Revolution, he revives once more the charm of the dying century (Plate 179B). But at the same time, the features of the beautiful young woman, who was to die young, express the spiritualized quality that was part of the essence of this noble age. Graff was even successful in overcoming the heroic style in landscape painting: there are small oil paintings of his in which landscape is characterized quite individually.

CHAPTER 29

AUSTRIA

Architecture

THROUGH her efforts to bring peace, the great Empress Maria Theresa endeared her-self to the hearts of her contemporaries far beyond the borders of Austria.[1] Her impact on the arts was considerable too. A feeling of solidarity swept all the peoples of her em-pire, including the artists. The cultural ties with Paris, then just beginning to be woven, gave to Vienna the character of a European centre; at this time Gluck was inaugurating the development that was to lead Austria to world leadership in the field of music. One of the greatest assets of Austria was the fact that, in spite of her international awareness, she maintained her German character. The empress wrote to her daughter Marie An-toinette in France: 'Remain a good German and count it an honour to be German.'

In view of the great tasks facing her and of the difficult position of her government, she could not, unlike Joseph I, who had once been a pupil of Fischer von Erlach, devote her energies limitlessly to the fine arts. She built for herself a magnificent and at the same time comfortable palace at Schönbrunn (Plate 180A) and a country house at Hetzendorf, and these fully reflect her character – but they only continue to a minor degree the grand tradition of Austrian architecture. The great Hildebrandt would still have been available for Schönbrunn, and after the death of Joseph Emanuel Fischer he had certainly hoped to ob-tain the surveyorship both there and at Laxenburg. He was unsuccessful, probably because the court accused him of a lack of conscientiousness in the administration of buildings.

When Archduke Franz I, Maria Theresa's husband, left his home in Lorraine and went to Vienna he was accompanied by Jean-Nicolas Jadot de Ville Issey (1710–61), an excellent architect who had been trained in France. At Würzburg in 1745, when Fried-rich Carl von Schönborn, referring to the Residenz, described Hildebrandt to the arch-duke as his 'stattlichen althen practicum' (magnificent old practitioner), the archduke replied that 'he knew nothing of this person'. It was Jadot who built the Vienna Aca-demy of Science and Letters in 1753, a building modelled on the French style of Ver-sailles.[2] He followed the same model for the charming menagerie at Schönbrunn, where the individual sectors of the circular area containing the animals' cages have as their centre an elegant pavilion based on a design by François Blondel.[3]

Jadot, however, was unable to acclimatize himself in Vienna. He left as early as 1753, and Nikolaus Paccassi (1716–90) was given the commission for the remodelling of Schönbrunn (1744–9; Plate 180A). As early as 1737, Joseph Emanuel Fischer had dis-carded the loggias in the roof and placed steep roofs with pediments over the projections. Paccassi removed these and placed a bare mezzanine floor over the central projection. He also demolished Fischer's outer flight of stairs, inserted an archway of modest dimen-sions, and replaced the large transversely placed hall by two galleries. As a result, instead of the five large arched windows in the centre there were now seventeen small ones. A dominant motif is thus lacking, especially as the pediment, designed in the first place by the elder Fischer and retained by his son, was discarded too. Maria Theresa had a very large retinue, which made it necessary to insert a half-storey, and this spoilt the fine elevation of Fischer's wings.

As opposed to Paccassi, who adhered to the classicist principle of simplification, Ferdinand von Hohenberg, who transformed and decorated the gardens from 1765, used a somewhat richer style.[4] In 1775 he built the Gloriette which, as an eye-catcher, crowns the height above the parterre. With its columns and arches it already foreshadows the neo-Renaissance of the nineteenth century.

For another building, too, Paccassi was appointed as Fischer's successor, with better results. During the 1760s he built the lateral façades of the Burg, facing the Josefsplatz. The Imperial Library thus became part of a completely closed square. This was scarcely in keeping with the Baroque as Fischer had conceived it; but it is a highly successful piece of town planning, and the monumental dignity is further enhanced by the Pallavicini Palace, closing the far side of the square. This was built in 1783 by Hohenberg.

The work of Joseph Hueber (1716–87) gave Styria, too, a share in the great building activity of the Theresan age.[5] The atmosphere, however, was entirely different from that in Vienna, and the association was less with Austria than with Bavaria, with which country she had had close ties ever since the Bavarian settlement there in the Middle Ages. Hueber, the son of a Viennese mason, had had the opportunity during his four journeyman years in the 1730s to see the great Baroque buildings of Bohemia, Saxony, and central and southern Germany. In 1740 he married the widow of Joseph Carlone in Graz, whereby, though he was only a country mason, he acquired Carlone's building business and position. In his most important work, the pilgrimage church on the Weizberg built in 1757–76, he found an excellent solution for the task facing south German architects at that time, which was to insert independent centralized spaces into a longitudinal building. He obtained an effect similar to a stage-set by projecting chamfered or hollow-chamfered internal buttresses so that they flank the vista towards altar and organ. His starting point was a transversely placed oval space in the middle, preceded and followed by two narrower bays formed by the internal buttresses, and enlarged laterally by elliptical chapels. The illusion of space was increased by Joseph von Mölk's wall paintings.

Styria already possessed a sound tradition of towers with richly sculptural caps; and in 1742–4 Hueber built the twin towers of the Mariahilfkirche at Graz in his own vigorous, clearly enunciated style (Plate 181). They stand in front of the Minoritenkirche built by Pietro de Pomis, which is beautifully sited on the bank of the river Mur. The gabled tower of the city church at Graz, built in 1780–1 by Joseph Steng, is still fully in the Baroque tradition. It is effectively placed at the end of the Herrengasse.

In southern Styria the centralized plan with a longitudinal ellipse surrounded by niches between internal buttresses, based on Viennese and south German models, was continued into the second half of the eighteenth century by the Marburg architect Johann Fuchs.

In upper Styria an important addition in the Late Baroque style was made to the abbey of Admont.[6] Gotthard Hayberger (1699–1764) of Steyr, who was called to Admont by Abbot Anton II in 1742, developed a gigantic plan. This was limited to the buildings lying behind the church, and among them only the library survived the fire of 1865 (Plate 180B). The details were not completed until 1774 (by Hueber). It is a magnificent, majestic room with a domed longitudinal ellipse as its centre. The ceiling fresco by Bartholomäus Altomonte and the sculpture by Veit Königer and Thaddäus Stammel blend with the Rococo of the bookcases to give a brilliant white and gold interior.

Hayberger also worked on the abbey of Seitenstetten in upper Austria, where he was responsible for the very dynamic main portal, and in 1765–78 he built the town hall of Steyr, still in a fully Baroque way, with ample forms and strong accentuation of the verticals.[7]

On the other hand, the more academic ideals of the age found an expression in upper Austria too – in much simpler but all the more impressive buildings. The Benedictines of Kremsmünster[8] rivalled the Jesuits in their zest for the education of the young. Between 1748 and 1760 they built the observatory, beautifully sited on a hill, near to the convent, as part of their Academy for Young Noblemen (Plate 182). The vertical lines of the pilaster strips on this tall building seem to be reminiscent of the forms of a modern frame building – except that, in accordance with Baroque aims, the dominant central tower creates an overall unity which is no longer sought in our own day.

In the Tyrol the relationship with southern Germany as shown in the parish church of Innsbruck[9] (see p. 103) was continued. The priest–architect Franz Penz (1707–72) used the flat saucer dome, generally of oval shape, for many buildings. In his most important work, the parish church at Wilten (1751–4), he placed two transversely set parts with oval vaults one behind the other, without as yet chamfering the internal buttresses.

The ties with Bavaria persisted also in domestic architecture; about 1775, for example, the Gothic Helblinghaus at Innsbruck received a rich, dynamic stucco façade resplendent with Rococo forms (Plate 183).

Sculpture

The Tyrolese sculptor Balthasar Ferdinand Moll (1717–85) followed closely in Donner's footsteps. He was born at Innsbruck, the son of Nikolaus Moll, a much-employed sculptor, who gave him his first training. Moll arrived in Vienna in 1741, the year of Raphael Donner's death. He received his further training at the Academy school run by Matthäus Donner (1704–56) who, as a teacher, transmitted the art of his elder brother to the younger generation of artists. In 1745 Moll won the academy gold medal, and from 1751 to 1759 held a professorship there. His sarcophagus for Franz I and Maria Theresa, commissioned by the empress in 1753, marks the peak of his artistic career (Plate 184B). It was to be placed in the domed crypt of the Capuchin church.[10] There is no classicism yet in this work; owing to his Tyrolese origins, Moll was close to Bavarian circles, and still used Rococo forms. But what interested his contemporaries most was the truth of his interpretations of the intellectual and physical qualities of the human being. Impressed by the great personality of Maria Theresa, Moll represented the imperial couple half reclining on the sarcophagus, instinct with vitality in the face of death. Moll did the sculpture for some twenty more sarcophagi, and the portraits on them represent on the whole his most personal achievement. In his allegories on the other hand he continued Donner's art of a classical representation of the human body. For all their softness and naturalism, they are not rendered with overmuch detail. This idealizing increases in Moll's late works; yet, though classicism came to dominate, the lifelikeness was never lost.

Donner's genius in composing beautiful, supple groups was successfully adapted for a small work by Johann Georg Dorfmeister (1736-86), the early so-called Memorial of 1761 in the Vienna Barockmuseum.[11] This charming piece was intended to gain for its maker the favour of the imperial couple who were represented in the form of Apollo and Minerva. The artist appears as a putto, presenting his petition.

How great the difference was between sculpture in Vienna under the influence of Donner and sculpture in Munich can be seen in the early work of Franz Xaver Messerschmidt (1736-83). He was born at Wiesensteig near Geislingen. At an early age (allegedly in 1745) he was sent to Munich to his uncle, Johann Baptist Straub, and immediately after, from 1750 to 1752, to Graz to his other uncle, Philipp Jacob Straub. He arrived in Vienna in 1752, where he became a pupil of Matthäus Donner at the Academy. His lead group of the *Immaculate Conception*, still in the Rococo style, was made for the Convent of the Savoyan Ladies in Vienna in 1768.[12] During the 1760s he was frequently employed by the court as a portraitist. His gilded lead bust of *Gerard van Swieten*, director of the Imperial Library and of the imperial health services (1769, Barockmuseum; Plate 185A), expresses in a still vigorous Baroque style the intellectual eminence and unusually energetic personality of the celebrated doctor. During a stay in Rome in 1765 Messerschmidt received a call to the Paris Academy, but turned it down. In the same year he visited London. On his return to Vienna in 1769 the Academy conferred on him the titles of Statuarius and Professor; but he was never elected to the chair, the objection being that he was confused in mind and had the most whimsical fancies. He was retired in 1774 and returned to his home town, but in 1775 was appointed sculptor to the court at Munich. There, too, he was unable to conform, and from 1777 until his death he lived as a recluse at Bratislava (Pressburg).

During this period of intellectual over-tension, though with his artistic ability not only undiminished but actually increased by the study of antique models, he produced his great series of character heads. They are in fact interpretations of actors' grimaces rendered with a realism and a deliberate intent to startle that are almost embarrassing, despite the high artistic quality in the structure of the heads[13] (Plate 185B). Lavater's studies of physiognomy and the healing by magnetism of the Viennese Doctor Mesmer found their immediate repercussions in Messerschmidt's art, and he endeavoured to classify like a scientist. His situation is characteristic of his age: in the absence of unifying concepts of religion and mythology, the artist is no longer in a natural contact with his fellow men. He isolates himself in his art, and suffers under this isolation.

Messerschmidt's fate was typical. During these years in the 1770s, when Mozart's music was approaching its zenith, the possibilities for sculpture in Vienna, despite adequate commissions and available talent, deteriorated. The sculptural decoration for the park of Schönbrunn was begun under the supervision of Wilhelm Beyer (1725–1806) and executed in the French classicist style.[14] Born in Gotha, Beyer was trained in Rome from 1751 to 1759 and came to Vienna in 1767. In his capacity as garden architect, painter, sculptor, and writer he represented an international style in the Winckelmann sense, and it was Winckelmann who 'first gave him an idea of Greek proportions, form, and expression'.

Among Beyer's many collaborators Johann Hagenauer (1732–1810)[15] does not stand out in any way, though his early works are not without importance. He was a native of upper Bavaria and first worked at Salzburg. His gilded bronze statuette of *Christ at the Column* (1756, Cleveland Museum) is still in the vigorous, expressive style of the Late Baroque. The sculpture for the New Gate of the Mönchsberg Tunnel and the column with the Immaculate Conception in front of the cathedral, done in 1766–71, are in the grand Salzburg manner. In 1773 he was called by Beyer to work on eight of the figures for the Schönbrunn Park. Further works followed, and these show the gradual stifling of a great talent under the barren wind of classicism. Two Tyrolese sculptors also collaborated at Schönbrunn – Veit Königer,[16] who worked at Graz (p. 296), and Franz Anton Zauner (1746–1822), the most important representative of Viennese classicism.[17] In his equestrian statue of Joseph II in front of the Imperial library in Vienna, Zauner showed a sensitive response to the beauty of the unique square.

In Styria Veit Königer (1729–92) successfully developed his work to the very limits of what Baroque sculpture could achieve. This was due to the unbroken line of Styrian Baroque sculptors[18] preceding him: Marx Schokotnigg (1661–1731), Johann Jakob Schoy (1686–1733), Joseph Schokotnigg (1700–55), and Philipp Jakob Straub (1706–74). The link was further strengthened by two of the customary intermarriages. Straub, who was born at Wiesensteig in Baden, a brother of the more famous Johann Baptist Straub, was trained at the Vienna Academy from 1730 to 1733. In 1733 he married Schoy's widow and took over his workshop. His excellent works in the Stadtpfarrkirche and on Mariahilf at Graz show an undiminished Rococo with a Bavarian note. Joseph Schokotnigg continued the work of his father Marx, who through his contact with Fischer von Erlach had inaugurated the Styrian development with its purely Baroque orientation. Presumably Joseph, like his father, had worked in Italy; this is suggested, for example, by his statues on the Stadtpfarrkirche. His work culminates in the sculpture for the high altar of the church of the Brethren of Mercy, which had been entrusted to him in 1732.

This was the starting-point for Veit Königer, the successor of Schokotnigg, who had died in 1755. Königer was born at Sexten in south Tyrol in 1729. He studied at the Vienna Academy from 1751 to 1755, and was in 1754 awarded first prize for his group of *Hercules fighting Antaeus*. He married Schokotnigg's daughter and thus acquired his workshop. Obviously the style that Königer had developed in his home town had only been temporarily modified by his academic studies, and is therefore not typical of the

Viennese school; nevertheless his idealized types and statuesque treatment of figures are also quite distinct from the Bavarian Rococo. This can be seen in his *Annunciation*, the masterpiece with which he began his activity at Graz in 1756 (Plate 184A).[19] Originally, following an ancient custom, the figures of the Virgin and the angel stood separated on either side of the chancel arch in the church of St Andrew. Although their effectiveness depends on their relationship to the arch, they were later removed to the Landesmuseum, where the lack of architectural support is especially noticeable in the raised arm of the angel. By comparing this work with the *Annunciation* by Ignaz Günther at Weyarn,[20] we can see that the Bavarian sculptor, who had studied at the same time as Königer at the Vienna Academy, retained the playful dancing gesture of the Rococo to a much greater degree than the Tyrolese artist working in Styria – even though Günther's work was done about seven years later (Plate 147). The trend towards generalization in Königer's work prevented him from attaining the heights reached by Günther's genuinely personal art, vibrating with life; but on the other hand the Tyrolese artist can claim a far greater religious intensity for his figures. His *Immaculate Conception* for Maria-Grün near Graz of about 1762–5, which originally stood in front of the Münzgraben-kirche, expresses the ideal of the Virgin Mary interceding for man with all the fervour of the Baroque. The qualities he had inherited from the Pustertal were later stifled by the conventional language of classicism, which led him to produce rather weary-looking figures such as those on the Column of the Trinity in the cemetery of St Peter at Graz of 1775.

Even in sacred art, the interest in physiognomy ousted the old Baroque language of form. The Tyrolese sculptor Franz Xaver Nissl (1731–1804), working at Fügen, attempted to give a purely human interpretation of the nature of holiness. Characteristic of this aim are the subjects of his figures on the four confessionals in the abbey of Fiecht, done in 1774. They represent *The Searching of Conscience, Repentance, Good Intentions*, and *Satisfaction*.[21]

Painting

It is a remarkable fact that in Austria in the second half of the eighteenth century, at a time when the arts in general were declining, painting continued to flourish. This was largely due to two great artists: Maulbertsch and Kremser-Schmidt, or Schmidt of Krems. In as far as they were not officially fostered by the Academy and by the court, they can be described as secessionists. The Academy refused to appoint Maulbertsch as a professor 'because his all too daring, undisciplined spirit does more harm than good to the young academy students'. He was not ennobled, as was then customary; he probably did not even want to be. On the other hand he remained in favour with the Church and with the people, as is proved by the many commissions he received. Criticism of his work cannot be traced farther back than 1780. At that time, while he was working on the frescoes of Pápa Cathedral, the bishop of Erlau requested him to eliminate all motifs that were 'horrifying and frightening' (*schräckend und schauerlich*). 'In place of the *sotto in sù* he was to give a more orthogonal rendering of architecture in profile' and 'a good view of the main figures'. Maria Theresa, who was probably influenced by her husband, preferred the international Rococo style, as can be seen from the very tasteful decoration of Schönbrunn, and she commissioned the Roman Gregorio Guglielmi (1714–73) to paint some of the large frescoes in the rooms. In four frescoes on the ceilings of the two galleries[22] he gave a remarkably realistic interpretation of army life in Austria, which presents the greatest conceivable contrast to Maulbertsch's visionary art. Although Maulbertsch owed much to Italy, and particularly to Tiepolo, as a result of his German origin he was essentially closer to the Bavarian and Swabian circles.

Franz Anton Maulbertsch, the son of a painter, was born in 1724 at Langenargen on Lake Constance. In 1739, when he was sixteen years old, we find him in Vienna as a pupil of van Roy, and in Vienna he remained until his death in 1796. In 1741 he became a student at the Academy, where he won a first prize in 1751. There, under the director-ship of Jakob van Schuppen, to whom in fact he owed much, he must have become familiar with the Viennese Baroque Classicism. It was due to Donner's prestige that even Maulbertsch, the most painterly of all Viennese painters, retained a three-dimen-sional conception of the human figure. He was critical of his own early style: when at an advanced age he examined the frescoes in the Piaristenkirche which he had painted at twenty-one, he admitted that he had been studying the errors of his youth, probably meaning chiefly the mistakes in the rendering of the figures. His *Venus and Adonis* (*c.* 1785; Plate 188A), an oil painting in grisaille in the Albertina, is conceived in a sculptural way. It formed part of an *Allegory on the Fate of Art* which Maulbertsch presented to the Schmutzer Academy in 1770 'on the occasion of his appointment as a professor'.

Despite the stylization of his figures, his starting-point was always a precise idea of position and movement, especially for foreshortenings, which he could paint in the most difficult positions with the utmost ease.[23] His studies, too, for example the one for a *St Francis receiving the Stigmata*, show how carefully he explored all the possible atti-tudes for a specific scene that demanded a maximum of expressive fervour. Fantastic as his art may appear, it was in that sense always based on solid foundations. The same applies to his representation of movement, where he also seems simply to give free rein to his fiery temperament. Under the inspiration of Rubens he produced the most vivid interpretations of mythological scenes, for example in his oil sketch with the *Rape of Deianira* (*c.* 1785/6; Plate 188B). His handling of paint, with patches of colour that seem to skim across the surface, conjures up an illusion of movement that surpasses every-thing until then achieved. A splendid prelude to this manner appears in his early fresco in the dome of the Piaristenkirche in Vienna (1752; Plate 186A), where the saints are no longer disposed on individual banks of clouds, but are swept into the atmospheric space. The single figures too are no longer, as they still were in Troger's work, carefully framed, but everything is caught up in a whirl, angels and saints, even God himself. Despite Maulbertsch's many links with Troger – such as the use of light colours, es-pecially white and blue, colours that are intensified by pink, or the striving for warmth and beauty – there are fundamental differences. These lie in his etherealizing of solid form, in his manner of linking the most varied objects in flowing movement, and in his avoidance of calm, static forms by means of a swift, sketchy execution. He was fully aware that imaginary events could only be made to come to life by methods which are themselves imaginative. Therefore the ceiling fresco which transcends reality is the ideal vehicle for his art.

In his oil paintings, too, the ground is often merely indicated – figures floating in space convey better his urgent sense of movement. Often the faces are fleetingly sketched, but the hands are eloquently expressive, for instance in the *Martyrdom of the Apostle Judas Thaddaeus* (c. 1760) in the Barockmuseum at Vienna.[24] The saint's left hand, stretched out to the torturer preparing to strike the blow, shows the merest hint of a defensive gesture. Far more emphatic is the movement of the right hand, raised to indicate the Heart of Jesus appearing in the clouds. In the *St Narcissus* in the same collection (c. 1754) the transfiguration is expressed not in the gnome-like face of the saint, but in the silvery colour of the alb, which is consciously contrasted with the rich brilliance of the vestments. Here again the spiritual life is eloquently expressed in the forward gesture of the left hand hovering over the sacred book. The sense of floating is further stressed by the two angels, who with the main figure form a lozenge-shaped group in which the saint and the large angel raising the massive codex read as a spiral. A similar composition is used by Maulbertsch in his group of the *Assumption* in the church of Heiligenkreuz-Gutenbrunn (1757). Here he expresses not the darkness and lowliness of the earthly life of the Virgin, but her glory and her beauty.

And yet his art is in no sense exclusively spiritual. The real and the unreal are interwoven as in a dream. But even reality seems strangely fantastic. On the ceiling fresco in the divinity school of the Old University in Vienna, the *Baptism of Christ* (c. 1766) is attended by magnificently attired Orientals with large turbans, by bathers, and, in the foreground right, by a gentleman and a lady in rich Rococo costumes[25] (Plate 187). These charming figures are without logical function, inserted where the composition called for them. Indeed Maulbertsch's whole *œuvre* is a passionate revolt against the rationalism of the age. The oil sketch in the Barockmuseum for the frescoes in the church of Schwechat (1765)[26] shows St James of Compostela, who resembles an ordinary soldier, mounted on a rearing horse and engaged in combat. A blue saddle-cloth is falling off the horse. Maulbertsch needed the gold edged with blue as a contrast for the white steed and the white clouds; this was of more importance for him than the fact that such a large and splendid cloth trailing behind the horseman is incongruous even in a legendary battle.

Elsewhere, too, broad draperies enhance the expressive painterly quality desired by the artist rather than appertain to the figures they cover, which are of secondary importance. On the ceiling fresco in the church of Heiligenkreuz-Gutenbrunn (1757; Plate 189) a strip of gold brocade winds upwards between the musician angels; this has no *raison d'être*, whereas the crosses which also appear are related to the scene represented, *The Invention of the Cross*. On the other hand the contours of Christ's Cross, which the painter felt to be too hard, are dissolved in clouds, but the drapery, to which no significance attaches, is clearly defined in all its rich painterly quality.[27] The extensive group of people at the foot of the rock on which St Helena is standing are less conspicuous than are the piles of drapery and the carpets. The billowing drapery round the holy empress herself recalls the fact that at that time the crinoline with its ample material was in fashion. The mounted knight emerging from the background on his fairy-tale white steed is a typical Maulbertsch invention. He seems like the embodiment of the vision of the captain beneath the Cross of Christ, a vision that has been translated into powerful movement. The eye is drawn farther to a downward-swooping angel carrying the Vernicle. Other figures are only lightly sketched in.

There can be no doubt that Maulbertsch appeals so much to us because he keeps so detached from his subject matter. However, he could maintain this detachment only to a limited degree, for his patrons desired clear legibility and fame for themselves.

Four scenes showing the history and the apotheosis of the bishopric of Olmütz are represented in the frescoes in the Feudal Hall of the castle at Kroměříž (Kremsier) (1758–60),[28] one of his most important works. It is a matter for speculation as to how far he wished all his figures to be taken seriously, in view of his frequent caricaturing. At Kroměříž St Martin spurring on his horse has all the appearance of a plump, pert, chubby-faced captain of cavalry. This conception is certainly rooted in Bavaria. Maulbertsch was obviously a follower of Asam, to whom he owes a great deal – for instance the use of large draperies as part of his compositions.[29] Furthermore, Maulbertsch, in common with his whole generation, was deeply influenced by Rembrandt, an influence which he received via Venice.

At the end of his life he felt himself that his brilliant talent had run its course.[30] He expressed this in his letters, saying that he now sought 'quiet and order' and a 'more effective interpretation of the Histories'. This suggests that he no longer rejected Winckelmann's condemnation of the Baroque. In his *Self-Portrait* of *c.* 1790 in the Barockmuseum at Vienna (Plate 186B),[31] he has abandoned brilliant colours. The dark-shadowed painting is laced with a blue that is without lustre and serves to enhance the melancholy character of the whole. Nevertheless even this portrait tells of the vitality of a fiery temperament. The hands, which had painted frescoes in fifty-nine different places, seem to be modelled in undulating forms out of a soft pasty substance. In this picture Maulbertsch retained the freedom of the Baroque.

He was not an isolated artistic phenomenon; on the contrary his art represents only the finest flower of a universal painterly culture and could strike a responsive chord in many people. Among his contemporaries were artists of distinction who worked in small country towns. To us their lives seem to have flowed uneventfully along narrow artisan lines. The portraits, however, tell a different story. The brilliance of the town and country traditions and the quality of the crafts as a whole were everywhere a reflection of the culture of the Rococo. In the churches and country houses which were scattered over the whole land the superlative quality went far beyond anything conceivable today.

It was thus possible for a much simpler and more popular artist such as Schmidt of Krems to produce an *œuvre* of enchanting quality that found its way to every part of Austria. The number of his surviving pictures is put at two thousand. His art has none of the heightened intensity of colour, none of the vibrant force that informs all parts of Maulbertsch's inspired *œuvre*. In keeping with his own status in life, Schmidt's art remains objective and realistic. A comparison between the two artists shows up the Mannerism in Maulbertsch's work. In the scene of *Christ Asking to be Baptized* in the fresco at the Old University in Vienna,[32] Maulbertsch represents Christ with his right foot raised. This movement is balanced by the counter-movement of the upper part of his body. The left shoulder is lifted, the head turns in the same direction, while the chest and the hands folded in prayer are again turned in the opposite direction. John the Baptist stands high up on a rock. His right foot, too, is drawn up and his left hand raised in amazement, in keeping with his words: 'Surely it is I who need to be baptized by thee and thou comest to me.' In the oil sketch for the *Baptism of Christ* by Schmidt in the Landesmuseum at Graz[33] it is not the tense dramatic moment that is depicted but the act of baptism itself, comprehensible to everyone. Christ and John the Baptist are represented approaching one another in a natural movement. Maulbertsch painted for theologians and experts in art – there were enough of them at this time – Schmidt for the community. To make another comparison, let us take Schmidt's frescoes in the nave of the parish church of Krems representing *The Triumph of the Cross* (1745):[34] St Michael, flying down from heaven, where the Cross surrounded by biblical figures is visible, is beginning to hurl its enemies into hell. Maulbertsch, like Troger, would have represented St Michael hurtling headlong from the sky. In the fresco in Krems, the movement has become calmer. The scene is interpreted in a simple, lucid manner to suit the needs of the times. In the ceiling frescoes, too, Schmidt reverts to customary compositions, and as a result the ceiling fresco begins to lose its universal significance. Soon it was to disappear altogether.

Ceiling painting forms only a comparatively small part of Schmidt's *œuvre*. Moreover it is also characteristic of the times that he favoured small pictures for devotional use in the home. Nevertheless he does not abandon the Baroque; he may tone down impetuous movement, but he does accentuate the unity of the work of art by a handling of light which illuminates all parts of his compositions with a silvery sheen, thus accomplishing one of the chief aims of the Baroque (Plate 190). It is, however, his piety that distinguishes his art in the first place from classicism. From the outset he wished to serve the Church, and he gave visual expression to what the faithful were to experience at Mass and at prayers by revealing the power of the emotions.[35] This was one reason why his art remained in favour over a long period, until the time when poetry and music found even more potent means of touching the human heart. The course of his own life was in itself sufficient to ensure the unswerving directness of his art.

Whereas the majority of artists in those years experienced a break in the continuity of their art, if only by the fact that in later life they worked right away from their homes, Schmidt's whole life flowed in one direction. It was centred in one of the loveliest spots in Austria, the Wachau, within sight of some of the greatest monuments of Austrian art: Göttweig, Dürnstein, Melk. Martin Johann Schmidt was born at Grafenwörth near Krems in 1718, and he was so closely associated with the area that he came to be affectionately known throughout Austria as 'Kremser-Schmidt'. His father Johann Schmidt was called by Abbot Hieronymus Übelbacher of Dürnstein, an enthusiastic builder and connoisseur, to do the sculpture for the interior of the abbey church and of the tower.[36] From childhood on the son was thus introduced into the type of surroundings that he was to find all his life in the many Austrian abbeys and churches whose protégé he was. His training as a craftsman was supervised by Gottlieb Starmayr at Stein, near Krems.

Schmidt must have familiarized himself with the art of Rembrandt through the collections of engravings at Dürnstein, Göttweig, and Vienna, and his whole later work moved within Rembrandt's orbit. In 1764 he took up etching himself, and this led him to make reproductions of his paintings for advertising purposes. He occupied various offices at Krems, and obviously made no effort to gain a footing in Vienna, though he was content to be elected a member of the Vienna Academy in 1768. His extensive practice made it necessary for him to organize a large workshop which, from 1786 onwards, had a growing share in the production of his pictures. In 1801 he died, a wealthy citizen, at Stein on the Danube, near Krems.

It is characteristic of his circumstances that he had a collection of two hundred and sixty-three pictures from the widest variety of schools. This, too, provided a link with the oil painting of the past. For instance, he continued to favour the dark-shadowed brown grounds popular in the High Baroque, but allowed significant figures or heads to stand out brilliantly in a shimmer of light, as in the painting of *The Martyrdom of St Catherine* at Dürnstein priory church (1767). The enchantingly lovely figure in a misty white robe, such as he loved to paint, is kneeling in prayer and receives the blow from the executioner's sword with the utmost tranquillity. The executioner as a contrasting figure is also fully illuminated. The expressive power of Schmidt's art is shown in the way in which the shadows flicker across the bare back of the executioner, giving an immediate sense of demoniac evil.

The altarpieces in the parish church of Schwechat near Vienna (1764) were outstanding works too.[37] In the one representing *St James Major*, the saint, with both arms raised, is swaying the multitude by the force of his sermon. In a characteristic manner, Schmidt strives to combine the spiritual and ascetic with physical beauty and purity; for at the feet of St James is a young and beautiful woman with her child in her arms. The *Immaculate Conception* in the same church shows to what lengths he went in his interpretation of beauty to satisfy an age which had revived the ideals of antiquity. Many people may consider the girlish appearance of the Virgin, clothed in white, to be rather too sweetly pretty – but we must remember that *dolcezza* is an essential part of the Catholic service. It would be difficult to find a contemporary painter who expressed this as clearly as did Schmidt.

He competed with Troger in representing the fervour of the dying saint praying and receiving holy communion. On the altarpiece of 1772 in the chapel of the Melkerhof in Vienna, the magic of light permitted him to show the praying soul of the saint being carried to heaven.[38] Here it is not putti who act as bearers, but personifications of the harmony and beauty of the world beyond. Despite the often heavy participation of the workshop and despite their popular appeal, Schmidt's works retain a refinement which can be considered one of the major assets of Austrian culture as a whole.

Alongside this individualized art flowed the broad stream of work rapidly produced by routine painters. Josef Adam Ritter von Mölk (1714–94) is a typical example. He was known in the Tyrol as 'Windbag-Mölk of Vienna'.[39] A *Fa Presto* of the eighteenth century, he worked in forty-four churches and palaces, helped by many assistants. He absorbed influences from all sides: from Pozzo, from the Venetians, and from Schmidt.

Owing to the skill and ingenuity with which he used his paintings to create the illusion of wider spaces, he was popular with architects, in spite of his hasty execution. He was comparatively successful with his decorations for the abbey church at Rein of 1766 and for the pilgrimage church of Weizberg of 1771, where he created the illusion that the painted saucer domes are real domes.

The quality of Austrian fresco painting survived better in the work of the widely diffused members of the Troger school. Of these Johann Wenzel Bergl (1718–89) extended the use of illusionistic painting from the ceiling to the walls, and favoured exotic landscapes. The visitor who enters the rooms he painted at Schönbrunn is meant to receive the impression that he has been transported into a fantastic garden in fairyland.[40]

In the second half of the eighteenth century there was a considerable expansion of fresco painting in the Tyrol. Franz Anton Zeiller (1716–94),[41] a member of a family of painters living at Reutte in the Lechtal, worked mainly in the Tyrol after receiving a thorough training at Augsburg, Naples, and Venice. In 1768 he was appointed court painter to the bishop of Brixen. Like Josef Anton Zoller (1730–91), who lived at Hall, he adhered to the Bavarian school that followed Tiepolo and favoured fantastic or popular features, surprising oblique views into rotundas or domed buildings, and a coarse Rococo ornament partly painted and partly in stucco.

As opposed to this, Martin Knoller (1725–1804),[42] a pupil of Paul Troger, continued the great and serious art of his teacher. Despite the fact that during his stays in Rome, in 1755 and again in 1760–5, he came under the classicist influence of Mengs and Winckelmann, he did not abandon the vigorous Baroque style of Troger. His fresco in the abbey church of Volders of 1766 is still composed to harmonize with the shape of the dome, and presents lively groups of angels and saints on dark clouds circling upwards into the ever-increasing light of the skies – certainly an effective and immediate manner in which to make the heavenly scene immediately credible. Nevertheless in the harder, more sculptural drawing of the figures Knoller did make a concession to classicist theory. Astonishingly enough this Baroque composition, even at such a late moment, had tremendous success far beyond the boundaries of the Tyrol. It almost seems as if patrons and their architects were only waiting for an artist who, as late as the eighth decade of the eighteenth century, could still successfully master the monumental task of designing such ceiling frescoes. Knoller was thus commissioned to paint the large fresco in the dome over the chancel of the abbey church of Ettal in Bavaria in 1769, the ceiling fresco in the Bürgersaal in Munich in 1774, and in 1770–5 the seven domes in the abbey church of Neresheim, a late work of the great Balthasar Neumann (Plate 160). In the Tyrol he painted the frescoes for the abbey church of Gries in 1771–3. In these works he successfully reverted to a style that was both dynamic and painterly in the colouring; and it was not until the 1780s that the blight of classicist theory descended on his art too. His pupil Josef Schöpf (1745–1822),[43] very talented in his handling of paint, was considerably less successful in avoiding this danger. But even he was encouraged by the church-minded Tyrolese people to keep away from a form of art that was already modelled on the example of David in Rome, in order to remain faithful to the old manner of fresco painting.

CHAPTER 30

HUNGARY

Architecture

UNDER the Empress Maria Theresa, who by her personality had won the feudal lords completely to her side, a great revival came about in Hungary. The nobles gave her the splendid royal castle in Budapest, which was probably begun to a plan by Jean-Nicolas Jadot de Ville Issey, in 1749. From 1766 the work was directed from Vienna by the court architect Franz Anton Hillebrandt (1719–97).[1] It was in fact roofed as early as 1752, but completion was not achieved until 1770, and in the nineteenth century the castle was entirely restored. The only other building work to be controlled by the Vienna court was at Bratislava (Pozsony, Pressburg).

Andreas Mayerhoffer and Jakob Fellner (1722–80) developed a style in harmony with the Hungarian character. According to Révhelyi, it was Mayerhoffer who designed the most noteworthy ecclesiastical building of the period, the university church at Pest.[2] He may also be responsible for the palace of Hofkammerpräsident Anton Count Grassalkovich (1760) and the roughly contemporary reconstruction of the archbishop's summer residence, both at Bratislava. The former shows the already much simplified style of the sixties, with pilaster strips and shallow segmental pediments running parallel to the round-headed arches of the windows. The former archiepiscopal palace (now the town hall) has a majestic, almost classicist articulation by pilasters.

In contrast to the Viennese style of many-storeyed palaces, people otherwise preferred low buildings of an intimate character. This is the case with the palace of Baron Johann Péterffy in the Lane of the Piarists in Pest (1756).[3] Mayerhoffer is documented as the architect. He provided the portal with two flanking atlantes on the Austrian model, though they are smaller than they would have been on an Austrian palace. There is a decorative transformation in the window pediments and double coat of arms on the upper storey. The palace of Georg Erdödy on the hill in Buda, erected in 1750, is much plainer, with its Tuscan pilasters and only slightly projecting centre bays. Slanting portal-pilasters carry the balcony, and a curved and broken pediment in the manner of Hildebrandt crowns the composition. The same pediment was used later at the castles at Gödöllö (1744–50; Plate 191A) and Ráday in Pécel (1747), due to the influence of Mayerhoffer, presumably a pupil of Hildebrandt. The charming Rococo palace of Gödöllö is definitely ascribed to him, and he also, in 1735, finished the picturesque Grassalkovics Palace in Pest, now unfortunately demolished.

Co-operation between patron and architect led Jakob Fellner to build for Count Jószef Esterházy a whole series of palaces of a very individual character, e.g. at Tata (1764–78), now a hospital (Plate 194). The same refinement is evident in the episcopal palace at Veszprém, erected by Fellner in 1765–6. The distinguished, plain, yet intimate and serene effect was typical, as was the predilection for rounded corners. The central part of the wonderful and magnificently restored castle of Fertöd (Esterháza) near Sopron (Ödenburg) was erected by Erhard Martinelli under Prince Jószef Esterházy in 1720 (Plate 191B). It was and is a worthy setting for Haydn's creations. The adjoining court with its rounded wings is the work of Miklos Jacoby (1733–84), with the collaboration of Melchior Hefele in the design of the façades (Plate 192). The transition to the central section is discordant. Finally, from 1763, Johann Ferdinand Mödlhammer rounded off the court with one-storeyed ranges – a Hungarian Schönbrunn!

Middle-class houses included some of a distinct type, such as the White Cross in the water-town of Buda (Batthyány tér. 4 Föhomlokgat; 1775–6; Plate 196). Two houses, formerly separate, have been made into one. In the centre of the main storey are three tall, round-arched windows, and above these three circular windows. The whole is covered with a web of Rococo ornamentation. This higher centre was connected with the lateral wings by a most remarkable cornice, descending gradually in a curve. Farmhouses keep to their idyllic type until the nineteenth century (Plate 195).

In 1762–4, at the instigation of Primas Franz, Count Barkóczy, a bold plan was developed by J. M. Amadeo Canevale and F. A. Hillebrandt for the castle hill at Esztergom (Gran). The model is to be found in the cathedral. Through Bishop Karl, Count Esterházy, Eger (Erlau), too, was in 1762–90 turned by Fellner and his school into the most handsome Baroque town in Hungary (Plate 193). Here, alongside buildings influenced by court and church architecture, there exist pleasing ones in a more middle-class, popular style.

Building activity was very lively among the orders too. The Premonstratensians had their abbey church at Jászó (Jasov) built by Anton Pilgram of Vienna from 1745 to 1763 (Plate 197B), and the Cistercian abbey church at Szentgotthárd is by the same architect. At Jászó, the front, consisting of a two-towered church façade in the centre of the long ranges of the monastic buildings, is an impressive example of the light and elegant Viennese style. It was also the Board of Works of the Viennese court which suggested the single tower rising from the gable at Szentgotthárd. In the interior of both churches, the arrangement whereby the columns converge towards the high altar, like the scenic wings of a theatre, derives from a Roman prototype of a hundred years earlier – the church of S. Maria in Campitelli. In the church of the Minorites at Eger (Erlau), built in 1758–63 by Matthias Gerl (Plate 197A), the architect continued to develop the motif of curving the centre by the insertion of colossal double columns. The strongly expressive horizontal lines of the two main cornices seem literally to bind the building together, in contrast to the soaring movement of the two towers of 1758–73.

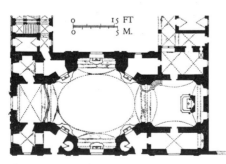

Figure 32. Christof Hamon and Martin Nepauer: Buda-Vezeváros, St Anne, 1740–72. Plan (1 : 375)

Oval churches with a cupola and twin towers, on the pattern of Hildebrandt's St Peter in

Vienna, are often found in Hungary. An example is St Anne at Buda-Vezeváros (1740–72), which was begun by Christof Hamon and continued by Martin Nepauer (Figure 32).

Painting

The frequently remarked revival of the Baroque at the very end of its life was particularly evident in the field of painting and sculpture. An important starting-point for painting was furnished by Troger's frescoes of 1742 in the church of the Elizabethans at Bratislava (Pozsony, Pressburg) and those of 1744–7 at Györ (Raab). Maulbertsch, too, had worked at the village church of Sümeg,[4] at the castle of Halbthurn (Féltorony)[5] (1774), at the parish church of Pápa (1781–3), and elsewhere, at a time when his form of Baroque was frequently meeting with rejection. However, although his Hungarian patrons, Bishops Esterházy and Szily, appreciated his brilliant art, their objections to his lack of clearness and lucidity contributed to impair the painterly force of his style.[6] The naturalistic frescoes of Stefan Dorfmeister (1729–97), a pupil of Troger, at Köszeg (1784) and Szigetvár (1788) already overstep the limit of 1780 set for this book.

Sculpture

Sculpture was particularly in thrall to the influence of Donner (cf. p. 110), who had spent the 'most fertile eleven years of his life in Pressburg' (Hekler). A distinguished native sculptor, Johann Anton Krauss, executed the high altar of the Cistercian church at Eger (contract of 1769) and the sculptural furnishing of the abbey church at Jászó of about five years later. The angels of the tabernacle there are on the pattern of Donner, i.e. they show a reversion to the Baroque. On the high altar of the same church, a representation of St Francis Borgia replaced a painted altarpiece. The figure is surrounded by a frame and set in a little stage, kneeling before the monstrance on a Rococo altar – a late example of the Baroque mixture of the arts.

*

As with Hungarian art as a whole, popular art did not reach its climax of achievement until the end of the eighteenth and beginning of the nineteenth centuries. Its forms and colours are highly original, owing almost nothing to the main stream of development. Only here is the independent and individual character of the people fully expressed, as fundamentally grand and noble as the shaping of their art is fine and expressive. It calls to mind their native tongue, which is melodious and strange to foreign ears. The arcaded farmhouses, so built because of the warm climate, have no architectural articulation in the way of piers and columns such as those further west in the Danube region possess. The mass of the masonry opens in semicircles that peep out like eyes from below the broad thatched roofs (Plate 195).

305

CHAPTER 31

POLAND

Architecture

In Poland, as in Saxony, Augustus the Strong's death meant the overt curtailment of projects which lack of money would probably have brought to a stop anyway. Nevertheless his successor, Augustus III, maintained to a limited extent the policy of exalting the Saxon domination of Poland by the erection of magnificent buildings. What the new king, in contrast to his father, lacked in initiative was supplied by Count Brühl, who was a passionate patron of building. The fact that Pöppelmann had died in 1736, at the critical moment when renewed building activity was beginning in Poland, decided the situation: the Dresden Rococo, inaugurated by Longuelune and developed by Knöffel, set the standard. Direct French influence is perceptible only in the interior decoration, and even architects of Italian origin frequently designed houses in the Saxon manner.

When the Royal Palace at Warsaw was being completed, the idea of deepening the front range facing the Vistula so as to increase the size of the rooms was in itself right; but to build the new wings without taking into account the compact pentagonal form of the palace required the self-confidence of an Italian, in this case Chiaveri (Plate 198B).[1] In his plans, dated 1740, the new middle pavilion was placed at the north-east corner of the old palace. Only the southern half of the new range corresponded to the northern river wing of the pentagon. The northern half of Chiaveri's structure stood at the point where the connecting link to the church of St John branched off from the palace. The visual impression was decisive. At one time Augustus the Strong had wanted to make the obtuse angle of the pentagon projecting towards the Vistula the centre of the building, but this had proved visually unsatisfactory. Now the main façade was shifted laterally to the north, in relation to the body of the palace. Since this was hidden from the eye, the impression received was that the new façade constituted the Vistula front, and that it ran in front of the entire body of the building. According to Chiaveri's plan, which was later altered, the elevation of the centre with its broken rhythm, the forward-curving middle part of three bays flanked by straight one-bay wings, and the whole crowned by a towering pediment intended to enclose the huge royal coat-of-arms of Saxony and Poland would most magnificently have represented the Polish Baroque in its sympathies with Italy. But during the execution of the building by Andrea Solari a plan was successfully imposed that was obviously inspired by Knöffel, in which the five-window centre projects with rounded corners – a characteristic feature of the Saxon Rococo.[2] The mansard roof of the middle pavilion, the increased height of the entire roofs, and the uniformity of the pilaster strips reflect the same style.

In 1750 Count Brühl purchased the palace of Prince Sanguszko in order to have a house at Warsaw suitable to his rank. It was probably erected by Lorenzo Serres, but was rebuilt after 1664 by Tylman van Gameren. Its position next to the Saxon Palace, with an entrance opening from a common forecourt, and the wedge shape of the building plot, appropriate for a Baroque layout, made the palace, which is still known as the Brühl Palace, eminently suitable for the count's princely establishment. The old palace was retained as the nucleus of the new building, and Tylman's architecture, with its characteristic rhythmic alternation of arches and sculptural decoration, has determined the appearance of the exterior down to the present day. The main range of buildings was covered by a powerful mansard roof to stress its importance. The proportions are so nicely calculated that the more recent parts harmonize perfectly with the older ones. Nothing of the interior decoration has survived from the Saxon period. The reconstruction was carried out in 1757–81 under the direction of Johann Friedrich Knöbel. The plans for the court were adapted to suit the extant ground plan. The gatepiers supporting the broad iron gates with their crowning groups of statues, and the narrow lodges with their simple pilaster-strip articulation and sculptural decoration above, represent the finest achievement of the Saxon Rococo in Warsaw.

Among the palaces built for the Polish aristocracy, Schloss Radzyń-Podlaski[3] for Count Eustachy Potocki was entirely transformed c. 1755 to a comprehensive plan in the Rococo style by Jakob Fontana to a design by Johann Friedrich Knöbel. The projecting central part of the palace dates from this later period, as do also the orangery (Plate 198A), the Rococo stucco decoration of the façade, and in particular the sculpture on the attics and cornices. The sculpture was produced by a team, among them Redler, who must have been in contact with Verschaffelt. The figure of a stag caught in a net which crowns the west wing recalls the similar group on Schloss Benrath (p. 257).

The first enlargement of the old palace at Białystok had been made at the end of the seventeenth century by Tylman van Gameren, who added a rectangular pavilion. The extension and addition of higher storeys was continued for Jan Clemens Branicki by Johann Siegmund Deybel from 1728 and c. 1750. Jakob Fontana constructed the staircase c. 1755. The main storey and the mezzanine above, articulated by giant pilasters, were once crowned by a roof with a parapet, a sculptured pediment, and two domes; the impression was thus much less meagre than it appears today, after the nineteenth-century alteration in which a plain new roof was built by Russian architects.

Under Augustus III church architecture continued to be dominated by Italian architects, who remained almost untouched by the Saxon Baroque. The only link arose through Francesco Placidi, who, having worked in Poland for twenty years, was made Konducteur under Chiaveri for the construction of the Hofkirche in Dresden (recorded in 1738) and was then commissioned by Augustus III to prepare plans for a sepulchral chapel for Augustus the Strong in the crypt of Cracow Cathedral.[4] The designs, which were in his consistent Italian Baroque style, were never executed. Like Chiaveri, he used the German motif of a west front with a pediment, for instance on the Cracow church of the Trinitarians (1752–8; an attribution) and on that of the Piarists (façade completed 1759).[5] The high, narrow interior of the Trinitarian church is reminiscent of the Cracow Gothic style. The façade of the church of the Salesian Nuns at Warsaw, built in 1754–63

(Plate 199), is attributed to Ephraim Schröger. The rest of the church is by Jakob Fontana, who with his father Jozef – first mentioned in 1709 – dominated ecclesiastical architecture in the capital.[6] The façade of the church of the Dominican Observants was erected by Schröger in 1760. St Peter in Vienna, with its diagonally placed towers between which projects the rounded end of the longitudinal oval nave, was a prototype that was used with modifications several times in Poland, for example probably by Thomas Resler in the former church of the Piarists at Chełm in the Lublin area (1753–63).

The painterly, irrational, fantastic element in the Baroque found a ready response in the Polish mind, especially at Lvov (Lemberg) and Vilna. Foreign artists too tried to do justice to it: in a first design for the (United) Greek–Catholic Cathedral of St George at Lvov, Bernhard Merderer sought to reproduce a Ukranian wooden church in monumental form in which three centrally planned parts are aligned. Since this would have proved too costly, he began in 1738 to erect the church on a cruciform plan with a shallow central dome and with the four obligatory subsidiary domes concealed behind an attic with lanterns. This motif, which had been borrowed from palace architecture, combined with the undulating façades provided the cathedral, beautifully sited on a hill, with the dynamic, painterly silhouette that the east was so fond of. The unique building culminates in the magnificent equestrian statue of St George which crowns the entrance front. After Merderer's death in 1759 the sculptural decoration of the interior and exterior of the church was completed by Fessinger, who worked on it until 1776. The German artists here found an unusual expression for the artistic genius of the east, where the attic in all forms had always been a popular feature. In addition, Fessinger designed the statues for the gallery in the Dominican church at Lvov in an exuberant Baroque style. The church, built by Jan de Witte from 1749 to 1764, has an elliptical plan and is crowned by a dome on a high drum.

A fundamentally different conception was expressed at Vilna, one-time capital of Lithuania. Here buildings with light, slender elevations producing flat painterly effects are given preference over curving three-dimensional forms. Characteristic of the desire for filigree effects are the wrought-iron decorative pieces on the pediments. Here, too, a German, Christoph Glaubitz, probably a native of Silesia, was the head of the school. He built the church of St Catherine after the fire of 1703. The missionary church, erected in 1757, still retains the same stylistic character.

In church architecture the Baroque persisted until the end of the eighteenth century, and in addition to Italian and native masters many Germans were employed. The plans for the great Ukrainian abbey and pilgrimage church at Poczajow near Kremenec in Wolhynia (1771–92) were furnished by Gottfried Hoffmann of Breslau. The twin towers are still set diagonally, and the front curves forward between them. Moreover the architects who came to Poland were accompanied by painters, for example Georg Wilhelm Neunhertz, who in 1731 painted the dome of the church at Ląd built by Pompeo Ferrari.

The election of Stanislas Augustus Poniatowski as king of Poland in 1764 brought classicism to the fore. Once again, as in the Renaissance, Poland accepted the ideals of antiquity earlier than did the German countries. It was characteristic of the personal attitude of Stanislas Augustus that during the very year when he came to the throne he called the French architect Victor Louis to Warsaw to rebuild and decorate the royal palace. Louis's designs were used even after he himself had returned to Paris in 1765. The king's favourite architect, however, was Domenico Merlini (1731–97), a native of Castello di Valsolda on Lake Lugano, who married in Warsaw in 1764. He completed the interior decoration of the royal palace (1770–86) and also erected the buildings for the Lazienki park (1774–80), excellent achievements in the classicist style. Even Saxon architects such as Ephraim Schröger (1727–83), Simon Gottlieb Zug (1733–1807), and Johann Kamsetzer (1753–95) followed this lead, though Schröger's Carmelite church in Warsaw (1777–80) still has a semi-Baroque character, and Zug's Pod Wietrami Palace (Palace of the Winds), built for a banker in 1769–80, bears *rocaille* ornament, owing to the influence of the French publications of Jean-François Neufforge. Elsewhere, however, Zug produced mature works in the classicist style, for example the circular domed Protestant church at Warsaw (1777–9) and the Villa Natolin, south of Warsaw, for Prince August Czartoryski (1780–3). Here he even succeeded in infusing some Greek spirit.

During the years before the final partition of the country the Polish people, who were engaged in a heroic struggle for freedom against overwhelming odds, continued an age-old tradition in their simple, one-storeyed farmhouses and manor houses, village halls and inns. The farmers retained their log houses with horizontally placed logs. These were also used for the large granaries of the estates, with their high hipped roofs frequently surrounded by arcades. The timber-saving frame house was introduced from Saxony, where it was frequently used. The beauty of rural Polish architecture lay in its close links with nature. Nothing could be more idyllic than a small Polish manor house (Plate 200). These one-storeyed houses, nestling in the ground and concealed beneath tall willows, seem to be an integral part of the landscape. The friendly white walls attract from afar; on approaching one is struck by the high roofs and the often broken and curved skyline. A small portico, and perhaps the shape of the roof, indicate that the owners were familiar with, and admired, the dynamic style of the time.

The hospitable character of the Poles was also expressed in the country inns, large, barn-like buildings with a big gateway for vehicles on the entrance side. On that side, too, were the two guest rooms, one for Christians and one for Jews. Thanks to the incredible toughness and hardiness of the horses and to the obligingness of the postilions, travelling in Poland, despite the bad roads, was often more agreeable than in the west. J. C. F. Schulz in his *Reise eines Livländers* says: 'We may compare this [he is referring to speedy travelling] in some respects to travelling in Saxony or Prussia, where the passenger appears to be there to suit the postilion and his horses rather than they to suit the passenger.'

Painting

Bernardo Belotto was fully equal to the task of giving in paint a vivid picture of Poland in the Baroque age. Born in 1720, he went to Warsaw in 1767 and resigned from his post in Saxony in 1768. Stanislas appointed him painter to his court in 1770. During the next ten years until his death Belotto gave in twenty-seven paintings a spirited interpretation of Warsaw and its magnificent palaces with ruins and humble cottages immediately adjoining them, and, more especially, of the population. He showed dashing young gentlemen on mettlesome horses, high officials in fine carriages, and ordinary people of every description. Nor did he confine himself to their outward appearance: he revealed their inner nature with the insight of the Italian, whose own people have so much in common with the Polish. The broad, impressionistic technique of the Venetian painter was still entirely Baroque, and his painterly use of light and shade did full justice to the three-dimensional character of the buildings he painted.

On the other hand Marcello Bacciarelli (1731–1818), the most celebrated painter at the court of Stanislas Augustus, came under French influence. His mythological, allegorical, and historical frescoes in the Royal Palace and in the Lazienki show the flaccid manner that characterizes the transition period from the Rococo to classicism. Nevertheless he, too, was competent as a portraitist, a branch of painting that was much in demand.

*

The dissolution of the patriarchal, feudal way of life is the reason underlying the gradual extinction of a great art that had flourished for three centuries, culminating in Central Europe in the Baroque. Since this way of life had formed a unified whole, it could inspire an art aimed in a similar way at unity. The pilgrimage church of Birnau, where all the arts were blended in harmonious orchestration, side by side with the unified social structure of the population round Lake Constance is one example. The crumbling of the close-knit social order of the past began in the second half of the eighteenth century, when the shape of the democracies of the future begins to appear, bent on struggle. Rifts also appeared in the body aesthetic. Specialization emerged, such as portrait painting and landscape painting. Once the true value of the human being had become the object of intensive search, the vast field of the individual opened up and consequently the artist turned his attention to the characteristic interpretation of the individual. As Christianity lost its hold, a change took place in the conception of nature. She was no longer subordinated to man but was considered in the spirit in which antiquity had approached her. In this way, as a prelude to the nineteenth century, a form of landscape arose in which the heroic ideal was modified in the light of realism.

These specialized categories apart, rationalism dominated wide fields of art and imposed on them a banal, philistine outlook. In conscious opposition to this, many of the most significant artists, such as Maulbertsch in Vienna and Schlaun in Münster, retained the formal language of the Baroque, as did also Goya in Spain – the opponent of the classicistically-minded Mengs.

The Baroque permitted the artist to give free rein to his imagination in a powerful, compelling expressiveness scarcely conceivable under classicism. Even music, which is more independent of social ties, reverted often to the older forms which had such a stirring emotional appeal.

NOTES TO PART ONE

CHAPTER I

2   1. Eberhard Hempel, *Geschichte der deutschen Baukunst* (Munich, 1949), plates 194–8.

2. *Op. cit.*, plate 217.

4   3. *Op. cit.*, plate 209.

4. *Op. cit.*, plates 214–16.

5. We learn from Endres Tucher's *Baumeister-buch der Stadt Nürnberg* (*Bibl. des lit. Vereins in Stuttgart*, LXIV) (Stuttgart, 1862) that special tasks were allotted for every day of the year.

5   6. E. Hempel, *op. cit.*, plate 231.

7   7. Anton Hekler, *Ungarische Kunstgeschichte* (Berlin, 1937), plate 119.

8. *Architektura Polska* (Warsaw, 1952), plates 178–80.

9. *Op. cit.*, plates 185–90.

8   10. W. Lübke and A. Haupt, *Geschichte der Renaissance in Deutschland*, 3rd ed. (Esslingen, 1914), I, figure 14, figures 250–2.

11. *Op. cit.*, II, figures 2–5.

12. Karl Swoboda, *Prag* (Berlin, 1941), 71.

9   13. E. Hempel, *op. cit.*, figure 260.

14. *Op. cit.*, plate 261.

0   15. *Beschreibende Darstellung der älteren Bau- und Kunstdenkmäler des Königreichs Sachsen*, VI (Dresden, 1886), 20 ff.

16. Ed. Vereinigung Berliner Architekten, *Der Kirchenbau des Protestantismus* (Berlin, 1895), figures 47–9.

17. Leo Gundermann and Heinrich Kreisel, *Würzburg* (Berlin, 1930), 64–7.

18. W. Lübke and A. Haupt, *op. cit.*, I, figure 210.

19. *Op. cit.*, I, figure 212.

20. *Op. cit.*, II, figure 211.

21. *Op. cit.*, II, figure 212.

22. *Op. cit.*, II, figures 325–7.

23. Paul Klopfer, *Baukunst und dekorative Skulptur der Renaissance in Deutschland* (Stuttgart, 1909), 107.

24. John Summerson, *Architecture in Britain* p. 17 *1530–1830*, 3rd ed. (London, 1958), 67.

25. Walter Buchowiecki, *Der Barockbau der* p. 18 *ehemaligen Hofbibliothek in Wien* (Vienna, 1957), 126.

26. *Kreisarchiv München H. R.*, 95, 4.   p. 19

27. Richard Benz, *Deutscher Barock*, I (Stuttgart, 1949), 10.

CHAPTER 2

1. When, in 1780 in Hamburg, Matthias p. 23 Claudius learned of the death of the Empress Maria Theresa, he wrote the following lines:

> Auf den Tod der Kaiserin
> Sie machte Frieden! das ist mein Gedicht.
> War ihres Volkes Lust und ihres Volkes Segen
> und ging getrost und voller Zuversicht
> Dem Tod als ihrem Freund entgegen.
> Das kann ein Welteroberer nicht.
> Sie machte Frieden! Das ist mein Gedicht.

> On the Death of the Empress
> She made her peace. That is my poem.
> She was her people's delight, her people's blessing,
> And went consoled and confident
> To meet death as a friend.
> No conqueror of worlds can do so:
> She made her peace. That is my poem.

2. Memorials on which large-scale figures of the p. 26 deceased kneel in front of biblical scenes with small figures in relief represent such an enhancement of the stress on personal, human values that it can only be called a reversal of the medieval size relationship between man and God (Plate 23A). The ecclesiastical rule of Protestant princes in particular is expressed in giant monuments, where the deceased sometimes appear behind the altar, as for example on the tomb of Landgrave Georg of Hessen in the Stadtkirche at Darmstadt (d. 1588, by Peter Ostens) and on that of Duke Johann Friedrich der Mittlere of Saxony (d. 1595, by Nikolaus Bergner) in the Moritzkirche at Coburg.

3. In 1717, at the instigation of Prince Eugene, p. 28 engineering academies were founded in Vienna and

Brussels for the instruction of officers and *Land-vasallen* in military and civil architecture, mathematics, statics, and mechanics. Such engineer-officers frequently attained high rank as architects, as for example Maximilian von Welsch, Balthasar and Franz Ignaz Neumann, Michael Küchel, and Johann Michael Fischer.

p. 29   4. In 1661 Fischer von Erlach's father, the sculptor Johann Baptist Fischer, had four journeymen and five apprentices in his workshop at Graz. For the column erected in honour of the accession of Leopold I his wife, too, helped.

5. In 1755 the court painter Joseph Anton Wunderer received the commission for the high altar of the collegiate church of St Andrew at Freising. Ignaz Günther prepared the model from Wunderer's sketches and delivered it in 1756. The contract was signed on the basis of this model. Günther was responsible for the statues, Wunderer for the setting. J. B. Zimmermann was to model the plaster curtain; the columns, main cornice, pilaster strips, brackets, frames for the altar panel, and the tabernacle were to be executed by the court carpenter Aichhorn from Günther's designs; A. Feulner, *Ignaz Günther* (Munich, 1947), 129.

6. Eberhard Hempel, *Gaetano Chiaveri* (Dresden, 1955), 98, 99.

7. Enrico Zuccalli had rented large and expensive premises so as to have sufficient room to execute models (letter to Elector Max Emanuel, October 1680); R. Paulus, *Henrico Zuccalli* (Strasbourg, 1912), 73. It took almost a year to produce the model for the church of Berg-am-Laim near Munich.

8. Jean-Louis Sponsel, *Der Zwinger* (Dresden, 1924), plates 10 ff.

p. 30   9. Cf. E. Hempel, *op. cit.*, 200 ff. In Nuremberg, Joh. Jak. Schübler (d. 1741), mathematician and student of the theory of architecture, demanded an architecture based on 'geometrical measurements' and not on 'fantasy, deceptive taste, and insinuating fashion'. His designs, especially those for interior decoration, are based on complicated mathematical calculations. The bookcase with revolving cylindrical racks invented by him has found a successor in our own day in the Munich central telegraph office. Cf. J. J. Schübler, *Interieurs und Mobiliar des 18. Jahrhunderts* (Vienna, 1885).

10. In his book *Das Gesetz der Baukunst* (Leipzig, 1955), I, 225 etc., Otto Schubert has shown that in Chiaveri's Catholic Baroque Hofkirche (begun in 1739) the figures are related not to the columns or to the pilasters on which they stand but to the body of the building. The proportion of the figure to the total height is $1:6$ or $1:5\cdot5$; on the other hand its proportion to the lower section of the column is $1:3\cdot53$, to the upper section $1:2\cdot66$. As opposed to this the Renaissance rule was again observed by Stengel in his Ludwigskirche at Saarbrücken (1762–75): figure to total height $= 1:8\frac{1}{4}$, figure to column $= 1:5$.

11. V. Fleischer, *Fürst Karl Eusebius von Liechtenstein als Bauherr und Kunstsammler* (Vienna and Leipzig, 1910).

12. Count Humprecht Johann Černín wrote of Johann de Capauli, the master mason who worked on his palace in Prague, that he had always treated him as affectionately as if he had been a blood relation (J. J. Morper, *Das Czernin-Palais in Prag* (Prague, 1940), 35). When the stone mason Giovanni Battista Pozzi died in 1677 Count Černín described him as 'this good, honest gentleman whom I love with all my heart' (*ibid.*, 48).

13. Sächsisches Landeshauptarchiv, Dresden. A roll with drawings by Augustus the Strong.

14. C. Gurlitt, *Andreas Schlüter* (Berlin, 1891), figures 44 and 45.

NOTES TO PART TWO

CHAPTER 3

35 1. Eberhard Hempel, *Geschichte der deutschen Baukunst*, 2nd ed. (Munich, 1949), plate 273.

2. W. Lübke and A. Haupt, *Geschichte der Renaissance in Deutschland*, 3rd ed. (Esslingen, 1914), I, plate 221.

3. Württembergische Landesbibliothek, Stuttgart, Cod. Hist. F.562, A148.

36 4. W. Lübke and A. Haupt, *op. cit.*, plate 221.

5. After its destruction in the Second World War, Freudenstadt was rebuilt in an exemplary manner and the market-place was cleared of its garden layout.

6. Hans Eberlein, *Augsburg* (Berlin, 1939), 161.

7. *Op. cit.*, 157.

8. Theodor Neuhofer, *Eichstätt* (*Grosse Kunst-führer*, xv) (Munich, 1954), 22.

9. Ingeborg Albrecht, 'Elias Holl', *Münchner Jahrbuch der bildenden Kunst*, N.F. XII (1937), figure 6.

37 10. Ulrich Christoffel, *Höhepunkte abendländischer Architektur* (Munich, 1960), figure 148.

11. Cf. I. Albrecht, *loc. cit.*, 101 ff.

12. I. Albrecht, *loc. cit.*, figures 10–11.

13. *Augsburg* (Lindau, 1953), plate 57. The town hall was bombed and burnt down, but has now been restored.

14. H. Eberlein, *op. cit.*, 167.

15. Heinrich Kreisel, *München* (Munich, 1950), plate 10.

38 16. *Op. cit.*, plate 44.

17. U. Christoffel, *op. cit.*, figure 151.

18. E. Hempel, *op. cit.*, figure 202.

19. Max Hauttmann, *Geschichte der kirchlichen Baukunst in Bayern, Schwaben und Franken 1550–1780* (Munich, 1923), 119, plate 7.

39 20. *Op. cit.*, 171, plate 6, 1.

21. T. Neuhofer, *op. cit.*, 18, plate 'Schutzengel-kirche'.

22. H. Kreisel, *op. cit.*, plates 36–54. The palace was bombed and burnt down, but has been faithfully restored.

23. *Op. cit.*, plate 58.

24. E. Hempel, *op. cit.*, plate 287.   p. 40

25. Rochus Kohlbach, *Die barocken Kirchen von Graz* (Graz, 1951), plates 20–7.

26. Anton Hekler, *Ungarische Kunstgeschichte* p. 42 (Berlin, 1937), figure 127.

27. Engelbert F. von Kerckerinck zur Borg and p. 43 Richard Klapheck, *Alt-Westfalen* (Stuttgart, 1912), plates 102–3.

28. Heinrich Kreisel, *Würzburg* (Berlin, 1930), 64–7.

29. Bodo Ebhardt, *Der Wehrbau Europas im Mittelalter*, I (Berlin, 1939), plate 68.

30. E. Hempel, *op. cit.*, 311, plates 277–8.   p. 44

31. W. Lübke and A. Haupt, *op. cit.*, I, plate 212.

32. *Op. cit.*, I, plate 189.   p. 45

33. R. Steche, *Beschreibende Darstellung der älteren Bau- und Kunstdenkmäler des Königreichs Sachsen*, VI (1885), 22 ff.

34. W. Lübke and A. Haupt, *op. cit.*, II, figure 344.

35. Cornelius Gurlitt, 'Die Kunstdenkmäler Dresdens', *Beschreibende Darstellung der älteren Bau- und Kunstdenkmäler des Königreichs Sachsen*, XXII (1901), figure 245.

36. *Ibid.*, supplement XXI.

37. Fritz Löffler, *Das alte Dresden* (Dresden, 1955), plate 57.

38. W. Lübke and A. Haupt, *op. cit.*, II, figure p. 46 308.

39. *Op. cit.*, II, figure 313.

40. E. Hempel, *op. cit.*, plate 285.

41. W. Lübke and A. Haupt, *op. cit.*, II, figure p. 47 273.

42. *Op. cit.*, II, plates 306–7.

43. Joseph Braun, *Die Kirchenbauten der deutschen Jesuiten* (Freiburg im Breisgau, 1908), plates 1, 2 ff.

44. Only in the church of St Peter at Münster i. W. do short sturdy columns with Renaissance forms support the lower arcades.

45. Eberhard Lutze, *Bremen* (Munich, 1953), p. 48 plate 60.

p. 48   46. *Architektura Polska: Wydanie drugie* (Warsaw, 1956), plate 200.

47. Ed. Vereinigung Berliner Architekten, *Der Kirchenbau des Protestantismus* (Berlin, 1893), figures 191–2.

p. 49   48. Information on the artistic activity of the Polish kings of the Vasa dynasty has been published by W. Tomkiewicz in the series of documentary publications of the Art Institute of the Republic. See W. Tomkiewicz, *Z dziejów polskiego mecenatu artystycznego wieku XVII* ('Notes on the History of Polish Art Patronage in the Seventeenth Century') (Wrocław (Breslau), 1952).

49. *Architektura Polska, op. cit., Wydanie drugie*, plates 173–6.

50. W. Tatarkiewicz has written two papers on Polish Late Renaissance churches: 'O pevnej grupie kościołów polskich z pocz. XVII w.' ('On a Group of Polish Churches of the Early Seventeenth Century'), *Sztuki Piękne*, II (1926); and 'Typ lubelski i typ kaliski w architekturze kościelnej XVII w.' ('The Lublin and Kalisz Types in the Ecclesiastical Architecture of the Seventeenth Century'), *Prace Kom. Hist. Szt.*, VII (1937–8). More recent discussions of this ecclesiastical style by J. Łoziński in his book *Sztuka polska czasów nowożytnych* ('Polish Art of Recent Centuries') (n.d.), 181–5.

51. *Architektura Polska, op. cit., Wydanie drugie*, plate 234.

52. *Op. cit., Wydanie drugie*, plates 253, 323–4.

53. *Op. cit.*, 1st ed., plate 256.

54. *Die katholische Kirche in Volkspolen* (Warsaw, 1953), 86.

p. 50   55. Dagobert Frey, *Krakau* (Berlin, 1941), plates 20–2; W. Husarski, *Attika polska i jej wpływ na kraje sąsiednie* ('The Polish Parapets and their Influence on Neighbouring Countries') (Warsaw, 1936), with a bibliography of the most important Polish, French, Swedish, Czechoslovak, and German works.

56. *Architektura Polska, op. cit., Wydanie drugie*, plate 192.

57. *Op. cit.*, plate 193.

58. *Op. cit.*, plate 194.

59. *Op. cit.*, plate 195.

60. Cf. W. Husarski, *Kazimierz Dolny* (Warsaw, 1953) and *idem*, 'Kamienice renesansowe w Kazimierzu Dolnym' ('Renaissance Houses in Kazimierz Dolny'), *Biblioteka Lubelska*, IX (1950).

61. *Architektura Polska, op. cit., Wydanie drugie*, plate 269. Andreas Hegner Abrahamowicz has until now been regarded as the architect of the palace at Warsaw. According to recent research, however, he was a civil servant, and the north Italian artists quoted were the real architects: W. Tomkiewicz, *op. cit.*, 16; *idem*, 'Zamek warszawski' ('The Palace at Warsaw') *Słownik historyczny sztuk Plastycznych zeszyt dyskusyjny* (Discussions) (Warsaw, 1951), 86–7.

62. Cornelius Gurlitt, *Warschauer Bauten aus der Zeit der sächsischen Könige* (Berlin, 1917), plate X, bottom. The appearance of the so-called Kasimir Palace and of the palaces of the Warsaw magnates dating from the first half of the seventeenth century has until now been known only from an engraving by Dahlberg of 1656 and from the poem with a description of Warsaw by A. Jarzębski, *Gościniec albo opisanie Warszawy 1643 r... wyd* ('Reminiscences of a Journey or Description of Warsaw 1643 . . .') (Warsaw, 1909). However, the primary source for the Kasimir Palace has recently been found by Walter Hentschel (Walter Hentschel, *Die sächsische Baukunst des 18. Jahrhundert in Polen*, MS, written in 1961, in the Kunstgeschichtliche Institut, Dresden, Technische Universität). It is a measured account dating from 1724 and belongs to the collection of the Sächsisches Landeshauptarchiv in Dresden. For the Kasimir Palace see Z. Rewski, 'Villa regia w Warszawie' ('The Villa Regia in Warsaw'), *Stolica*, VII/321 (1954).

63. Cornelius Gurlitt, *op. cit.*, 59, plates XI, XXXV.

64. *Architektura Polska, op. cit., Wydanie drugie*, plate 261.

65. *Op. cit.*, plate 273.

66. The house at Podhorce, with a reconstruction of its seventeenth-century state, was published by A. Szyszko-Bohusz, 'Podhorce', *Sztuki Piękne*, I (Warsaw, 1925).

CHAPTER 4

p.   1. Norbert Lieb, *Augsburg* (Lindau, 1953), plates 60–3.

2. *Op. cit.*, plate 65.

3. *Op. cit.*, plate 64.

4. Adolf Feulner, *Die deutsche Plastik des 17. Jahrhunderts* (Florence and Munich, 1926), plate 8.

5. *Op. cit.*, plate 22.

6. Heinrich Kreisel, *München* (Munich, 1950), plate 11; A. Feulner, *op. cit.*, plates 41–2.

52 7. Friedrich Kriegbaum, in *Jahrbuch der Kunsthistorischen Sammlungen in Wien*, N.F. V (1931), plate 203.

8. *Loc. cit.*, plates 208 ff.

9. A. Feulner, *op. cit.*, plate 19.

53 10. Cf. *Sitzungsberichte der kunstgeschichtlichen Gesellschaft in Berlin*, report of Dr Claus Zoege von Manteuffel, 13 January 1961: 'Studien zu Martin und Michael Zürn'. I am much obliged to the author for information and for the loan of photographs. However, his attribution must still be cleared up. Erich Herzog published a *St George* in the Historisches Museum at Frankfurt on Main which is doubtless by the same master as work of Justus Glesskher; cf. *Münster*, XIII (1960), 227.

11. A. Feulner, *op. cit.*, plate 52.

12. *Op. cit.*, plate 29.

13. Albert Erich Brinckmann, *Barockskulptur* (Berlin, 1917), figure 160.

4 14. Robert Bruck, *Die Sophienkirche in Dresden* (Dresden, 1912), plates 22–3; *Zeitschrift für bildenden Künste*, LXIV (1930), 59–67, with nine illustrations.

15. *Die Kunstdenkmäler des Freistaates Sachsen* (Dresden, 1929), figure 76, a and b, and plates 20–6.

16. At Strehla the customary relationship between the retable and the funeral monument has not yet been achieved, in so far as the two large figures of the donors on either side of the altar stand away from it.

17. The plan presented in 1623 by Bernhard Ditterich seems to be the basis for Albert Freyse's engraving in Martin Gosky, *Arbustum etc.* (1650). It obviously shows the preliminary stage of the retable. See Eberhard Hempel, 'Der Altar der Marienkirche zu Wolfenbüttel', *Festschrift Friedrich Winkler* (Berlin, 1959), 254.

5 18. A. E. Brinckmann, *op. cit.*, figures 204–5.

19. *Op. cit.*, figures 168–70.

20. Whereas the retable or reredos is no longer used in church architecture today, the slab supported by angels or by the symbols of the Evangelists has retained its significance for a Protestant altar, because in the absence of relics no solid altar is needed: cf. e.g. the altar in the Heiliggeistkirche at Heidelberg, which was restored by Otto Bartning.

21. A. Feulner, *op. cit.*, plate 50.

22. A book on Münstermann by Dr Herbert Wolfgang Keiser, the director of the Landesmuseum in Oldenburg, is ready for press. I am indebted to him for help.

23. A. Ulbrich, *Geschichte der Bildhauerkunst in*   p. 56
Ostpreussen (Königsberg, 1926–9), I, 77, figure 55, plate III.

24. Adolf Holm, *Lübeck* (Bielefeld and Leipzig, 1900), figure 91.

CHAPTER 5

1. At that time Uffenbach was very close to p. 57
Dürer, as can be seen from his *Ascension of Christ* (1599) now in the Historisches Museum at Frankfurt, which comes from Dürer's *Ascension*. Furthermore, thanks to his teacher Grimm, Uffenbach belonged to the line of succession of Grünewald. He later acquired the drawings which Grünewald had left at his death. The decoration of the altars in the Dominican church at Frankfurt contained works by the elder Holbein, by Dürer, Grünewald, and Hans Baldung Grien. Among the Netherlandish artists exiled from their country as Protestants and who had settled at Frankfurt, Martin van Valckenborgh, especially as a painter of night pieces, must have been of some importance for the young Elsheimer. Contact with Coninxloo is probable too, since Coninxloo, after the fall of Antwerp, had gone to Frankental in the Palatinate and worked there from 1587. When he moved to Amsterdam in 1595, the school he had established remained.

2. Willy Drost, *Adam Elsheimer* (Potsdam, 1933), plate IV.

3. H. Weizsäcker, *Adam Elsheimer* (Berlin, 1936 and 1952), I, plate II.

4. Otto Fischer, *Geschichte der deutschen Malerei* (Munich, 1942), 315.

5. W. Drost, *op. cit.*, figure 8.

6. *Op. cit.*, plate 2.   p. 58

7. *Op. cit.*, plate II.

8. H. Weizsäcker, *op. cit.*, II, no. 8, pp. 12 etc. Engraved by Goudt in 1608.

9. With regard to the version in the National Gallery, London, Weizsäcker (*op. cit.*, II, no. 9, p. 14) leaves the problem open as to whether or not this is a studio replica. Davies (*Burlington Magazine*, LXIV (1934), 290) regards it as a 'damaged original'. Engraved by Goudt in 1613.

p. 58   10. H. Weizsäcker, *op. cit.*, II, plate 5–5c.

p. 59   11. Domestic Archives of the Medici, II B 2d. Florence.

12. W. Drost, *op. cit.*, figures 36–8.

13. *Op. cit.*, plate XII.

14. *Op. cit.*, plate V.

p. 60   15. According to Sandrart and others, Elsheimer suffered from melancholia and lost all desire to work. He got into debt, and his pupil Hendrick Goudt exploited him – lent him money, seized his works, and finally had him sent to prison. Although Elsheimer was released, he died shortly after.

16. Kurt Steinbart, *Johann Liss* (Vienna, 1946), plate 39.

17. *Op. cit.*, plate 37.

18. Vincenzo Golzio, *Il Seicento e il Settecento* (Turin, 1950), 569 ff.

19. The replica in the Kassel gallery is more coarsely painted.

CHAPTER 6

62 1. Josef Weingartner, *Die Kirchen Innsbrucks* (Vienna, 1921), 29, plate 27.

2. B. Reifenstein and D. Frey, *Wien in Bildern* (Vienna, 1928), plate 24.

63 3. Martin Riesenhuber, *Die kirchliche Barock-kunst in Österreich* (Linz, 1924), plates 38, 49.

4. *Op. cit.*, plates 39, 70.

5. Hans Sedlmayr, *Österreichische Barockarchitektur* (Vienna, 1930), plate 22.

6. Kardos György, *Magyar építéstörténet a XV századtól* (Budapest, 1956), 15.

64 7. Dagobert Frey, *Das Burgenland* (Vienna, 1929), figure 2, plates 9–12.

8. Anton Hekler, *Ungarische Kunstgeschichte* (Berlin, 1937), plate 138.

9. Kurt Blauensteiner, *Georg Raphael Donner* (Vienna, 1944), plates 19, 22.

10. It might be argued that buildings by north Italian architects should not be included in a book on Central European architecture; but it should be remembered that the Bohemian milieu did imprint a common character on people of different nationalities. The basic quality came from the overwhelmingly Czech population. However, owing to the existing political and cultural conditions, Austrian influence was so strong that, to take one example, correspondence on building matters was carried on in German. Two languages were in current use, Czech and German, and the architects were expected to know both.

11. Karl Swoboda, *Prag* (Berlin, 1941), 92.

55 12. *Topographie der historischen und Kunstdenkmale des politischen Bezirkes Raudnitz*, II, *Raudnitz Schloss* (Prague, 1910).

56 13. In a letter of 1673, Count Johann Humprecht Černín describes his collaboration with his architect Caratti for the drawing of the plans as follows: '... and on occasion I leave my other work and watch him, and at times give him my own opinion'.

14. Johann Joseph Morper, *Das Czernin-Palais in Prag* (Prague, 1940), plates 25–7.

15. Rausch, *Ausführliche Nachrichten aus Böhmen* (Salzburg, 1749), 156.

16. Gerhard Franz, *Die deutsche Barockkunst Mährens* (Munich, 1943), plate 3.

17. *Op. cit.*, plates 4–5.

18. *Op. cit.*, plates 26–8.

19. *Op. cit.*, plates 23–5.

20. Hans W. Hegemann, *Die deutsche Barockbaukunst Böhmens* (Munich, 1943), plate 69. p. 67

21. *Op. cit.*, plate 68.

22. *Op. cit.*, plates 66–7. In 1691 Fischer had asked permission in Prague 'to make a *brouillon* of the plan of the Kreuzherrnkirche, seeing that he [Fischer] had a particular affection for the above-mentioned Mathieu, because of his great experience in architecture'. (On Mathey see Morper, 'Der Prager Architekt Jean Baptiste Mathey', *Münchner Jahrbuch der bildenden Kunst*, N.F. IV (1927), 221.)

23. Gerhard Franz, *Bauten und Baumeister der Barockzeit in Böhmen* (Leipzig, 1962), 47 ff.

24. *Die Kunstdenkmäler des Königreichs Bayern*, II, 14, *Oberpfalz, Tirschenreuth*, plates VIII–XV. p. 68

25. Alfred Wiesenhütter, *Der evangelische Kirchenbau Schlesiens* (Breslau, 1926), plates 29–37.

26. Poncini, who had also worked at Łowicz and Poznań, was recognized as the architect by N. Miks: 'Architektura des Bischofspalastes in Kielce', *Biul. Hist. Szt.*, XIV (1952). In the same paper the group of buildings related to the bishop's palace is discussed. The paper also contains the most important bibliography on the group. p. 69

27. *Architektura Polska, Wydanie drugie* (Warsaw, 1956), plate 214.

28. *Op. cit.*, plate 264.

29. Paul Weber, *Wilna* (Vilna, 1917), figures 66–70. p. 71

30. Hermann Weidhaas, 'West-östliche Beziehungen in der Baugeschichte', *Wissenschaftliche Zeitschrift der Hochschule für Architektur und Bauwesen Weimar*, III (1955/6), 55–6.

31. *Architektura Polska, op. cit., Wydanie drugie*, figure 48, plates 304–5.

32. *Architektura Polska, op. cit.*, 1st ed., plates 34–48.

p. 71   33. Fritz Löffler, *Das alte Dresden* (Dresden, 1955), plate 47.

p. 72   34. About 320 sheets of sketches, numerous letters, and three handwritten manuscripts on artillery matters and pyrotechnics by Klengel survive in the Nicolai Collection at the Württembergische Landesbibliothek at Stuttgart; E. Hempel, 'Unbekannte Skizzen von Wolf Caspar von Klengel', *Abhandlungen der Sächs. Akademie der Wissenschaften*, XLIX, no. 4 (Berlin, 1958).

35. Cf. the engraving of 1676 by D. Conrad showing Heinrich Schütz and his choir in the chapel of the Dresden Schloss (F. Löffler, *op. cit.*, plate 45). At Moritzburg, the singing gallery above the altar had to be removed when the altar was reconstructed in 1728. The singing gallery above the pulpit has survived.

p. 73   36. On 16 May 1684 Starcke wrote to Johann Georg III that 'for the eighth year he had had to inspect and supervise the Great Garden and the construction of the palace and to organize and arrange everything in accordance with the elector's commands, following the drawing that the latter had condescended to make'; W. Bachmann, 'Entstehung und Frühgeschichte des Grossen Gartens', *Sitzungsberichte und Abhandlungen der Flora in Dresden*, N.S. XXXVI–VIII (1931–3), 87 ff.

37. Hans Heubach, *Geschichte des Schlossbaues in Thüringen 1620–70* (Jena, 1927), figures 4–16.

38. *Op. cit.*, figures II–IV.

39. G. Dehio, *Handbuch*, I, *Mitteldeutschland*, 6th ed. (Berlin, 1940), 384–5.

p. 74   40. Martin Wackernagel, *Die Baukunst des 17. und 18. Jahrhunderts*, II, *Baukunst des 17. und 18. Jahrhunderts in den germanischen Ländern* (Berlin, 1915), figure 52.

41. *Kunstdenkmäler der Provinz Hannover*, IV (Osnabrück, 1907), figures 227, 231.

p. 75   42. M. Wackernagel, *op. cit.*, figure 75.

p. 76   43. Max Hauttmann, *Geschichte der kirchlichen Baukunst in Bayern, Schwaben und Franken 1550–1780* (Munich, 1921), 155.

44. Karl Atz, *Kunstgeschichte von Tirol*, 2nd ed. (Innsbruck, 1909), figure 873.

p. 77   45. M. Hauttmann, *op. cit.*, figure on p. 117, plate 6, I.

p. 78   46. Joseph Braun, *Die Kirchenbauten der deutschen Jesuiten*, II (Freiburg im Breisgau, 1910), plate 4.

47. *Op. cit.*, plate 6.

48. *Op. cit.*, plates 7, 8.

CHAPTER 7

1. Rudolf Kautzsch, *Der Mainzer Dom*, II p. (Frankfurt on Main, 1925), plates 184–5.

2. Erika Tietze-Conrat, *Osterreichische Barockplastik* (Vienna, 1920), plate 8.

3. Adolf Feulner, *Die deutsche Plastik des 17. Jahrhunderts* (Florence and Munich, 1926), plates 58–9.

4. *Die Kunstdenkmäler der Provinz Niederschlesien*, p. *Breslau*, II (Breslau, 1933), figure 26.

5. H. A. Gräbke, 'Tobias Wilhelmi und die Magdeburger Barockskulptur', *Jahrbuch für Kunstwissenschaft* (1927), plate I.

6. *Loc. cit.*, plate 3.

7. *Loc. cit.*, plate 2.

8. *Beschreibendes Verzeichnis der älteren Bau- und Kunstdenkmäler des Königreichs Sachsen*, XIV, plate I.

9. *Op. cit.*, XXXIX, figure 553.

10. A. Ulbrich, *Geschichte der Bildhauerkunst in* p. *Ostpreussen* (Königsberg, 1926), vol. I, plate 12, figure 260, p. 235.

11. Albert Erich Brinckmann, *Barockskulptur* (Berlin, 1917), figure 210 ff.

12. Brinckmann assumes that Gudewerth, during a long period as a journeyman, had worked in Münstermann's shop and had introduced a softer, more classical note into Münstermann's figures, inspired by the Romanesque style. He dismisses G. Brandt's theory that Gudewerth had had a Netherlandish training. It should, however, be pointed out that Gudewerth's adoption of Rubens' compositions proves some Netherlandish influence. Moreover, his Baroque realism is in such contrast to Münstermann's Mannerism that it is impossible to accept Brinckmann's view that Gudewerth was of importance for the spread of the Münstermann style in Holstein.

13. A. E. Brinckmann, *op. cit.*, figure 222.

14. *Die Kunst- und Geschichtsdenkmäler des Grossherzogtums Mecklenburg-Schwerin*, IV (Schwerin, 1901), 218.

CHAPTER 8

1. Latin edition of the *Teutsche Akademie* of 1683, p. ch. 28, fol. 69. This was preceded by an exchange of letters.

2. In recent literature on Willmann doubts are expressed as to whether he really was taught by Backer. But in view of the authenticity of Sandrart's information, there is no justification for doubt.

3. E. Kloss, *Michael Willmann* (Breslau, 1954), plate 7.

4. *Op. cit.*, plate 35.

5. Angelus Silesius wrote the text for the Hymns on the Thirty-Two Stations of the Cross which were erected in 1672 etc. in the surroundings of Krzeszów by Abbot Bernhard Rosa. The drawings were engraved by Melchior Küsell, Georg Andreas Wolfgang, and Joachim von Sandrart.

6. *Op. cit.*, plates 14 ff.

7. *Op cit.*, plate 21.

8. *Op. cit.*, plate 25.

9. Georg Biermann, Deutsches Barock und Rokoko Leipzig, 1914), 85.

10. *Op. cit.*, plates 161–5.

11. *Meisterwerke der österreichischen Barockmalerei* p. 84 *in der Alten Galerie des Landesmuseums Joanneumin Graz* (Graz, 1961), plate 172.

12. Jaromír Neumann, *Malířství XVII. Století v* p. 85 *Čechách* (Prague, 1951), 157.

CHAPTER 9

p. 87   1. Hans Sedlmayr, *Johann Bernhard Fischer von Erlach* (Vienna, 1956), plates 1, 2, 4, 6.

p. 88   2. See Note 4 to Chapter 6.

3. An instructive example of this kind of ceiling decoration is at Graz, the paintings in wide stucco frames by Hans Adam Weissenkirchner in the large saloon of Schloss Eggenberg (dated 1684/5).

4. The richness of the sculptural decoration is further enhanced at St Florian by giant Corinthian demi-columns in the nave (Plate 46). Moreover, the north Italian architect seems to have been inspired more by Palladio than by the Roman art of, say, Rainaldi, even though Rainaldi was closer in time to him. Rainaldi sought to reinstate free-standing columns, and this the architect of St Florian did not wish to follow. In fact the height and width of the nave were modelled on S. Ignazio in Rome, as were also the columns of the arcades and their composite capitals. Compared with the Gesù and Salzburg Cathedral, both earlier buildings, the proportions at S. Ignazio and at St Florian are more elongated.

5. Cf. Hans Reuther, 'Das Platzlgewölbe der Barockzeit', *Deutsche Kunst und Denkmalpflege* (1955), 121 ff. The geometrical construction is a hemisphere with an inscribed square, the parts of the sphere projecting beyond the square being sliced off vertically so that four round arches form the boundary of the vault. The German terms *Hängegewölbe* and *Stutzkuppel* mean the same as *Platzlgewölbe*. Instead of round, the initial plan can be elliptical. Furthermore the *Platzlgewölbe* can also be depressed, in which case the German term is *Böhmisches Kappengewölbe*. In the latter the inscribed square does not touch the basic circle. That the idea of ceiling paintings to increase the apparent space came from Rome was fully appreciated in the north, as can be seen from the French expression 'à la romaine'.

6. Vincenzo Golzio, *Il Seicento e il Settecento* (Turin, 1950), figure 463.

p. 89   7. *Op. cit.*, figure 456.

8. *Op. cit.*, figures 590–3.

9. H. Sedlmayr, *op. cit.*, plate 8.

10. *Op. cit.*, plates 30–2.

11. *Op. cit.*, plates 35–6.

12. *Op. cit.*, plate 34.

13. *Op. cit.*, plates 37–40.

14. *Op. cit.*, plates 90–3.

15. In 1725 an edition with French text was published at Leipzig and in 1730 one with English text in London, bearing the title, 'A Plan of Civil and Historical Architecture, in the Representation of the most Noted Buildings of Foreign Nations, both Ancient and Modern'. The editor, Thomas Lediard (1685–1748), had excellent engravings made from the plates in the Leipzig edition.

16. H. Sedlmayr, *op. cit.*, plates 132–3.

17. *Op. cit.*, plate 131.

18. Scenes from the Life of St Charles Borromeo are depicted in relief on the scroll bands. Old Testament prototypes of the columns are those of the temple of Solomon. III Kings vii. 23 of the Vulgate contains a reference to Hiram of Tyre, skilled in the arts: 'Et statuit duas columnas in porticu templi'.

19. In Fischer's *Entwurf einer Historischen Architektur*, Book III, 'Of some buildings of the Arabs and Turks', with engravings of mosques surrounded by minarets, is followed by Book IV with engravings of his own works including the Karlskirche. When he was in Rome Fischer will certainly have seen the plans made for Alexander VII (1655–67) in which the two columns are intended to be displayed symmetrically in a great town-planning scheme (drawings in the Palazzo Chigi). Subsequently, in 1690, he himself used the motif for the Triumphal Arch 'der fremden Niederleger'.

20. The Baroque character was also gradually intensified in the development of the plans. Thus, as E. Böck has shown ('Die Frontalperspektive der Karlskirche in der "Historischen Architektur" von J. B. Fischer von Erlach', *Alte und Neue Kunst*, VII (1955), 65 ff.), Fischer had the dome drawn about twenty feet higher than built, when the sheet with the frontal perspective in the *Historische*

Architektur was prepared (xII). This is in accordance with the Roman prototypes. In the same year George Bähr gave a steep outline to the dome of the Frauenkirche in Dresden. Early classicist buildings in Paris must also have exerted some influence, for instance François Mansart's façade of the Église des Minimes (1636) and Levau's Collège des Quatre Nations (begun in 1661), the latter on Fischer's smaller dome over the choir behind the larger one.

21. Karl Swoboda, *Prag* (Berlin, 1941), plates 96–7.

22. On the drum the wide rectangular windows are replaced by narrower round-arched ones, and the columns of the 'Verkröpfungen' by demi-columns. In 'Studien zur Wiener Karlskirche', *Alte und Neue Kunst*, IV (1955), 75 ff., Liselotte Popelka submits evidence to show that the alterations were already decided upon by the elder Fischer von Erlach. She regards notes in the accounts for 1719 and 1720, which mention partial payments for the columns, as proof that the later form of the drum was already established at that time. This, however, can only refer to the columns which still appear in the *Historische Architektur* published shortly afterwards, and not to the demi-columns which were indeed added later by Fischer's son. It remains true, however, that as early as 1722 the younger Fischer supervised the execution of buildings begun by his father, who was sick and very old at that time. The flatter articulation of the drum may have been in part due to the son's taste, though he must have had his father's sanction for it, seeing that the latter (and in this instance Miss Popelka is certainly right) was still alive when it was completed.

23. H. Sedlmayr, *op. cit.*, plates 172–3.

24. Bruno Grimschitz, *Wiener Barockpaläste* (Vienna, 1944), plates 12–15.

25. H. Sedlmayr, *op. cit.*, plates 74–9.

26. *Op. cit.*, plates 134–5.

27. *Op. cit.*, plates 136–44.

28. *Op. cit.*, plates 155–60.

29. *Op. cit.*, plates 186–93.

30. A convincing attribution of the design of the Imperial Library to the elder Fischer von Erlach is only possible on the basis of stylistic analysis. The contemporary sources are silent. The plan does not occur e.g. in Fischer's *Historische Architektur*. One can only draw attention to the inscription on the engravings in S. Kleiner and J. J. Sedlmayr's *Dilucida Repraesentatio Bibliothecae Caesareae*

(Vienna, 1737), according to which the younger Fischer executed the building (*exstruxit*). If the latter had also designed it, Kleiner would certainly have credited him with *invenit*, especially as he was still alive. For the attribution to Fischer Junior is Justus Schmidt, for instance in Dehio's *Handbuch der deutschen Kunstdenkmäler*; and against it are the traditional opinions and the most recent investigations by H. Sedlmayr (*op. cit.*) and W. Buchowiecki (*Der Barockbau der ehemaligen Hofbibliothek in Wien*, Vienna, 1957).

31. B. Reiffenstein and D. Frey, *Wien in Bildern* (Vienna, 1928), plate 55. p. 95

32. *Op. cit.*, plate 56.

33. H. Sedlmayr, *op. cit.*, plate 246.

34. Karl Reinöhl, *Wien anno 1786* (Vienna, 1947), plates 4, 27–9.

35. Bruno Grimschitz, *Johann Lucas von Hildebrandt* (Vienna, 1932), 31. p. 96

36. *Op. cit.*, 30, plates 25–6.

37. The building was begun for the Obersthof-marschall Count Heinrich Franz Mansfeld, Fürst Tondi. After his death the palace passed in 1716 to Prince Adam Franz von Schwarzenberg. Around 1720 Fischer von Erlach was entrusted with its completion. Into the semicircular projection towards the garden he inserted large round-arched windows which rise into the entablature. The doors below were given a similar form. Thus the centre is vigorously emphasized, in characteristic contrast to the even rhythm of Hildebrandt's façade. p. 97

38. B. Grimschitz, *op. cit.*, plates 46–52.

39. *Op. cit.*, plates 60, 62–9.

40. *Op. cit.*, plates 97–139.

41. *Op. cit.*, plates 84–9.

42. *Op. cit.*, plates 76–81.

43. *Op. cit.*, plates 202–19. p. 98

44. *Op. cit.*, plates 141–52.

45. *Op. cit.*, plates 186–95.

46. *Op. cit.*, plates 57, 167.

47. *Op. cit.*, plates 234–8.

48. *Op. cit.*, plates 229, 231–3.

49. Hans Sedlmayr, *Österreichische Barockarchitektur* (Vienna, 1930), 74, plate 53.

50. *Op. cit.*, plates 64–5.

51. In his diaries Übelbacher calls Prandtauer 'that distinguished architect from St Pölten, perhaps the most distinguished in the whole of Austria'. p. 99

p. 99   52. On 25 December 1718 the Elector Lothar Franz von Schönborn wrote to his nephew Friedrich Karl '. . . building is a delight and costs a lot of money, everyone has his own taste and this will also be true of the prelate of Mölk, although I have no doubt the monk will peep out everywhere'; Hugo Hantzsch, *Jakob Prandtauer* (Vienna, 1926), note 19.

53. *Op. cit.*, plates 2–31.

p. 100   54. *Op. cit.*, plates 32–48.

55. *Op. cit.*, plates 96–9.

p. 101   56. H. Sedlmayr, *op. cit.*, plate 22.

57. *Op. cit.*, plate 70.

58. *Op. cit.*, plate 68.

59. That the tower was designed by Steinl and executed by Munggenast is evident from an inscription on a contemporary engraving which states: 'Matthias Steinl invenit, Josephus Mungenast aedificavit'. This also suggests that at Dürnstein too the inventive Steinl had done the designs and thus controlled the execution. A comparison between Steinl's model of 1722 for the high altar of Zwettl (figure 67 in H. Sedlmayr, *op. cit.*), and Munggenast's design for the same altar of 1729 can help us to assess the shares of the two artists in a joint work. Steinl not only adapted the proportions to the Gothic east end but also wanted to place the Baroque retable beneath a high Baroque canopy resting on a kind of clustered Gothic piers. It is hard to visualize what this would be like in the execution. On the heavily pierced retable two of the diagonally placed corner columns were to be detached from the retable itself. In opposition to this, Munggenast's model, which was followed in the execution, was much more architectonic. He formed a semicircle opening in three arcades with grilles. The crowning volutes are similar to those of Steinl. Following the arrangement at Vorau, Steinl had suggested the *Coronation of the Virgin* as the subject for the painting and the *Holy Trinity* as a sculptural group. When he executed the work, Matthias Götz, like Egid Asam at Rohr, represented the Coronation of the Virgin in relief.

60. H. Sedlmayr, *op. cit.*, 78, 79, plates 86, 88–91.

p. 102   61. H. Hantzsch, *op. cit.*, plate 55.

62. H. Sedlmayr, *op. cit.*, 72, plate 44.

63. M. Hauttmann, *Geschichte der kirchlichen Baukunst in Bayern, Schwaben und Franken 1550–1780* (Munich, 1921), plate 36, IV.

64. H. Sedlmayr, *op. cit.*, plate 102.

65. Fr. Krauss and R. Meeraus, *Die Oststeiermark* (Graz, 1930), 174 ff.

66. H. Sedlmayr, *op. cit.*, plate 23.

67. *Op. cit.*, plate 24.

68. Erika Tietze-Conrat, *Österreichische Barockplastik* (Vienna, 1920), plate 8.

69. Heinrich Decker, *Barockplastik in den Alpenländern* (Vienna, 1943), plates 87–8.

70. *Op. cit.*, plates 15 ff.

71. Franz Martin, *Die Kunstdenkmäler Österreichs, Salzburg (Dehio Handbuch)*, 4th ed. (Vienna, 1954), plates 73–4.

72. According to Franz Martin, *op. cit.*, 99.

73. *Die kirchlichen Denkmale der Stadt Salzburg (Österr. Kunsttopographie)* (Vienna, 1912), figures 107–8.

74. *Op. cit.*, plate XXXVI.

75. *Op. cit.*, figures 9–10.

76. This is the opinion of W. Boeckelmann, *Balthasar Permoser* (Graunstein, 1951), 10 ff.

77. The Italians, who were not very accurate in this respect, also called him Belmosel, Belmossel, and Delmosel.

78. Ernst Michalski, *Balthasar Permoser* (Frankfurt on Main, 1951), plates 2, 4.

79. G. Richa, *Notizie istoriche delle chiese fiorentine*, III (Florence, 1775), 211.

80. 'Der Donner wurde von Julien [Giuliani] in Heiligenkreuz als ein Knab von 13 Jahren beiläufig aufgenommen. Er zeigt ein besonderes Genie. Er raubte die Kerzen und Zinnernen Kriegeldeckel [Krügeldeckel] und stach mit seinem Griffel bei nacht.'

81. E. Tietze-Conrat, *op. cit.*, plate 30; Eberhard Hempel, *Gaetano Chiaveri* (Dresden, 1955), plates 11–32.

82. Kurt Blauensteiner, *Georg Raphael Donner* (Vienna, 1944), plate 6.

83. *Op. cit.*, plate 8.

84. *Op. cit.*, plate 9.

85. *Op. cit.*, plates 10–11.

86. *Op. cit.*, plate 7.

87. *Op. cit.*, plates 19–22.

88. *Op. cit.*, plates 27–8.

89. *Op. cit.*, plates 47–75. The original figures are now in the Museum der Stadt Wien. They were replaced by bronze copies on the fountain in 1873.

90. *Op. cit.*, plates 78–87.

112 91. *Kunstdenkmäler Bayern*, II, 14, pp. 127–31, plate XIV.

92. Rochus Kohlbach, *Der Dom zu Graz* (Graz, 1948), figures 45–9.

113 93. Anton Mayr, *Josef Thaddäus Stammel* (Vienna, 1912), plate 56d.

114 94. Not accepted as by Rottmayr by H. Schüller (Thieme-Becker). In his opinion only the cartouches for the destroyed ceiling of the large central room can be regarded as documentarily certain. On the other hand they are accepted as by Rottmayr by Feulner, Tietze, Tintelnot, and others (see Bibliography).

95. Max Dvořák, *Die Entwicklungsgeschichte der barocken Deckenmalerei in Wien* (Vienna, n.d.), plates 3–4.

96. Hans Tietze, 'Johann Michael Rottmayr', *Jahrbuch der Zentralkommission*, N.F. IV (1906), 81 ff.

115 97. M. Dvořák, *op. cit.*, plate 9.

98. Hans Tietze, *Wien* (Leipzig, 1918), figure 99.

116 99. Max Dvořák, *op. cit.*, plate 11.

100. W. Buchowiecki, *Der Barockbau der ehemaligen Hofbibliothek in Wien* (Vienna, 1957), plate 27.

117 101. H. Hammer, *Die Entwicklung der barocken Deckenmalerei in Tirol* (Strassburg, 1912), 303; R. Jacobs, *Paul Troger* (Vienna, 1930), illustration on p. 89.

118 102. *Das Wiener Barockmuseum* (Vienna, 1923), plate 152.

103. H. Tintelnot, *Die barocke Freskomalerei in Deutschland* (Munich, 1951), figure 56.

104. H. Hammer, *op. cit.*, plates 34–5.

105. H. Tintelnot, *op. cit.*, plate 301.

119 106. G. Agath, *Das deutsche Gesellschaftsbild von 1650–1750: Johann Georg Platzer* (Dissertation, Breslau university, 1923).

107. O. Kernstock, *J. C. Hackhofers Festenburger Gemälde*, 3 vols, *Kirchenschmuck*, XXXIV (1903), with seven illustrations.

108. H. Hammer, *op. cit.*, plates 16–17.

120 109. H. Tintelnot, *op. cit.*, figures 30–2.

110. H. Hammer, *op. cit.*, plates 26–7.

111. *Op. cit.*, plates 31–2.

112. *Op. cit.*, plates 34–5.

CHAPTER 10

1. Kardos György, *Magyar építéstörténet a XV szazadtól* (Budapest, 1956), 37; B. Grimschitz, *Johann Lucas von Hildebrandt* (Vienna, 1932), 44, 45, plates 33–5. p. 122

2. A. Hekler, *Ungarische Kunstgeschichte* (Berlin, 1937), plate 139.

3. *Op. cit.*, plate 134. p. 125

4. G. Biermann, *Deutsches Barock und Rokoko* (Exhibition, Darmstadt, 1914) (Leipzig, 1914), I, 38 ff.

CHAPTER 11

1. Dientzenhofer's importance is evident from p. 126 this passage. In spite of this, Czech art historians of the twentieth century deny the importance of Christoph Dientzenhofer as a designer of buildings. It must however be pointed out that in contemporary literature the two most important buildings of the period, sv. Mikuláš in Prague and the abbey church at Břevnov, are unanimously attributed to him. For Břevnov the documents published in 1934 by B. Menzel also indicate that it is a work by Christoph Dientzenhofer (H. G. Franz, *Die Kirchenbauten des Christoph Dientzenhofer*, Brünn, 1941, 10).

2. Franz emphasizes the difference between p. 127 Dientzenhofer's architecture and the architecture of Guarini. He maintains that the former represents an entirely new start when compared with the latter (*op. cit.*, 89). Dientzenhofer used spherical forms to vitalize the whole interior, Guarini only to stress individual spatial compartments. These differences have their origin in contrasts between generations and nations. Nevertheless, in my opinion, the architectural ideas in Bohemia go back to Guarini and would not have arisen without him. It was only through him that such fruitful motifs as the placing of the pilasters diagonally and using three-dimensional curves in the transverse arches of vaults were introduced into the Bohemian Baroque. New is the idea of a contrast between bays below and vaults above.

3. J. J. Morper, *Der Prager Architekt J. B. Mathey* (Munich, 1927), figures 19–25.

4. Hans W. Hegemann, *Die deutsche Barockbaukunst Böhmens* (Munich, 1943), plate 68 ff. On the staircase of the Villa Troja are a great number of

figures made by members of the Heermann family at Freiberg in Saxony, which are preliminary studies for the Dresden Zwinger.

p. 128   5. *Op. cit.*, 28, plate 88.

p. 130   6. G. Franz, *Die deutsche Barockbaukunst Mährens* (Munich, 1943), plates 50–6.

p. 131   7. *Op. cit.*, figures 7–10, plates 32–4.

8. E. Hempel, *Geschichte der deutschen Baukunst* (Munich, 1949), plate 334.

p. 132   9. G. Franz, *op. cit.*, figure 25.

10. H. W. Hegemann, *op. cit.*, 24, plate 81.

11. E. Hempel, *op. cit.*, plate 341.

12. Karl M. Swoboda, *Prag* (Berlin, 1941), 132.

13. H. W. Hegemann, *op. cit.*, figure on p. 36 ff, plates 98–116.

p. 134   14. Kamil Novotny and Emanuel Poche, *The Charles Bridge of Prague* (Prague, 1947), plates 23, 23a.

p. 136   15. *Op. cit.*, plate 16.

p. 137   16. Olga Strettiová, *Das Barockporträt in Böhmen* (Prague, 1957), plates 34–46.

p. 138   17. *Op. cit.*, plate 51.

p. 139   18. E. Hempel, *Gaetano Chiaveri* (Dresden, 1955), plates 72–3.

19. Georg Biermann, *Deutsches Barock und Rokoko* (Leipzig, 1914), I, plates 64–7, II, 222.

CHAPTER 12

p. 140   1. Cf. T. Makowiecki, *Archiwum Planów Tylmana z Gameren* ('Archive of the Designs of Tylman van Gameren') (Warsaw, 1938); Dagobert Frey, *Krakau* (Berlin, 1941), plates 90–1.

2. J. Zachwatowicz, *Architektura Polska* (Warsaw, 1952), plate 331.

3. *Op. cit.*, plates 332, 334.

4. *Op. cit.*, plates 327, 328.

5. *Op. cit.*, plate 287.

6. *Op. cit.*, plate 284.

7. In addition to his work on the Krasiński Palace in Warsaw and on that of Wilanów, Palloni also worked on the following churches: the former Camaldulensian church at Pozajście, the Kasimir Chapel at Vilna, the Camaldulensian church at Bielany, the chapel of St Charles Borromeo at Łowicz, and the parish church at Wegrów.

p. 141   8. J. Zachwatowicz, *op. cit.*, plate 354.

9. D. Frey, *op. cit.*, plate 93.

10. C. Gurlitt, *Warschauer Bauten aus der Zeit der sächsischen Könige* (Berlin, 1917), plate 8.

11. *Op. cit.*, plate 19.   p. 1

CHAPTER 13

1. Richard Konwiarz, *Alt-Schlesien* (Stuttgart, p. 1 n.d.), plate 187.

2. *Op. cit.*, plate 41.

3. *Op. cit.*, plate 13.

4. *Op. cit.*, plate 102.

5. G. Klimpel, *Kollegienbauten der Jesuiten in Schlesien* (Breslau, 1923).

6. In 1700 Johann Georg Knoll of Memmingen p. 1 furnished designs for the Jesuit house of Liegnitz. He had been at Breslau since 1662 and, from 1689 onwards, was in charge of the building operations of the church of the Sacred Name of Jesus there. The designs show the influence of Fischer von Erlach. In 1701 he began the construction of the Jesuit College at Liegnitz, but his death in 1704 put an end to his work. It was obviously from him that Frantz, his successor in the service of the Jesuits, derived the Austrian elements. (Cf. Grundmann, *Die Baumeisterfamilie Frantz*, Breslau, 1937.)

7. R. Konwiarz, *op. cit.*, plate VII, 140.

8. Alfred Wiesenhütter, *Der evangelische Kirchenbau Schlesiens* (Breslau, 1926), plates 67–73.

9. R. Konwiarz, *op. cit.*, plate XXV, 67, 113–19.

10. *Op. cit.*, plates 113, 127, 224.

11. *Op. cit.*, plates 120–6, 158.

12. *Op. cit.*, plates 103–6, 108–10.   p.

13. *Op. cit.*, plates 190–4.

14. For reproductions of Schloss Kunewald and of the Schreyvogelhaus, see B. Grimschitz, *Johann Lucas von Hildebrandt* (Vienna, 1932), plates 168, 45; of the Hatzfeld Palace, E. Hempel, *Geschichte der deutschen Baukunst* (Munich, 1949), figure 361.

15. R. Konwiarz, *op. cit.*, plates 47–50.

16. *Die Kunstdenkmäler der Stadt Breslau* (Breslau, 1933), II, figure 66.

17. Erich Wiese, in *Jahrbuch der preussischen* p. *Kunstsammlungen*, LV (1934), 57–88, attributes the six statues from the former high altar of the Kreuzkirche at Wrocław, now in the Unterkirche, to Weissfeld, but the *St Andrew* he reproduces definitely derives from the Bernini tradition, in contrast to Weissfeld's documented statues.

18. Hans Tintelnot, *Die barocke Freskomalerei in Deutschland* (Munich, 1951), plates 25–7.

19. Ernst Kloss, *Michael Willmann* (Breslau, n.d.), plate 85.

20. *Op. cit.*, plate 132.

21. *Op. cit.*, plate 111.

22. H. Tintelnot, *op. cit.*, plate 39.

23. Cornelius Gurlitt, 'Die Kunstdenkmäler Dresdens', in *Beschreibende Darstellung . . . des Königreichs Sachsen*, XXI (Dresden, 1900), figure 170.

CHAPTER 14

148 1. Hans Reuther, 'Beiträge zur Natursteinverwendung in der mainfränkischen Barockarchitektur', *Deutsche Kunst- und Denkmalpflege*, II (1956), 128 ff.

2. Josef Morper, 'Zur Geschichte des osteuropäischen Wallfahrtskirchentypus. Heilige Berge und marianische Gnadenburgen in Böhmen und Mähren', *Die christliche Kunst*, XXII (1926), 121 ff.

3. L. Gundermann and H. Kreisel, *Würzburg* (Berlin, 1930), plate 106.

149 4. *Op. cit.*, plate 74.

5. Heinrich Kreisel, *Burgen und Schlösser in Franken* (Munich, 1955), plates 48–51.

6. Max Hauttmann, *Geschichte der kirchlichen Baukunst in Bayern, Schwaben und Franken 1550–1780* (Munich, 1921), figure on p. 148, plate 14.

7. *Op. cit.*, plate 16, II.

8. *Op. cit.*, 147, plate 12, II.

151 9. Karl Lohmeyer, *Die Baumeister des rheinisch-fränkischen Barocks*, I (Vienna and Augsburg, 1931), figure 49.

10. *Op. cit.*, figure 52.

11. Heinrich Kreisel, *Fürstenschlösser in Franken* (Berlin, 1936), 65–6.

152 12. Theodor Neuhofer, *Eichstätt* (Munich, 1954), unnumbered plate.

13. H. Popp, *Die Architektur der Barock- und Rokokozeit in Deutschland und der Schweiz* (Stuttgart, 1913), plate 20.

14. *Op. cit.*, plate 82.

15. *Op. cit.*, plate 88.

153 16. Max H. v. Freeden, *Balthasar Neumann* (Munich, 1953), plate 30.

17. *Op. cit.*, plate 70.

18. K. Lohmeyer, *op. cit.*, figure 9. p. 154

19. Richard Sedlmaier and Rudolf Pfister, *Die fürstbischöfliche Residenz zu Würzburg* (Munich, 1923), plates 68–74. p. 156

20. *Op. cit.*, plates 75 ff.

21. Max H. von Freeden, *Balthasar Neumann als Stadtbaumeister* (Berlin, 1937). p. 157

22. Max H. v Freeden, *Balthasar Neumann* (Munich, 1953), plate 49.

23. The town hall at Bamberg is attributed to Neumann by Max v. Freeden, *op. cit.*, 31 and plate 31.

24. *Op. cit.*, plates 24–5.

25. Hauttmann, *op. cit.*, figure on p. 197, plate 28.

26. *Op. cit.*, figure on p. 198. p. 158

27. Max H. v. Freeden, *Balthasar Neumann* (*op. cit.*), plate 33.

28. *Op. cit.*, plate 55.

29. *Op. cit.*, plate 59.

30. *Op. cit.*, plates 36–40.

31. Martin Wackernagel, *Baukunst des 17. und 18. Jahrhunderts in den germanischen Ländern*, Handbuch der Kunstwissenschaft (Berlin-Neubabelsberg, 1915), figure 141. p. 159

32. H. Popp, *op. cit.*, plate 143.

33. *Op. cit.*, plate 98, bottom.

34. *Op. cit.*, plate 106.

35. *Op. cit.*, plates 144–5.

36. *Op. cit.*, plate 98, top.

37. *Op. cit.*, plate 21.

38. Joseph Braun, *Die Kirchenbauten der deutschen Jesuiten* (Freiburg im Breisgau, 1910), II, 310, plate 14. p. 160

39. A. Holtmeyer, *Altkassel* (Marburg, 1913).

40. Theodor Demmler, in *Jahrbuch der preussischen Kunstsammlungen*, XLIII (1922), 137.

41. Heinrich Mayer, *Bamberger Residenzen* (Munich, 1951), 99 ff., plates 31–3. p. 161

42. Johann Leo Broder, *Johann Rudolf Byss* (dissertation, Zürich) (Basel, 1940). p. 162

CHAPTER 15

1. Norbert Lieb and Franz Dieth, *Die Vorarlberger Barockbaumeister* (Munich and Zürich, 1960). p. 163

2. Sebastian Hyller, abbot of Weingarten, was the son of a baker at Pfullendorf; Rupert Ness,

abbot of Ottobeuren, who carried out the magnificent reconstruction, was the son of a hammersmith at Wangen.

p. 163 3. N. Lieb and F. Dieth, *op. cit.*, plates 28, 63, 87, figure 149.

4. *Op. cit.*, 31. According to the chronicle of 1683, the architect Heinrich Meyer, a Jesuit, improved the building in several respects 'especially regarding the height of the church'.

5. *Op. cit.*, plates 65, 66, 149.

p. 165 6. Heinrich Hammer, 'Die St Jakobs-Pfarrkirche in Innsbruck und die süddeutschen Wandpfeilerkirchen', *Zeitschrift d. deutschen Vereins f. Kunstwissenschaft* (1938).

7. Mosbrugger was christened Andreas and was given the name Caspar in the monastery.

8. Recent research, especially by Linus Birchler (*Einsiedeln und sein Architekt Bruder Caspar Mosbrugger*, Augsburg, 1924), has been very liberal in the attribution of a large number of churches to Mosbrugger. Presumably a number of them will have to be dropped.

p. 166 9. G. Spahr, 'Bruder Andreas Schreck. Planentwerfer und Bauleiter der Barockbasilika in Weingarten', *Das Münster*, II (1958), 133 ff. Schreck never worked outside the Weingarten estates. When drawing up the plans for the church at Weingarten, he probably made use of designs already extant.

p. 167 10. W. Hermann, *Münchner Jahrbuch*, N.F. III (1926); J. H. Drissen, *Die Barockarchitektur der Abtei Weingarten* (dissertation, 1928); F. Dieth (Münster, 1950); O. Sandtner (Münster, 1951); H. Schnell (Weingarten, 1950). As opposed to this, Norbert Lieb rightly considers that it is not possible to ignore the traditional names of Herkommer and Beer (*Barockkirchen zwischen Donau und Alpen*, Munich, 1953, 27).

p. 168 11. L. Birchler, *op. cit.*; H. Schnells Kleine Kirchenführer, no. 538 (1951); A. Reinle in *Zeitschrift für schweizerische Archäologie und Kunstgeschichte*, XIII (1952), 170 ff; R. Henggeler in *Zeitschrift für schweizerische Archäologie und Kunstgeschichte*, XV (1954), 103 ff.

p. 170 12. Professor Edgar Lehmann has written a comprehensive book on monastic libraries of the Baroque period in Germany which will be published by the Deutscher Verein f. Kunstwissenschaft, Berlin.

p. 171 13. Karl Lohmeyer, 'D. E. Rossi und seine Schlossbauten in Deutschland', *Rep. f. Kunstwissenschaft*, XL (1917), 193–211.

14. Karl Lohmeyer, *Die Baumeister des rheinischfränkischen Barocks* (Vienna and Augsburg, 1931), 184 ff.

15. The theatre is marked in Krohmer's plan of 1762.

16. Ernst Fiechter, *Schloss Ludwigsburg* (Stuttgart, 1924).

17. A. E. Brinckmann, *Stadtbaukunst* (Berlin, 1920), 40 ff. p. 1

18. Wilhelm Boeck, *Josef Anton Feuchtmayer* p. 1 (Munich, 1948).

19. Johann Caspar Füssli, *Leben und vorzügliche* p. 1 *Werke von Georg Philipp Rugendas und Johannes Kupezki* (Zürich, 1758), 41.

20. Hans Tintelnot, *Die Barocke Freskomalerei in Deutschland* (Munich, 1951), plate III, 60, 61.

21. E. Neustätter, *Johann Evangelist Holzer* (dis- p. 1 sertation) (Munich, 1933), 56; H. Tintelnot, *op. cit.*, plates 88, 89.

CHAPTER 16

1. In 1674, the dean of Altötting writes to the p. 1 Elector Ferdinand Maria that Zuccalli attacked him after divine service in the House of Canons with such disgracefully sneering and mocking words, treating him so contemptuously, that he was not able to tell his Electoral Grace all that the architect's presumption committed against him. Thrice he stamped his foot on the earth into the mud saying he cared no more for him than for that mud.

2. Erich Hubala regards Zuccalli's plan as a p. repetition of Fischer's plan for the castle of Niederweiden and its Milan summer-house (*Kunstchronik*, IV, 1957, 350 ff.). However, it is to be pointed out that the conception of an oval central hall occurs also elsewhere during this period, e.g. in a sketch of Wolf Caspar von Klengel (d. 1691). Cf. E. Hempel 'Unbekannte Skizzen W. C. v. Klengel's', *Abhandlung der sächsischen Akademie der Wissenschaften zu Leipzig, Phil.-hist. Klasse*, XLIV, 4 (1958).

3. The stairs were executed only in 1847–8, when p. the originally planned iron railing was replaced by a heavy marble balustrade.

4. A. Feulner, *Bayrisches Rokoko* (Munich, 1923), p. plate 1.

5. Norbert Lieb, *München* (Munich, 1952), 107 ff.

6. A. Feulner, *Münchner Barockskulptur* (Munich, 1922), plates 3–5.

7. N. Lieb limits the co-operation of the joiner ('Kistler') Dietrich to the execution of the architectural parts of the high altar which was designed by Cuvilliés and conjectures that the figures may have been the work of the Munich court-sculptor Jakob Gerstens the elder, who came from Brussels (*Barockkirchen*, Munich, 1953, 149 and 162).

8. A. Feulner, *Bayrisches Rokoko* (*op. cit.*), plate before p. 135.

9. In his valuable work *Die barocke Freskomalerei in Deutschland* (Munich, 1951), Hans Tintelnot treats Cosmas Damian Asam before Rottmayr in the third chapter, whereby the relationship is reversed.

10. H. Tintelnot, *op. cit.*, 30–2.

11. In the church of the Invalides in Paris (completed in 1706), Hardouin Mansart, following Italian models, left an opening in the internal dome so that the painted higher outer dome, lit from the sides, becomes visible.

12. *Geschichte der besten Künstler in der Schweiz* (Zürich, 1770). Füssli had met Asam at Ettlingen.

CHAPTER 17

1. Presumably the architecture is based on designs by Klengel, who died in 1691 while the building was under construction. He had increased the height of the tower and also remodelled the adjacent chapel. It is quite certain that the military exploits of Johann Georg III were to be celebrated in the triumphal architecture. His undistinguished successor Johann Georg IV did, it is true, have his own name put up, but the only credit he can claim is that he completed the gate.

2. J. L. Sponsel, *Der Zwinger* (Dresden, 1924), plates 5 and 11. A considerable number of sketches, presumably by Dietze, are in the Landesbibliothek in Stuttgart, Nikolai Collection; cf. E. Hempel, 'Unbekannte Skizzen von Wolf Caspar von Klengel', *Abhandlung der sächsischen Akademie der Wissenschaften zu Leipzig, Phil.-hist. Klasse*, II, 4 (1958).

3. J. L. Sponsel, *op. cit.*, 162 ff. and plates 11, 2, and 12. Wolfgang Pfeiffer in his unpublished thesis on the palaces of Dresden suggests that these drawings be removed from the œuvre of Pöppelmann and given to Karcher, but in view of their severely

architectural, disciplined character, this does not seem convincing to me.

4. Eberhard Hempel, *Der Zwinger zu Dresden* p. 192 (Berlin, 1961), figure 62 ff.; J. L. Sponsel, *op. cit.*, 96 and 200, plate 24.

5. The Zwinger was destroyed in 1945, but a p. 193 large portion is being rebuilt.

6. Heinrich Gerhard Franz, *Zacharias Longuelune* p. 194 (Berlin, 1953), 25 ff.

7. According to Klaus Mertens (*Der Park von Gross-Sedlitz*, thesis 1962, Techn. Univ. Dresden, not yet printed), not Longuelune, but Pöppelmann (fountain called 'Stille Musik') and Knöffel laid out the park. Nearly all the known plans for the palace, however, are the work of Longuelune.

8. Bähr was one of the experts called in to give p. 197 an opinion on Viscardi's Mariahilfkirche at Freystadt, which was to be of the utmost importance for the history of architecture (cf. p. 180). See Otto Höver, *Vergleichende Architekturgeschichte* (Munich, 1923), 158.

9. The recession of the galleries in a concave curve occurs already at Weingarten and Einsiedeln.

10. S. W. Henn, 'Die Sicherung und der Wieder- p. 198 aufbau historischer Bauwerke', *Baumeister*, XLV (1948), 305–20. Dresden's historic buildings were, without exception, burnt out when the town was destroyed in 1945. The Hofkirche, the Kreuzkirche, and the Annenkirche, the Zwinger and the Japanisches Palais have been partially rebuilt. The Frauenkirche is a gigantic heap of ruins.

11. The combination of a columned hall with a Greek cross, which was Bähr's starting point, is already to be found in the Noorderkerk in Amsterdam, begun in 1620 by Hendrik de Keyzer and completed in 1623 by Hendrik Staats. In the Katharinakyrka in Stockholm, built between 1656 and 1676 by Jean de la Vallée on a cross plan with four stair-towers inserted in the angles, the dome, like that of the Frauenkirche, did not originally stand on a drum. The drum was not inserted until after a fire in 1724.

12. Built by Oberlandbaumeister Johann Erhard Strassburger of Gotha; Vereinigung Berliner Architekten, *Der Kirchenbau des Protestantismus* (Berlin, 1893), figures 244–6.

13. Eberhard Hempel, *Gaetano Chiaveri* (Dres- p. 199 den, 1955).

14. Sigfried Asche, *Drei Bildhauerfamilien an der* p. 200 *Elbe* (Vienna, 1961), plates 68–85.

p. 200   15. *Op. cit.*, plates 86–110.

p. 201   16. *Beschreibende Darstellung der älteren Bau- und Kunstdenkmäler des Königreichs Sachsen*, XXI (1906), plates 64 ff.

p. 202   17. S. Asche, *op. cit.*, plates 116–43.

18. Ernst Michalski, *Balthasar Permoser* (Frankfurt on Main, 1927), plates 88, 89, 92, 93.

CHAPTER 18

p. 208   1. *Studieresor* (1914), ed. O. Sirén, 228.

p. 210   2. The only contemporary information is given by Peter Schenk in 1702. On his engraving *Arx Berolinensis* he describes Schlüter as being from Danzig.

3. Under Clement X (1670–6) the statue of the *Dying Gaul* had been brought from the Villa Ludovisi to the Capitol. Schlüter may have had an opportunity of seeing it in Rome.

p. 211   4. The sculpture of the Arsenal has survived. The sculpture of the royal palace that was not destroyed during the war was saved when the building was pulled down. The Kamecke House was destroyed in the Second World War, but the four figures from the roof were saved and are now in the museum. The old post office was pulled down as early as the nineteenth century. The equestrian statue of the Great Elector was rescued and, at the time of writing, stands in front of Schloss Charlottenburg. The pulpit in the Marienkirche, the tomb of Männlich in the Nikolaikirche, and the bust of Landgrave Frederick II of Hesse-Homburg at Schloss Homburg have all survived.

5. Humbert stresses the fact that the building of the Arsenal could not be assigned to a single architect, because the plans were continually being altered, both before and during the execution

(*Bibliothèque germanique*, 1734, 172). He mentions François Blondel (*Bibliothèque germanique*, XXVII, 1773, 72) and Nering (*Humberts Nachrichten*, ed. von Heinecken, 1768), both of whom furnished designs.

6. In 1743, at the request of Pope Benedict XIV, p. three mathematicians made an examination of cracks in the dome of St Peter's.

CHAPTER 19

1. According to Johann Georg Burckhardt, p. *Epistola ad amicum* (Hanover, n.d.) (16 June 1710), 'the building that had just been erected at Salzdahlum provided no opportunity for Korb to show his keenness until after his return, when the duke had it enlarged and embellished'. Cf. August Fink, 'Die Baumeister von Schloss Salzdahlum', *Zeitschrift für Kunstwissenschaft*, IV (1950), 187. This, however, is contradicted by other witnesses, for example Christian Heinrich Erndl, *De itinere suo anglicano et batavo annis 1706 et 1707 facto relatio o.O.* (1710): 'His Grace the Duke has employed a joiner named Hermann Korb for this building from its very foundations.'

CHAPTER 20

1. Vereinigung Berliner Architekten, *Der* p. *Kirchenbau des Protestantismus* (Berlin, 1893), figures 115–16.

2. *Op. cit.*, figures 191–2.

3. *Op. cit.*, figures 212–14.   F

4. H. Popp, *Die Architektur der Barock- und Rokokozeit in Deutschland und der Schweiz* (Stuttgart, 1913), plates 4, 169.

CHAPTER 21

229 1. Much of the decoration of the Reichen Zimmer had been safeguarded and in this way escaped destruction. It was thus possible for the excellent Munich restorers to bring the rooms back to their original state, so that the public can again be admitted in 1963. A large part of the stucco work, wood-carving, and the fabrics covering the wall has been supplemented. The Residenz Theatre could also be reconstructed, not, it is true, on the original site but in the block containing the dispensary. The Amalienburg has survived.

31 2. French history of art considers Cuvilliés a provincial representative of French Rococo.

3. Zimmermann belongs both to Bavarian and to Swabian art. Wessobrunn, his birthplace, is in upper Bavaria, but he became a resident of Landsberg in Swabia, near to it. Of his most important buildings the church at Steinhausen is in Swabia, the Wieskirche in upper Bavaria.

33 4. I owe to the kindness of Dr Woeckel of the Zentralinstitut für Kunstgeschichte the new plan of St Anna am Lehel from the Hauptarchiv at Munich. This has never before been published.

39 5. A small wooden relief of *John the Baptist Praying*, in the Bayrisches Nationalmuseum in Munich, testifies to the close relationship between Günther and Egell. On the back is the inscription: 'Copied from Paul Egel in Mannheim. Ignaz Gündter 1751.'

CHAPTER 22

45 1. This was rectified by Ernst Michalski, who in his book *Joseph Christian* (Leipzig, 1926) proved that the models for the statues were produced at Zwiefalten by Christian and then executed in plaster by Feuchtmayer. The only works of sculpture that can be attributed to the latter are the statues over the cornice and the stucco reliefs beneath it.

47 2. In the contract of 1741 with reference to the decoration of the Schlosskapelle at Meersburg,

Cardinal Damian Hugo von Schönborn instructed Feuchtmayer: 'As regards the colours, agreement must be reached with the painter who does the fresco, and sweet colours are always the best.' Boeck, *Joseph Anton Feuchtmayer* (Tübingen, 1948).

CHAPTER 23

1. Fritz Scholl, in his book *Leopoldo Retti* (Ansbach, 1930), describes him as the creator of the decoration in the elector's apartments at Ansbach, which seems doubtful to me. On the other hand Scholl's clarification of the history of this decoration, which had already been made famous by the plates in Otto Lessing, *Schloss Ansbach* (Leipzig, 1908), is very valuable. Previously they had been erroneously dated much too early: 1725–32. *p. 250*

2. Max Sauerlandt, *Die deutsche Plastik des achtzehnten Jahrhunderts* (Florence and Munich, 1926), plates 84–8; Hans Konrad Röthel, *Ferdinand Tietz. Der Figurenschmuck des Parkes von Veitshöchheim. Der Kunstbrief* (Berlin, 1944). *p. 258*

3. Hermann Schneider, *Das frühklassizistische Werk des Johann Peter Wagner* (Würzburg, 1936); M. Sauerlandt, *op. cit.*, plates 103–4. *p. 259*

4. A. Beringer, *Peter Anton von Verschaffelt* (Strasbourg, 1902). *p. 260*

5. Adolf Feulner, *Die Zick* (Munich, 1920). *p. 261*

6. Max H. von Freeden and Carl Lamb, *Das Meisterwerk des Giovanni Battista Tiepolo. Die Fresken der Würzburger Residenz* (Munich, 1956).

7. Oefeleana (manuscript, Staatsbibliothek, Munich). *p. 262*

8. G. Biermann, *Deutsches Barock und Rokoko* (Leipzig, 1914), 271. *p. 263*

9. Famous for his idealized portrait of *Goethe in the Campagna* (Frankfurt, Staedelsches Institut). Cf. Friedrich Rintelen, *Reden und Aufsätze* (Basel, 1927), 104, 'Uber Tischbeins Goethe-Porträt'.

10. G. Biermann, *op. cit.*, plate 912.

11. *Op. cit.*, plates 919 ff.; F. Novotny, *Painting and Sculpture in Europe: 1780–1880* (Pelican History of Art) (Harmondsworth, 1960), 44 f. and plate 27.

12. Four of them passed to the Neue Pinakothek in Munich. *p. 264*

CHAPTER 24

p. 266   1. Obituary for Knobelsdorff by Frederick II (*Œuvres*, VII, Berlin, 1846–57, 32–6).

p. 267   2. Frederick II soon permanently separated from his wife.

3. Margarete Kühn (*Schloss Charlottenburg*, Berlin, 1953) suggests that Jean de Bodt may have designed the staircase. Frederick I described the Charlottenburg staircase as 'the most beautiful ornament in the whole house'.

p. 274   4. G. Biermann, *Deutsches Barock und Rokoko* (Leipzig, 1914), 254 ff.

p. 275   5. Friedrich Bleibaum, *Johann August Nahl* (Baden bei Wien, 1933).

CHAPTER 26

p. 280   1. G. Biermann, *Deutsches Barock und Rokoko* (Leipzig, 1914), 453.

CHAPTER 28

p. 289   1. M. C. F. Prange, *Mengs-Werk*, I (Halle, 1786), 25; cf. F. Novotny, *Painting and Sculpture in Europe: 1780–1880* (Pelican History of Art) (Harmondsworth, 1960), 23 ff. and plate 1.

CHAPTER 29

p. 291   1. The popularity of the empress, as shown for example by the poem by Matthias Claudius quoted there, has been remarked in Note 1 to Chapter 2.

2. Guglielmi's ceiling fresco in the great hall was destroyed by fire in 1961. An attempt will be made to reconstruct it, with the help of numerous coloured photographs taken during the war.

3. In summer, Maria Theresa liked to take breakfast in the pavilion of the menagerie. This was the central point at which the cages and enclosures met, so that she was surrounded by the animals and could see everything. This plan is artistically far superior to those of modern zoological gardens.

p. 292   4. E. H. Hainisch, 'Der Architekt Johann Ferdinand Hetzendorf von Hohenberg', *Wiener Jahrbuch für Kunstgeschichte*, XII/XIII (XVI/XVII) (1949), 19–90.

5. H. Reuther, *Der steirische Baumeister Josef Hueber* (Weinbergkirche, 1947); *idem*, 'Die Entwicklung und Bedeutung der Vierungskuppel im steirischen Sakralbau des Barock', *Festschrift W. Sas-Zaloziecky* (Graz, 1956); *idem*, 'Eine Gruppe

elliptischer Zentralraumkirchen des 18. Jahrhunderts in Steiermark', *Zeitschrift für Kunstgeschichte*, XIX (1956).

6. J. Wichner, *Kloster Admont und seine Bezie-* p. 29 *hungen zur Kunst* (Vienna, 1888); A. Krause, *Die Stiftsbibliothek in Admont* (Linz, 1948).

7. P. Petrus Ortmayr and P. Aegid Decker, *Das Stift Seitenstetten* (Wels, 1955).

8. H. Schachner, *Das Benediktinerstift Kremsmünster* (1909).

9. J. Weingartner, *Die Kirchen Innsbrucks* (Innsbruck, 1921).

10. D. Frey, *Wien in Bildern* (Vienna, 1928), plate 74. Until the time of Franz Joseph, the Habsburgs were buried in the modest church of the Capuchins. The sarcophagi, however, show nothing of Capuchin humility.

11. *Das Barockmuseum im Unteren Belvedere* p. 29 (Vienna, 1923), plate 33. Dorfmeister did not receive an imperial stipend on account of this work, as he had hoped.

12. E. Tietze-Conrat, *Österreichische Barockplastik* (Vienna, 1926), plate III ff.; cf. F. Novotny, *Painting and Sculpture in Europe :1780–1880* (Pelican History of Art) (Harmondsworth, 1960), 218 and plate 182.

13. At his death Messerschmidt left 69 heads, of which 49 were finished: 32 in lead, 16 in stone, and 1 in wood.

14. E. Tietze-Conrat, *op. cit.*, plate 84.   p. 2

15. *Op. cit.*, plates 87–8.

16. Eduard Andorfer, *Veit Königer* (Vienna, 1925).

17. Hermann Burg, *Der Bildhauer Franz Anton Zauner und seine Zeit* (Vienna, 1915).

18. Rochus Kohlbach, *Die barocken Kirchen von Graz* (Graz, 1951), with much information about their furnishings.

19. E. Andorfer, *op. cit.*, plate 1.   p. 2

20. J. Feulner, *J. Günther* (Vienna, 1920), plate 5; *idem* (1947), plates 186–9.

21. Nissl remained untouched by classicism. About 1755 he opened a workshop of his own at Fügen, which at times seemed almost like a factory. From then on, the art of carving became more and more industrialized in the Tyrol, and the peasant children learned carving as soon as they began to make Christmas mangers.

22. J. Zykan, 'Deckengemälde des Gregorio p. Guglielmi in Wien und ihre Wiederherstellung',

Österreichische Zeitschrift für Denkmalpflege, IV (1950), 14–24. The frescoes were severely damaged. They have, however, been successfully restored according to present-day principles for the preservation of ancient monuments, which allow the restorer a good deal of freedom where the fresco is in a very bad state.

23. He avoids showing legs as much as he can, and legs in movement appear only in his early works. Cf. the *Allegory of Light and Truth* in the Wallraf-Richartz Museum in Cologne (*c.* 1750); K. Garas, *Franz Anton Maulbertsch* (Vienna–Budapest, 1960), plate 17.

298 24. See *Das Barockmuseum im Unteren Belvedere* (*op. cit.*), plates 70–1.

25. H. Tintelnot, *Die barocke Freskomalerei in Deutschland* (Munich, 1951), plate 131. Sometimes Maulbertsch's biblical pictures are conceived humorously. An example is the one in the Moravian Museum at Brno (Brünn) where Rebecca, offering drink to Eleazar and his animal, wears a fashionable feathered hat (K. Garas, *op. cit.*, plate 44). That the artist means to be funny is proved by the comic faces of the camels. The picture, painted in 1754, shows the eighteenth century taking up the mannered style of the sixteenth, when the old faith was deeply shaken and biblical themes were no longer necessarily treated seriously. Maulbertsch did, however, remain faithful to the Church, though at the end of his life – witnessed above all by the frescoes at Strahov in Prague – the foundation of his faith rested more on a general Protestant philosophy than on that of the Roman Catholics. It is characteristic that the Roman Catholic basis for art was preserved to a greater extent in Hungary.

26. K. Garas, *op. cit.*, plates 146–7. The frescoes at Schwechat, near Vienna, were destroyed during the last war.

27. *Op. cit.*, plate 85. As the frescoes are in the country, away from the polluted air of the city, they remain extremely well preserved.

99 28. *Op. cit.*, plates 110–17. The contract was signed on 19 March 1759. The influence of Tiepolo is evident.

29. It is to be remembered, on the other hand, that such draperies already play a great role in Rottmayr's frescoes, which were painted about forty-four years earlier; one can in fact speak of an Austrian tradition.

30. Even Maulbertsch was unable to escape classicism: the fresco of 1794 at Strahov in Prague is cold and dead, and there is nothing of Baroque vivacity or painterly conception. The blame lies largely with those who carried out the work. See K. Garas, *op. cit.*, 302–10, who says on p. 159: 'Maulbertsch, then aged seventy, was no longer capable of more than crystallizing painterly conceptions in nimble sketches and masterly outlines, in a light manner.'

31. K. Garas, *op. cit.*, frontispiece.

32. *Op. cit.*, plate 187.

33. See F. Dworschak, R. Feuchtmüller, K. p. 300 Garzarolli-Thurnlackh, and J. Zykan, *Der Maler Martin Johann Schmidt, genannt der 'Kremser Schmidt'* (Vienna, 1955).

34. H. Tintelnot, *op. cit.*, plate 149.

35. Kremser-Schmidt would never have depicted saints in a comic fashion, as Maulbertsch did.

36. In Dürnstein, besides the altar-paintings of Kremser-Schmidt, there is carving on the choir-stalls, on the pulpit, and in the vestibule done by his father, Johann Schmidt.

37. They were destroyed by bombing. p. 301

38. A similar deeply touching representation of the death of St Joseph is in the Museum of Fine Arts in Budapest. See K. Garas, *op. cit.*, plate 201.

39. The painter Anton Zoller spoke indignantly of the painting of the Servitenkirche at Innsbruck having been entrusted to the 'windbag Mölk from Vienna' (H. Hammer, *Die Entwicklung der barocken Deckenmalerei in Tirol*, Strasbourg, 1912, 333).

40. H. Tintelnot, *op. cit.*, plate 123. p. 302

41. H. Hammer, *op. cit.*, 318 ff.

42. *Op. cit.*, 365.

43. *Op. cit.*, 369 ff.

CHAPTER 30

1. G. Kardos, *Magyar építéstörténet a XV századtól* p. 303 (Budapest, 1956), 54.

2. A. Hekler, *Ungarische Kunstgeschichte* (Berlin, 1937), plates 129 and 132.

3. E. Réh, 'Das ehemalige Péterffy-Palais und sein Meister', *Henszlmann-Blätter*, VIII (1930).

4. K. Garas, *Franz Anton Maulbertsch* (Vienna– p. 305 Budapest, 1960), plates 88–104.

5. B. Grimschitz, *Johann Lucas von Hildebrandt* (Vienna, 1932), 62.

p. 305   6. K. Garas, *op. cit.*, plates 254–61, p. 132. Maulbertsch emphasized his having kept scrupulously to the text which, in itself, has a classicist flavour.

CHAPTER 31

p. 306   1. C. Gurlitt, *Warschauer Bauten aus der Zeit der sächsischen Könige* (Berlin, 1917), plate 25.

2. *Op. cit.*, plate 26a.

3. *Architektura Polska*, pt 1 (Warsaw, 1952), plate p. 297.

4. C. Gurlitt, *op. cit.*, plate 28a.

5. D. Frey, *Krakau* (Berlin, 1941), plate 91.

6. C. Gurlitt, *op. cit.*, 98.   p.

BIBLIOGRAPHY

The classification is of two kinds. (1) In accordance with the historical frontiers of the seventeenth and eighteenth centuries. This is the case, e.g., with upper Saxony and Bavaria. (2) In accordance with the inclusion of a place in the territory of a tribe, e.g. Swabia or Franconia. Thus Augsburg is under Swabia, Munich and Regensburg are under Bavaria, and Nuremberg under Franconia.

In addition, Holl is included among the Swabian artists; Westphalia in north-western Germany; the North counts as 'North', not as 'Prussia'; Magdeburg is included in Upper Saxony; and the Imperial Towns are always included in the surrounding territory.

The detailed classification of the material is as follows:

I. *General*
   A. General Works
   B. Special Topics
   C. Sources
   D. Patrons

II. *Individual Countries*
   A. Austria
      1. General
      2. Places
      3. Artists
   B. Bavaria
      1. General
      2. Places
      3. Artists
   C. Czechoslovakia
      1. General
      2. Places
      3. Artists
   D. Denmark

   E. Franconia and Rhineland
      1. General
      2. Places
      3. Artists
   F. Germany
      1. General
      2. Places
   G. Hungary
   H. North Germany
      1. General
      2. Artists
   I. North-West Germany
      1. Artists
   J. Poland
      1. General
      2. Places
   K. Prussia
      1. General
      2. Places
      3. Artists

   L. Saxony, Lower
      1. General
      2. Places
      3. Artists
   M. Saxony, Upper
      1. General
      2. Places
      3. Artists
   N. Silesia
      1. General
      2. Artists
   O. Swabia
      1. General
      2. Places
      3. Artists
   P. Switzerland
      1. General
      2. Artists
   Q. Thuringia
      1. General
      2. Artists

I. GENERAL

A. GENERAL WORKS

Allgemeines Künstlerlexikon. Zürich, 1779–1819.

ANGYAL, A. *Slavische Barockwelt.* Leipzig, 1961.

Cambridge Modern History, II–VI. Cambridge, 1907–25.

CHRISTOFFEL, U. *Höhepunkt abendländischer Architektur.* Munich, 1960.

GRIMMELSHAUSEN, H. J. C. VON. *Der abenteuerliche Simplicissimus.* Mompelgart, 1669.

GRÜN, K. *Kulturgeschichte des Siebzehnten Jahrhunderts.* Leipzig, 1880.

HEINECKEN, C. H. VON. *Nachrichten von Künstlern und Kunstsachen.* Leipzig, 1768–71. Continuation, vol. I, Leipzig, 1786.

Inventories of Historical Monuments in Austria, Czecho-Slovakia, Germany, Hungary, Switzerland. 1870–.

KASER, K. *Das Zeitalter der Reformation und Gegenreformation von 1517–1660.* Gotha-Stuttgart, 1922.

Die Kunstformen des Barockzeitaltars (Sammlung Dalp, LXXXII). Berne, 1956.

MARPERGER, J. G. *Historie und Leben der berühmtesten europäischen Baumeister nach Félibien und mit den drei hinterstelligen Seculis ausgeführt.* Hamburg, 1711.

335

Neueste Reisen durch Deutschland, Böhmen, Ungarn, die Schweiz, Italien und Lothringen. Hanover, 1740–; 3rd ed. 1776.

The New Cambridge Modern History, II, *The Reformation 1520 to 1559*, ed. G. R. Elton, Cambridge, 1958; VII, *The Old Regime 1713 to 1763*, ed. J. O. Lindsay, Cambridge, 1957.

SANDRART, J. V. *Teutsche Academie der edlen Bau-, Bild- und Mahlerey-Künste.* 1st ed. Nuremberg, 1675; ed. A. R. Peltzer, Munich, 1925.

SCHMITT, O. *Reallexikon zur deutschen Kunstgeschichte.* Stuttgart, 1937–.

Schrifttum zur Deutschen Kunst. Berlin, 1937–.

THIEME, U., and BECKER, F. *Allgemeines Lexikon der bildenden Künstler.* Leipzig, 1908–50.

B. SPECIAL TOPICS

BIERMANN, G. *Deutsches Barock und Rokoko. Im Anschluss an die Jahrhundert-Ausstellung deutscher Kunst 1650–1800.* Darmstadt, 1914; 2 vols., Leipzig, 1914.

BOCK, E. *Die deutsche Graphik.* Munich, 1922.

BRINCKMANN, A. E. *Barockskulptur.* Berlin-Neubabelsberg, 1917.

BRINCKMANN, A. E. *Barock-Bozzetti (Deutsche Bildhauer*, IV). Frankfurt a.M., 1924–5.

DROST, W. *Barockmalerei in den germanischen Ländern (Handbuch der Kunstwissenschaft).* Berlin-Neubabelsberg, 1926.

FEULNER, A. *Die deutsche Plastik der siebzehnten Jahrhunderts.* Munich, 1926.

FEULNER, A. *Skulptur und Malerei des 18. Jahrhunderts in Deutschland.* Wildpark-Potsdam, 1929.

FEULNER, A., and MULLER, T. *Geschichte der deutschen Plastik.* Munich, 1953.

FRITSCH, K. E. O. *Der Kirchenbau des Protestantismus.* Berlin, 1893.

HAUTTMANN, M. *Geschichte der kirchlichen Baukunst in Bayern Schwaben und Franken 1550–1780.* Munich, 1921.

JESSEN, P. *Katalog der Ornamentstich-Sammlung.* Berlin, 1894.

JESSEN, P. *Meister des Ornamentstiches.* 4 vols. Berlin, 1922–4.

KOHLHAUSEN, H. *Geschichte des deutschen Kunsthandwerkes.* Munich, 1955.

LIEB, N. *Barockkirchen zwischen Donau und Alpen.* Munich, 1953.

REUTHER, H. 'Das Platzlgewölbe der Barockzeit', *Deutsche Kunst- und Denkmalpflege*, XIII (1955), 121.

SAUERLANDT, M. *Die deutsche Plastik des achtzehnten Jahrhunderts.* Munich, 1926.

STURM, L. C. *Architektonische Reise-Anmerkungen.* Augsburg, 1719.

TINTELNOT, H. *Die barocke Freskomalerei in Deutschland.* Munich, 1951.

C. SOURCES

BROEBES, J.-B. *Vues des palais et des maisons de plaisans de S.M. le roy de Prusse.* Augsburg, 1733.

CUVILLIÉS, F. DE. *Opus of prints.* Munich, 1738–. Newly ed. and completed by his son, F. de Cuvilliés the younger, as *Architecture bavaroise.*

DECKER, P. *Fürstlicher Baumeister oder Architectura civilis.* 3 pts. Augsburg, 1711 and 1716.

DIEUSSART, C. P. *Theatrum architecturae civilis.* 1st ed. Güstrow, 1679.

DLABAČ, G. J. *Allgemeines historisches Künstlerlexikon für Böhmen.* Prague, 1775–.

FISCHER VON ERLACH, J. B. *Entwurf einer historischen Architektur.* Vienna, 1721.

FURTTENBACH, J. *Architectura civilis.* Ulm, 1628.

FURTTENBACH, J. *Kirchengebäw.* Augsburg, 1649.

FÜSSLI, J. A. *Geschichte der besten Künstler in der Schweiz.* Zürich, 1769–74.

FÜSSLI, J. A. *Allgemeines Künstlerlexikon.* Zürich, 1779–1819.

[GOLDMANN, N.] *Vollständige Anweisung zu der Zivil-Baukunst durch Nicolaus Goldmann*, published by L. Sturm. Wolfenbüttel, 1696.

GRIMMELSHAUSEN, H. J. C. VON. *Der abenteuerliche Simplicissimus.* Mompelgart, 1669.

HEINECKEN, C. H. VON. *Nachrichten von Künstlern und Kunstsachen.* Leipzig, 1768–71. Continuation, vol. I, Leipzig, 1786.

KEYSSLER, J. G. *Neueste Reisen durch Deutschland, Böhmen, Ungarn, die Schweiz, Italien und Lothringen.* Hanover, 1740–; 3rd ed. 1776.

LEUTHNER, A. *Grundtliche Darstellung der fünff Seullen etc.* Prague, 1677.

MARPERGER, J. G. *Historie und Leben der berühmtesten europäischen Baumeister nach Félibien und mit den drei hinterstelligen Seculis ausgeführt.* Hamburg, 1711.

PÖPPELMANN, M. D. *Vorstellung und Beschreibung des Zwingergartens zu Dresden.* Dresden, 1729.

POZZO, A. *Prattica della perspectiva.* 2 vols. Rome, 1693 and 1698.

SANDRART, J. V. *Teutsche Academie der edlen Bau-, Bild- und Mahlerey-Künste.* 1st ed. Nuremberg, 1675; ed. A. R. Peltzer, Munich, 1925.

STURM, L. C. *Architektonische Bedenken von Protestantischen kleinen Kirchen Figur und Einrichtung.* Hamburg, 1712.

STURM, L. C. *Civil-Baukunst.* Augsburg, 1718.

STURM, L. C. *Architektonische Reise-Anmerkungen.* Augsburg, 1719.

D. PATRONS

Augustus the Strong

GURLITT, C. *August der Starke.* Dresden, 1924.

Frederick the Great

SEIDEL, P. *Friedrich der Grosse und die bildende Kunst.* 2nd ed. Leipzig-Berlin, 1924.

Liechtenstein, Karl Eusebius von

FLEISCHER, V. *Fürst Karl Eusebius von Liechtenstein.* Vienna, 1910.

Schaumburg, Ernst von

BRUCK, R. *Ernst von Schaumburg.* Berlin, 1917.

Sporck

PAZAUREK, G. *Franz Anton Reichsgraf von Sporck, ein Mäzen der Barockzeit, und seine Lieblingsschöpfung Kukus.* Leipzig, 1901.

II. INDIVIDUAL COUNTRIES

A. AUSTRIA

1. General

DECKER, H. *Barockplastik in den Alpenländern.* Vienna, 1943.

FLEISCHER, V. *Fürst Karl Eusebius von Liechtenstein.* Vienna, 1910.

GARZAROLLI-THURNLACKH, K. *Die barocke Handzeichnung in Österreich.* Zürich, 1928.

GINHART, K. *Die bildende Kunst in Österreich: Renaissance und Barock, 1530–1690; Barock und Rokoko, 1690–1780.* Baden bei Wien, 1939.

HAMMER, H. *Die Entwicklung der barocken Deckenmalerei in Tirol.* Strassburg, 1912.

Meisterwerke der österreichischen Barockmalerei in der Alten Galerie des Landesmuseums Joanneum in Graz. Graz, 1961

MICHAILOW, N. *Österreichische Malerei des 18. Jahrhunderts.* Frankfurt a.M., 1935.

RIEHL, H. *Barocke Baukunst in Österreich.* Vienna, 1930.

RIESENHUBER, M. *Die kirchliche Barockkunst in Österreich.* Linz, 1924.

SEDLMAYR, H. *Österreichische Barockarchitektur.* Vienna, 1930.

TIETZE-CONRAT, E. *Österreichische Barockplastik.* Vienna, 1920.

2. Places

Dürnstein

PÜHRINGER-ZWANOWETZ, L. *Stift Dürnstein.* Vienna, 1948.

Innsbruck

HAMMER, H. *Paläste und Bürgerbauten Innsbruck.* Vienna, 1923.

Salzburg

HAGEN-DEMPF, F. *Die Kollegienkirche in Salzburg.* Vienna, 1949.

PRETZELL, L. *Salzburger Barockplastik.* Berlin, 1935.

Vienna

SCHMIDT, J. *Wien.* Vienna, 1938.

3. Artists

Allio

PAUKER, W. *Donato Felice Allio. Beiträge zur Baugeschichte des Stiftes Klosterneuburg.* Vienna, 1907.

Donner

BLAUENSTEINER, K. *Georg Raphael Donner.* Vienna, 1944.

Fischer von Erlach

BUCHOWIECKI, W. *Der Barockbau der ehemaligen Hofbibliothek in Wien, ein Werk J. B. Fischers v. Erlach.* Vienna, 1957.

FISCHER VON ERLACH, J. B. *Entwurf einer historischen Architektur.* Vienna, 1721.

FREY, D. *Johann Bernhard Fischer von Erlach. Eine Studie über seine Stellung in der Entwicklung der Wiener Palastfassade.* Vienna, 1923.

FREY, D. 'J. B. Fischer von Erlach', *Jahrbuch für Kunstgeschichte des Bundesdenkmalamtes,* I (1955), 93.

ILG, A. *J. B. Fischer von Erlach*. Vienna, 1895.

KUNOTH, G. *Die historische Architektur Fischers von Erlach*. Düsseldorf, 1956.

SEDLMAYR, H. *Johann Bernhard Fischer von Erlach*. 2nd ed. Vienna, 1956.

Hildebrandt

GRIMSCHITZ, B. *Johann Lucas von Hildebrandt*. Vienna, 1932.

Kremser-Schmidt

DWORSCHAK, F., FEUCHTMÜLLER, R., GARZA-ROLLI-THURNLACKH, K., and ZYKAN, J. *Der Maler Martin Johann Schmidt, genannt der 'Kremser Schmidt'*. Vienna, 1955.

Maulbertsch

BENESCH, O. 'Maulbertsch. Zu den Quellen seines malerischen Stiles', *Städel-Jahrbuch*, 3/4 (1924), 107.

GARAS, K. *Franz Anton Maulbertsch*. Vienna-Budapest, 1960.

Pozzo

POZZO, A. *Prattica della perspettiva*. 2 vols. Rome, 1693 and 1698.

Prandtauer

HANTSCH, H. *Jakob Prandtauer*. Vienna, 1926.

Rauchmiller

HAENCKE, B. 'Mathias Rauchmüller, der Bildhauer', *Repertorium für Kunstwissenschaft*, XXV (1902), 96.

Rottmayr

TIETZE, H. 'J. M. Rottmayr', *Jahrbuch der Zentralkommission*, N.F. IV (1906), 81.

Stammel

MAYR, A. *Die Werke des Plastikers Josef Thaddäus Stammel*. Vienna, 1912.

Steinl

PAUKER, W. 'Der Bildhauer und Ingenieur Steinl', *Jahrbuch des Stiftes Klosterneuburg*, II (1909), 275, 347.

Troger

JACOBS, R. *Paul Troger*. Vienna, 1930.

Weissenkirchner

ROSENBERG-GUTMANN, A. *Hanns Adam Weissenkirchner*. Vienna, 1925.

B. BAVARIA

1. General

FEULNER, A. *Bayrisches Rokoko*. Munich, 1923.

HAUTMANN, M. *Geschichte der Kirchlichen Baukunst in Bayern Schwaben und Franken 1550–1780*. Munich, 1921.

SCHNELL, H. M. *Der baierische Barock, die volklichen, die geschichtlichen und die religiösen Grundlagen*. Munich, 1942.

2. Places

Munich

FEULNER, A. *Münchner Barockskulptur*. Munich, 1922.

LIEB, N. *Münchner Barockbaumeister*. Munich, 1941.

Nymphenburg

HAGER, L. *Nymphenburg*. Munich, 1955.

Wies

LAMB, C. *Die Wies*. Berlin, 1937.

3. Artists

Asam Brothers

HANFSTAENGL, E. *Die Brüder Cosmas Damian und Egid Quirin Asam*. Munich, 1955.

Cuvilliés

BRAUNFELS, W. *François de Cuvilliés*. Würzburg, 1938.

CUVILLIÉS, F. DE. *Opus of Prints*. Munich, 1738–. Newly ed. and completed by his son, F. de Cuvilliés the younger, as *Architecture bavaroise*.

Effner

HAUTTMANN, M. *Der kurbayrische Hofbaumeister Josef Effner*. Strassburg, 1913.

Fischer, J. M.

HAGEN-DEMPF, F. *Der Zentralbaugedanke bei Johann Michael Fischer*. Munich, 1954.

Günther

FEULNER, A. *Ignaz Günther*. Munich, 1947.

SCHÖNBERGER, A. *Ignaz Günther*. Munich, 1954.

Schwanthaler

GUBY, R. 'Der Bildhauer Thomas Schwanthaler und seine Zeit', *Kunst und Kunsthandwerk*, XXII (1919), 228.

Straub

GIEDION-WELCKER, C. *Johann Baptist Straub*. Munich, 1922.

Zimmermann

MUCHALL-VIEBROOK, T. *Dominicus Zimmermann*. Leipzig, 1912.

Zuccalli

PAULUS, R. *Henrico Zuccalli*. Strasbourg, 1912.

C. CZECHOSLOVAKIA

1. General

BLAŽIČEK, O. J. *Sochařství Baroku V. Čechách Plastika 17. a 18. věku* (with German and French résumé). Prague, 1958.

DLABAČZ, G. J. *Allgemeines historisches Künstlerlexikon für Böhmen*. Prague, 1775–.

FRANZ, H. G. *Bauten und Baumeister der Barockzeit in Böhmen*. Leipzig, 1962.

FRANZ, H. G. 'Die "böhmische Wandpfeilerhalle" im 18. Jhdt.', *Zeitschrift für Ostforschung*, II. Jahrgang (1962).

FRANZ, H. G. *Die deutsche Barockbaukunst Mährens*. Munich, 1943.

FRANZ, H. G. *Studien zur Barockarchitektur in Böhmen und Mähren*. Munich-Vienna, 1943.

HEGEMANN, H. W. *Die deutsche Barockbaukunst Böhmens*. Munich, 1943.

PAZAUREK, G. *Franz Anton Reichsgraf von Sporck, ein Mäzen der Barockzeit, und seine Lieblingsschöpfung Kukus*. Leipzig, 1901.

PROKOP, A. *Die Markgrafschaft Mähren in kunstgeschichtlicher Beziehung*, III. Vienna, 1904.

STEPHAN, O. *Pamálky archaeologicke a mistopsné, Praha*, XXXV (1927), 79 and 468.

STEPHAN, O. 'Contributions to the History of Bohemian Baroque Architecture' (in Czech), *Pam. arch.*, XXXV (1928), 79 and 468 ff.

STRETTIOVÁ, O. *Das Barockporträt in Böhmen*. Prague, 1957.

2. Places

Kuks

LUKAS, J. *Sporkuv Kuks*. Prague, 1950.

Prague

MORPER, J. J. *Das Czernin-Palais in Prag*. Prague, 1940.

STEPHAN, O. *Pražské kostely*. Prague, 1936.

3. Artists

Dientzenhofer

FRANZ, H. G. *Die Kirchenbauten des Christoph Dientzenhofer*. Brno, 1941.

Leuthner

LEUTHNER, A. *Grundtliche Darstellung der fünff Seullen, etc.* Prague, 1677.

Mathey

MORPER, J. J. 'Der Prager Architekt Jean Baptiste Mathey', *Münchner Jahrbuch der bildenden Kunst*, N.F. IV (1927), 79, 468.

Santin-Aichel

FRANZ, H. G. 'Gotik und Barock im Werk des Johann Santini Aichel', *Wiener Jahrbuch der bildenden Kunst*, N.F. IV (1927), 99.

D. DENMARK

WEILBACH, W. *Dansk Bygningskunst*. Copenhagen, 1930.

E. FRANCONIA AND RHINELAND

1. General

HAUTTMANN, M. *Geschichte der kirchlichen Baukunst in Bayern Schwaben und Franken 1550–1780*. Munich, 1921.

KREISEL, H. *Burgen und Schlösser in Franken*. Munich-Berlin, 1955.

LOHMEYER, K. *Die Baumeister des rheinischfränkischen Barocks*. Vienna–Augsburg, 1931.

Quellen zur Geschichte des Barocks in Franken unter dem Einfluss des Hauses Schönborn, pt 1, in 2 vols. Augsburg, 1931 and 1955.

2. Places

Banz and Vierzehnheiligen

TEUFEL, R. *Banz und Vierzehnheiligen*. Berlin, 1936.

Kassel

KRAMM, W. *Kassel, Wilhelmshöhe, Wilhelmstal*. Berlin, 1933.

Pommersfelden

KREISEL, H. *Das Schloss Pommersfelden*. Munich, 1953.

Würzburg

BRUHNS, L. *Würzburger Bildhauer der Renaissance und des werdenden Barock.* Munich, 1923.

SEDLMAIER, R., and PFISTER, R. *Die fürstbischöfliche Residenz zu Würzburg.* Munich, 1923.

3. Artists

Decker

DECKER, P. *Fürstlicher Baumeister oder Architectura civilis.* 3 pts. Augsburg, 1711 and 1716.

Dieussart

DIEUSSART, C. P. *Theatrum Architecturae civilis.* 1st ed. Güstrow, 1679.

Egell

LANKHEIT, K. *Die Zeichnungen des kurpfälzischen Hofbildhauers Paul Egell.* Karlsruhe, 1954.

Elsheimer

DROST, W. *Adam Elsheimer und sein Kreis.* Potsdam, 1933.

WEIZSÄCKER, H. *Adam Elsheimer.* 2 vols. Berlin, 1936 and 1952.

Neumann

FREEDEN, M. H. VON. *Balthasar Neumann.* Munich–Berlin, 1953.

REUTHER, H. *Die Kirchenbauten Balthasar Neumanns.* Berlin, 1960.

Zick

FEULNER, A. *Die Zick.* Munich, 1920.

F. GERMANY

1. General (see also I. B, SPECIAL TOPICS)

BENZ, R. *Deutscher Barock, Kultur des 18. Jahrhunderts,* pt 1. Stuttgart, 1949.

BRAUN, J. *Die Kirchenbauten der deutschen Jesuiten.* 2 vols. Freiburg i.Br., 1908–10.

DEHIO, G. *Handbuch der deutschen Kunstdenkmäler.* Berlin, 1924–.

GERSTENBERG, K. *Deutsche Sondergotik.* Munich, 1913.

GURLITT, C. *Geschichte des Barockstiles und des Rococo in Deutschland.* Stuttgart, 1889.

HAGER, W. *Die Bauten des deutschen Barocks.* Jena, 1942.

HEMPEL, E. *Geschichte der deutschen Baukunst.* 1st ed., Munich, 1949; 2nd ed., 1956.

KELLER, H. *Das Treppenhaus im deutschen Schloss- und Klosterbau des Barock.* Munich, 1936.

LÜBKE, W. *Geschichte der Renaissance in Deutschland.* Hirth ed., revised by A. Haupt. Esslingen, 1914.

PINDER, W. *Deutscher Barock. Die grossen Baumeister des 18. Jahrhunderts.* Düsseldorf–Leipzig, 1912.

POPP, H. *Die Architektur der Barock- und Rokokozeit in Deutschland und der Schweiz.* Stuttgart, 1913.

STANGE, A. *Die deutsche Baukunst der Renaissance.* Munich, 1926.

WACKERNAGEL, M. *Baukunst des 17./18. Jahrhunderts. Germanische Länder.* Berlin–Neubabelsberg, 1915.

ZÜLCH, W. K. *Entstehung des Ohrmuschelstiles.* Heidelberg, 1932.

2. Places

See II. INDIVIDUAL COUNTRIES

G. HUNGARY

GYÖRGY, K. *Magyar építéstörténet a XV. századtól.* Budapest, 1956.

HEKLER, A. *Ungarische Kunstgeschichte.* Berlin, 1937.

H. NORTH GERMANY

1. General

ULBRICH, A. *Geschichte der Bildhauerkunst in Ostpreussen.* 2 vols. Königsberg, 1926–9.

2. Artists

Gudewerth

BRANDT, G. *Hans Gudewerth.* Leipzig, 1898.

Liss

OLDENBOURG, R. 'Jan Lys', *Jahrbuch der preussischen Kunstsammlungen,* XXXV (1914), 136.

STEINBART, K. *Johannes Liss.* Vienna, 1946.

Matthieu

STEINMANN, E., and WITTE, H. *Georg David Matthieu.* Leipzig, 1911.

Münstermann

RIESEBIETER, M. 'Ludwig Münstermann', *Jahrbuch für Kunstwissenschaft,* I (1929), 60.

Ziesenis

KUNTZE, F. F. *Johann Georg Ziesenis.* Charlottenburg, 1932.

I. NORTH-WEST GERMANY

1. Artists

Gröninger

KOCH, F. 'Die Gröninger', *Beiträge zur west-fälischen Kunstgeschichte*, I (1905).

Schlaun

HARTMANN, H. *Johann Conrad Schlaun*. Münster, 1910.

RENSING, T. *Johann Conrad Schlaun*. Munich-Berlin, 1954.

J. POLAND

1. General

ZACHWATOWICZ, J. *Architektura Polska do połowy XIX wieku. Wydanie drugie*. Warsaw, 1956. (Contemporaneous German translation entitled *Polnische Architektur bis zur Mitte des XIX. Jahrhunderts*.)

2. Places

Lvov (Lemberg)

PIOTROWSKI, J. *Lemberg und Umgebung*. Lemberg, n.d.

Warsaw

GURLITT, C. *Warschauer Bauten aus der Zeit der sächsischen Könige*. Berlin, 1917.

(*See also* the Notes to the text)

K. PRUSSIA

1. General

BROEBES, J.-B. *Vues des palais et des maisons de plaisans de S. M. le roy de Prusse*. Augsburg, 1733.

SEIDEL, P. *Friedrich der Grosse und die bildende Kunst*. 2nd ed. Leipzig–Berlin, 1924.

SCHMITZ, H. *Preussische Königsschlösser*. Berlin, 1926.

WIESENHÜTTER, A. *Protestantischer Kirchenbau des deutschen Ostens*. Leipzig, 1936.

2. Places

Berlin

HERZ, R. *Berliner Barock*. Berlin, 1928.

WERNER, A. *Der protestantische Kirchenbau des friderizianischen Berlin*. Berlin, 1913.

Charlottenburg

KÜHN, M. *Schloss Charlottenburg*. Berlin, 1953.

Potsdam

KANIA, M. *Potsdamer Baukunst*. 3rd ed. Berlin, 1926.

MANGER, H. L. *Baugeschichte von Potsdam, besonders unter Regierung König Friedrichs II*. 3 vols. Berlin, 1789–90.

3. Artists

Knobelsdorff

KNOBELSDORFF, W. v. *Georg Wenzeslaus von Knobelsdorff*. Berlin, 1861.

STREICHHAN, A. *Knobelsdorff und das Friderizianische Rokoko*. Burg, 1932.

Schlüter

GURLITT, C. *Andreas Schlüter*. Berlin, 1891.

LADENDORF, H. *Der Bildhauer und Baumeister Andreas Schlüter*. Berlin, 1935.

LADENDORF, H. *Andreas Schlüter*. Berlin, 1937.

L. SAXONY, LOWER

1. General

BRUCK, R. *Ernst von Schaumburg*. Berlin, 1917.

STURM, L. C. *Architektonische Bedenken von Protestantischen kleinen Kirchen Figur und Einrichtung*. Hamburg, 1712.

STURM, L. C. *Civil-Baukunst*. Augsburg, 1718.

STURM, L. C. *Architektonische Reise-Anmerkungen*. Augsburg, 1719.

2. Places

Salzdahlum

FINK, A. 'Die Baumeister von Schloss Salzdahlum', *Zeitschrift für Kunstwissenschaft*, VI (1950), 183.

3. Artists

Goldmann

Vollständige Anweisung zu der Zivil-Baukunst durch Nicolaus Goldmann, published by L. Sturm. Wolfenbüttel, 1696.

Korb

ALVENSLEBEN, U. v. *Die Braunschweigischen Schlösser der Barockzeit und ihr Baumeister Hermann Korb*. Berlin, 1937.

Lauterbach

THÖNE, F. 'Der Wolfenbütteler Barockbau-meister Johann Balthasar Lauterbach', *Zeitschrift für Kunstwissenschaft*, VI (1950), 197.

M. SAXONY, UPPER

1. General

GURLITT, C. *August der Starke*. Dresden, 1924.

2. Places

Dresden

BARTH, A. *Zur Baugeschichte der Dresdner Kreuz-kirche*. Dresden, 1907.
DÖRING, A. *Die Neue Königstadt*. Dresden, 1920.
HEMPEL, E. *Der Zwinger in Dresden*. Berlin, 1961.
LÖFFLER, F. *Das alte Dresden*. 3rd ed. Dresden, 1958.
SPONSEL, J. L. *Der Zwinger*. Dresden, 1924.
SPONSEL, J. L. *Die Frauenkirche zu Dresden*. Dresden, 1893.
SPONSEL, J. L. *Das Grüne Gewölbe zu Dresden*. 4 vols. Leipzig, 1925–32.

Leipzig

PEVSNER, N. *Leipziger Barock*. Dresden, 1928.

Meissen

ZIMMERMANN, E. *Die Erfindung und Frühzeit des Meissner Porzellans*. Berlin, 1908.

3. Artists

Chiaveri

HEMPEL, E. *Gaetano Chiaveri*. Dresden, 1955.

Kändler

GRÖGER, H. *Johann Joachim Kändler, der Meister des Porzellans*. Dresden, 1956.

Klengel

HEMPEL, E. 'Unbekannte Skizzen von Wolf Caspar von Klengel', *Abhandlung der Sächsischen Akademie der Wissenschaften zu Leipzig*, Phil.-hist. Klasse, XLIX, 4 (1958).

Longuelune

FRANZ, H. G. *Longuelune und die Baukunst des 18. Jahrhunderts in Dresden*. Berlin, 1953.

Nosseni

MACKOWSKY, W. *Giovanni Maria Nosseni*. Berlin, 1904.

Permoser

BESCHORNER, H. *Permoser Studien*. Dresden, 1913.
BOECKELMANN, W. *Balthasar Permoser*. Traun-stein, 1951.
MICHALSKI, E. *B. Permoser*. Frankfurt a.M., 1927.

Pöppelmann

PÖPPELMANN, M. D. *Vorstellung und Beschreibung des Zwingergartens zu Dresden*. Dresden, 1729.

Walther

HENTSCHEL, W. 'Der Dresdner Bildhauer Se-bastian Walther', *Zeitschrift für bildende Kunst* (1930/1), Heft 3/4, 59.

Wilhelmi

GRÄBKE, H. A. 'Tobias Wilhelmi und die Magde-burger Barockskulptur nach dem dreissigjährigen Kriege', *Jahrbuch für Kunstwissenschaft*, IV (1927), 223.

N. SILESIA

1. General

KLIMPEL, G. *Kollegienbauten der Jesuiten in Schlesien*. Breslau, 1923.

2. Artists

Frantz

GRUNDMANN, G. *Die Baumeisterfamilie Frantz*. Breslau, 1937.

Willmann

KLOSS, E. *Michael Willmann*. Breslau, 1934.

O. SWABIA

1. General

HAUTTMANN, M. *Geschichte der kirchlichen Bau-kunst in Bayern Schwaben und Franken 1550–1780*. Munich, 1921.

2. Places

Ludwigsburg

SCHMIDT, R. *Schloss Ludwigsburg*. Munich, 1954.

Neresheim

NEUMANN, G. *Neresheim*. Munich, 1947.

Ottobeuren

LIEB, N. *Ottobeuren.* Augsburg, 1933.

Weingarten

HERRMANN, W. 'Zur Bau und Künstlergeschichte von Kloster Weingarten', *Münchner Jahrbuch der bayrischen Kunst*, N.F. III (1926), 232.

3. Artists

Christian

MICHALSKI, E. *Joseph Christian.* Leipzig, 1926.

Feuchtmayer

BOECK, W. *Joseph Anton Feuchtmayer.* Tübingen, 1948.

Furttenbach

FURTTENBACH, J. *Kirchengebäw.* Augsburg, 1649.

Holl

BAUM, J. *Die Bauwerke des Elias Holl.* Strassburg, 1908.

INGEBORG, A. 'Elias Holl', *Münchner Jahrbuch der bildenden Kunst*, N.F. XII (1937), 101.

PFISTER, R. 'Die Augsburger Rathaus-Modelle des Elias Holl', *Münchner Jahrbuch der bildenden Kunst*, N.F. XII (1937), 85.

Schickhardt

BAUM, J. *Heinrich Schickhardt.* Strassburg, 1916.

Schreck

SPAHR, G. 'Bruder Andreas Schreck. Planentwerfer und Bauleiter der Barockbasilika in Weingarten', *Münster*, XI (1958), 133.

Wink

FEULNER, A. *Christian Wink.* Munich, 1912.

P. SWITZERLAND

1. General

JENNY, H. *Kunstführer der Schweiz.* 2nd ed. Berne, 1934.

LANDOLT, H. P., and SEEGER, T. *Schweizer Barockkirchen.* Frauenfeld, 1948.

LIEB, N., and DIEDL, F. *Die Vorarlberger Barockbaumeister.* Munich and Zürich, 1960.

2. Artists

Gessner

LEEMANN-VAN ELCK, P. *Salomon Gessner.* Zürich, 1930.

Mosbrugger

BIRCHLER, L. *Einsiedeln und sein Architekt Bruder Caspar Mosbrugger.* Augsburg, 1924.

DIETH, F. 'Andreas Mosbrugger', *Münster*, III (1950), 1.

Q. THURINGIA

1. General

HEUBACH, H. *Geschichte des Schlossbaues in Thüringen: 1620–1670.* Jena, 1927.

2. Artists

Krohne

MÖLLER, H. H. *Gottfried Heinrich Krohne und die Baukunst des 18. Jahrhunderts in Thüringen.* Berlin, 1956.

THE PLATES

Konrad Heinzelmann: Nuremberg, St Lorenz, 1439–77. Interior of choir; tabernacle by Adam Kraft, 1493 (damaged in the war and since restored)

I

(A) Arnold von Westfalen: Meissen, Albrechtsburg, begun 1470. Interior

(B) Cologne, Gürzenich, 1437–44. Exterior (destroyed in the war and externally reconstructed)

2

Greifswald, house in the Marktplatz, fifteenth century

(B) Konrad Krebs: Torgau, Schloss Hartenfels, hall range, 1532–44

(A) Sterzing (Vipiteno), town hall, completed 1524. Exterior

4

Prague, Belvedere, 1535–60. Exterior

(A) Rothenburg on the Tauber, town hall, *c.* 1570. Exterior

(B) Heidelberg, Schloss, Ottheinrichsbau, 1556–9. Exterior

Wendel Dietterlin: Plate 108 from *Architectura und Austheilung der V Seulen*, 1593

Lucas Kilian: Portrait of Elias Holl, 1619

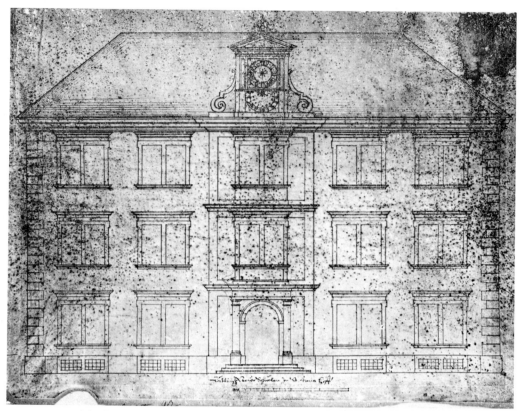

(A) Elias Holl: Augsburg, St Anne's School, design for façade, 1613

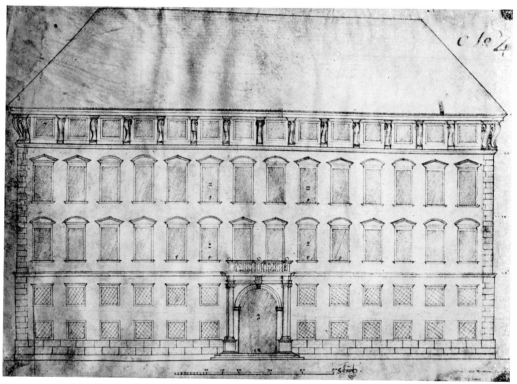

(B) Elias Holl: Augsburg, town hall, first design for the façade, 1614

9

Elias Holl: Augsburg, town hall, 1615–20. Façade (destroyed in the war and since rebuilt)

Munich, St Michael, interior of nave, 1583–97, and chancel by Friedrich Sustris, 1592

Santino Solari: Salzburg Cathedral, 1614–28. Façade

(A) Laurenz van der Sype: Eggenberg, Schloss, begun 1623. Exterior

(B) George Ridinger: Aschaffenburg, Schloss, 1605–14. Exterior (before destruction)

Jakob Wolff the Elder and Peter Carl: Nuremberg, Pellerhaus, 1602–7. Exterior (before destruction)

(A) Jakob Wolff the Younger: Nuremberg, additions to the town hall, 1616–22. Exterior
(partly restored, destroyed in the war and since rebuilt)

(B) Johannes Schoch: Heidelberg, Schloss, Friedrichsbau, 1601–7. Exterior

(A) Lüder von Bentheim: Bremen, town hall, 1608–13. Exterior

(B) Paul Francke: Wolfenbüttel, St Mary, 1604–26. Interior

(A) Paolo Romano: Lvov (Lemberg), church of the Bernardine Fathers, 1600–30. Exterior

(B) Kazimierz, Przybyła Houses, early seventeenth century

(B) Hubert Gerhard: Patrona Bavariae,
1613. *Munich, in front of
the town hall*

(A) Lvov (Lemberg), Boimów Mausoleum, 1609–17

(B) Georg Petel: Salvator Mundi, c. 1633. *Augsburg, St Moritz*

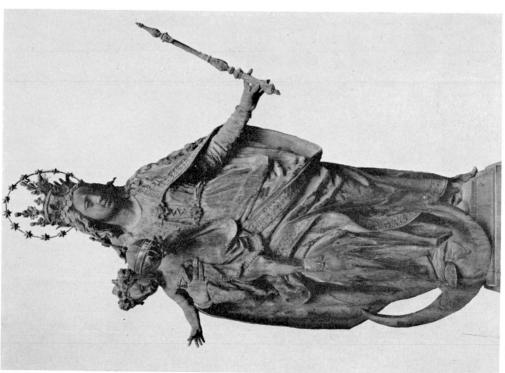

(A) Hans Krumper: Patrona Bavariae, 1616. *Munich, Residenz*

Jörg Zürn: The Virgin from the high altar, 1613–19.
Überlingen Minster

(A) Jörg Zürn: High altar, 1613–19. *Überlingen Minster*

(B) Sebastian Walther: Relief with the Annunciation to
the Shepherds, 1640. *Dresden, Grünes Gewölbe*

21

Zacharias Hegewald: Altar, 1638. *Kötzschenbroda, church*

(A) Franz Ditterich: High altar, 1605. *Strehla, church*

(B) Ebert Wolf the Younger: Altar, *c.* 1608. *Bückeburg, palace chapel*

Ludwig Münstermann: Adam and Eve, *c.* 1624. *Oldenburg, Landesmuseum*

Ludwig Münstermann: Altar, *c.* 1623. *Insterburg, Lutheran parish church*

(A) Adam Elsheimer: The 'Small Tobias', *c.* 1607.
London, Lady Martin

(B) Adam Elsheimer: The Flight into Egypt, *c.* 1609.
Munich, Bayerische Staatsgemäldesammlungen

(A) Adam Elsheimer: Jupiter and Mercury visiting Philemon and Baucis, *c.* 1607.
Dresden, Gemäldegalerie

(B) Adam Elsheimer: Landscape, *c.* 1600–10. *Edinburgh,*
National Gallery of Scotland

27

(A) Adam Elsheimer: Bathsheba, *c.* 1608. Gouache. *Berlin, Kupferstichkabinett*

(B) Johann Liss: Soldiers' Camp, *c.* 1625. *Nuremberg, Germanisches National-Museum*

Johann Liss: The Toilet of Venus, 1625–6. *Pommersfelden, Galerie*

(A) Carlo Antonio Carlone: Vienna, church of the Nine Angelic Choirs, 1662. Façade

(B) Philiberto Luchese: Vienna, Hofburg, Leopold Range, 1661–8. Exterior

(A) Francesco Caratti: Prague, Černín Palace, begun 1668. Exterior

(B) Vienna, Starhemberg Palace, 1661 (?). Exterior

Carlo Lurago: Passau Cathedral, nave, after 1668

(A) Antonio Petrini: Würzburg, Haug church, 1670–91. Exterior (before destruction)

(B) Thomas Poncini: Kielce, episcopal palace, 1638. Façade

Zamość, town hall, 1639–51, staircase eighteenth century. Exterior

(A) Turka (Galicia), timber church, 1746

(B) Wolf Caspar von Klengel: Dresden, opera house, 1664–7. Ceiling painted by Harms, 1675–82. Engraving. *Dresden, Stadtmuseum*

(A) Johann Georg Starcke: Dresden, Palace in the Grosser Garten, 1679–83.
Façade (before partial destruction)

(B) Oranienburg, orphanage, 1650–60. Exterior (before partial destruction)

36

Michael Beer (?): Kempten, abbey church, 1652–66. Façade

Hans Georg Kuen (?): Solothurn, Jesuit church, 1680–8. Interior

(A) Matthias Rauchmiller: Tomb of Bishop Karl von Metternich,
c. 1675. *Trier, Liebfrauenkirche*

(B) Hans Gudewerth: St Mark from the high altar,
1640. *Eckernförde, church*

(B) Valentin Otte: High altar, 1664.
Leisnig, Matthäuskirche

(A) Hans Gudewerth: Memorial to Heinrich Ripenau, c. 1653.
Eckernförde, church

(B) Michael Willmann: The Kiss of the Virgin, 1682.
Wrocław (Breslau), Museum

(A) Hans Gudewerth: Putto from the high altar, 1640.
Eckernförde, church

Johann Heinrich Schönfeld: The Life-Class in the Augsburg Academy, after 1660.
Graz, Johanneum

(A) Johann Heinrich Schönfeld: Christ with his Disciples on the Lake of Genezareth, c. 1670–80. *Augsburg, Museum*

(B) Michael Willmann: St Bernard of Clairvaux appearing to the Abbot of Cîteaux, 1661–1700. *Lubiąż (Leubus), collegiate church*

(B) Joachim von Sandrart: Self Portrait, *c.* 1670.
Frankfurt, Historisches Museum

(A) Heinrich Christoph Fehling: Wolf Kaspar von Klengel, *c.* 1675.
Moritzburg

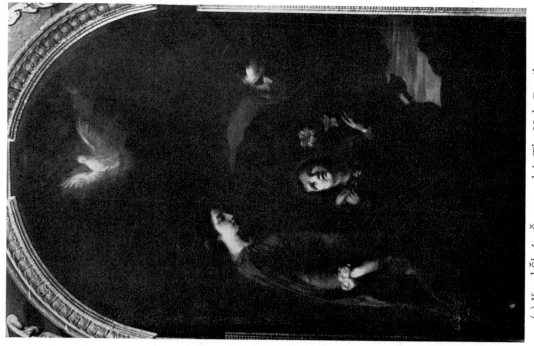

(B) Karel Škréta Šotnovoský: The Holy Family, 1664.
Prague, Teyn church

(A) Karel Škréta Šotnovoský: Bernard de Witte, 1651.
Prague, Národní Galerie

Carlo Antonio Carlone: St Florian, abbey church, 1686–1708. Interior

Johann Bernhard Fischer von Erlach: Vranov (Frain), Castle, 1690–4. Interior of great hall

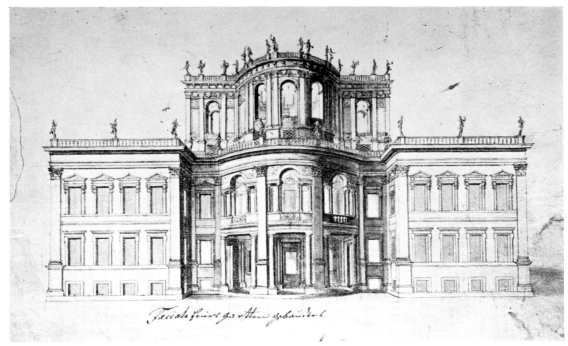

(A) Johann Bernhard Fischer von Erlach: Design for a summer house, *c.* 1699.
Vienna, University Library

(B) Johann Bernhard Fischer von Erlach: Design for a palace for Frederick I,
King of Prussia, 1704. *Vienna, Albertina*

(A) Johann Bernhard Fischer von Erlach: Salzburg, Dreifaltigkeitskirche, 1694–8. Engraving

(B) Johann Bernhard Fischer von Erlach: Salzburg, Kollegienkirche, 1696–1707. Engraving

49

(A) Johann Bernhard Fischer von Erlach: Vienna, Karlskirche, begun 1716. Façade

(B) Johann Bernhard Fischer von Erlach: Vienna, Imperial Library,
begun 1722. Exterior

Johann Bernhard Fischer von Erlach: Vienna, Imperial Library, begun 1722. Interior.
Dome painted by Daniel Gran, 1726–30

51

(A) Johann Lucas von Hildebrandt and Johann Bernhard Fischer von Erlach: Vienna,
Schwarzenberg Palace, begun 1697. Garden front

(B) Johann Lucas von Hildebrandt: Vienna, Daun-Kinsky Palace, 1713–16. Façade

(A) Johann Lucas von Hildebrandt: Vienna, Daun-Kinsky Palace, 1713–16. Detail of balustrade

(B) Johann Lucas von Hildebrandt: Vienna, Upper Belvedere, 1721–2. Exterior

Jakob Prandtauer: Melk Abbey, begun 1702. Exterior

Joseph Munggenast: Altenburg Abbey, 1730–3. Interior of library.
Ceiling by Paul Troger, plasterwork by Michael Flor

Joseph Munggenast: Altenburg Abbey, church, 1730–3. Interior

(A) Matthias Steinl and Joseph Munggenast: Dürnstein Priory, church,
1721–5. Interior

(B) Georg Anton Gumpp: Innsbruck, Landhaus, façade, 1725–8

Matthias Rauchmiller and Johann Bernhard Fischer von Erlach: Vienna,
Pestsäule, 1682–94

58

Matthias Steinl: Joseph I, *c.* 1710. Ivory.
Vienna, Kunsthistorisches Museum

(B) Michael Bernhard Mandl: Horse Pond Monument, 1695. *Salzburg, Archiepiscopal Stables*

(A) Meinrad Guggenbichler: St Benedict from the Holy Ghost Altar, 1682–4. *Mondsee Abbey, church*

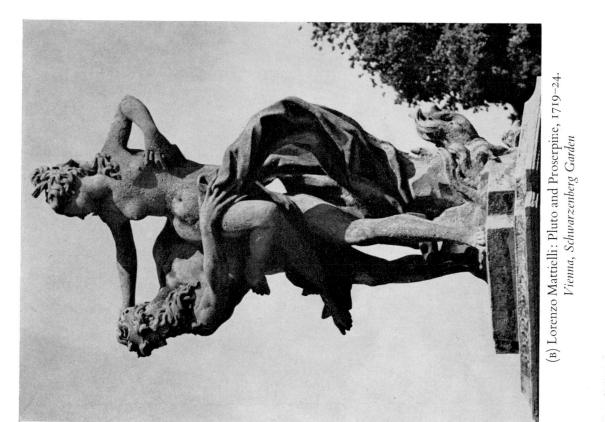

(B) Lorenzo Mattielli: Pluto and Proserpine, 1719–24.
Vienna, Schwarzenberg Garden

(A) Lorenzo Mattielli: Winter, 1719–24.
Vienna, Schwarzenberg Garden

Georg Raphael Donner: Angel from the altar, *c.* 1735. *Bratislava (Pozsony, Pressburg)*
Cathedral, chapel of St Elemosynarius

(A) Georg Raphael Donner: The River March, 1737–9. *Formerly Vienna, Mehlmarkt*

(B) Georg Raphael Donner: The River Enns, 1737–9. *Formerly Vienna, Mehlmarkt*

Georg Raphael Donner: St Martin from the high altar, *c*. 1735.
Bratislava (Pozsony, Pressburg) Cathedral

Josef Thaddäus Stammel: St Martin, high altar, 1738–40.
St Martin, near Graz

(A) Johann Michael Rottmayr: Ceiling fresco, 1704–6.
Wrocław (Breslau), *St Matthias*

(B) Paul Troger: Ceiling fresco in the nave, 1732–3.
Altenburg, *St Lambert*

Daniel Gran: Design for the ceiling fresco in the dome of the Schwarzenberg Palace, Vienna, 1724. *G. Engelhardt collection*

Paul Troger: The Feeding of the Five Thousand, design for the ceiling fresco in the summer refectory at Geras, 1738. *Vienna, Barockmuseum*

Cseklész, castle, 1711–23. Wings by Jakob Fellner, 1756

(B) Pest, university church, executed by Andreas Mayerhoffer,
1730–42. Interior

(A) Christoph Dientzenhofer: Prague, sv. Mikuláš Malá Strana
(St Niklas on the Kleinseite), 1703–11. Interior

(B) Christoph Dientzenhofer: Prague, sv. Mikuláš Malá Strana. Detail of façade, 1709–11

(A) Christoph Dientzenhofer: Prague, sv. Mikuláš Malá Strana. Façade, 1709–11

(B) Christoph Dientzenhofer: Břevnov (Breunau), Benedictine church, 1708–21. Interior

(A) Christoph Dientzenhofer: Břevnov (Breunau), Benedictine church, 1708–21. Exterior

(A) Johann Santin-Aichel: Kladruby (Kladrau), Benedictine church, enlarged 1712. Vault

(B) Johann Santin-Aichel (?): Křtiny (Kiritein), Premonstratensian church, before 1712–1735. Vault

Johann Santin-Aichel: Kladruby (Kladrau), Benedictine church, enlarged 1712.
Interior of nave

Johann Santin-Aichel: Žd'ár nad Sázavou (Saar), abbey church, *c.* 1710. Organ

(A) Johann Santin-Aichel (?): Lomec (Lometz), chapel, 1692–1702. Vault

(B) Kilian Ignaz Dientzenhofer: Počaply (Potschapl), church, 1724–5. Exterior

Johann Bernhard Fischer von Erlach: Prague, Clam-Gallas Palace. Portal by Braun, *c.* 1713.

(B) Mathias Bernhard Braun: Lightheartedness, c. 1719.
Kuks (Kukus), hospital church

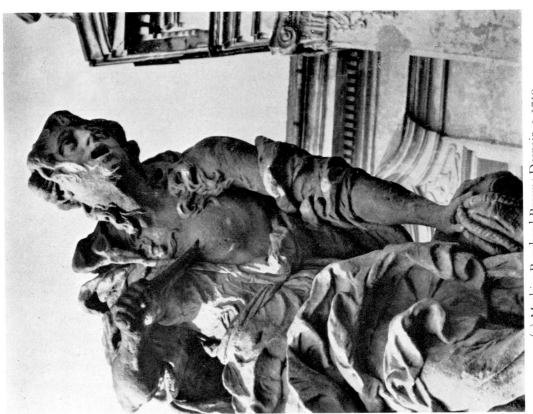

(A) Mathias Bernhard Braun: Despair, c. 1719.
Kuks (Kukus), hospital church

(B) Matej Vaclav Jökl: The Virgin with St Bernard, 1709.
Prague, Charles Bridge

(A) Mathias Bernhard Braun: Charity, *c.* 1719.
Kuks (Kukus), hospital church

(B) Johann Kupecký: Self Portrait, c. 1740.
Prague, Hradshin

(A) Johann Kupecký: Franziska Wussin, c. 1716.
Prague, Národní Galerie

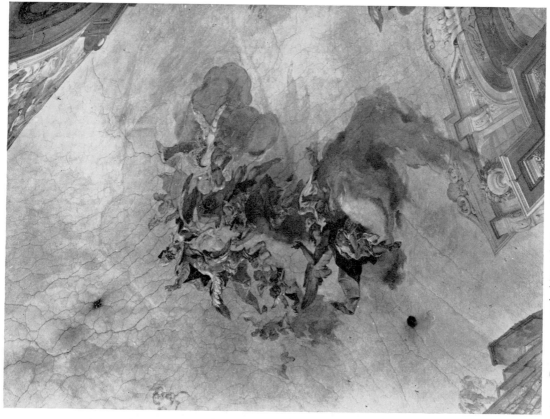

(A) and (B) Johann Lucas Kracker: Ceiling fresco in the nave (details), 1760–1. *Prague, sv. Mikuláš Malá Strana (St Niklas on the Kleinseite)*

Antonio Petrini: Würzburg, Julius Hospital, court wing, 1699. Exterior

(A) Agostino Locci: Wilanów, palace, 1677–96. Exterior

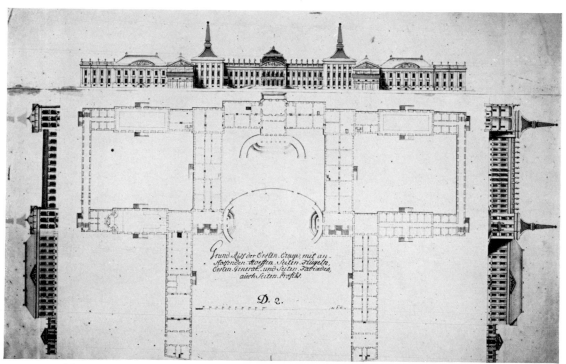

(B) Mathaes Daniel Pöppelmann: Design for the Saxon Palace, Warsaw, *c.* 1730.
Dresden, Sächsisches Staatsarchiv

Anton Jentsch: Krzeszów (Grüssau), abbey church, 1728–35. Façade

Martin Frantz: Jelenia Góra (Hirschberg), Gnadenkirche, 1709–18. Exterior

(B) Michael Willmann: Abbot Rosa, c. 1695.
Wrocław (Breslau), Museum

(A) Leonhard Dientzenhofer: Schöntal, Cistercian church,
1700–17. Interior

Michael Willmann: Landscape with Jacob's Dream, *c. 1690. Wrocław (Breslau), Museum*

Antonio Petrini: Würzburg, University Church, tower, 1586–91, restored 1696 etc.

Georg Dientzenhofer: Bamberg, St Martin, façade, 1681–91

(A) Johann Dientzenhofer: Banz, abbey church, 1710–18. Interior

(B) Johann Dientzenhofer: Pommersfelden, Schloss, 1711–18. Marble Saloon

Johann Dientzenhofer: Pommersfelden, Schloss, 1711–18. Exterior

Balthasar Neumann: Würzburg, Residenz, begun 1719. Exterior (before partial destruction)

(B) Antonio Bossi: Würzburg, Residenz, plasterwork in the White Salon, 1744

(A) Balthasar Neumann: Würzburg, Residenz, begun 1719. Garden front

95

Balthasar Neumann: Würzburg, Residenz. Staircase, 1737–50

Balthasar Neumann: Werneck, Schloss, 1734–45. Chapel, interior

(A) Balthasar Neumann: Werneck, Schloss, 1734–45. Garden front

(B) Paul du Ry: Kassel, Oberneustadt, begun 1688, with the Karlskirche, 1698–1706

Bamberg, town hall, 1732–7. Exterior

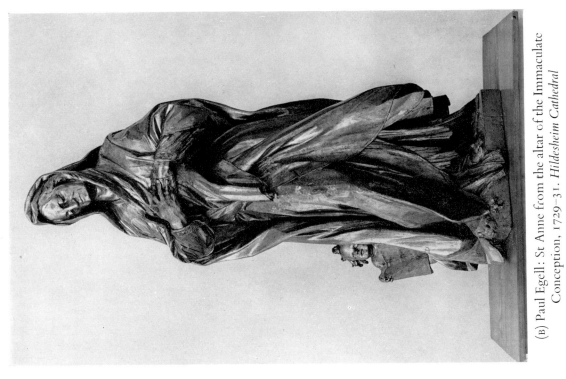

(B) Paul Egell: St Anne from the altar of the Immaculate
Conception, 1729–31. *Hildesheim Cathedral*

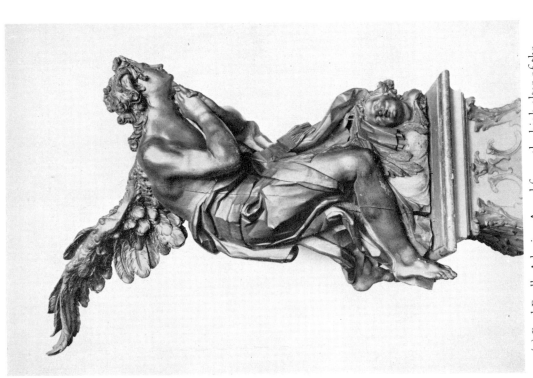

(A) Paul Egell: Adoring Angel from the high altar of the
Unterpfarrkirche, Mannheim, c. 1735. *Berlin (East), Staatliche Museen*

(B) Paul Egell: Judas Thaddaeus, c. 1735. Bozzetto.
Mainz, Altertumsmuseum

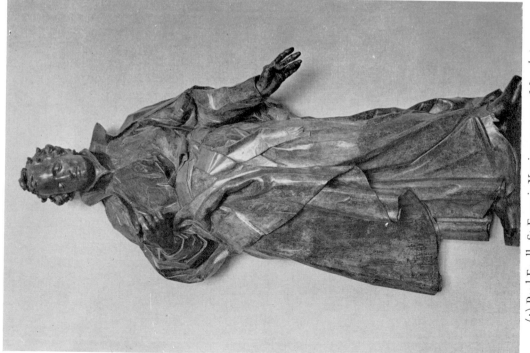

(A) Paul Egell: St Francis Xavier, c. 1735. *Mannheim,
Stadtgeschichtliches Museum*

Franz Beer: Rheinau, abbey church, 1704–11. Interior

Franz Beer: St Urban, abbey church, 1711–15. Interior

(B) Weingarten, abbey church, 1715–23. Façade

(A) Weingarten, abbey church, 1715–23. Interior

(B) Michael Thumb: Schönenberg, near Ellwangen, pilgrimage church, begun 1682. Façade

(A) Hans Georg Kuen and Caspar Mosbrugger: Einsiedeln, abbey church, designed 1703. Interior

Caspar Mosbrugger: Einsiedeln, abbey church, façade

Philipp Joseph Jenisch, Johann Friedrich Nette, and Donato Frisoni: Ludwigsburg, palace, 1704–19. Garden front

(B) Johann Evangelist Holzer: Ceiling fresco, 1739.
Partenkirchen, St Anton

(A) Johann Evangelist Holzer: Sketch for ceiling fresco at Münsterschwarzach
abbey church, executed 1737–40. *Augsburg, Museum*

Johann Evangelist Holzer: Peasants dancing, sketch for a fresco on the façade of an inn at Augsburg, *c.* 1735.
Augsburg, Museum

(A) Enrico Zuccalli: Schleissheim, Lustheim, 1684–9. Exterior

(B) Enrico Zuccalli: Ettal, monastery, church begun 1709. Exterior

Giovanni Antonio Viscardi: Freystadt, Mariahilfkirche, 1700–8. Exterior

(A) Enrico Zuccalli and Giovanni Antonio Viscardi: Schloss Nymphenburg,
1663–1723. Exterior

(B) Joseph Effner: Schleissheim, west front, 1701–26

Cosmas Damian and Egid Quirin Asam: Munich, St Johannes Nepomuk, 1733–46. Exterior

Egid Quirin Asam: Assumption of the Virgin, 1718–22. *Rohr, monastery church*

Egid Quirin Asam: The Trinity, 1733. *Munich, St Johannes Nepomuk*

(B) Cosmas Damian Asam: Ceiling fresco,
1735. *Ingolstadt, St Maria Victoria, Bürgersaal*

(A) Cosmas Damian Asam: The Finding of the True Cross,
ceiling fresco, 1733. *Legnickie Pole (Wahlstatt),
abbey church*

(B) Marcus Conrad Dietze: Dresden, Schloss, Grünes Tor, designed 1692–3

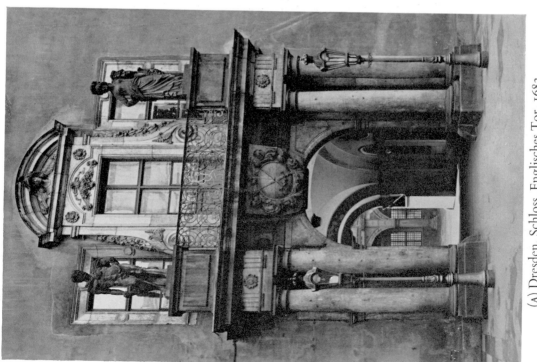

(A) Dresden, Schloss, Englisches Tor, 1682

Mathaes Daniel Pöppelmann: Dresden, Zwinger, Kronentor, 1713 (severely damaged and rebuilt)

(A) Mathaes Daniel Pöppelmann: Dresden, Zwinger, Wallpavillon, begun 1716 (severely damaged and under reconstruction)

(B) Dresden, Altstadt, with the Frauenkirche (*left*) and the Hofkirche (*right*) (before partial destruction)

(B) Hans Georg Roth: Carlsfeld, church, 1684–8. Exterior

(A) Mathaes Daniel Pöppelmann: Pillnitz, Wasserpalais, 1720–3. Exterior

(B) George Bähr: Dresden, Frauenkirche, 1725–43. Interior
(before destruction)

(A) George Bähr: Dresden, Frauenkirche, 1725–43. Exterior
(before destruction)

Balthasar Permoser: Head of one of the Damned, c. 1720. *Leipzig, Museum der bildenden Künste*

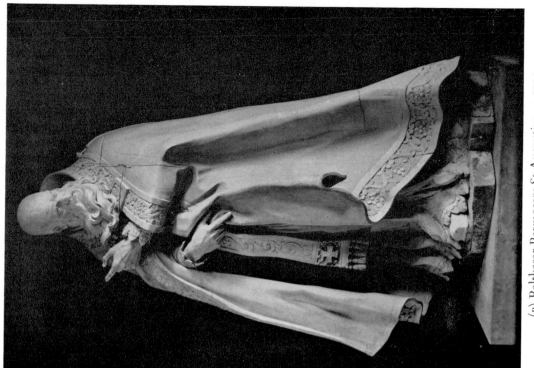

(B) Balthasar Permoser: St Augustine, *c.* 1720.
Bautzen, Stadtmuseum

(A) Balthasar Permoser: Flora, 1724.
Formerly Wiederau, now Dresden, Zwinger

(B) Johann Joachim Kändler: Singer, *c.* 1744.
Celle, Schloss

(A) Johann Joachim Kändler: Piece from the Swan Set, 1737–41.
Dresden, Porzellansammlung

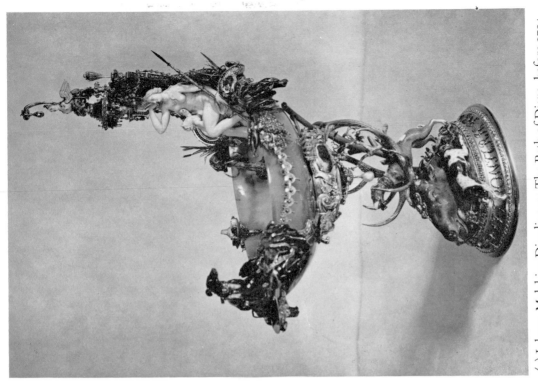

(B) Johann Melchior Dinglinger: The Bath of Diana, before 1704. Chalcedony bowl with ivory and gold. *Dresden, Grünes Gewölbe*

(A) Johann Melchior Dinglinger: The Household of the Grand Mogul of Delhi (detail), 1701–9. *Dresden, Grünes Gewölbe*

Johann Arnold Nering, Andreas Schlüter, and Jean de Bodt:
Berlin, Arsenal, 1695–1717. Façade (before destruction)

Andreas Schlüter: Berlin, Schloss, 1698–1707. Garden side (before destruction)

(B) Andreas Schlüter: Keystone with Medusa head, 1696.
Berlin, Arsenal

(A) Andreas Schlüter: Keystone with the head of a Dying Warrior, 1696.
Berlin, Arsenal

Andreas Schlüter: Monument to David Männlich (detail), 1700. *Berlin, St Nicholas* (portrait medallion now missing)

Andreas Schlüter: Berlin, Schloss, 1698–1707. Courtyard (before destruction)

Andreas Schlüter: The Great Elector, 1696–1709. *Charlottenburg, Schloss*

Andreas Schlüter: Berlin, Kamecke House, 1711–12. Exterior (before destruction)

(B) Andreas Schlüter: Amphitrite, 1711–12.
Formerly Berlin, Kamecke House, now Museum

(A) Andreas Schlüter: Poseidon, 1711–12.
Formerly Berlin, Kamecke House, now Museum

(A) Hermann Korb: Hundisburg, Schloss, 1694–1702. Exterior

(B) Hermann Korb: Wolfenbüttel, Holy Trinity, 1705–19. Interior

(A) Hermann Korb: Wolfenbüttel, library, 1706–10. Exterior.
After a painting by Andreas Tacke

(B) Hermann Korb: Wolfenbüttel, library, 1706–10. Interior.
After a painting by Andreas Tacke

Johann Conrad Schlaun: Münster, St Aegidien, 1724–9. Façade

(A) Johann Conrad Schlaun: Clemenswerth, 1736–50. Exterior

(B) François de Cuvilliés: Nymphenburg, Amalienburg, 1734–9. Exterior

François de Cuvilliés: Nymphenburg, Amalienburg, 1734–9. Interior

Dominikus Zimmermann: Steinhausen, pilgrimage church, 1728–31. Interior

Dominikus Zimmermann: Steinhausen, pilgrimage church, 1728–31. Exterior

(A) Dominikus Zimmermann: Die Wies, pilgrimage church, 1745–54. Interior

(B) Johann Michael Fischer: Ingolstadt, St Mary, 1736–9. Interior (before destruction)

Simpert Kramer and Johann Michael Fischer: Ottobeuren, abbey church,
begun 1737. Interior

Johann Michael Fischer: Rott am Inn, abbey church,
1759–63. Interior

(B) Johann Baptist Straub: St Catherine of Siena, c. 1760.
Munich, Bayerisches Nationalmuseum

(A) Ignaz Günther: Raphael, c. 1760.
Munich, Bayerisches Nationalmuseum

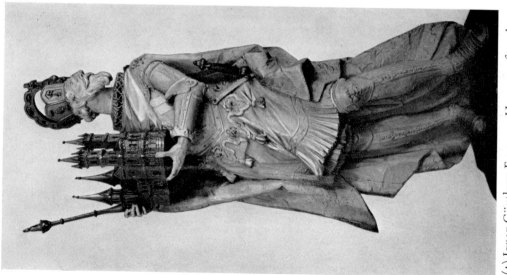

(A) Ignaz Günther: Emperor Henry, as founder of the church of Rott, 1760–2. *Rott am Inn, abbey church*

(B) Ignaz Günther: Guardian Angel, 1763. *Munich, Bürgersaal*

Ignaz Günther: The Trinity, from the high altar, 1760–2.
Rott am Inn, abbey church

Ignaz Günther: The Annunciation, 1764. *Weyarn, Stiftskirche*

(A) Hagenberg, Jodlbauerhof, 1786, with paintings on façade

(B) Johann Baptist Zimmermann: Ceiling fresco, 1730–1. *Steinhausen, pilgrimage church*

Christian Wink: Ceiling fresco, 1769. *Dietramszell, St Leonhard*

(B) Johann Georg Edlinger: Peasant, late eighteenth century.
Augsburg, Städtisches Kunstsammlung

(A) George de Marées: Countess Maria Anna von Holnstein, c. 1755.
Munich, Städtische Galerie

(B) George de Marées: Elector Max III Joseph of Bavaria with his Intendant Count Seau, c. 1760. *Nymphenburg, Schloss*

(A) Johann Georg Übelherr: Detail of wall decoration in a bedroom, c. 1734. *Kempten, Residenz*

(B) Peter Thumb and Giovanni Gaspare Bagnato: St Gallen, abbey, 1748–70. Exterior

(A) Peter Thumb: St Gallen, abbey, library, 1758–67. Interior

Peter Thumb (master mason), Joseph Anton Feuchtmayer (plasterer), and Gottfried Bernhard Göz (painter): Birnau, pilgrimage church, 1746–58. Interior

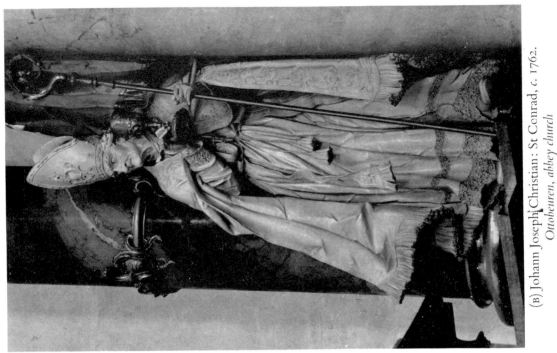

(B) Johann Joseph Christian: St Conrad, c. 1762.
Ottobeuren, abbey church

(A) Joseph Anton Feuchtmayer: Figure from the stables,
c. 1742. *Salem, abbey*

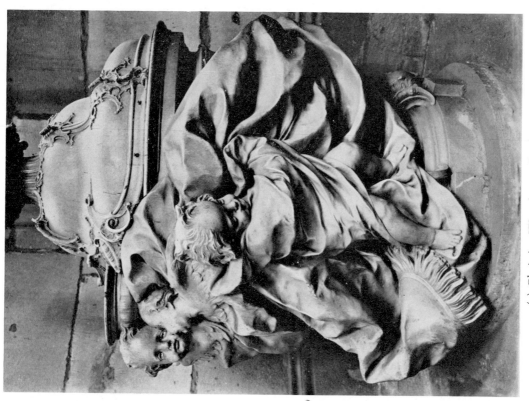

(B) Christian Wenzinger: Font, 1768.
Freiburg im Breisgau Minster

(A) Joseph Anton Feuchtmayer: Honey-licking Putto,
c. 1750. Birnau, pilgrimage church

Franz Joseph Spiegler: Ceiling fresco, 1751. *Zwiefalten, abbey church*

(A) Gottfried Bernhard Göz: Ceiling fresco, 1749–50. *Birnau, pilgrimage church*

(B) Salomon Gessner: Hylas and the Nymphs, 1771. *Munich, Staatliche Graphische Sammlung*

(A) Balthasar Neumann: Vierzehnheiligen, pilgrimage church, 1743–72. Model.
Bamberg, Sammlung des Historischen Vereins

(B) Balthasar Neumann: Etwashausen, parish church, 1741–5. Interior

Balthasar Neumann: Vierzehnheiligen, pilgrimage church, 1743–72. Interior

Balthasar Neumann: Neresheim, abbey church, 1747–92. Interior

(A) Friedrich Joachim Stengel: Saarbrücken, St Ludwig, 1762–75. Exterior

(B) Trier, No. 39 Krahnenstrasse, mid eighteenth century. Façade

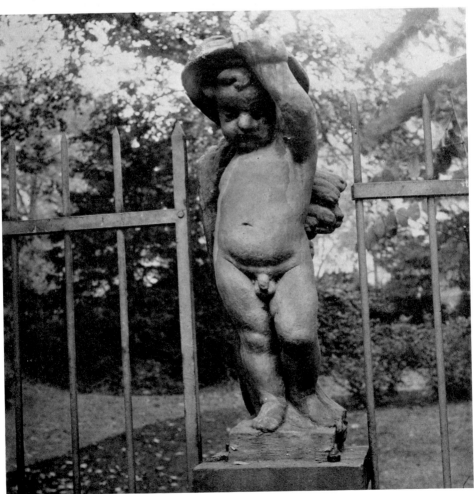

(A) and (B) Kassel, Johann August Nahl's house in the Friedrichsplatz,
reliefs and putto by Nahl, 1771

Ferdinand Tietz: Pegasus, 1765–8. *Veitshöchheim, gardens*

(B) Johann Peter Wagner: Flora, after 1771. *Veitshöchheim, staircase*

(A) Ferdinand Tietz: A Dancer, 1765–8. *Veitshöchheim, gardens*

Johann Zick: The History and Glorification of the Bishopric of Speyer, ceiling fresco, 1752. *Bruchsal, Schloss, staircase (before destruction)*

Januarius Zick: Saul and the Witch of Endor, 1752. *Würzburg, Museum*

(B) Ferdinand Kobell: Rocky Landscape, c. 1780.
Schwerin, Staatliches Museum

(A) Johann Heinrich Tischbein the Elder: The Artist's Wife.
Wrocław (Breslau), Museum

(A) Georg Wenzeslaus von Knobelsdorff: Charlottenburg, Schloss, dining room, completed 1742
(before partial destruction, now under restoration)

(B) Georg Wenzeslaus von Knobelsdorff: Charlottenburg, Schloss, Golden Gallery, 1740–6
(before partial destruction, now under restoration)

(A) Georg Wenzeslaus von Knobelsdorff: Potsdam, Stadtschloss, 1744–51. Court side (before destruction)

(B) Georg Wenzeslaus von Knobelsdorff: Potsdam, Stadtschloss, 1744–51. Music room (before destruction)

Georg Wenzeslaus von Knobelsdorff: Berlin, opera house, 1741–3. Exterior

(A) Georg Wenzeslaus von Knobelsdorff: Potsdam, Sanssouci, 1745–7. North side

(B) Johann Gottfried Büring and Heinrich Ludwig Manger: Potsdam, Neues Palais, 1763–6. Exterior

Daniel Nikolaus Chodowiecki: Girl writing, *c.* 1760. Chalk.
Weimar, Schlossmuseum

(A) Daniel Nikolaus Chodowiecki: The Artist's Daughter Jeanette at her Mother's Breast, 1761. Pencil. *Leipzig, Museum der bildenden Künste*

(B) Daniel Nikolaus Chodowiecki: Evening Party at the house of Parson Bocquel, 1773. *Berlin (East), Kupferstichkabinett*

Wehdel, Wehlburg, 1750. Exterior

(A) Johann Conrad Schlaun: Rüschhaus, 1745–8. Court side

(B) Johann Conrad Schlaun: Rüschhaus, 1745–8. Garden side

(B) Johann Georg Ziesenis: Countess Maria zu Schaumburg-Lippe, c. 1770. *Formerly collection of the Prince of Schaumburg-Lippe (destroyed)*

(A) Georg David Matthieu: Johann Völler, Groom of the Chamber, c. 1770. *Schwerin, Staatliches Museum*

(A) Johann Christoph Knöffel: Dresden, Kurländer Palais,
1728–9. Exterior (before destruction)

(B) Johann Georg Schmidt, Christian Friedrich Exner, and Gottlieb
August Hölzer: Dresden, Kreuzkirche, 1763–1800.
Façade. Engraving. *Dresden, private collection*

(B) Anton Raphael Mengs: The Infanta Maria Theresa, c. 1776.
Vienna, Kunsthistorisches Museum

(A) Anton Raphael Mengs: Domenico Annibali, 1750–2. *Milan, Brera*

(B) Anton Graff: Louise Elisabeth von Funcke, c. 1795.
Leipzig, Museum der bildenden Künste

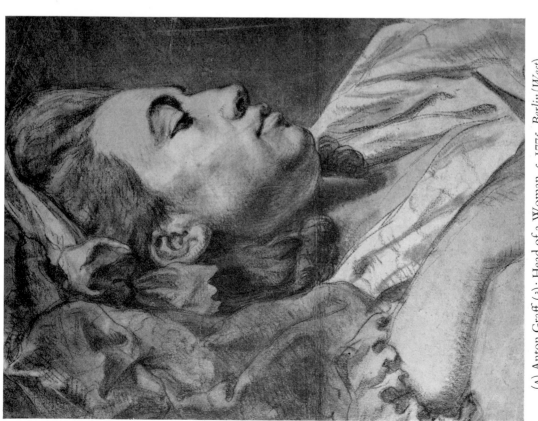

(A) Anton Graff (?): Head of a Woman, c. 1775. Berlin (West),
Kupferstichkabinett

(A) Johann Bernhard Fischer von Erlach and Nikolaus Paccassi: Schönbrunn, 1695–1749. Exterior

(B) Gotthard Hayberger: Admont, abbey, 1742–74. Interior of library

Joseph Hueber: Graz, Mariahilfkirche, façade, 1742–4

Kremsmünster, Benedictine Academy for Young Noblemen, observatory, 1748–60

Innsbruck, Helblinghaus, façade, *c.* 1775

(B) Balthasar Ferdinand Moll: Sarcophagus of Franz I and Maria Theresa, begun 1753. *Vienna, Capuchin church*

(A) Veit Königer: Virgin of the Annunciation, 1756. *Graz, Landesmuseum*

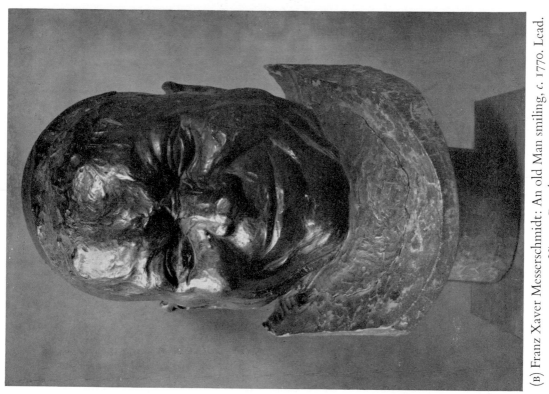

(B) Franz Xaver Messerschmidt: An old Man smiling, c. 1770. Lead.
Vienna, Barockmuseum

(A) Franz Xaver Messerschmidt: Gerard van Swieten, 1769. Lead.
Vienna, Barockmuseum

(B) Franz Anton Maulbertsch: Self Portrait, *c.* 1790.
Vienna, Barockmuseum

(A) Franz Anton Maulbertsch: Dome fresco, 1752–3.
Vienna, Piaristenkirche

Franz Anton Maulbertsch: Baptism of Christ, ceiling fresco, c. 1766. *Vienna, Old University, Divinity School*

(B) Franz Anton Maulbertsch: The Rape of Deianira, *c.* 1785–6. Oil sketch. *Vienna, Albertina*

(A) Franz Anton Maulbertsch: Venus and Adonis, *c.* 1785. Oil sketch. *Vienna, Albertina*

Franz Anton Maulbertsch: The Invention of the Cross, ceiling fresco, 1757–8.
Heiligenkreuz–Gutenbrunn, church

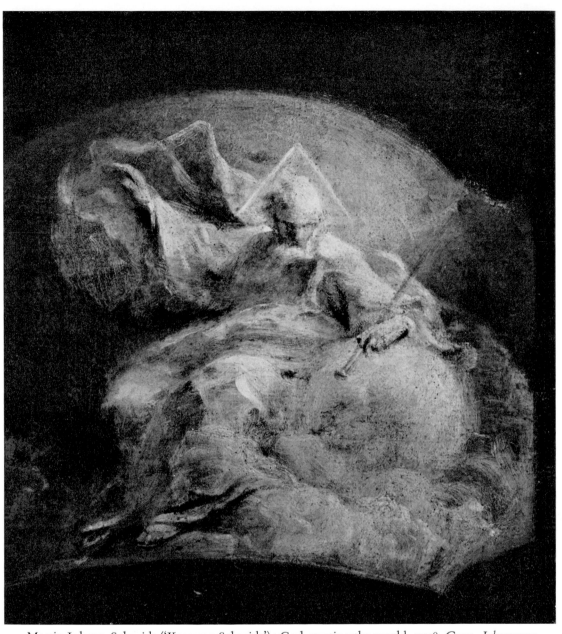

Martin Johann Schmidt ('Kremser-Schmidt'): God creating the world, 1778. *Graz, Johanneum*

(A) Andreas Mayerhoffer: Gödöllö, palace, 1744–50. Exterior

(B) Erhard Martinelli: Fertöd, Schloss Esterháza. Exterior, 1720

Miklos Jacoby: Fertöd, Schloss Esterháza. Courtyard, 1762–6

Jakob Fellner: Eger (Erlau), Pedagogical Seminary (formerly Episcopal Lyceum), 1765–83

Jakob Fellner: Tata, District Hospital (formerly Esterházy Palace), 1764–78

Balatonakali, farmhouse, 1834

Buda, No. 4 Batthyány Tér., 1775–6. Exterior

(B) Anton Pilgram: Jászó (Jasov), abbey church, 1745–63. Interior

(A) Matthias Gerl: Eger (Erlau), church of the Minorites, 1758–73. Façade

(A) Jakob Fontana: Radzyń, palace, *c.* 1755. Orangery, exterior

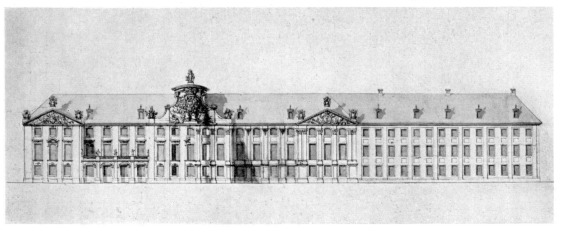

(B) Gaetano Chiaveri: Design for additions to the royal palace, Warsaw, 1740. Engraving

Ephraim Schröger: Warsaw, church of the Salesian Nuns. Façade, 1754–63

Modlnica, manor house, eighteenth century. Exterior

INDEX

Numbers in *italics* refer to plates. Main references appear in **bold** type. References to the notes are given only where they indicate matters of special interest or importance: such references are given to the page on which the note occurs, followed by the number of the chapter to which it belongs and the number of the note. Thus $313(2)^1$ indicates page 313, chapter 2, note 1. Artists' names are always indexed under the final element of the surname: thus Sir Anthony van Dyck will be found under Dyck. Where names of places or buildings are followed by the name of an artist in brackets, the entry refers to work by that artist in such buildings or places; thus Vienna, Barockmuseum (Troger) refers to the paintings by Troger in the Barockmuseum.

H